COUNSELING: THEORY AND PROCESS

THIRD EDITION

JAMES C. HANSEN

State University of New York at Buffalo

RICHARD R. STEVIC

State University of New York at Buffalo

RICHARD W. WARNER, JR.

East Carolina University

ALLYN AND BACON, INC.

Boston   London   Sydney   Toronto

Library of Congress Cataloging in Publication Data

Hansen, James C.
    Counseling: theory and process.

    Includes bibliographies and index.
    1. Counseling.   I. Stevic, Richard R.   II. Warner,
Richard W.   III. Title.
BF637.C6H324 1982   158'.3   81-12855
ISBN 0-205-07640-8   AACR2

Printed in the United States of America.

10 9 8 7 6 5 4 3 2 1   86 85 84 83 82

CONTENTS

PREFACE

Counseling is a process that assists individuals in learning about themselves, about their environment, and ways to handle their roles and relationships. Although individuals seek counseling because they are experiencing problems, counseling is not necessarily remedial. The counselor may assist an individual with the decision-making process in educational and vocational matters as well as with resolving interpersonal concerns. Counseling is an applied field in which the counselor uses behavioral knowledge to help the client. Theory is helpful in understanding the development of behavior patterns, the manner and extent of undesirable behavior, and the development of procedures for changing client behavior.

The purpose of this book is to provide a base from which students aspiring to be counselors or counselors working in the field can build a personal theory of counseling, ideally a theory that will guide their own practice. We realize that no one text can do justice to all the theories in the field of counseling. Our goal is not to present an exhaustive treatment of each theory, but rather to provide the tools and general background to enable an individual to build his or her own counseling theory. To achieve this goal, we begin, in Chapter One, with a general discussion of theory and theory development. The next nine chapters are an overview of the contributions to counseling from various theoretical positions. Chapters Two through Five are devoted to psychoanalytic theory, ego-counseling, Adlerian theory, and transactional analysis. These are followed by chapters on the self-theory approach and the Gestalt approach to counseling. The behavioral theory and the rational approaches of Glasser and Ellis are discussed in the remaining chapters on theory. Chapter Eleven assesses the present status of counseling theory and compares the various theoretical approaches.

From the theoretical base presented in Part One, the second part of the book moves to the process of counseling. The section begins with a chapter describing counseling as a relationship between counselor and client, and examining the dimensions that occur in that relationship. In Chapter Thirteen the focus is on initiating counseling, and in Chapter Fourteen we illustrate how the counseling process evolves through various stages to termination. Chapter Fifteen presents concepts related to the diagnostic processes in counseling. The next three chapters are concerned with specific topics in counseling: decision making, use of tests in counseling, and vocational counseling. The final chapter deals with ethics, legalities, and values that may confront a counselor during the counseling process. Case material and interview typescripts are presented to illustrate the counseling process. Obviously a professor's use of tape recordings and films as illustrations is an excellent way to make counseling come alive.

We have drawn the material in this book from the theories and research of many writers in the field of counseling. We also acknowledge the stimulation of our colleagues and students as an important contribution to the completion of the book.

PART ONE

COUNSELING THEORY

PART ONE
INTRODUCTION

The major premise of this book is that counselors must understand both the why and the how of counseling. A counselor who has knowledge of one but not the other is lacking as a professional. Therefore we focus in this text on both the theory and the process of counseling. The study of counseling theory addresses the question *why*; the study of the counseling process addresses the question *how*.

Our second major assumption is that each counselor must develop a personal theory of counseling. In most cases we expect that this personal theory will be eclectic, a systematic combination of bits and pieces from several existing theories. There is evidence that this systematic eclecticism is increasingly necessary and useful. Garfield and Kurtz (1977) reported the views of 154 clinicians that no single current theory applied adequately to the many kinds of clients seen in counseling and therapy.[1] Our aim is to help the reader build a personal systematic eclectic approach.

Because we believe that this process must begin with an examination of the current thinking within the profession, Part One presents theories that are currently receiving the most attention by counselors themselves. Each chapter describes the theoretical background and examines the actual counseling procedures advocated by that approach. The second part of the book will examine the general concepts and methods through which theories are translated into the counseling process.

Part One begins with a chapter devoted to the process of developing a personal counseling theory. The purpose of Chapter One is to provide a system that will facilitate the development of a theory as the reader moves through the text and subsequent training.

Our examination of counseling theory begins with approaches that have been influenced directly by psychoanalytic theory, then moves to theories that represent a clear departure from Freudian thought. Few approaches to counseling or therapy have not been influenced in some way by Freudian psychoanalytic theory. Freud's theories have affected the work of psychiatrists, psychologists, counselors, social workers, and others involved in the helping professions. Chapter Two presents only the major Freudian concepts, for the psychoanalytic approach is used largely in traditional psychotherapy, not in counseling.

Following Chapter Two are discussions of three approaches that have been greatly influenced by Freudian thought and are particularly important to the field of counseling: ego counseling, Adlerian counseling, and transactional analysis, a relative newcomer to the field. Chapter Three examines the ego-analytic approaches to counseling. Although in many respects there is only a slender distinction between psychoanalytic theory and ego-analytic theory, that difference makes the latter approach more appropriate to counseling. The Adlerian approach, in Chapter Four, and the transactional analysis approach, in Chapter Five, both have ties to Freudian thought but are further removed from it than is the ego-analytic position. Much of Adler's theoretical position is in direct contrast to Freud's. Transactional analysis has also been influenced by Freudian thought

1. S. L. Garfield and R. Kurtz, "A Study of Eclectic Views," *Journal of Consulting and Clinical Psychology*, 1977, 45, 78–83.

even more than its founder, Eric Berne, would admit, but many of its positions contrast sharply with traditional analytic theory.

Chapters Six and Seven discuss two approaches that represent clear breaks with Freudian thought. Adherents of self-theory (Chapter Six) and Gestalt therapy (Chapter Seven) share a belief in the capacity of individuals to be self-directing. These are not only the approaches with this focus: others include Kelly's notion of personal constructs or Gendlin's experiential counseling. But our purpose is not to present all the theories in a given area, only those that are most representative of particular orientations to counseling.

Chapters Eight, Nine, and Ten present theories that place much more emphasis on counseling as a special type of learning situation. Chapter Eight describes the broad range of behavioral approaches to counseling. Although there are many differences among those who refer to themselves as behaviorists, all share a belief in use of the laws of learning to bring about behavioral change. Because the behavioral field is so broad, the chapter focuses on the basic laws of learning adhered to by most behaviorists and on how many of these laws are translated into specific counseling techniques.

Chapter Nine discusses reality therapy, and Chapter Ten rational-emotive counseling. Both approaches share the behaviorist belief that counseling is a learning process, but both place more faith in human capacity for reasoned thought than do the behaviorists.

Advocates of the theories presented in Chapters Three through Ten are continually modifying and updating their approaches; the theories are not final products. The reader who is interested in any of these approaches is encouraged to go beyond the basic information presented here to read original material.

Chapter Eleven, the final chapter, in Part One, compares the material presented in Chapters Two through Ten, to provide the reader with both a framework for developing a personal eclectic position and a starting point for the material on the counseling process presented in Part Two.

TOWARD A PERSONAL THEORY OF COUNSELING

CHAPTER ONE

8

**CHAPTER
ONE**

TOWARD A
PERSONAL
THEORY OF
COUNSELING

The profession of counseling, begun by Frank Parsons in the 1900s, experienced tremendous growth in the 1960s, a modest but profound change in direction during the 1970s, and has entered the 1980s striving to retain what has been of value while being responsive to new needs. In the 1960s, an influx of federal funds into programs for the preparation and training of counselors created not only more counselors, but also more and generally better programs. New social programs in the 1970s broadened the work setting of counselors. The changing populations and social needs of the 1980s have further increased the demand for competent professional counselors. Counselors graduating today are better prepared to fulfill their functions than those who graduated a scant ten years ago, but the demands are so complex that training programs must continually strive for further improvement.

Although this growth has produced positive results, it is also true that many counselors today seem to lack definite direction or purpose. The current demand for accountability, long overdue, will force those already in the field and those about to enter it to develop a more systematic approach to the provision of counseling. Each counselor must develop a personal counseling model as a framework for operating. Some may admire the methods of Perls or the theories of Krumboltz, but no one can be a duplicate of anyone else. A counselor must be faithful to herself or himself and must have a personally tailored model, a personal counseling theory that provides both a rationale for counseling and guidelines for the actual process of counseling. This chapter is designed to help start that process, by examining first what counseling is and, second, the process of personal theory building, to provide the necessary framework for integrating theory and process into a personal theory of counseling.

COUNSELING

WHAT IS COUNSELING?

As Tyler (1969) points out, *counseling* is a word that everyone seems to understand, but it is quite apparent that no two people understand it in exactly the same way. The rapid growth of the profession has confused the issue of what counseling means. Part of the confusion may also stem from the fact that counseling as we now know it had its beginnings in related but separate fields.

An Interdisciplinary Background

Counseling is an applied social science with an interdisciplinary base composed of psychology, sociology, cultural anthropology, education, economics, and philosophy (Glanz, 1974). Each of these disciplines has made and continues to make its own, unique contribution to counseling. From psychology we learn about human growth and development; sociology provides insight into social structure and institutions; anthropology helps us understand the importance of culture; and from economics we learn about the dynamics involved in the world of work. For readers who wish to investigate how each of these disciplines has affected the base of knowledge on which counseling rests, Hansen's *Explorations in Sociology and Counseling* (1969) is an excellent source.

The purpose of counseling makes it clear why such varied disciplines have influenced the profession. The purpose of counseling is to provide for the individual's optimum development and well-being, but the individual functions in a social context, not in isolation. If counselors are to enhance the well-being of the individual, they must understand as many as possible of the factors that affect people; they must adopt an interdisciplinary approach. Such an approach is a product both of our past and of the current demands made by the publics we serve.

There have been several stages in the development of the current broad conception of counseling. Miller's outline (1961) is summarized below by category of emphasis.

Vocational Guidance

The vocational guidance movement, whose founding is generally attributed to Frank Parsons, was the original form of counseling. Parsons's primary concern was to develop a method for matching individuals with appropriate occupations. During this period, counseling was seen as being concerned with gathering data about the individual and about occupations, then matching the two. Many writers have suggested that the Parsonian period's main contribution to counseling was that its emphasis on gathering data about individuals led to the use of psychological techniques for analyzing individual differences. Although this development has had a positive influence on knowledge about human behavior, two outcomes of this period tended to restrict the development of counseling. During this period and for many years afterward, counseling was often perceived as an event limited to one or two sessions that took place before entering the world of work. Second, it came to be regarded as a profession involved solely with vocational matters (Shertzer & Stone, 1971).

Educational Guidance

The next stage, which emphasized the educational nature of counseling, originated with the work of Brewer, who was troubled that schools were concerned chiefly with translating knowledge and did not relate this knowledge to the world that students would enter. In Brewer's view, education should provide "guidance" for young people in living. Jesse B. Davis was also instrumental in developing the concept of educational guidance as moral guidance or guidance for living. These developments broadened the scope of counseling activities beyond concern with a prospective occupation; counseling came to include the total life of the individual. So conceived, counseling services were seen as "a series of activities and actions permeating all educational activity" (Shertzer & Stone, 1971, p. 64). This approach had the advantage of identifying counseling with the concept that each child has a right to be his or her own person and to receive an education attuned to that individuality. The prime disadvantage was that counseling became synonymous with teaching. Many schools still provide formal classes on occupations and so-called group guidance or counseling. If restricted to didactic presentations without personalized information, such classes are probably irrelevant to most participants.

Adjustment

10

CHAPTER
ONE

TOWARD A
PERSONAL
THEORY OF
COUNSELING

A third emphasis that prevailed for a time was counseling for adjustment. This developed from two sources: those concerned with mental health and those concerned with education. In 1908 Clifford Beers, in his book *The Mind That Found Itself*, called attention to the problem of mental illness in the United States. Coupled with the emergence of the field of psychoanalysis, Beers's work led to increased interest in both the concept of mental illness and methods for helping those afflicted. This movement promoted rapid expansion in psychiatry and clinical psychology. Many people in these fields referred to what they were doing as counseling, like the people in the vocational guidance movement. Those in education most often referred to the process as "life adjustment," defined as "that which better equips all American youth to live democratically with satisfaction to themselves and profit to society as home members, workers, and citizens" (U.S. Office of Education, 1950, p. 1). The mental health movement was also emphasizing adjustment, defined as a state of good mental health. Both groups regarded counseling as a means of helping people adjust to themselves and society. This position contributed to the notion that counseling should help the individual understand himself or herself in relation to the world. It also tended to increase the importance of counseling as an effective intervention when people are in difficulty. This attitude could also be a disadvantage, for it tended to focus attention on the crisis role of counseling rather than its developmental role. A second disadvantage was that it led to a general belief that the function of counseling was to get people to conform to the society.

Developmental Counseling

In reaction to the emphasis on counseling for adjustment, developmental counseling emerged in the early 1950s. This stage coincided with an increasing emphasis in psychology on developmental tasks. As defined by Havighurst,

> A developmental task is a task which arises at or about a certain period in the life of an individual, successful achievement of which leads to his happiness and to success with later tasks, while failure leads to unhappiness in the individual, disapproval by society, and difficulty with later tasks (1952, p. 2).

The role of counseling in this process was to facilitate individual movement along the developmental path. Counseling services were seen as extending over a long period and focusing on enhancing the individual's inherent ability to move toward maturity. This was in sharp contrast to the crisis-intervention approach implied by the emphasis on adjustment.

Related to the developmental approach was an emphasis on counseling as an aid in decision making. This approach held that counseling was necessary only when individuals needed help in making decisions; hence, counseling should be concerned with helping people learn the decision-making process as well as helping them with individual decisions. Although its rationale is valid—in our society all individuals need to know how to make decisions—by itself this approach implies that counseling takes place only at certain times, usually in connection with some form of crisis or problem.

Manpower Needs versus Social Reconstruction

In the 1960s counseling evolved two, sometimes conflicting, emphases. In 1958, passage of the National Defense Education Act (NDEA) put counseling under pressure to meet national manpower needs. The purpose of NDEA was to recruit more young people into science. Counselors were to be trained to help channel bright students in that direction. In some ways this was a return to the old Parsonian method of finding the best people and matching them to appropriate occupations, or to the life adjustment approach in which counseling was to help people make adaptations to the society. At the same time other pressure was developing for counseling to serve as an agent for social reconstruction. This approach recognized that many of an individual's difficulties derive from the inadequacies of the society, and perceived counseling as a means of righting these wrongs. The obvious advantage of such an approach is that it places great importance on the individual; its disadvantage is the overwhelming nature of the proposed task.

More recently there has been strong pressure on the profession to recommit itself to career development counseling. This pressure emanates from the career education movement. "Few concepts introduced into the policy circles of American education have ever been met with such instant acclaim as career education" (Hoyt, Evans, Macklin, & Mangum, 1972, p. 1). This movement is largely a response to the problems created by a rapidly changing, complex society. As Herr (1974) suggested, "As societies become developed (industrial) the concomitant magnitude of opportunities poses a 'burden of decision' for the young and displaced" (p. ix). As professionals, career education specialists and counselors need to respond to these needs in a productive way.

Recent Emphasis

During the 1970s there was increasing reliance on counselors as part of mental health teams working in community mental health centers. In these settings counselors provided a variety of therapeutic services to a wide range of clients, including those with alcohol and drug problems, those with marital and family problems, adolescents, the handicapped, and the occupationally displaced. These new settings forced the development of counselor training programs that would prepare a different kind of counselor. These new counselors represented a radical departure from the traditional educational counselor.

This examination of the major influences on the development of counseling implies the existence of rather simplistic, separate models. Helping someone select an occupation or the appropriate educational courses appears to be a relatively easy task. If, however, counseling is defined as a process concerned with an individual's optimum development and well-being, both personally and in relation to the larger society, the task involves a complex model that comes close to encompassing all the emphases that have been discussed. The evolution of the definition of counseling has involved additions rather than substitutions. Far more important, the growth of counseling has involved growth not simply in the number of emphases but also the scope of their focus.

12

CHAPTER
ONE

TOWARD A
PERSONAL
THEORY OF
COUNSELING

A second source of confusion about what counseling is stems from the attempt to differentiate counseling from psychotherapy. This has been particularly true recently, when counselors and psychologists have functioned in the same or similar work settings. Most counseling authorities regard psychotherapy and counseling as a continuum of services. According to Vance and Volsky (1962), counseling deals with so-called normal individuals whose problems are developmental in nature, whereas psychotherapy is concerned with those who are in some way deficient. Their continuum is based on the kind of people with whom the two services work. Similarly, for Brammer and Shostrom (1977) counseling is largely concerned with the so-called normal individual and is characterized by terms such as conscious awareness, problem solving, educative, supportive, and situational; psychotherapy, on the other hand, is concerned with reconstruction, depth emphasis, analysis, and focusing on the unconscious and especially on neurotic and emotional problems. They suggest that counseling and psychotherapy are generally used interchangeably.

A special committee of the American Psychological Association suggested that counseling involves helping individuals plan for a productive role in their social environments. "Whether the person being helped with such planning is sick or well, abnormal or normal, is really irrelevant. The focus is on assets, skills, strengths, and possibilities for further development. Personality difficulties are dealt with only when they constitute obstacles to the individual's forward progress" (APA Report, 1961, p. 6). Hence, the focus of the APA continuum is not the individual, but the manner in which the counselor and psychotherapist work with their respective clients. Wolberg (1954) attempted to differentiate counseling from psychotherapy by defining three kinds of approaches: supportive, insight-reeducative, and insight-reconstructive. He considered the first two approaches appropriate for counselors, the third for psychotherapists. As with other attempts to delineate function, Wolberg appeared to regard counseling and psychotherapy as elements of a continuum. According to English and English (1958), "While usually applied to help the normal counselee, [counseling] merges by imperceptible degrees into psychotherapy" (p. 127).

Let us concede that counseling and psychotherapy indeed exist along a continuum. Although they are at opposite ends of the continuum, they are related ways of helping people in need. Both exist because our complex technological society has placed many demands on individuals, demands that involve the roles they are expected to fulfill in society. In some cases the transition from the demands of one role to the demands of another causes intrapersonal difficulties: the individual experiences internal value conflicts. In other cases, the difficulty arises from the nature of the roles themselves; the individual has difficulty assuming a particular role. The continuum is discernible in these two interrelated but somewhat different problem areas. At one end are intrapersonal conflicts; at the other are conflicts that involve role definitions.

This continuum, shown in Figure 1-1, illustrates that an individual's difficulty may occur in the development of personality, in the destruction of the personality through role demands, in role transition, in role choice, in conflicts among roles, or in contradictions between values and role expectations (Perry, 1955). In these cases either psychotherapy or counseling can be useful.

FIGURE 1–1 COUNSELING–PSYCHOTHERAPY CONTINUUM

CHAPTER
ONE   13
TOWARD A
PERSONAL
THEORY OF
COUNSELING

Intrapersonal Problem ⟶ Role Definition Problem

Given this dimension of the continuum, it is clear that problems vary in intensity and are often related. However, an individual can have very serious role problems without any intrapersonal disturbance. Likewise, an intense intrapersonal conflict can exist independently of role demands. In large part, a person's ability to deal with any problems that arise from role conflict is related to the degree of intrapersonal conflict: someone who is experiencing intense intrapersonal difficulties will be unable to deal with any role-related concerns. Thus, the type of assistance that can best serve a particular individual is related to the degree to which that person suffers from some internal disturbance. We can assume that the smaller the degree of internal disturbance, the better able the individual will be to deal with difficulties surrounding role. In effect, someone with minimal internal disturbance will be more apt to respond to shorter-term, direct guidance (Perry, 1955).

Although everyone needs to understand her or his personality, people with minimal internal conflicts require no complete restructuring of personality in order to deal with problems of role. Restructuring personality is not necessary in order to make a vocational choice or to deal with a marital problem. In contrast, those with an intense intrapersonal conflict will be unable to deal with problems created by role. These people require an intense therapeutic relationship over an extended period, an experience designed to restructure the personality.

As the sample situation in Figure 1–2 indicates, most psychotherapy occurs

FIGURE 1–2 A SAMPLE SITUATION ON AN INTERPERSONAL/ROLE PROBLEM CONTINUUM

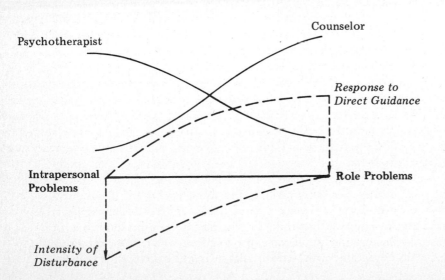

14

CHAPTER
ONE

TOWARD A
PERSONAL
THEORY OF
COUNSELING

in the area of intrapersonal conflict of high intensity. The counselor works at the other end of that continuum with people who are more likely to respond to short-term, more direct kinds of learning experiences. The difference, then, is that counseling works toward helping people to understand and develop their personality in relation to specific role problems; psychotherapy aims at reorganization of the personality through interaction with a therapist.

Counseling, then, as we define it, is

> a therapeutic and growth process through which individuals are helped to define goals, make decisions, and solve problems related to personal-social, educational and career concerns. Specialized counseling provides assistance with concerns related to physical and social rehabilitation, employment, mental health, substance abuse, marital and family problems, human sexuality, religious and value choices, career development, and other concerns (Warner, 1980, p. 2).

Counseling does not attempt to restructure personality, but to develop what already exists. It is chiefly concerned with individuals' adjustments to themselves, to significant others in their lives, and to the cultural environment in which they find themselves.

THEORY

WHAT IS A THEORY?

We can now examine the role of theory in counseling. As each of us finds all too often, our memories are not infallible. Confronted with vast arrays of information, we need a framework for organizing that information. Solving a problem, even with a great deal of applicable information, is almost impossible without a plan or model. A theory provides such a model. It is a structure on which information necessary to the solution of a problem can be organized. This framework enables us to assign various kinds of data to their proper places and to develop a sense of the relationship between each piece of data. Wolman (1973) defines a theory as a system composed "of empirical data derived from observation and/or experimentation, and of their interpretation" (p. 383). Thus, a theory grows out of a systematic analysis of past events.

According to Stefflre and Matheny (1968), a theory is a model that the theorist uses to blend the reality of experiences with ideas about plausible explanations for these experiences. The theorist attempts to make sense out of life through constructing a framework that permits a logical and reasonable explanation of events. A theory, then, is an explanation of events on which future courses of action can be based.

Thus, a theory provides a standard by which to measure progress toward a desired outcome. This view assumes that a theory should influence the approach to a problem. If it does not, the theory is useless (Polster & Polster, 1973). To function without theory is to operate without placing events in some order and thus to function meaninglessly. Those who claim they can operate without theory generally hold some vague and implicit assumptions about the nature of events; in reality they are working from a theoretical frame of reference. The danger of this approach is that an implicit or hidden theory is subject to the interjection of personal biases into the interpretation of experience. To state a theory in explicit terms runs the risk of dogmatism, but it also minimizes the intrusion of bias.

In summary, a theory is an explanation for events that can be tested by events; it is useful only to the extent that it influences behavior; and it is better stated explicitly than held implicitly.

HOW DOES A THEORY DEVELOP?

If a theory is a structure, we must assume it is based on several smaller pieces of information. In building a theory about human behavior we begin by examining current theories on the topic. Then we attempt to verify those theories through observation. In attempting to understand why a child is often absent from school, for example, we might first offer several reasons based on what has been written about children's behavior in school. To authenticate these explanations, we observe the child. If we note that the child is absent every time there is to be a math test, we might infer a relationship between the two events. If we observe these events for some time, our inferences may become a hypothesis: the child is afraid of failure. At this point we have made a statement about what we believe to be the relationship between the two events. If we observe the behavior of this child in several situations, we are likely to see several kinds of events and may make several additional inferences about the relationship among these events. We may observe that this child does come to school to take tests in other subjects. Further, we may see that the math teacher is extremely intolerant of students who fail, whereas the other teachers are much more tolerant and encouraging. As many of these events are observed and several inferences are made, a series of separate but related hypotheses may emerge. These related hypotheses are the bases for a theory about the child's behavior. Thus, in this example, as in all theory development, we started with existing possible explanations, observed actual events, and made inferences about the relationship between these events. Over time these inferences became hypotheses; assumptions about the relation of these hypotheses followed; the structure for a mini-theory was formed. If we observed many children and began to combine all the mini-theories, we would be developing a theory about one facet of children's behavior.

In line with this procedure, this text is designed to help in building a personal theory of counseling. Part One, which examines current theories, is designed to provide a general framework for understanding human behavior. Part Two, which focuses on the actual process of counseling, should help develop counseling strategies that fit a general framework. As you read and discuss each chapter in Part One you should begin observing human behavior, ideally in a setting similar to one in which you work as a counselor. As you move through Part Two you should begin to try different process strategies in a supervised setting. Our hope is that as you finish the text you will have developed a tentative approach to counseling.

The process does not end here. A theory is not a law. A theory is always in the process of being formulated; it is not static or stable. With new observations of events, new inferences and hypotheses may develop that will affect the basic structure of the theory. A genuine theory is only a provisional formulation of a position or interpretation, subject to some form of verification and testing and followed by reformulation (Williamson, 1965). A theory is based on observations of events, but continuing observations are necessary, either to verify assumptions and hypotheses or to generate new hypotheses when the original ones cannot be verified.

A theory, then, is a framework of inferences and hypotheses made about the plausible relationships between a series of events. But a theory is generated by people in a certain culture at a particular time. As Stefflre and Matheny (1968) pointed out, a theory is derived from bases that are personal, historical, sociological, and philosophical. Seldom is it truly scientific; both the individual theorist's personal needs and societal needs tend to dictate which questions are asked and which answers are acceptable.

Personal Need

The element of personal need is present in both the adoption and construction of a theory. Shoben (1962b) suggested that it is our own psychological need structure, not what research tells us, that dictates what theory we will adopt as our own. Thus, both the theory builder and the person selecting a theory should look closely at their need structures to determine their reasons for choosing one theory instead of another. In this process it is essential to examine one's basic personal philosophy about the nature of humans and human development.

Philosophy

To some degree, the prevailing philosophy of the time or of the place where the theorist works or where the theory is to be applied dictates the kind of theory that is used or developed. It is, in part, philosophy that defines which goals people should strive for. Philosophy defines what the good life is or what the acceptable answers are. These definitions change with place and time. Hence, a theory that is developed or used at a particular time tends to reflect the dominant philosophy of the time.

Historical Period

The development of theory is also tied to the period in which it is developed. A theory too far ahead of its time is nearly useless because it does not fit contemporary requirements; its answers to problems are unlikely to be considered plausible. History is full of examples of theorists who were far ahead of their times and thus found few people who would even listen to them, let alone try to implement the theory. The early troubles of men like Freud and Rogers are examples of this phenomenon.

Cultural Framework

Similarly, sociological and cultural elements affect the development of theory. U.S. society is based on order, yet at the same time promotes the concept of people's unique individuality. We strive to find order in all things so that we can understand events and behaviors, but we also want to feel that each person has some freedom of choice. Thus, we try to blend these two sometimes contradictory feelings in the development of most of our personality theories. Recently, for example, many writers in counseling have been discussing an approach called humanistic behaviorism. These writers are attempting to blend two seemingly divergent views.

Applicability

In the United States the prevailing concern is with what works. We are generally not interested in theories that dwell in the past; we are concerned with what is happening now. As a pragmatic people, we expect our theories to relate to and give plausible reasons for events and behaviors occurring in today's world.

In summary, theories do not grow in isolation. Because so many factors influence their development, they are rarely completely scientific. They are in fact a product of their time and place. To understand why certain theories are developed and used, we must know something about the personal needs of the theorists and of those who adopt the theory for use. We can understand the development of a theory only if we understand the context in which the theory was developed. This does not necessarily mean that the theory is tied to the period in which it was developed. A good theory is always evolving; it is receptive to the formulation of new hypotheses based on observations of new events.

WHAT ARE THE REQUIREMENTS OF A GOOD THEORY?

The first requirement of a good theory is that it be clear. It must be easily understood and communicable. Its assumptions or hypotheses must be stated so as not to contradict one another. Often a theory is difficult to understand, not because the concepts are so difficult, but because they have not been carefully and thoughtfully related to one another.

Second, a good theory is comprehensive. It does not deal with exceptions or with isolated cases, but supplies plausible explanations for a variety of phenomena in a variety of situations.

A good theory also is heuristic in nature; it is stated in terms explicit enough to generate research. If it is a vague accumulation of thoughts, it is inaccessible to testable hypotheses. It must be so designed that it can be subjected to the rigors of scientific inquiry.

A good theory should relate means to the desired outcomes, stating techniques for achieving the end product. Defining outcomes without stating the means of achieving them is not a formulation of theory, but a mere statement of objectives (Williamson, 1965).

Finally, a good theory is useful to its intended practitioners. To the scientist, the best theory is one that can be subjected to experimental testing; to the counselor it is one that supplies adequate guidelines for the use of specific techniques with individual clients.

In our discussion of theory so far, we have dealt with the general concept apart from any one discipline. Shertzer and Stone (1974) have delineated the four major functions of theory:

1. A theory synthesizes a particular body of knowledge. It brings together a

18

CHAPTER
ONE

TOWARD A
PERSONAL
THEORY OF
COUNSELING

body of related knowledge and, in shorthand fashion, attempts to organize the separate findings into a meaningful and useful whole.

2. A theory increases the understanding about a particular body of knowledge. It attempts to order data and to demonstrate the pieces of the puzzle that are the most important.

3. A theory provides tools for making predictions. Like a diagram, it depicts various points and what may be expected to occur at these points. For the practitioner it acts as a guide to pathways that are possible and what may result from following certain routes. It points out the relationship between means and ends.

4. A theory encourages further research in the area. It makes no difference whether the theory is proved correct or incorrect; its importance is that it stimulates further investigations into the phenomena with which it is concerned. Thus, a theory is always in the process of becoming. As new research evidence is accumulated the theory is substantiated, revised, or simply rejected (pp. 236–237).

THEORY IN COUNSELING

How does this concept of theory relate to counseling? What do we mean when we talk about counseling theory or theories? Where do these theories come from? How are they developed? Of what value are they to the practitioner? How does a counselor decide which of the vast array of theories to adopt? How does one counselor develop a personal theory of counseling?

A counseling theory is a model on which plans of action are developed. This model enables counselors to distinguish normal or rational behavior from what is abnormal or irrational. A counseling theory also provides a frame of reference for understanding the possible causes of behavior that are typical and damaging to the client. For a client having problems with, say, interpersonal relations, this frame of reference enables the counselor to understand the possible causes of such difficulty.

This is not to say that the counselor will have a definitive set of answers for each problem that clients present, or that all clients with similar problems will share identical causes of behavior. A theory, however, does enable the counselor to make some assumptions about the general causes of such behavior. If, for example, the counselor concludes that the client's interpersonal difficulties are caused by some events in early childhood, the counselor may try to help the client gain insight into how these events are affecting present behavior, and through this process the counselor will assume that the client's behavior will be changed. On the other hand, the counselor may view the client's problem as the result of learning inappropriate responses to the situation and will try to help the client learn more appropriate ways of behaving. In either case the counselor makes assumptions about the causes of the behavior and, based on those assumptions, tries to help the client. In speaking of counselors and theory, Schwebel (1962) stated, "What we listen for here and respond to . . . depends in part on us as persons and part on our orientation, that is on a theory which has made particular assumptions about the causes of problems and the methods of treatment" (p. 328).

Whether the counselor's theory is implicit or explicit, some theory does exist. As soon as a counselor begins to confer with a client he or she is making some assumptions about what kinds of behavior are maladaptive and what kinds can be corrected; hence, the counselor is operating from some theoretical position. A counselor who operates without asking what is happening, without some model for action or some assumptions about counseling, is likely to do the client more harm than good.

Counseling theories provide a means of organizing what people have learned about the process of counseling. They are designed to serve as guides to indicate possible causes of a client's difficulties, alternative courses of action, and the desired counselor behavior in the counseling process. The theories themselves grow out of concepts of human nature and what people should be, and out of assumptions about how behavior is changed in the desired directions.

THE BASES OF COUNSELING THEORY

Personality Development

A counseling theory needs to be based on or in some way derived from a theory of personality. Counselors must have some knowledge of the manner and means of personality development from its infant forms to elaborate and more complex adult forms (Williamson, 1965). Not only must they have some knowledge of the development of the normal personality, but they must also understand how maladaptive behavior develops. Only when they understand the development of adaptive and nonadaptive behavior can counselors hope to formulate ways to help their clients. Counselors' views of the nature of humans largely determine which theory of personality, and thus, which counseling theory, they adopt. A counselor who views human behavior as basically determined will counsel from one perspective; one who believes that people basically possess free choice will counsel from a completely different frame of reference.

Behavior Change

A counseling theory also needs to incorporate a concept of how human behavior is changed. Most counseling theorists agree that counseling is really a learning experience, but theories differ as to how this learning occurs. Some theorists argue that the nature of the counseling relationship itself causes client learning to take place; others argue that client learning takes place because the counselor uses reinforcement techniques. Both theoretical positions include a procedure for effecting change.

End Product

A counseling theory must also include some idea of what the desired end product is. Every society develops methods for attempting to change undesirable behaviors and for encouraging desired ones. That is, society determines what the "good life" is. A good counseling theory includes similar notions. In essence it creates a hierarchy of values toward which the counseling process is aimed. This hierarchy of values ultimately becomes the goal of counseling.

20

CHAPTER
ONE

TOWARD A
PERSONAL
THEORY OF
COUNSELING

Role of Counselor

Finally, a counseling theory must include notions about the counselor's appropriate role. The theoretical frame of reference will determine, for example, how much control of the interview the counselor will undertake, how much faith to put in testing and other diagnostic devices, and the extent to which he or she uses directive techniques and interpretative statements. Perhaps most important, the theory will determine the counselor's position on specific techniques.

SUMMARY

Counseling theory, then, must be based on knowledge of human development and personality. From these a counseling theory must derive notions about human nature and how individuals learn. Because counseling is an applied field, the task of counselors and counseling theory is to define how behavior change is brought about and, more important, how this change is brought about in the counseling context. Because the counselor's role or behavior in counseling is in large part determined by theoretical orientation, each counselor needs to evolve his or her own particular theory.

THEORY AND PRACTICE

One of the criteria of a good theory is that it be useful; yet many practicing and prospective counselors seem to question the efficacy of applying theory in their day-to-day work. The reason may be that many of the presently constructed theories of counseling are not useful; it may be that many of our theories are only descriptive, providing no real plans for action; or it may be that counselors simply have not understood the theories as presented. Whatever the reason, the day is rapidly approaching when counseling from no frame of reference will not satisfy our various publics. Counselors must begin to ask some very pertinent questions of themselves. First, they must ask: What is the basic purpose of what I am doing? Once they have determined the answer, they need to ask: What are the means to reach those goals and how are these means different from what other people do? In determining these means they need to know what assumptions they are making about human nature and its development. As Kehas has said, "How do we build knowledge and test it if not by inquiring systematically into experience, making some generalizations about it, and then testing those generalizations to see if our explanations are accurate and help us understand what is happening. Surely we need to know in order to do" (1972, p. 1).

As Brammer and Shostrom (1977) indicate, a counselor who does not have a solid foundation in the current thinking and research in the field, as well as a solid personal counseling theory, is only applying cookbook techniques to help clients solve their problems. This situation tends to occur when a counselor works from some implicit rather than explicit theory. "Without (an explicit) theoretical orientation . . . action is vulnerable to oversimplified and glib imitativeness—even mimicry—and to use of the gimmick" (Polster & Polster, 1973, p. 3). When a theory is explicit, a counselor has a better opportunity to test and evolve a personal theory based on experiences and perhaps some personal research efforts.

If we can accept the suggestion of John Dewey (1859–1952) that creative thinking is essentially a matter of seeing events and concepts in a unique or new pattern (1959), then we can make the next assumption that every counselor has the potential for developing a personal counseling theory. The logical place to begin is with a theory that has made some assumptions about the nature of counseling and been submitted to some empirical testing. This theory can then be subjected to counseling experience, and out of this process should grow new hypotheses and assumptions or verification of the previously held assumptions. The original theory is helpful to the extent that it provides the counselor with a base from which to explore her or his world and an opportunity to develop a tentative personal theory, which in turn gives meaning and direction to his or her counseling.

Theory is in fact integral with practice. Most great theorists, among them Freud and Rogers, evolved their theories from their practices and continuously revised their theories on the basis of new findings. In essence, a theory is practical because of, not in spite of, its heuristic nature. It enables the counselor to make systematic observations about counseling experiences; it encourages the combination of various concepts; and it helps the counselor to predict, to evaluate performance, and to improve outcomes (Brammer & Shostrom, 1977).

Figure 1–3 illustrates a systems approach to conceptualizing the relationship between theory and practice and to developing a personal theory of counseling. The figure demonstrates the relationship between theory and practice; they are components of a system. Any successful system has built-in mechanisms that permit it to adjust itself. The system shown in Figure 1–3 contains feedback loops from counseling practice and client outcomes to observations of human behavior, indicating that theory should have a direct bearing on practice. The feedback of counseling practice and client outcomes into the system permit a theory to be modified by practice.

Most important, the system shown in Figure 1–3 demonstrates the process of personal theory building. It moves from abstract ideas through observations to actual practice and back again. The first stage represents developmental processes that occur in prospective counselors prior to entering a counseling program. Because it is going to affect their attitude to existing counseling theories, a necessary first step is to examine their philosophical view of people.

The second state is roughly equivalent to the training process of a prospective counselor. This text is designed to facilitate movement through this stage; Part One covers the first step, examining existing counseling theories at an abstract level. The trainees then evaluate these data through their own observations of human behavior. These observations lead to inferences about relationships between events and then to general hypotheses about human behavior. All the data then begin to crystallize into a primary or basic theory of counseling, a theory that now contains concepts about how personality develops, how it can be changed, and what the objectives of counseling should be. Part Two of the text, which focuses on process, is designed to help develop specific counseling skills within the framework of personal characteristics and the personal approach to counseling. Ideally, as trainees move through the material in Part Two they have an opportunity through a prepracticum or practicum to try various approaches and to receive feedback about their efforts, both from those conducting the training and from peers who are also going through the process. This feedback permits continual modification and updating of approaches to counseling.

22

FIGURE 1-3 BUILDING A THEORY OF COUNSELING: A SYSTEMS APPROACH

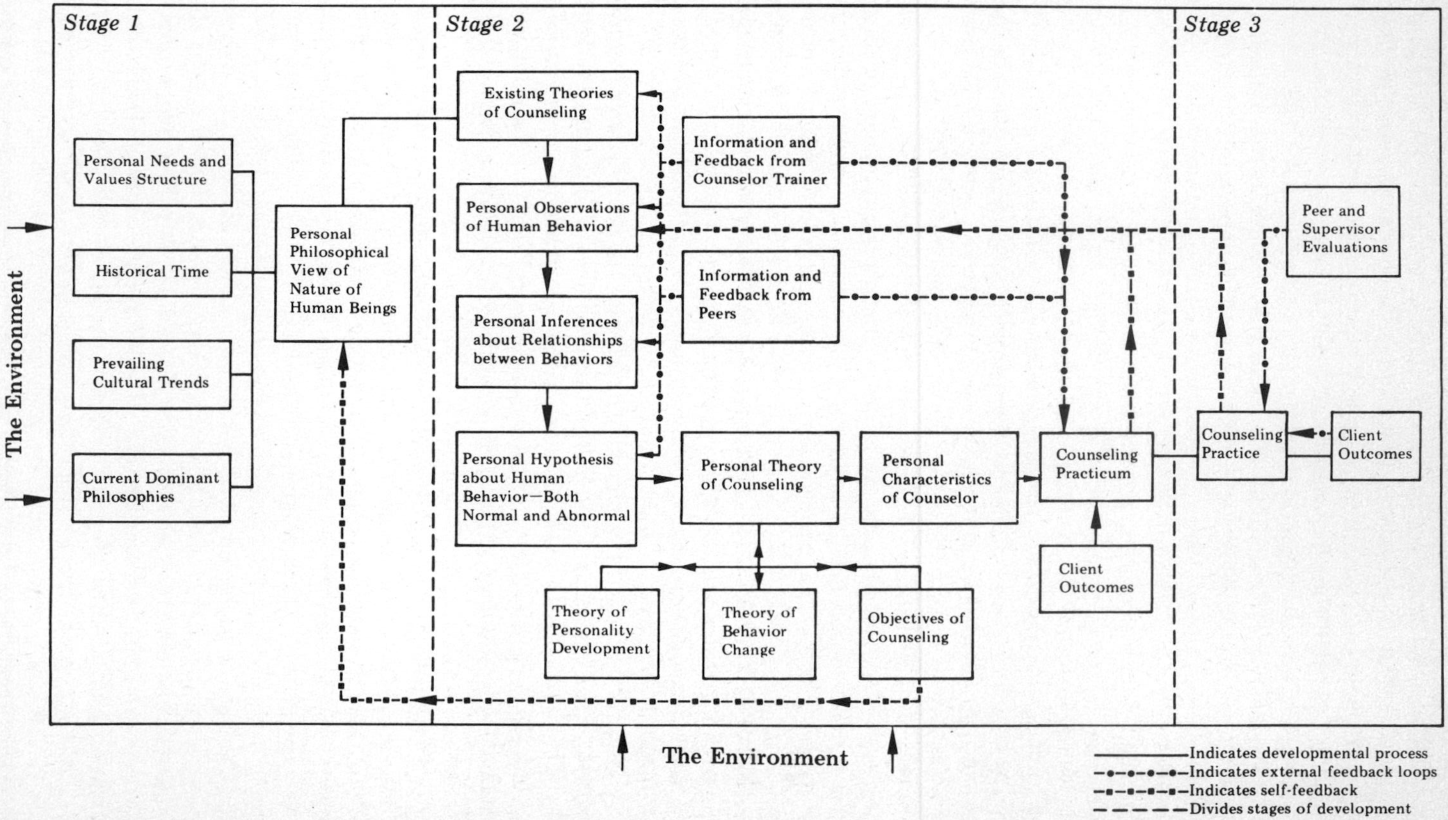

Stage three represents the professional counseling process. In this stage the most important feedback comes from what happens to clients, but the counselor should also continue to seek feedback from peers and supervisors. This information flows back into the system and helps the counselor modify and update the whole system.

The process outlined in Figure 1-3 is really a subsystem of the world in which we live. As such, it is affected by events in that larger world. What is most vital to each counselor is the encouragement to develop a theory that is explicitly formulated, regularly evaluated, and subsequently subjected to modification (Ford & Urban, 1963).

Rotter (1954) summarized the principal values of theories in clinical work; this summary is equally useful to the field of counseling. He suggested that theories serve as the basis for constructing new instruments and methods as well as for testing old methods. In addition, they provide a means of evaluating counseling techniques and ideas and problems in counseling practice, provide encouragement for the development of consistent assumptions, and aid the counselor in recognizing and resolving contradictions in the theory and inconsistencies between theories and practice. Only as counselors recognize the need for and the value of counseling theory will the field progress. We need to know what it is we are about.

SUMMARY

In this chapter we have discussed what counseling is and how it differs from psychotherapy. We concluded that counseling is chiefly concerned with the individual's adjustment to himself, the significant others in his life, and the cultural environment in which he finds himself.

Next we considered how theory is developed, why it is developed, the necessary ingredients for a good theory, and the functions it can serve.

Third, we discussed what counseling theory means and how the theory should relate to actual practice. Counseling theory provides a structure from which the counselor can work in meaningful ways; by itself counseling theory has no meaning.

Finally, we discussed the need for counselors to develop their own theory of counseling, based on a study of present theory, but modified and developed through their own counseling experiences and research. To begin this process we now turn to an examination of some contributions to counseling theory.

REFERENCES

American Psychological Association. *The current status on counseling psychology: A report of a special committee of the division 17 of the counseling psychology.* Washington, D.C., 1961.

Brammer, Lawrence M., & Shostrom, Everett L. *Therapeutic psychology* (2nd ed.). Englewood Cliffs, N.J.: Prentice-Hall, 1968.

————. *Therapeutic psychology* (3rd ed.). Englewood Cliffs, N.J.: Prentice-Hall, 1977.

Creative inquiry. John Dewey Centennial, *Saturday Review*, November 21, 1959, *42*, 22-23.

English, Horace B. & English, Ava Champ-

24   CHAPTER
ONE
TOWARD A
PERSONAL
THEORY OF
COUNSELING

ney. *A comprehensive dictionary of psychological and psychiatric terms.* New York: McKay, 1958.

Ford, D. H., & Urban, H. B. *Systems of psychotherapy: A comparative study.* New York: John Wiley and Sons, 1963.

Glanz, E. G. *Guidance foundations, principles and techniques* (2nd ed.). Boston: Allyn and Bacon, 1974.

Hansen, D. A. *Explorations in sociology and counseling.* New York: Houghton Mifflin, 1969.

Havighurst, R. J. *Developmental tasks and education* (2nd ed.). New York: Longman's Green, 1952.

Herr, E. L. (ed.). *Vocational guidance and human development.* Boston: Houghton Mifflin, 1974.

Hoyt, K. B., Evans, R. N., Macklin, E. F., & Mangum, G. L. *Career education: What it is and how to do it.* Salt Lake City: Olympus Publishing, 1972.

Kehas, C. D. What research says about counselor role. *Focus on Guidance,* 1972, *4*(9), 1–10.

Miller, C. H. *Foundations of guidance.* New York: Harper & Row, 1961.

Patterson, C. H. *Theories of counseling and psychotherapy.* New York: Harper & Row, 1966.

Perry, William G. The finding of the commission in counseling and guidance on the relation of psychotherapy and counseling. *Annals of New York Academy of Sciences,* November 7, 1955, *63,* 396–407.

Polster, E., & Polster, M. *Gestalt therapy integrated: Contours of theory and practice.* New York: Brunner/Mazel Publishers, 1973.

Rotter, J. B. *Social learning and clinical psychology.* Englewood Cliffs, N.J.: Prentice-Hall, 1954.

Schwebel, Milton. Some missing links in counseling theory and research. *Personnel and Guidance Journal,* December 1962, *41,* 328.

Shertzer, B., & Stone, S. C. *Fundamentals of guidance* (2nd ed.). Boston: Houghton Mifflin, 1971.

———. *Fundamentals of counseling* (2nd ed.). Boston: Houghton Mifflin, 1974.

Shoben, Edward J., Jr. New frontiers in theory. *Personnel and Guidance Journal,* 1953, *32,* 80–83.

———. The counselor's theory of a personal trait. *Personnel and Guidance Journal,* 1962, *40,* 617–621. (a)

———. Guidance: Remedial Function or social reconstruction? *Harvard Educational Review,* Fall 1962, *32,* 431–443. (b)

Stefflre, Buford (ed.). *Theories of counseling.* New York: McGraw-Hill, 1965.

Stefflre, Buford, & Matheny, Kenneth (eds.). *The function of counseling theory.* Guidance Monograph Series, Boston: Houghton Mifflin, 1968.

Strupp, H. H. The psychotherapist's contribution to the treatment process. *Behavioral Science,* January 1958, *3,* 34–67.

Sundland, D. M., & Barker, E. N. The orientations of psychotherapists. *Journal of Consulting Psychology,* June 1962, *26,* 201–212.

Tyler, Leona. *The work of the counselor* (3rd ed.). New York: Appleton-Century-Crofts, 1969.

U.S. Office of Education. *Report on the national conference on life adjustment,* Washington, D.C., 1950.

Vance, Forrest L., & Volsky, Theodore C., Jr. Counseling and psychotherapy: Split personalities or Siamese twins. *American Psychologist,* 1962, *17,* 565–570.

Wallach, M. S., & Strupp, H. H. Dimensions of psychotherapists' activity. *Journal of Consulting Psychology,* April 1964, *28,* 120–125.

Warner, R. W., Jr. *Individual counseling.* Atlanta, Ga.: Georgia Department of Education, 1980.

Williamson, E. G. *Vocational counseling: Some historical, philosophical and theoretical perspectives.* New York: McGraw-Hill, 1965.

Wolberg, Lewis R. *The technique of psychotherapy.* New York: Grune and Stratton, 1954.

Wolman, Benjamin B. *Dictionary of behavioral science.* New York: Van Nostrand Reinhold, 1973.

CHAPTER ONE

25

TOWARD A
PERSONAL
THEORY OF
COUNSELING

CLASSICAL PSYCHOANALYTIC THEORY

CHAPTER TWO

Sigmund Freud (1856–1939), the founder of classic psychoanalytic theory, was primarily a practitioner of psychoanalysis; his theory grew out of his practice with people who had psychosomatic illnesses. He believed that an individual's behavior is determined by both interpersonal and intrapsychic factors; he called this assumption psychic determinism. Human beings, in Freud's view, are not masters of their own destinies; rather, their behaviors are directed by the need to gratify basic biological needs and instincts. Behavior is not random, but is determined by past experiences.

LEVELS OF AWARENESS

Freud (1935) held that three different levels of awareness influence personality development: the conscious, the preconscious, and the unconscious. At any one time we can be aware, or conscious, of only a very limited number of things. A particular thought, idea, or feeling may occupy the conscious for only a limited time, but while it is there we are unaware of other stimuli around us. The person who focuses attention upon a particular task while an array of events is occurring around her or him is an example of this phenomenon.

The second level of awareness described by Freud is the preconscious. Many ideas or thoughts, though not a part of the conscious, can be brought to the conscious level. When we are asked to recall a past meeting or event, we are calling into consciousness some ideas or events in the preconscious.

The third level of awareness is the unconscious. In Freud's view, this is the most important portion of the mind because it largely determines human behavior. We are not aware of the mental activities that occur in this part of the mind, nor can we bring them to the conscious level. In fact, we unknowingly resist doing so. The traditional example is the man who hates his mother yet is unaware that he has these feelings. In psychoanalytic theory, the importance of these unconscious feelings is that they constantly strive to become conscious and the individual must expend energy to keep them in the unconscious. Thus, Freud regarded people as being in a constant state of internal conflict of which they are not aware.

STRUCTURE OF PERSONALITY

In his later work, Freud retained the concept of the conscious, preconscious, and unconscious in his view of the individual as composed of three subsystems: the id, ego, and superego. These three elements interact to such a great extent that it is difficult to measure their separate effects on behavior. One subsystem seldom operates independently from the other two; rather, an individual's behavior should be considered the result of interaction among the id, ego, and superego.

ID

Freud regarded the id the original system of the personality. In the classic psychoanalytic sense, a newborn infant is all id. The id consists of the constitution of the infant—all the infant brings into the world. It is the source of a fixed reservoir of sexual energy, which Freud referred to as libido.

Within the domain of the id Freud included human instincts, the two most important of which are sex and aggression. The basic function of the id is to maintain the organism in a comfortable, or low-tension, state. Thus, when an infant is hungry and demands to be fed, the id seeks immediate gratification of hunger in order to return the organism to a comfortable state.

Freud believed that this "pleasure principle" governs the id into adult life. Most of the id processes occur at an unconscious level and influence overt behavior without the individual's being aware of that influence. In the example of the man who hates his mother, we can see the id in operation. The feeling toward his mother may affect his relationship with other women although he may be unaware of this influence on his behavior. Generally, id impulses come into consciousness only when the ego is in a weakened state.

EGO

Unlike the id, the ego is not present at birth but develops as the individual interacts with the environment. Its function is to develop muscular and sensory control of the body and to sort out and understand the outer world. In the early stages of development, the infant cannot distinguish among objects, which is the primary reason a hungry baby will put anything it touches into its mouth. At this stage of development there is no sense of the reality of the world, and the infant must learn to discriminate between images in its mind and objective reality. In this process the infant soon learns that to form an image in its mind will not satisfy its need; as a result the infant is forced to begin to differentiate itself from the outer world, learning to find something there that matches the internal image. This matching process that separates the ego from the id is referred to as identification and is one of the most important concepts in psychoanalytic theory.

Thus, the primary function of the id is to satisfy the needs of the organism without regard to external realities. The ego develops out of the id because of the organism's need to deal with those realities. The object of the ego is to mediate between the pleasure principle, by which the id operates, and the outer world. The ego, then, operates on the reality principle and attempts to contain the discharge of energy until there is an appropriate external object to satisfy the need. In the example of the hungry child, the development of the ego alters behavior. As the infant learns to identify objects in the outer world that will satisfy hunger, it ceases putting everything into its mouth. The ego, then, functions as the executive of the individual's personality.

SUPEREGO

The process of identification is likewise important in the development of the superego. The earliest objects in the external world that satisfy the infant's needs are its parents. Early in its development the child learns that important others are likely to look with disfavor on direct expressions of his or her impulses. The parents act as disciplinary agents, and through a process of rewards and punishments of varying degrees the child learns what is acceptable and what is unacceptable behavior. As this process continues through the child's early development, the superego not only adopts the parents' values and customs but also incorporates the accepted values, traditions, and customs of the society.

The superego is a form of individual internal control. When a child's behavior is appropriate even when no one else is there to watch, the superego has emerged. In Freud's view, the superego is made up of two subsystems: the conscience and the ego-ideal. The conscience represents things the individual believes she or he should not do. The ego-ideal represents things the individual would like to be. Either of these subsystems often comes into conflict with the id impulses.

The superego is a built-in control mechanism whose principal function is to control the primitive impulses of the id, which would not lead to accepted behavior. This control occurs largely in the unconscious part of the mind, not in the individual's awareness. The superego represents what is ideal within the individual; it strives for perfection.

In Freud's view the dynamics of personality center on the interaction among the id, ego, and superego. He described psychoanalytic theory as "a dynamic conception which reduces mental life to the interplay of reciprocally urging and checking forces" (1910, p. 107). The id, operating on the pleasure principle, constantly seeks gratification of needs, while the energies of the ego and superego operate both to meet the needs of the individual and to hold in check some of the impulses of the id. The ego must not only interact with the real world, but also must be able to mediate between the id and the superego. An individual dominated by the id will tend to be impulsive; a person dominated by the superego will be overly moralistic. The function of the ego is to keep the individual from these two extremes. The actual form or pattern of interaction among the three subsystems is a product of the individual's development through the psychosexual stages. We now turn to the process of development through these stages.

PSYCHOSEXUAL STAGES OF DEVELOPMENT

Freud contended that an individual's personality is basically formed during the first five years of life, as the individual attempts to learn new ways of reducing tension that emanates from four basic sources: physiological growth processes, frustrations, conflicts, and threats (Hall & Lindzey, 1957). Much of the latter three are products of the growth process of the individual.

In Freud's view, the development of personality, including the various defense mechanisms and how an individual uses them, is largely dependent on the course of her or his psychosexual development. Much of this development occurs during the first five years of life, after which there is a period of relative calm for six years. Then, during adolescence the process becomes very active once again. Another of Freud's major assumptions is that at any one point in a person's development, one body area predominates as a source of pleasure. In normal development a person moves through an orderly sequence in which one body area gives way to another; the order of this sequence is the same for everyone. The third major assumption is that failure to complete this normal sequence will result in serious personality problems.

PREGENITAL STAGES

Freud labeled the first three stages of development the pregenital stages. These are the oral, anal, and phallic stages.

Oral Stage

Freud believed that the infant sucks not just to take in food, but also because sucking produces a pleasurable sensation. This stage of development usually lasts through the first year of life, during which the relationship with the mother is extremely important. As the infant identifies with the mother, it turns from self-love or narcissism to love of others. Freud contended that there are two dangers at this stage of development. If the infant's relationship with the mother becomes too comfortable, the child becomes too dependent and will fixate at this stage, resulting in an overly dependent personality in adult life. At the other extreme, the child who experiences a great deal of anxiety in interaction with its mother may feel insecure, and this insecurity will continue into adult life.

Anal Stage

During the second year of life the source of pleasure shifts to the anal zone of the child's body. During this stage the manner in which toilet training is conducted is extremely important. A child who is dealt with very strictly during this stage may develop into a very retentive personality type. A person who is cruel, obstinate, or stingy is said to have been fixated at the anal stage. During this stage the child first attempts to achieve control over himself or herself and others.

Phallic Stage

From age three to five or six the child is in the phallic stage of development. This stage often produces maladaptive behavior later in life. Freud asserted that during this period the child receives pleasure chiefly through self-manipulation. As the importance of the genital area increases, several psychological developments may occur: castration anxiety, penis envy, and the famous Oedipus complex.

Castration anxiety arises from a boy's fear that he may lose his penis. His parents, in an attempt to stop him from masturbating, may make him fear the loss of his penis, particularly if he has an opportunity to see a girl, who does not have a penis. He may conclude that he will be punished just as she has been punished. Similarly, a girl may develop penis envy when she observes her lack of a penis. She may feel that hers has been removed because of some wrongful act on her part. In either case, Freud asserted that serious problems of personality development are attributable to these developments.

The last development during the phallic stage is what Freud called the Oedipus or Electra complex. Briefly, the Oedipus complex involves the boy's desire to possess his mother and remove his father from the scene. The Electra complex is the desire of the girl to possess her father and remove her mother from the scene. Because this relationship cannot be consummated, resolution of this conflict is extremely important for later personality development. The child must abandon the parent object and become sexually motivated toward others. Subsequent attitudes toward people of the opposite sex and toward those in authority are largely determined by the individual's success in working out the Oedipal complex. This is accomplished largely through the child's identifying with the parent of the same sex; then, through the processes of incorporation and sublimation, the child is able to redirect his or her libidinal energies.

LATENCY STAGE

In Freud's view, from the end of the fifth or sixth year of life until puberty the child is in a stage of latency during which the child spends time developing skills with no sexual implications.

GENITAL STAGE

The first three stages of development can be characterized as narcissistic; during the genital stage self-love begins to change into love of others. With the beginning of puberty the child enters a stage that normally culminates in mature heterosexual behavior; the individual is transformed from a self-loving individual into a socialized adult. In this ultimate stage of development, the normal individual does not get pleasure from oral, anal, or autoerotic activities and is not affected by castration anxiety or an unresolved Oedipus or Electra complex. Rather, the greatest pleasure comes from a relationship with a member of the opposite sex.

DEFENSE MECHANISMS

Each stage of psychosexual development is fraught with the potential for producing frustrations, conflicts, and threats. Freud believed that individuals deal with these tensions through identification, displacement, and other defense mechanisms.

One of the most important roles of the ego is to deal with events that arouse anxiety within the individual. The ego may approach this problem by realistic problem solving, or it may attempt to deny, falsify, or otherwise distort reality. If the ego approaches the problem realistically, the individual's personality stands to be enhanced; however, if the latter choice is made the development of personality is impeded. Although Freud classified identification, displacement, and sublimation as defense mechanisms, these three are realistic problem-solving procedures and differ substantially from other defense mechanisms, which tend to deny, falsify, or distort reality, and which operate in the unconscious. Although defense mechanisms may operate effectively for a time, the more they are used the more rigid the individual's personality becomes.

In the early stages of development, the threats to the self that create anxiety are external. An example is people who are physically larger and who have complete control over the individual, such as parents. As the superego develops, threats to the self can also occur from within: an individual's fears that the id impulses will assume control can result in great anxiety. The defense mechanisms develop to cope with both internal and external threats. They occur primarily at the unconscious level.

IDENTIFICATION

In an earlier section, identification was mentioned as a process whereby the ego and superego develop. That process is extended later in life to include functions much like imitation: the individual, in an attempt to reach a certain goal (such as reduction of tension), incorporates the characteristics of another person into her or his own personality. Most of this occurs at the unconscious level and consists in trial and error; that is, if the behavior taken on reduces the tension, the individual retains the behavior. If the new behavior is not successful in reducing tension, the individual discards it. Although parents are the first and usually the most important people with whom the individual identifies, the adult personality is the result of numerous identifications made throughout his or her development.

DISPLACEMENT

One uniquely human characteristic is the ability to transfer the object of psychological energy from one object to another. If an object that served to reduce tension is no longer available or loses some of its power, another object can and will take its place. This process of redirecting energy from one object to another is called displacement. The development of personality depends to a great extent on this process of energy displacement or object substitution: because the new object is not likely to satisfy the need for tension reduction as well as the original object did, the individual is constantly seeking new and better methods of reducing tension. Displacement accounts for constant human striving and the variability in our behavior.

Freud felt that the most significant form of displacement in the development of civilization is sublimation. Sublimation is the process whereby the individual modifies the expression of a primitive impulse to conform with behavior that is socially acceptable. Sublimations usually take the form of channeling aggressive or sexual energy into intellectual, humanitarian, cultural, and artistic pursuits. Hence, as an individual matures, she or he sublimates or displaces energy to objects that not only yield personal satisfaction but also contribute to the larger society.

REPRESSION

One of the earliest concepts developed by Freud is that of repression. Repression is the act of forcing from consciousness an impulse that causes anxiety. The individual attempts to do away with the impulse by refusing to acknowledge its existence. An individual experiencing repression may not see an object that is in plain sight, or the repression may actually have a physical effect: a man afraid of the sexual impulse may become impotent. Although repression is necessary for normal personality development and occurs to some extent in everyone, some people become overly dependent on repression as a defense. Such people tend to withdraw from contacts with the world and generally are tense and rigid in personality. In such individuals the superego is said to predominate over the ego; the ego has lost some of its controlling power to the superego.

To deal with a repressed impulse, an individual must believe that the impulse no longer constitutes a danger. A child who represses sexual impulses during adolescence may find that her or his adult ego can cope with these impulses, and the repression will cease. In many cases, however, the individual never learns that a repression is no longer necessary.

PROJECTION

Anxiety that originates externally is easier to deal with than anxiety that comes from the id impulses. Hence, if an individual can attribute anxiety to an object in the external world, he or she is likely to feel some relief. This defense is called projection. It consists, first, in not recognizing a characteristic within oneself and, second, in attributing the same characteristic to another person. Instead of saying, "I hate my sister," the individual using projection says, "My sister hates me." Projection is a favorite defense among those who try to enhance their self-esteem. The individual attempts to make herself or himself look good and at the same time to downgrade others.

REACTION-FORMATION

When an individual has an impulse that produces anxiety, the ego may attempt to deal with the impulse by concentrating upon the direct opposite. If an individual feels hate for someone else, the ego may attempt to deal with the hate impulses by showing great outward signs of love toward that person. This form of defense is called reaction-formation. Extreme forms of any behaviors such as a phobia, usually can be attributed to reaction-formation.

FIXATION

In Freud's view normal personality development occurs through a series of well-defined stages of psychosexual development. Moving from one stage to the next involves many frustrations and anxieties. If this anxiety becomes too great, the normal pattern of psychological growth halts at least temporarily, because the individual is afraid to move on to the next stage. He or she experiences fixation. In such cases the individual does not want to give up a behavior pattern that has been satisfying and adopt new behaviors that might not provide the necessary satisfaction.

REGRESSION

Similar to the defense of fixation is the mechanism known as regression: a person may revert to an earlier phase of development instead of moving forward to another stage. This usually occurs when the individual is faced with a severe threat. A little child may revert to infant behavior in a situation in which he or she feels threatened by a loss of love. An adult may withdraw from heterosexual activities because she or he feels inadequate, and through withdrawal from these activities avoids the situation that causes the anxiety. It is generally held that an individual who regresses returns to a stage of development at which he or she was once fixated.

Occurrences of either regression or fixation are relative in degree. Fixation at a particular stage of development is rarely complete; likewise, regression to an earlier stage of development is rarely total.

In summary, Freud believed that individual personality develops as a result of two major factors: maturation by moving through a natural growth pattern; and learning to overcome tension and anxiety that result from conflicts, frustration, and threats by utilizing identification, displacement, and the defense mechanisms. All these processes rechannel the original impulses into more accessible and acceptable sources or objects. This development of personality occurs in an orderly manner and is related to the areas of the body from which the individual derives pleasure. Finally, the Freudian model of personality is a dynamic one, in which the constant interaction of the id, ego, and superego determines the way in which the personality develops. Good mental health is a product of a good balance among the id, ego, and superego.

ABNORMAL PERSONALITY DEVELOPMENT

Classic psychoanalytic theorists view the causes of abnormal personality as rooted within the individual: a behavioral disorder is caused by some disturbance in the internal dynamic equilibrium. The two possible causes of this imbalance are: (1) ineffective dynamics among the ego, id, and superego; and (2) inappropriate childhood learning. In the first case the ego for some reason has failed in its role as executor of the organism. Instead of serving an integrative function, the ego allows the individual to overuse the defense mechanisms. This overuse, primarily of repression, begins in early childhood. The child uses repression to deal with impulses that cause anxiety, pushing them into the unconscious. There they remain, only to arise at later stages of development to cause increased difficulty. If the ego had been able to deal with these impulses when they first developed, the potential for a healthy personality would have been increased.

A second factor in the development of maladaptive behavior is early learning. Freud believed that behavior is acquired either to reduce psychological energy so that it will be socially acceptable or to control drives that might produce pleasure but would be accompanied by severe penalties. Hence, most of these learned behaviors are products of an approach-avoidance situation: there is internal motivation to engage in the behavior, but external forces inhibit it. Such a conflict can produce problems such as anxiety neurosis, obsessive compulsive behavior, or schizophrenia.

In Freud's view, the nature of a neurosis is determined largely by early learning experiences, the defense mechanisms the individual has used against tension, and the stage of psychosexual development at which the person has fixated or to which he or she has regressed. After attempting to cope with a situation and failing, the individual resorts to regression to satisfy her or his needs. This regression brings forth earlier anxieties and tensions that have been repressed. Neurotic behavior develops in the attempt to deal with this tension. This behavior requires increasing amounts of energy to deal with the anxiety; hence, the individual has less and less energy left for dealing with the realities of the world. A vicious cycle is established.

GOALS OF THERAPY

The major goal of the psychoanalytic method is to bring to the conscious level the repressed impulses that are causing anxiety. These are the impulses of the id with which the ego has been unable to deal successfully. In therapy people receive a chance to face situations with which they have been unable to cope. The therapist establishes a nonthreatening context in which the client learns to express thoughts and feelings without fear of being condemned. This freedom allows the individual to explore the appropriateness or inappropriateness of current behavior and to consider new behaviors.

TECHNIQUES IN THERAPY

The basic techniques used in therapy are free association, transference, and interpretation. Because traditional psychoanalysis is seldom used by counselors, discussion of the techniques will be brief and highly simplified.

Free association is simply the practice of letting—indeed, making—clients verbalize whatever is on their mind. Although this sounds simple, it is most difficult to get clients to engage in this behavior. Trying to verbalize everything that comes into one's mind is generally a socially discouraged behavior.

The transference phenomenon is quite complex. It consists in the individual's directing emotional feelings toward the therapist as though the therapist were the original object that caused the feelings. This process enables the client to work through the original conflict.

The therapist uses interpretation to help the individual intellectualize, and to replace superego functions with ego functions. Thus, interpretation is designed to bring the patient step by step back to the world of reality. The therapist may base interpretations on material presented by the client in free association, from dream analysis, or from transference.

SUMMARY

Despite its impact on psychiatry and counseling, classic psychoanalytic theory needs more concrete formulations about how behaviors are acquired and modified. Its influence on the study and modification of human behavior would be even greater if all the concepts and propositions could be integrated into a comprehensive theory of human behavior (Ford & Urban, 1967).

The basic psychoanalytic concepts of personality development presented in this chapter have influenced many approaches to counseling, particularly the ego-analytic approach presented in Chapter Three. The actual therapy process, presented only briefly, generally is not applicable to the functions of most counselors. Readers who wish to study Freudian theory in more detail can examine some of his work in translation.

REFERENCES

Ford, D. H., & Urban, H. B. *Systems of psychotherapy: A comparative study.* New York: John Wiley and Sons, 1967.

Freud, S. Psychogenic visual disturbance according to psycho-analytical conceptions. In *Collected Papers* (Vol. 2). London: Hogarth Press, 1924. (Originally published, 1910.)

————. *A general introduction to psychoanalysis.* New York: Liveright, 1935.

Hall, C. S., & Lindzey, G. *Theories of personality.* New York: John Wiley and Sons, 1957.

EGO-COUNSELING

CHAPTER THREE

Freud's development of psychoanalytic theory provided the impetus for the work of many other theorists, referred to collectively as neoanalysts. This group includes Adler, Horney, Jung, Rank, Sullivan, and Fromm. The theories of all these thinkers are related to classical Freudian thought but are also distinctive enough to warrant separate consideration. Because it is impossible to include all their theories, this book presents only the three neoanalytic theories we believe are most applicable to counseling. The first of these is ego-counseling.

Ego-analysts vary greatly in the degree to which they accept Freudian theory. Their concepts are, however, an extension of psychoanalytic thought, with major emphasis on the functions of the ego. According to Hartmann, "Ego psychology represents a more balanced consideration of the biological and the social and cultural aspects of human behavior" (1967, pp. 158–159). Ego-analytic counselors are concerned "with the ego as organization—with ego-strength" (Hummel, 1962, p. 464). Freud believed the individual's ego is formed out of the energy of the id as the infant interacts with its world. What begins as all id becomes id and ego. The ego-analysts believe the ego develops independently from the drives of the id and, once developed, resists being reattached to the id (Hartmann, 1967). The ego is not viewed as dependent on the impulses of the id; rather, it is viewed as a rational entity that is largely responsible for an individual's intellectual and social accomplishments. The ego has its own source of energy apart from the id, and its own motives, interests, and objectives.

Ego-analyst counselors focus on what they term normal or healthy behavior. They contend that because most of Freud's ideas were based on work with the abnormal personality, the validity of his assumptions about normal behavior is doubtful. The ego-analysts also believe the antecedents of behavior are more complex and varied than the simple instinctual drives expounded in classic psychoanalytic theory. In their view, people are also influenced by the events with which they come in contact.

Hartmann, one of the leading exponents of ego-analytic theory, believes learning plays a role in the development of the individual. In his view, the ego is composed of inherited ego characteristics, instinctual drives, and the influences of external reality (1964). This balanced approach has led to "an improved understanding of man's relations to his environment, and to the most significant part of it, his fellowmen . . . " (Hartmann, 1967, p. 158). Ford and Urban (1967) have pointed out that essentially the ego-analysts have developed Freudian psychoanalytic theory into a broader, more adequate theory of psychology. The ego-analysts, though not making major revisions in classical psychoanalytic theory, give more importance to the effects of environmental events and learned responses. Although they acknowledge the importance of situational events, they are equally concerned with the role played by the psychological energy of the ego.

THEORY OF PERSONALITY

The ego-analysts, unlike Freud, maintain that much human behavior is independent of innate drives. In their view an individual is born with the capacity to respond to different kinds of stimuli, only some of which can be attributed to innate energy. In early infancy the individual responds instinctually to satisfy such needs as hunger. These response patterns soon lose dominance as the individual begins to develop response patterns for his or her environment. Most adult behavior is related not to instinct, but, to the manner in which an individual responds to events. Ego-analysts have devoted most of their studies to the learned behaviors of the individual. As described by Brammer and Shostrom (1977), ego psychology is concerned with the adaptive functions of individuals.

STAGES OF DEVELOPMENT

Freud conceived of personality development as a sequence of psychosexual stages. The ego-analytic position regards personality as the product of a wider variety of factors over a longer period. Erikson's (1963) eight stages of ego development are probably the best example of this view. The first four stages of psychosocial development are roughly equivalent to Freud's first four. In line with the belief that the ego, in the form of conscious thought, becomes more important as the individual matures, the first four stages are dominated by unconscious drives, the last four by conscious thought processes.

In each of Erikson's stages of psychosocial development there are critical periods through which an individual must pass. As Table 3–1 illustrates, success or failure at these critical points produces opposite effects on the personality. Failure at any one stage jeopardizes, but does not preclude, full development at the later stages. Success at these critical points demonstrates that an individual's ego "is strong enough to integrate the timetable of the organism with the structure of social institutions" (Erikson, 1963, p. 246).

Erikson warns against the assumption that the sense of trust or identity

is an achievement, secured once and for all at a given state. . . . The assumption that on each stage a goodness is achieved which is impervious to new inner conflicts and to changing conditions is, I believe, a projection on child development of that success ideology which can so dangerously pervade our private and public daydreams and can make us inept in a heightened struggle for a meaningful existence in a new, industrial era of history (1963, pp. 273–274).

In effect, the ego is always in a state of evolution and open to both forward and backward change through the stages. Furthermore, at each stage the question is not one of either/or. A child does not develop trust to the exclusion of mistrust; rather, it is hoped that individuals will develop a reasonable balance between the two dimensions so that they will trust those things they should and mistrust those things they should. Keeping in mind the importance of this balance, we can turn to how it is maintained through the individual's developmental process.

PROCESS OF PERSONALITY DEVELOPMENT

Of initial importance in the development of the ego is the infant's relationship with his or her mother. Through this relationship the infant begins to develop a sense of ego and non-ego, a concept of what is self and what is outside of self, that is the environment. If the child is frustrated in this relationship, then further development of the ego may be impaired because the infant is mistrustful of those things that are outside the self. If, as is usually the case, this relationship is good,

TABLE 3-1 ERIKSON'S PSYCHOSOCIAL STAGES OF DEVELOPMENT

	SUCCESS		FAILURE
I. Early infancy (birth to one year)	**Trust** Child received affection and need satisfaction.	vs.	**Mistrust** Child abused or neglected.
II. Later Infancy (one to three years)	**Autonomy** Child encouraged to develop self-control and is provided respect by parents.	vs.	**Shame and Doubt** Child made to feel inadequate and not worthy of respect.
III. Early Childhood (four to five years)	**Initiative** Child encouraged to use imagination and test reality on his own.	vs.	**Guilt** Child made to feel guilty for his fantasies, which are often sex-related. Reality testing is discouraged.
IV. Middle Childhood (six to eleven years)	**Industry** Child has developed sense of duty and accomplishment.	vs.	**Inferiority** Child does not value accomplishment. Exhibits sense of failure.
V. Puberty and Adolescence (12 to 20)	**Ego Identity** Individual has now developed a sense of self-concept, a sense of what he is not, can do, and cannot do.	vs.	**Role Confusion** Individual has no real sense of being. Confused about himself and his relation to the world.
VI. Early Adulthood	**Intimacy** Individual has ability to form close relationships.	vs.	**Isolation** Individual remains apart from others. May even be antagonistic toward them.
VII. Middle Adulthood	**Generativity** Time of productivity in work and family.	vs.	**Stagnation** Time of nonproductivity and wandering. No real accomplishments in any area.
VIII. Late Adulthood	**Integrity** Approaches state of self-actualization.	vs.	**Despair** Loss of faith in self and others. Fearful of approaching death.

Adapted from *Childhood and Society*, 2nd ed., revised, by Erik H. Erikson. By permission of W. W. Norton & Co., Inc. Copyright 1950, © 1963 by W. W. Norton & Co., Inc.

then the individual's trust and interest in things that are outside the self are increased and the chances for further normal development of the ego are enhanced. This, then, is the beginning stage for the development of the ego functions. It is important to remember that, according to the ego-analysts, the ego develops from its own energy source and thus is not dependent upon energy from the id, which is what the classic psychoanalytic model says.

With the development of an awareness of ego and non-ego in a non-frustrating atmosphere, the child begins to explore the outer world. Trial-and-error learning first appears during this period as the individual attempts different types of coping behavior for the situations that arise in the child's environment. Hartmann (1964) places great importance on this period, for during this stage of development physical maturity allows the child to manipulate things within the environment as well as the self. This development, in turn, causes the child to come in contact with more stimulation, to which responses must be learned. The ego-analyst's contention is that most of an individual's behaviors are consciously focused toward specific objectives. Hartmann (1961) contends that the individual derives pleasure or satisfaction not only from fulfilling innate drives, but also from developing mastery over problems presented by the environment. The child learning to manipulate a particular toy receives satisfaction, not of some inner need, but of the desire for success in accomplishing a particular task. As Ford and Urban (1967) have indicated, it is this attention to behavior initiated through thoughtful, conscious planning that separates the ego-analysts from the classical psychoanalysts. The ego-analysts acknowledge that some behavior is caused by events of which the individual is not aware, but they also maintain that most behavior is caused by events in the individual's environment.

One of the most important events in the development of the normal ego is the development of communication skills, which allows the child to deal in abstractions. The child learns to differentiate between the symbol for apple and the apple itself by learning that the latter will satisfy the need for food but the symbol will not. Development of this skill allows the child to think about events without actually experiencing them. Hence, the individual can imaginatively experience a trip to the moon without actually facing the dangers of such a trip.

The development of language skills also increases the individual's ability to differentiate among objects within her or his environment by formulating abstractions. According to King and Neal (1968), the child now has the power to understand that being bitten by one dog does not mean that all dogs will bite, and thereby avoids the overgeneralization that all dogs are bad. If the individual cannot make such an abstraction after being bitten by a dog, he or she will fear all dogs.

Equally important is development of the ability to delay termination or satisfaction of some behavior elicitor. As Erikson (1946) pointed out, it is the individual's ability to retain habitual patterns of behavior to bring satisfaction that provides identity. In the face of deprivation of satisfaction, the individual must be able to recall times when satisfaction occurred after a similar period of deprivation and, following that, learn to anticipate a future event that will lead to satisfaction. This calls for the development of control over one's drives. The individual who continually seeks immediate gratification of needs will be constantly subjected to situations that cause tension and anxiety.

One of the major influences on the development of the ego and its functions is the significant others with whom the individual comes in contact. According to

Hartmann (1964), the child learns from these others certain methods for coping with and solving problems. Fromm (1947) suggested that personality develops through the process of relating oneself to the world, by acquiring and assimilating things from the world in order to satisfy one's needs and by relationships with other people. Fromm called this process of identification with other people in the environment the socialization process. It begins with the childrearing practices of the parents and then is extended to others with whom the child interacts. This process plays a dominant role in the development of the individual's life-style in that it provides the individual with a pattern of behaviors that will allow him or her to operate within the society (Fromm, 1947).

Thus, the ego-analysts tend not to emphasize the negative effects of society on the individual as Freud did, but acknowledge the equal importance of its positive effects. This emphasis on the importance of the society in shaping behavior allows the ego-analysts to be more optimistic about the individual's potential for modifying behavior later in life. They accept the premise that the basic patterns of behavior are established during the first six years of life, but they regard them as only a base on which new behaviors are built throughout life. The key to the development of normal personality is the ability to develop new patterns of behavior or modify old ones to cope with new demands. As Kubie (1958) pointed out, the development of a normal personality requires that the individual be flexible. This flexibility confers the freedom to learn through experience; the ability to listen, evaluate, reason, feel, and adapt to changing internal and external demands; the freedom to respond to rewards and punishments; and the ability to recognize the achievement of satisfaction. A person lacking this flexibility will cease to develop or will regress to earlier patterns of behavior in the hierarchy. Either way, she or he can then be said to be behaving abnormally.

Ego-analytic theory implies that people, through conscious effort, learn new patterns of behaving. They select ways of behaving that seem appropriate. People are not subject solely to behavior elicitors outside their awareness, but are instead active agents in choosing and directing personal behavior. These behaviors, used often enough, become automatic and do not require conscious thought. For instance, a child learning the complicated behavior pattern of hitting a baseball with a bat must at first think about what she or he is doing; with increasing proficiency, however, the child no longer gives conscious thought to all the procedures required, but perhaps to where to hit the ball. This, too, with repetition becomes an automatic behavior. Patterns of behavior build upon one another in a related network or system (Rapaport, 1951). According to Ford and Urban (1967), these patterns of behavior may become quite independent of the original reason for their existence. A behavior originally used to respond to a physiological need may subsequently be used to respond to an event unrelated to the original need. In this situation the ego has made an active choice of a behavior to reach a particular goal. This is just one way in which the ego functions in an active, adaptive fashion. The following section deals with those functions in more detail.

EGO FUNCTIONS

Ego-analysts tend to view the functions of the ego in a broad, positive manner. In the traditional analytic view, ego functions involve the use of repression, projection, and other Freudian defense mechanisms that emphasize protective or regressive behavior. In the ego-analytic view, the ego functions are employed to cope with the environment through the use of reasoning and conscious thought processes. The analytic processes look to the past, the ego-analytic ones to the future. According to Kroeber (1964), the defensive functions of the ego are dominated by rigidity and the distortion of present reality, whereas the conscious coping functions of the ego are dominated by the reality of the situation and are flexible. The ego-analytic approach emphasizes the individual's ability to deal with the environment and personal needs positively instead of defensively.

The three categories of ego functions established by Kroeber (1964) are impulse economics, cognitive functions, and controlling functions.

Impulse Economics

Impulse economics is the ability to control impulses and channel them into acceptable and usable behavior. In classic psychoanalytic theory, the individual deals with impulses by displacement, repression, or reaction-formation. The latter two processes amount to denying the impulse; displacement involves finding another outlet for it. Even in displacement, however, the ego is being reactive. If, instead of these behaviors, an individual chooses to deal with impulses in a more positive way, she or he will cope with the impulse by redirecting its expression or by delaying satisfaction of the impulse until a more appropriate time. Functioning thus, the ego is being active and positive, not reactive. An example is a male and female who delay sexual gratification with each other until marriage because they believe it is the right action to take.

Cognitive Function

Like impulse economics, the cognitive function of the ego can be used either defensively or positively. A person who uses the cognitive function negatively distorts reality through such mechanisms as intellectualization and rationalization. In contrast, a person who chooses to deal with his or her feelings copes with the situation by developing objectivity. In this instance the individual is exercising the ability to analyze the situation and logically think through a solution (Kroeber, 1964).

Controlling Functions

The controlling functions of the ego allow the individual to develop ability to concentrate on the current task without being affected by personal feelings. They permit the development of flexible behavior rather than regression to past behaviors. They also promote awareness of others' feelings. On the other hand, an individual using the controlling functions in a defensive manner will ascribe her or his feelings to others, will regress to earlier patterns of behavior when confronted by a difficult situation, and will simply deny awareness to feelings that are painful.

There are two keys to the ego-analysts' view of personality development and use of the ego functions. One is the importance they assign to people's ability to respond to external situations. The other is the exercise of conscious control in responding to behavior elicitors. In the ego-analysts' view, people often direct their behavior through active cognition and may respond either in a rigid, defensive manner or in a more positive, coping manner. The ego-analysts regard personality as a structure, or pattern, of behaviors interrelated with a network of independent systems. Some of these patterns are developed in response to innate psychological needs. As individuals mature, they develop more and more of these patterns through conscious thought processes in response to new situations.

THE DEVELOPMENT OF ABNORMAL BEHAVIOR

Ego-analysts contend that abnormal behavior results from a breakdown in the normal ego functions.

In an individual with a normal pattern of behavior, the ego functions establish patterns of behavior that cope successfully with the demands of environmental experience. These patterns develop into a network of behaviors that constitute the person's life-style. The behaviors are increasingly under the conscious, thoughtful control of the individual. When a situation or a series of events causes the individual to lose this self-control, the result is a behavioral breakdown. That is, when an individual is threatened or overwhelmed by a situation and behavior moves from conscious control to unconscious control, the potential exists for a behavioral disorder (Rapaport, 1958). This occurs, the ego-analysts believe, when the ego functions have not been strong enough to cope with the demands of the particular situation, and the ego functions surrender control of behavior to the id. In their view, this breakdown in the ego functions generally results from inadequate ego development during some phase of the psychosocial stages of development. A breakdown in one of the ego functions, however, or the ego's failure to exert control in a particular kind of situation, does not necessarily indicate a total breakdown of the ego. Some behavior patterns may continue to operate normally. Because all patterns of behavior are interrelated, however, it is necessary to understand the whole system of behaviors (Hartmann, 1953). The malfunction of one pattern of behavior in response to a particular situation is related to the function of the entire system. In battle, for example, one person will react to the stress abnormally, while another will not. Individual differences in reacting to stress reflect the different patterns of stable behavior that the individuals have developed.

What causes an individual to lose control over his or her behavior? What renders the ego unable to deal with situations that it handled adequately earlier? According to Rapaport (1958), a particular pattern of behavior can be maintained only as long as the behavior receives some reward. For example, a child who has developed a basic trust in individuals (Erikson's first stage) will interact with others in a trusting and open fashion. This pattern of behavior will continue as long as it is rewarded by others. If, however, at some period the trusting behavior consistently encounters rejection or hostility from others, the trusting behavior will begin to disappear; the ego loses its ability to behave in a trusting fashion. This loss is the germination of maladaptive behavior, for now the individual, even when presented with a situation calling for trust, will be unable to respond, because the behavior has been eliminated. As Erikson stated, the fact that the ego learns the appropriate behavior at one stage does not mean that the behavior is permanent. Individual behaviors are continually modified through encounters with the problems of existence (Erikson, 1963).

Abnormal patterns of behavior, then, develop when the individual loses the capacity to respond appropriately. This may happen because previously adequate behavior has not been reinforced and the pattern of behavior is no longer usable. An extreme example is a sustained period of stimulation deprivation such as the U.S. hostages experienced in Iran. A second cause of abnormal behavior is the inadequacy of current patterns of behavior to meet the demands of a situation: the individual loses control because the ego has not developed sufficiently to cope in an appropriate way. Rapaport cited the emergence of puberty as an example of a new situation for which a person may not have built an adequate pattern of behavior. In this case the sexual urge will dominate until the individual has learned patterns of behavior that will bring the sexual urge under conscious control.

In the ego-analytic view, then, abnormal behavior does not reflect a total failure of the ego but a breakdown in a particular pattern of behavior. The normal individual has an ego that is flexible and capable of changing with the demands of the environment as well as the demands of internal drives; the abnormal individual has patterns of behavior that are inflexible to the demands of environment or to internal demands.

The ego-analysts attribute more conscious control of behavior to the individual than do the Freudians. The ego-analysts also attribute more power to external events in eliciting and affecting individual behavior. In their view the behavior, and indeed the personality, of the individual are affected not only by early childhood experiences, as in the Freudian view, but also by environment and the subsequent strength of ego functions as they develop throughout life.

THE GOALS OF COUNSELING

The goals of ego-counseling are, in a sense, more limited than those of classic psychoanalytic therapy. Ego-counselors attempt to help clients with one or two specific ego defects that are causing difficulty. According to Kroeber (1964), counselors do not view clients in terms of their defense mechanisms, but instead attempt to help them divert their energy from maladaptive to adaptive behavior. Ego-counselors, then, look for specific maladaptive ego functions within the individual, not for unconscious evidence of a traumatic event in infancy. Ego-counselors try to help clients see and understand their maladaptive behavior, and then to help build new ego functions that are more adaptive. The chief goal is to help each individual develop what Erikson (1963) might call a sense of ego-integrity.

THE COUNSELING PROCESS

Ego-counseling focuses on normal and conscious characteristics rather than on unconscious motivations or internal causes of behavior. To this end the counseling relationship is reality and present oriented. The emphasis is on the cognitive rather than the conative domain. This does not mean that during counseling certain material that the client has repressed will not be brought out and dealt with, nor that strong affective feelings are not expressed in ego-counseling. What it does mean is that the ego-counselor tends to be more concerned with today's behaviors than with past ones. The goal is to help the client with today's situation, not yesterday's.

In discussing the prime concerns of the ego-counselor, Hartmann (1961) emphasized the need to understand the whole behavior system of the client, both habitual behavior patterns that are functioning normally and those that are functioning abnormally. The counselor must strive to understand both parts of the ego: those that are strong, and those that are weak and unable to cope with either innate needs or the demands of the individual's environment. The ego-counselor acknowledges that innate needs or drives may cause discomfort, and thus abnormal behavior. However, the emphasis is on the situational threats that cause the individual to deal ineffectively with such events. The counselor attempts to help the client understand in what respect his or her behavior is not functional and what the client can do to change.

Ego-counseling, then, is much less intense and of shorter duration than psychoanalysis. Although both counseling and psychotherapy are concerned with personality, the ego-counselor is not concerned with reshaping the whole personality. As Bordin pointed out, "Personality is dealt with only as it bears on the decision or problem situation and the client is not encouraged to go much further afield (1955, p. 336). In Hummel's view, "It seems foreign to the concept of a counseling process intended to further normal (ego) development, to commit this process to extensive efforts at personality reorganization" (1962, p. 466). The counselor's tasks are to keep the specific goals of counseling in mind and to direct the counselor relationship so that its emphasis is on the current problem. Consequently, "the counselor influences the counseling deliberations as early as his assessment of a counselee warrants, so that a gradual focus is made on a set of counselee constructs with relation to some (significant) role or relationship in reality" (Hummel, 1962, p. 469). The counselor accomplishes this task by giving selective attention to the client and by defining the counseling relationship. The emphasis of counseling is on rational thought processes and on the cognitive dimensions of the relationship.

In essence, then, the counselor, not the client, controls the nature of the relationship. This control, however, is not mechanistic. The counselor must be warm and spontaneous, and the client must perceive the counselor as someone not only professionally competent but also concerned with the client and willing to make some commitment. This requires that the counselor be a good and objective listener. A counselor must communicate both acceptance and a willingness to help; at the same time the counselor must maintain an objective frame of reference in order to help. Without this objectivity, the counselor's own need pattern may intrude itself. If a counselor responds to a client by suggesting solutions that have worked for herself or himself, it is likely that the counselor has become too involved to be effective. On the other hand, as Bordin (1955) pointed out, some involvement is necessary; it is difficult to understand the feelings of others without relying to some extent on personal emotional experience. The important concern is not to let those emotional experiences intefere with meeting the needs of the client. According to Hummel (1962), the ego-counselor is aware of the power of the relationship, but is also aware that not only feelings, but also facts, alternatives, and decisions must be examined and resolved.

The counseling relationship, then, is one in which one individual, the client, comes to another, the counselor, seeking help with a problem. The counselor is a professionally trained individual who should be able to give this aid. For counseling to be effective, both people must be committed to solving the particular concern. A solution is best accomplished in an atmosphere of mutual trust, understanding, and acceptance. The counselor, by virtue of professional training, is responsible for controlling the relationship so that the client can achieve optimum growth. The emphasis of the counseling process is upon helping the client understand how her or his behavior in certain situations has been maladaptive, and then helping the client develop new patterns of behavior that are adaptive.

Because ego-counseling is concerned with relatively normal individuals who function adequately in most situations but are troubled by specific concerns, the duration of counseling is relatively short, usually five to six sessions. "We are assuming that a relatively well-integrated person can make use of a brief counseling experience to set in motion a learning process that carries far beyond the relationship itself" (Bordin, 1955, p. 334). By the end of the counseling period, the client should feel capable of dealing effectively with new situations as he or she encounters them. The counseling process is best terminated on a positive note, so that when new difficulties arise, the individual will not feel the need for a counselor.

TECHNIQUES OF EGO-COUNSELING

The techniques utilized in ego-counseling are not a set of prescribed, inflexible methods. They are a set of preferred attitudes and stategies for the counselor to use while respecting the client's right to be an individual (Hummel, 1962).

INITIAL BEHAVIOR OF COUNSELOR

The process of counseling begins when a client comes to the counselor seeking assistance with a difficulty. In the initial stages of counseling it is the responsibility of the counselor to try to develop an understanding of the client and to tell the client the rules by which they will operate. In this respect ego-counseling resembles other theoretical approaches. Bordin (1955) emphasized that the counselor must allow as much freedom to the client as possible in these early stages. Given this freedom, the client can express her or his concerns, which in turn will enable the counselor to define the task before them. In ego-counseling it is essentially the counselor who defines the task, after careful attention to what the client has presented. As Bordin (1955) indicated, the inexperienced counselor is often not patient enough to listen carefully and completely to the client before defining the problem area or task.

CONTROL OF PROCESS

Once the client and counselor have established a relationship that permits them to define the client's difficulty, it is the responsibility of the counselor, as the professionally trained person in the relationship, to maintain focus on the task. The counseling is designed to build the ego strength of the individual, but the expertise of the counselor facilitates the process. The counselor selects the aspects of the individual's problem to work on and keeps the relationship focused on this goal. "The counselor does this by selective responsiveness and by helping the client to establish greater intellectual control over other conflicting responses" (Bordin 1955, p. 340). The counselor discourages wide digressions, in the belief that the best course is to work on one concern at a time. Once that concern is resolved, investigation of another area of concern is appropriate.

The counselor also guides the relationship by controlling the cognitive and conative dimensions of the client's expressions. The cognitive dimension refers to overt behaviors or expressions; the conative dimension refers to the individual's emotions. The aim of the counselor is to keep a balance between the two dimensions. Counseling cannot be geared only to the expression of emotion, because most client problems also have a cognitive or reality component. Nor can counseling be geared only to the cognitive aspects of the problem while ignoring the client's feelings about the problem. The ego-counselor strives for a balance between the dimensions by not letting the client communicate in one dimension to the exclusion of the other.

CONTROL OF AMBIGUITY IN THE RELATIONSHIP

The counselor's use of ambiguity is another technique designed to facilitate the counseling process. Ambiguity, or lack of structure within a particular situation, is necessary in counseling so that a client does not feel compelled by the situation to behave or respond in prescribed ways. In general, the counselor should strive to establish a highly ambiguous situation in the early stages of counseling so that the client will feel free to express herself or himself. The counselor must define some areas of the relationship, such as what topics are appropriate and what the limits are on the client-counselor relationship, but the counselor should keep in mind that the more defined the relationship, the less ambiguous the situation. Nondirective techniques, which involve little talking by the counselor, increase the ambiguity of the relationship; directive techniques, in which the counselor takes the lead in the interaction process, decrease ambiguity.

It is important that the degree of ambiguity offered be appropriate to the client's problem. Generally, the more cognitive the problem, the less ambiguity needed. Bordin (1955) suggested three specific purposes for the use of ambiguity in the counseling relationship. First, an ambiguous counseling context provides a background against which the feelings of the client can be contrasted. Second, ambiguity elicits responses from the client that represent unique aspects of his or her personality. Third, the eliciting of these responses facilitates the deveopment of transference through projection. Transference enables the counselor to understand the reasons for the client's behavior. Thus, ambiguity facilitates the process whereby the counselor comes to understand the personality of the client and the accompanying behavioral patterns, both those that are appropriate and those that are inappropriate.

The inexperienced counselor often will present a very ambiguous situation to a client without realizing its implications. This may leave the client with so few guidelines that he or she becomes uncomfortable with the process and quickly terminates, or it may act to encourage a very intense relationship, which the client may not be equipped to handle.

TRANSFERENCE

Although ego-analysts acknowledge that transference may occur in counseling, they do not ascribe to it the importance that Freud did. In the classic sense, transference occurs when the client displaces feelings from previous situations onto the therapist; the therapist becomes a substitute figure for a person from the client's past. The ego-analysts believe that a phenomenon resembling transference occurs, but they describe it only as a feeling developed by the client for the counselor. In general, they believe the essentially normal individual can work through his or her problems in the counseling relationship without relying on a full-fledged transference. Hummel (1962), for example, contended that for most clients the use of transference is unnecessary and is, in fact, inappropriate for those who are relatively free of crippling neurotic defenses. Nevertheless the counselor must be aware of the possibility and sensitive to the potential use of phenomena resembling transference, if they occur. Often, carefully confronting the client with what is happening will lead to positive therapeutic exchanges about the event.

COUNTERTRANSFERENCE

Countertransference is essentially the opposite of transference. It is a counselor's feeling for a client, based on past or external events. As such, it is a disruptive force that the counselor must control. The counselor cannot allow personal feelings toward the client to enter into the counseling process. Sexual attraction to a client, for example, could interfere with the process of counseling, and the counselor must be carefully attuned to reactions to the client to prevent their interference with the process.

DIAGNOSIS AND INTERPRETATION

The counselor's control of the dimensions of the counseling relationship facilitates the client's self-exploration, which in turn enables the counselor to achieve a full understanding of the client. Based on that understanding, the counselor makes a tentative diagnosis of the problem. Although this diagnosis should not be imposed on the client, the counselor is responsible for defining the problem, sharing the diagnosis with the client, and helping him or her to understand it fully. The primary technique for helping the client achieve this understanding is interpretation. The counselor uses interpretation to help the client crystallize thoughts or feelings, to compare conflicting ideas, and to point out the defense mechanisms that are being misused. Through interpretation, the counselor attempts to put what the client has said into a more understandable perspective so that the latter can see the reasons for her or his behavior or feelings. "The counselor introduces new meanings into the discourse as one who is trying not to convert the counselee, but to join him in a mutual effort at comprehension" (Hummel, 1962, p. 475). Even though the counselor is the acknowledged expert, she or he must take care not to impose an interpretation or diagnosis on the client or to use interpretation too early in the process. In either case the client may resist the interpretation by establishing defense mechanisms even more firmly. Thus, the timing of the interpretation is extremely important, and the counselor must be aware of the client's readiness to deal with it. Only when the client is ready will the interpretation be meaningful and help in the counseling process.

BUILDING NEW EGO FUNCTIONS

Once the client understands the problem, counseling focuses on development of new behaviors—new ego functions. This part of the process may be very cognitive in nature; the counselor may actually instruct the individual in the proper way to behave, utilizing a role rehearsal technique in which the client practices new behaviors within the safe confines of the counseling office before trying them in a real situation. The counselor may also assign homework in which the client must try some new behaviors to strengthen the ego so that it can function more appropriately in the situations that were causing difficulty.

SUMMARY

The ego-counselor's principal techniques are methods for controlling the counseling relationship. These consist chiefly in balancing the cognitive-conative dimension and in controlling the amount of ambiguity offered to the client. Within this context the counselor comes to understand the client's difficulties from the expressions and behaviors the latter exhibits in the counseling relationship. These behaviors and expressions are often elicited through the use of modified or moderate transference phenomena. Once the counselor understands the client's difficulty, he or she attempts to bring the client to that understanding through the use of interpretative statements, taking into account the client's readiness to accept the interpretation. Once the client understands the problem, the counselor and client begin to discuss, and then practice, new modes of behaving.

Hummel (1962, pp. 479–480) outlined a series of steps that a typical ego-counselor and client might follow. The client's problem in this example is academic study.

1. The counselor first helps the client examine feelings about his or her life, and performance in school, and other school-related tasks.
2. The counselor encourages the client to project herself or himself into the future, to discuss career and life goals. The counselor then attempts to get the client to see some relationship between present behavior and future goals.
3. The counselor attempts to discuss with the client obstacles to the client's reaching those goals and how these obstacles might be removed.
4. As the discussion of obstacles continues, the counselor through interpretation and reflection attempts to get the client to examine herself or himself and external circumstances. In addition, the counselor attempts to get the client to see the interrelated nature of his or her feelings and behaviors.
5. Finally, the counselor helps the client establish a revised set of intentions in relation to academic study, and then, if possible, to rehearse new behaviors. The rehearsal involves getting the client to envision how she or he will behave in various hypothetical situations, such as setting up a study schedule.

In effect, the purpose of ego-counseling is to produce changes not only in specific behavior—in the example, better grades—but also in "the complex of meanings and organizing principles which guide the counselee in his transactions within the sector of academic study" (Hummel, 1962, p. 479).

Although ego-counseling is based largely on classic psychoanalytic theory, ego-counselors believe that ego functions control or account for more of individual behavior than the psychoanalysts indicate. They attribute a large part of a person's behavior to conscious control. Hence, they tend to give more credit to the role of environment in a person's development and subsequent behavior. Ego-counseling is also much more concerned with relatively normal individuals and with helping these develop stronger, more fully functioning egos, instead of placing emphasis on the abnormal and complete personality reorganization.

Ego-counseling is designed to help individuals develop the coping aspects of the personality. It is designed to help people cope with the realities of the world through building ego functions. As Grossman (1964) pointed out, ego-counseling is concerned with getting the ego to the point that it can deal with problems in the real world, while helping the individual to eliminate the defense mechanisms that hinder interaction with the real world.

REFERENCES

Bordin, E. S. Psychological counseling. New York: Appleton-Century-Crofts, 1955.

Brammer, L. M., & Shostrom, E. L. Therapeutic psychology: Fundamentals of counseling and psychotherapy (3rd ed.). Englewood Cliffs, N.J.: Prentice-Hall, 1977.

Erikson, E. H. Ego development and historical change. In The psychoanalytic study of the child (Vol. 2). New York: International Universities Press, 1946.

———. Youth: Change and challenge. New York: Basic Books, 1963.

Ford, D. H., & Urban, H. B. Systems of psychotherapy: A comparative study. New York: John Wiley and Sons, 1967.

Fromm, E. Man for himself. New York: Rinehart, 1947.

Grossman, D. Ego activating approaches to psychotherapy. Psychoanalytic Review, 1964, 51, 65–68.

Hartmann, H. Contribution to the metapsychology of schizophrenia. In The psychoanalytic study of the child (Vol. 8). New York: International Universities Press, 1953.

———. The mutual influence in the develop-ment of ego and id. Psychoanalytic Quarterly, 1961, 20, 31–43.

———. Essays on ego psychology. New York: International Universities Press, 1964.

———. Psychoanalysis as a scientific theory. In T. Millon (Ed.) Theories of psychopathology. Philadelphia: W. B. Saunders, 1967.

Hummel, R. C. Ego-counseling in guidance: Concept and method. Harvard Educational Review, 1962, 32, 461–482.

King, P. T., & Neal, R. Ego-psychology in counseling. Boston: Houghton Mifflin, 1968.

Kroeber, T. C. The coping functions of the ego-mechanisms. In R. W. White (Ed.), The study of lives. New York: Atherton Press, 1964.

Kubie, L. The neurotic distortion of the creative process. Manhattan, Kansas: University of Kansas Press, 1958.

Rapaport, D. The organization and pathology of thought. New York: Columbia University Press, 1951.

———. The theory of ego autonomy: A generalization. Bulletin of Menninger Clinic, 1958, 22, 13–35.

INDIVIDUAL PSYCHOLOGY OF ALFRED ADLER

CHAPTER FOUR

Alfred Adler, though often thought of as a student of Freud, was more of a colleague; younger than Freud by 14 years, he was already a practicing physician when he joined Freud and others to form the Vienna Psychoanalytic Society. In 1911, however, Adler's thinking had evolved to the point that he broke with Freud and the Vienna Psychoanalytic Society. Adler's development of what became known as individual psychology "had an immediate influence on people outside the analytic professions: on teachers, doctors, criminologists, and the man in the street" (Munroe, 1955, p. 355). This probably was because Adler's concepts were both less shocking and easier to understand than Freud's (Munroe, 1955). Over the years, however, Adler's influence seemed to diminish; in 1955 Munroe wrote, in her text, *Schools of Psychoanalytic Thought,* "Adlerian theory is no longer vivid" (p. 335). She did add in a footnote that she had been told a renaissance was beginning, and that statement proved true. In the last twenty years individual psychology has experienced a rebirth. Individual psychology societies today are believed to number more than 20,000 lay and professional members (Allen, 1971). Other approaches have incorporated many of the concepts originally developed by Adler. According to Ellenberger, "It would not be easy to find another author from which so much has been borrowed from all sides without acknowledgment than Alfred Adler" (1970, p. 645). Given this renewed, widespread influence, let us examine the thinking that generated it.

THEORY OF PERSONALITY DEVELOPMENT

STRUCTURE OF PERSONALITY

Adler's split with Freud centered on Freud's theory that humans are social beings driven by aggressive and sexual drives. Adler came to believe that the individual is not driven solely to satisfy personal pleasure but is also motivated by a sense of social responsibility and a need to achieve. Adler's concept of this need to achieve has often been misunderstood. Basically, it amounts to a common humanistic notion that "the individual is engaged in the striving for self-realization, in contributing to his fellowman, in making the world a better place to live" (Mosak & Dreikurs, 1973, p. 40).

Adler saw each individual as a consistent and unified entity striving toward a chosen life goal. Each individual chooses a goal and develops unique, characteristic ways of attempting to reach it. Adler believed that the way to understand an individual is to find out what her or his goal is, then to determine the life-style the individual has developed to reach it.

The Adlerian position emphasizes the interaction of the environment, heredity, and the individual as the determinants of behavior. Adler contended that the individual's perception of events, not the event itself, determines behavior. An objective event in an individual's life—a physical deficiency, broken home, or an intolerable teacher—influences the individual's responses only indirectly. The actual event may affect the likelihood that a particular behavior will develop, but in itself does not determine behavior. Most important is how an individual perceives and interprets such events, and there are innumerable ways of perceiving any given event. Adler referred to these individual perceptions as fictions and emphasized that they are not to be confused with reality. Nevertheless, each individual behaves as though the fictions are reality. This is a phenomenological rather than deterministic view of personality and behavior.

Life Goal

Adler believed that in addition to creating fictions of real events each individual develops a personal fictional goal as part of an effort to overcome inherent weaknesses in relation to the world. The attainment of the goal represents overcoming this inherent weakness and securing ultimate happiness. Just as the individual's interpretations of events are fictions, so the goal he or she chooses is a fiction. In Adler's view, this fictional goal serves as the unifying force for each individual; all individual behavior is directed toward the accomplishment of the chosen goal and is an operating force in day-to-day behavior. "[The individual] will continuously interpret the daily happenings of life in the perspective of his fictional goal" (Bischof, 1970, p. 181). Adler referred to this pattern of the individual's behavior as his life-style.

Life-Style

Adler felt that if an individual is to achieve superiority, it is necessary to live in accordance with her or his unique directional pattern, or life-style. This life-style is a product of the person's inner, self-driven and determined direction of behavior and of his or her environment, which influences the direction the inner self will take (Bischof, 1970). "Schematically the life-style may be seen as a syllogism: 'I am. . . . The world is. . . . Therefore. . . .'" (Allen, 1971, p. 5). What follows the *therefore* dictates what the individual will do with his life. Adler believed that everyone goes through this process of judging the status of self and the status of the world and, based on those perceived judgments, begins to form a pattern of behavior that becomes the life-style.

Social Interest

Adler also emphasized the importance of the social context of human behavior. He believed that individuals are born with an interest in other humans. Like other drives, social interests need contact to be activated, but in this case the activation is automatic (Bischof, 1970). The child's interactions, first within the family and then with others, establish certain conditions for the types of behaviors that may develop (Ansbacher & Ansbacher, 1956). All human behavior is interaction with other beings. "For this reason, we can presume one basic desire in all human beings; the desire to belong, which Adler called 'social interest' " (Dreikurs, 1961, p. 60). Hence, whatever a person does is done in relation to a social group. Consequently, Adler believed, the only way to study human behavior effectively is within the social context. For this reason Adler considered his theory of human behavior a social psychology (Ansbacher & Ansbacher, 1956). To understand how these concepts affect the development of the individual, we need to examine Adler's sequence of personality development.

Adler believed that most of what an individual becomes in adult life is formed during the first four or five years of existence. During this time the child develops a notion of self, a pattern of behavior, and a life-style and begins to select a life goal, the attainment of which represents all that is good and toward which all behavior will be directed.

Adler believed that every individual is born with a feeling of inferiority. The infant is helpless in its environment. Even if it is born perfectly developed and normal, it is completely dependent on others. Almost everything it perceives is bigger and more competent. An additional burden exists if the infant has a physical defect. Adler contended that the infant soon perceives this inferiority and that this results in an uncomfortable internal state. This feeling is extended through early childhood as the child continually confronts his or her inability to be self-sufficient and people who can play ball, tie shoes, button shirts, and the like better than she or he. This process is normal, inevitable, and occurs in everyone to some degree. Adler contended that this basic feeling of inferiority is the ultimate driving force of humans. The child, perceiving its inferiority, begins to try to find ways to reduce the uncomfortable feelings caused by its subjective evaluation of self. The direct consequence of this feeling of inferiority is a striving for superiority. This concept should not be confused with a drive toward social eminence or leadership. Rather, it is a basic drive within each individual to master her or his environment. This force, Adler contended, causes a person always to be moving forward and improving his or her situation. "All our functions follow its direction. They strive for conquest, security, increase, either in the right or in the wrong direction. The impetus from minus to plus never ends. The urge from below to above never ceases" (Adler, 1930, p. 398). Essentially, each individual has two types of goals: immediate and long-term (life goal). Immediate goals are related to the life or long-term goals and are easily observed in day-to-day interaction. The long-term goals reflect private inner logic and the individual's basic outlook on life (Dreikurs, 1957).

The child, in its search for ways of dealing with a world in which it feels inferior, first creates some internal order by using an inherent capacity to attend to certain events in the environment and then interpreting these events. In effect, the child builds a world of perceptions about events. This process involves active participation. Adler did not believe that people are simply blank screens on which life experiences are drawn. Rather, an individual's perceptions of experience are affected by internal expectations. Thus, someone suffering from paranoia will perceive even the most favorable intentions from others as somewhat hostile. This concept is much like what we commonly refer to as the self-fulfilling prophecy. A person who expects hostility will probably behave in ways that will generate hostility. Throughout childhood the individual develops an increasing number of these perceptions, and they become habitual as well as interrelated. Soon the child has an organized picture of his or her world, a picture that is partly accurate and partly inaccurate. Some of these perceptions, or fictions, involve future objectives, the attainment of which will allow the child to value herself or himself as superior, removing the unpleasant feelings created by the feeling of inferiority.

In conjunction with the fictional goal, the child's innate social interest is also developed. In Adler's view, favorable conditions in the child's early interactions with family members encourage this social interest (Dreikurs, 1957). Because these responses are developed in conjunction with other behaviors, striving for superiority becomes fused with social interests. In this way the child becomes a social being, seeking to attain her or his goal in ways that will also benefit others. One of the best ways to overcome the uncomfortable feeling created by feelings of inferiority is to believe that one is contributing to the welfare of others and is therefore valuable (Ansbacher & Ansbacher, 1956).

As the child matures, he or she begins to focus on one particular goal, which serves as the organizing element for all personal behavior. The child projects this goal in the belief that its attainment will overcome all obstacles and bring perfect security. This unique goal determines the individual's interests, the situations that summon involvement, and the kinds of behaviors he or she is most likely to develop.

Once the child has selected a goal to work toward and established habitual patterns of behavior designed to reach it, she or he has developed a life-style, the most comprehensive level of behavior. The individual's life-style dictates all that is considered his or her personality; "it is the whole that commands the parts" (Hall & Lindzey, 1957, p. 123). Everyone has the same ultimate goal of superiority, but the objective and the manner of seeking it are unique. In this way Adler accounted for human individuality.

The development of life-style conforms with the three basic tenets of Adlerian psychology: self-determination, teleology, and holism (Dreikurs, 1971). Adlerians hold that individuals determine their own behavior; external events do not. They also believe that the chosen behavior is goal directed; it is purposeful, not random. Finally, unlike Freud, they believe that individuals cannot be subdivided into parts; people behave holistically. Adlerians, then, perceive individuals as self-controlled people who move toward their chosen goal as unified wholes.

This life-style, once formed, rarely undergoes change, but the specific behaviors an individual uses to bring about the desired end often do change as situations demand. For example, a young child may use whining behavior to achieve a certain goal, but later in life finds that whining no longer works and so changes behaviors, perhaps asking for things in a favorable way. The goal has not changed, only the means used to achieve it. Once the individual has selected a life goal and developed a life-style to achieve that goal, it is very difficult, and even painful, to change it. She or he may change elements within the system, but is reluctant to abandon the system itself.

In Adler's view, people's life-styles have developed by about the age of five years. From that time on, their personality retains the same basic form and dictates everything they do (Ansbacher & Ansbacher, 1956). Adler believed, however, that people are not fully aware of their life-style: they cannot explain it to themselves because much of it has been formed before they developed the ability to symbolize events through language. This explains not only why people do not understand all of their behavior, but also why their patterns of behavior remain relatively unchanged throughout life. It is difficult for someone to change behavior that cannot be verbalized. This is one of the prime reasons why people who are experiencing difficulty need someone else to explain their life-style to them.

In summary, Adler viewed personality development in terms of the child's struggle to remove herself or himself from a position of inferiority to a place of superiority. To accomplish this task, the child forms fictions as a means of bringing some sense of order out of the environment. Part of these fictions are the goals toward which the individual moves in order to remove a feeling of inferiority. Gradually the individual selects one goal around which he or she organizes behavior and fuses this with an innate social interest to form a unique life-style. At this point the primary personality of the individual develops. This primary personality may undergo minor changes during the person's lifetime, but its basic form remains stable.

We now consider what happens within this normal progression to account for abnormal behavior.

ABNORMAL DEVELOPMENT

In Adler's view, the basic cause of abnormal or maladaptive behavior is a heightened sense of inferiority. Abnormality, as he saw it, is a result of developing heightened feelings of inferiority early in life; in an attempt to deal with the overwhelming tension created by these feelings, the individual develops inappropriate patterns of behavior to overcompensate for the inferiority. Adler contended that the three main reasons an individual develops increased feelings of inferiority are being born with a physical or mental defect, being pampered by parents, and being subjected to neglect.

PHYSICAL AND MENTAL DEFECTS

Adler believed that children who are born physically defective do not necessarily develop increased feelings of inferiority. The original, organic inferiority does, however, play a central role in development. Some individuals never overcome their feelings of inferiority and develop failure life-styles. Others somehow compensate for their physical defects and achieve normal life patterns. Still others may overcompensate; these and the people who have adopted failure life-styles are most apt to develop abnormal patterns of behavior.

Mental defects are much more difficult to overcome than physical ones. Compensation is difficult in a world that relies on and gives highest esteem to brain power. This, Adlerians claim, is the reason for more maladaptive behavior in the mentally defective than in those with a physical defect (Bischof, 1970).

For a child born with either a physical or mental defect the important factor is not the defect itself. It is the child's reaction to the event and the reactions of others that influence the path of development. If the child's reaction is positive, development may follow a normal course. If, on the other hand, the child and those around him or her react to the defect as a serious liability, the probability of abnormal development increases.

DEFECTS IN CHILDREARING

Adler also stressed that abnormal or maladaptive behavior is often a product of environmental forces, generally parental behaviors, acting upon the young child. He felt that a child who is pampered and constantly cared for will come to see himself or herself as lacking self-sufficiency, which increases feelings of inferiority.

A child who is given no opportunity to try things and to experience her or his own successes and failures will not develop autonomy and self-control. Such a child is likely to become egocentric, seeking a sense of superiority by taking from others. In Adler's view, this is the personality development most harmful for both the individual and society.

Similarly, the child who is neglected is not likely to develop normally. The neglected child, given no direction, must rely completely on trial and error in order to learn; even when the child achieves some minimal success, the parents provide no reward for accomplishment. As a result the individual develops a lackadaisical life-style that brings neither personal satisfaction nor happiness to others (Bischof, 1970). Such a person causes society less harm than the pampered child but is just as harmful to himself or herself.

Once the individual has developed an unusual amount of tension because of increased feelings of inferiority, the likelihood of subsequent abnormal behavior increases. One form this behavior takes is an overstriving for superiority. In an attempt to deal with tension, the individual establishes an extremely high fictional goal, and the behavior for reaching that goal will probably be extremely rigid. Adler likened it to seeking a godlike state of perfection.

Another result of intense feelings of inferiority is inadequate development of social interest. The child who is pampered, neglected, or in some way treated as different is not likely to have human encounters that encourage expectations of satisfactory interactions with others. This leads the child to conclude that cooperation with others in pursuit of her or his goals is unlikely to prove fruitful (Ansbacher & Ansbacher, 1956). As a result the child selects objectives designed to satisfy personal needs without any consideration of common objectives that may also serve others. Developing selfish goals and behavior in turn affects the amount of interaction he or she has with others. Although Adler did not elaborate this concept, he believed that the individual who develops abnormally has a lower activity level than that of a normal person.

In Adler's view, then, abnormal behavior development is the result of the same factors that account for normal personality development. The differences lie with the abnormally high feelings of inferiority created within the individual and the subsequent development of inappropriate patterns of behavior in the attempt to deal with the heightened tension.

APPROACH TO COUNSELING

"Adlerian counseling deals with the whole person—one's physical, emotional-interpersonal, intellectual, and spiritual aspects as they interact within the unity of the self" (Garfinkle, Massey, & Mendell, 1980, p. 63).

> We do not attempt primarily to change behavior patterns or remove symptoms. If a patient improves his behavior and finds it profitable at the time, without changing his basic premises, then we do not consider that as a therapeutic success. We are trying to change goals, concepts, and notions (Dreikurs, 1967, p. 79).

This may seem a rather global goal, but Adler considered the development of abnormal behavior to be directly related to the individual's feeling of inferiority. The more specific goals involve taking the client back along his or her developmental path in an attempt to restructure that development and help the client understand his or her life-style and current social situation. The first of these goals is to help the individual reduce the negative evaluation of self, feelings of inferiority. The second is to help the client correct her or his perceptions of events and, at the same time, develop a new set of objectives toward which to direct behavior. The final goal is to redevelop the individual's inherent social interest with its accompanying social interaction. Adler felt that this last step was crucial, for "not belonging is the worst contingency that man can experience; it is worse than death" (Dreikurs, 1957, p. 173). If the goal of increasing social interest and participation is not reached, the rest of the process is largely wasted (Ansbacher & Ansbacher, 1956).

THE PROCESS OF COUNSELING

Adler was one of the first to recognize the importance of the relationship between counselor and client. He believed that the counseling situation establishes an "interpersonal relationship in which the client's lifestyle can become apparent" (Garfinkle et al., 1980, p. 63). In his view, therapy is essentially a social relationship, and the whole process of counseling is a process of socialization. The client's problems are largely a result of lack of socialization, and counseling can be a powerful tool in redeveloping this process. The counseling process has this potential largely because of the social interaction between the counselor and the client. For many clients this relationship is unique; it is the first time they do not have to be afraid in a situation with someone else. Given a permissive and warm atmosphere by the counselor, the client feels accepted and able to deal openly with feelings of inferiority for the first time.

Sonstegard and Dreikurs (1973) contended that a counselor's sincerity is of paramount importance in establishing a client's feeling of trust. In addition, the counselor must be an objective and attentive listener who can communicate a liking and concern for the client. The counselor must also be able to remain patient, even in the face of hostility and resistance. In Adler's view, the client should never in any way be offended by the counselor. Thus, the counselor must be able to state things in a manner acceptable to the client. This last ability is extremely important, for it is the counselor, not the client, who will develop an understanding of what is causing the difficulty. If the counselor cannot communicate this understanding in ways that the client will accept, the latter will never come to understand her or his own behavior and its logical consequences. And if there is no understanding by the client, there will be no change in behavior.

Adler also believed that it is important in the counseling process to treat the client as a responsible individual. The counselor must communicate that it is the client's responsibility to act and that from acting in a responsible way he or she can expect success. Moreover, Dreikurs (1961) pointed out, the counselor needs to maintain the human quality in interaction with the client; anything that detracts from the spontaneous nature of the relationship can only harm the counseling process.

In Adler's view, once the proper relationship has been established, counseling proceeds through three stages. In the first stage the counselor strives to develop an understanding of the client's goals and life-style. Once this analysis is completed, the counselor tries to interpret the client's behavior to her or him. In effect, the counselor is explaining the individual to himself or herself. Central to this process is helping the client understand the goal of his or her behavior and how that goal determines disturbing attitudes, thoughts, and behavior. Once this understanding is achieved, the client will be able to select new goals, which in turn will result in new behaviors. Finally, Adler believed in the importance of developing the client's social interest. Adler saw the therapist's role as similar to that of a mother, giving the client the experience of a loving contact with another human being and then helping her or him to transfer this heightened social interest to positive feelings toward others. Ultimately this would bring the client's private goals in line with goals of the larger society and give him or her confidence that any problem can be solved in cooperation with others. Adler assumed that going through this process would change the client's behavior. This was the real test of counseling for Adler: an individual cannot develop a true understanding of self without a subsequent change in behavior. If there is no change, then there has been no self-understanding, and counseling has not been successful.

TECHNIQUES OF COUNSELING

Adler elaborated few specific techniques to be used in counseling. This may account for the relatively infrequent use of his therapy system for many years, in contrast with the widespread use of many of his concepts. Others such as Dreikurs, however, have recently developed Adler's concepts into specific techniques.

From Adler's perspective, the first and most important task of therapy is for the counselor to develop an understanding of the client's life-style. To come to that understanding, the counselor must first examine the client's current behavior, asking the client to describe events in his or her current existence and his or her reactions to them. At the same time, the counselor is observing the behavior of the client within the counseling situation. The permissive atmosphere is designed not only to enhance social interaction, but also to permit the client to behave in an open fashion. In this way the counselor can gain firsthand knowledge of the client's behavior patterns. Once the current situation is understood, the counselor tries to understand the individual's entire life-style.

Adler identified two general techniques to be used by the counselor during this analysis stage: empathy and intuitive guessing. The counselor needs empathy to understand the feelings that are guiding the client's behavior. Intuitive guessing is the ability to interpret the client's mind. Dreikurs (1961) referred to this technique as finding the "hidden reason" for a client's behavior. These techniques keep the counselor from having to rely entirely on the self-reports of the client, who is unable to verbalize all reasons for her or his behavior (Ford & Urban, 1967).

Gushurst (1971) has specified four things the counselor must know in order to develop an understanding of life-styles. First, the counselor must be aware of the factors that Adlerians believe have a significant influence on personality: organic inferiority, pampering, and neglect. Second, the counselor must be able to recognize patterns of behavior, to infer, from the presence of two or more specific behavioral traits, that certain related aspects of behavior are likely to be there also. For example, the counselor can expect that the pampered child will utilize a variety of behaviors to get things from others. Third, the counselor must be able to compare patterns within the client's family constellation to determine areas of similarity and difference. Finally, the counselor must be able to interpret the material accurately so that the client will understand her or his life-style and its logical outcomes.

One of the first steps in the process is to have the client describe his or her family constellation, listing all family members, with particular emphasis on siblings. The client is then asked to describe each family member, to rate each one on several dimensions (such as intelligence, temper, femininity, being spoiled), to describe differences and similarities in family members (such as who is most different from or similar to the client; who played together). These data are used to establish what factors exist in the individual's environment and may be contributing to certain patterns of behavior. By examining this constellation, the counselor can begin to understand the unique interactions between individuals that may have affected the client's life-style. This particular technique is receiving increasing attention in the field of counseling, particularly at the elementary school level. Counselors are increasingly turning to observations in both home and school settings in order to understand the causes of a child's difficulty.

Rudolf Dreikurs, a student of Adler, believed it is possible to distinguish between counseling and psychotherapy at this point. Dreikurs believed there is no need to analyze the entire life-style in order to provide vocational counseling, marriage counseling, and child guidance. Instead, these problems can be solved by an examination and understanding of current behavior. To solve a problem in a marriage, for example, it is not necessary to explore the complete life-style of each individual, but to change the two partners' erroneous behaviors toward each other (1961).

EARLY RECOLLECTIONS

To understand the complete life-style, the counselor must engage the client in a discussion of early recollections. Adler believed that memory is biased and that the individual remembers only events that have meaning in his or her current life-style. Hence, if the counselor can understand which events have formed the basis for the client's life-style, she or he will be in a position to present a new understanding of these events to the client.

Early recollections are specific events that the client remembers from childhood, preferably before the age of ten. They are things that the client can recall clearly, not only the incidents but also the feelings that went with them (Gushurst, 1971). These recollections are good indicators of current attitudes and desires. According to Mosak (1958), the counselor interprets these early recollections in terms of both themes and specific details; characters who appear should not be treated as specific individuals, but as prototypes. The specific character may represent men in general, authority figures, and the like. The counselor brings the various themes of the early recollections together to understand their unity and pattern in terms of the client's life-style (Nikelly & Verger, 1971). All the material from the early recollections can provide the counselor with a picture of how the client sees herself or himself and other people, and of the client's life-style in general.

INTERPRETATION

Once the counselor has come to understand the client's life-style through analysis of family constellation and early recollections, she or he needs to interpret this understanding to the client in such a manner that the client will accept the information. In general, this is a process of pointing out the "basic mistakes" in the client's approach to life. Adler never said exactly how this was to be done, only that the counselor must be flexible and use whatever methods he or she feels will develop new understanding in the client.

In Adler's view, once clients have developed a new understanding of their behavior, that behavior will change. Dreikurs (1961) believed the counselor can enhance this process by providing encouragement. In large part, this encouragement consists in helping clients understand that they were causing their own difficulty and are also responsible for improving the situation. This awareness of power over self tends to free individuals. Once clients realize they can exert control over the direction and quality of their life, counseling can terminate.

ADLERIAN CONSULTATION

One major area of development in the Adlerian movement is in consultation procedures for parents and teachers. Bernice Grunwald, a public school teacher and member of the Alfred Adler Institute of Chicago, suggested that if all children were brought to realize that every class in school is a working–problem-solving unit, with every individual responsible for his or her own behavior, many problems in schools would not exist. Grunwald believed this kind of realization is possible only if the teacher believes it too and is willing to learn group dynamics and procedures (1971). It is safe to say that parents, too, might benefit from approaching the home as a working–problem-solving unit, and their children as responsible partners in it. To establish this kind of environment, parents and teachers often need specific training. The counselor is often in a position to offer such consultative services.

One Adlerian-based approach to consultation with parents and teachers has been developed by Dinkmeyer (1971). Dinkmeyer, long associated with the Alfred Adler Institute of Chicago and the field of elementary counseling, refers to his procedures as "C" groups. The psychological foundations for these groups are:

1. Behavior is holistic and can be understood only in terms of its unity.
2. Behavior is significant only in relation to the consequences it produces.
3. An individual's behavior as a social being can be understood only in terms of its social context.
4. Individual motivation is best understood through observation of how the individual seeks to be recognized.
5. Behavior of individuals is goal directed.
6. A feeling of belonging is basic to human existence.

7. Behavior can be understood only in terms of the internal frame of reference of the individual.

These seven principles are directly related to Adlerian concepts of human growth and development. Dinkmeyer's "C" group is a way of teaching Adler's principles and the means of implementing them in the home and school. The approach is based on creating environments in which children are encouraged, not discouraged, and where they learn both that they are responsible for their own behaviors and how those behaviors affect others. The actual procedures used to train teachers and parents are discussed in Dinkmeyer and Carlson's *Consulting: Facilitating Human Potential and Change Processes* and in Dinkmeyer's *Raising a Responsible Child*.

SUMMARY

From this brief discussion it is clear that Adler's philosophy has had a great influence on the field of counseling. Adler's theory of personality is perhaps the first of the phenomenological approaches. Many of the concepts that he first used, such as inferiority, life-style, compensation, empathy, and respect, are now found in a variety of counseling approaches. In some ways it is unfortunate that he did not write as much about his theory of therapy as he did his theory of personality, for his concepts are clearly understood, but there are few guidelines for counselors attempting to implement his theory. Fortunately, as interest in Adlerian procedures increases, many others are developing therapy procedures from Adler's basic concepts. The Alfred Adler Institute of Chicago is an excellent resource for material, as are the many publications by Dreikurs and Dinkmeyer.

REFERENCES

Adler, A. Individual psychology. In C. Murchison (Ed.), *Psychologies of 1930*. Worcester, Mass.: Clark University Press, 1930.

Allen, J. W. The individual psychology of Alfred Adler: An item of history and a promise of a revolution. *The Counseling Psychologist*, 1971, *3*(1), 3–24.

Ansbacher, H., & Ansbacher, R. *The Individual psychology of Alfred Adler*. New York: Basic Books, 1956.

Bischof, L. J. *Interpreting personality theories* (2nd ed.). New York: Harper & Row, 1970.

Dinkmeyer, D. The "C" group: Integrating knowledge and experience to change behavior an Adlerian approach to consultation. *The Counseling Psychologist*, 1971, *3*(1), 63–72.

———. *Raising a responsible child: Practical steps to successful family relationships*. New York: Simon and Schuster, 1973.

Dinkmeyer, D., & Carlson, J. *Consulting: Facilitating human potential and change processes*. Columbus, Ohio: Charles E. Merrill, 1973.

Dreikurs, R. Group psychotherapy from the point of view of Adlerian psychology. *International Journal of Group Psychotherapy*, 1957, *7*, 363–75.

———. The Adlerian approach to therapy. In M. I. Stein (Ed.), *Contemporary psychotherapies*. New York: The Free Press, 1961.

———. *Psychodynamics, psychotherapy, and counseling*. Chicago: Alfred Adler Institute, 1967.

——. *Social equality: The challenge of today.* Chicago: Henry Regrery, 1971.

Ellenberger, H. F. *Discovery of the unconscious: The history and evolution of dynamic psychiatry.* New York: Basic Books, 1970.

Ford, D.H., & Urban, H.B. *Systems of psychotherapy: A comparative study.* New York: John Wiley and Sons, 1967.

Garfinkle, M.I., Massey, E., & Mendell, W.M. Two cases in Adlerian child therapy. In Gary S. Belkin (Ed.), *Contemporary psychotherapies.* Chicago: Rand McNally, 1980.

Grunwald, B. Strategies for behavior change in schools. *The Counseling Psychologist*, 1971, *3*(1), 55–57.

Gushurst, R. S. The techniques, utility, and validity of life style analysis. *The Counseling Psychologist*, 1971, *3*(1), 30–40.

Hall, C. S., & Lindzey, G. *Theories of personality.* New York: John Wiley and Sons, 1957.

Mosak, H. Early Recollections as a projective technique. *Journal of Projective Techniques*, 1958, *22*, 302–311.

Mosak, H., & Dreikurs, R. Adlerian psychotherapy. In R. Corsini (Ed.), *Current psychotherapies.* Itasca, Ill.: F. E. Peacock, 1973.

Munroe, R. L. *Schools of psychoanalytic thought: An exposition, critique, and attempt at integration.* New York: Dryden Press, 1955.

Nikelly, A. G., & Verger, D. Early recollections. In A. G. Nikelly (Ed.), *Techniques for behavior change.* Springfield, Ill.: Charles C Thomas, 1971.

Sonstegard, M., & Dreikurs, R. The Adlerian approach to group counseling of children. In M. M. Ohlsen (Ed.), *Counseling children in groups.* New York: Holt, Rinehart and Winston. 1973.

TRANSACTIONAL ANALYSIS

CHAPTER FIVE

Transactional analysis is often classified as a neoanalytic approach, even though Eric Berne, who began to develop TA around 1954, denied that it was related to traditional Freudian thought. Although transactional analysis differs in many ways from traditional analytic thought, there is little question that, at the very least, many of its concepts are an outgrowth of Freudian thought. For example, Henry Stack Sullivan's basic ideas about interpersonal interactions have been largely adopted by TA, and Sullivan is classified as a neoanalyst.

Transactional analysis is, for the most part, a procedure involving individuals within a group context. Counselors should therefore have some knowledge of group procedures before attempting to implement TA principles in counseling. The basic TA principles of personality theory can be an aid to understanding the dynamics of clients, and these dynamics in turn can be useful in individual counseling.

Transactional analysis as an approach to counseling grew out of Berne's clinical practice. Berne believed that an individual is a composite of separate entities, each with its own patterns of behavior, speech, and movement. Each of these entities exercises control over the individual at various times. Berne referred to these entities as ego states, they are a cornerstone of TA theory.

As Berne formalized his thoughts, he started a series of weekly meetings at Carmel, California, with colleagues interested in his approach. Later he formed a similar group that became the San Francisco Transactional Analysis Society. Since 1958 the TA movement, described by English (1973) as a populist movement, has won an impressive number of converts among both professionals and the lay public. Berne's death in 1970 does not appear to have affected the movement. People like Kupfer, Steiner, Karpman, Crossman, Maxwell, and Schiff have carried on his work in transactional societies across the country.

Certainly part of the reason for this growth is the receptivity of the lay public to the concepts of transactional analysis. Several books on the subject have become popular best sellers, including two by Berne, *Games People Play* (1964) and *What Do You Say After You Say Hello?* (1972), and Harris's *I'm O.K., You're O.K.* (1969). *Born to Win* (1971), by James and Jongeward, has also done much to popularize transactional analysis concepts.

THEORY OF PERSONALITY

STRUCTURE OF PERSONALITY

Berne (1966) contended that there are three definitive ego states, which he called Parent, Adult, and Child. Each ego state has its own gestures, mannerisms, and speech pattern. Each also has the capacity to be in charge of the individual at any given time. When the Child ego state is in control, for example, the individual will exhibit behaviors and speech associated with that ego state. TA theorists maintain that although there is some relation between the Freudian concepts of id, ego, and superego and the ego states of Child, Adult, and Parent, they are in reality quite different. It is true, however, that the id and the Child are both concerned with pleasure, the ego and the Adult with reality testing, and the superego and

Parent, in part, are controls on the other personality components. The Parent, Adult, and Child, however, represent forms of actual observable behavior rather than implied psychological constructs. According to Berne, "Super-ego, ego, and id are inferential concepts, while ego states are experiential and social realities" (1966, p. 220). In short, when an individual is in the Adult ego state, an observer sees and hears an adult. This fact demonstrates a clear distinction between traditional Freudian thought and transactional analysis: the focus of psychoanalytic thinking is on the unconscious, whereas the focus of TA is on observable, conscious behavior. We now turn to specific discussion of each ego state.

Child Ego State

"The Child ego state is a set of feelings, attitudes, and behavior patterns which are relics of the individual's own childhood" (Berne, 1976, p. 477). It is composed of three parts, known as the Adapted Child, the Natural Child, and the Little Professor. The Natural Child contains the young, impulsive, untrained, emotionally expressive child; the Adapted Child is formed as the child interacts with parents and is more controlled; and the Little Professor is the forerunner of adultlike reasoning.

The Child ego state is crucial in normal development, for it is the foundation on which an individual builds his or her concept of self. "It is important for the individual to understand his Child, not only because it is going to be with him all his life, but also because it is the most valuable part of his personality" (Berne, 1972, p. 12). In a mature adult the Child ego state represents the individual's development until around the age of seven. It is important in adulthood as the part of the individual that can really experience pleasure.

Spontaneity, creativity, charm, and joy are characteristics of the Child ego state. An individual operating from the Child will use childish words such as "wow" and "gee whiz," and her or his behavior can be typified as loud, active, and unpredictable. Society acts to inhibit Child ego state behavior in adults, so adults must seek out and structure situations in which they can exhibit such behavior. Sporting activities and parties are two situations that permit this behavior, and that is the prime reason for their existence.

Because the Child ego state is formed earliest, before the development of a full vocabulary, much of it consists of feelings. Many are joyful and exciting feelings, springing from such experiences as finding that one can exercise control over one's body by picking up and throwing a ball, seeing one's first butterfly. These are the experiences and feelings of the Natural Child. On the other hand, the dependent and initially helpless child may be caught between personal needs to explore, to experience pleasure, to act, and to know and the demands and restrictions of the environment, principally in the form of parents. This is most often a frustrating period, for the child must give up some of the behaviors that bring pleasure in order to satisfy his or her parents. "The predominant by-product of the frustrating, civilizing process is negative feelings. On the basis of these feelings the little person early concludes, " 'I'm not OK' " (Harris, 1969, p. 48). This is the process that forms the Adapted Child. The third part of the Child, the Little Professor, is a product of the child's first attempts to reason things out for herself or himself. It becomes the part of the Child that is evaluative, intuitive, and creative.

Parent Ego State

Like the Child ego state, the Parent ego state is largely formed by the time a child enters first grade. Unlike the Child, however, the Parent is subject to continual adaptation as the individual interacts with authority figures throughout life. This process is extremely important, for the information stored in the Parent ego state must be appropriate to the individual's current life situation if the Parent is to be productive. This updating process can occur only if the individual's Adult ego state is fully operative.

Parent behavior is characteristically nonreasoning and nonperceptive-based. Behavior and thinking are based on commands made to the individual in the past that were incorporated into the Parent. Most of these injunctions or commands contain words such as "never," "always," and "never forget that" (Harris, 1969). The individual, when operating from the Parent level, does not evaluate current information but lets past commands guide current behavior. When operating from the Parent the individual feels, talks, and acts in the way she or he, when a child, perceived her or his parents behaving.

The Parent state, then, is a product of the child's recording material from his or her actual parents. This is not a simple linear transfer because, first of all, there are generally two parents and, second, each parent possesses and behaves from three different ego states. Thus, the child is recording material into her or his Parent from six ego states. Injunctions or rules such as "Never lie" or "You just can't trust those kinds of people" are recorded from the parents' Parent ego state. Childlike behavior is recorded when the parents are in their Child ego states. Becuase so much of this material is often inconsistent, the Parent ego state is subject to malfunctioning in later adult life.

Although it may appear that the Parent ego state is a detrimental component because of its inconsistencies and backward-looking orientation, it is, in fact, very necessary. The Parent state functions as the transmitter of cultural values and mores, and it acts "to conserve energy and diminish anxiety by making certain decisions 'automatic' and relatively unshakable" (Berne, 1976, p. 476).

Adult Ego State

In the process of exploring her or his world, the child accumulates data from experiences. The child's evaluation of these experiences marks the first appearance of the future Adult ego state. In this early stage the Adult is very fragile and can be easily overridden by commands from the Parent and the emotions of the Child. The emergence of the Adult is observable when a child is told not to do something because he or she will get hurt, but nevertheless has to test the statement. In doing so, the child is using evaluative skills, and evaluation is an Adult ego state behavior.

"The Adult ego state is characterized by an autonomous set of feelings, attitudes, and behavior patterns which are adapted to the current reality" (Berne, 1976, p. 476). It acts as an assimilator and evaluator of information. It is not concerned with feelings, but with facts; it asks "What?," "Where?," "How?" Feelings are, for the most part, absent from the Adult state, although it does have the capacity to evaluate them. As such, the Adult is best thought of as a regulatory mechanism that evaluates data from external sources and from the other ego states, processes those data, evaluates possible outcomes, and makes decisions about what action to take.

In a fully functioning individual, the Adult ego state is always changing, unlike the fairly static Child and Parent. It has the capacity to evaluate the data in the Parent or Child and to support or change those data. The Adult does not attempt to rule the personality, but it does seek to keep the Parent and Child ego states current, appropriate, and in balance.

MOTIVATION

In the TA view, each individual possesses two primary needs: physiological and psychological nurturing. The physiological needs are food, air, water, and the like for physical survival. The psychological needs, in TA terminology, are *stimulus hunger and strokes, structure hunger, and position hunger.* The personality of the individual is a product of interactions with his or her world, particularly as it relates to other people, in attempts to satisfy these needs. According to TA theorists, these needs can be met only through transactions with other individuals.

Stimulus Hunger and Strokes

One of Berne's basic beliefs, based on his review of research, was that all individuals have a basic need for stimulation, or recognition, in the form of physical or psychological attention from others in the individual's environment. Berne came to call this recognition strokes. A stroke is a form of recognition, either physical or psychological, that one person gives another. "The work of Rene Spitz and H. F. Harlow has shown that without adequate stroking, the organism, infant or monkey, shows retarded growth in all areas, physical, emotional, and mental" (Kambly, 1971, p. 9). Initially, this need is met through physical stroking. As an individual matures, physical stroking is increasingly replaced by symbolic strokes, in the form of words, facial expressions, and other nonverbal communications.

Strokes can be either positive or negative and either conditional or unconditional. Conditional strokes, either positive or negative, are for doing. A parent may praise a child for hitting a home run (positive) or slap the child for disobeying (negative). Both are dependent on the individual's *doing* something. An unconditional positive or negative stroke is simply for being: "I like you because you are you" (positive) or "I don't like you because you are you" (negative). Even though negative strokes are painful, if they are the only kind of recognition available from the environment, the individual will seek them out in preference to no strokes at all.

Strokes can also be mixed. For example, the statement "Helen, everything looks so great. I just can't believe you were able to do it" is a stroke that is overtly positive, but the second part of the sentence contains a covert negative stroke. It is therefore a "crooked" or mixed stroke. Most often the real intention of a crooked stroke is negative.

Each individual learns to seek out the kinds of strokes he or she came to expect as a child. A child who receives primarily negative and conditional strokes will continue to seek those kinds of strokes in the belief they are the only kind available. A person motivated in this direction often develops what others consider maladaptive behavior. A child who receives positive and unconditional strokes has a much better chance of becoming a fully functioning adult. In either case, the search for strokes is a prime motivating force.

Structure Hunger

"Structure hunger recognizes a dilemma of man through the ages—what to do with 24 hours a day, 168 hours a week" (Holland, 1973, p. 359). Structure hunger is the individual's need to utilize time to maximize the number of strokes received. "People are willing to pay almost any price to have their time structured for them, since few are capable of structuring their own time automatically for very long" (Berne, 1966, p. 230). The ways in which an individual attempts to structure time depends on how comfortable she or he is with feelings. A person who is afraid of close emotional relationships will make minimal investments in others and will receive minimal strokes (Kambly, 1971). One who is not afraid of intimate relationships will generally receive a high number of very rewarding strokes. In either case, people seek to structure their time within the level of risk at which they feel comfortable. There are six ways in which people can structure their time. They are listed below in relative order, from time structure with the least risk to structure with the highest risk.

1. **Withdrawal** Individuals who cannot take any risk may withdraw into themselves. They may actually withdraw physically like a hermit, or they may simply retreat psychologically. These individuals receive strokes mainly through fantasy and self-talk. Payoff is minimal.

2. **Rituals** Highly structured ways to receive strokes are called rituals. These often take the form of social courtesies exchanged between individuals, permitting them to give and receive strokes without any real investment. The following interchange is illustrative of such rituals.

Roth	Milo
How are you today?	Fine, and you?
Good. See you later.	O.K. Later!

In this interchange, both Roth and Milo are able to exchange strokes, but neither has really invested much energy. Stroke value is low and transactions at this level do not last long.

3. **Pastimes** Pastimes structure time in a larger segment than rituals. They consist in nongoal-oriented discussion with others. Children, sports, cars, and gardening are typical topics used in pastimes. The use of an external subject permits individuals to interact without much personal risk.

4. **Activities** An activity is most often work, or other goal-oriented behavior. In activities, individuals set up a situation in which the accomplishment of the task brings them the strokes they need. Many individuals become workaholics in an attempt to receive their strokes.

5. **Games** This is without doubt the means of structuring time that has been most written about. The "games people play" make up the majority of social activity. They consist in a series of orderly transactions between two individuals that provide a payoff in strokes to both parties. "The payoff of a game is the chronic familiar feeling of depression, anger, frustration, jealousy, or

righteousness, triumph, etc." (Kambly, 1971, p. 10), that the people desire. The feeling they seek is called their "racket" or basic life-style. The payoff is often called a "trading stamp" because game players collect them much as other people collect trading stamps. People who have a jealousy racket engage in games that have the payoff of letting them feel jealous. Games can be entered into only by two people who will both receive the payoff they desire. Games have no losers.

6. **Intimacy** Intimacy as a way to structure time has the highest potential for rewards, but also the greatest risks. "Intimacy is a game-free exchange of internally programmed affective expressions . . ." (Berne, 1966, p. 231). Only individuals who are able to be open and sincere with one another can enter into intimate relationships.

Although most people use all six means of structuring time to some degree, trouble can occur when they overuse one procedure to the exclusion of others.

Position Hunger

The third psychological motivator is the individual's need to have his or her chosen life position confirmed. This need is related to the person's racket, life script, and counterscript. The types of strokes received in childhood influence the life positions, the life script, counterscript, racket, and games an individual adopts. Position hunger is the need to behave in ways to reaffirm these choices continually. To understand position hunger as a motivating force, we must examine the formation of life position, life script, and counterscript.

Life Position The way people feel about themselves and others is reflected in their chosen life position. Berne held that the individual makes this decision early in life, based on perceptions of her or his world. "The destiny of every human being is decided by what goes on inside his skull when he is confronted with what goes on outside his skull" (Berne, 1972, p. 31). An individual may choose one of four life positions:

1. **I'm OK—You're OK** This position is the optimal one and is often called the evolutionary position (Kambly, 1971). It is the basic position of trust that all individuals possess initially in life. As the best position for a meaningful life, it is the desired position of everyone. However it is the least maintained position. Berne held that unless this position was adopted early in life, it would be very difficult to attain later in life. He described it as "the position of genuine heroes and princes and heroines and princesses" (1972, p. 86).

2. **I'm OK—You're Not OK** This position is the paranoid position, often called the revolutionary position (Kambly, 1971). Harris (1969) contended that the position develops as an overreaction to feelings of I'm Not OK; people use it as a defense to keep from feeling I'm Not OK. It is very difficult for individuals who adopt this life position to be objective about themselves or others. Harris (1969) indicated that people with this life position drift into criminal behavior and surround themselves with yes-men to receive strokes. Even these strokes are not accepted as authentic because the individual does not believe that anyone is OK.

3. **I'm Not OK—You're OK** Kambly (1971) referred to this position, which is the most common one chosen, as the devolutionary position. Harris

(1969) contended that it is the position most often forced on children, and Berne (1972) described it as the self-abasement of depressive position. Because the people who adopt this position are constantly feeling unworthy, they are constantly in search of strokes. This leads them to be deferential to everyone. The constant need to please others often leads to a productive but unhappy life. Because of the constant pressure this position often leads to depression, and in several cases, suicide (James & Jongeward, 1971).

4. **I'm Not OK—You're Not OK** This is the helpless or obvoluntionary position (Kambly, 1971) and is often adopted by rejected children. Receiving no strokes from their parents, the children first feel they are not OK and later come to believe others are not OK either, because they don't give strokes. These people have a hopeless outlook on life and live only on a day-to-day basis. They often develop schizoid behavior (James & Jongeward, 1971).

The individual's choice of a life position is a product of the injunctions and permissions received in childhood, primarily from parents, before the age of six.

Injunctions Injunctions are orders that parents give their child to behave in prescribed ways. The long-term effect of these commands depends both on the form they take and the manner in which they are enforced. Berne (1972) listed three kinds of injunctions:

1. Straight commands, or first-degree injunctions, are commands that are enforced either through approval or nonapproval. Such injunctions are part of normal parent-child interactions; their use does not prohibit the development of a positive life position and script in the child.
2. Commands in which the parents send both an overt and covert message to the child are called second-degree injunctions. These injunctions usually are enforced by threats and blackmail and, because of the double message, they leave the child confused. They lead to the adoption of the I'm Not OK life position.
3. Commands enforced by severe punishment are third-degree injunctions. These injunctions also lead to the adoption of an I'm Not OK life position but are more damaging than second-degree injunctions because they make the child feel like a real loser.

First-degree injunctions do not prohibit the development of a positive, I'm OK life script; second- and third-degree injunctions do prohibit such development. All are negativistic, and the more severe they are, the stronger the likelihood of the child's adopting an I'm Not OK position.

Permissions Parents who give a child freedom to make her or his own decisions are using permissions. The more permissions a child receives, the higher the probability that she or he will choose a positive life position and life script. As we shall see, permissions are an important tool for the counselor.

Life Script Having chosen a life position as a result of the injunctions and permissions received, the child begins to implement a life plan, or script. This plan is designed to meet a need for position hunger. The script enables the child to re-affirm continually the life position he or she has chosen, regardless of how faulty the position is. The script outlines the way in which the individual will structure time and the ways in which she or he will try to get the strokes necessary to exist. In this way the script interferes with the Adult ego state's capacity to evaluate current data accurately. Thus, the script is a means of rationalizing irrational or inappropriate behavior.

Counterscript In addition to a life script, an individual often develops a counterscript as a way to give up a largely unhappy life script for a short time in favor of a happier one, after which she or he returns to the original life script. Steiner (1973) described the counterscript of an alcoholic as a short period of sobriety or, for a person whose life plan is to commit suicide, a brief period of happiness in a relationship with a lover. In all cases there is a cyclical pattern: the individual spends most of the time implementing the life script, but for short periods may engage in the counterscript, only to return once again to the life script.

Understanding the basic motivating force of an individual is essential to transactional analysis. In most cases, this understanding results from analysis of the person's life script. The life script reveals the way in which the individual structures time, the life position chosen, and the means of maintaining that position. The means by which the individual seeks to meet basic needs are called *transactions*.

TRANSACTIONS

Transactions, the ways in which individuals meet their survival needs, are forms of communications between individuals. They can take place between any one of the ego states of one individual—Parent, Adult, or Child—and any one of the ego states of another individual. It is through transactions between parents and the child that the foundations of the child's personality are formed. They also become the means by which the individual seeks to receive the kinds of strokes she or he needs for survival.

There are three types of transactions between individuals: complementary, crossed, and ulterior.

Complementary

If communication between two individuals is to continue, it must be complementary. As shown in Figure 5–1, a complementary transaction is one in which the

FIGURE 5–1 COMPLEMENTARY TRANSACTION

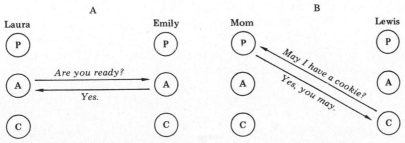

Source: Games People Play, by Eric Berne, M.D. Copyright © 1964 by Eric Berne. Reprinted by permission of Random House, Inc.

FIGURE 5–2 CROSSED TRANSACTIONS

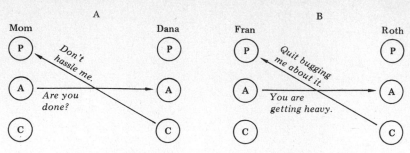

Source: *Games People Play*, by Eric Berne, M.D. Copyright © 1964 by Eric Berne. Reprinted by permission of Random House, Inc.

vectors do not cross. Transaction A illustrates a complementary transaction between the Adult ego states of Laura and Emily, transaction B a complementary transaction between the Parent ego state of Mom and the Child ego state of Lewis. The transaction is complementary in both cases because the ego state that is being addressed is the ego state that responds.

Crossed

A response from an ego state not being addressed causes a crossed transaction. Figure 5–2 shows two examples of this type of transaction. In both cases, the Adult of one individual tried to address the Adult of the second individual, but the Child responded instead. Such a transaction halts meaningful communication.

Ulterior

In an ulterior transaction, one thing is being said at an overt level, but a second message is being sent at a covert level. Generally, the overt message is one that is socially acceptable, whereas the covert message is a more basic psychological one. Two such transactions are shown in Figure 5–3. In the transaction between Dick and Jane four ego states are involved, with the important part of the transaction being what is communicated at the psychological level. In transaction B, the salesperson sends an overt message to the customer's Adult, but "hooks" the Child with the covert message. This, of course, is a typical sales technique. Because of their double message, ulterior transactions often cause frustration between individuals, particularly between a parent and a child.

Because transactions are the ways in which individuals seek to meet their needs, they are fundamental to the development and final shape of personality. We turn now to how these factors interact in the process of development.

PROCESS OF PERSONALITY DEVELOPMENT

Transactional analysis holds that in every individual there is an essentially positive potential that, given proper nourishment, will become a reality (Dusay & Steiner, 1971). Although physiological, psychological, and socioeconomic factors affect

FIGURE 5-3 ULTERIOR TRANSACTIONS

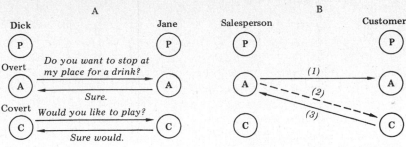

A

Dick   Jane
(P)   (P)

Overt   *Do you want to stop at*
         my place for a drink?
(A) ←——————————————————→ (A)
                Sure.

Covert   *Would you like to play?*
(C) ←——————————————————→ (C)
              Sure would.

B

Salesperson   Customer
(P)   (P)

                        (1)
(A) ——————————————————————→ (A)
          - - - - - - (2) - - - - →
                 (3)
(C)   (C)

1. This is our top line, but you probably
   want to see our cheaper model.
2. You can't afford this.
3. I want this one.

Source: Games People Play, by Eric Berne, M.D. Copyright © 1964 by Eric
Berne. Reprinted by permission of Random House, Inc.

everybody, they determine only the broad limits within which a person may
develop.

TA theorists believe that personality development begins prior to birth: such
factors as size of the family, whether the child is to be welcomed or unwanted, and
whether the parents want a boy or a girl determine the environment into which
the child is born. As such, these factors affect the kinds of strokes the child
receives at birth and, in turn, the child's adoption of one of the four basic life positions. In some cases these prenatal factors have a positive effect; in others, the effect is detrimental.

The initial life position of infants is the natural trust position, I'm OK—
You're OK. If that position is to be maintained, parents must provide the child
with unconditional positive strokes. Along with care for the infant's basic
physiological needs, these strokes are all that is needed to maintain positive
development during the infant's first half year of life. As the child begins to move
about and explore on his or her own, helping the child maintain the I'm OK position becomes more difficult. Falzett and Maxwell (1974) described the kinds of
parent behaviors that either enhance or hinder healthy development from the age
of six months through the age of twelve. Table 5-1 outlines this sequence.

The basic premise of Falzett and Maxwell's general guideline is that the
parents should respect the child and encourage self-development and self-control.
Given good parenting, the child will be able to maintain the natural I'm OK position; unhealthy parenting will lead to adoption of one of the I'm Not OK positions. Good parenting will also help the child develop means of receiving strokes
that are not based on games and rituals, and to form ego states that are functional
and uncontaminated.

Each of the three ego states—Parent, Adult, Child—can be subdivided according to where the data came from during the development of that ego state.
Given normal development, each of the ego states has the potential to control the
physical and psychological behavior of the individual. Only one ego state can be
in charge at any one time. In TA terms, only one ego state can be cathected at a
time, "that is, imbued with the energy necessary to activate muscular complexes

involved in behavior . . ." (Dusay & Steiner, 1971, p. 201). It is true, however, that one ego state may be cathected while another ego state has enough energy to be aware of what the other ego state is doing. In this case, it is usually the Parent or Child that is cathected, with the Adult being partly energized. At a sporting event, for example, caught up in the excitement of the game, the Child may be in control, but the Adult may be saying, "You are making a spectacle of yourself."

A child who receives healthy parenting will be able to cathect each of the ego states when the use of that ego state is appropriate. In TA terms, this means that there is sufficient permeability among ego states. The Parent is often appropriate when the individual must exercise control over subordinates or children. The Adult is best when some rational decision is necessary, and the Child is appropriate for the expression of emotions or creativity (Dusay & Steiner, 1971).

Normal personality development, then, is a product of healthy parenting behavior. It is characterized by the maintenance of the I'm OK life position, by the adoption of a life script relatively free of the need to play games to receive strokes,

TABLE 5-1 FALZETT AND MAXWELL'S DEVELOPMENTAL SEQUENCE

	HEALTHY PARENTING	UNHEALTHY PARENTING
6–18 mos.	Parents give children permission to explore his or her world. Parents provide protection for this exploration, and unconditioned positive strokes. Discipline is generally inappropriate. Communication should be largely between parents' Child and child's Child.	Parents refuse to give either protection or permission for child to explore. They place restrictions on movement and may institute severe toilet training.
18 mos.–3 yrs.	Parents help child develop capacity to control self and to consider others' feelings and needs. Child's reasoning powers are encouraged with some Adult-to-Adult transactions, even though majority of transactions are still Child-to-Child. Toilet training and some discipline are now appropriate.	Parents provide the child with neither discipline nor expectations, or expectations are too high and severely enforced. Child is not encouraged by Adult-to-Adult transactions to be a problem solver.
3–6 yrs.	Parents continue encouraging problem-solving behavior, help child understand own feelings, and examine ways of getting strokes. Parents encourage socially approved behavior and discourage game playing.	Parents tease child, exclude child's thinking. In essence, child is left very much on his own, with no encouragement of problem-solving behavior.
6–12 yrs.	Emphasis is on Adult-to-Adult transactions. Parents really listen to child's ideas and respect his right to believe as he does. Child is provided with a broad base of experiences in order to develop personal skills.	Parents impose rigid sets of rules and values, or none. No respect for child's ideas or reasoning power.

and by sufficient permeability among the ego states that the individual can utilize each when appropriate.

ABNORMAL DEVELOPMENT

An individual who has been constantly subjected to unhealthy parenting is likely to choose a life position of I'm Not OK and a life script designed to maintain that position. The person will lack the full use of the ego states. The severity of the maladaptive behavior depends on the position chosen and how severely the ego state development has been impaired.

If the individual has given up the I'm OK—You're OK position for the most common position, I'm Not OK—You're OK, her or his life will probably be fairly normal and productive, but it will contain little joy or real happiness.

The person who adopts the position I'm OK—You're Not OK will have a life script dominated by paranoid thinking and is most likely to engage in antisocial behaviors.

Adoption of the I'm Not OK—You're Not OK position leads to a life of hopelessness and despair. The individual generally will not cause anyone else difficulty but will not be very happy with himself or herself or with life.

In addition to affecting the selection of a life position that leads to an inappropriate life-style, unhealthy parenting can lead to two problems in ego state development, contamination and exclusion.

CONTAMINATION

When one ego state is affected by data from another ego state, contamination has occurred. Most often it is the Adult ego state that suffers contamination from either the Child or the Parent. "It occurs when the Adult accepts as true some unfounded Parent beliefs or Child distortions and rationalizes and justifies these attitudes" (James & Jongeward, 1971, p. 231). The effect is to keep the Adult from accurately processing data. Instead of evaluating current data, the Adult behaves as though data from either the Parent or the Child are accurate. Most often, contamination involves the Adult's accepting irrational Parent beliefs. Prejudices that have passed from the Parent's Child to the Child's Parent are a form of contamination. Delusions occur with severe contaminations but, more often, contaminations simply distort the individual's perception of reality, thus producing inappropriate behavior.

EXCLUSIONS

In normal situations an individual develops the capacity to move from one ego state to another when appropriate. In abnormal development, however, the ego boundaries may become either too flexible or too rigid. When the ego boundaries are too flexible, the individual moves from one ego state to another in response to very minute stimuli. Such an individual appears to lack identity and the ability to deal meaningfully with life. This individual is unable to tell what he or she may do next.

At the other extreme are very rigid ego boundaries, which do not permit the free flow of psychic energy. Generally, rigid boundaries act to hold most energy within one ego state and thus prevent the other ego states from operating. As a result, the individual with rigid boundaries responds to most stimuli with one ego state, always behaving as a Parent or as a Child or as an Adult. The person at a party who cannot really enjoy herself or himself is excluding the Child. The effect of exclusions is that the person is unable to respond with the appropriate ego state.

Inappropriate life positions, contaminations, and exclusions are all products of childrearing practices in which parents make their strokes conditional upon the child's behaving as they desire. The child is rarely given permission to explore or to develop. Instead, the parents issue injunctions, never permitting the development of functional ego states or the choice of an I'm OK—You're OK position. Inappropriate behavior, like normal development, is the product of parent behaviors. In one case the parents provide unconditional positive strokes; in the other, all strokes are conditional.

SUMMARY

Transactional analysis sees personality development, both normal and abnormal, as influenced primarily by transactions between the ego states of the parents and the ego states of the child. The individual's choice of a life position is a product of these transactions and once a choice is made, the individual sets about living in a way to confirm this position and to bring the strokes he or she has learned to need. In many cases, the chosen life position and subsequent life script lead to inappropriate patterns of behavior and establish the need for counseling.

TRANSACTIONAL ANALYSIS IN COUNSELING

Transactional analysis is primarily a contractual system for treating individuals within the group context. The general goal of transactional analysis "is social control in which the Adult retains the executive in dealings with other people . . ." (Berne, 1976, p. 478). Individuals who seek counseling are people who for one reason or another are not in control. For working with such individuals Berne (1966) set forth four general objectives.

1. The first objective is to help the client decontaminate any damaged ego state.
2. The second is to develop the client's capacity to use all ego states when appropriate. This involves getting rid of exclusions and excessive permeability between ego states.
3. The third goal is to help the client develop full use of the Adult; in effect, to establish a thoughtful, reasoning individual with the capacity to govern her or his own life.
4. The final goal is to help the client replace the inappropriately chosen life position and life script with an I'm OK position and a new, productive life script.

In addition, individual client objectives are established on a contractual basis. The contracts between counselor and client spell out the specific objectives the client is seeking through the counseling process. Dusay and Steiner (1971) stated that the contract must meet the following requirements:

1. Both the counselor and the client, through Adult-Adult transactions, must mutually agree on the objectives.
2. The contract must call for some consideration: from the counselor, professional skill and time; from the client, either money or time and effort.
3. The contract must define the competencies of both parties. On the one hand, it establishes that the counselor has the skill to help with this problem; on the other, it establishes that the client is of appropriate mind and age to enter the contract.
4. Finally, the objective(s) of the contract must be legal and within the ethical limits of the counselor.

Transactional analysis counseling includes both the four global objectives, which are appropriate to some degree for all clients, and the specific objectives elaborated in each counselor-client contract.

THE COUNSELING PROCESS

Transactional analysis focuses on individuals, but within a group context. TA counselors regard the group process as a means of analyzing and supplying feedback to members about the kinds of transactions they engage in. The counseling group is seen as a microcosm of the real world, the basic difference being that each member is there to work on specific objectives and the counselor is there as the leader of the group.

Berne (1966) felt that careful preparation of members for the group process was essential, but also that transactional analysis could be effective with all types of clients and problems, and that only very rarely should anyone be excluded from a group.

It is clear from Berne's (1966) writing that the TA counseling process is leader centered. Although member-member transactions are important, the counselor-member transactions are the most important part of the group process. As such, more responsibility for success rests with counselor behavior than with the dynamics of the group.

Berne (1966) saw the counseling process as a series of four steps. He assumed that an individual comes to counseling in order to restructure her or his entire life, which would involve going through all four stages. This may indeed be the case in long-term therapy, but in counseling the goals may be more limited. It may be helpful to think of counseling as being primarily concerned with the first two stages and therapy with the last two, even though it is clear that such a distinction is never complete.

Structural Analysis

Structural analysis is the part of the TA process designed to help individuals understand their own ego state structures. Its goal is to help the client develop fully functioning ego states free of contaminations and exclusions (Berne, 1966). Once the client has achieved this healthy state, the final goal of structural analysis is that the client place the Adult ego state in charge of his or her life.

Transactional Analysis

The second stage of TA counseling focuses on understanding the transactions in which the client normally engages. Such an analysis can help improve the client's ability to communicate with others. The understanding of transactions is a prerequisite to the third stage, game analysis.

Game Analysis

At this stage, transactional analysis requires the counselor to determine what payoff a client receives for playing a certain game, interpret the game to the client and, if necessary, confront the client with it. Once this is achieved, the counselor can give the client permission to quit the game.

Script Analysis

Ordinarily, counselors do not enter into script analysis, for this final stage of the TA process involves getting the client to see that the whole life script has been a mistake. The depression that accompanies such a revelation can be very dangerous, and only experienced and fully trained TA counselors should attempt this stage.

CHARACTERISTICS OF THE COUNSELOR

A transactional analysis counselor is much more than a facilitator of the group process. She or he is a leader who must be skilled in the analysis of ego states, transactions, games, and life scripts. The counselor should also be able to interact with clients in an open, warm, and sincere fashion and to listen and observe. As Berne stated, "Any well-read student or properly programmed computer can make correct interpretations, given properly weighted findings; the real skill lies in collecting and evaluating data" (1966, p. 66). Berne (1966) suggested two additional requirements for counselors. First, they must be able to recognize from which ego state the client is operating at any time. Second, they must demonstrate sincere commitment to the client and faith in the latter's ability to overcome difficulties. In summary, the TA counselor is best viewed as a warm, empathic expert who assumes at least equal responsibility, and perhaps more, for the outcomes of counseling.

TECHNIQUES OF COUNSELING

There are four techniques to be used by the TA counselor. Three of these, permission, protection, and potency, relate to establishing the necessary counseling atmosphere. The fourth, operations, defines more specific counselor behaviors.

Permission

Most individuals who come to counseling are still behaving on the basis of many parental injunctions. One of the first things a counselor must do is give clients permission to do what their parents told them not to do (Steiner, 1973). Dusay and Steiner (1971) listed three other areas in which permissions are given in counseling:

1. The counselor gives the client permission to use their time together effectively by not letting the client enter into nonproductive time structuring, such as rituals or withdrawal.
2. The counselor gives the client permission to experience all ego states, usually by encouraging the client to use the Adult's ability to reason and the Child's ability to enjoy life. This is often accomplished through role playing, in which the client is asked to act out the Child or the Adult.
3. The counselor gives permission not to play games by not letting the client play them. The client does not get the strokes needed and therefore gives up the game.

Protection

When a client receives permission to give up the parental injunction and use the Adult, the Child is likely to become frightened (Steiner, 1973). This is why protection is necessary. As the client prepares to abandon part of the life script, the counselor must convince him or her that counseling is a safe environment in which to do so. Protection is a supporting statement, such as "Don't be scared" or "Don't worry—you won't be hurt" from the counselor's Parent to the client's Child. The Parent (counselor) tells the Child (client) that everything will work out fine.

Potency

"Good therapists [counselors] are not magicians, they just know what to do and when to do it" (Steiner, 1973, p. 24). This is what potency is: a measure of the counselor's ability to use all his or her skills at the best times so that those skills are maximally effective. As Dusay and Steiner (1971) suggested, the ultimate test of a counselor's potency is whether the client is able to do away with the parental injunction.

Operations

Berne (1966) proposed a list of eight techniques that he had found helpful in counseling. This list is not comprehensive, but it does provide the prospective TA counselor with some guidelines.

1. **Interrogation** Many clients have difficulty using their Adult ego state. A counselor confronted with this behavior must question, or interrogate, the client until the latter produces an Adult response. Because it is a forcing technique, it must be used carefully.

2. **Specification** Specification takes place when the Adult of the counselor and the Adult of the client agree on where a particular client behavior comes from. For example, both may agree that a particular client behavior comes from the Parent ego state. Being specific is important in developing a complete understanding of the client's three ego states.

3. **Confrontation** In confrontation the counselor points out to the client discrepancies or inconsistencies in behavior or statements.

4. **Explanation** Explanation is a counselor teaching behavior, an Adult-to-Adult transaction in which the counselor explains why the client has been behaving in a given way.

5. **Illustration** Illustration is a way of both breaking tension and instructing. The humor of the illustration pleases the client's Child while the message gets through to the Adult. It also serves to indicate to the client that both Adult and Child behaviors are appropriate.

6. **Confirmation** Confirmation is pointing out to a client the reappearance of behavior that had ceased when first confronted by the counselor. In this way the counselor attempts to get the client to see that he or she really has not given up the behavior and must work harder to do so.

7. **Interpretation** Through interpretation the counselor tries to help the client see the reasons behind a given behavior. In this sense, it is very similar to a traditional psychoanalytic procedure.

8. **Crystallization** In crystallization the counselor tells the client that the latter is now ready to give up the game she or he has been using to receive strokes. In effect, the counselor says, "You now have a better way of receiving your needed strokes."

Two relatively new procedures developed by followers of Berne have been effective in helping clients develop understanding of their ego states and the games they are playing.

Ego-grams

According to Dusay (1977), the developer of the ego-gram procedure, an individual possesses a fixed amount of energy. Therefore, a person who is utilizing a great deal of energy in the Child has little left for the Parent or Adult. "The ego-gram was created in order to symbolize the amount of energy that a person exudes in each of his or her ego states at any time. After considering his or her ego-gram, a person becomes clear about what he or she wants to change, raise, lower, or develop in certain ego states" (Dusay, 1977, p. 40).

Figure 5–4 shows a sample ego-gram. The individual represented in Figure 5–4 is spending most energy in the ego states of Controlling Parent and Adapted Child. This indicates that the individual is a rather controlled person. To be able to enjoy life more, the client must transfer energy to the Free Child ego state. By using an ego-gram, the counselor can help clients see where they need to go in order to accomplish their goal(s).

FIGURE 5-4 EGO-GRAM

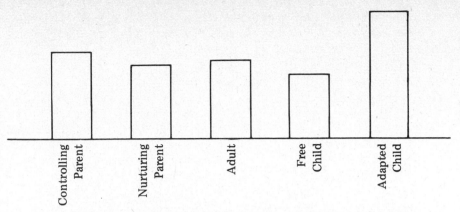

Source: Transactional Analysis after Eric Berne: Teachings and Practices of Three TA Schools, edited by Graham Barnes. Copyright © 1977 by Graham Barnes. Reprinted by permission of Harper & Row, Publishers, Inc.

Karpman Triangle

The Karpman Triangle (Figure 5–5) was developed to help people understand the games that dominate their life. It is based on the assumption that game players assume one of three roles: persecutor (P), rescuer (R), or victim (V). Generally, individuals have one favorite role even though in any given game they may adopt any of the three roles (Wollams, Brown, & Huige, 1977). People who feel superior to others most often adopt the persecutor role; those who feel they are more knowledgeable adopt the rescuer role; and the victim role is adopted by those who like to feel helpless. As with the ego-gram, the Karpman Triangle can help both the client and the counselor understand the games the client is playing in order to receive the strokes needed for survival.

To use either the ego-gram or the Karpman Triangle, the counselor must have an in-depth understanding of transactional analysis. A superficial understanding can lead to gross errors that could be very harmful to the client.

SUMMARY

This chapter has presented an overview of the transactional analysis approach to personality development and counseling. Additional material is available in the books and articles referred to in this chapter, particularly those by Berne.

FIGURE 5-5 KARPMAN TRIANGLE

Source: Transactional Analysis after Eric Berne: Teachings and Practices of Three TA Schools, edited by Graham Barnes. Copyright © 1977 by Graham Barnes. Reprinted by permission of Harper & Row, Publishers, Inc.

Because transactional analysis basically focuses on the individual within the group, counselors interested in using this approach should obtain a solid foundation in group dynamics and then seek more training in TA principles. Regional transactional analysis societies across the United States and Canada provide extensive training programs.

REFERENCES

Berne, E. *Transactional analysis in psychotherapy.* New York: Grove Press, 1961.

———. *Games people play.* New York: Grove Press, 1964.

———. *Principles of group treatment.* New York: Oxford University Press, 1966.

———. *What do you say after you say hello?* New York: Bantam, 1972.

———. *Transactional analysis psychotherapy.* In W. S. Sahakian (Ed.), *Psychotherapy and counseling: Techniques in intervention* (2nd ed.). Chicago: Rand McNally, 1976.

Dusay, J. M. *The evolution of transactional analysis.* In G. Barnes (Ed.), *Transactional analysis after Eric Berne: Teachings and practices in three TA schools.* New York: Harper's College Press, 1977.

Dusay, J. M., & Steiner, C. *Transactional analysis in groups.* In H. I. Kaplan, & B. J. Sadock (Eds.), *Comprehensive group psychotherapy.* Baltimore, Md.: Williams and Wilkins, 1971.

English, F. T.A.'s Disney World. *Psychology Today,* 1973, 6(11), 45–50, 98.

Falzett, W., & Maxwell, J. *O.K. childing and parenting.* El Paso: Transactional Analysis Institute of El Paso, 1974.

Harris, T. *I'm o.k., you're o.k.: A practical guide to transactional analysis.* New York: Harper & Row, 1969.

Holland, G. A. Transactional analysis. In Raymond Corsini (Ed.), *Current psychotherapies.* Itasca, Il.: F. E. Peacock, 1973.

James, M., & Jongeward, D. *Born to win: Transactional analysis with Gestalt experiments.* Reading, Mass.: Addison-Wesley, 1971.

Kambly, A. *An introduction to transactional analysis.* Ann Arbor, Mich.: The University Center, 1971.

Steiner, C. *Transactional analysis made simple.* Berkeley, Calif.: T. A. Simple, 1973.

Wollams, S., Brown, M., & Huige, K. *What transactional analysts want their clients to know.* In G. Barnes (Ed.), *Transactional analysis after Eric Berne: Teaching and priorities in three TA schools.* New York: Harper's College Press, 1977.

SELF-THEORY

CHAPTER SIX

The basic concepts that underlie current concepts of self-theory have been expressed in the literature of psychology for many years. However, self-theory has received most attention in the last quarter-century. As with psychoanalytic theory, there are many interpretations of self-theory, including those of Snygg and Combs, Sarbin, Mead, and Koffka. No theorist, however, has had as much influence on self-theory and its relation to counseling as Carl Rogers. Rogers's concepts and their extensions by theorists like Truax and Carkhuff are the most fully developed and most extensively researched positions on self-theory.

The ideas of Carl Rogers have had a profound and controversial influence on the field of counseling. Since the publication of his book *Counseling and Psychotherapy* in 1942, Rogers has been willing and eager to have his ideas tested by evaluative research, and he continues to maintain that his theoretical formulations are in no way final. It is evident that Rogers has been serious about the continuing evolution of his theory. As we examine the original theoretical statements that appeared in the 1942 book and trace their development through his texts, *Client-Centered Therapy* (1951), *A Theory of Therapy, Personality, and Interpersonal Relationships, as Developed in the Client-Centered Framework* (1959), *On Becoming a Person* (1961), *Freedom to Learn* (1969), *Carl Rogers on Encounter Groups* (1970), and *On Becoming Partners: Marriage and Its Alternatives* (1972), we can see a number of significant changes in his position. In his view, theory is "a fallible, changing attempt to construct a network of gossamer threads which will contain the solid facts . . . a stimulus to further creative thinking" (1959, p. 191). Perhaps Rogers's willingness to revise his position and his desire that it be questioned and tested account for the impact of his self-theory, called client-centered theory, upon the field of counseling. As Hart (1970) indicated, Rogers introduced the experiential approach to the professions of counseling and therapy.

BACKGROUND

From his work as a therapist, Rogers incorporated elements of his own experience and the influences of other theorists into a theory of personality and therapy. Rogers was influenced by Thorndike at Columbia and by his first practical experience at the Institute for Child Guidance, which was dominated by Freudian thought. While on the staff of the Child Guidance Center in Rochester, Minnesota, Rogers was influenced to some degree by the thinking of Otto Rank. In 1940 he moved from a clinical setting to a position on the faculty of Ohio State University, where he began to crystallize his experiences into a theory of therapy.

In 1945, Rogers moved to the University of Chicago, where he organized the Counseling Center, coined the term *client-centered therapy* to describe his approach to counseling, and conducted a great deal of research. He continued this research at the University of Wisconsin, focusing on hospitalized schizophrenics. In 1964 Rogers went to the Western Behavioral Sciences Institute in La Jolla, California, and in 1968 with some colleagues formed the Center for Studies of the Person in La Jolla, where he is currently a Resident Fellow. Since then, Rogers has focused on using client-centered therapy to help normally functioning individuals, largely through the group process.

Although much of his work is a synthesis of theorists such as Snygg and Combs, Rank, and Sullivan, Rogers's major hypothesis came from his own experiences: "I feel that if I subtracted from my work the learnings I have gained from deep relationships with clients and group participants, I would be nothing" (1974, p. 120). His first formulations concerned the process of therapy. Only later did he broaden this theory of personality. In his Distinguished Professional Contribution Award address to the American Psychological Association in 1973 he expressed his continued desire to learn and improve his ideas: "I should stop here, but I cannot. It is always a strain for me to look backward. It is still the present and the future which concern me most" (Rogers, 1974, p. 122).

THEORY OF PERSONALITY

Rogers believes that his theory of therapy is on stronger ground than more general theories of personality: "Although a theory of personality has developed from our experience in client-centered therapy, it is quite clear to anyone closely associated with this orientation that it is not our central focus" (1959, p. 194). Nonetheless, it suits our purpose better to discuss his notions about personality, its development, and the nature of normal and abnormal behavior before examining the client-centered approach to counseling.

Rogers rejected the Freudian concept of the individual as basically an irrational, unsocialized, and self-destructive being who has little control over self. In Rogers's view, people are positively motivated: individuals are rational, socialized, and largely determine their own destiny. ". . . The individual has the capacity to guide, regulate, and control himself, providing only that certain definable conditions exist. Only in the absence of these conditions, and not in any basic sense, is it necessary to provide external control and regulation of the individual" (1959, p. 221). Thus, given a reasonable situation in which to grow and mature, the individual will develop to full potential, and along constructive lines, relatively free from internal anxiety.

THE STRUCTURE OF PERSONALITY

Rogers's theory of personality involves three essential ingredients: the organism, the phenomenal field, and the self.

The Organism

The term *organism* refers to the total individual. "The organism is at all times a total organized system in which alteration of any part may produce changes in any other part" (Rogers, 1951, p. 487). The organism, then, is all that a person is: thoughts, behaviors, and physical being. Furthermore, the organism acts holistically in relation to the phenomenal field; that is, the individual always acts as an organized entity in an effort to satisfy needs. The organism's one basic motive is the need to become actualized: "the urge to expand, extend, develop, mature" (Rogers, 1961, p. 351). That is, the organism desires to develop fully and to be free of external controls. Finally, the organism allows some experiences to become symbolized in the consciousness while denying or ignoring other experiences. What the organism tends to be aware of and to symbolize are products of learning, and the individual who is able to symbolize most experiences in awareness is likely to experience normal development.

Phenomenal Field

The *phenomenal field* is all that a person experiences. "Every individual exists in a continually changing world of experience of which he is the center" (Rogers, 1951, p. 483). The phenomenal field is the individual's ever-changing world of experience, internal as well as external. Some events are consciously perceived, some are not. It is also what the individual perceives in the phenomenal field that is important, not the actual reality: what the individual perceives to be occurring is his or her reality.

The Self

The most important of Rogers's principles of personality is his concept of the *self*. In Rogers's view, the self is a differentiated portion of the phenomenal field composed of a series of perceptions and values about "I" and "me." In the structure of personality, the self is the center around which the personality evolves. The self develops out of the organism's interaction with the environment. As it develops, it tends to integrate as well as distort some of the values of other people. The self strives to maintain both the organism's consistency of behavior and its own consistency. Experiences consistent with the concept of self are integrated; those not consistent with the self are perceived as threats. The self is always in process; it grows and changes as a result of continuing interaction with the phenomenal field.

Summary

Rogers's concept that the personality is always in a state of development is central to his theory: the three components of personality continue to interact and produce changes in individuals as they constantly strive toward self-actualization. Human behavior is goal directed toward control of the environment and the individual's place in that environment. It is innately good and need not be subject to control under normal circumstances; each individual is capable of "a balanced, realistic, self-enhancing, other-enhancing behavior" (Rogers, 1961, p. 105).

In Rogers's concept of reality, it makes little difference what actually happens in an event; it is people's perception of their experience that affects their choice of a response. Hence, people respond actively to events through thought, not passively.

Personality, then, is a product of continuing interaction among the organism, the phenomenal field, and the self. Human behavior is a unitary and positive movement toward the goal of self-actualization. Finally, people are basically good and, given normal conditions for development, are responsible for their own actions.

We now turn to how this structure develops in individuals. First we will examine the course of normal personality development; then we will consider ways in which this normal development is impaired.

PERSONALITY DEVELOPMENT

Organismic Valuing Process

In Rogers's view each individual is born with a tendency toward actualization. This inherent tendency is the motivational system for the infant and continues throughout life. Thus, from the outset the infant's behavior is goal directed, focused on the need to satisfy the organism in interaction with reality. The infant exists in an environment of its own creation and can be understood only from its internal frame of reference (Rogers, 1959). If an infant perceives a new situation as frightening, it makes no difference that in reality no threat exists. The infant's perception of that situation constitutes its real world. Cumulative experience of this situation may change the infant's perception of reality; but it is the perceived reality that affects behavior, regardless of whether that perception is accurate. The infant interacts with perceived reality as a unit and begins to evaluate experiences by the criterion of whether they meet the need for self-actualization. Experiences perceived as failing this need acquire a negative value; those perceived as fulfilling it are given a positive value. This constitutes the organismic valuing process (Rogers, 1959). It is "an ongoing process in which values are never fixed or rigid, but experiences are being accurately symbolized and continually and freshly valued in terms of the satisfactions organismically experienced . . ." (Meador & Rogers, 1973, p. 137). Through this valuing process the individual begins to pay attention to positively evaluated experiences and to avoid those valued negatively.

Positive Regard from Others

The self develops from the organism's interaction with perceived reality as the individual's experiences begin to be differentiated and symbolized in awareness as self-experience. As the infant interacts with its environment, most importantly with significant others, this awareness of self-experiences develops into a concept of self, which is a differentiated part of the phenomenal field. Up to this point in its development, the infant has been concerned only with satisfying its own need for actualization and has been able to operate on its own internal locus of control, the organismic valuing process. As awareness of self develops, a universal and pervasive need for positive regard develops (Rogers, 1959). This need "can only be satisfied by others, and his need for positive regard from significant others is particularly important" (Meador & Rogers, 1973). In the growing process, the infant learns that certain behaviors cause people to respond in warm and loving ways that are innately satisfying. Likewise, it learns that certain behaviors are responded to with anger and rejection, which are not satisfying to it. Because of the need for positive regard from others, the infant begins to respond with behaviors that will elicit satisfying responses from others and to avoid behaviors that do not elicit those responses. The individual is beginning to accept the values of others instead of its own. This leads the infant to adopt a set of self-evaluative thoughts based on behaviors that are valued by others.

Self-Regard

Through this process the infant develops a need for self-regard, "a learned sense of self based on his perception of the regard he has received from others" (Meador & Rogers, 1973, p. 130). The infant begins to judge its own behavior as good or bad in terms of what others value, regardless of whether the behavior is personally satisfying. Given this development, the infant now has two processes for evaluating its own behavior: the innate organismic valuing process and the adopted values of others. Often the evaluations of others become so important that the individual's behavior is dominated not by what will be innately satisfying, but by what will cause others to respond in favorable or positive ways. If this process is carried far enough, the individual begins to like or dislike herself or himself based on the evaluations of others. In this case the need for self-regard causes the child to introject the values of others into the self.

Conditions of Worth

At this point the individual cannot value himself or herself in a positive light unless he or she behaves in terms of these introjected values, regardless of whether the behavior is innately satisfying. Because many of the experiences that the organismic valuing process has valued positively do not receive positive regard from others, the individual begins to avoid or deny those experiences. At this point the person has developed conditions of worth. The individual gives positive value to some experiences that are not innately satisfying, and negative value to some that are (Rogers, 1959).

Proper Conditions for Normal Development

It is possible that the sequence described above does not have to take place. Earlier in this chapter we noted that the need for positive regard from others and self-regard play a large part in establishing the proper conditions for normal personality development. Given constant unconditioned positive evaluation by the significant others in their environment, people will develop a healthy personality. In this situation they constantly experience positive evaluation from others, which is satisfying even though some of their behaviors may not be accepted. If a child always feels loved by others even though they do not accept some of her or his behavior, no conditions of worth will develop. In this situation the child experiences unconditioned positive regard, which results in unconditional self-regard. These conditions lead to the development of a healthy personality, for if no conditions of worth are developed, the organismic valuing process and needs for self-regard and positive regard are congruent: hence, people will evaluate their behavior on the basis of an anticipated positive or negative effect. In Rogers's view, behaviors that bring positive results will not only be personally satisfying but, because of the nature of people, will be basically accepted and positively valued by society. Thus, as a result of the sequence just described, individuals will be well-adjusted and socialized (Rogers, 1959).

SUMMARY

In Rogers's view, people who are given the proper conditions for growth will develop into fully functioning individuals. Under these conditions they will be open to all their experiences and will have no need to apply defensive mechanisms. They will be aware of all their experiences and will be able to symbolize them accurately. The organismic valuing process will determine behavior, and individuals will be in a continual state of change as they have new experiences. They will be able to deal with new situations in creative and adaptive ways because there is no need to distort or deny awareness of any experiences. As socially effective individuals they "will live with others in the maximum possible harmony, because of the rewarding character of reciprocal positive regard" (Rogers, 1951, p. 234). Rogers does not describe such people as "well adjusted," but as "fully functioning," to imply a continuing process instead of a static state. "The fully functioning person would be a person-in-process, a person continually changing. Thus, his specific behavior cannot in any way be described in advance. The only statement which can be made is that the behaviors would be adequately adaptive to each new situation, and that the person would continually be in a process of self-actualization."[1]

THE DEVELOPMENT OF MALADAPTIVE BEHAVIOR

Given that everyone is born with the potential for good and with the one basic motive of actualizing the organism, how does the individual develop psychological maladjustment; that is, how is he or she prevented from becoming a fully functioning person?

In the normal course of development individuals have a need for self-regard. This need, which is based on their personal perception of the regard given by others, leads individuals to perceive their experiences in a selective fashion in terms of self-introjected conditions of worth. These conditions of worth, developed because of others' reactions, are not necessarily congruent with the organismic valuing process, for they are not based on the innate valuing system but on the values of others. In this situation, individuals perceive and symbolize in awareness only experiences that are in agreement with their conditions of worth. Those experiences not in agreement are either distorted or denied to awareness. As this process takes place, individuals alter their perceptions of events to meet the requirements of the conditions of worth. Self-experiences not consistent with the conditions are not brought into the structure of the self in accurate form. Hence, from the time people first develop conditions of worth and perceive experiences based on these conditions of worth, the possibility exists for incongruence between the self and the organism's experience. This incongruity leads to vulnerability and psychological maladjustment. The individuals can no longer act as a unified whole. Sometimes behavior is controlled by the organismic valuing process, but at other times it is controlled by introjected conditions of worth. In essence, the individual is trying to keep two masters happy.

CHARACTERISTICS OF THE MALADAPTIVE PERSONALITY

Estrangement

In Rogers's view this is the basic estrangement of man. "He has not been true to himself, to his own natural organismic valuing of experience, but for the sake of

---

1. From Rogers, C. R., A theory of therapy, personality, and interpersonal relationships as developed in the client-centered framework, in S. Koch (ed.), *Psychology—A study of a science*, vol. 3, *Formulation of the person and social context.* Copyright © 1959, McGraw-Hill. Used by permission of McGraw-Hill Book Company.

preserving the positive regard of others has now come to falsify some of the values he experiences and to perceive them only in terms based upon their value to others" (Rogers, 1959, p. 226). This development occurs early in infancy, when the individual has learned certain values that cause betrayal of the self. A child does many things that are innately satisfying but cause rejection or anger from others. The child may be noisy when parents want quiet; may fight when he or she should not; may show too much interest in sexual activities. When the child loses this important positive regard, she or he begins to develop the conditions of worth that lead to incongruity between self and experiences.

Incongruity in Behavior

As a result of the development of incongruity between self and experiences, the individual develops incongruities in behavior. Some behaviors will be consistent with the self-concept and will act to maintain and enhance it (the process of self-actualization). Other behaviors will be based on the conditions of worth and will maintain and enhance aspects of experience that are not a portion of the self-structure. To maintain itself, the self will distort these experiences or deny them as part of its self-experiences. The behavior of the individual in this state may take the form of having sexual relations at one time because it is innately satisfying, yet at other times avoid sexual relations because others may feel this behavior is inappropriate. This inconsistent pattern of behavior will probably cause anxiety.

Anxiety

If the individual's behavior is not distorted or denied, but instead is accurately symbolized in her or his awareness, the self-concept will be exposed to inconsistency and develop feelings of anxiety. "The conditions of worth would be violated, and the need for self-regard would be frustrated" (Rogers, 1959, p. 226). "Experiences which seem to the behaver to be threatening to his existing concepts of self are likely to be rejected with great vigor" (Combs & Snygg, 1959, p. 113). The individual who feels threatened has no choice but to defend the self. Combs and Snygg, Hilgard (1949), and Rogers have suggested that the common defense mechanisms outlined in psychoanalytic theory are means of dealing with this threat. They keep experiences that are inconsistent with the self-concept from being accurately symbolized in the awareness.

Defense Mechanisms

Defense mechanisms act to keep individual perceptions of experiences consistent with self-structure, through selective perception or distortion of the experience, or through denial of the experience to awareness. As Hilgard stated, "The need for self-deception arises because of a more fundamental need to maintain or restore self-esteem" (1949, p. 376). With defense mechanisms, however, neither the actual behavior that causes the anxiety or threat to the self nor the conditions that caused the individual to deny or distort the experiences change. Thus, the individual is forced into an inflexible and maladaptive pattern of behavior and becomes increasingly rigid as more and more perceptions of self-experiences are distorted. The individual is prevented from fully functioning because experiences are not assimilated into the structure of the self.

Maladaptive Behavior

To some degree almost all people employ defenses to protect their self-image. But when there is a high degree of inconsistency between the concept of self and experiences, and the individual is suddenly confronted with this inconsistency by some experience he or she cannot deny or distort, the defense mechanism will be unable to cope with the situation. This situation causes anxiety in the individual in proportion to the threat to the self.

In such a state the individual will sometimes behave in ways consistent with experiences that have previously been distorted or denied to awareness, at other times in ways that are consistent with the self-concept. For example, the person may sometimes behave in an openly hostile way to other people, at other times in a socially acceptable manner. Thus, the behavior of individuals in a state of disorganization is unpredictable to both themselves and those around them.

In Rogers's view, individuals experiencing personal difficulty or maladaptive behavior are generally in a constant state of anxiety or tension. Behavior tends to be rigid because of inaccurate perceptions of experiences. These people are unable to adopt new behaviors to meet new situations or to assimilate new experiences into the self-structure. Such individuals tend to misjudge many situations and to avoid new ones; they are unaware of much of their behavior because they tend to deny the experience to awareness or to distort it to fit the self-concept. Behavior is unpredictable and often irrational, and the individuals frequently feel their behavior is out of their control. People trying to serve two masters are unable to satisfy either one, and the result is dysfunction.

Before considering how self-theorists attempt to help people return to a position of self-actualization, we will examine the objectives of self-theory, or client-centered counseling.

THE GOALS OF COUNSELING

One of the most important aspects of client-centered counseling is that the counselor allows the client to set the goals. If the counselor were to set the goals for the client, he or she would be interfering with the individual's basic motivating force, the need for self-actualization. Each individual, given the proper circumstances, can develop and regulate his or her behavior, and this behavior will be positive and socially acceptable. In essence, the goal of the client-centered counselor is to establish the proper conditions whereby the client can resume a normal developmental pattern.

In a more specific sense, however, the goal of the client-centered counselor is to help the individual reinstitute the process toward self-actualization by removing the obstacles to this process. The objective is to free the client of learned behaviors that hinder the innate tendency toward self-actualization, to help the client redevelop his or her own resources and potential (Boy & Pine, 1963). Hence, although the global goals for all clients are the same, it is expected that each client will establish individualized goals (Rogers, 1970). The counselor strives to help the client remove obstacles trapped within that hinder a true perception of experiences and thus gain new insight into her or his experiences and self-structure. In Rogers's view, counseling is a process of releasing an already existing force in a potentially adequate individual.

In the client-centered view, the complete goals of counseling have not been accomplished when the person leaves counseling; only the patterns for future change have been established. The obstacles to growth have been removed and new ways of perceiving experiences established so that the individual can proceed toward self-actualization. Rogers did not believe the counseling experience, "no matter how uplifting, to be an end in itself, but finds its significance primarily in the influence it has on later behavior . . ." (1970, p. 70).

THE COUNSELING PROCESS

The client-centered approach to counseling has been described as an *if-then* approach. If certain conditions exist, then a process will take place that has certain definable characteristics. If this process occurs, then the counselor can expect certain changes in the client. The basic hypothesis is that given the establishment of the proper conditions for growth, the client will be able to gain personal insight and take positive steps toward solving his or her difficulties. We now turn our attention to these necesary conditions.

NECESSARY AND SUFFICIENT CONDITIONS

In the client-centered approach, the conditions set forth as necessary for counseling are also assumed to be sufficient for counseling. If the conditions exist or are provided, then change will take place in the client. In the client-centered view, the following conditions are both necessary and sufficient.

Psychological Contact

The first condition in the counseling process is that two people be in contact. Earlier, Rogers used the word *relationship*, but replaced it with the word *contact*. In Rogers's terms, this need for the counselor and client to be in at least a minimal state of psychological contact constitutes the least experience between two people that could be referred to as a relationship.

Minimum State of Anxiety

The second condition is that the client be in at least a minimum state of anxiety, vulnerability, or incongruence, that is, experiencing incongruity between self-concept and behavior. The more anxious the individual is about this incongruity, the more likely it is that successful counseling will take place. The individual has to be uncomfortable enough to want to make some changes in himself or herself.

Counselor Genuineness

The third essential condition is that the counselor be congruent or genuine in the relationship. The counselor must be an integrated or whole person whose concept of self allows cognizance of all his or her behaviors and accurate awareness in experiencing them. The more closely the counselor approaches the state of a fully functioning individual, the more effective he or she will be. This state of congruity allows the counselor to be aware of and honest about the kinds of feelings the client is eliciting. "Congruence in the therapist's own inner self is his sensing of and reporting his own felt experiencing as he interacts in the relationship" (Meador & Rogers, 1973, p. 139).

Unconditioned Positive Regard

The fourth necessary and sufficient condition is that the counselor experience unconditioned positive regard toward the client. To have unconditioned positive regard for an individual means to respect the person regardless of differential values one might place on the other's various behaviors. The counselor does not judge one behavior as positive and another as negative; rather, the counselor accepts the individual regardless of his or her behaviors. It is much like the feeling a parent has toward a child, valuing and loving the child for herself or himself, even though the parent may not place equal value on all the child's behaviors. Provided with this condition, the client comes to believe he or she is a person of worth, a person capable of growth.

Empathic Understanding

The fifth essential condition is that the counselor experience empathic understanding of the client's internal frame of reference. In Rogers's view, no one can ever fully understand another person's internal frame of reference. *Empathic understanding* means that the counselor is able to understand the client's internal frame of reference as accurately as another person can. It is an attempt to try to understand the client as if the counselor were the client. "This exclusive focus in therapy [counseling] on the present phenomenal experience of the client is the meaning of the term 'client-centered' " (Rogers, 1959, p. 191).

Client Perception

The final necessary and sufficient condition is that the client perceive, to some degree, the existence of the counselor's empathic understanding and unconditioned positive regard. It is not sufficient for the counselor to have unconditioned positive regard or empathic understanding for the client; these conditions must be communicated and the client must perceive that they are present.

If the counselor provides these conditions to the client, then the process of counseling will take place, and if the process of counseling takes place, certain definable outcomes will occur. These outcomes aim at returning the individual to self-actualization. According to Rogers (1959), the greatest flaw in his statement of necessary and sufficient conditions is that they are stated in all-or-none terms. All the conditions, except possibly the first, exist on a continuum. Recent research, to be discussed in detail later, appears to indicate that these conditions do exist on a continuum, and that the degree to which they exist is perhaps even more crucial.

Given these six conditions, what can a counselor expect to happen in the process of counseling? What changes will occur in the transactions between client and counselor, and what changes can we expect in the client?

Given the proper conditions, clients should feel increasingly free to express their feelings. In the threat-free, nonpossessive, accepting atmosphere of the counseling situation, clients feel valued by the counselor regardless of the kinds of thoughts they express. The counselor's provision of unconditional positive regard eliminates any threat to receiving positive feedback from statements. They will not receive negative feedback from the counselor for expressing socially unacceptable feelings. As clients come to feel comfortable in the counseling situation, more and more of their statements will become self-referential, moving from nonself matters, which are safer to discuss, to "I" or "me" statements. For example, a client may move from discussing how difficult it is for brothers to get along to how difficult she or he finds it to get along with her or his brother.

As the number of self-referential statements increases, clients begin to see their experiences and feelings in a more realistic light. They are able to symbolize experiences accurately in their consciousness and to examine feelings and experiences in an objective manner without threat to the self. They can examine the incongruity between experiences and concept of self because there is no threat in doing so in the counseling situation. There, they can express socially unacceptable feelings without the self's being threatened by another's reactions.

In the counseling situation clients are able to express their true feelings and to examine objectively experiences that have been denied or distorted in the past because of the threat to the self. As they examine these experiences objectively, their concept of self is reorganized by assimilating these experiences. As the reorganization of self-concept continues, experiences and self-structure become increasingly congruent. This lessening of incongruity means that there are fewer threatening situations to the self, and, in turn, clients behave less defensively. They no longer have to protect the self by denying or distorting experiences, because more experiences are congruent with self-concept. Clients learn to feel an unconditional positive self-regard, and they redevelop the ability to react to experiences based on the organismic valuing process rather than on the introjected conditions of worth. In short, they become their own person once again, not only able to deal with situations that have caused difficulty in the past, but also open to new situations. With flexible and adaptive behavior, they are becoming fully functioning individuals.

Those who follow the client-centered approach or, as some now call it, the relationship theory approach, make no attempt to explain the process or the reasons for its success. As Rogers (1959) pointed out, no one really knows why, when a piece of steel is rubbed by a magnet, it will point north if it is allowed to rotate freely. Likewise, why the individual goes through this process is really not important; what is important is that, given the proper conditions, this process will occur in the counseling situation and will lead to certain outcomes; namely, the client will be able to perceive experiences accurately, evaluate them in terms of the organismic valuing process, and act accordingly.

IMPLEMENTING THE PROCESS

Rogers's first exposition of his theory in 1942 placed great importance on specific techniques derived from his experience as a practicing therapist. He described concrete procedures that a therapist or counselor should use, and these were accompanied by partial transcripts of actual therapy situations. By 1951, Rogers had rejected this approach; his second book emphasized that two different therapists could use the same technique but get different results. Rogers had shifted the emphasis to the importance of the therapist or counselor in the relationship. Currently, he talks less about technique and more about the attitudes of the counselor. Given the proper attitude, the counselor in the client-centered framework has a great deal of freedom in the counseling interview. It is the counselor's role to create the conditions that make it possible for the counseling process to take place; the counseling process, in turn, will result in changes in the client.

Worth of the Individual

Of prime importance in implementing the process of relationship or client-centered counseling is the counselor's attitude toward the worth and integrity of the individual. The counselor attempts to implement the process of counseling by being as perceptive and sensitive as possible to the client and his or her experiences. In essence, the counselor must perceive the internal frame of reference of the individual as accurately and completely as possible, and then feed these perceptions back to the client. In one sense the client-centered counselor becomes an alter ego for the client, a self out of the self. This allows the client to see and examine his or her own attitudes, feelings, and perceptions as worn by another. As a result the counselor can view clients more objectively without the complications of emotion. The counselor assumes that the client, having perceived these elements more closely in a nonthreatening and nonjudgmental atmosphere, will come to welcome her or his feelings into the structure of the self.

Nature of the Counseling Relationship

The nature of the relationship is of major importance in establishing the counseling process. This relationship has been initiated by the client's coming to the counselor to seek help. Hence, the major responsibility for the relationship is the client's, not the counselor's. In defining the nature of the relationship to the client, the counselor must make it clear that he or she does not have all the answers; it is the client who has the answers. The counselor is there to help the individual find her or his own solutions. The major responsibility for the success of counseling rests with the client. The unique aspect of self-theory or client-centered counseling is this emphasis on client responsibility.

Time Limit

The counselor should place a time limit on the relationship, specifying the length of each session, and perhaps also the number of sessions. There are two primary reasons for establishing these limits. The first is the obvious reality that a counselor has a limited amount of time available. But perhaps more important is the belief that, given certain time limits, the client may sense a need to make the sessions as productive as possible. Although the counselor sets this limit, it must be made clear that the client is basically responsible for what occurs within the allotted time.

Focus on Individual, Not Specific Problem

The emphasis in the counseling relationship is on the individual, not on a particular concern or problem. This is in line with the self-theory belief that one aspect of behavior is related to the whole system of behavior. Hence, the entire system requires attention, not just one aspect of it. Within this context, it is expected that the counseling relationship will help the client develop better ways of dealing with life in general and that she or he will become a more mature, more socialized, and more self-enhancing person. Specific problems or concerns will be resolved as a by-product of growth toward self-actualization. All of this implies that specific goals for counseling are less important than the overall goal of restoring the personal growth process through the provision of the necessary conditions to bring about meaningful change.

Here and Now

The self-theory position also puts emphasis on the individual's current existence, both inside and outside the counseling relationship. Self-theorists believe that knowledge of the nature and background of the client's difficulties is unnecessary. What is important is not what has happened in the past that may have led to the client's current difficulties; rather, the manner in which the client is now operating concerns the counselor. In the example of a client's feeling hatred for a brother, the client-centered position is that it makes little difference that this hatred developed because the brother usurped attention from the client; current feelings toward the brother and how they affect the client's whole pattern of behavior are important. One of the counselor's roles is to help the client focus on current feelings by expressing them verbally.

Diagnosis

In self-theory, emphasis on the individual's situation replaces diagnosis in counseling. Diagnosis is considered undesirable because it implies that a few have the power to decide what is right for the many. It also violates the assumption that individuals are self-determining beings, responsible for their own actions. Second, diagnosis in counseling is inappropriate because only clients can diagnose their difficulty. Only the clients can accurately see their internal frame of reference; thus, it is dangerous for the counselor to attempt a diagnosis. Finally, diagnosis implies a denial of the unique qualities of each man or woman. To diagnose is to place people in categories, and the client-centered counselor wishes to avoid this. Rather than diagnosing the client's difficulty, the counselor should respond to the individual as a unique person with a potential for self-diagnosis and remediation.

Emotional versus Intellectual Content

In addition to focusing on the client's current situation and denying the need for diagnosis, the client-centered approach emphasizes the need for concentrating on the emotional rather than the intellectual elements in the relationship. Pure knowledge of intellectualization does not help the client, because the impact of the knowledge is blocked from awareness by the emotional satisfactions that the individual achieves through current behavior. The individual may know intellectually what the real situation is, but emotional responses prevent the client from using this knowledge to change behavior.

Regardless of what the real situation is, the individual's feelings about that situation are most important, and these are what must concern the counselor. Thus, in client-centered counseling the counselor attempts to help the client focus on feelings about himself or herself, other people, and events in his or her world. It is the counselor's role to feed back to the client as accurately as possible the feelings the latter is expressing at that time, in the hope that the client will be able to view these feelings more objectively.

Role of Information

The focus on the emotional aspects of the counseling process is coupled with the client-centered view of the role of information in counseling. In general, the client-centered approach does not hold that the counselor should bring information into the counseling process. This approach does not deny the importance of information; rather, it proposes that it should be the client who brings information into the counseling process—information that has been gathered outside of counseling, perhaps under the counselor's direction. Thus, the actual counseling experience is devoted to helping the individual sift through the information, with the emphasis again being placed on the client's feelings toward that information. The counselor is responsible for helping the client focus on her or his feelings about the information. It is the feeling about the information, not the information per se, that is important.

Testing

This view on the use of information in the counseling process also applies to a specific kind of information: testing. Current client-centered thinking does not completely exclude the use of tests in counseling, but their use may be somewhat limited. As with other types of information, what is important is how the client feels about the test and its information. In speaking about the use of tests in counseling, Rogers stated that "The client may, in exploring his situation, reach the point where, facing his situation squarely and realistically, he wishes to compare his aptitudes and abilities with those of others for a specific purpose. When tests come as a real desire from the client, they may enter into the situation" (1946, p. 142). Even in this situation it may be more important to discuss why the client wishes to take a particular test. If, for example, a client were to ask, "Do you have a test that will tell me what occupation I should enter?" the counselor, instead of listing all the tests that might do the requested job, should first focus on why the client feels he or she needs a test in order to make this decision.

SUMMARY

It is clear that the self-theory, client-centered, or relationship approach to counseling does not place much emphasis on counseling techniques. The emphasis is almost exclusively on the importance of the relationship. The focus is on the ability of the counselor to establish a relationship in which the six necessary conditions outlined earlier are present. To the degree that these conditions are present and are perceived as being present by the client, the counseling process will be effective.

The key elements in establishing these conditions are the counselor and the counselor's relationship with the client. The counselor must be a patient and expert listener who fully accepts each individual by offering an atmosphere of unconditional positive regard and empathic understanding. In an attempt to help the client develop insight into her or his difficulty, the counselor encourages free expression from the client and then reflects these feelings. In a very real sense the counselor becomes an alter ego for the client. In this process no specific problem, information, or other intellectual elements are discussed; the focus is on the individual in her or his current state.

If the counselor follows this process, then the necessary and sufficient conditions for counseling will be established. The client will be able to go through the process of articulating feelings, developing insight and self-understanding, and finally developing reoriented goals and new modes of behavior. Although counseling may end at this stage, it is not the end of the process. The client has simply been returned to a state where he or she is able independently to continue the lifelong process toward self-actualization. The individual is in control of his or her own behavior once again. The conditions of worth, the introjected values of others, have disappeared and the organismic valuing process has taken its proper place as the evaluator of experiences and controller of behavior.

RECENT EXTENSIONS OF SELF-THEORY

One of the outstanding contributions to the field of counseling by self-theorists has been their willingness to submit their methods of counseling to the test of research. Since the inception of self-theory, client-centered or relationship counselors, led by Rogers, have made it clear that their hypotheses should be submitted to research and then reformulated on the basis of that reasearch; Rogers's own theory has undergone several changes since 1942. Whereas initial research consisted mainly in analyzing tapes from counseling sessions, it now covers a wide range of techniques, most of them based on client self-reports. This approach fits with the theory's basic assumption that only the client can really tell whether or not the counseling has been beneficial.

Studies on the actual process of counseling include early research by Rogers and Dymond (1954), Hogan (1948), and Raskin (1949). These studies indicated that as counseling progressed, the defensiveness of the client decreased, congruence btween the self and experience increased, and the client tended to see himself or herself as the locus of evaluation. Later studies by Traux and Carkhuff (1967) and Carkhuff and Berenson (1967) demonstrated that, given the necessary and sufficient conditions, a client will move into self-exploration, which will lead to positive changes in the individual.

The research on the outcomes of counseling is perhaps both the most interesting and the most important. Theorists ask: Given the conditions and the process of counseling, what kinds of outcomes can be expected? A review of the research in this area shows that this aspect of the theory has received the least confirmation. Studies by Cowen and Combs (1950) and Grummon and John

(1954) tended to support the hypothesis that individuals who have gone through client-centered counseling do have better overall adjustments. A similar study, conducted by Carr (1949), found no evidence of better adjustment following counseling. Much of this research is based on self-reports and is extremely difficult to evaluate. However, more studies are now appearing that lend support to the effectiveness of counseling based on the process described above.

An early study by Seeman (1954) found that therapeutic success was related both to the degree that the counselor felt liking for the client and the degree to which the client felt liked by the counselor. More recent research by Truax (1961b), Carkhuff (1967a), and Carkhuff and Berenson (1967) indicated that in many cases these conditions are sufficient to bring about change in the client. Truax and Carkhuff (1967) concluded that a person who can communicate warmth, genuineness, and accurate empathy is more effective in helping others. It appears that these conditions can be measured in the counseling process, at least to some degree, and that the conditions do have a beneficial effect on the client.

Truax (1963) found that schizophrenic clients who had therapists offering high levels of the necessary conditions showed improvement after counseling, but that those who had therapists offering low levels of these conditions tended to show negative personality changes. Truax and Carkhuff (1965) also reported that changes in the level of the conditions offered affected the amount of the client's self-exploratory behavior. A study by Holder, Carkhuff, and Berenson (1967) found that the depth of self-exploration of a low-functioning client was related to the amount of the necessary conditions offered by the counselor. A study by Truax, Wargo, and Silber (1966) found that when high levels of the necessary conditions were provided, counseling could be effective with the culturally disadvantaged. This research seems to indicate that not only are the conditions necessary, but also the levels of the conditions offered affect the outcomes of counseling. This research has been coupled with the development of scales to measure the requisite conditions (Truax, 1961b, 1962a, 1962b; Carkhuff, 1967a). These developments led to an extension of Rogerian thinking usually referred to as the Carkhuff Model.

THE CARKHUFF MODEL

In 1969 Carkhuff published a two-volume text, *Helping and Human Relations: A Primer for Lay and Professional Helpers*, in which he set forth a model for helping based on the necessary and sufficient conditions. Carkhuff renamed many of the conditions, added some, and produced a standardized set of scales to measure the level of the conditions being offered by one person (helper) to another (helpee). Since then Carkhuff and his associates have continued to modify and extend the model, but the basic model and its rationale remain essentially the same.

The model developed by Carkhuff (1971) prescribes three goals for the helping (counseling) process.

1. **Client self-exploration** The first goal of counseling must be to provide conditions that facilitate the client's self-exploration. Before anything else can happen, both the counselor and the client must explore all dimensions of the presented difficulty.
2. **Client self-understanding** If the client is enabled to explore his

problem and his feelings in depth, he will come to understand exactly what is causing his difficulty.

3. **Client action** Once understanding is achieved, the client is ready to begin what is perhaps the most difficult part of the process—taking action. Understanding without action is generally nonproductive. In this stage, the counselor helps the client consider the available alternatives and then helps the client plan a series of steps that will lead to a successful outcome.

Carkhuff's counseling process (1971) utilizes six conditions or dimensions that are provided to the client. The counseling process is also seen as a two-stage process: facilitation and action. During facilitation, the primary objective is to establish a working relationship with the client so that she or he feels free to enter into self-exploration, which in turn leads to self-understanding. During this stage the dimensions of empathy, respect, concreteness, and genuineness are most important; in the action stage confrontation and immediacy are most important.

Empathy

Carkhuff (1969a) contended that empathy is the most important element in the counseling process. According to Carkhuff and Berenson, "We must emphasize that empathy is not the client-centered mode of reflection with which it is most often confused" (1977, p. 8). In their view, it combines reflection and accurate diagnosis.

Respect

"Respect is the ability to respond to the other person in such a way as to let him know that you care for him and that you believe in his ability to do something about his problem" (Carkhuff, 1971, p. 170). Respect means recognizing the uniqueness of each individual and conveying to the client the belief that he or she is a unique individual. The notion of respect goes beyond Rogers's unconditional positive regard in that it is to be conveyed throughout counseling (Carkhuff & Berenson, 1977).

Concreteness

This is the ability of the counselor to get the client to be specific about her or his concerns. "Specifically, concreteness refers to the helpee (client) pinpointing or accurately labeling his feelings and experiences" (Gazda, 1973, p. 26). The counselor helps the client accomplish this by being concrete himself or herself. An early study of Truax and Carkhuff (1967) indicated that a counselor's ability to be concrete may be even more important than empathic understanding.

Genuineness

Genuineness means that the counselor is able to be himself or herself in the relationship. The counselor does not wear a facade and is able to let personal feelings operate in counseling when appropriate. The counselor must always, however, keep in mind what will benefit the client; this will sometimes make it necessary to withhold a genuine expression (Carkhuff, 1971).

Confrontation

Often in counseling, the counselor will note discrepancies, either between things the client is saying, or between what the client is saying and doing. In such circumstances, the counselor must be able to point out these discrepancies to the client. Carkhuff (1969a) describes three general types of confrontations. They point out a discrepancy:

1. between what the client says she or he wants to be and what the person is;
2. between the client's statement about himself or herself and actual behavior;
3. between the way the client describes herself or himself and how the counselor perceives the client.

The counselor must use confrontations of any type with caution, particularly early in the counseling process. They are action oriented and involve some risk, but often are necessary to move clients forward.

Immediacy

Immediacy is the ability of the counselor to get the client to focus on what is currently going on in the counseling relationship. This generally involves some dynamic between the counselor and the client.

Carkhuff has developed scales to measure the levels of counselor performance on each of the six dimensions. His scale contains five points, and the minimum level at which a counselor must perform on each dimension in order to be helpful is level three. Carkhuff and others have conducted a great deal of research with these scales and the dimensions. Generally, the research supports the hypothesis that the dimensions are, at the least, necessary conditions for counseling; they may not be sufficient. Because of their importance in counseling, however, they are discussed in more detail in Chapter Twelve.

SUMMARY

The recent developments in self-theory, though based on Rogers's thinking, represent a movement toward eclecticism. Rogers has contributed to an understanding of some basic requirements for effective counseling regardless of a counselor's particular theory.

REFERENCES

Boy, A. V., & Pine, G. J. *Client-centered counseling in the secondary school.* Boston: Houghton Mifflin, 1963.

Carkhuff, R. *The counselor's contribution to facilitative processes.* Urbana, Ill.: Parkinson, 1967a.

———. Toward a comprehensive model of facilitative interpersonal processes. *Journal of Counseling Psychology*, 1967b, *17* 62–72.

———. *Helping and human relations: A primer for lay and professional helpers (Vol. 1).* New York: Holt, Rinehart and Winston, 1969a.

———. *Helping and human relations: A primer for lay and professional helpers (Vol. 2).* New York: Holt, Rinehart and Winston, 1969b.

———. Helping and human relations: A brief guide for training lay helpers. *Journal of Research and Development in Education*, 1971, *4*(2), 17–27.

Carkhuff, R. R., & Berenson, B. G. *Beyond counseling and therapy.* New York: Holt, Rinehart and Winston, 1967.

———. *Beyond counseling and therapy* (2nd ed.). New York: Holt, Rinehart and Winston, 1977.

Carr, A. C. An evaluation of nine non-directive psychotherapy cases by means of Rorschach. *Journal of Consulting Psychology*, 1949, *13*, 196–205.

Combs, A. W., & Snygg, D. *Individual behavior: A perceptual approach to behavior* (rev. ed.). New York: Harper & Row, 1959.

Cowen, E. L., & Combs, A. W. Follow-up study of 32 cases treated by nondirective psychotherapy. *Journal of Abnormal Social Psychology*, 1950, *45*, 232–258.

Gazda, G. M. *Human relations development: A manual for education.* Boston: Allyn and Bacon, 1973.

Grummon, D. L., & John, E. S. Changes over client-centered therapy evaluated on psychoanalytically based thematic apperception test scales. In C. R. Rogers & R. F. Dymond (Eds.), *Psychotherapy and personality change: Co-ordinated studies in the client-centered approach.* Chicago: University of Chicago Press, 1954.

Hart, J. T. The development of client-centered therapy. In J. T. Hart and T. R. Tomilerson (Eds.), *New directions in client-centered therapy.* Boston: Houghton Mifflin, 1970.

Hilgard, E. R. Human motives and the concept of self. *American Psychologist*, 1949, *4*, 374–382.

Hogan, R. The development of a measure of client defensiveness in the counseling relationship. Unpublished doctoral dissertation, University of Chicago, 1948.

Holder, T., Carkhuff, R. R., & Berenson, B. G. The differential effects of the manipulation of therapeutic conditions upon high and low functioning clients. *Journal of Counseling Psychology*, 1967, *16*, 139–144.

Meador, B. D., & Rogers, C. R. Client-centered therapy. In R. Corsini (Ed.), *Current psychotherapies.* Itasca, Ill.: F. E. Peacock, 1973.

Raskin, N. J. An analysis of six parallel studies of the therapeutic process. *Journal of Consulting Psychology*, 1949, *13*, 206–220.

Rogers, C. R. *Counseling and psychotherapy.* Boston: Houghton Mifflin, 1942.

———. Psychometric tests and client-centered counseling. *Educational Psychological Measurement*, 1946, 6, 139–144.

———. *Client-centered therapy: Its current practice, implications, and theory.* Boston: Houghton Mifflin, 1951.

———. A theory of therapy, personality, and interpersonal relationships, as developed in the client-centered framework (unpublished manuscript, 1955).

———. A theory of therapy, personality, and interpersonal relationships as developed in the client-centered framework. In S. Koch (Ed.), *Psychology—A Study of a Science (Vol. 3).* New York: McGraw-Hill, 1959.

———. *On becoming a person: A therapist's view of psychotherapy.* Boston: Houghton Mifflin, 1961.

———. *Freedom to learn: A view of what education might become.* Columbus, Ohio: Charles E. Merrill, 1969.

———. *Carl Rogers on encounter groups.* New York: Harper & Row, 1970.

———. *On becoming partners: Marriage and its alternatives*. New York: Delacourt, 1972.

———. In retrospect: Forty-six years. *American Psychologist*, 1974, 29(2), 115–129.

Rogers, C. R., & Dymond, R. F. (Eds.). *Psychotherapy and personality change: Coordinated studies in the client-centered approach*. Chicago: University of Chicago Press, 1954.

Seeman, J. Counselor judgments of therapeutic process and outcome. In C. R. Rogers & R. F. Dymond (Eds.), *Psychotherapy and personality change*. Chicago: University of Chicago Press, 1954.

Truax, C. A. Clinical implementation of therapeutic conditions. In C. R. Rogers, *Therapeutic and research progress in a program of psychotherapy research with hospitalized schizophrenics*, 1961a.

———. A scale for the measurement of accurate empathy. Discussion paper no. 20, Wisconsin Psychiatric Institute. University of Wisconsin, 1961b.

———. A tentative scale for the measurement of unconditional positive regard. Discussion Paper no. 26, Wisconsin Psychiatric Institute. University of Wisconsin, 1962a.

———. A tentative scale for the measurement of therapist genuineness of self-congruence. Discussion paper no. 35, Wisconsin Psychiatric Institute. University of Wisconsin, 1962b.

———. Effective ingredients in psychotherapy: An approach to unravelling the patient-therapist interaction. *Journal of Counseling Psychology*, 1963, 10, 256–263.

Truax, C. B., & Carkhuff, R. R. Personality change in hospitalized mental patients during group psychotherapy as a function of the use of alternate sessions and vicarious therapy pretraining. *Journal of Clinical Psychology*, 1965, 21, 327–329.

———. *Toward effective counseling and psychotherapy: Training and practices*. Chicago: Aldine, 1967.

Truax, C. B., Wargo, C. G., & Silber, I. D. Effects of high accuracy empathy and nonpossessive warmth during group psychotherapy with female institutionalized delinquents. *Journal of Abnormal Psychology*, 1966, 71, 267–274.

GESTALT COUNSELING

CHAPTER SEVEN

In 1951 Fritz Perls predicted that within twenty years there would be an explosion in interest in Gestalt therapy (Perls, 1969b). The prediction was accurate: the explosion has been occurring since the 1960s. "Dynamic, dramatic, intensive, and absorbing Gestalt therapy already has exerted a powerful influence upon therapeutic counseling, encounter group therapy, marathon groups, family therapy, school counseling, psychiatric social work, and rehabilitation counseling with delinquents and drug addicts" (Belkin, 1980, p. 239). The Esalen Institute at Big Sur, California, is perhaps the best-known center for Gestalt approaches. But there are Gestalt training institutes in at least fifteen cities, and more than twenty-five books on Gestalt procedures have been published since 1969 (Fagan, 1975). In some ways the popularization of Gestalt therapy is unfortunate. Any bookstore offers several books loosely based on Perls's writings, and "Gestalt weekends" of various kinds are widely advertised. Many of these publications and events tarnish the image and credibility of Gestalt counseling and that is too bad because it has much to offer.

Fritz Perls began his career in Germany. In 1921 he received an M.D. from Friedrich Wilhelm University. Then he went into psychoanalytic training in Berlin, Frankfurt, and Vienna. The rise of Nazism drove him from Germany in 1933 and from Amsterdam in 1935. From 1935 to 1946 he worked in South Africa; in 1946 he moved to the United States and established a private practice. His first major statement on Gestalt psychology, *Ego, Hunger, and Aggression*, was published in 1947. This was followed by the publication of *Gestalt Therapy: Excitement and Growth in the Human Personality* (Perls, Hefferline, & Goodman, 1951) and *Gestalt Therapy Verbatim* (Perls, 1969b). From 1964 to 1969 Perls conducted training institutes at Esalen.

Perls developed the Gestalt approach to counseling and therapy from a psychological theory of perception known as Gestalt psychology, founded by May Wertheimer, Wolfgang Kohler, and Kurt Koffka in Germany around 1910. The three psychologists formulated their ideas in opposition to a current emphasis in psychology on seeking to understand human experiences by reducing them into component parts. They argued that most often the component parts cannot be understood separately, but must be considered as organized wholes. They chose the German word *Gestalt*, which English and English have defined as signifying "a unified whole, properties which cannot be derived by summation from the parts and their relationships" (1958, p. 225), to describe their point of view.

BASIC CONCEPTS

Before examining the Gestalt approach to counseling and therapy, it will be helpful to understand some of the basic tenets of Gestalt psychology.

Gestalt psychologists believe that human behavior is much more than a product of unrelated stimuli. A picture, for example, is a whole that has meaning: a Gestalt. Isolated, the splashes of color or shading will probably have no meaning. The parts have meaning only in relation to the whole in which they exist. Similarly, a series of musical notes tends to have meaning only in the perspective of an organized whole, a song. These examples illustrate the principle that individuals always act to organize stimuli into wholes, or Gestalts.

FIGURE 7-1 PRINCIPLE OF CLOSURE

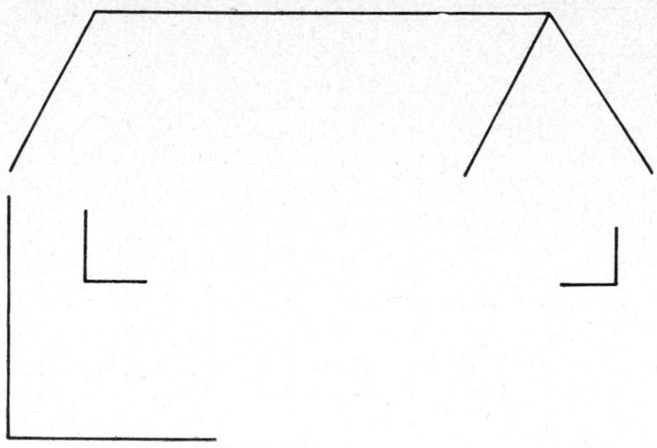

Gestalt psychologists have developed several principles to explain how this process occurs. Three of these principles illustrate the process.

- **Principle of Closure** When people perceive a figure that is incomplete, their minds act to finish the figure and perceive it as complete. Most people would perceive the series of lines in Figure 7-1 as a house.
- **Principle of Proximity** The relative distance of stimuli from each other within the perceptual field determines how they are seen. In Part *a* of Figure 7-2 people are most likely to perceive a series of related dots, whereas the dots in Part *b* generally would be seen as unrelated.
- **Principles of Similarity** The similarity of stimuli in the perceptual field causes people to group them together. Figure 7-3 would be seen as columns of squares and columns of circles, not as rows that contain both circles and squares.

Each of these principles illustrates how the mind seeks to make sense of the

FIGURE 7-2 PRINCIPLE OF PROXIMITY

a.   b.

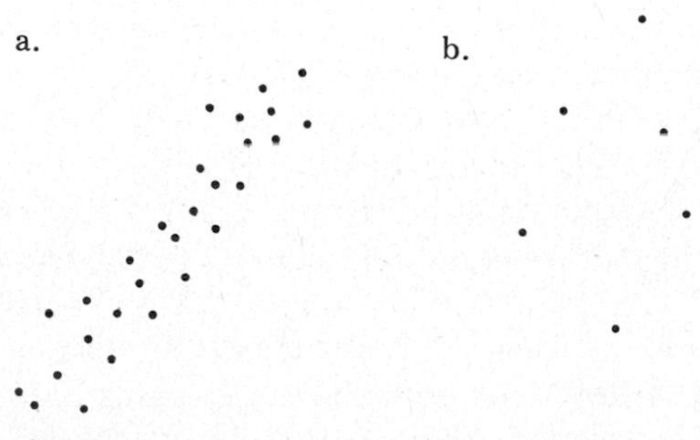

FIGURE 7-3 PRINCIPLE OF SIMILARITY

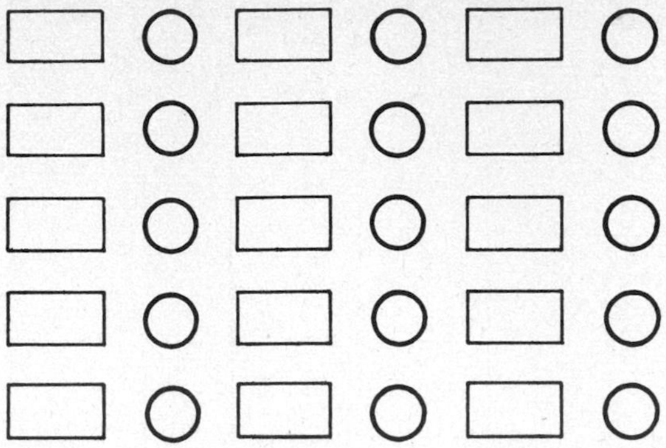

vast array of stimuli in the phenomenal field by pulling things together. The important point is that the stimuli have meaning only as they are organized in the mind by the individual. Out of the vast array of possibilities, what determines what people attend to in their phenomenal field? At any one time a person can be aware of only a single cluster of these stimuli, which form a Gestalt. The person reading this text might from time to time, transfer concentration from the printed page to other Gestalts in the setting, such as a couch or bed, or become aware of a favorite song on the radio. These examples illustrate the basic figure-ground principle so important in Gestalt psychology. The individual is always acting to organize his or her phenomenal field to meet his or her needs (Coleman, 1960). The things people are focusing on in their field are referred to as the *figure*; the rest of the field is called the *ground*. Anything within the field, including bodily sensations, thoughts, pain, pleasure, or external objects, can become figures; however, two events may not be figures at the same time (Coleman, 1960).

The particular meaning the individual gives to a figure is a function of its relationship to the total ground of which it is a part. This is not as simple as it sounds, for the phenomenal field of each person depends on the individual's level of awareness. A person driving on a highway at 65 mph may casually be aware of another car at the side of the road. Her or his awareness is not acute enough to detect the fact that the car is a patrol car; the result is a ticket for speeding. Given another person with a higher level of awareness in a similar situation, the individual might see the car for what it is and might change his or her behavior and not get a ticket. In both cases the patrol car is in the phenomenal field, but the two individuals gave it different meanings, depending on their levels of awareness. When people perceive clearly and sharply, their behavior is similarly efficient and accurate, but when awareness is vague, behavior is also likely to be vague, inappropriate, and disorganized (Coleman, 1960).

In summary, the major assumptions of Gestalt psychology are:

1. People actively seek to form meaningful wholes out of their phenomenal fields.
2. Any event in the phenomenal field can become differentiated at any time from the ground and become the figure.

3. Whether the event does become a figure depends upon the need(s) of the individual.
4. The meaning given to the figure depends upon the perceived ground in which it exists.
5. The level of awareness of the individual in relation to his or her phenomenal field will determine the accuracy of perception and her or his behavior.

Traditional Gestalt psychology never applied these principles beyond explaining the perceptual process in humans. As Wallen indicated, original Gestalt theorists never extended these basic assumptions "to organic perceptions, to the perceptions of one's own feelings, emotions, and bodily sensations" (1970, p. 8). Perls and others developed what became known as Gestalt therapy and counseling from this point.

THEORY OF PERSONALITY

Although Perls was trained as a psychoanalyst and part of Gestalt counseling is influenced by this training, the Gestalt view of people is very similar to both existential and humanistic positions.

Passons (1975b) listed eight assumptions about the nature of human beings that act as the framework for Gestalt counseling:

1. Individuals are composite wholes made up of interrelated parts. None of these parts—body emotions, thoughts, sensations, and perceptions—can be understand outside the context of the whole person.
2. Individuals are also part of their own environment and cannot be understood apart from it.
3. People choose how they respond to external and internal stimuli; they are actors,not reactors.
4. People have the potential to be fully aware of all their sensations, thoughts, emotions, and perceptions.
5. Individuals are capable of making choices because they are aware.
6. Individuals have the capacity to govern their own lives effectively.
7. People cannot experience the past and the future, they can experience only themselves in the present.
8. People are neither basically good nor bad.

MOTIVATING FORCE

It is clear from these eight assumptions that Gestalt theory views people as capable of directing their own development. In fact, Perls felt that individuals must take responsibility for their own lives. The motivation for this process, according to Perls (1969b), springs from the fact that everyone has only one inherent goal: to self-actualize. This sounds similar to the Rogerian or self-theory position, but there is a striking difference. Rogers described the process of actualization as striving to become all that one is capable of becoming. The perspective is future oriented. The Gestalt position is much more present oriented. According to Kempler, "Becoming is the process of being what one is and not a process of striving to become" (1973, p. 262). This striving to be is the basic motivating force for all behavior. All other needs are a part of this overriding need to actualize oneself. These needs include the basic biological needs that must be satisfied if the individual is to survive and what might be termed secondary needs, developed through interaction with the environment. This level of needs is generally related directly to behavior, but all behaviors revert to the basic need to actualize oneself.

An individual's behavior at any given time is explained by the Gestalt theorists in terms of the figure-ground relationship. As Passons indicated, "Needs move in and out of the figure and ground field. At a given moment a particular need may emerge and direct the person's behavior. The need moves from ground to figure" (1975b, p. 15). After the individual has met this need, the figure moves back into the ground and a new one captures and directs the individual's behavior. This is a very flexible and flowing process, and for each individual a different need may dominate (become figure) in a particular situation. In fact, for the same individual in two apparently similar situations, a different need can dominate at various times. So it is almost impossible to predict behavior. All that can be said with certainty is that even in situations in which two or more needs are in conflict, one need will become dominant; at that time and in that situation, the meeting of that need is most important to the individual. It cannot be predicted that in a future similar situation the same need will dominate. The individual cannot deal with the past or the future, only the present.

Having examined the Gestalt view of human nature and the basic motivating force, we can now turn our attention to the process of personality development.

PERSONALITY DEVELOPMENT

Perls conceptualized personality development as a product of the individual's striving to maintain a balance between conflicting inner forces. At every moment the individual is confronted with either an external demand or an internal need, either one of which activates action to restore balance. This striving for balance is designed to reduce tension within the individual and the process is referred to as "organismic self-regulation" (Perls, 1969a). This inherent ability for self-regulation develops in the evolving personality in three phases: social, psychophysical, and spiritual (Kempler, 1973). Kempler described these stages as sequential and also as representative of the individual's potential level of awareness. In the social stage the infant is aware of others without having an awareness of self. This stage is dominated by required interactions with others that simply permit the organism to survive. The infant is unable to secure the food needed for survival and so must rely on those around it.

During the second, psychophysical, stage, the child develops a sense of self, or self-image. "The psychophysical stage, characterized by awareness of one's own person, is described in terms of personality and is divided into three components; self, self-image, and being" (Kempler, 1973, p. 262). Whereas being exists from birth, the other two parts of the personality develop as the individual interacts with his or her environment. Generally, by the time the individual reaches midadolescence these three subsystems of the personality are in full operation. According to Kempler (1973), this development occurs through three processes: adaptation, acknowledgment, and approbation.

Adaptation

Adaptation is the process whereby the individual discovers the boundaries to her or his existence, becoming aware of what is self and what is nonself. No evaluative judgments are made; rather, it is a becoming aware of one's world and adapting one's behavior to it. The child who touches a hot stove and burns herself or himself establishes a boundary and adapts to it. Early childhood in particular, and life in general, is replete with these encounters with the universe, and in each case the individual adapts his or her behavior. This adaptation leads to a growing differentiation and appreciation of the boundaries in which the person exists (Kempler, 1973).

Acknowledgment

Through acknowledgment individuals discover themselves. "Watch me" is the child's password to the parents as he or she plays. "In his innocent wisdom he knows that he must be acknowledged" (Kempler, 1973, p. 263). Personal acknowledgment leads children to develop a sense of self and an appreciation of their own existence.

Acknowledgment is similar to adaptation in that both are processes of establishing certain truths without an accompanying judgment. Whereas adaptation defines boundaries of the universe, acknowledgment is the process of validating self and others. Children who ask a parent to watch them are asking for validation, not approval or disapproval. The proper response of the parent is a simple acknowledgment such as "OK" or "Not right now" (Kempler, 1973). In both responses there is no approval or disapproval, simply acknowledgment. Acknowledgment given in this fashion permits children to develop a personal valuing system for their own behavior. Unfortunately, most parents respond with a kind of validation that is accompanied by a notion of approval or disapproval. This process is what the Gestaltists refer to as approbation.

Approbation

Approbation is the process whereby people develop splits within their personalities. Acknowledgment leads to awareness of self, but approbation creates a self-image that is a notion of self based on external standards. As children seek acknowledgment of their existence and instead receive approbation, they soon learn to seek approval rather than acknowledgment. Instead of "Watch me," they now ask, "Didn't I do that well?" Once this process is instituted, individuals develop a polarization in their personality. On one hand there are feelings of self that represent things they want to do, and on the other hand is the self-image that represents all that individuals feel they should do because of external standards.

As Kempler (1973) pointed out, children must receive acknowledgment to survive, and if they cannot receive pure acknowledgment, they will seek approval. In effect, they will choose to change their own being and develop an acceptable self-image that indirectly gets them the acknowledgment they need to survive. As individuals move through the developmental years, they encounter myriad situations, and at each point there is possibility for the development of notions of self and notions about the proper self-image. Thus, the personality becomes a system with being at the center, and at the point where being encounters the external world there is potential for developing the beginnings of a continuing conflict between self and self-image; a battle between forces that want the individuals to be what they are and forces that want them to be what they should be.

From a Gestalt viewpoint, approbation interferes with the development of a sound and healthy notion of self. The self is responsible for "formulating the creative adjustment contacts within the environment. Thus, the self is active, dynamic, and changing according to emergent needs and environmental presses" (Passons, 1975b, p. 16). The self acts to move the individual to self-actualization. The self-image acts to hinder that process.

The actual development of the self occurs as the individual interacts with her or his environment. As Harman and Franklin stated, ". . . Growth occurs when a person is willing to make contact with people, objects, and situations in the environment" (1975, p. 363). As this process takes place, the individual is bound to meet frustration, which from a Gestalt perspective is positive. "Without frustrations there is no need, no reason, to mobilize your resources, to discover that you might be able to do something on your own" (Perls, 1969b, p. 32). Frustration, which is painful, causes the infant to learn how to do things that remove the frustration. This is the process of growth as the individual learns to rely on the self rather than on others; it is the move from a dependent status to an independent one. Such an individual identifies more with the self than with the self-image, and thus is able to be creative and self-regulating. "This allows for situations to be finished, problems to be solved, and environmental contacts to be focused on those things which have interest and excitement for him" (Passons, 1975b, p. 16). A person who reaches this stage of development is ready to move to the spiritual phase of personality development.

Few people achieve the spiritual stage, although most acknowledge its existence. Kempler (1973) described this phase as the movement from "sensory-sensing" to "extra sensory-sensing" awareness. "From intellectual, physical, and emotional activity, man manifests himself as what might be called a sensitive-intuitive person" (p. 262). This is the stage of awareness many try to achieve through artificial means such as drugs. The only true way of achieving this stage, however, is through development of a fully functioning self during the second phase of development, and this does not happen very often. Most individuals lead their lives within the second phase; thus, it is the psychosocial phase with which we should be most concerned.

Personality, then, is a product of individuals' interactions with their perceived environment from the moment of birth onward. Growth takes place through assimilating material from the environment, utilizing the processes of adaptation, acknowledgment, and approbation. Throughout the social, psychophysical, and spiritual stages of development, people strive to meet their needs by forming Gestalts, the wholes that allow them to organize behavior within the environment in order to meet current needs. Because these needs are always changing, even from moment to moment, the process of Gestalt formation is a continuous process. It causes some events in the environment to become figure, which recedes into ground when that need has been met.

Each individual's personality is a composite of three separate entities: self, self-image, and being. Being is the essential existence of the organism; the self is the creative process that leads the individual to actualizing behaviors; the self-image is the part of personality that hinders creative growth. Whenever being comes into contact with the world, the potential exists for development of self and self-image. Thus, an internal conflict is established between what the self wants to do and what the self-image says she or he should do. In normal growth and development people develop some balance between the self-image and the self that permits them to operate in a relatively effective way. In most cases these patterns emerge as the "character" of the individual. Unfortunately, it is the very fact that a character is established that Gestalt theorists believe keeps people from being actualized. Character leads individuals to play the same roles over and over again, and this is the basic conflict (Perls, 1969a): to be actualized the self has to be free to interact creatively with the environment. If character is established, implying the influence of the self-image, the self is no longer free to be creative. Most individuals exist this way, in what amounts to basic estrangement. It is also this division within the self that leads people to experience difficulty and eventually may bring them to the counseling situation.

MALADAPTIVE BEHAVIOR

Most people exist by maintaining some balance between the desires of the self and the shoulds of the self-image. According to Kempler (1973), however, often an experience or series of experiences occurs that upsets this balance. In such cases, either the self or the self-image acts to challenge the other. In effect, an internal war erupts that causes the individual to experience anxiety and often produces ineffective behaviors. The nature of the difficulty will depend on the general state of the individual's psychological health and the kind of experience that sets the internal war in motion. The individual who is behaving in maladaptive ways is generally attempting to actualize the self-image rather than the self. Such an individual is more subject to the opinions of others than to the self-control mechanisms (Ward & Rouzer, 1975). Passons (1975a) divided the kinds of problems individuals experience into the following six areas: (1) lack of awareness, (2) lack of self-responsibility, (3) loss of contact with environment, (4) inability to complete Gestalts, (5) disowning of needs, and (6) dichotomizing dimensions of the self.

1. **Lack of awareness** is usually related to rigid personality. The character people establish to maintain the delicate balance between self and self-image causes them to lose contact with the what and how of their behavior. They lack creative ability to deal with the environment: they simply exist, moving through life from day to day with an uneasy feeling of nonfulfillment.

2. **Lack of self-responsibility** is related to lack of awareness, but takes the form of trying to manipulate the environment instead of the self. Instead of striving for independence or self-sufficiency, which is the hallmark of maturity, individuals strive to remain in a dependency situation.

3. **Loss of contact with the environment** is also related to lack of awareness. This problem can take two forms. In the first, individuals become so rigid in their behavior that no input from the environment is accepted or incor-

porated. In effect, they withdraw from contact with the environment, including other people. Such withdrawal into self prohibits individuals from meeting their needs and from moving toward maturity. The other form is manifested in people who need so much approbation that they lose themselves by trying to incorporate everything from the environment. The self becomes almost totally subsumed by the self-image.

4. **Inability to complete Gestalts** or to complete business is another kind of problem. As Polster and Polster (1973) indicated everyone has the capacity to tolerate internally the persistence of many unfinished situations, but if they become powerful enough they will cause difficulty. The person who gets angry with a spouse but does not express that anger directly, kicking the dog instead, is not completing the business. Such uncompleted business always seeks to be completed. When unfinished business becomes strong enough "the individual is beset with preoccupation, compulsive behavior, wariness, oppressive energy, and much self-defeating activity" (Polster & Polster, 1973, p. 36). The unfinished business causes the individual to continue to strive to complete it in current activities. Polster and Polster (1973) list the following examples of typical complaints representing unfinished Gestalts or business that clients bring to counseling: "I never told my father how I felt; I was humiliated when I wanted attention; I wanted to be an artist and they made me become a doctor" (p. 36). An individual who is preoccupied with unfinished business cannot bring his or her full awareness to bear on the current situation.

5. **Disowning of needs** occurs when people act to deny one of their own needs. Passons (1975a) pointed out that in our society individuals commonly deny their need to be aggressive. This need is generally socially unacceptable, so individuals tend not to express it. Instead of channeling the energy into constructive behavior, people deny the existence of the need and thereby lose the energy it produces.

6. **Dichotomizing dimensions of the self** takes the form of people perceiving themselves at only one end of a possible continuum such as "strong or weak, masculine or feminine, powerful or powerless" (Passons, 1975b, p. 17). Individuals who perceive themselves at only one end of the continuum never realize the full value of the continuum. As Passons (1975b) indicated, people who cannot admit any weakness cannot fully appreciate the strength they do have. The most popularly known split is what Perls (1969b) called "top dog–underdog." The top dog is that part of the individual characterized as moralistic, perfectionistic, and authoritarian. It is the top dog who strives to get the individual to behave as others expect. The underdog represents the desires of the individual and operates as the defensive and dependent part of the personality. As Perls stated, "The underdog is the Mickey Mouse. The top dog is the Super Mouse" (1969b, p. 18). The resulting personality fragmentation into "controller" (top dog) and "controlled" (underdog) produces an internal conflict that is incapable of completion (Ward & Rouzer, 1975, pp. 25–26). As long as the person continues to listen to the top dog, this internal conflict will remain, for the needs of the individual will not go away.

All six categories of behavioral disturbances are directly related to the conflicts within the self. This conflict usually occurs as a direct result of dissonance between the expression of individual needs and environmental demands. Instead of relying on the self and the capacity for self-regulation, people become caught in trying to maintain an externally imposed self-image. Instead of utilizing energy to interact with and assimilate the environment, they direct energy toward playing roles. As the roles demand more and more energy, individuals have less and less energy to devote to fulfilling the needs of self. Because these needs never go away, such people experience continual anxiety, which in turn generally leads to patterns of inappropriate and unsatisfying behaviors. It is at this point that many individuals seek some assistance.

GOALS OF COUNSELING

The overriding objective of Gestalt counseling is to bring about integration of the individual. People who come to counseling suffer from the split caused by the formation of self-image concepts. This split keeps them from utilizing their energy in appropriate ways to meet personal needs and to grow, develop, and actualize. Given that the self-image is a product of the demands of others, a specific aim of counseling is to help clients discover that they do not have to depend on others, but that they can do many things for themselves (Perls, 1969b). Since a significant element of a healthy individual is the ability to regulate the self, the objective of counseling is to move the individual from dependence on others' judgments to reliance on self-regulation. This process leads to an integration of self as the need to play the roles demanded by the self-image begin to disappear. The ultimate goal is for the individual to be true to himself or herself. As Perls suggested, this goal is never totally achieved. "Integration is never completed; maturation is never completed. It's an ongoing process forever and ever" (Perls, 1969b, p. 64). The goal of Gestalt counseling is a global one; although a client may present a specific concern to the counselor, the Gestalt counselor holds that the specific concern is only a representation of a more generalized problem, the inability to be self-regulating.

Of central importance in the achievement of self-regulation is increasing the individual's awareness. According to Perls, awareness itself is curative. Given awareness, "the organism can work on the healthy Gestalt principle: that the most important unfinished situation will always emerge and can be dealt with" (1969a, p. 51). Consistent with this belief, much of what the Gestalt counselor does is designed to help the client achieve an improved level of awareness that leads to integration and organismic self-control.

THE ROLE OF THE COUNSELOR
AND THE COUNSELING PROCESS

According to Perls (1969b), the role of the counselor is to provide an atmosphere in which the client has the opportunity to discover her or his own needs; to discover those parts of the self that the client has given up because of environmental demands; and to provide a place in which the client can experience growth. Such an atmosphere is created as the counselor acts to facilitate the client's awareness of self in the now (Passons, 1975a). "The now is the present, is the phenomenon, is what you are aware of, is that moment in which you carry your so-called memories and your so-called expectations with you. Whether you remember or anticipate, you do it now" (Perls, 1969a, p. 44). So defined, the now is a continuous process; it is never stationary; it exists and immediately gives way to a new now. As the now moves, so does the individual's awareness, for "being aware of one's now means staying aware of one's flow" (Passons, 1975b, p. 22). Being aware means being able to focus on or attend to what one is currently doing.

To facilitate this process, counselors utilize the most important tool they have: themselves. A counselor, fully aware of herself or himself in the now, engages the client in a here-and-now interaction. The counselor does not interpret, probe, preach about reality; rather, he or she interacts with the client in the now. "Gestalt counseling is active, confrontative, and concerned with what is experienced in the 'now.' The past is a memory, the future is a fantasy, and are important only as they are experienced in the present as such" (Pietrofesa, Hoffman, Splete, & Pinto, 1978, p. 83).

The Gestalt counselor must view himself or herself as a catalyst, acting in whatever ways necessary to help the client increase his or her awareness. According to Polster and Polster (1973), the counselor above all else must be an exciting, energetic individual who brings his or her full humanity to the counseling session. Only in this way will the counselor be able to enter into the client's now and react to it. "He does not interpret behavior, but rather focuses on the 'what' and 'how' of the person's (client's) now, the assumption being that the most pressing need will eventually emerge to be dealt with" (Passons, 1975b, p. 22). As soon as the client is able to express this need the counselor can begin the process Fagan (1970) referred to as patterning, the process whereby the counselor helps the client see the ongoing pattern of her or his life. Awareness of these patterns is the first step in the move toward reintegration of the self and healthy functioning.

TECHNIQUES OF COUNSELING

Of the many techniques that might be utilized by Gestalt counselors, the most commonly used techniques employ "how" and "what" questions focusing attention on current functioning. With both types the counselor is seeking to get the client to become more aware of feelings, behaviors, emotions, and sensations in the now. At the same time, the counselor is attempting to discover what things the client is trying to avoid and in what areas of functioning he or she is suffering from internal conflicts. "Awareness is an attempt to get the patient in touch with all of himself so that he can utilize all of his potential" (Harman & Franklin, 1975, p. 259).

FRUSTRATING THE CLIENT

People who come to counseling generally suffer from a lack of self-sufficiency and full awareness. As Perls (1969b) suggested, individuals who are experiencing difficulty cannot see the obvious; they are full of avoidances and resistances that prevent full awareness. Perls suggested also that clients are at an impasse that they really do not want to work through. "Very few people go into therapy to be cured, but rather to improve their neuroses" (1969b, p. 39). The impasse involves an unsatisfied need or some unfinished business that individuals believe they do not have the resources to resolve. In effect clients come to counseling hoping the counselor will provide an answer that will permit them to exist but will not require them to work through the difficulty. Instead of providing the answer, the counselor seeks to force clients to work through the impasse, first by permitting or, indeed, structuring the situation so that the impasse comes into the open, and then frustrating the clients by refusing to give them what they seek.

> This is what we are again and again trying to do, to frustrate the person until he is face to face with his blocks, with his inhibitions, with his way of avoiding having eyes, having ears, having muscles, having authority, having security in himself (Perls, 1969b, p. 38).

The counselor's goal is to help clients recognize that the impasse exists in the mind and that they have the ability to resolve their own impasse. In effect, the counselor is telling the client, "You can and must be responsible for yourself."

EXPERIENTIAL TECHNIQUES

The preceding general techniques are utilized in Gestalt counseling to establish an appropriate working environment and then to bring the impasses of clients into the open. In addition to these generalized techniques, Gestalt counselors also utilize a variety of experiential games, designed basically to increase individuals' awareness of themselves and their impasses and then to help them reintegrate themselves. Perls (1969b) indicated that this last step is the most crucial, for stripping the individual of all defenses and giving him or her no new ways of behaving, make the client even more vulnerable to outside forces than he or she was prior to counseling.

Levitsky and Perls (1970) and Passons (1975a) suggested a variety of these specific techniques. The following list is a summary of the techniques from both lists that appear to be most appropriate for use by counselors.

1. **Use of personal pronouns** Clients are encouraged to use "I" and "thou" to personalize communication. This is one way of helping clients to acknowledge their behavior. For example, the client might be asked. "How are you feeling right now?" and the client might respond with "Fine." The counselor might then say, "What is fine?" in an attempt to get the client to respond, "I am fine."

2. **Converting questions to statements** Often clients use questions to keep the focus off themselves or to hide what they are really thinking. The client who asks, "Do you really believe that?" is generally saying, "I don't think you believe that." Forcing clients to use the second statement makes them declare their own belief system.

3. **Assuming responsibility** Clients are asked to end all expressions of feelings or beliefs with "and I take responsibility for it." Another way to help clients assume responsibility for their own behaviors is to have them change "can't" to "won't." Instead of saying, "I can't do ＿＿＿," clients are encouraged to say, "I won't do ＿＿＿." Assumption of responsibility helps clients see themselves as having internal strength rather than as relying on external control.

4. **Sharing hunches** Counselors have a tendency to interpret what they see as the meaning of a particular client's behavior or statement. A better ap-

proach is to present the material to the client as though it were a hunch. "I see you tapping your foot and I imagine it means you are nervous." This behavior on the part of the counselor is less threatening, and it has the strong advantage of helping clients understand that all people imagine more than they know. That is, individuals see, and imagine the meaning of what they see: they project meaning. Having clients use the "see—imagine" statements helps them recognize their projections.

5. **Playing the projection** Related to sharing hunches is the technique of asking clients to play their projections. When clients project something onto other individuals, the counselor asks them to play the role of the person upon whom they have projected.

6. **Expressing resentments and appreciations** Many clients express strong negative feelings about people with whom they interact. The Gestalt position is that the clients would not continue to interact with these people unless some positive feelings existed. The counselor tries to get the client to express some of these feelings, believing that the client has become dominated by the negative and, to improve that relationship, should focus on some positive aspects. In this way clients can see both ends of the continuum. When a husband and wife come to counseling, for example, they generally have patterns of behavior that keep them focused at the negative end of the continuum. One of the tasks of the counselor is to get them to see, by expressing them, that there are some positive aspects of the relationship.

7. **Role rehearsal and reversal** As in the strategy for playing the projection, clients are often asked to play a role. In this case they may be asked to act out a behavior that is the opposite of the one in which they normally engage. This role reversal helps them get in touch with a part of themselves they were either unaware of or have denied existed. Clients may also be asked to rehearse in counseling a new role they are going to try outside of counseling. The rehearsal strengthens the belief that the new behavior can be carried out.

8. **Game of dialogue** When clients are caught between conflicting parts of their personalities (top dog–underdog; passive–aggressive), the counselor may instruct them to play both roles and to carry out a verbal dialogue between the two parts. Such a dialogue brings the conflict into the open so that it may be inspected and resolved.

The techniques presented here, particularly the first three generalized ones, are commonly used and representative of many others. The writings of Perls provide a fuller discussion; the book by Passons (1975b) is also helpful.

SUMMARY

Gestalt counseling is an outgrowth of a theory of perception known as Gestalt psychology. Its major tenets are that people behave in holistic fashion and that they have the capacity to regulate themselves. Individuals experience difficulty because they have come to depend too much on external events rather than on their internal self-regulation mechanisms. Such a situation probibits them from having full awareness of themselves and of the environment in which they exist. The purpose of counseling is to restore individuals' ability to be fully aware of themselves and their world. The process is an active, confrontative one, with an emphasis on how and what clients are experiencing. The counselor strives, through a variety of techniques, first to help clients recognize the strength they have, and then to help them utilize that strength in daily experience.

REFERENCES

Belkin, G. S. Contemporary psychotherapies. Chicago: Rand McNally, 1980.

Coleman, J. C. Personality dynamics and effective behavior. Chicago: Scott, Foresman, 1960.

English, H. D., & English, A. C. A comprehensive dictionary of psychological and psychoanalytical terms. New York: David McKay, 1958.

Fagan, J. Gestalt therapy introduction. Counseling Psychologist, 1975, 4, 3.

———. The tasks of the therapist. In J. Fagan & I. L. Shepherd (Eds.), Gestalt therapy now. Palo Alto: Science and Behavior Books, 1970.

Harman, R. L., & Franklin, R. W. Gestalt, instructional groups. Personnel and Guidance Journal, 1975, 54(1), 49–50.

Kempler, W. Gestalt therapy. In R. Corsini (Ed.), Current psychotherapies. Itasca, Ill.: F. E. Peacock, 1973.

Levin, L. S., & Shepherd, I. L. The role of the therapist in Gestalt therapy. Counseling Psychologist, 1975, 4, 27–30.

Levitsky, A., & Perls, F. S. The rules and games of Gestalt therapy. In J. Fagen and I. L. Shepherd (Eds.), Gestalt therapy now. Palo Alto: Science and Behavior Books, 1970.

Passons, W. R. Gestalt therapy interventions for group counseling. Personnel and Guidance Journal, 1975a, 51, 183–189.

———. Gestalt approaches in counseling. New York: Holt, Rinehart and Winston, 1975b.

Perls, F. S. Ego, hunger, and aggression. New York: Random House, 1969a. (Originally published 1947.)

———. Gestalt therapy verbatim. Lafayette, Calif.: Real People Press, 1969b.

———. In and out of the garbage pail. Lafayette, Calif.: Real People Press, 1969c.

Perls, F. S., Hefferline, R., & Goodman, P. Gestalt therapy: Excitement and growth in the human personality. New York: Julian Press, 1951.

Pietrofesa, J. J., Hoffman, A., Splete, H. H., & Pinto, D. V. Counseling: Theory, research, and practice. Chicago: Rand McNally, 1978.

Polster, E., & Polster, M. Gestalt therapy integrated: Contours of theory and practice. New York: Brunzer/Mazel, 1973.

Wallen, R. Gestalt therapy and Gestalt psychology. In J. Fagen and I. L. Shepherd (Eds.), Gestalt therapy now. Palo Alto: Science and Behavior Books, 1970.

Ward, P., & Rouzer, D. L. The nature of pathological functioning from a Gestalt perspective. Counseling Psychologist, 1975, 4, 24–27.

BEHAVIORAL APPROACHES TO COUNSELING

CHAPTER EIGHT

Behavioral theories have been in existence for some time, but their application to counseling is a rather recent development. Early efforts to apply learning theory principles to counseling centered largely on attempts to put the existing theories of counseling into a behavioral framework. The work of Dollard and Miller (1950) and of Pepinsky and Pepinsky (1954) are examples of this kind of effort. It was not until the Cubberley Conference at Stanford University in 1965 that behavioral counseling really gained momentum and national attention. John Krumboltz played a major role in that conference and has continued to play ". . . a major sustaining role in the development of the behavioral counseling approach" (Barclay, 1980, p. 457).

The early period of development is best characterized by the now-classic debate in 1956 between B. F. Skinner and Carl Rogers. Skinner, as the leading spokesperson of behaviorism, argued that the environment was the sole determiner of behavior. He saw humans as completely reactive beings whose behavior is controlled by external events. Rogers represented the humanistic notion that humans are self-determining. Although these two people would probably continue to hold opposite views, the approaches to counseling that they originally represented have changed markedly over the last quarter-century. Increasingly self-theorists are discussing the need for the counselor to utilize action strategies in counseling, and behaviorists are talking about the internal feelings of individuals. Two of the most exciting recent developments in behavioral counseling have been in the areas of covert reinforcement and self-management programs. Early critics of behavioral approaches contended that it is a system for manipulating others, but the recent developments have escaped that criticism. As indicated by the title of the Mahoney and Thoresen (1974) text, *Self-Control: Power to the Person*, a major emphasis in current behavioral approaches is on helping people control their own lives. It is unfortunate that many critics of behavioral approaches are still basing their arguments on behaviorism as it was structured twenty or thirty years ago, for the dichotomy between behavioral and humanistic approaches to counseling no longer exists. "Behavioral Counseling is no longer a partisan movement. It is part of the basic repertory of counseling" (Barclay, 1980, p. 457). The work of a host of individuals—Salter, Wolpe, Bandura, Krumboltz, Thoresen, and Hosford—has greatly broadened the early behavioral approaches to counseling.

It is still true that the behavioral approach to counseling makes the basic assumption that most client problems are problems in learning. As such, behavioral counselors view their task as an attempt to help those who come to them to learn new, more adaptive behaviors. In effect, the counselor is one kind of learning specialist (Krumboltz, 1966). This approach is not a conglomeration of techniques applied mechanically to clients, but one that places a great deal of faith in the laws of learning established through scientific investigation (Michael & Meyerson, 1962).

The rapidity of development and change within behaviorism and the divergences among individual theorists make it difficult to discuss all aspects of the field in a single chapter. The focus of this chapter is on the central concepts and beliefs with which most behavioral theorists would agree. Detailed discussions of the broad field of behavioral counseling are available in the works of such theorists as Krumboltz (1966), Hosford and deVisser (1974), Bandura (1969, 1977), Lazarus (1972), Wolpe (1959), Krumboltz and Thoresen (1969, 1976), and Mahoney and Thoresen (1974).

BEHAVIORIST PRINCIPLES OF LEARNING

The behavioral position is that most, if not all, of a person's personality can be attributed to the effects of the laws of learning as the individual interacts with his or her environment. Most of these principles of learning come within three general categories: (1) classical or respondent conditioning, (2) operant conditioning, and (3) imitative learning. Most current behavioral approaches to counseling utilize some combination of these models.

CHAPTER
EIGHT
131
BEHAVIORAL
APPROACHES
TO
COUNSELING

CLASSICAL OR RESPONDENT CONDITIONING

Ivan Petrovich Pavlov (1849–1936) is usually credited with the founding of classical conditioning. Classical conditioning makes use of the fact that some events in an individual's environment are related to some human neuromuscular and glandular responses (Michael & Meyerson, 1962). The taste of a lemon, for example, causes most people to salivate. The lemon is a stimulus that causes an automatic reaction in the organism, which is a response. Many such unconditioned stimulus-response connections are present at birth, and most of them are concerned with maintaining the existence of the organism.

A neutral stimulus that has not been part of an innate stimulus-response relationship can become a conditioned stimulus that creates a response by being paired with an original unconditioned stimulus. An infant's natural response to a loud noise (unconditioned stimulus) is fear (unconditioned response). As Watson and Rayner (1920) demonstrated with Albert, this fear response could eventually be elicited by a previously neutral stimulus in the form of a rat once the appearance of the rat (conditioned stimulus) had been paired with the loud noise several times. The response (fear) to the conditioned stimulus (rat) is called a conditioned response. This is the chain of learning from a classical conditioning standpoint. This new relationship will not remain as part of the organism's behavior if the conditioned stimulus is presented often enough without the introduction of the unconditioned stimulus. In the case of Albert, if the rat was presented frequently without any accompanying presentation of the loud noise, the conditioned stimulus, the rat, would lose its power to evoke a fear response. This is the process of extinction.

Although classical conditioning may explain the way in which some behavior is learned, many learning theorists believe that much of an individual's behavior cannot be explained by the classical model. To explain how most of an individual's behavior is learned, these theorists turn to the assumptions of operant conditioning.

OPERANT CONDITIONING

The basic principles of operant conditioning were outlined by B. F. Skinner (1938). Skinner's contention was that most human behavior occurs at random; the critical question is: What are the environmental consequences of the behavior? This type of behavior operates on the environment, in contrast with behavior that responds to prior stimuli (Michael & Meyerson, 1962). Basic to operant conditioning is a law of learning postulated by Skinner (1938): If a certain behavior is followed by an environmental event that brings satisfaction to the individual, then the probability of the behavior's recurrence is increased. An example is the child who sucks his or her thumb. At some time the infant randomly stuck its thumb in its mouth, and the sensations generated were pleasurable, and so, rewarding. Because the behavior was rewarding, the probability of that behavior's recurring is increased. In short, the child has learned the behavior of thumb sucking. Thus, learning through operant conditioning is the opposite of learning through classical conditioning. Operant conditioning occurs because of what happens after a particular behavior, whereas classical conditioning occurs in response to a stimulus in the environment. In operant conditioning the organism first must behave in a certain manner, and this behavior is shaped by the consequences of the environmental events that follow it.

IMITATIVE LEARNING

Most learning theorists contend that some of an individual's behavior is learned through a process that does not involve directly receiving a reward. Such learning is said to take place through the process of imitation or vicarious learning: an observer learns a particular response by watching some other person (the model) perform the response. Hosford (1980) believes that most human behavior is learned through observation and that this view is substantiated by psychological and anthropological research. Miller and Dollard (1941) referred to this process as "matched dependent behavior": the individual learns the response only if she or he matches the behavior of the model. Mowrer (1960) felt that the observer could learn the response of the model simply by seeing the model rewarded; in this view, the reward given the model is a vicarious reward for the observer. Work by Bandura (1962, 1965, 1969) has suggested that imitative learning can take place without either the model or the observer being rewarded. Bandura referred to this as a contiguity-mediational theory, which holds that imitative learning can take place simply through one individual's observing another respond. Bandura pointed out, however, that although the pattern of behavior may be learned simply through observation, reinforcement may be necessary in order for the observer to perform the behavior. In a sense, the behavior may lie dormant until it is called forth through reinforcement.

It is obvious how important this notion of imitative learning is to the learning theory position. Everyone has observed children modeling their behavior on someone they admire, such as holding a bat just like a famous ballplayer. Aspiring counselors also learn much of their own counseling behaviors, good or bad, through modeling based on their supervisors. Recent research indicates that this imitative learning is an extremely important factor, integral with the other laws of learning.

Classical/respondent, operant, and imitative learning are the basic models used in some combination by most behaviorists. No specific theory constitutes the one best representation of the whole field. However, some basic concepts have been developed as part of these models, upon which most behaviorists would agree. These concepts are essential to the behavioral approach to counseling, and we will now examine them.

ESSENTIAL CONCEPTS OF BEHAVIORISM

Reinforcement

CHAPTER
EIGHT
BEHAVIORAL
APPROACHES
TO
COUNSELING

133

Primary and Secondary Reinforcement   In general, there are two classifications of reinforcements. Primary reinforcements are such things as food, water, and air that are vital to life maintenance. Very few of the reinforcements an individual seeks or receives beyond infancy are primary. As soon as a young child begins to interact with the environment, he or she begins to learn that other stimuli can be reinforcing. These secondary, or learned, reinforcers, such as money, praise, blame, and love, are stimuli that the individual has learned to value. Generally, these occur as neutral stimuli until they are associated with a primary reinforcer. For example, initially the only reinforcement the infant recognizes when being held by its mother is food. The mother at this period is neutral. If the mother is warm and pleasant, however, getting attention from her soon becomes desirable, and this attention becomes a secondary reinforcement. Although the term *secondary* implies that these reinforcers are less important than primary ones, this is not true; not only do secondary reinforcements far outnumber primary ones in adult life, but many of them share equal importance with primary reinforcements and sometimes exceed them in importance, as when a person sacrifices his or her life to save others.

Positive and Negative Reinforcement   "The operation of presenting a positive reinforcer contingent upon a response is called positive reinforcement. The operation of removing an aversive stimulus contingent upon a response is called negative reinforcement" (Michael & Meyerson, 1962, p. 4). Positive and negative reinforcers are not absolutes; they are relative to the person receiving the reinforcement. Although it is often assumed that most people perceive certain events (such as praise, money) as positive reinforcements and others (such as scorn, ridicule) as negative, the individual's evaluation of an event as positive or negative depends on how the individual receiving the reinforcement perceives the event. In positive reinforcement, the individual receives something pleasurable or desirable as a consequence of behavior. In negative reinforcement, the consequence of a behavior is the removal of something undesirable or painful to the individual. Negative reinforcement is not synonymous with punishment. Punishment is the *application* of an aversive event as a result of the behavior; negative reinforcement is the *removal* of the aversive event as a result of the behavior. Generally, negative reinforcement is effective in changing behavior; punishment may have short-term effects but very few long-term ones.

Many positive and negative reinforcers become generalized secondary reinforcers. Money often becomes a positive generalized secondary reinforcement, because people learn that money can be used to bring many other kinds of pleasurable consequences. Similarly, the force of the negative reinforcement of social rejection may cause individuals to respond in certain ways in many situations.

Either positive or negative reinforcement may take place without the receiver's being consciously aware of it. Although there are many times when the individual is aware of having been rewarded, there are other times when he or she will not realize that any reinforcement, positive or negative, has occurred. In the operant model, however, it makes little difference whether the individual is consciously aware of the reinforcement.

Schedules of Reinforcement

Skinner and his followers have concentrated much research on the importance of the rate and timing of reinforcement. The schedule of reinforcement is the particular pattern of reinforcement applied to a particular response. The simplest schedule is continuous reinforcement: after every response of a given nature, a reward or reinforcement is applied. This is the simplest form and is very effective in developing new behavior, but it is the least effective for the maintenance of long-term behavior. If the reward is given continuously, the effects of the reward are soon lessened. If a parent gives a child a cookie to keep the child quiet, the reinforcement will work at first, but if the parent does this every time, the cookie soon loses its effect. Reinforcement on an intermittent basis is much more effective than continuous reinforcement.

Intermittent reinforcement can be subdivided into two rather large categories: ratio reinforcement and interval reinforcement. The former involves the rate of responses: after so many correct responses a reward is applied. An interval schedule of reinforcement is based on the passage of a given amount of time; it does not make any difference how many responses are made; the reward is delivered only after the proper amount of time has passed. Most people who have been exposed to either of the intermittent schedules will retain the learned responses longer than if they had been on a continuous schedule. The response is more difficult to extinguish. When trying to instill a particular response in an individual it is most effective to begin with a continuous reinforcement pattern and then shift to an intermittent schedule once the behavior has been acquired. The child who is rewarded for good behavior on an intermittent basis will maintain that behavior over longer periods of time without an additional reward.

Developing Complex Behaviors

In the behaviorist view, one of the basic models of learning—imitative learning—relates directly to the development of some complex behaviors. Others, however, are learned through the processes of extinction, generalization, discrimination, and shaping.

Extinction Behavior is said to occur for as long as it receives some intermittent reinforcement. If the behavior ceases to be reinforced either positively or negatively, it will eventually disappear. If, for example, a person ceased to be paid for going to work, it is doubtful that she or he would continue on the job very long. A person who had worked there only a short time would probably quit immediately; someone who had been there for some time would probably take longer to quit. The importance of this law of learning is that people's behavior is continuously able to change and they are instrumental in changing it. Often, for example, a person learns a behavior that is appropriate to one stage of development, but not at a later stage. Without the process of extinction, the behavior would persist and become inappropriate.

Generalization   Generalization, an extremely important principle of learning, is the assumption that a reinforcement that accompanies a stimulus increases the probability not only that the particular stimulus will elicit a particular response, but also that other, similar stimuli will, too. Hence, an individual will respond to any new situation in the environment as he or she would to a similar situation. If an infant receives satisfaction from being held by its mother and responds accordingly, the infant may generalize this satisfaction to the stimulus of being held by its father and will respond in the same manner. The process of generalization is extremely important because no two stimuli or stimulus situations are exactly the same. Having the ability to generalize allows individuals to move from one similar situation to the next without always having to learn completely new behaviors. People are able to carry a core of behavior with them. It is also true, however, that even similar situations may require small changes in behavior; therefore, the ability to discriminate among situations is also important.

Discrimination   It is apparent that people cannot go through life responding in the same way to related but different stimuli. For example, although a student might feel quite comfortable about openly disagreeing with one instructor, it might be a disaster to disagree with another instructor. To survive, individuals must learn the difference between two given situations. The law of discrimination states that relationships between stimuli and responses that have been generated through the process of generalization may be broken down separately. This occurs through combining reinforcement with extinction. In this process the correct response to a stimulus receives reinforcement, but the incorrect response to a similar situation does not. In the case of the two instructors, in one class the student would receive positive reinforcement for disagreeing and negative reinforcement for not participating; in the other class, the opposite would be true. Because of this pattern of reinforcement the individual will learn to make the correct response only in the presence of the correct stimulus; that is, he or she learns to tell the difference between two similar situations. The level of discrimination required depends in large part on how important the stimulus situation is to the person. The ability to discriminate between good and bad art is important to some, but relatively unimportant to others. The fact that each person is forced to make many thousands of discriminations in everyday life proves the importance of discrimination in the learning process.

Shaping   The laws of reinforcement, extinction, generalization, and discrimination all come together in a process referred to by Skinner as shaping. Shaping is the process of moving from simple behaviors that are approximations of the final behavior to a final, complex behavior. Through this process certain behaviors that are close approximations of the final behavior are reinforced, while other behaviors are not. At each stage of the process a closer approximation of the final behavior is required before reinforcement is given.

For example, the behavior of a child who does not interact with other children in class might be changed so that the child could interact in a positive fashion. The first step would be to help the child see the desirability of interacting with others. Then an environmental situation could be established in which the child was required to interact with another child. This could be accomplished by giving the child and one or two other children a common learning task to work on together. During interaction in this small group, even at minimal levels, the child would receive some form of reinforcement from the teacher or counselor. Once some interaction is developed, the degree of interaction required to receive reinforcement can be increased. Upon reaching a satisfactory level of interaction in this small group, the child could be made part of a larger group and the process utilized in the smaller group repeated. The final stage would be to reinforce the child's interaction in the context of a classroom activity, the desired behavior. In this process a teacher or a counselor may use external reinforcement to start the process, but the child's self-reinforcement will quickly become the chief motivation for the new behavior. As the child begins to interact in a controlled situation and finds that interaction pleasurable, she or he can be expected to seek out other interactions.

Shaping, then, uses situations and external reinforcement in a planned way to help people begin or learn a new behavior, but the ultimate goal is for individuals to reinforce themselves for behaviors that bring them pleasure. Someone has had to help them begin or learn any one of numerous complex behaviors, but people continue it because they find it rewarding.

Mediating Responses

The principles of learning outlined above apply to both humans and other animals. In addition, however, humans have the capacity to develop mediating responses. They can respond to their environment in new ways through planning and evaluation. These "higher mental processes" (Dollard & Miller, 1950) consist largely in the use of language and symbolization.

Because humans have the capacity to use symbols and language, they can label stimuli and can mediate their effects. By means of language individuals can go through a reasoning process when confronted with a particular stimulus, and delay any immediate response to the stimulus. A person who sees a symbolization of food, despite the drive that it calls forth, is able to delay the response to that stimulus until it is time to eat. That person is mediating her or his response to a given stimulus. Much of human behavior is governed this way; indeed, most adult human behavior involves a process of mediation, and it is this process that makes humans not only different from other animals, but also more complex. Even Skinner acknowledged that individuals may have some capacity to mediate the effects of environmental events and that psychologists need to be aware of that capacity (1971).

These mediating events have received increased attention in behavioral counseling and therapy. Homme referred to them as *coverants*. "Coverants are events the laymen call mental. These include thinking, imagining, reflecting, ruminating, relaxing, day-dreaming, fantasizing, etc." (Homme, 1965, p. 502). Osgood (1953) explained these internal events in his two-stage theory of learning. Osgood's model is represented by S–r–s–R, the first S is the external stimulus, which produces a covert response (r), which in turn creates an internal stimulus (s), causing the external response (R). It is the S–R we see; the r–s occurs internally. Many behavioral counselors who place emphasis on helping individuals develop self-management programs utilize procedures that focus on these internal processes.

SUMMARY

This overview of the basic principles of learning is in no way an exhaustive treatment. Our attempt, rather, has been to provide the notions of learning theory that form the basis for behavioral counseling. We now consider how all of these specific principles of learning come together to form what we normally refer to as personality, either normal or abnormal.

THEORY OF PERSONALITY

The basic assumption of the learning theory approach to personality is that behavior is learned as individuals interact with their environment. People are not innately bad or good; they are born neutral, like the Lockian idea of a tabula rasa (Hosford, 1969), and how they develop their personalities depends upon interaction with the environment. From the learning theory perspective, individuals are reactive beings; they react to stimuli as the stimuli are presented to them. In the process, patterns of behavior and ultimately personalities are formed. Most learning theorists would concede that some behavior may be a result of the interaction of an individual's innate characteristics with the environment. However, because innate characteristics cannot be controlled or defined, behaviorists focus on things that can be controlled or explained, the observable interactions between the individual and the environment, especially in terms of the significant others in that environment.

Within the framework of learning theory, human behavior is determined by the goals people set for themselves and or as sometimes imposed by society. Behavior is always directed to these goals. "An individual responds with those behaviors that he has learned will lead to the greatest satisfaction in a given situation" (Rotter, 1964, p. 57). Human motives for behaving are developed through experience, and gradually the individual develops a set of differentiated motives or needs. The interaction between a mother and a child illustrates this process. The initial stages of the infant's interaction with its mother result in satisfaction through feeding. This satisfaction gradually becomes generalized to the extent that the infant receives pleasure simply by being in the presence of the mother. The infant learns to want attention from its mother, a goal or motive that is separate from the first goal of reducing feelings of hunger. Through continuing interaction with the mother, the child learns that some behaviors result in pleasurable attention from her and other behaviors do not. In order to receive this pleasurable attention, the child will strive to do things that will please the mother and gain her attention. Finally, this process may generalize to the extent that the child behaves in certain ways even when the mother is not present; the child has learned that she would approve of these behaviors, and this in itself is satisfying. Thus, motives or drives or needs are developed, not through instincts or other innate characteristics, but through the individual's interaction with the environment.

LEARNED NEEDS

As the individual continues to interact with the environment, he or she develops a network of motives or needs that act to guide behavior. These needs or motives will vary from being very specific, like a need for a mother's love, to very general, such as the need for good interpersonal relationships. The more specific the need, the more possible it is to predict the pattern of behavior in a given situation (Rotter, 1964). Rotter (1964) outlined three broad characteristics of these learned needs: need potential, freedom of movement, and need value.

Need Potential

Need potential involves a set of behaviors that are directed toward a particular need, such as receiving attention from others, and the probability of their occurrence in a given situation. For example, an individual confronted with a choice between going to class or going off with some friends has the option of responding to either the need to please friends or the need to please an instructor. If the need to please friends has a higher need potential than the need to please the instructor, then the behavior of going off with friends is the one most likely to occur.

Freedom of Movement

Freedom of movement relates to the belief of the individual that certain patterns of behaviors will lead to certain satisfactions or rewards. The child learns that crying will bring attention from others, but this same behavior in a teenager will likely bring not attention, but rejection. This principle accounts for the fact that individuals do not behave like robots. They choose behaviors that they have learned will bring them the reinforcements they desire.

Need Value

Finally, each need of the individual has value. In any given situation one need or goal may have more value than some other goal. As in the preceding illustration, a student may have a need to please the instructor, but also a need to be seen in a favorable light by his or her peers. The relative value the student attaches to these two needs in a given situation will in part determine what patterns of behavior she or he chooses. Thus, a type of need hierarchy develops. Each individual has an innate hierarchy of needs, such as food and water. Most needs, however, are formed through learning. The existence of a needs hierarchy serves to explain the fact that in any given situation an individual may have the potential for several responses, and each of these responses has a probability for occurrence that can be ranked in order of importance. In the example of students in the classroom, one student may place more value on pleasing the instructor and his or her response is governed by that need. To another student in the room the need to please peers may have more value, and she or he will respond accordingly. Yet another student may value neither of these needs and may behave quite differently from the other two. Once the needs have been established, however, individuals actively make decisions designed to satisfy their needs. They become something more than simply reactors.

According to behaviorists, then, human personalities are determined largely by interaction with the environment. Once it is possible to understand a person's psychological situation, it becomes possible to understand the structure of that individual's personality and to predict his or her behavior. The individual learns through experience that certain situations will present certain satisfactions or dissatisfactions; through this experience, the person develops different patterns of needs that lead to different patterns of behavior. Individual differences develop because individuals perceive specific situations differently. The child who has received love from a parent will react to the latter's presence in certain predictable ways, and this pattern of behavior will be different from that of the individual who has been rejected by a parent. In essence, each individual has learned through experience to attribute a certain meaning to a given situation, and reacts to the situation on that basis.

The basis for the structure of an individual's personality, then, is learned patterns of behaviors. Obviously, much of this learning takes place early in the individual's development. Hence, not unlike other theoretical approaches to personality, the learning theory approach recognizes the importance of early childhood experiences in the development of personality. Unlike other approaches, however, the learning theory approach does not attribute much of personality to innate characteristics, but ascribes the individual's needs to experiences that he or she has learned would bring satisfaction.

As individuals interact with their environment, they are subject to the laws of learning; thus, personality is a product of learning. As the individual receives reinforcements from the environment, some behaviors are strengthened or learned, while others are weakened or extinguished. Many of these reinforcements are self-reinforcements, which take on increased importance as the individual matures. The person who receives satisfaction from looking in a mirror after being on a diet is engaging in self-reinforcement. Reinforcement can be understood only through the eyes of the recipient; what is perceived as a positive or negative reinforcement may be quite different for each individual. Premack (1965) suggested that almost any event has the potential to be reinforcing, and to determine what is reinforcing it is necessary to observe the activities in which an individual normally engages. Behaviors that for some reason bring the individual satisfaction are reinforcing. This important principle has specific use in counseling.

People may also learn some patterns of behavior through imitating others. This learning in turn leads to generalizations and discriminations and the gradual shaping of simple responses into complex behaviors. In addition, as people mature, they develop the ability to make mediating responses, largely through the use of language. These mediating responses allow individuals to plan and formulate responses to various stimuli, or to withhold an immediate response to a particular stimulus. This is the process of personality development. Although the form of personality depends largely on the environment in which the individual develops, behaviorists are increasingly aware of the influence of the internal state on the organism.

ABNORMAL PERSONALITY DEVELOPMENT

Like normal, or adaptive, patterns of behavior, abnormal or maladaptive behaviors are learned largely through the interaction of the individual and the environment. "Man's personality consists of both his positive and his negative habits. Those habits which are inappropriate (i.e., deviant) are learned in much the same way as appropriate behaviors" (Hosford, 1969, p. 2). Inappropriate behavior has been learned because it has been rewarded at various times. Children who are constantly disruptive in a classroom may behave that way because they have learned that only with such behavior can they receive attention. When the teacher shouts at them, they are receiving satisfaction or a reward for the behavior. Thus, this behavior has brought a valued reward—attention. Likewise, children who are withdrawn, who might be termed social isolates have learned to behave in that manner. By being social isolates they may be avoiding a situation or people with whom they are uncomfortable. The reward is not having to participate in a situation that causes fear, a fear that has also been learned through experience. Because learning theory is mainly concerned with observable behavior, it does not try to take into account any inner reason for maladaptive behavior. Both the attention-seeking children and the social isolates are examples of individuals who have simply learned bad habits.

Maladaptive behavior is different from normal behavior, not in terms of how it was learned, but only to the degree that the behavior is atypical or maladaptive to the observers (Hosford, 1969). In other words, maladaptive behavior is behavior that either no longer brings satisfaction to the individual or that will ultimately bring the individual into conflict with the environment. In the case of a social isolate, the child is engaging in a pattern of behavior that is bringing temporary satisfaction but will ultimately cause him or her difficulty. In this case the objective of counseling would be to help the child learn to enjoy interpersonal interactions, thus helping her or him engage in behaviors that will bring both immediate and long-term rewards.

GOALS OF COUNSELING

Given that adaptive and maladaptive behaviors are learned in the same ways, what do behaviorists hope to accomplish through the process of counseling? Blackham and Silberman (1971) suggested four specific steps to be followed in establishing the goals of counseling and the methods to be used to bring about changes.

1. **Problem definition** It is important to take the initial statement of the client and to determine where, when, and with whom the inappropriate behavior occurs. This analysis should attempt to determine the events that lead to the inappropriate behavior. If possible, the behavior of the client should be observed in the actual situation that is causing the difficulty.

2. **Developmental and social history** Taking a developmental history of the client may be helpful in terms of identifying areas of success or failure, competencies and deficiencies, interpersonal relationship patterns, adjustive behaviors, and problem areas. It is also useful in determining whether there are any physical or organic reasons for certain behaviors.

3. **Establishing specific goals of counseling** Many counselors who adhere to other theories consider behavioral procedures helpful if a client has a very specific concern, but inappropriate for individuals with such feelings as inferiority, inadequacy, despair, and alienation (Marquis, 1972). Most behaviorists, however, would agree with Marquis's statement that "such highly generalized problems are usually the result of an inadequate diagnosis of the specific areas of anxiety . . ."

(1972, p. 47). Thus, behaviorists' overall goals differ little from those of other counseling approaches. Behaviorists believe, however, that careful analysis of the general concern will reveal a number of specific concerns. Behaviorists would say that the general concern is too global to work with in counseling and that counselors and clients need more specific goals with which to work if counseling is to be productive.

Krumboltz (1966) contended that the goal of counseling must be stated in specific terms, that is, in terms of particular behaviors that need to be changed. People come to counseling because they have particular problems they cannot resolve by themselves, and they believe the counselor will be able to help them. The goal of counseling must be to help individuals resolve the problems they bring to the counseling situation. Clients will rarely come to a counselor saying they need a better self-concept; rather, a client is more inclined to say he or she feels inadequate with a group of people. Although feeling inadequate in a group of people may indicate a poor self-concept, the behavioral counselor would deal with the specific concern, not the global feeling; other aspects of the self-concept may also need some work, but the behavioral position is that the counselor needs to work on one specific concern at a time. Only in this manner can appropriate behavior changes be brought about.

The goals of counseling, then, must be stated in specific terms, and the specific short-term goal of counseling may be different for each client. The ultimate goal is always to help each client develop a system of self-management so that the individual can control his or her destiny. If the client's goal is out of the counselor's realm of interests, competency, or ethical considerations, the counselor must tell her or him that this goal is personally inappropriate and uncomfortable. In essence, the counselor and the client must agree on the goal they want to achieve and concur that through counseling there is a possibility of achieving it.

4. **Determine methods to be used to bring about desired change** The methods by which the counselor will operate are not rigid. Rather, a counselor responds within her or his own limits to the goal the client presents, and the accomplishment of that goal is of the utmost importance. The methods the counselor utilizes to help each client may be quite different, depending upon the client and the problem that he or she brings to the counseling situation.

THE PROCESS OF COUNSELING

In the behaviorist view, the counseling process is a special type of learning situation. Both the client and the counselor should recognize the situation as such, and the counselor should view himself or herself as an aid in this learning process (Krumboltz, 1966). Any changes that come about as a result of the counseling process are a direct result of the same laws of learning that apply outside the counseling situation.

This does not entail a mechanistic approach in counseling. Wolpe (1958) emphasized the need for the counselor to be accepting, to try to understand the client and what she or he is communicating, and to be nonjudgmental: "All that the patient says is accepted without question or criticism. He is given the feeling that the therapist is on his side" (1958, p. 106). Krumboltz likewise believed that it is essential for a counselor to be understanding and to communicate this understanding to the client. The counselor must be warm and empathic and hold each individual in high regard. Without these conditions it would not be possible to determine the client's difficulty or to gain the necessary cooperation of the client (Krumboltz, 1966). Even classic behaviorists such as Pepinsky and Pepinsky (1954) and Dollard and Miller (1950) stated the need for the counselor to be personal and to establish a warm, permissive atmosphere for the client.

This phase of counseling is crucial. If the client does not perceive the counselor as a warm, caring, receptive person, it will make little difference what techniques the counselor uses. For example, a counselor might try to use praise or attention as positive reinforcement for certain behaviors. That praise or attention, however, will be effective only if the client values them from the counselor. If the client perceives the counselor as essentially noncaring, that praise or attention may not act as positive reinforcement, but may, indeed, be negative reinforcement.

A second reason for establishing a facilitative atmosphere is to give clients freedom to express their concerns. In such an atmosphere clients discover that the counselor is someone who will listen to their concerns, and perhaps for the first time in their lives they feel they have found someone with whom they can really talk (Dollard & Miller, 1950). Their statements are not received with a judgmental or shocked attitude, but are accepted. When this kind of atmosphere is established, clients' problems can be clarified and their feelings about the problem understood by the counselor. At this point the two participants in the relationship begin to work on resolving the client's difficulty. Unless the problem is sharply defined so that both the counselor and the client understand the problem clearly, however, counseling will not progress.

Central to the process of counseling, then, is defining the client's particular concern. From a learning theory framework it is not enough to relate a client's difficulty to having a poor self-concept. Instead, the behavioral counselor attempts to have the client define the concern in specific terms such as, "I am unable to relate to individuals of the opposite sex," or, "I stutter in front of a group of people." These are examples of specific behaviors and can be dealt with through counseling. This does not mean that behavioral counselors are not concerned with an individual's having a good self-concept or with self-actualization, but they contend that these global concepts must be translated into specific behaviors desired by the client. Only after the appropriate behaviors have been defined can the counselor and client work toward achieving them. Successful achievement of these behaviors may indeed lead the client to have a better self-concept, which is of course desirable, but it is not a workable original goal. As Bijou (1966) indicated, global attempts are doomed to failure because there is just too much behavior to deal with at one time. It is far better to work on one concern and, once that has been resolved, to move to another concern, if one exists. In this way both the counselor and the client have a clear notion as to their goal and when it is accomplished.

The counselor is an active participant in the counseling process. He or she helps the client define the specific concern that has brought the latter to the counseling situation and decides whether the kind of aid she or he can offer will help the client. In addition, the counselor has the major responsibility for deciding what techniques will be utilized in the counseling process. Once the client and the counselor have defined and agreed upon the concern, the counselor controls the process of counseling and accepts responsibility for its outcome. It is the counselor's responsibility to launch the client on a course of action that will eventually help the latter resolve his or her difficulty. To accomplish this, the counselor must control the counseling process. This is not an arbitrary manipulative control that goes against the client's wishes; it is specifically designed to meet the goals of the client and is done with her or his full consent. In the exercise of this control the counselor may use whatever ethical techniques she or he feels will lead the client to the desired behavior. Some of these techniques will be applied in the counseling situation itself, but the counselor may also involve himself or herself in the individual's environment outside the counseling office by working with significant others in the client's life. The entire process is directed to providing each client with the necessary skills to manage his or her own life.

TECHNIQUES OF COUNSELING

Although most behaviorists would be in general agreement about what constitutes the process of counseling, even though their emphases might differ, the differences among actual techniques of counseling are somewhat greater. Some follow a basically traditional model; others operate from a broadly conceived behavioral base. Those who adhere to a more traditional approach (such as Wolpe) rely on techniques rooted in the basic principles of learning. Those who operate from a basic behavioral position (such as Krumboltz, Thoresen, and Lazarus) also acknowledge the importance of procedures that are not directly tied to the principles of learning. As Lazarus stated, "In the practical details of my day to day work with clients, I have found it necessary to broaden the base of conventional behavior therapy" (1972, p. vi). According to Krumboltz and Thoresen, "There is no 'approved list' of techniques the use of which enables one to call himself a behavioral counselor. The door must be kept open to all procedures that might be helpful" (1969, p. 3). In effect, these people are advocating behavioral eclecticism. This section focuses on procedures that are related to the basic principles of learning designed to either increase and strengthen or to decrease and weaken certain behaviors. The procedures designed to develop new behavior or to increase some behaviors include shaping, modeling, contracting, and assertive training. Those designed to eliminate or weaken behaviors include desensitization, extinction, and reinforcement of incompatible behaviors. Other techniques, such as covert sensitization, can be used either to increase or to decrease behavior.

In this section, we will discuss first the techniques most directly related to traditional learning theory and move to those less closely related to a strict learning theory approach. Many of the techniques are useful both in the actual process of counseling and in client self-management programs carried out outside of the actual counseling sessions. Self-management procedures have become an important addition to the field of behavioral counseling. They utilize the same laws of learning that the counselor uses in the counseling relationship, but the important difference is that the client is put in charge of his or her own behavioral change program. The plan is established by the counselor and the client in counseling, but the client has the chief responsibility for the implementation of the plan, with the counselor acting in a supporting role. Throughout this section we will mention specific techniques that are often used in self-management or self-control programs.

The person most closely identified with the traditional model of conditioning in counseling is Joseph Wolpe. According to Wolpe's theory of reciprocal inhibition (1958), the fundamental aim of counseling must be to remove the feelings of anxiety caused by stimuli that are objectively harmless. Counseling is judged effective to the degree that it breaks down this learned response to the stimuli so that a more appropriate response may occur.

To accomplish the counseling goals, the client and counselor usually meet from one to a dozen times. During this period the counselor strives to establish a relationship in which the client feels that the counselor likes and is not judging him or her, while the client is giving the counselor all the information possible about childhood, family, school experience, vocational plans, and anything else that may relate to the client's current status as a person. This information is helpful to the counselor in attempting to understand the client in her or his current state; however, it is not essential to bring a great deal of the past into the counseling situation. What is important is an understanding of how the client behaves at the current time.

After the initial interviews, the client may take some inventories designed to give information about the kinds of activities that elicit inappropriate responses. This information is used in conjunction with information from the interviews. The information is combined to establish a hierarchy of conditions that cause anxiety in the individual and to which the client responds in an inappropriate manner. The formation of this hierarchy might proceed in the following way. An individual may tell the counselor that he or she is fearful or anxious when being observed by others. The counselor attempts to establish the hierarchy of needs by ascertaining what kinds of people observing the client cause him or her the most anxiety. The counselor may find that the client is quite comfortable at home being observed by family, a little less comfortable in the company of friends, a little more uncomfortable in the company of strangers, and quite uncomfortable when alone with another strange individual. This evidence of increasing anxiety in different situations helps the counselor form the hierarchy, which is the basis for the counseling process. The techniques used are assertive training, sexual responses training, relaxation training, and systematic desensitization.

Assertive Training

"In general, assertive responses are used for anxieties evoked in the course of direct interpersonal dealings" (Wolpe, 1958, p. 113). These responses are very similar to what Salter (1949) called excitatory responses. A person in need of assertive training is one who has an inappropriate anxiety response in interpersonal relationships. This anxiety inhibits expression of assertive statements and behavior. The individual internalizes the feelings generated by the situation, which can lead to the development of such symptoms as ulcers and high blood pressure. Assertive training simply involves trying to get the client to express these feelings during interactions with others. A person who has been hurt by something someone else has done to him or her is encouraged to tell that person her or his feelings. In effect, the client is told that there is no reason not to express these feelings and that anxiety over expressing them is groundless. Wolpe and Lazarus (1966) contended that the expression of the assertive response acts to inhibit any anxiety created by the interpersonal situation, and that because the assertive behavior will be self-rewarding, the anxiety will continue to be inhibited.

CHAPTER
EIGHT
BEHAVIORAL
APPROACHES
TO
COUNSELING

145

The counselor first attempts to get the client to be assertive in the counseling interview; that is, to state his or her feelings to the counselor. In this initial stage the counselor uses the operant principles of reinforcement, extinction, and shaping to develop the desired assertive responses. Once this is accomplished the client is instructed to attempt the same kinds of responses outside of counseling. The principle of conditioning involved here is that in expressing assertive responses to the counselor the client finds that there is no punishment or anxiety accompanying the response. Hence, the expression of the assertive response is teamed with a relaxed situation rather than an anxiety-producing situation. The counselor must use as much pressure as is necessary to get the client to perform the assertive behavior outside the counseling situation. In some cases the counselor will be unable to motivate the client to do this and may have to resort to role playing in the interview (Wolpe, 1958).

As the client engages in assertive behaviors outside of counseling, it is to be expected that general positive feedback from others will act as positive reinforcement for the behavior. This will lead the client to feel better about herself or himself and her or his interpersonal relations, an extremely important self-reinforcement for continuing the behavior. Thus, once the behavior has been established the client engages in self-management by feeling rewarded or satisfied as he or she engages in the desired behavior.

Sexual Training

Sexual counseling, although counselors will not need to use this technique, is included here as another technique from the traditional model. This procedure is used when the client has anxiety connected with sexual situations. According to Wolpe, "the key to the problem of impaired sexual performance is the subtraction of anxiety from the sexual encounter" (1969, p. 74). The first step in the process is to define as exactly as possible the actual situation that creates the anxiety. Starting at this point, a hierarchy of increasing anxiety situations is determined. The client may simultaneously receive relaxation training. At this point the individual is instructed to engage in the activity that produces the least anxiety only when he or she is completely relaxed. Once the client can engage in that activity without any anxiety, he or she is instructed to engage in the next behavior, and so on. Thus, all this procedure involves is instructing the client to participate in sexual activities only when there is no anxiety accompanying the situation. Like the assertive technique, the critical issue is to motivate the client to follow the instructions of the counselor. In this way only pleasurable feelings are generated by sexual situations because the client avoids sexual situations that cause anxiety. Gradually, these pleasurable feelings will extend to other sexual situations.

Relaxation Training

Relaxation training is appropriate for any kind of anxiety, but is most applicable when the stimulus causing the anxiety is an inanimate object. The technique, originally developed by Jacobsen (1938), involves instructing the client in muscle relaxation. The client is told that relaxing is a way of combating anxiety. When an individual relaxes systematically, all tension in the muscular structure of the body is eliminated. This situation is incompatible with feelings of anxiety, which create tension in the muscular structure. This is a form of counterconditioning, referred to as reciprocal inhibition. Relaxation of the muscles is most often used by Wolpe in conjunction with systematic desensitization.

Systematic Desensitization

"Systematic Desensitization is a form of classical conditioning in which anxiety-provoking situations are paired with inhibitory responses" (Belkin, 1980, p. 130). The technique of systematic desensitization, based on Wolpe's theory of reciprocal inhibition, uses both the hierarchy of anxiety-producing situations developed from the initial interviews and the techniques of relaxation. An extensive analysis of the behavior of the individual establishes an anxiety hierarchy. Once the hierarchy has been established, the client is trained in deep-muscle relaxation. The training sessions are roughly twenty minutes long, focusing in order on the muscles in the arms, head, neck, and shoulders, and finally the trunk and legs. At this point the actual presentation of the items from the hierarchy begins. The client, in a relaxed state, is asked to imagine the least anxiety-producing item in the hierarchy. Once the client can put herself or himself in that situation without feeling any anxiety, the next item on the list is presented. The process continues until the client can imagine the most fear-producing situation in the hierarchy without feeling anxiety. In essence, the client is being conditioned to a new response to the formerly fear-producing stimulus situations. Instead of an anxiety response he or she is being conditioned to a relaxed response, and the two are incompatible. "The essential principle of reciprocal inhibition is that an organism cannot make two contradictory responses at the same time . . . if the response that is contradictory to anxiety results in a more pleasant state or more productive behavior for the subject. The new response to anxiety-evoking stimuli will gradually reinforce the anxiety response" (Bugg, 1972, p. 823).

Each of the techniques outlined above has in common the goal of changing an old, inappropriate response to a stimulus to a response that is more appropriate. This is accomplished in large part through counterconditioning procedures, in which an incompatible and more desirable response is teamed with a stimulus that previously produced an undesirable one. The list of techniques presented here is not exhaustive, but does include the ones most frequently used by therapists following the traditional model. A more detailed account of these techniques can be found in the writings of Joseph Wolpe (1958, 1969), Andrew Salter (1949), and Lazarus (1972).

IMPLOSIVE THERAPY

A modified form of classical conditioning that has not been as widely known or used as other classical techniques is implosive therapy (Belkin, 1980). This approach combines some characteristics of classical conditioning and extinction. According to Belkin (1980), implosive therapy is unlike systematic desensitization in that ". . . the subject is not given simultaneous anxiety-inhibiting stimuli. Rather, by intensely concentrating on the fearful stimulus, the client is taught to associate 'neutral stimuli' with the anxiety-evoking ones" (p. 133). The client is taught to imagine the feared thing or event in a situation in which nothing negative will or can happen. The repeated imagining in the face of a neutral response acts to extinguish the previous anxiety response. Belkin (1980) suggests that implosive procedures may be most effective when the target client behavior is characterized by avoidance, such as in phobias.

BROAD-BASED BEHAVIORAL COUNSELING

Like those who generally follow the traditional model of behavioral counseling, practitioners of the broader-based model place great emphasis on establishing a relationship between counselor and client. As Krumboltz pointed out, "The client is likely not to describe the totality of his problems unless he thinks his listener will understand things from his point of view" (1969, p. 224). Second, "the counselor's ability to communicate his understanding of the client's problem to him establishes the counselor as an important person in the client's life and therefore one able to be an influential model and effective reinforcing agent" (Krumboltz, 1969, p. 224). Hence, the first goal of the behavioral counselor is to establish a relationship with the client in which the latter feels free to express herself or himself to the counselor and views the counselor as an individual genuinely interested in attempting to help with the difficulty.

Once this relationship has been established, the counselor's actual techniques will vary, depending upon the client and the nature of the concern. The techniques used will most often include shaping, extinction, contracting, time out, imitative learning, and cognitive learning. The behavioral counselor may, however, rely on more than the face-to-face meetings with the client. Because of their belief in the importance of the environment in establishing and maintaining behaviors, behavioral counselors will often attempt to make changes in the individual's environment. Thus, in some cases the counselor becomes a behavioral engineer manipulating the individual's environment to provide one that will aid the process of behavioral change. Although some may object to this manipulation, behaviorists point out that the manipulation is used to enhance the probability that the client will accomplish her or his desired behavior. The client, not the counselor, establishes the goals of counseling.

Shaping

The most frequently used technique of the broad-based model is that of shaping. This technique involves modifying behavior through reinforcement, helping clients acquire desired behaviors through a series of approximations of the desired behavior. If the desired behavior is present and the goal is simply to increase its occurrence, the counselor uses direct positive reinforcement of the behavior within the counseling situation. In addition, the behavioral counselor attempts to structure the real world of the client so that the latter receives positive reinforcement for the behavior in the real situation.

If, however, the desired behavior has not been a part of the client's behavioral repertoire, the counselor must reinforce initial behaviors that are approximations of the final behavior. Gradually the counselor requires the client to make finer discriminations by reinforcing behaviors that are increasingly closer to the desired behavior and not reinforcing other behaviors. The actual reinforcement used to encourage further responses in the desired direction may consist in the counselor's giving particular attention to a statement or by inattention to certain statements. The counselor may express verbal approval of certain statements and disapproval of others by not responding or responding negatively. Through the reinforcement, whether verbal or nonverbal, positive or negative, certain responses are reinforced and certain responses extinguished. In this way the client's behavior is shaped in the direction that both he or she and the counselor have agreed upon.

Hosford (1969) outlined four crucial considerations in the use of reinforcement in counseling. First, the counselor must be sure that the reinforcement is strong enough to motivate the client to perform the desired behavior; the same kind of reinforcement does not work equally well for all clients, and the counselor must find the reinforcement that has the greatest potential for increasing the desired behavior. At this point the Premack principle is of extreme importance: to determine what may be reinforcing for the client, the counselor must find out what the individual really likes to do. These highly desirable behaviors are used as reinforcers for the behavior being worked on in counseling. If, for example, a client has entered counseling in order to develop better study habits and the counselor determines that the individual really enjoys certain TV programs, the counselor might establish with the parents (or directly with the client) a system in which the client is permitted to view those programs contingent upon spending a predetermined amount of time studying. If the agreement, or contract, is made directly with the client, the counselor has established a self-management program: the client is chiefly responsible for shaping her or his own behavior.

Hosford's second point is that the counselor must use reinforcement in a systematic manner. As Krumboltz stated, "The question is not whether the counselor should or should not use reinforcement—the question is how the counselor can time his use of reinforcement in the best interests of his client" (1966, p. 15). In the initial stages of counseling it is important that each response indicating movement in the desired direction be reinforced; as counseling progresses, however, the reinforcement should be applied on a systematic but intermittent basis because the intermittent schedule of reinforcement tends to have the most long-lasting effect on behavior.

The third consideration is the contingency between the demonstration of the desired response and the application of the reward. For greatest effectiveness the reinforcement must follow closely the demonstrated desired response. The fourth factor is closely related to this contingency: the desired response must first be elicited by the counselor. This often involves the use of cue statements. A cue statement is a statement so designed that the client can hardly avoid responding in the desired direction. In effect, the counselor is giving a verbal prompting to the client. This prompting, or giving of cue statements, may be particularly important in the early stages of counseling; as reinforcement begins to show results, however, there should be less need for this kind of statements.

The technique of shaping in counseling, then, involves gradually molding the client's current behavior toward the desired behavior through the use of positive and negative reinforcement. This reinforcement can be verbal or nonverbal; it must be strong enough to motivate the client, and it must be applied consistently soon after the desired response.

Extinction

Whereas shaping is a process of increasing a desired behavior, extinction is the process of decreasing the frequency of an undesirable behavior. Extinction involves withholding any reinforcement, positive or negative. It involves ignoring a specific behavior. In counseling this means a nonresponse to undesirable verbal or motor behavior of the client. When trying to extinguish behavior the counselor will often find that the target behavior of the client increases in an attempt to receive the usual previous reinforcement—perhaps attention. Gradually, if the reinforcement continues to be withheld, the behavior will decrease and eventually be eliminated. Bandura (1969) listed several factors that affect the rate of extinction:

1. the degree to which the behavior was reinforced on an irregular basis;
2. the degree of effort required to engage in the behavior;
3. the level of deprivation sustained during extinction;
4. the degree to which changes in reinforcement conditions are distinguishable;
5. the degree to which alternate modes of responding are available.

Because extinction procedures are not as easy to use as it may first appear, the counselor must develop full understanding of the factors listed by Bandura in relation to each specific client before attempting the procedure with that client.

Reinforcing Incompatible Behaviors

Similar to the process of systematic desensitization, this technique involves reinforcing one response to block the appearance of the undesired behavior. For example, a client may desire to decrease the number of self-doubting thoughts. The client cannot think positively and negatively about herself or himself at the same time. Hence, the counselor utilizes positive reinforcement to reward the client's expression of positive self-thoughts. This in itself blocks the appearance of negative thoughts; if they do occur, the counselor uses extinction techniques. This technique is also often used in self-management programs. The client with negative self-thoughts might be instructed to carry a series of cards on which positive self-thoughts are written. As soon as the client experiences the onset of a negative thought, she or he takes out the cards and reads three of the positive statements to herself or himself. Gradually this process will reduce or eliminate the undesired negative thoughts by replacing them with positive ones. As with shaping, the client is controlling his or her own behavior change plan. The behavioral counselor's role has been to help the client develop a systematic plan for desired behavior change.

Modeling

A second technique that is receiving increasing attention from behavioral counselors is modeling, or imitative learning. Imitative or vicarious learning is one of the principal means by which people learn new behaviors. The use of imitative learning in counseling involves the presentation of a model or models to the client who demonstrate the desired behavioral outcome, and with whom the client can easily identify. In the counseling situation the client may be so ignorant of ways to modify behavior or to develop new ones that reinforcement techniques may be inappropriate and ineffectual in the early stages. Instead, it may be more appropriate to present some type of model to the individual that represents the desired behavior. The client may learn the new behavior simply through observing the behavior of the model. According to Bandura (1969), whether the client learns the new behavior or not will depend on four factors: (1) attention, (2) retention, (3) motor reproduction, and (4) incentive. Certainly, if an individual is to learn from observing a model, his or her attention must be focused on the target behavior of the model. Second, if the client is to reproduce the modeled behavior, she or he must have the capacity to retain the behavior mentally; no amount of modeling is going to help an individual with a mental deficiency to learn certain complex behaviors. Third, the client must have the physical capacity to reproduce the behavior. Finally, the client must see some incentive for engaging in the behavior. Kagen addressed this last point when he stated that the model's behavior must represent some desirable goal that the client would like to obtain. "The most salient of these include: (a) power over the environment . . . ; (b) competence and instrumental skills; (c) autonomy of action; and (d) the receipt of love, affection, and acceptance from others" (Kagen, 1963, p. 82). The model presented to the client may demonstrate more control over personal destiny than the client does; may have greater ability to deal with certain situations; may be more accepted by other individuals; and, because of these strengths, may be able to be more independent in behavior. The effectiveness of presenting a model or models to a client, then, depends upon how closely the client can identify with the behavior of the model: the closer the identification, the more incentive there will be to acquire the behavior.

Four basic types of models have been used in counseling: filmed, taped, live, and self-as-a-model. In the first three cases the model is presented to the client as an example of the desired behavior. After presenting a taped or filmed model, the counselor uses cue statements that lead the client to a discussion of the model's behavior. During this discussion the counselor can employ verbal reinforcement techniques to shape the client's behavior further in the desired direction. Seldom in counseling is imitative learning used by itself. More often, it is used in conjunction with the technique of shaping.

Live peer models who actually take part in the counseling process usually appear in group counseling. In this case the models are there to be themselves and to share the means they have used to deal with the problems confronting the clients. In this way the clients can actually engage the models in discussion, and at the same time the counselor can use positive reinforcement in the same way as with a filmed model. In general, live peer modeling appears to be most effective with personal and social problems, and filmed and taped models with more cognitive problems.

Hosford (1980) has been developing a procedure he refers to as self-as-a-model. "Similar to standard modeling, it relies principally on client imitation of demonstrated examples to promote behavioral change rather than on cognitive mediation of the response contingencies, which is the stimulus for change in self-observation. During the self-as-a-model procedure, clients do not observe instances of their inappropriate behavior as is often the case in self-observation"

(1980, p. 469). In the self-as-a-model procedure, the counselor takes a client through the following steps (Hosford & deVisser, 1974):

1. Clients are taught self-monitoring and self-observation skills.
2. Clients develop a list of behaviors they wish to eliminate and/or develop.
3. Clients select specific skills or knowledge they wish to change.
4. Counselor and client make a model audio- or videotape of the target behavior or hierarchy of behaviors.
5. Clients are taught positive self-imagery in order to call forth in their memory the view of themselves engaging in the behavior on the tape.

CHAPTER
EIGHT

151

BEHAVIORAL
APPROACHES
TO
COUNSELING

Hosford (1980) presents evidence of the effectiveness of this procedure with such problems as self-acceptance, interpersonal skills, improving teaching skills, and improving counselor attending behavior. Warner, Valine, Higgins, and McEwen (1980) have found a similar procedure effective in teaching counselor responding behavior.

Contracting

A comparatively recent development in the field of behavioral counseling, particularly in self-development programs, is the use of behavior contracts. Contracting is based on the assumption that it is helpful for a client to specify the behavioral change that is desired. Like other contracts, the behavioral contract is a negotiated agreement between two parties—in this case, between the client and the counselor—in which both parties get something out of the contract and give something to the other individual involved in the contract.

Contracting is a logical extension of behavioral principles, for it establishes reinforcement contingencies for desired behaviors in advance (Dustin & George, 1973). As Mahoney and Thoresen (1974) indicated, these consequences may be either concrete material or social rewards. In the former case, the client, as party to the contract, may deposit some amount of money or other valuable with the counselor and sign a contract that specifies how these reinforcers are to be used. For example, a client who desires to lose weight might deposit fifty dollars with the counselor and agree that for every day he or she consumes only a prescribed number of calories, fifty cents will be returned, and for every violation fifty cents will be lost. Or, a client who wishes to improve school work habits might agree that when school work is completed, her or his teacher and parents will praise the behavior, and when it is not completed, they will either ignore (extinguish) the behavior or criticize (punish) it. In either case, the response consequences of both the desired and undesirable behaviors are specified in advance and agreed to by all parties.

The following list is a summary of the desirable characteristics for effective behavioral contracts cited by Dustin and George (1973) and Mahoney and Thoresen (1974):

1. **Clear expectations** All requirements of the contract for both parties are stated clearly and objectively. If possible, the expectations and goals should be stated in positive terms.

2. **Level of behavior and consequences** Both parties to the contract must agree on how much of a certain behavior will lead to how much of a positive consequence. It is very important for these two elements to be in balance.

3. **Monitoring system** The contract should specify how the parties will determine when the desired behavior has been completed so that the positive consequences can be delivered.

4. **System of sanctions** Some procedure of penalties for failure to engage in desired behavior must be written into the contract.

5. **Reachable goals** The contract must be written so that the goals are something the client can achieve. In some cases this means writing one contract that calls for a minimum level of performance. Once that level has been maintained for a period of time, the contract is renegotiated to require a higher level of performance. There must be a clause in the contract that will permit renegotiation downward if the goals have been set too high.

6. **Bonus systems** Each contract should have a bonus system that rewards a long period of contract compliance by the client with extra payoffs.

Cognitive Learning

Another technique that may be used by counselors following a behavioral model is cognitive learning. In some respects cognitive learning is very similar to contracting and assertive training. There may be occasions when the client knows what the desired behavior is, but not how to accomplish the behavior. In such cases it may be appropriate for the counselor to suggest what to do. In essence, this technique involves an oral contract between the client and the counselor. Having agreed on the desired behavior, the client agrees to try what the counselor suggests for a certain period. This simple technique may be very effective in some cases. Like other techniques, it should not be used in a mechanical manner, but as one of several techniques in the process of counseling.

Covert Reinforcement

Covert reinforcement presents positive reinforcing consequences in the form of mental imagery. This procedure involves either pairing an image of the undesired behavior with a second image that is extremely negative, or pairing an image of a desirable behavior with an image of an extremely positive consequence. Used in a negative fashion, an individual who desires to lose weight might first imagine eating a box of candy and then pair this with an image of getting violently ill. Used in a positive fashion with the same problem, the client might first imagine turning down the box of candy and then pair it with the positive image of receiving all kinds of attention from the opposite sex. As in the technique of desensitization, the images are first utilized within counseling while the individual is in a state of muscle relaxation. Eventually the images have been paired (classical conditioning) often enough so that the actual behavior outside counseling will produce the paired image. The person in the example will not eat candy either because of the image or thought of getting ill, or because of the thought of getting a lot of attention. As Mahoney and Thoresen (1974) pointed out, the negative imagery is very adversive, although it has been shown to be effective. For this reason, the use of positive covert reinforcement is advisable whenever possible.

The behavioral counselor will probably use several techniques in combination. With some clients the counselor may employ all the techniques at various times during counseling, or particular combinations of techniques. Each of the many theorists and practitioners in behavioral counseling has variations not only of the basic techniques described here, but also other techniques. All, however, find their rationale for counseling in the laws of learning discussed in this chapter.

SUMMARY

A wide variety of approaches operate within the framework of behaviorism. This chapter has presented material that most behaviorists could support. Most, for example, have moved away from the extreme position of Skinner. They have, like practitioners of other theories, become more eclectic in approach.

Many practitioners who do not philosophically agree with the behavioral position find that some behavioral techniques are effective aids in their own counseling. Prospective counselors should not confuse behavioral approaches with strict Skinnerian doctrine, nor should they dismiss any techniques simply because of their association with behaviorism.

REFERENCES

Bandura, A. Social learning through imitation. In M. Jones (Ed.), *Nebraska Symposium on Motivation.* Lincoln: University of Nebraska Press, 1962.

———. Behavioral modification through modeling procedures. In L. Krasner & L. Ullmann (Eds.), *Research in behavior modification.* New York: Holt, Rinehart and Winston, 1965.

———. *Principles of behavior modification.* New York: Holt, Rinehart and Winston, 1969.

———. *Social learning theory.* Englewood Cliffs, N.J.: Prentice-Hall, 1977.

Barclay, J. R. The revolution in counseling: Some editorial comments. *Personnel and Guidance Journal,* 1980, *58,* 457.

Belkin, G. S. *Contemporary psychotherapies.* Chicago: Rand McNally, 1980.

Bijou, S. W. Implications of behavioral science for counseling and guidance. In J. D.

Krumboltz (Ed.), *Revolution in counseling: Implication of behavioral science.* Boston: Houghton Mifflin, 1966.

Blackham, G. J., & Silberman, A. *Modification of child behavior.* Belmont, Calif.: Wadsworth Publishing, 1971.

Bugg, C. A. Systematic desensitization: A teaching worth trying. *Personnel and Guidance Journal,* 1972, *50,* 823–828.

Dollard, J., & Miller, N. E. *Personality and psychotherapy.* New York: McGraw-Hill, 1950.

Dustin, R., & George, R. *Action counseling for behavior change.* New York: Intext, 1973.

Homme, L. E. Perspectives in psychology: XXIV. Control of coverants, the operants of the mind. *Psychological Record,* 1965, *15,* 501–511.

Hosford, R. E. Behavioral counseling: A contemporary overview. *The Counseling Psychologist,* 1969, *1,* 1–33.

———. The Cubberley conference and the evolution of observational learning strategies. *Personnel and Guidance Journal*, 1980, 467–472.

Hosford, R. E., & deVisser, L. *Behavioral approaches to counseling: An introduction.* Washington, D.C.: APGA Press, 1974.

Jacobsen, E. *Progressive relaxation.* Chicago: University of Chicago Press, 1938.

Kagen, J. The choice of models: Conflict and continuity in human behavior. In E. Lloyd-Jones & E. M. Westervelt (Eds.), *Behavioral science and guidance: Proposals and perspectives.* New York: Columbia University Press, 1963.

Krumboltz, J. D. Changing the behavior of behavior changers. *Counselor Education and Supervision*, 1967, 46 (6), 222–229.

Krumboltz, J. D. (Ed.), *Revolution in counseling.* Boston: Houghton Mifflin, 1966.

Krumboltz, J. D., & Thoresen, C. E. *Behavioral counseling: Cases and techniques.* New York: Holt, Rinehart and Winston, 1969.

———. *Counseling methods.* New York: Holt, Rinehart and Winston, 1976.

Lazarus, A. A. *Clinical behavior therapy.* New York: Bruner/Mazel, 1972.

Mahoney, N. J., & Thoresen, C. E. *Self-control: Power to the person.* Monterey, Calif.: Brooks-Cole, 1974.

Marquis, J. D. An expedient model for behavior therapy. In A. A. Lazarus (Ed.), *Clinical behavior therapy.* New York: Bruner/Mazel, 1972.

Michael, J., & Meyerson, L. A behavioral approach to counseling and guidance. *Harvard Educational Review*, 1962, 32, 382–402.

Miller, N. E., & Dollard, J. *Social learning and imitation.* New Haven: Yale University Press, 1941.

Mowrer, O. H. *Learning theory and the symbolic processes.* New York: John Wiley and Sons, 1960.

Osgood, C. E. *Method and theory in experimental psychology.* New York: Oxford University Press, 1953.

Pepinsky, H. B., & Pepinsky, P. N. *Counseling: Theory and practice.* New York: Ronald Press, 1954.

Premack, D. *Reinforcement theory.* In D. Levine (Ed.), *Nebraska Symposium on Motivation.* Lincoln Nebraska Press, 1965, pp. 123–180.

Rotter, J. B. *Clinical psychology.* Englewood Cliffs, N.J.: Prentice-Hall, 1964.

———. Some implications of a social learning theory for the practice of psychotherapy. Mimeographed paper, 1962.

Salter, A. *Conditioned reflex therapy.* New York: Creative Age Press, 1949.

Skinner, B. F. *The behavior of organisms.* New York: Appleton-Century-Crofts, 1938.

———. *Science and human behavior.* New York: Macmillan, 1953.

———. *Beyond freedom and dignity.* New York: Knopf, 1971.

Warner, R., Valine, W., Higgins, E., & McEwen, M. An investigation of two approaches to pre-practicum training for counselors. *Journal of Counseling Services*, 1980, 3, 31–36.

Watson, J. B., & Rayner, R. Conditioned emotional reaction. *Journal of Experimental Psychology*, 1920, 3(1), 1–14.

Wolpe, J. *Psychotherapy by reciprocal inhibition.* Stanford: Stanford University Press, 1958.

———. *The practice of behavior therapy.* New York: Pergamon Press, 1969.

Wolpe, J., & Lazarus, A. A. *Behavior therapy techniques.* New York: Pergamon Press, 1966.

REALITY
THERAPY

CHAPTER NINE

William Glasser developed Reality Therapy as an approach to working with institutionalized delinquents (Belkin, 1980). It is often considered one of a group of
cognitive approaches, including rational emotive therapy (RET), which is discussed in Chapter Ten as a cognitive-dynamic approach. As Belkin noted,
"Although there are substantial differences among these approaches, they all rely,
to a greater or lesser degree, on the individual's mobilization of logical faculties to
overcome his or her emotional difficulties" (1980, p. 341). They also share a lack of
emphasis on the etiology, or causes, of normal and abnormal development, focusing instead on the counseling process. This makes it possible to teach both approaches to clients, classroom teachers, and other human service professionals
and paraprofessionals in a relatively short time. Because of these similarities, some
counselors who utilize techniques from both the reality and RET approaches as
well as some old trait and factor concepts prefer to call themselves rational or
cognitive therapists (Belkin, 1980). Even though these approaches are treated in
separate chapters, they have numerous similarities, summarized at the end of
Chapter Ten.

Glasser was trained in traditional psychoanalytic procedures but became
disenchanted with this narrow approach during his work with female offenders at
the Ventura School for Girls in California. Out of that work Glasser (1965) came
to believe that all human behavior was motivated by people's striving to meet
basic needs that are generally the same for all individuals. He suggested that
people may label the needs differently, but no one really disagrees that all people,
regardless of location or culture, share the same essential needs. Some of their
needs are the traditionally defined physiological needs that maintain the organism. Beyond basic needs, Glasser contended, there are "two basic psychological
needs: the need to love and be loved and the need to feel that we are worthwhile
to ourselves and to others" (1965, p. 9). Moreover, "when a man acts in such a
way that he gives and receives love, and feels worthwhile to himself and others, his
behavior is right or moral" (Glasser, 1965, p. 57). These two basic psychological
needs have now been incorporated into one, which Glasser calls *identity*. "Reality
Therapy views identity as a single, basic requirement of all mankind" (Glasser &
Zunin, 1973, p. 294). "It means that we must see ourselves as somehow being different from everything else, that no matter where we go we will not find another
person who thinks, looks, acts, and talks exactly as we do. This need is universal
and transcends all cultures" (Glasser & Zunin, 1973, p. 292).

PERSONALITY DEVELOPMENT

Glasser sees personality development as a function of how well individuals learn to
meet their needs: the degree to which they are capable of meeting their needs
largely determines whether they function appropriately or inappropriately. Those
who can meet their needs are termed responsible, those who cannot irresponsible.
Responsible behavior is behavior that leads to the satisfaction of personal needs
without depriving others of their ability to fulfill their needs (Glasser, 1965).
Responsible behavior results in the formation of a personality that has at its core a
"success identity"; irresponsible behavior results in a personality that incorporates
a "failure identity."

The ability to behave responsibly is difficult to learn. As Glasser suggested, all people share basic innate needs that cause them problems if left unsatisfied. People are not, however, endowed with the natural ability to satisfy these needs; it must be learned (Glasser, 1965). This learning process begins early, but becomes critical around the time children are ready to enter school and are developing social, verbal, and intellectual skills (Glasser & Zunin, 1973). These skills begin to provide the tools people need to define themselves in terms of success or failure. Glasser (1965) maintained that those who develop a success identity (responsible) do so through a loving relationship with responsible parents. Responsible parents establish an involvement with their children through love, teaching, discipline, and modeling. The prime prerequisite for this involvement is that the child feel loved for what he or she is. Children want to be responsible, but they will not "accept discipline and learn better ways unless they feel the parents care enough to show them actively the responsible way to behave" (Glasser, 1965, p. 18). A second prerequisite is that the child feel worth. As Glasser and Zunin (1973) suggested, a child may be so showered with apparent love that the child is never allowed to do anything for herself or himself. A child who never has to accept responsibility for his or her own actions cannot experience self-worth. Self-worth comes from being able to carry out tasks to a successful conclusion.

Parents and significant others who wish to teach their children responsible behavior must constantly act in responsible fashion with them. They must be willing to hold a child to a responsible course of action even when the child becomes angry with them. To back off in such a situation is to teach the child irresponsibility. Only through interactions with parents and significant people who are themselves worthwhile and responsible can children learn to love, to feel worth, and to behave responsibly. Given such a growth environment, children will be able to satisfy their needs and will subsequently develop success identities. These people will be able to govern their lives using the three Rs of reality therapy: right, responsibility, and reality.

Right refers to Glasser's (1965) belief that there is an accepted standard or norm against which behavior can be compared. Fully functioning individuals have the capacity to correct themselves when they do things that compare unfavorably with that standard, and the ability to praise themselves when they behave in ways that are acceptable. If people fail to evaluate their behavior and to change it when they are wrong, they will not fulfill the basic need to be worthwhile and will suffer psychologically.

Responsibility is the ability to satisfy personal needs without interfering with other individuals' desires to meet their own needs. It is the ability to meet personal needs within the given social and cultural context. This does not mean that people must always agree with the status quo, but they mean that if they disagree with the status quo they work to change it within the prescribed system.

Reality is the final R. People must understand that there is a real world and that they must fulfill their needs within that framework. The reality of the world from Glasser's standpoint is not a perceived reality that is different for each individual but one composed of hard facts. Fully functioning individuals recognize this and are able to meet their needs within those constraints.

In sum, personality is formed as the individual strives to meet both physiological and psychological needs. The most important needs are to love and be loved and to feel self-worth and see worth in others. In order to meet these needs people need to learn what is right, to behave responsibly, and to understand

and face reality. This learning takes place only through involvement with responsible, loving parents and significant others, who love and discipline the child in proper fashion and permit the child to develop personal responsibility. Such a process leads the child to develop a success identity that is synonymous with healthy functioning.

MALADAPTIVE BEHAVIOR

Reality therapy dispenses with the labels usually associated with abnormal or maladaptive behavior, such as psychosis or neurosis (Glasser, 1965). From the reality therapy standpoint, individuals who are behaving inappropriately are doing so because they have been unable to satisfy their needs. When people are unable to meet their needs they will generally lose touch with objective reality: they are unable to perceive things as they really are. In effect, they are unable to operate on the basis of right, responsibility, and reality.

The key to maladaptive functioning is simply that some individuals, because of lack of involvement with others, have never learned to act responsibly. Although a large part of this defect can be attributed to the failure of parents to become involved with their children, in *Schools without Failure* (1969) Glasser pointed out that peers and the school environment play an important role in the development of a failure identity. He pointed out that teachers meet an overwhelming number of children whose needs for love and worth are not being met and that the ways schools are presently constituted lead many to confirm the failure identity that had begun to be formed in the home. In most classes, for example, children are judged on what they fail to learn rather than on the success they achieve.

Maladaptive behavior, then, basically results from the children's never learning to meet their needs through involvement with others. It is also true, however, that even if individuals have learned how to meet their needs at one point, later circumstances can change and thoroughly alter their ability to do so. Glasser (1965) maintained that this is always a function of an individual loss of involvement. He maintained that all people who are suffering from some type of psychological difficulty "are at that time lacking the proper involvement with someone . . . a person whom he genuinely cares about and who he feels genuinely cares about him" (Glasser, 1965, p. 12).

GOAL OF COUNSELING

Counseling from a reality therapy perspective is simply a special form of teaching or training an individual, in a fairly short time, what she or he should have learned during normal growth (Glasser, 1965). The more irresponsible the individual, the more she or he has to learn in order to perform responsibly. The overriding goal of reality therapy counseling is to teach the client through involvement how he or she can meet needs, using the three Rs of right, responsibility and reality as a guide. As with the behaviorist and R.E.T. counselor, the reality therapist focuses on changing the behavior of the client, and only indirectly any underlying causes for the behavior, if such underlying causes do in fact exist. As

Rachin stated, "Reality Therapy differs from conventional therapy in that it labels behavior as either responsible or irresponsible (not the person as mentally ill) and it emphasizes dealing with his behavior in the present (not the person's psychological history)" (1974, p. 47).

PROCESS AND TECHNIQUES OF COUNSELING

Glasser (1965) listed the necessary characteristics of a reality counselor.

1. The counselor must first of all be an individual who is responsible, who is able to fulfill his or her own needs.
2. The counselor must be strong, never expedient. She or he must be able to withstand the client's request for sympathy or justification of behavior, never condoning any irresponsible behavior by the client.
3. The counselor must be a warm, sensitive human being who has the ability to understand human behavior.
4. The counselor must be able to share his or her own struggles with the client so that the latter can see that all individuals can act responsibly even though it is sometimes difficult.

Reality therapy views counseling as a rational process. The counselor must establish a warm, understanding environment, but most important is initially giving the client the notion that she or he has the capacity to be responsible for herself or himself. The client is happy or unhappy because of his or her own behavior and decisions, not because of any external events. As counseling proceeds the counselor must also make it clear that it is responsible behavior, not counseling, that makes people happy. Only the client can make himself or herself happy, and only if the client is willing to face reality and take responsibility for herself or himself.

Beyond describing counseling as a special kind of learning situation, Glasser did not discuss specific techniques. Rather, he presented some general procedures to be used flexibly by counselors to meet the clients' needs. Glasser and Zunin (1973) listed eight of these procedures, summarized below.

1. **Focus on the Personal** The first essential procedure is that the counselor communicates concern to the client. This concern plus warmth and understanding are the keys to successful counseling. The counselor can facilitate this process by using personal pronouns (I, you, we) and by encouraging the client to use them. The personal principle also means that the counselor is willing to be self-disclosing when that is in the client's best interests and that the counselor conveys a belief in the client's ability to help herself or himself.

2. **Focus on Behavior, not Feelings** Many approaches to counseling contend that to help clients, counselors must first focus on helping them feel better, on the hypothesis that feeling better leads to behavior that is more satisfying. Glasser maintains that just the opposite is true: people feel better after they behave more satisfactorily. Therefore, the focus of the counseling process is on what

clients are currently doing that makes them feel the way they do. If a client says, "I'm not feeling very well" the counselor does not say, "Can you tell me a little more?"; rather, the counselor says, "What are you doing that makes you feel that way?" The belief is that as the client begins to describe his or her behavior it becomes apparent to both the client and the counselor why she or he feels that way. The counselor can sometimes heighten this awareness by telling the client, "Now that you have described your current behavior I can understand why you feel the way you do. What keeps you from feeling even worse?" The question is designed to focus attention on the behavioral assets the client does have. Thus, the second procedure is designed to help clients become aware of both self-defeating behavior and behavioral assets. Through this they become aware that they may be their own worst enemy and best friend.

3. **Focus on Present** The emphasis in counseling should be on current functioning. If past events are discussed, the past experience is related to current functioning; or the client is asked to consider alternative ways he or she could have behaved; or the counselor asks what assets kept the client from behaving in even worse fashion. In discussing the present, as much emphasis is given to an individual's assets as to the maladaptive behavior: understanding only the client's failures is only half an understanding. Clients often know their failures all too well; what they do not recognize are their strengths, and strengths are the foundations for future responsible behavior. These first three principles as described by Glasser and Zunin (1973) are designed to facilitate responsible involvement between counselor and client. According to Glasser, "The ability of the therapist to get involved is the major skill of doing Reality Therapy" (1965, p. 22). Once this involvement occurs, the counselor can begin helping the client see how the latter's behavior is unrealistic, rejecting the irresponsible behavior, and finally, teaching the client better ways to meet her or his needs within the real world (Glasser, 1965). The final five principles described by Glasser and Zunin (1973) are designed to accomplish these objectives.

4. **Value Judgment** All clients must eventually be forced to evaluate their own behavior. After the current behavior is fully described, the counselor insists that clients evaluate the behavior in terms of whether it is responsible; that is, whether it is helping or hurting themselves and others. If it is hurting, it should be changed. The reality counselor does not make the value judgments for clients, but neither does he or she condone irresponsible behavior. "We feel that it's irresponsible for a therapist to excuse misbehavior, that is behavior which the patient has judged is wrong" (Glasser & Zunin, 1973, p. 301).

5. **Planning** Once clients have evaluated their irresponsible behavior they are ready to proceed with planning. This stage involves making specific plans to change irresponsible behavior to responsible behavior. It is extremely important for the counselor to help clients develop realistic plans. The tendency in counseling is for the clients to make grandiose plans. Often counselors need to help clients plan their changes in sequence so that they experience success at progressively difficult levels. A client who has experienced unsuccessful dating behavior might be started on a plan that simply calls for engaging a member of the opposite sex in conversation; then, having experienced success there, to plan for engaging in some informal dates, then a formal date, and so on. It is far better to have successes in smaller stages than to try a big change and experience failure. "Successes breed

successes, and failures breed gloom and defeatism" (Glasser & Zunin, 1973, pp. 301–302).

6. **Commitment** Simply having a plan is not enough. "A plan that does not have the client's firm commitment is likely to fail . . ." (Barr, 1974, p. 67). The reality counselor strives to get clients to make a commitment to carry out their plans. Often, particularly with early plans, clients are asked to sign a contract that commits them to carrying out this behavior. As these plans are made and carried out, gradually the focus moves from the clients' making a commitment to the counselor to the clients' making a commitment to themselves. As they become able to keep the commitment, the clients will gradually gain a sense of self-worth and maturity.

7. **No Excuses** Obviously, not all plans that clients commit themselves to will be carried out successfully. When a client returns and reports that the plan was either not carried out or did not work, the counselor refuses to accept excuses. Instead of exploring with the client the reasons why the plan failed (excuses), the reality counselor concentrates on helping the client draw up and make a commitment to a new plan. The new plan will often be a modification of the original one, perhaps with a smaller but more attainable goal. This stage of reality counseling requires strong self-discipline in the counselor, for most clients really do want to discover why a plan failed. The counselor must be able to say, "I'm not asking why your plan failed. What I want to know is when and how you are going to do what you want to do." This communicates the counselor's belief that the client can carry out a reasonable plan.

8. **Eliminate Punishment** In Glasser's view, eliminating punishment is as important as not accepting excuses. The counselor should not punish, through verbal statements, clients' failures to carry out a plan. Such punishment does not change the behavior; it only reinforces the clients' failure identity. The counselor must let the clients simply experience the natural consequence of failure to carry out their plan. Such a procedure once again tells clients that they can and must be responsible for their own plans.

Glasser maintained that through these procedures clients will become more responsible, realistic individuals, able to meet their needs.

Reality therapy is a more complex process than it may seem. The reality counselor must be empathic, involved, and able to provide evidence that he or she is willing to suffer through the client's struggle to change inappropriate (nonresponsible) behavior. Wubbolding (1975) suggested several specific reasons for counselor difficulty in carrying out this approach, summarized below.

1. The counselor may not take enough time to become really involved with the client and to convey that involvement convincingly to the client. This problem is particularly prevalent among beginning or action-oriented counselors who are in a hurry to get on with the task. Such individuals must remember that without involvement there is little chance for real change.

2. The plans and/or contracts developed by the counselor and the client may be too vague. Counselors must remember that establishing small goals that are achievable by the client is much more

therapeutic than establishing vague, lofty goals that the client has a low probability of achieving.

3. A third problem, related to the first, is that the counselor may have become so involved in getting the client to change that he or she forces a contract on the client before the client is really committed to changing. Contracts entered into under these circumstances are destined to failure.

NONCOUNSELING UTILIZATION OF REALITY THERAPY

Principles of reality therapy are being utilized increasingly in public school classrooms. Glasser (1969) maintained that children can be taught responsible behavior in the schools if schools will commit themselves to a program that fosters involvement and relevance. Guided interaction in the classroom can move the school in that direction. In guided interaction the teacher leads the students in discussion of a topic that has some meaning to them. They may focus on problem-solving issues, intellectual issues, or curriculum matters. According to Glasser (1969), such meetings should take place every day in elementary school and at least twice a week in high school. Details about this use of reality principles are found in Glasser's *Schools without Failure* (1969).

SUMMARY

Reality therapy holds that people can be responsible for their behavior. Those who come to counseling do so because they lack involvement with others and are not behaving in ways that fulfill their needs. The task of the reality counselor is to become involved with the client and to get her or him to face reality. Confronted with reality, the client is forced to decide whether to behave in responsible or irresponsible ways. "Reality may be painful, it may be harsh, it may be dangerous, but it changes slowly. All any man can hope to do is struggle with it in a responsible way by doing right and enjoying the pleasure or suffering the pain that may follow" (Glasser, 1965, p. 41).

REFERENCES

Barr, N. I. The responsible world of reality therapy. *Psychology Today*, 1974, 7(9), 64–68.

Belkin, G. S. *Contemporary psychotherapies.* Chicago: Rand McNally, 1980.

Glasser, W. *Reality therapy.* New York: Harper & Row, 1965.

———. *Schools without failure.* New York: Harper & Row, 1969.

Glasser, W., & Zunin, L. M. Reality therapy. In R. Corsini, (Ed.), *Current psychotherapies.* Itasca, Ill.: F. E. Peacock, 1973.

Rachin, R. L. Reality therapy: Helping people help themselves. *Crime and Delinquency*, 1974, 20, 45–53.

Wubbolding, R. E. Practicing reality therapy. *Personnel and Guidance Journal*, 1975, 54(3).

RATIONAL-EMOTIVE THERAPY

CHAPTER TEN

Rational-emotive therapy (RET), originally developed by Albert Ellis, is an approach to counseling that is continuing to evolve. As Ellis stated, ". . . although RET did emphasize (and perhaps overemphasized) cognitive disputing in its early years, as my own experience with RET increased and as other therapists all over the world began to employ it and revise and add to its procedures, our joint efforts produced a good many other cognitive (not to mention emotive and behavioral) procedures" (1977, p. 73). This evolution has moved Ellis to refer to his approach as a cognitive-behavior approach. Although many of the new procedures outlined in Ellis's 1977 article are clear departures from RET, this chapter focuses on the original, basic concepts that make RET unique.

Ellis was originally trained in classic psychoanalytic procedures, but in the course of private practice began to question this approach. Subsequently he began to take on a more active role, incorporating into his therapy advice, homework, bibliotherapy, behavioral principles, and direct confrontations. By 1955 he had rejected psychoanalytic principles entirely and was concentrating on changing clients' behaviors by confronting them with what he termed their irrational beliefs and persuading them to adopt a rational thought process. In 1959 he started the Institute for Rational Living in New York City and now operates a state-approved training program called the Institute for Advanced Study in Rational Psychotherapy. While other individuals such as Maultsby at the University of Kentucky have developed training programs, the institute remains the major training location for those wishing advanced training in RET procedures.

Ellis (1962) contended that people have an inherent capacity to act either rationally or irrationally. The former leads to effective behavior and a productive life-style; the latter leads to unhappiness and a nonproductive life-style. The irrational pattern begins early and is reinforced by parents and the general society. According to Ellis, thinking and emotions are closely interrelated: "among adult humans raised in a social culture, thinking and emoting are so closely interrelated that they usually accompany each other . . . [they operate in circular fashion] so that one's thinking becomes one's emotion and emoting becomes one's thought" (1958, p. 36). Because humans are largely verbal animals, this thinking and emoting take the form of self-talk, and this self-talk directs an individual's behavior in either rational or irrational directions.

PERSONALITY DEVELOPMENT

Because Ellis focused on the development of maladaptive behavior, it is difficult to discuss his concepts of normal development except at a superficial level. Essentially, Ellis's position is that the individual is born with the "powerful predisposition to be self-preserving and pleasure-producing . . . and to actualize some of his potentials [but] he also has exceptionally potent propensities to be self-destructive, to be a short-range hedonist . . . and to avoid actualizing his potentials for growth" (1973a, p. 171). These bipolar tendencies exist in all people, but each individual has inherent tendencies in one direction or the other.

Ellis also viewed people as extremely gullible and suggestible. This suggestibility is greatest during childhood. Because children are social beings with a basic need for love and attention, they quickly learn behaviors designed to elicit responses from those around them. In the course of this learning children begin to behave in ways that are pleasing to others because that is what brings them the love and attention they need. Soon children evaluate themselves on the basis of what others say. To a certain extent this is necessary, for children have to exist in a world with other people, but Ellis (1973a) maintained that "emotional disturbance is almost always associated with the individual's caring too much about what others think of him" (1973a, p. 176). Emotionally mature individuals are able to maintain a fine balance between caring about what they themselves feel and caring about others' evaluations. The degree to which a child's interactions with parents and significant others encourages the development of this behavior will have a direct bearing on the degree to which the individual develops rational or irrational patterns of thinking. Ellis believed that this process is best explained through a principle he calls ABC. Ellis contended that whenever an event (A) occurs and is followed by some unpleasant consequence (C), all individuals have two possible ways of thinking (B): rational or irrational. First, they generally convince themselves of a reasonable, sane, or rational belief (rB) such as "I do not like this event (A). I wish it had not occurred. I feel sorry, angry, and frustrated because it did." If people keep this rational belief they probably will do something in a realistic way that will prevent the event from recurring. This is the procedure that occurs if optimum functioning is to be obtained (Ellis, 1973a).

CHAPTER
TEN
RATIONAL-
EMOTIVE
THERAPY

169

Most often, however, when people are upset by (C) they convince themselves of a second set of beliefs that is inappropriate and irrational (iB) such as "I can't stand this event, it is awful, it shouldn't have happened, I am worthless for letting it happen and you are terrible for doing it to me" (Ellis, 1973a). These beliefs are inappropriate because:

1. They cannot be validated or disproven.
2. They lead to needlessly unpleasant feelings such as anxiety.
3. They prevent the individual from going back to the event (A) and changing or resolving it (Ellis, 1973a).

Ellis (1973a) maintained that these irrational beliefs are magical and impossible to validate because (1) individuals can stand the unpleasant event (A) even though they might not like it; (2) it is not awful, for awful has no real meaning, although it may be inconvenient or unbeneficial; (3) by holding that the event should not have occurred the individuals are playing God, in that whatever they want not to exist should not exist; and (4) by stating that they are worthless because they could not stop the event, individuals are stating that they should be able to control the universe and that anyone who cannot is obviously worthless.

It is this second set of beliefs (iB) that Ellis believed is most often reinforced as individuals develop. All the ways in which parents, schools, and other people and institutions make children feel worthless furnish proof for Ellis's contention. Being made to feel worthless reinforces children's irrational belief systems. Thus, even though "man has vast untapped resources for the growth of his potential" (Ellis, 1973a, p. 175), it is most often people's potential for irrational thinking that is reinforced.

Most individuals, then, develop personalities that are composed of both belief systems. Those who operate effectively do so most of the time on the basis of their rational (rB) belief system; those who experience difficulty are usually operating on the basis of their irrational (iB) belief system.

MALADAPTIVE BEHAVIOR

In Ellis's view, "human beings are the kind of animals who, when raised in any society similar to our own, tend to fall victim to several major fallacious ideas" (1972, p. 220). These irrational ideas became ingrained or imprinted at an early age before "later and more rational modes of thinking were given a chance to gain a foothold" (Ellis, 1972, p. 220). Once irrational ideas are part of the belief system, individuals continue to reindoctrinate themselves through self-talk and so, continue to behave in inappropriate ways.

Ellis postulated that there are eleven "major illogical and irrational ideas which are presently ubiquitous in Western civilization and which would seem inevitably to lead to widespread neurosis" (1962, p. 61). These eleven ideas, originally published in 1962 in *Reason and Emotion in Psychotherapy*, are summarized below.

1. **It is absolutely essential for an individual to be loved or approved by every significant person in his or her environment.** Although it is desirable for individuals to be loved, the idea is irrational because it is impossible to be loved or approved by everyone, and striving to attain the goal leads to behavior that is not self-directing.

2. **It is necessary that each individual be completely competent, adequate, and achieving in all areas if the individual is to be worthwhile.** It is impossible for any individual to be competent in every endeavor, and an individual who feels she or he must be is doomed to a sense of failure. Such an idea also leads a person to view every situation in competitive terms. The individual strives to outdo others rather than simply enjoying the activity itself.

3. **Some people are bad, wicked, or villainous and these people should be blamed and punished.** This idea is irrational because everyone makes mistakes. These mistakes are a result of stupidity, ignorance, or emotional unbalance, not of someone's being a certain way. Furthermore, blame and punishment are not effective ways of changing behavior. The rational idea is to admit that everyone makes mistakes and that making mistakes does not make anyone worthless. The objective should be to correct the mistake.

4. **It is terrible and catastrophic when things are not the way an individual wants them to be.** The reality of life is such that not all situations are as people would like. This reality may be unpleasant or bothersome, but it is not a catastrophe. Treating an event as a catastrophe does not change the situation; it only makes people feel worse. If a person does not like something, she or he can try to change it. If the person cannot do anything about it, he or she should accept it.

5. **Unhappiness is a function of events outside the control of the individual.** People and events can do very little actual harm other than physically abusing an individual or depriving an individual of such things as food. This seldom happens in North American society; most events that people perceive as harmful are only psychologically harmful: it is the perception of the event that is harmful.

6. **If something may be dangerous or harmful an individual should constantly be concerned and think about it.** This is irrational because simply thinking about it (a) doesn't change it, (b) may in fact lead to its occurrence, (c)

and may make it worse than it actually is. The rational person tries to evaluate the event objectively and do what he or she can to alleviate its dangerous or fearful elements.

CHAPTER
TEN
RATIONAL-
EMOTIVE
THERAPY

171

7. **It is easier to run away from difficulties and self-responsibility than it is to face them.** This is irrational because running away does not solve the situation. Usually the situation remains and must eventually be dealt with.

8. **Individuals need to be dependent on others and have someone stronger than themselves to lean on.** Depending on others leads to insecurity and nongrowth. Such individuals never learn self-regulation and are always at the mercy of others.

9. **Past events in an individual's life determine present behavior and cannot be changed.** The past may influence the present but does not necessarily determine it. People have the capacity to change the way they now behave even though they cannot change the past.

10. **An individual should be very concerned and upset by other people's problems.** This is irrational because often those problems have nothing to do with the concerned individual, and even if they do, getting upset usually prevents someone from helping others do anything about their problems.

11. **There is always a correct and precise answer to every problem, and it is catastrophic if it is not found.** This is irrational because there is no perfect solution to any situation. The search only produces continued anxiety. As a result the individual is never satisfied and is always searching for the one lost solution.

Although there are many corollaries to these postulates, Ellis maintained that they are the major causes of emotional problems. In his view, once people believe these ideas they become inhibited, hostile, defensive, guilty, anxious, ineffective, inert, uncontrolled, and unhappy (Ellis, 1972). Ellis contended that most of these ideas are more or less specifically taught by parents and the culture, and that most adults in our society believe in most of them. "It must consequently be admitted that the neurotic individual we are considering is often statistically normal" (Ellis, 1972, p. 225). Ellis's contention implies that U.S. culture produces individuals who are to some degree emotionally disturbed. This is not necessary, but is the current state of affairs. Hence, the task is to help individuals recognize their illogical thinking and to develop rational ways of thinking.

GOALS OF COUNSELING

RET counselors have one primary objective for all clients, "namely, that of finally inducing the [client] to internalize a rational philosophy of life just as he originally learned and internalized the irrational view of his parents and his community" (Ellis, 1962, p. 95). Thus, a client may come to counseling with a presenting concern, such as getting along with peers, that is causing him or her difficulty. While dealing with this concern, the RET counselor also seeks to effect a change in the whole underlying pattern of illogical thinking. In Ellis's view, if only the presenting symptom is attacked, the client will probably return later with other symptoms. Therefore, the counselor must attack the "basic irrational thinking processes, which underlie all kinds of fears" (Ellis, 1962, p. 96).

The RET counselor operates from an authoritative position (Ellis, 1962) justified by the counselor's training and experience. "Even if he does not look upon himself in this manner, the members of his clientele almost invariably do. And whether he likes it or not, a considerable portion of his effectiveness with patients results from his being or appearing to be something of an authority figure to them" (Ellis, 1962, pp. 364–365). In Ellis's view, initially clients may need to be approached in a supportive, warm fashion and be allowed to express feelings, "but the rational therapist does not delude himself that these relationship-building and expressive-emotive methods are likely to really get to the core of the (client's) illogical thinking" (Ellis, 1962, p. 95). Relationship techniques are viewed simply as preliminary techniques, and "the rational therapist goes beyond that point to make a forthright, unequivocal attack on the client's general and specific irrational ideas and to try to induce him to adopt more rational ones in their place" (Ellis, 1972, p. 226).

The counselor needs to understand the client's world and see the client's behavior from the latter's point of view, but it is the ability to understand the client's irrational behavior "without getting involved in or believing in it that enables him to induce the [client] to stop believing in or feeling that his behavior is necessary" (Ellis, 1962, p. 115). The counselor "must keep pounding away, time and again, at the illogical ideas that underlie the client's fears" (Ellis, 1972, p. 227). She or he must use the most direct, persuasive, suggestive, active, and logical techniques possible to help the client move from irrational to rational thinking (Ellis, 1962).

TECHNIQUES OF COUNSELING

"All the techniques in rational-emotive therapy are designed to do more than change behavior and help the client feel better. They are also used to change basic philosophies and to give him or her specific means of restructuring these philosophies" (Ellis, 1973b, p. 62). There are essentially two ways of doing this: (1) the counselor acts as a frank counterpropagandist who directly confronts and contradicts the irrational self-talk and beliefs of the client; and (2) the counselor encourages, persuades, cajoles, and commands the client to engage in behavior that will act as a forceful counterpropaganda instrument (Ellis, 1972).

According to Ellis (1973a), these processes take place via three basic modalities: cognitive, emotive, and behavioristic.

Cognitive counseling is designed to show the client "that he is an errant demander and that he had better give up his perfectionism if he wants to lead a happier, less anxiety-ridden existence" (Ellis, 1973a, p. 182). This is essentially a teaching process in which the client learns to recognize shoulds, oughts, and musts, and how to distinguish irrational beliefs from rational ones. The assumption is that the counselor is simply teaching the client how to use her or his cognitive ability more skillfully (Ellis, 1973a). During this stage all kinds of teaching devices are used (such as pamphlets, books, tape recordings, films, and filmstrips).

Emotive-evocative counseling is designed to change the client's basic value system. During this stage various techniques are used to demonstrate to the client the differences between truths and falsehoods (Ellis, 1973a). For example, the counselor might use role playing to show the client that the latter's ideas are false; modeling to show the client more appropriate ways of behaving; unconditional acceptance and humor to show that the client is accepted even though some of her or his ideas are absurd; and exhalation to get the client to give up irrational ideas and replace them with more rational thinking (Ellis, 1973a).

The behavioral stage is basically designed to help the client develop new modes of thinking and behaving once he or she recognizes the errors in past thinking and behavior. These techniques may include homework, role-playing, and operant conditioning procedures (Ellis, 1973a). Ellis has used some behavioral techniques since the early 1960s, and "there are indications of an increasing rapproachment between behavioral techniques and RET theory, which has been termed cognitive behavioral therapy" (Dolliver, 1977, p. 61). A former student of Ellis's, Maxie Maultsby (1975), described his derivative of RET as rational behavior therapy. Ellis (1973c) himself stated that there is increasing similarity between RET and behavioral techniques. In a 1977 article, Ellis raised the question whether RET really has anything that clearly distinguishes it from other cognitive-emotive-behavior therapy approaches. His answer was: "That depends on whether we consider what I now call 'general' or 'inelegant' RET and what I call 'elegant' RET" (Ellis, 1977, p. 74). He characterized his early formulations as "general" or "inelegant" RET and his current thinking as "elegant" RET. The essential difference between the two is that Ellis no longer restricts himself to the basic ABC principles of RET, but uses techniques drawn from a variety of approaches. Despite this apparently eclectic position, he has maintained that "general" RET is still the heart of his approach.

In essence, the techniques utilized in RET counseling may come from almost every other theoretical approach; it is truly an eclectic position. "Probably fifty or sixty different kinds of cognitive procedures in therapy now exist, and more appear all the time. RET tries to use, in various ways, almost all of these methods . . ." (Ellis, 1977, p. 73). According to Ellis (1973a), the key is what can best help the client. In his view, an efficient system of counseling considers (1) economy of client and counselor time spent in counseling; (2) the rapidity with which a client can be helped with immediate concerns; (3) the ability of a counseling approach to be effective with a wide variety of clients; and (4) the depth and lasting effect of solutions. According to Ellis, RET is best able to meet all these criteria.

SUMMARY OF RET

The basic assumption of the RET approach to counseling is that most people in our society develop many irrational ways of thinking. These irrational thoughts lead to irrational or inappropriate behavior. Therefore, counseling must be designed to help people recognize and change these irrational beliefs into more rational ones. The accomplishment of this goal requires an active, confrontative, and authoritative counselor who has the capacity to utilize a great variety of techniques.

REALITY THERAPY AND RATIONAL-EMOTIVE THERAPY

It is clear that both Glasser and Ellis place major responsibility for an individual's actions with that individual. When someone is experiencing difficulty, it is because she or he is behaving either irresponsibly (Glasser) or irrationally (Ellis). In either case the individual is viewed as having the capacity to change. In both approaches the counselor's role is largely one of confronting clients with what they are doing and then teaching them to think and behave in more appropriate fashion. To accomplish this the counselor may use many different techniques.

There is one key difference between the two approaches. In Glasser's view, there is an external standard of right and wrong against which individuals must judge their behavior. Ellis's position is more existential: individuals are presumed capable of establishing their own criteria of right and wrong and are expected to do so. This difference can result in an important difference in the actual process of counseling. Ellis might push a client to develop her or his own standards and to disregard everyone else's. Glasser, on the other hand, would confront a client with the latter's need to consider external reality.

Despite this difference, the two approaches are very similar and both have demonstrated some effectiveness with a variety of clients. Both approaches seem most appropriate when clients can be expected to have a high intellectual capacity and least appropriate for clients who have difficulty in reasoning.

REFERENCES

Dolliver, R. H. The relationship of rational-emotive therapy to other psychotherapies and personality theories. *Counseling Psychologist*, 1977, 7 (1), 57–63.

Ellis, A. Rational psychotherapy. *Journal of General Psychology*, 1958, 59, 35–49.

——. *Reason and emotion in psychotherapy.* New York: Lyle Stuart, 1962.

——. Rational-emotive psychotherapy. In J. T. Huler & H. L. Millman (Eds.), *Goals and behavior in psychotherapy and counseling.* Columbus, Ohio: Charles E. Merrill, 1972.

——. Rational-emotive therapy. In R. Cor-

sini (Ed.), *Current psychotherapies.* Itasca, Ill.: F. E. Peacock, 1973a.

——. The no-cop-out therapy. *Psychology Today*, 1973b, 7, 56–62.

——. Are cognitive behavior therapy and RET synonymous? *Rational Living*, 1973c, 8 (2), 8–11.

——. Rejoinder: Elegant and inelegant RET. *The Counseling Psychologist*, 1977, 7, (1) 73–82.

Maultsby, M. C. Rational behavior therapy for acting-out adolescents. *Social Casework*, 1975, 56, 35–43.

TOWARD A THEORY OF COUNSELING: WHERE ARE WE NOW?

CHAPTER ELEVEN

178 CHAPTER
ELEVEN

TOWARD A
THEORY OF
COUNSELING:
WHERE ARE
WE NOW?

Chapters Two through Ten have presented several basic theoretical approaches to counseling. Although there are many other variations, the approaches presented are representative of the continuum of theories currently being practiced. The diversity in counseling perspectives causes concern to many in the field of counseling. Some feel that the profession of counseling is doomed because of the many differences; others view the situation as a healthy climate in which to test new ideas and assumptions. A realisitic attitude probably lies somewhere between the two extremes, for despite the variety of theoretical approaches to counseling, there are many similarities.

The purpose of this chapter is to examine the areas of agreement and disagreement among the positions presented. This is in line with our belief that each counselor must develop his or her own theoretical position. As the systems model presented in Chapter One indicated, part of the process of developing one's own theory is synthesizing preexisting theories into a personal eclectic position. As Robinson (1965) stated, the eclectic counselor examines various theories, takes from them valid and testable ideas, and molds them into a consistent approach that works for him or her. This procedure is very different from that of Robinson's syncretic counselor, who simply utilizes ideas from many positions without attempting to integrate them; or that of the pragmatic counselor, who believes that theory has no place in counseling; or finally, that of the personality theorist, who advocates one single position as the answer to everyone's problems. The weight of evidence indicates that the eclectic position described by Robinson should be the choice of counselors. "As treatments useful in one area of human disturbance are found to be less valuable in another, efforts are made to arrive at better criteria for selecting patients for particular forms of therapy and for modifying existing forms. Here the stated task for the future is to achieve greater specificity concerning the effects of particular kinds of intervention" (Karasu, 1977, p. 852). The true eclectic must choose techniques based on evidence that they believe will work with a particular client with a particular problem. This chapter presents material that may help the prospective counselor move toward the kind of eclectic position described by Robinson. A conceptual model developed by Frey (1972) provides a framework for this material by showing some relationships among the various theoretical approaches.

INTERRELATIONSHIP OF COUNSELING THEORIES: A MODEL

As Frey (1972) indicated, several people have attempted to develop a model that would show the relationship among various theoretical approaches to counseling. Patterson (1966) used a single linear division that placed theories on a dimension ranging from rational approaches to affective approaches. More recently, Marmor (1975) and Karasu (1977) have studied the similarities and differences among approaches to counseling. All of these models failed to be meaningful because they were either based on a single dimension, and a single dimension could not adequately show the complexity of interrelationships among theories; or like Barclay's (1968), they were based on philosophical orientations too far removed from actual practice. The model developed by Frey (1972) appears to master these problems.

Frey (1972) combined the unidimensional (rational-affective) model of Patterson (1966) and the unidimensional (insight-action) model of London (1964) into a four-celled model. This model is capable of showing the relationship among theories both in terms of the actual process of counseling (Patterson) and the objectives of that process (London).

We will use the insight–action dimension of the Frey model to describe the objectives of each approach to counseling. Some approaches hold that counseling must deal with the totality of the individual and that insight is a prerequisite for any change in behavior, and these approaches are placed in one of two cells emphasizing insight (for example, the client must develop an understanding of her or his life script). More specific and action-oriented positions will be placed in one of two cells emphasizing action (for example, the client will be able to be assertive in appropriate social situations).

The second dimension of Frey's model, the rational–affective, will be used to describe the actual process of counseling. Approaches that emphasize conative or affective expression within the counseling process will be placed in one of two cells emphasizing affect. These approaches encourage the expression of feelings about situations. Conversely, approaches that emphasize counseling as a rational learning process will be placed in one of two cells indicating an emphasis on rational thought. Here the emphasis is on clients' thinking about situations.

The basic dimensions of Frey's model (1972) are shown in Figure 11-1. The closer a particular theory is to the intersection of the four cells (such as Adlerian), the more similar it is to approaches in the other quadrants; conversely, the farther out an approach is from the intersection (such as self-theory), the more dissimilar it is from all other approaches. Those that share a quadrant, may use different vocabulary to describe their approach but are similar in terms of both the process of counseling and the objectives of that process.

Figure 11-1 shows two theories in the rational–insight quadrant, three in the insight–affective quadrant, only one in the affective–action quadrant, and two in the action–rational quadrant. The remaining theory (RET) straddles the rational–insight and action–rational quadrants.

Theories in the rational–insight quadrant share a belief that a rational thought process leads clients to insight, which in turn leads to a change in emotional status and then to actual change in behavior. Of the three approaches in this quadrant, RET is the most rational and, together with Adlerian, is very close to the axis, indicating a real balance among all four dimensions of the model. The T.A. and Adlerian approaches, though placing slightly more emphasis on insight, are also close to the action quadrant.

Approaches in the insight–affective quadrant maintain that clients develop insight into their difficulties by coming to understand their emotions and their internal drives and motivations. As Frey (1972) indicated, emphasis is on feeling, knowing, and understanding. It should be noted how close the ego-counseling position is to the axis. In actuality, although it is in a different quadrant, it is probably closer to the Adlerian approach than to the self-theory approach, which is in the same quadrant. The self-theory position is the farthest from the axis. It differs not only from other approaches in the same quadrant, but also from all other approaches. This is due largely to the almost total reliance of the self-theory position on insight that comes through focusing on the here-and-now feelings of

180   CHAPTER
ELEVEN

TOWARD A
THEORY OF
COUNSELING:
WHERE ARE
WE NOW?

FIGURE 11–1 FREY'S FOUR-CELLED MODEL OF
COUNSELING THEORIES

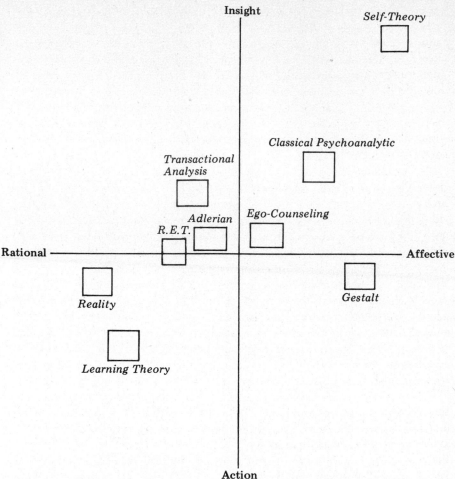

Source: Frey, David H., Conceptualizing counseling theories: A content analysis of process
and goal statements. *Counselor Education and Supervision,* 1972, *11,* 4. Copyright © 1972 American Personnel and Guidance Association. Reprinted with permission.

the client. The psychoanalytic position, in contrast, focuses on insight derived
from exploration of past emotional events.

    The Gestalt position is the only one shown in the affective–action quadrant.
This approach is very close to the insight–affective quadrant, but it places more
emphasis on feeling and its relationship to action or behavior change. Gestaltists
acknowledge that insight is necessary but represents only half the counseling task;
the other half involves planning for how this insight can change behavior. The
Gestalt position is often thought to be very similar to the self-theory position, and
in some ways it is, but a clear distinction exists in their respective emphases on
planning for action. Gestaltists are much more concerned about actual behavior
change, although Carkhuff's recent modifications in self-theory would move the
latter very close to the intersection of all four quadrants.

In the last quadrant, action–rational, are the behaviorists, the reality counselors, and, to a somewhat lesser degree, the RET counselors. These approaches emphasize the role of a rational process in producing specific behavioral changes. The approaches shown in this quadrant maintain that feelings change after behavior changes, not the other way around: if individuals feel bad it is because of something they are doing; if they change what they are doing then they will feel better. Within the quadrant, behaviorists are more concerned than reality counselors about specific behaviors; hence, it can be said that they are the most action oriented.

One of the most striking things about this model is that six of the nine positions presented in Chapters Two through Ten are grouped in close proximity to the intersection of the four quadrants. Only the behaviorists, Gestaltists, and self-theorists are at any extremes, and many counselors within each of these groupings would probably appear closer to the center if their actual practices were analyzed. This indicates that even most formally stated positions are more eclectic in nature than they might initially appear. It also lends credence to our view that each individual can develop his or her eclectic position as described by Robinson. It is interesting to note that the older the profession of counseling becomes and the more sophisticated its procedures, the closer toward the axis all approaches move. Keeping this conceptual model in mind, we can now examine the similarities and dissimilarities among the approaches in the following areas: nature of individuals, personality development, abnormal development, the counseling process—including the goals of counseling, the counseling relationship, and the role of the counselor—and the techniques of counseling.

NATURE OF INDIVIDUALS

One of the most difficult questions that must be addressed by every approach to counseling concerns the nature of human beings. Counselors must decide what people's role is in the world before they can hope to help them. Yet, human beings are the most complex organisms known, and this complexity is reflected in the diversity of answers to the question.

In the ego-counseling, psychoanalytic, and TA views, people are reactive beings. They react to their own innate drives and needs. Those drives and needs are developed and profoundly influenced by early childhood experiences and frustrations. In these views, human nature is largely determined during the first five years of existence. During these five years children have many emotional experiences, and these experiences form the basis for later behavior.

Learning theorists take a similar approach: they also view people as reactive. In the learning theory view, people do not react to their own innate drives, but to the world around them. In the view of behaviorists, people are biological beings who react to the stimuli in their environments. Human behavior is determined, but it is determined by the environment in which people exist. People do not control their own destinies, but are controlled by external forces. Adult behavior is a direct result of early childhood environment, for children learn patterns of behavior in reaction to their environment. These learned patterns determine later reactions to stimuli in the environment.

In contrast with these theories, the other positions presented in this text

182   CHAPTER
ELEVEN

TOWARD A
THEORY OF
COUNSELING:
WHERE ARE
WE NOW?

maintain that individuals are beings in the process of becoming, beings with potential for controlling their own behavior. In this view, human behavior is not determined by forces outside of people's control, but is controlled by the individual through a conscious and thoughtful process. People are not irrational, controlled individuals, but rational beings who largely determine their own destinies.

Although it appears that the approaches to counseling have little in common in terms of their conception of the nature of people, there is an implied commonality among them. This commonality is implied by the fact that all these approaches to counseling were developed in order to help people bring about changes in their behavior. Hence, all the approaches acknowledge that human behavior has the capacity to change. Related to this common assumption is the common belief that certain events in an individual's life can cause difficulty and that these difficulties are serious enough to need some kind of change. Thus, all the approaches share the belief that sometimes individuals are in situations that cause them to need help, and that help can be offered with the expectation that a change in the situation will occur.

PERSONALITY DEVELOPMENT

Virtually every approach to counseling acknowledges the importance of the first five years of life. The approaches based on analytic principles tend to agree what an individual becomes is largely a function of internal dynamics. These internal drives move people to try to satisfy needs that for the most part exist outside awareness. Similarly, the behaviorists believe that personality is a function of individuals' reactions to stimuli in their environment. Those reactions (behaviors) that bring satisfaction are retained as part of the personality and those that do not are discarded. Both of these general approaches, then, hold that people acquire behaviors either in an attempt to satisfy inner drives or to bring some feeling of satisfaction. In both cases personality development is viewed as a reactive process not under thoughtful, rational control.

Conversely, the Gestalt, Adlerian, reality, RET, and self-theory positions to varying degrees share a belief in people as actors. They contend that people may have internal needs and that they are indeed subject to certain environmental constraints, but that these factors do not determine entirely what people do. The emphasis is on how individuals perceive and evaluate the internal needs and external events. In these views people act on the world rather than reacting to it. It is through this action, a large part of which is interpersonal interaction, that personality is formed.

In all approaches, the process of personality development is a function of the individual's needs being met. In the first case, this process is largely out of control of the individual; in the second, the individual is accorded a great deal of credit for what he or she ultimately becomes. All these concepts agree on the importance of early childhood experiences. All emphasize the influence of these experiences on the adult personality. Whereas the analytic and learning theory positions both maintain that individuals are reactive beings, they differ to some extent about what people react to. In the analytic view, people react to both innate drives and, to a lesser degree, the environment; in the learning theory view, individuals basically react to stimuli in their environment. In both views, individuals do not have much conscious control over their own behavior. At the other extreme are approaches that attribute all of human behavior to thoughtful control: individuals are able to evaluate their own experiences and then to act accordingly. These approaches subscribe to the rather optimistic notion that individuals act on the environment and are in control of their own personality development, whereas the analytic and learning theory approaches take the comparatively pessimistic view that individuals react to stimuli, innate or external, and that personality development is largely outside of conscious control. Regardless of this central difference, it is clear that all approaches agree on the importance of the environment in the shaping of personality. The differences center on how theorists view the interaction between the individual and the environment.

ABNORMAL DEVELOPMENT

All approaches to counseling acknowledge that during early childhood the individual can have experiences that lead to maladjustment or maladaptive behavior later in life. Analytic theorists maintain that this type of behavior results from a breakdown in the functioning of the ego: in some way the ego was unable to cope with some situations in a meaningful and positive fashion, and these experiences were suppressed in the unconscious. They may arise later and cause difficulty because the individual never learned to deal with the experience in the first place. In contrast, self-theory, Gestalt, Adlerian, reality, RET, and transactional analysis theorists believe that perception is the key to inappropriate behavior. In the self-theory view, the memory of these events is pushed into the unconscious; the individual either distorts the original experience or denies its existence because it does not fit with the conception of self. Thus, both the analytic and self-theory approaches to counseling view maladaptive behavior as stemming from experiences that have been denied awareness, and this denial in turn prevents the individual from learning how to cope with them in a positive fashion. From this perspective, then, maladaptive behavior is only a symptom of some underlying cause. Gestaltists, on the other hand, while agreeing with the self-theorists about the importance of perception, believe that maladaptive behavior results from individuals' trying to deny what they are and at the same time trying to be something they are not.

Reality therapists consider maladaptive behavior a result of an individual's being frustrated in the attempt to meet personal needs. This frustration leads the individual to lose contact with or to misperceive the real world. Similarly, RET views maladaptive behavior as a function of the individual's distorting the world and continually telling himself or herself that these distortions are true.

In the Adlerian view, maladaptive behavior is formed early in life, when the child perceives her or his inferiority to be so great that the child feels rejected by others and adopts a completely self-centered life-style.

Similarly to the Adlerian viewpoint, TA theorists believe that the individual's perception of early events is a determiner of inappropriate behavior. Transactional analysts believe that individuals' perceptions of events lead them to adopt a particular life position and script, and that individuals gear their lives to confirm and maintain the chosen life position and script. If the position and script are inappropriate then so, too, will be the behavior of the individual.

The learning theory position is quite different from the preceding approaches. In the behaviorist view, maladaptive behavior is acquired in the same manner as normal behavior. The inappropriate behavior is learned because it has been rewarded at various times. The learning theorist is concerned not with underlying causes, but only with the maladaptive behavior. Maladaptive behavior differs from normal behavior, not in the manner in which it has been developed, but only to the degree that it is atypical or maladaptive to the observer. Hence, behavior is not caused by hidden motives or drives or by inaccurate perceptions, but occurs because it brings some satisfaction to the individual. As we shall see, differences in opinion about the nature of maladaptive behavior are reflected in the various approaches to counseling.

THE COUNSELING PROCESS

GOALS OF COUNSELING

Basic to the counseling relationship are the goals of counseling. Psychoanalysts, ego-analysts, Adlerians, Gestaltists, self-theorists, and transactional analysts tend to state these goals in global fashion: the goals involve reorganizing the whole structure of the individual. Adherents to these theories believe that the presenting problem is only a symptom of an underlying cause and that the cause itself must be the focus of counseling. To some extent, RET and reality counselors would agree, but they are also concerned about helping the individual to develop new behaviors. The behavioral counselors maintain that the goals of counseling must be stated in specific terms, and they focus directly on the presenting problem. The analysts, ego-counselors, Adlerians, Gestaltists, and TA counselors tend to view the goals of counseling as basically the same for everyone; the reality and RET counselors occupy an intermediate position and are concerned with a global attitude that affects specific behaviors; and the behavioral counselors believe that different goals should be established for each individual.

Despite these general differences, all approaches have in common the goal of facilitating changes in behavior. Some counselors view this goal holistically; others see it in terms of some combination of global and specific goals; and learning theorists see it in terms of specific behaviors. The goals move from very global to very specific, and the differences in degree affect the way in which the counseling relationship is handled.

COUNSELING RELATIONSHIP

As Figure 11-1 shows, self-theorists, Gestaltists, psychoanalysts, and ego-counselors tend to view the counseling relationship as a basically affective or emotional process, whereas the other approaches regard the relationship as a rational one. Certainly none of the approaches excludes either emotion or reason. They do, however, vary in the degree to which they encourage rational or emotional expressions by the client. A self-theorist counselor, for example, is much more likely than a behavioral one to respond to expressions of affect. Such a pattern of responding indicates to the client the kinds of things to which the counselor will respond.

In addition, the Adlerian, analytic, TA, and ego-analytic approaches are more concerned with the client's exploring the past, whereas the other approaches emphasize current functioning. Once again, the counselor's orientation will indicate to the client the kinds of material the counselor will attend to. As with the affect–rational dimension, few counselors emphasize one end of this continuum exclusively.

ROLE OF COUNSELOR

Central to the differences among the approaches is the role of the counselor in the counseling process. The ego-analytic, analytic, TA, reality, RET, and learning theory positions hold that the counselor is an expert to whom the client has come with a problem that she or he cannot resolve alone. This assumption leads to the view that the counselor must take a somewhat active role in the counseling relationship. The ego-analysts, analysts, and TA counselors see themselves as controlling the relationship, balancing it between the affective and cognitive domains. Further, they consider the counselor responsible for making a diagnosis of the problem and then presenting a plan for resolving the situation to the client. Likewise, reality, RET, and learning theorists counselors prescribe the method of treatment once a diagnosis has been determined. All approaches emphasize the need for the client to feel confidence in and be respected by the counselor. In addition all maintain that the client must agree with the diagnosis before any particular treatment will be effective. Nevertheless, these approaches tend to regard the counselor as the controlling agent in the relationship. Their model of the relationship is quite similar to the medical model.

In contrast, the self-theorists, Gestaltists, and Adlerians argue that because of man's inherent growth tendency, the client has the capacity and the motivation to solve her or his own problem if provided with a nonthreatening atmosphere. The self-theorists emphasize that the counselor's presence or behavior in the counseling relationship does not directly influence the client's behavior. In their view, then, there is no need for the counselor to make a diagnosis and, indeed, diagnosis is detrimental to the process of counseling. In self-theory, the locus of evaluation belongs with the client; moreover, diagnosis by a counselor creates dependency needs in clients, whereas they should be helped to develop their own strength. The self-theorists believe that if the counselor controls the relationship and sets the goals for the client, she or he is interfering with basic human nature. From this perspective, the counselor's role is simply to provide the conditions so that the client may reinstitute the self-actualizing tendency. The counselor controls only the conditions, not what the client does.

Neither the Gestalt or Adlerian counselors go as far as the self-theorists, although they do agree that people basically have the potential to look into themselves and change their behavior. The Adlerians do believe, however, that the counselor can provide direct assistance to the client that will facilitate insight. This assistance often takes the form of interpretation and diagnosis. Gestalt counselors are probably the most active; the action is not interpretive, but is designed to confront the client with current behavior and (particularly) inconsistencies in that behavior.

186 CHAPTER
ELEVEN

TOWARD A
THEORY OF
COUNSELING:
WHERE ARE
WE NOW?

The counseling relationship is viewed somewhat differently by the various approaches, ranging from the very cognitive, action-oriented learning theory approach through the somewhat balanced ego-analytic approach to the affective, insight-oriented self-theorists. The self-theorists believe that insight, by itself, will lead the client to change, whereas the ego-analysts contend that the counselor must in effect prescribe the necessary changes for the client. On the other hand, the learning theory approach is exclusively action oriented. To behaviorists, the client's problem needs to be dealt with directly, not as a symptom of some hidden difficulty. The degree to which an approach is insight or action oriented directly affects the degree to which the counselor assumes responsibility for the outcome of counseling. The behaviorist, action-oriented counselor is not only more active in the actual counseling relationship, but may also take an active role in the outside life of the client.

Despite these differences there are some common factors among the approaches to the counseling relationship. All share a belief in the necessity for a good relationship. All stress the need for the client to feel accepted and understood in the relationship; for the client to feel that the counselor is concerned and able to help; and for the counselor to be genuine or honest with the client. In effect, the counselor must come across to the client as a real person, one deserving of the client's trust. This topic is so important that Chapter Twelve, which begins Part Two of this book, is devoted exclusively to the counseling relationship.

A second element common to all approaches is the notion that the counseling process will lead to some change on the part of the client and that this change can be aided through the use of the counseling interview. Although some behavioral, reality, and RET counselors stress the need for manipulation of the outside environment of the client, they also place a great deal of importance on the counseling interview. In terms of the amount of change expected through use of the counseling process, there are differences in degree but not in expectation. Some theorists expect a complete change in personality, others want changes only in particular areas. Most theorists take the latter position.

Most approaches, then, agree on the necessity of an appropriate counseling relationship built on the assumptions that counseling can lead to behavioral change; that this change is facilitated through the interview process; that the relationship must be based on mutual trust and understanding between the counselor and the client; and that both members of the relationship must have confidence in the ability of the relationship to bring about changes in the client.

Using the conceptual model presented in Figure 11-1, we will now examine how differences in the views of the counseling relationship are translated into the actual techniques used in counseling.

TECHNIQUES OF COUNSELING

RATIONAL–INSIGHT

The approaches in the rational–insight quadrant share a belief that insight, if not necessary, is at least helpful in bringing about behavior change and that techniques employed by the counselor facilitate this insight. Like the insight–affective counselors, they maintain that a client must understand why he or she is experiencing difficulty before any change can be expected. Unlike the insight–affective practitioners, however, they regard the process of discovering as more of a rational than an emotional one. As Figure 11–1 shows, the Adlerian counselor and the TA counselor tend to approach a balance in their emphases on rationality and affect, whereas the RET counselor, as the name implies, places much more emphasis on the importance of reason in the process, and is also more concerned about behavior. In fact, the RET counselor will often try to change behavior before working on developing client insights.

RET is basically a teaching procedure that attempts to bring the client to understand both the rational and affective components of behavior. Ellis (1973) divided counseling into three separate stages: cognitive, emotive, and behavioristic. In the cognitive stage the techniques are designed to confront the client's expressions so that the latter can distinguish rational thoughts from irrational ones. In the emotive stage the counselor may use role-playing techniques to help the client perceive irrational beliefs; may model how the client can adopt different values; and may use exhortation to get the client to replace old thoughts with new, more appropriate ones. In the final stage the counselor seeks to help the client establish "habits" of behavior that are based on rational thinking about events. In this stage the counselor may use such techniques as homework and even some behavioristic reinforcement. It is apparent that RET, although it emphasizes rational thinking that leads to insight, is also concerned with the emotive aspects of client problems and with having the client take some positive action. It is very close to a true eclectic approach, as Ellis himself has often acknowledged.

The Adlerian approach is also very close to an eclectic position. Unlike the RET counselors and like the transactional analysts, the Adlerians are interested in the effects of early life impressions on individuals. Thus, early recollection, memories of childhood, plays an important role in Adlerian counseling. Equally important are individuals' perceptions of their current life space. Developing these perceptions may involve analysis of family structure and, sometimes, the work structure. This analysis is designed to determine the patterns of behavior the clients have used and are using in the attempt to reach their chosen life goals. Once these are understood, the counselor presents the patterns to the clients. The counseling process then shifts to the development of a more appropriate life goal. As with all the approaches in this quadrant, the process is counselor directed.

The TA counselor places great reliance on the ability to develop an understanding of the client. To do this, during the early stages of counseling the counselor uses game analysis, script analysis, and analysis of ego structure, focusing mainly on the individual's current interactions with others. Because it is important to understand interaction patterns, TA counselors most often work with individuals within a group setting. Next, the TA counselor seeks to interpret this understanding to the client. In this part of counseling the emphasis is very similar to the Adlerian position.

Once clients understand the ways in which they are behaving, the counselor tries to get them to take positive action by assuring them of permission to engage in new behaviors, and of protection if things should not go well.

The traditional TA counseling process is not only counselor centered; it also focuses on counseling as a rational rather than an affective process. Like the

188   CHAPTER
ELEVEN
TOWARD A
THEORY OF
COUNSELING:
WHERE ARE
WE NOW?

rational-emotive therapists traditional TA counselors are concerned with the specific new behavior in which the client will engage. As such, both positions are more action-oriented than the Adlerian approach. Neither, however, is as concerned with specific actions as the theorists in the rational–action quadrant. It is worth noting that many of the new TA theorists call for a great deal of Gestalt procedures that are highly "affect" oriented.

INSIGHT–AFFECTIVE

All three approaches in the insight–affective quadrant (psychoanalytic, ego-counseling, and self-theory) consider insight a necessary prerequisite to behavior change. The psychoanalytic and self-theory positions are that a client must understand the total self and all the underlying dynamics of behavior. The ego-counselors, while believing insight is necessary, focus more on understanding parts of oneself than on the total self. All agree, however, that a client who cannot get along with others must know the reasons before behavior can improve. They differ markedly, however, on the kinds of counselor behaviors that lead the client to this insight, and the degree to which the client's total personality must be involved. The ego-counselor, as the most action oriented of the group, is concerned with helping the client change specific behaviors. Psychoanalytic and self-theory counselors are more inclined to believe that the total personality must be the focus.

The psychoanalytic counselor, believing that profound exploration of the past is necessary for understanding the present, acts to facilitate free association and transference. This procedure is designed to help the counselor develop an understanding of the client. Through interpretations, the counselor then presents this understanding to the client. Having expressed the repressed needs of the client, the sources of difficulty, the counselor assumes that the client will be able to develop new ways of behaving. It is clear that the psychoanalytic counselor places much more faith in her or his own therapeutic potential than does either the self-theory counselor or the ego-counselor.

Of the three approaches in this quadrant, and perhaps in the whole model, the self-theory counselor uses the fewest techniques. The emphasis is on the counselor's ability to establish the proper conditions for therapeutic change. In this view the counselor, by providing the "necessary and sufficient conditions," acts to facilitate client exploration of self, which leads to self-understanding and ultimately to changes in behavior. No other techniques are needed. In contrast, the more eclectic approaches derived from Rogers's work do use specific techniques to accomplish certain goals.

Ego-analysts emphasize the ability of the counselor to control the dimensions of the relationship, largely by controlling the amount of ambiguity offered to the client, and through the use of partial interpretations. With these techniques the counselor first provides the structure necessary for the client to express her or his feelings and then leads the client to an understanding of the problem. In effect, the counselor, having made a diagnosis, leads the client to self-awareness through the use of interpretation. After the client achieves self-awareness, the counselor and client plan specific steps to implement new behaviors. This stage often involves role playing, role rehearsal, and sometimes homework assignments.

This last stage makes ego-counseling the most action oriented of the approaches in this quadrant.

CHAPTER 189
ELEVEN
TOWARD A
THEORY OF
COUNSELING:
WHERE ARE
WE NOW?

AFFECTIVE-ACTION

The affective–action quadrant contains only the Gestalt approach. According to Perls (1969), the responsibility of the Gestalt counselor is simply to provide an opportunity for the client to discover what her or his needs are and then to supply an atmosphere in which the client can grow. As such, the approach is generally without techniques. The Gestalt counselor is concerned with interacting with the client in the here and now. In doing so, the counselor focuses as much on the client's nonverbal expressions and gestures as on the verbal. Perls (1969) felt that clients must be made aware of this "psychosomatic language" in order to understand the totality of their being—their Gestalt. This awareness leads to the discovery of needs and then to the process of growth.

To bring about this awareness, the counselor seeks always to keep the client in the present, by confronting the client with current behavior in the counseling relationship. For example, the client may be saying positive things and at the same time be moving around in a chair. The Gestalt counselor would focus the client's attention on this inconsistency. The use of games also forces clients to deal with current feelings. Even dreams are utilized actively. Dreams are not interpreted or simply recalled; the Gestalt counselor makes the client act out dreams, in effect, to relive them. All these processes are designed to bring the client to full awareness of her or his total being, which includes both the client's needs and his or her resources for dealing with them. The Gestalt approach, then, is both insight and action oriented.

Unlike the approaches in the insight–affective quadrant, Gestalt counseling emphasizes achieving insight into current functioning, not into past causes. Also, unlike other insight approaches, Gestalt counselors are more concerned with the client's taking positive action. These goals require Gestalt counselors to be much more active in the relationship than the self-theory counselors, with whom they are often confused. Pure Gestaltists are difficult to find; many counselors use Gestalt techniques, but few use them exclusively.

RATIONAL-ACTION

The two approaches found solely in the rational–action quadrant work for actual behavior change. They tend to be more cognition oriented than any other approach in the model. This does not mean that they ignore the necessity for establishing a relationship with the client, but it does mean that they work more directly with specific behaviors rather than with feelings. The client's presenting concern is the focal problem of counseling. The importance of the past and/or underlying dynamics are underplayed, and the counselor tries to help the client change the specific behavior. Whereas other approaches tend to maintain that changes in feelings lead to changes in behavior, the reality and behavioral approaches tend to maintain the reverse. The dichotomy is not as simple as it sounds, but it does illustrate the difference in emphasis.

Reality therapy is shown as more rationally oriented than RET because the latter emphasizes both the rational and emotive aspects of personality. Reality

190   CHAPTER
ELEVEN
TOWARD A
THEORY OF
COUNSELING:
WHERE ARE
WE NOW?

therapy, on the other hand, is most concerned about teaching people the importance of reality. As Glasser stated, "The therapist must not only be able to help the client accept the real world, but he must then further help him fulfill his needs in the real world so that he will have no inclination in the future to deny its existence" (1965, p. 32). According to Glasser, people are more interested in behavior than in attitudes.

Reality therapists' techniques are intended to force clients to see and understand the conditions of their reality and to accept the fact that they are responsible for their behavior in that world. It is essentially a confrontative, teaching process. In Glasser's view, sympathy has no place in counseling; what is important is that the client adopts more productive behavior.

Similarly, the behaviorists are concerned with specific behavioral changes rather than attitudes. They differ from the reality position in that they place less faith in the individual's rational thought process. Learning theorists view counseling as simply a type of learning experience. Thus, their counseling techniques rely on the same laws of learning that apply in everyday life: reinforcement, shaping, imitative learning, and cognitive learning. The counselor decides which principles of learning will be most effective with a particular client and then applies those laws to the counseling process. The counselor must help the client decide on the desired behavioral change, must help the client understand what consequences are maintaining the current behavior, and then help the client develop behaviors that will also bring desired consequences.

Both approaches, then, place emphasis on behavioral changes, on counseling as a teaching process, and on the counselor as the director of the process. They differ somewhat in the techniques they use to teach the new behaviors and in their belief in individuals' capacity to reason for themselves.

While each of the approaches to counseling applies different techniques, they all require that some form of verbalization take place between the client and the counselor. If this kind of exchange does not occur, neither does the process of counseling. One persistent criticism of counseling is that it is basically designed, regardless of the theory used, for those who can verbalize. In fact this criticism may be valid, and more attention should be paid to how counselors can operate with potential clients who possess limited verbal skills.

This examination of the various approaches has shown that among them there are many similarities as well as differences. The differences appear to stem from different concepts about the nature of human beings and how the events around people influence their lives. Some differences are the result of different interpretations of similar events; some, of a difference in semantics. Although these differences may in some cases be extremely important, they are often magnified out of proportion. They are not so great, or indeed, so important that some type of unity cannot be achieved among the various approaches to counseling. To that end, it may be appropriate to examine some research comparing different theoretical approaches to counseling.

RESEARCH

Some of the differences among various theoretical approaches to counseling have been demonstrated in research literature. Sundland and Barker (1962), using a

Therapist Orientation Scale, conducted a survey of 139 psychotherapists. The questionnaire contained sixteen subscales; on nine of them there were significant differences among the therapists classified as Freudians, Sullivanians, and Rogerians. In the development of the Therapist Orientation Scale, however, items on which therapists agreed were discarded. When the same therapists were grouped by level of experience, differences were found only on one scale.

Wallach and Strupp (1964) examined the differences among Freudian, general psychoanalytic, Sullivanian, and client-centered counselors. Using a scale of usual therapeutic practices, they found that the four groups could be differentiated on the amount of personal distance maintained in the counseling relationship.

McNair and Lorr (1964), using a scale based on the Therapist Orientation Scale, surveyed 265 therapists. Like the previous studies, the results showed differences on three separate dimensions.

Although these studies indicated that there are differences in counseling practice, it must be remembered that these researchers were looking for differences. Perhaps an even more important question concerns the outcomes of counseling. Did the use of different approaches produce any differences in the outcome of counseling? To a large extent this question has not been answered by the research. Hence, we really do not know whether the differences that were found have any significance.

Just as there is evidence of differences among various theories, there is a growing body of evidence that there are many similarities. Fiedler's classic studies (1950a, 1950b, 1951) demonstrated that there was little difference among various approaches to counseling. Much of the evidence has demonstrated some approximation between the self-theory and behavioral or learning theory positions. Sapolsky (1960) found that the effectiveness of reinforcement techniques was related to the success of the relationship. Ullmann and Krasner (1965) also emphasized the importance of the relationship regardless of the theoretical approach of the counselor.

In one investigation of how theory affects proactive children, Truax (1966) analyzed a single, long-term, successful case handled by Carl Rogers. Truax concluded that the data from this case indicated that Rogers was quite successful in using the techniques of reinforcement. This investigation indicates that perhaps the positions of the self-theorists and the learning theorists are really not far apart, at least in actual practice. In a later study, Truax (1968) found that when three of the necessary self-theory conditions for counseling—accurate empathy, nonpossessive warmth, and genuineness—were used as reinforcers, clients increased their amount of self-exploration. Like the previous study, this investigation indicates that actual counseling may have elements of both learning theory and self-theory.

In an investigation by Anderson, Douds, and Carkhuff (1967) there was a further indication that although theories may be different, practices at the very least overlap. In listening to forty taped counseling interviews they found that counselors who were operating at a high level of functioning, offering high levels of the necessary conditions for counseling, were more effective in the use of confrontations with their clients. The technique of confrontation is one that is more typically associated with the action approaches to counseling (learning theory or ego-counseling), yet it was found to be effective in a self-theory context.

An extensive review of research by Ellis (1977) demonstrated quite clearly that there is increasing similarity among all approaches. However, there is as yet little evidence as to whether these differences or similarities make any real differences in counseling outcomes.

192 CHAPTER
ELEVEN

TOWARD A
THEORY OF
COUNSELING:
WHERE ARE
WE NOW?

SUMMARY

At this point one may wonder whether there will ever be one unified theory of counseling. Rogers believes the profession of counseling must develop a broader perspective if differences are to be reconciled. In a similar vein, Allport (1961) suggested that the main trouble with counseling theories is that they are partial rather than whole theories. In effect, both said that we need to develop further the theories we now have, and that as this development occurs, we may see a rapprochement among them. There is already some indication of basic agreement on some crucial issues.

There is little question that most approaches to counseling recognize the importance of the relationship in counseling. Although some argue that it is not sufficient by itself, all agree that it is necessary. It is also clear that all approaches to counseling recognize that difficulties do arise in a person's life and that these difficulties can be overcome through the process of counseling. Given these basic agreements, perhaps the differences that exist are not insurmountable. After all, a theory is only a set of assumptions that is in the process of testing. It is not something final and static, but should always be changing.

As we stated in Chapter One, it is most important that counselors strive to develop a theory for themselves that is based on certain assumptions but are also open to revision. After studying current theories and the research that relates to them, the counselor is ready to try these theories in his or her own practice and research and to develop a personal theory from these experiences. The counselor's development of self-understanding is crucial to the successful development of her or his own mode of counseling.

REFERENCES

Allport, A. W. Psychological models for guidance. *Harvard Educational Review*, 1961. *32*, 373–381.

Anderson, S., Douds, J., & Carkhuff, R. B. The effects of confrontation by high and low functioning therapists. Unpublished paper, University of Massachusetts, 1967.

Barclay, J. *Counseling and philosophy: A theoretical exposition.* In B. Shertzer & S. C. Stone (Eds.), *Guidance Monograph Series.* Boston: Houghton Mifflin, 1968.

Ellis A. Rational emotive therapy. In R. Corsini (Ed.), *Current psychotherapies.* Itasca, Ill.: F. E. Peacock, 1973.

——. Rational-emotive therapy: Research data that supports the clinical and personality hypotheses of RET and other modes of cognitive behavior therapy. *Counseling Psychologist*, 1977, *7* (1), 2–42.

Fiedler, F. The concept of an ideal therapeutic relationship. *Journal of Consulting Psychology*, 1950a *14*, 235–245.

——. A comparison of therapeutic relationships in psychoanalytic non-directive and Adlerian therapy. *Journal of Consulting Psychology*, 1950b, *14*, 436–445.

——. Factor analysis of psychoanalytic, non-directive, and Adlerian therapeutic relationships. *Journal of Consulting Psychology*, 1951, *15*, 32–38.

Frey, D. H. Conceptualizing counseling theories: A content analysis of process and goal statements. *Counselor Education and Supervision*, 1972, *11* (4), 243–250.

Glasser, W. *Reality therapy: A new approach to psychiatry.* New York: Harper & Row, 1965.

Karasu, T. B. Psychotherapies: An overview. *American Journal of Psychology*, 1977, *31*, 134.

London, P. *The modes and morals of psychotherapy.* New York: Holt, Rinehart and Winston, 1964.

Marmor cites common factors in therapies. *Psychiatric News*, 1975, 1–15.

McNair, D. M. & Lorr, M. An analysis of professed psychotherapeutic techniques. *Journal of Consulting Psychology*, 1964, *28*, 265–271.

Patterson, C. *Theories of counseling and psychotherapy.* New York: Harper & Row, 1966.

Perls, F. S. *Gestalt therapy verbatim.* Lafayette, Calif.: Real People Press, 1969.

Robinson, F. P. Counseling orientations and labels. *Journal of Counseling Psychology*, 1965, *12*, 338.

Rogers, C. R. Divergent Trends. In R. May (Ed.), *Existential psychology.* New York: Random House, 1961.

Sapolsky, A. Effect of interpersonal relationships on conditioning. *Journal of Abnormal and Social Psychology*, 1960, *60*, 241–246.

Sundland, D. M., & Barker, E. N. The orientation of psychotherapists. *Journal of Consulting Psychology*, 1962, *26*, 201–212.

Truax, C. B. Reinforcement and nonreinforcement in Rogerian psychotherapy. *Journal of Abnormal Psychology*, 1966, *71*, 1–9.

———. Therapist interpersonal reinforcement of client self-exploration and therapeutic outcome in group psychotherapy. *Journal of Counseling Psychology*, 1968, *15*, 225–231.

Ullmann, L. P., & Krasner, L. *Case studies in behavior modification.* New York: Holt, Rinehart and Winston, 1965.

Wallach, M. S., & Strupp, H. H. Dimensions of psychotherapists' activities. *Journal of Consulting Psychology*, 1964, *28*, 120–125.

CHAPTER ELEVEN
TOWARD A THEORY OF COUNSELING: WHERE ARE WE NOW?

193

PART TWO

COUNSELING PROCESS

PART TWO
INTRODUCTION

Theory and process are closely interrelated. A counselor begins with some general assumptions about personality, moves to more specific assumptions about behavior changes, and then forms a counseling theory that indicates procedures to be implemented. A counselor may start with a theory that feels comfortable and then modify and reformulate it through experience and evaluation. Such procedures help counselors know where they are going and what they are doing with a client. Theory in the counseling process provides both a method of helping counselors understand their clients and a set of guidelines for counseling behaviors.

Part Two focuses on the process of counseling. No one theory is followed; instead, concepts about the process from various positions and research are interwoven into eclectic procedures. Generally, the frame of reference is psychobehavioral, based on insight-oriented procedures that integrate broadly defined, behaviorally oriented approaches. The chapters present the general counseling process, permitting counselors to add techniques consistent with their theory.

We present the counseling process as a relationship between the counselor and the client rather than as a set of techniques. The counseling process consists of establishing a cooperative interaction and using that relationship to help clients explore themselves and their situations, gain a clearer understanding of both, and then try out appropriate actions. The counseling process can cover a wide range of client needs, from therapeutic personal changes to developmental decisions. The therapeutic process extends over a considerable period with numerous interviews that gradually produce changes in how clients view themselves and lead to overt or covert behavior change. In a more developmental process, counseling involves fewer sessions in helping comparatively self-directed clients resolve conflicting ideas, obtain information, or work through decisions. The basic processes are similar, with emphasis differing according to client needs.

This section begins with a chapter on counseling as a relationship. It focuses on the variables that contribute to the relationship and on how these variables also function as techniques to foster client self-exploration, understanding, and appropriate action. Chapter Thirteen is devoted to initiating the counseling process. It discusses the importance of the counselor's approach to client expectations and preferences and describes the counselor's behaviors throughout the initial interview. The following chapter presents a model of the various phases through which a counseling relationship may pass. The model discusses the goals and the behaviors between the counselor and client as the counseling process moves from the initial interview to self-exploration to working through to termination.

Chapter Fifteen discusses the role of diagnosis in the counseling process, both as a concept of classification and as a procedure in understanding the client. We present some models for using diagnosis as a procedure in understanding the client.

Chapters Sixteen through Eighteen are concerned with decision making in counseling, using tests, and vocational counseling. Although these elements may appear in any counseling relationship, they are most likely to be included for clients experiencing developmental problems. The chapter on decision making reviews several models and presents a step-by-step process of decision making in counseling. The chapter on testing describes the types of tests that may be used with clients and provides some guidelines for test interpretation. The vocational counseling chapter discusses the counselor's conceptualizing the vocational development process and using educational and vocational information to assist clients in making decisions that can prevent problems as well as help with placement or remediation.

The final chapter examines the roles of ethics, values, and legalities in counseling. It raises ethical considerations that can improve counselors' behavior and treats the significant relationship of counselors' values to their behavior. Likewise, counselors' awareness of the legal ramifications of their role can serve as a guide for appropriate behavior in the counseling process.

COUNSELING AS A RELATIONSHIP

CHAPTER TWELVE

Many in the field of counseling consider the counselor-client relationship the most important aspect of counseling. In recent years techniques have been superseded in theory by tones of feeling. Technique has become more flexible to allow concentration on the relationship between the counselor and client. Actually, the counselor's use of the relationship dimensions is the technique of counseling. Counseling is a process of establishing a cooperative relationship and then using it to help the client learn his or her desired appropriate behavior.

What differentiates the counseling relationship from any other helping relationship or friendship? Patterson (1969) stated that counseling is a special application of the principles of good human relations and described why this relationship is so significant. First, the counseling relationship is established and continues because the client feels a need for a special help or assistance with a problem she or he has been unable to resolve independently or through other relationships. Thus, the emphasis is on the client's desire for special help regarding feelings of dissatisfaction with himself or herself. Although friendships are beneficial to individuals in need of special help, they are often not sufficient to enhance the individual's self-esteem or resolve a particular problem. Second, the counseling relationship is formal and structured in that it is not continued on a casual social basis. It is characterized by special arrangements for a specified duration, privacy, and confidentiality. Third, the counseling relationship is limited to the therapeutic hour. Although this practice has been challenged by those who want to make the counselor an agent for social change, the counseling relationship usually does not extend beyond the professional relationship. The counselor may see the client in settings other than the office but the principle of the therapeutic hour still holds. Fourth, although the counseling relationship is limited in time, it is a closer and deeper relationship than ordinary social friendships. The relationship is carefully established as nonthreatening. This atmosphere permits client self-disclosure and self-exploration so that the counselor comes to know the client better than anyone else does. Fifth, the counseling relationship is powerful and thus effective because the principles of good human relationships are applied consciously and purposefully without the banalities of ordinary social interaction. The counseling relationship can develop rapidly and focus on the essentials.

AN OVERVIEW OF THE COUNSELING RELATIONSHIP

The counselor's techniques are actually the manner in which he or she works with the many variables in the counseling relationship. Horwitz (1974), in explaining how change occurs in psychotherapy, maintained that client change occurs through supportive aspects of the interpersonal relationship, which he termed a therapeutic alliance.

The counseling relationship is an alliance formed to help the client move toward a goal: more appropriate behavior. The client is able to try changes through an internalization of this therapeutic alliance. The internalization is made possible by the counselor's acceptance of the client as a person and by the former's help in resolving a problem. Feeling accepted despite inappropriate behavior may be a corrective emotional experience for the client. This experience helps enhance the client's self-esteem and encourages her or him to work for improvement, sometimes in an attempt to please the counselor. Although at first the client may merely identify with the counselor's attitudes, the client can eventually internalize the concepts and personalize these new attitudes and behaviors.

This is a global view of counseling as a relationship. This chapter examines the specific variables of the relationship. To help the client feel accepted and understood, the counselor will use differential levels of facilitative communication. While being genuinely herself or himself, the counselor will communicate a positive regard and empathic understanding of the client. These facilitative conditions have been found to be imperative in a counseling relationship and help to enhance the client's self-esteem.

The relationship does not develop automatically. A client may exhibit some form of resistance to the process or to an aspect of the problem. The counselor may use varying degrees of ambiguity by controlling the topic and process or by permitting the client to define the situation. The topics and the client's feelings about them will influence the degree to which the client reacts intellectually or emotionally. At times the client may transfer to the counselor attitudes or feelings that were experienced with other significant people. The counselor may experience a countertransference by having some emotional reactions and projections toward the client. The counselor should recognize all these relationship dimensions and work to help the client function in the most effective manner. The counselor recognizes these dimensions through the client's verbal and nonverbal communication and uses his or her own communication skills to help the client explore herself or himself, improve self-understanding, and begin more appropriate behaviors.

The counselor's skill in understanding these relationship dimensions and in communicating can facilitate the client's entry into the therapeutic alliance and movement through the stages of counseling that make up the counseling process. Therefore, counseling is a relationship consisting of various dimensions.

Although the relationship dimensions are presented separately in this chapter, many occur simultaneously. They are discussed independently to provide adequate coverage of each topic; however, they must be seen as an integrated process in counseling. We begin with a thorough examination of the therapeutic alliance and the general counseling process. This will be followed by discussion of the specific dimensions of the counseling relationship.

THE THERAPEUTIC ALLIANCE

The therapeutic alliance is characterized by the conviction of both the client and counselor that the primary goal of working together is to help the client. Two major readiness factors, one in the client and the other in the treatment process, permit a therapeutic alliance to develop. The client must possess a disposition or positive expectation of the counselor on which to build and strengthen an internal conception of a good significant other. Within the counseling process, there must be sufficient need gratification geared to the individual client to foster the latter's perception of the counselor as a helpful and constructive person.

A general model of successful counseling suggests that if the client is positively disposed to the experience with a good counselor and receives sufficient need gratification in the counseling process, the desired internalization of the therapeutic alliance will take place. Numerous stable changes associated with the development of a favorable therapeutic relationship result from this internalization. Internalization is the process whereby the representation of the counselor and a more gratifying relationship between the client and this significant other person become assimilated into the client's inner world of object relations. This dynamic is similar to the ordinary maturation and development process of infancy and childhood, when crucial internalized self and object representations become imprinted upon the personality of the individual. The counselor attempts to achieve an imprinting of psychological reactions; when it is successful, a significant change occurs in the client's inner and object world.

SUBPROCESSES OF INTERNALIZATION

Internalization involves several subprocesses that act reciprocally to enhance the counseling relationship: they contribute to the growth of the therapeutic alliance and in return tend to be enhanced by a growing positive relationship. Horwitz (1974) proposed four factors as subprocesses that will contribute to internalization: a corrective emotional experience, enhanced self-esteem, a transference improvement, and identification with the counselor.

Corrective Emotional Experience

The counselor's commitment to the client and the client's capacity to perceive this relationship not only produces a heightened self-esteem but also can modify the client's special problem behaviors. In a corrective emotional experience, the counselor responds differently to certain aspects of the client's behavior than the latter had expected; that is, retaliation is not forthcoming after the client's inappropriate behavior. Such an experience contributes to the growth of the relationship, engendering trust in the counselor's intentions and fostering hope that this relationship will fare better than others in the past. The growing alliance contributes to the client's capacity to experience and perceive helpful responses, which in turn enhances the growth of a good self-other relationship. Such a relationship permits the client to feel safe enough to explore himself, increase understanding, and internalize enough learning from the counselor to try new behaviors. In contrast, parents and significant others have generally responded with criticism and lack of acceptance to the client's inappropriate behaviors. The client's internalization of these feelings and denial of self-acceptance result in a reduced level of self-esteem. This earlier experience also leads the client to expect that the counselor will not accept her or him. When the client gradually learns that those expectations are unrealistic, he or she can modify misperceptions and reduce defensiveness. Although the counselor and client are trying to help the latter behave more appropriately, the counselor is accepting the client as a person.

Enhanced Self-Esteem

Horwitz's research team (1974) observed that every client who improved had more positive feelings about himself or herself and that these changes were clearly related to experiencing the counselor's interest, concern, and valuing. The affective bond between the client and counselor was strengthened.

Heightened self-esteem is more intense when experienced in a context of being accepted and valued despite the expression of inappropriate wishes or behaviors. The counselor's ability to accept the "badness" of the client's behavior reduces the pressure on the client to defend herself or himself, provides an opportunity for the client to internalize the counselor's attitudes, and enhances the client's self-regard. Enhanced self-esteem and the corrective emotional experience are reciprocal processes.

CHAPTER
TWELVE
COUNSELING
AS A
RELATIONSHIP

203

Transference Improvement

Another concomitant of an internalized good relationship is the client's effort to please the counselor by engaging in improving adaptive behaviors. The concept of a transference cure is frequently deprecated by analysts as being only the demonstration of a fleeting and transitory behavior. Such changes in behavior may be temporary and unstable when they are not based on a sufficiently strong and positive internalization. However, when a client has a positive reaction to the counselor and tries new appropriate behaviors in an attempt to please the counselor, the client can receive sufficient internal and external reinforcement to stabilize the new behavior. Thus, the transference improvement that develops in the context of a trusting relationship can be expected to persist.

Identification

Another cause and product of the internalization process is identification with the counselor's attitudes. At first, the client may identify with some of the attitudes and feelings the counselor has demonstrated toward him or her. The identification is based on the counselor's sense of commitment and feelings of responsibility and concern for the client. The client assimilates the essential ingredients of the therapeutic relationship into feelings about herself or himself. The process of identification is a basic ingredient of normal development; in counseling, it represents an acquisition in an area where normal development failed either because of conflict relationships with the parents or because the parents represented an inappropriate model.

Strupp (1978, pp. 3–22) also stressed the importance of client identification with the counselor, which occurs in all forms of counseling. While superficially resembling any good human relationship, the therapeutic alliance provides a unique situation for increased identification with the counselor. Given that the internalization of "bad objects" has contributed to the client's problems, counseling succeeds to the extent that the counselor can become a "good object." However, because the client tends to cling to objects of early childhood, defending them against modification, the counseling process involves a struggle. The ability of the counselor and client to form a therapeutic alliance is an important aspect of the client's growth.

The process of identifying with certain specific attitudes exemplified in the counselor is a by-product of internalization. This does not mean that the counselor imposes values on the client but that the counselor exemplifies attitudes and behaviors consistent with the client's goals for herself or himself. Identification refers to the process of becoming like an external model, in this instance, taking on certain qualities of the counselor or of other significant individuals. Identification involves a modification of the self-representation.

SUMMARY

Strupp (1978) concluded that the quality of the client-counselor relationship and of the alliance as it manifests itself throughout the interaction appears to be a highly significant prognostic indicator of progress. The internalization of the therapeutic alliance is both process and outcome and occurs through the interrelated processes of corrective emotional experience, heightened self-esteem, transference change, and identification with the counselor's values.

The counselor's attitudes are influential factors in creating the kind of relationship that leads to client improvement. Factors that foster development and maintenance of an effective relationship are of primary importance. What are the factors or dimensions of the counseling relationship that makes it effective? Several factors or dimensions in the interaction between counselor and client influence the effectiveness of the counseling. One of these, the facilitative conditions that the counselor communicates to the client, seems to serve as a base for the development of a relationship.

FACILITATIVE CONDITIONS

Rogers's (1957) statement of the necessary and sufficient conditions for therapeutic personality change—the specific counselor attitudes that he believed to be essential to the development of a counseling relationship—is a comprehensive and systematic conception of the change-producing ingredients of the counseling process. In Rogers's view, significant change does not occur except in a relationship. Two people must be in psychological contact; both client and counselor must be aware of the presence of the other. The other necessary and sufficient conditions include the counselor's positive regard for the client, the experience of unconditional positive regard, empathic understanding, and congruence in the counselor-client relationship.

The counselor must be congruent or integrated in the relationship, without any facade, role, or pretense. What the counselor says is not only honest, but also congruent with the counselor's feelings. The counselor's willingness to be genuine in words, behavior, feelings, and attitudes is the only way to guarantee reality in the relationship.

The second facilitative condition in a relationship is the counselor's experiencing an empathic understanding of the client's world and being able to communicate some of this understanding to the client. The counselor senses and experiences the client's private feelings and personal meanings as if they were his or her own. When the counselor can perceive these internally as they seem to the client and can successfully communicate some of this understanding to the client, then this condition is fulfilled.

The third condition for growth and change is the counselor's experiencing a warm, positive, accepting attitude toward the client. Although Rogers listed this condition third, it probably is the first thing the counselor is able to communicate to the client. It means that she or he likes the client as a person and cares for the latter in a nonpossessive way as a person with potential. This condition means that the counselor respects the client as an individual; it is usually termed positive regard.

The last condition for personal change in the relationship is called unconditionality of regard. Rogers hypothesized that the relationship will be effective to the degree that the positive regard is unconditional. The counselor does not accept certain feelings in the client and disapprove of others; there is a consistently positive feeling without reservation and without evaluations. The counselor's acceptance of the client is unconditional in the sense that it is nonjudgmental; there are no conditions or strings attached. It means an acceptance of and regard for the person's current attitudes no matter how negative or positive they may be. This acceptance of fluctuating feelings in the client makes for a relationship of warmth and safety. The client does not have to conceal aspects of self, behave in certain ways, or play certain games to gain the counselor's attention or positive valuation.

COMPARISON OF CONDITIONS

Rogers considered these variables so important in the counseling relationship that he has based his whole counseling approach on these conditions. The assumption that they are indeed necessary and sufficient conditions for change has become almost synonymous with client-centered counseling. Most approaches to the counseling relationship, however, include similar variables. Table 12–1 presents a comparison of these conditions across several theoretical approaches.

Psychoanalytic Theorists

Psychoanalytic theorists do not name specific attitudes that are necessary for successful counseling. However, Adler, Horney, and Alexander, examples of counselors with psychoanalytical orientations, seem to stress two similar variables in their writings. They say that understanding and friendly interest in the client are necessary for successful counseling to take place.

Adler, the first of Freud's colleagues to break away, cited the two main attitudes of the counselor as understanding and friendly interest. According to Horney (1942), by friendly interest the analyst gives the client a good deal of what may be called general human help, similar to what one friend might give to another: emotional support, encouragement, interest in the person's happiness. This may be the client's first experience of human understanding, the first time another person has bothered to see that he or she is not simply spiteful, suspicious, demanding, but with a clear recognition of such traits still likes and respects him or her as a striving human being. Sullivan (1954) used the word *awareness* instead of *understanding*, and *respect* instead of *friendly interest*. He believed that respect for the other person and awareness for the other person's feelings were elements of the expertness in interpersonal relations that any client would look for in an interviewer. Sullivan is probably most noted for his concept of the participant observer. He believed the counselor could not stand off to one side and apply his sense organs without becoming personally implicated in the operation. This concept of being personally implicated appears to be similar to Rogers's concept of congruence. Although Alexander (1963) did not mention a condition equivalent to congruence, he did present some similar ideas. He maintained that the counselor's objective, emotionally nonparticipating attitude is artificial for it does

TABLE 12-1 A COMPARISON OF THE FACILITATIVE CONDITIONS OF COUNSELING, BY THEORY

ROGERS	ADLER	HORNEY	SULLIVAN	ALEXANDER
1. Congruence	——	——	Personally implicated	——
2. Empathy	Understanding	Understanding	Awareness	Understanding
3. Positive regard	Friendly way	Friendly interest	Respect	Friendly interest
4. Unconditional regard	——			
5. ——	Intuitive guessing	——	——	——

DOLLARD AND MILLER	WOLPE	SHOBEN
1. ——	——	
2. Empathy	Empathy	Understanding
3. Acceptance Positive outlook	Respectful Seriousness	Warmth
4. ——	——	Nonretaliatory permissiveness
5. Mental Freedom Restraint	Communicate desire to serve	Honesty of communication

VAN KAAM	DREYFUS	MAY
1. Sincerity	Openness	Encounter
2. Acceptance	Understanding	Empathy
3. Gentleness		
4. Nonjudgmental attitude	Letting be	Nonthreatening atmosphere
5. Flexibility	——	

FIEDLER	TRUAX	CARKHUFF
1. ——	Genuineness	Genuineness
2. Understanding	Accurate empathy	Empathy
3. Warm interest	——	Positive Regard
4. ——	Nonpossessive warmth	——
5. ——	——	Concreteness, Immediacy, Confrontation

not exist between human beings in actual life. Alexander believed that the client reacts to the counselor as a concrete person, not only as a representative of transferred feelings. He also believed that the counselor's reactions exceed what is called countertransference; that they may also include behaviors based on conscious deliberations and on the counselor's spontaneous, idiosyncratic attitudes. Therefore, although Alexander did not state that being oneself in the interview is necessary, he was aware that it occurs frequently. He also discussed the conditions of understanding the client and of providing friendly interest.

Learning Theorists

Three learning theory orientations are included in Table 12-1. Of these, Dollard and Miller (1950) maintained that the client finds in the counselor someone with prestige who, by paying favorable attention and listening sympathetically, gives the client faith that some help will be forthcoming. The counselor shows excessive permissiveness, encourages the client to express feelings, does not condemn, and tolerates discussions of matters that have caused the client's friends to show anxiety and disgust. The anxious client tends to imitate the counselor's composure, and this activity is reassuring to the client. When the client has always received severe disapproval, the counselor's calm, accepting manner provides both great relief and a striking intervention. "It may be worthwhile to name four attributes of the therapist as a teacher in the situation of psychotherapy: We suggest that the therapist should be mentally free, empathic, restrained, and positive" (Dollard & Miller, 1950, p. 230). Although Dollard and Miller do not mention acceptance specifically, it is apparent from their writings that they expect the counselor to be accepting of the client. Their description of the counselor as calm, accepting, non-condemning may not include unconditional positive regard but probably involves a concept of positive regard for the client. Having a positive outlook means that the counselor has faith in the client and in the latter's ability to solve the problem and eliminate the conflicts. By mental freedom, Dollard and Miller mean the counselor must have much less anxiety than the client about the worst things that bother clients; she or he must be able to work with what the client says without anxiety. The counselor must also use some restraint and resist the strong tendency to conduct the interview as a conversation. He or she must subordinate self to the strategy of cure and say nothing that does not further this strategy. This exercise of restraint may inhibit the counselor from really being congruent or genuine in the relationship.

The action-oriented counselors who use conditioning approaches in counseling are frequently perceived as cold and inhuman. Wolpe (1966), however, described relationship variables that are quite similar to those of other approaches to counseling. He stated that whatever else the counselor may do, it is of first importance to display empathy and establish a trustful relationship. The client must feel fully accepted as a human being and not less worthy or less fortunate than the counselor. In Wolpe's view, the specific techniques used in therapy must be administered by people who are able to treat their clients with respectful seriousness and who can communicate a sincere desire to be of service.

Shoben discussed similar variables for the counseling relationship (Shaffer & Shoben, 1956). He believed the counselor should express a genuine concern for the client as a human being and devote total attention during the interview to understanding the client's feelings as fully as possible. The counselor should communicate friendliness or warmth to the client without condemnation. The counselor will also interpret the feelings of the client. In this area Shoben stressed honesty of communication, using the term nonretaliatory permissiveness in a sense very similar to that of unconditional positive regard. He maintained that the client should be free to discuss any subject and is never rejected or criticized for her or his beliefs or feelings.

Existential Theorists

Table 12–1 also presents the views of three existential counselors. Van Kaam (1966) included sincerity, acceptance, gentleness, and flexibility among the attributes of the relationship. His use of the term *sincerity* is very similar to Rogers's term *congruence*. Van Kaam believed the counselor's attitude should be straightforward, honest, and truthful. His term *acceptance* expresses a very broad concept. In Van Kaam's view, acceptance will generate in the client an experience of feeling truly understood in his or her unique personal world. Acceptance does not imply personal agreement with the client's strivings and decisions but a coexperience and a nonjudgmental attitude. The counselor's special function is not to judge to what extent the client is personally responsible for attitudes and feelings, but to understand the depth of the existence that they reveal.

Under the term *acceptance*, then, Van Kaam really included understanding, which is quite similar to empathy, and also a nonjudgmental attitude similar to unconditional positive regard. He described gentleness in terms similar to those of positive regard for the client. Gentleness is a basic orientation that reveals itself in respectful, sensitive, considerate, and tolerant modes of existence. The counselor respects the client because human nature is a gift of being that is fundamentally good and, therefore, lovable no matter how overgrown or veiled it may be by attitudes and feelings with which the counselor may not agree. Van Kaam used the word *flexibility* in the same way as the quality of creativity. He stated that counseling should not be a rigid observation of learned rules but that the counselor should be convinced that every client is unique and that everything the counselor says or does is a creative outgrowth of participation in the unique experience of the here and now.

Dreyfus (1962) contended that the counselor should be human or open, understanding, and maintain an attitude of "letting be." The counselor tries to understand the client's being-in-the-world, the client's self-perception environment, and reactions to both. It is through the counselor's understanding that the client attains self-knowledge. *Letting be* means affirmation of the other person by permitting the free emergence of inherited creative potentialities. The counselor does not evaluate, judge, or condemn. When the counselor allows herself or himself to be open to the client without trying to treat the latter as an object, then the counselor will be able to understand the client.

According to May (1967), empathy is the key to the counseling process. He described empathy as "feeling into" another person. The counselor feels into the client's personality until some state of identification is achieved. Real understanding occurs through this process, and understanding the client's unique pattern is a major goal. In May's view, both the client and counselor merge into a common psychic entity that works on the client's problem. He also believed the encounter is a real, here-and-now relationship, and that therefore the counselor must be wholly present in the relationship. Through this encounter both the counselor and client are somehow changed. May (1961) believed this type of relationship can exist only in a nonthreatening atmosphere in which the client experiences his or her existence.

Research

Two research studies are also included in Table 12–1. Fiedler's much-quoted studies from the 1950s compared experts with nonexperts and conclude that experts from different theoretical orientations provide a similar relationship, whereas nonexperts differ in the kinds of relationships they provide. In Fiedler's view, his investigation supported the "theory that relationship is therapy, that the goodness of therapy is a function of the goodness of therapeutic relationship" (1950, p. 344). The expert counselors of any of the three orientations created a relationship more closely approximating the ideal therapeutic relationship than the relationships created by nonexperts. Fiedler found that the variables that differentiate the relationships included an ability to understand the client's meanings and feelings, sensitivity to the client's attitudes, and warm interest without emotional over-involvement. Fiedler concluded that the ability to understand the client is the most important criterion of a counselor's expertness.

In one of the most significant research studies in the field of counseling, Truax concluded that "counseling can be for better or for worse" (1963). He reported that counselors who provided high levels of accurate empathy, understanding, nonpossessive warmth, and genuineness induced greater self-exploration throughout the process of counseling and also produced constructive behavioral and personality change in clients. He also reported that low levels of these factors led to client deterioration; in other words, counseling could be detrimental as well as beneficial for the client. Truax stated that genuineness means that the counselor is natural in the moment instead of presenting a professional facade: at any given moment, the counselor really is whatever her or his response denotes. Truax cited accurate empathy as an important variable. Accurate empathy involves more than empathic understanding, the ability of the counselor to sense the client's private world as if it were her or his own. It also involves more than the ability to know what the client means. Accurate empathy involves both the counselor's sensitivity to the client's current feelings and verbal facility to communicate this understanding in a language attuned to the client's feelings. The dimension of nonpossessive warmth or unconditional positive regard ranges from a high level—warmly accepting the client experience without imposing any conditions—to a lower level, at which a counselor evaluates the client or the client's feelings in a selective and evaluative way.

Carkhuff's Eclectic Approach

The last entry in Table 12–1 presents the facilitative conditions that Carkhuff and his associates have developed through extensive research into an eclectic approach to counseling. Although these concepts grew out of the client-centered orientation, they have been refined, extended, and researched to the point that they are proposed as a model for counseling. In 1967 Carkhuff and Berenson described a comprehensive model of facilitative processes. In 1969 Carkhuff published two volumes on the process of helping in human relations. To the core conditions of empathy, regard, and genuineness he added concreteness, immediacy, and confrontation.

Concreteness, or specificity of expression, demonstrates an increased level of client and counselor understanding regarding the specific feelings and the content of the discussion. Concreteness involves focusing not only on the feelings and experiences the client is expressing, but also on the immediate interaction between the client and the counselor. The critical criterion of this dimension is that the material be personally relevant to the client. The dimension of concreteness contributes by requiring complete comprehension of the specifics of the relevant material and the client's problem. It also serves to implement specific courses of action to help the client overcome the problem area. Therefore, concreteness is emphasized during the early stages of counseling, when the counselor is helping the client focus on specific aspects of the problem, and in the late phases, when the counselor is helping the client focus on specific courses of action.

The highest level of action within the facilitative communication is incorporated in interpretations of immediacy. The dimension of immediacy involves the question, "What is the client really trying to tell me that he cannot tell me directly?" Therefore, the counselor interprets directly to the client the messages he or she thinks the client is trying to communicate.

Confrontation is one of the more assertive communications used by the counselor. Confrontation involves communicating an undistorted observation and evaluation of the client's behavior. The confrontation focuses on the client's discrepancies in self versus ideal, insight versus behavior, and self versus other experiences. The client can choose to continue present behavior or make a commitment to change it. Effective confrontation will assist the client toward making the change. The effect of the confrontation is not necessarily immediately observable; evidence of the effects occur over time. Following effective confrontation by high-level facilitative responses, the client will engage in deeper self-exploration and demonstrate positive movement toward better understanding and eventually more appropriate behavior.

ASSESSING LEVELS OF FACILITATIVE COMMUNICATION

Carkhuff (1967) developed a five-point scale to assess the facilitative dimensions related to improved functioning in all interpersonal processes. On all scales, level three is defined as a minimally facilitative level of interpersonal functioning. At level three, the counselor's response of empathic understanding is essentially interchangeable with that of the client: they express essentially the same affect and meaning. The counselor communicates positive respect for the client's feelings, experiences, and potential and allows no discrepancies between what he or she states and other cues that indicate what he or she is feeling. Concreteness is defined as the counselor's enabling the client to discuss personally relevant material in a specific and concrete terminology.

Below level three the counselor's responses detract from the client's. Thus, at level two, the counselor does respond to expressed feelings of the client, but in such a way that he or she detracts noticeably from the client's affective communication. The counselor's response communicates little respect and concern for the client's feelings and experiences, and there are indications that the responses are only slightly related to what other cues indicate the counselor is feeling at the moment. The counselor frequently leads the discussion or allows material that is relevant to be dealt with on a somewhat vague and abstract level.

At the lowest level, level one, counselor responses communicate clear lack of respect or negative regard for the client, the counselor's expressions are clearly unrelated to other cues indicative of what he or she is feeling at the moment, and general responses are negative. At level one the counselor's responses either do not attend to or detract significantly from the client, communicating lack of understanding of the latter. The counselor allows all discussions to deal only with vague and anonymous generalizations.

Above level three, the counselor's responses are additive; thus, at level four the responses add noticeably to client expression and result in deeper expressions of feeling than the client is expressing himself. The counselor communicates deep respect and concern for the client and presents positive cues indicating a human response to the client (whether it is positive or negative) in a nondestructive manner. The counselor frequently helps the client to express fully almost all events of concern in concrete and specific words.

At the fifth level, counselor responses add significantly to the client's feelings and meanings in such a way as to express accurately feelings beyond what the person is able to express. The counselor communicates the deepest respect for the client's worth as a person and potential as a free individual. These expressions indicate that the counselor is acting freely and deeply in the relationship. He or she is completely spontaneous in interaction and open to all experiences. The counselor's communications are always helpful in guiding discussion so that the client may discuss specific feelings and experiences fluently, directly, and completely.

Although some research has demonstrated that counselors can offer differential levels of positive regard, empathy, and congruence, there is usually a high correlation between these dimensions, suggesting that one principal factor accounts for the communication. Typically, a counselor who offers a higher level of empathy will be offering a similar level of positive regard and genuineness. This has led to a more global rating and descriptions of counselors as high-, moderate-, or low-functioning counselors.

EVALUATION OF FACILITATIVE COMMUNICATION RESEARCH

In a review of research conducted up to 1970, Truax and Mitchell (1971) concluded there was clear evidence that therapists who are accurately empathic, warm, and genuine provide the necessary and sufficient conditions for effective counseling, regardless of the kind of problem or the theory of counseling. They also concluded that clients who receive low levels of the facilitative conditions tend not only to fail to improve but even to become worse. Parloff, Waskow, and Wolfe (1978) pointed out that some of the research included in that survey has been seriously questioned, and that the earlier assessment did not give sufficient weight to obvious inconsistencies among the reports cited. Parloff et al. went on to review some studies providing evidence that challenges both the idea that empathy, warmth, and genuineness are prerequisites for positive change and the trend for correlation of low ratings with deterioration.

In a more recent review Mitchell, Bozarth, and Krauft (1977) concluded that there is conflicting evidence regarding the existence of a direct relationship between facilitative conditions and outcome. Although a number of studies suggest that one or more of the dimensions are related to positive outcomes, other studies report little or no evidence of such a relationship. They concluded that "the recent evidence, although equivocal, does seem to suggest that empathy, warmth, and genuineness are related in some way to client change but that their potency and generalizability are not as great as once thought" (p. 181).

Parloff et al. (1978) suggested that the different measures used from study to study may have been a source of the inconsistencies in the findings; different measures of the same criterion repeatedly failed to show high correlations. The research evaluating the facilitative conditions has specified the characteristics of each of the conditions. However there has not been a comparable attempt to specify the nature of outcomes to be effected by the therapeutic conditions. According to Parloff et al. (1978), the importance of the therapeutic relationship conditions is not dismissed but should be considered as one of a number of important factors. The field of counseling is slowly beginning to study a broader range of activities in counselor interaction with different client populations under a variety of specified treatment conditions.

CONCLUSION

It is apparent that the facilitative conditions of empathic understanding, respect for the client, and honest counselor communications with the client have been an important variable in all counseling approaches. Although Freudians have not defined the counselor's function as genuine or congruent, they have prescribed friendly interest and understanding. Learning theorists also have relied heavily on acceptance and understanding, although they have been less concerned with the counselor as a person in the relationship. More recently, with the writings of Rogers, the existential orientation, and research on the relationship variables, the concept of the counselor as a person in the relationship has become prominent. Orlinski and Howard (1979) concluded from a review of the research on facilitative conditions that warmth and empathy are highly desirable qualities of counselor behavior. They suggested that although there are inconsistent findings in the research, if the facilitative conditions alone do not guarantee a good outcome, their presence probably adds to the mix of unofficial therapeutic ingredients.

DIMENSIONS OF THE COUNSELOR-CLIENT RELATIONSHIP

Although the facilitative conditions are a foundation, there are numerous other dimensions that contribute to a good counseling relationship. Interpersonal interaction involves variables that are intangible but nevertheless constitute the real process of counseling. Attitudes, thoughts, feelings, and perceptions between people, as well as within each person, are an integral part of the process. Ambiguity, the expression of feelings and thoughts, transference and countertransference, resistance, and confrontations are frequently involved, through both verbal and nonverbal communication. Instead of thinking about counseling in terms of techniques, it seems appropriate to conceptualize counseling as an interpersonal relationship. It is important for a counselor to be familiar with some of the significant dimensions that exist in varying degrees in most interviews.

RESISTANCE

Resistance is the tendency of a client's defenses to oppose the purposes of counseling, and it must be overcome in building and maintaining an effective relationship. In the psychoanalytic view, resistance represents the client's unconscious opposition to bringing subconscious material to consciousness; resistance, then, mobilizes the repressive and protective function of the ego. In the traditional psychoanalytic interview, resistance is related to the procedure of free association. The analyst assumes that the client's free association will not in fact be free: the client's desire to change will motivate her or him to talk about areas of importance, but when approaching strongly defended areas the client will block or distort communication. Resistance is the client's inability to deal directly and constructively with his or her impulses as they appear during therapy. Resistance is also associated with transference: in directing some of his or her impulses toward the counselor, the client also will defend against these impulses. Therefore, the reactions to the therapist are interwoven with the resistance process (Bordin, 1968).

Resistance typically implies that the client is experiencing a barrier that prevents verbalizing and moving toward specific goals. This force is not considered an agent of the self but as an opponent to the self. Gestalt theory suggests that the resistance is not just a passive barrier to be removed but a creative force in coping with a difficult world. Instead of seeking to remove the resistance, it is appropriate to focus on it assuming that, at best, a person grows through examining the resistance and, at worst, the resistance is nevertheless part of the person's identity. The resistance is part of the client's behavior style. "Labeling the original behavior merely resistant is misleading. To remove the resistance in order to return to the preresistant purity is a futile dream because the person who has resisted is a new person and there is no way to return. Every step in the development of resistance becomes part of a new formation of the individual's nature. He does not become the old person plus a resistance which can be removed as soon as he gets brave enough to remove it. He is a new person altogether" (Polster & Polster, 1973, p. 52).

Resistance generally arises in counseling when the client perceives a topic or situation as threatening. The client is compelled to defend himself or herself against further anxiety. The client may feel anxious about examining patterns of behavior or the personality structure; she or he fears growth and does not wish to change the self. "Viewing man as a composition of characteristics rather than merely a resister leads to a picture of man in trouble when he is divided within himself rather than against himself. The war within, frequently either stale or stalemated, is a war for existence waged by each part of the person, each with its own energy, its own supports, and its own opponents" (Polster & Polster, 1973, p. 57).

This composite nature of people is evident in the Gestalt work with personal polarities. The Gestalt perspective assumes that each individual is a never-ending sequence of polarities. When a client recognizes one aspect of himself or herself, the presence of its antithesis is implicit. To resolve the polarity, the Gestalt counselor seeks to aid each part of the person to live to the fullest while at the same time making contact with its polar counterpart. This reduces the chance that one part will remain impotent, clinging to the status quo. Instead, it is energized into making a vital statement of its own needs and wishes, asserting itself as a force that must be considered in the total person.

The client sometimes fears that by expressing feelings he or she will make the condition real; consequently, the client is reluctant to talk about death or losing love. In one view, resistance comes from within the client; when approaching a topic that causes anxiety, the client defends herself or himself by avoiding the topic or possibly the whole counseling situation. In another view, resistance is caused by an external threat, such as when the counselor interprets material before the client is prepared to handle it. Rogers (1942) believed that resistance is not necessarily a part of counseling and that it is present because of the counselor's behavior. He suggested that attempts to accelerate or abbreviate the counseling process may cause resistance in the client. The suggestion may make the client feel anxious about carrying it out, and may generate resistance to change. A counselor views resistance as interfering with progress and problem solving, and attempts to reduce the resistance.

Resistance probably exists to some degree in all interviews and may be viewed as the opposite of coping with emotional expression. Resistance varies from outright rejection of counseling to subtle forms of inattention. Although it is present to some degree in all interviews, the client usually does not recognize it. Therefore, it is mostly an unconscious phenomenon. It is an ambivalent attitude toward counseling: the client wants help yet resists it. According to Brammer and Shostrom "This ambivalent client attitude is one of the most baffling situations confronting the inexperienced counselor. Even experienced counselors occasionally cite resistance as an excuse for not establishing an effective relationship" (1968, p. 12).

Kell and Mueller (1966) viewed resistance as both a counselor and a client activity reflecting ambivalence. The client's inappropriate behavior receives sufficient reinforcement to make the prospect of giving it up for uncertain rewards a difficult process. Therefore, many clients enter counseling with mixed feelings about wanting to change. For example, a client may project onto the counselor the attributes of significant others who were helpful or hurtful. In assessing, understanding, and reacting to the client's ambivalence, the counselor's own ambivalence may become activated if the latter uncritically believes either side of the client's projections. The client may become ambivalent and immobilized because the counselor feels confused by inability to cope with the client's double messages. The client struggling with ambivalence will be particularly sensitive to the counselor's.

Bordin (1968) regarded two types of reactions as resistance. One type is the client's unwillingness to give up autonomy, or the tendency to fail to live up to the social standard of acting independently. The other type involves the client's defenses against inner conflicts when the nature of the counseling relationship tempts her or him to express conflicting impulses. Both types of resistance are significant for the counselor in the relationship. In the first, the counselor must avoid encroaching on the client's feelings of independence and learn to regard the latter's desire to differentiate himself or herself as a positive development rather than a problem in their relationship. When the client is resisting internal conflicts, the counselor should try to reduce the self-defeating behavior and continue to try to provide a relationship in which the client can be free to explore herself or himself. If the second type of resistance does not appear, the counselor must consider whether his or her own behavior has resulted in an alignment with the client to prevent the expression of impulses that underlie the difficulty.

Brammer and Shostrom (1968) offered five techniques for dealing with resistance, to be used for different levels of resistance in the client. Before handling resistance, however, a counselor must be aware both of any external causes that may be contributing to the resistance and of the influence of her or his techniques. The first technique entails being alert to the client's resistance but not responding to it. The fact that the client is experiencing a mild resistance does not indicate the counselor must do something about it. The counselor recognizes that this level of resistance is natural and concentrates on understanding the client's unique defensive style.

When the client shows a more pronounced disinterest in counseling by giving short answers or not hearing or seeing certain things, the counselor may feel it necessary to do something to reduce the client's resistance. There are some minor adaptations to reduce the client's defensiveness and keep the latter focused on exploring the problem further. One adaptation is to lessen the emotional impact of the discussion by moving to a more intellectual level. Another technique is to change the pace of the interview by shortening the degree of lead, by just shifting physical position, or easing the tension with a judicious use of mild humor. If a good relationship exists between the counselor and the client, supportive and accepting techniques may help clarify the situation and reduce the resistance.

If the resistance is stronger, the counselor may wish to redirect the interview to a less threatening area. This temporary diversion takes the pressure off the client and reduces the intensity of the interview. When the client appears to be aware of the resistance and a good working relationship exists, the counselor may wish to use some direct manipulation techniques. The counselor may offer an explanation of what the client is doing. This interpretation may help the client develop a tolerance and acceptance of the resistance as well as an intellectual understanding of it. A reflection of the feelings of resistance is also an effective technique, particularly in earlier interviews, when the relationship is not so well established. The strongest technique is direct confrontation, or questioning centered on the resistance.

After assessing his or her own confidence and examining the defenses of a highly resistant client, the counselor may wish to refer this person to another counselor who can remove the source of external resistance that has been inhibiting their relationship.

SELF-DISCLOSURE

The term *self-disclosure* was coined by Sidney Jourard (1958), who defined it as a process of making the self known to other persons by revealing personal information. Self-disclosure has traditionally been considered part of the client's therapeutic treatment; for counseling to be even minimally successful, the client must disclose personal information. Self-disclosure is a desirable client behavior because it has been positively related to personal adjustment and to successful therapy. Moreover, the level of counselor self-disclosure is as important as a client's, for the literature suggests that self-disclosure occurs in a reciprocal fashion. The dyadic effect describes a phenomenon in which there is a high correlation between self-disclosure to a person and the amount of disclosure received from that person (Jourard, 1964). According to Lazarus (1971), the verbal self-disclosure of the counselor will open the therapeutic channels of communication.

Halpern (1977) reported support for Jourard's idea that a client's past tendency to self-disclosure is related to the client's tendency to self-disclosure in counseling and that the disclosure is strongly affected by situational variables. Two of the situational variables that Halpern reported to be important are the degree to which the counselor is perceived as self-disclosing and the client's perception of the counselor as facilitative.

Other situational variables that may affect self-disclosure include the race and sex of the individuals; Casciani (1978), however, found that whereas in some studies sex or race has been a significant factor, in others it has not been shown to be significant.

In recent years, there has been considerable research investigating the use of models to elicit self-disclosure. These studies may have relevance to the counselor serving as a model for the client. The research has shown that individuals are more willing to self-disclose following exposure to a model who reveals personal thoughts or attitudes than are individuals who are not exposed to such models. Vondracek and Vondracek (1971) and Blackburn (1970) demonstrated that a counselor's behavioral modeling of self-disclosure can increase client disclosures. Likewise, client behaviors such as resistance or defensiveness may be the result of a client's use of an inappropriate model for counseling behavior. Hoffman-Graff (1977) found that counselors who disclosed negative information about themselves were perceived as significantly more empathic, warm, and credible than interviewers who disclosed only positive information. Clients interviwd by negative disclosing counselors perceived that they procrastinated significantly less after the interview than before, whereas the opposite was true for individuals in a positive disclosing situation. Casciani (1978) reported that the client's depth of disclosure, length of speech, and number of self-references were not related to the model's race, the length of the interview, or scores on the Self-Disclosure Questionnaire. Clients did, however, disclose at greater depths and for longer periods after observing models of the same sex.

It appears that counselor self-disclosure also acts as a reinforcement for the client's disclosure. Worthy (1969) found that self-disclosure from the counselor acts as a reinforcer, thereby increasing the likelihood of reciprocal self-disclosure. He also found that the more intimate disclosure, the more potent it is as a reinforcer. Gary and Hammond (1970) tested this concept of reciprocity of self-disclosure with alcoholics and drug addicts and found additional support for it. A study by Graff (1970) found that self-disclosing counselors were more effective than other counselors because their self-disclosure served as reinforcements for the client's self-disclosure. Vondracek and Vondracek (1971) suggested that the counselor's self-disclosure may also serve as a stimulus for immediate recall of personal experiences and thereby increase the client's self-disclosing behavior.

Giannandrea and Murphy (1973) found that a counselor's self-disclosure plays a positive role in interviews by increasing counselor attractiveness and client attendance and participation. An intermediate number of counselor self-disclosures was found to result in significantly more client returns for a second interview than when the counselor made few self-disclosures.

Although much of the literature has demonstrated the effectiveness of the counselor's self-disclosure, there is some evidence that it can be detrimental in the counseling relationship. Weigel, Dinges, Dyer, and Straumfjord (1972) investigated the relationship of perceived self-disclosure by both clients and counselors, their liking for each other, and their evaluation of each other's mental health. The findings indicate that clients' and counselors' role image of clients were positively related between liking and mental health and liking and self-disclosure. However, clients perceived counselor self-disclosure as a negative indicator of the counselor's mental health. Dies (1973) also found that openly disclosing counselors were viewed by their clients as less relaxed, strong, stable, and sensitive than were their less transparent colleagues.

The counselor's self-disclosure may evoke negative evaluations of the counselor or even lead some clients to feel that the counselor is guilty of unprofessional conduct by not remaining in a professional role. The findings of Weigel et al. suggest that the self-disclosing counselor violates the client's role expectations for the former's behavior, which are based on decades of cultural exposure. The best explanation may be Jourard's hypothesis that the relationship between self-disclosure and mental health is nonlinear (Jourard, 1971). This suggests that there is an optimum level for self-disclosure, beyond which it may be destructive of either an individual's feelings or the interpersonal relationship. Too little counselor self-disclosure may fail to produce client disclosures; too much may decrease the time available for the client or cause the latter to be concerned for the counselor. Even so, most research suggests that there is a reciprocal effect in the interpersonal relationship, indicating that as counselors increase their self-disclosures so will the clients.

McCarthy and Betz (1978) pointed out that definitions of self-disclosure have failed to distinguish self-disclosing responses from another potentially important kind of counselor response: self-involving responses. Both self-disclosing and self-involving responses may be classified as self-referent; differences between them, however, suggest that they may have different effects on the client. A self-disclosing response is a statement of factual information by the counselor about himself or herself; a self-involving response is a statement of the counselor's personal response to statements by the client. Therefore, self-disclosing responses are statements referring to the history or personal experiences of the counselor, whereas self-involving ones are present expressions of the counselor's feelings about or reactions to the client's statements or behaviors. McCarthy and Betz conducted a study to determine if the two different counselor responses had different effects on clients. They reported that self-involving counselors were rated as significantly more expert and trustworthy than the self-disclosing ones. The client responses to self-disclosing counselor statements contained significantly more references to the counselor; responses to self-involving counselor statements had more self-reference. In addition, client responses to the self-involving counselor were more likely to be phrased in the present than in the past or future. This refinement of the concept of self-disclosure certainly adds to its potential uses. At some times the counselor may wish to communicate information about himself or herself; on others, to communicate how she or he feels about the client's statement in a way to keep the client focused in the present.

AMBIGUITY

The degree of ambiguity in the counselor-client relationship ranges from an incomplete and vague stimulus situation with no predetermined response, to one with definite guidelines. In counseling the degree of ambiguity is related to the degree to which the counselor gives structure to the counseling situation for the client. The degree of ambiguity is controlled by the counselor's way of defining herself or himself and the situation. Part of this may be achieved directly, but frequently the definition is indirect. Bordin cited three areas in which the counselor communicates the degree of ambiguity: "(a) the topic he considers appropriate for the client to discuss; (b) the closeness and other characteristics of the relationship expected; and (c) the counselor's values in terms of the goal he sets up toward which he and the client should work as well as his values in general" (1968, p. 150). The counselor may structure the relationship with different degrees of clarity in these areas; one or two may be clearly defined while the others are left vague.

What is the function of ambiguity in the counseling relationship? Counselors assume that an individual's reaction to a stimulus situation is the result of a larger motivational organization. Thus, when a client reacts to the counselor in the counseling relationship, it is usually an amplification of the needs of the client. This behavior forms a basis for inferences about the client's personality. The counselor can highlight the inner determinants of the client's actions by weakening the external demands. This is seen most clearly in the theory of projective techniques.

The control of ambiguity in counseling rests on the principle that people invest into ambiguous stimuli the responses that are most heavily laden with the unique aspects of their life history. This permits a client to bring out major conflicted feelings, no matter how unaware of them he or she may be. This investment of the client's motivational and emotional structure into the relationship enables the counselor to understand more fully and deeply the core of the client's actions. For example, inferences about the nature of the client's defenses can be made from the latter's reactions to the ambiguous situation. From the content and sequence of responses, the counselor can understand the client's conflicts and the types of relationships she or he has with other people. An ambiguous situation may also provide a background for bringing the client's irrational feelings to awareness.

Ambiguity in the counseling relationship can be very useful, but it must be controlled for several reasons. First, ambiguity produces anxiety. Although anxiety is an important part of effective therapy, there is an optimal level that each person can tolerate. If anxiety exceeds this point, the person will be so overwhelmed by anxiety that all energies will be used in self-preservation efforts, leaving no energy for therapeutic progress. The counselor should relate the degree of ambiguity to the client's level of anxiety. Second, a person with schizoid tendencies needs less ambiguity because she or he is trying to maintain contact with reality; hence, a more structured situation is called for. Third, a relatively well-adjusted person who comes to counseling primarily for positive consultation has not made the decision to place his or her entire welfare in the counselor's hands. The amount of ambiguity the counselor can introduce into the relationship is extremely limited. Fourth, the counselor, too, is subject to anxiety produced by ambiguity. There is less certainty and less control of the client's reactions in an ambiguous counseling relationship. Ambiguity can lead to increased anxiety or to a greater expression of feelings by the client. A direct expression of feelings toward the counselor is also possible. Finally, a counselor can use ambiguity to serve her or his own needs rather than the client's. This can take the form of avoiding self-revelation to the client or, in the case of an inexperienced counselor, an expression of uncertainty and fear about making a wrong move.

Although ambiguity is a powerful tool in the relationship, it can lead to incorrect inferences. Epstein's (1966) writings about the use of ambiguity in projective testing are applicable also to the counseling situation. Epstein assumed that the greater the ambiguity, the more revealing is the information about the personality. This assumption fails to consider that individual differences can reflect random, inconsequential information as well as significant personality material.

Most drives and responses are latent, awaiting appropriate stimuli to arouse them. Thus, the more ambiguous a stimulus is, the greater the likelihood that it will bypass ego defenses and allow an opportunity for all drives to be expressed. Also, the more ambiguous the stimulus, the less its potency for activating specific drives. An unresponsive client is often assumed to be defensive when the possibility also exists that he or she hasn't been aroused in the first place.

The "blank screen" hypothesis, which states that reactions to a specific stimulus can be generalized to all stimuli, can be refuted. A highly ambiguous stimulus may not arouse specific drives but nevertheless has stimulating characteristics of its own. The nature of the stimulus may vary from person to person. For example, some people fear the loss of control that an unstructured stimulus provides, whereas others welcome the opportunity to use their imaginations.

Finally, as Bordin also warned, the more ambiguous the stimulus, the more the counselor as well as the client can lose control of it, which may lead to problems in interpretation. Epstein also agreed with Bordin that it is crucial to use the most effective level of ambiguity, not to assume that because ambiguity is good, the counselor should use more of it.

THE COGNITIVE-CONATIVE DIMENSIONS

Bordin (1968) discussed the cognitive-conative balance that exists in the relationship. The conative aspects of behavior include a person's feelings, strivings, and emotions; the cognitive aspects include conceptual, perceptual, and motor processes. The affective aspects of behavior are generally related to the release of energy. The infant's release of energy involves disorganized and unintegrated motor discharge. As a child develops perceptual and motor skills, energy is released in a more organized manner to express the child's needs. Therefore, the cognitive processes are particularly important in modifying and controlling most complex and meaningful behavior. Bordin suggested that the cognitive process serve two purposes in the cognitive-conative balance of behavior. "The cognitive aspects may either serve the purpose of controlling affect in the sense of leading to less or no expression, or may serve a truly instrumental function through the fullest possible successful expression of the affect" (1968, p. 169). Therefore, cognitive processes function to control and organize energy. To understand the client fully, the counselor must understand both aspects of the client's communications by applying his or her own cognitive and conative capacities.

The counselor can control cognitive-conative balance in the counseling relationship by her or his actions and communications with the client. To do this effectively the counselor must understand the client and know when each tactic is appropriate. For example, a client who expresses emotions through over-intellectual or over-rational examination needs to be encouraged to express feelings more freely and to relax the efforts to control them. On the other hand, a client who expresses feelings freely needs to be encouraged to introduce more conceptual aspects into her or his own communications.

A major assumption in counseling is that insight leads to changed behavior. The counselor's role is to help the client explore affective regions, to gain cognition of the relationship between feelings and actions, and with this new cognition change his or her behavior to meet personal goals more appropriately. The counselor usually transmits cognition to the client through an interpretation, applying two considerations: first, interpretation, whether accepted or rejected, will be ineffective before defenses are loosened. Second, the amount of emphasis on cognitive aspects of the interaction should be related to the intensity of affect that the client expresses. The greater the client's affective expression, the more cognitively the counselor can respond. Interpretation can be useful only when the client is ready for it.

Cognition, or giving information and calling attention to particular behaviors, will be most effective when introduced during a period of low resistance. It is best for the client to make the final interpretation, with the counselor leading up to but not stating it. If the client is defensive and fearful, however, any effort to introduce cognitions that are not specifically related to the avoidance will be seen and distorted by the defenses. When feelings are built up and the reasons for avoidance are near the surface, the interpretation of resistance may be made.

As a client begins to see successive examples in which her or his defenses have operated, an awareness of distorted actions develops. This process, called working through, refers to the repetitive process of rediscovery. The client finds in different incidents the need to defend the self and sees how these affect his or her interpersonal relationships. The number of times the counselor must work through incidents with the client depends on how well-integrated the client is. Some people understand with awareness of one or two experiences; others need more examples.

The counselor must also be aware of her or his own needs and take care not to impose on the client interpretations and cognitions that are not relevant to the latter's problems. These interpretations may be part of the counselor's defenses against a particular conflict. Finally, counselors seem to overemphasize the use of verbal reasoning and should remember that interpretation can advance the therapeutic process only when it is relevant to the client's needs.

TRANSFERENCE

Some clients' expectations are realistic; others may be distorted and even tinged with magic. The more troubled the client is, the greater the tendency to view the counselor as having superior powers. In such cases, the clients' tendency to view themselves as persons in need of help may place them in a dependent relation to someone else. Therefore, they may relate to the counselor in a transference relationship. This tendency to turn the counseling relationship into a quasi-parent-child relationship is of particular interest to psychodynamic counselors, who are interested in analyzing that relationship. While recognizing the importance of the counseling relationship, others, such as the behavior-oriented counselors, regard it primarily as a vehicle for effecting behavioral or cognitive change and are not concerned with the transference phenomenon (Strupp, 1978). Freud found that when a client in analysis proceeded to a successful outcome there was a time of intense personal attachment to the therapist. During the analytical relationship, the client never really knew the therapist as a person: he or she lay on a couch and did not see the therapist; between hours there was no other contact between them. With such an unstructured "blank screen" on which to picture the therapist, the client reacted during therapy in the same way as to most significant persons in her or his past; the client transferred the whole relationship to the therapist and was able to reenact earlier struggles of which no clear memory remained. According to Freud, this experience made profound personality reorganization possible. The process of transference permitted the client to relive developmental periods in which the basic personality patterns were established and to modify these patterns through the new emotional experience. It was this experience that was frequently termed transference neurosis, and resolution of this neurotic attachment to the counselor was of major importance. The working through process is another aspect of transference that has become prominent. The insights achieved in therapy do not automatically transfer to all areas of the client's life. There is much to discuss even after significant unconscious material has been brought to light. It takes considerable time to resolve a deep transference to the analyst and also to translate this attachment to other relationships with significant persons (Sundberg & Tyler, 1962).

A twenty-year longitudinal research study conducted at the Menninger Clinic focused in part on transference. The research team assumed that the client's reactions to the counselor would be more consistently determined by intrapsychic needs that were active at the time than by the actual behavior and intentions of the therapist. The research confirmed this prediction about transference content. Even so, the researchers made some revisions in their assumptions following the evaluation. First, they found that the introduction of more supportive parameters in the counseling relationship reduced transference manifestations, particularly negative views of the counselor. Second, they discovered that the more supportive the treatment mode, the greater was the tendency of the transference to conform to the actual personality attributes of the counselor.

A rather strongly held concept in psychoanalytic theory is that a client will tend to displace transference reactions to other individuals in the environment when she or he is unable to tolerate the figures generated in the counseling relationship. Usually a counselor will redirect such behavior into the counseling relationship by interpretation, depending on the assessment of the client's ability to handle such feelings. Research reported by Horwitz (1974) confirmed that in all the cases in which this assumption was used, there was a reciprocal relationship between the intensity directed toward the counselor and the fulfillment of psychological needs in the individual's life outside counseling.

In another view of transference, Dollard and Miller (1950) equated the word *transfer* with *generalize*. Whereas transference suggests that something is transferred, and in psychoanalytic theory it is not always clear what that is (although it usually seems to be a feeling or an emotion), generalization implies that any of a variety of similar stimuli may evoke the "same" response even though the response has been habitually associated with only one of these stimuli.

Transference is also viewed as "the degree of involvement the client feels with the therapist" (Rotter, 1954, p. 363). From the social learning point of view, the degree of involvement the client feels is a direct function of the amount of direct reinforcement the client has received (or expects to receive) from the counselor. This involvement is also a function of the degree to which the client sees future satisfactions as dependent upon the counselor's behavior. In Rotter's view, transference and countertransference are natural and helpful to the relationship as long as the counselor and client are aware of their existence.

Existential therapists believe that the client does not really transfer his feeling to the therapist but ". . . the neurotic is one who in certain areas never developed beyond the limited and restricted forms of experience characteristic of the infant. Hence in later years he perceives [spouse] or therapist through the same restricted, distorted 'spectacles' as he perceived father or mother" (May, Angel, & Ellenberger, 1958, p. 79).

Rogers (1951) acknowledged that transference occurs in a majority of client-centered relationships. "If one's definition of transference includes all affect toward others, then transference is obviously present in the relationship, if the definition is being used in the transfer of infantile attitudes to a present relationship, and very little if any transference is present" (p. 200). How is such transference to be handled? Rogers suggested that the client-centered counselor's reaction to transference is the same as any other attitude to the client: an attempt to understand and accept. Such acceptance will lead the client to perceive the transferred attitudes as coming from within and not from the counselor. Rogers also suggested that the transference does not become a problem because of the interpersonal nature of the therapeutic relationship. "The whole relationship is composed of the self of the client, the counselor being depersonalized for the purpose of therapy into being the client's other self" (1951, p. 208).

Although they did not discuss transference as such, Kell and Mueller (1966) examined the transfer of feelings. In their view, when the client is under stress and the relationship becomes intense, the client may choose events from the past and symbolically present them to the counselor as a means of communicating some of the feelings about current relationships and possibly some doubts about the counselor's adequacy to meet his or her needs. At one level the client may communicate faith and confidence in the counselor's ability to satisfy needs, but at another level the client may also communicate fears, concerns, and doubts. "A client may assure the counselor, for example, that he is succeeding in helping him, but at the same time the client may talk about how weak his father is. We believe that at such times, the counselor should consider the probability that the client is also concerned about the counselor's weakness" (Kell & Mueller, 1966, p. 40).

According to Brammer and Shostrom (1968), transference lies midway between the classic Freudian view, with emphasis on the past, and the position that all feelings currently expressed toward the counselor are transference. In their view, transference is a type of projection of a client's past or present unresolved and unrecognized attitudes toward authority figures and love objects; the client responds to the counselor in a manner similar to the way she or he responds to other significant persons. Through this transference process, the client builds certain expectations of the counselor and the latter's role. Transference, then, describes how the client construes and behaves toward the counselor. It is a largely irrational part of the counseling relationship in which the client projects onto the counselor self-regarding attitudes and unresolved feelings from earlier relationships. The intensity of transference is a function of the type of client, the setting, the length of counseling, the extent of emotional involvement, the counselor's personality, and the counselor's technique.

Holland (1965) assumed that the client has a problem or is functioning unsatisfactorily because some of the conditions required for development were inadequately or improperly supplied. The client has not been able to understand the nature of her or his deficiency or has been unable to find conditions that would enable him or her to complete or correct inadequate development. The client comes to a counselor hoping to complete or improve confidence in obtaining satisfaction. The client's need for help and selection of a counselor as a helper automatically place the counselor *in loco parentis*. Therefore, cognitive and emotional responses to the counselor frequently begin at a point where previous helping relationships have left off.

In Holland's view, transference is related to the client's level of maturity, and the extent to which transference responses create problems in the therapeutic relationship is determined by the developmental status of the client. If the client is relatively mature and relatively competent, the distortion involved in the perception of the counselor may be relatively slight. The transference problems of such a client are not likely to involve intense feelings, but there may be ambivalence resulting from the desire for assistance and a reluctance to accept a dependent role relative to the counselor.

In this developmental concept of transference, the client may look at the counselor as "the good parent." The immature client may resist many aspects of the working relationship in counseling, including the reality of his or her demands on the counselor or the counselor's requirement that the client grow or develop competence in order to insure continuation of the relationship. When the counselor does not provide direct emotional gratification that the client has expected, the latter may also be frustrated and angry.

An analyst uses transference feelings to help a patient recognize what she or he is trying to do in the relationship with the therapist. The client's transference helps the therapist understand him or her and provides valuable clues for later interpretation on the quality of the client's interpersonal relationships. In studying brief psychoanalytically oriented counseling, Malan (1976) found that directed interpretations—that is, those that refer to actual people— had strong positive correlations with outcome, especially transference interpretations that pointed out similarities between client reactions toward the counselor and earlier family reactions. Impersonal, or undirected, interpretations were found to be negatively related to client improvement.

The counselor does not depend upon the transference relationship for effective therapy, but is aware that transference is present in varying amounts. In brief forms of counseling, counselors rarely attempt to interpret transference feelings, trying to analyze a client's deep feelings in the same way that they manipulate life relationships. Counselors in this context reflect the client's feelings and accept the client in an attempt to help the latter see that the transference feelings reside within the client's own inadequate perceptions. Such counselors should regard expressions of negativism and hostility as resistance in an incomplete growing-up process.

Holland (1965) stated that the client will persist in believing in these attributes so long as she or he "needs" to believe in them to allay anxieties and feelings of inadequacy. In Holland's view, the counselor usually accepts the client's transference initially and uses it to help the client develop competence and confidence. If the counselor is successful, the client will more or less spontaneously relinquish illusions about the counselor and accept the latter as just another human being, though often with gratitude for the valuable services performed.

Kell and Mueller (1966) suggested that when the client begins to speak in metaphorical or symbolic ways about experiences that seem to be related to the present relationship, the counselor may find it necessary to expose the underlying implications to enter the experiences more meaningful to the current counseling relationship. The counselor's response is to release the client so that the latter can continue to express the feelings that are related in the basic conflict. If, for example, the client repeatedly expresses doubt about others and the counselor suggests, "Perhaps you are doubtful of me," the underlying dynamic is that the counselor is not fearful of the client's feelings, but that the counselor is perceptive and not punishing. According to Kell and Mueller, the counselor's adequacy is a function of the ability to recognize and respond directly to feelings, no matter what the feelings are.

Holland (1965) used the term *cognitive transference* to refer to the client's tendency to think about the counselor as having the same characteristics as persons known previously. He used the term *emotional transference* to refer to the feeling qualities of the cognitive responses plus the corresponding behavioral tendencies that are generalized from previous to new relationships. The term *working through the transference* appears often in the psychoanalytic literature, but its meaning is not very clear. The concept may be understood as the extent to which the client perceives and thinks about the counselor in terms of the latter's actual characteristics and the extent to which feelings toward the counselor represent a reasonable response to the counselor's actual behavior. Working through the transference therefore is not so much a general description of the counselor's efforts as it is a description of the ultimate goal. Because feelings and thoughts may be generalized to many people, the ultimate goal of counseling would be to have the client adequately and realistically handle all relationships in terms of the individual.

Brammer and Shostrom (1968) suggested that although transferences may complicate the counselor's task, they serve significant functions for the client. Transference helps build the relationship by allowing the client to express distorted feelings without the usual counterdefensive responses; when a client becomes irritated with the counselor, the counselor accepts these feelings instead of countering with irritation. Another function of transference is to promote the client's confidence in the counselor who is handling these feelings. Third, transference permits the client to become aware of the origin and the significance of feelings in his or her present life through the interpretation of the transference feelings.

Brammer and Shostron (1968) suggested that the counselor's main task in regard to transference is to encourage free expression of feeling while keeping the transference attitudes from developing into a deep transference relationship. They made several suggestions for handling and resolving transference feelings at various depths.

1. The usual technique for resolving transference is simple acceptance, which permits the client to live out projected feelings and to feel free in the interview.
2. The counselor may ask clarifying questions about the forms of anxiety that the client seems to be manifesting.
3. The counselor may reflect the client's level of feeling.
4. A stronger technique is to interpret the transference feeling directly, communicating information to the client that the latter has not already stated and that therefore may be rejected.

5. The counselor may focus on what is currently happening with the client's feelings rather than on why the client is having these feelings.
6. Frequently, calling attention to feelings causes the client to react in the opposite manner; therefore, a counselor may want to call attention to negative feelings but not to the positive transference.
7. The counselor may test the idea that the client is projecting feelings by asking her or him to reverse the projection and by encouraging repetition until the client feels the statement represents what he or she is really feeling.
8. The counselor may interpret transference feelings as an expression of "being deficiency," in which the client is seeking environmental support, instead of viewing the feeling as a transference from the past to the counselor.
9. The counselor may refer the client to a counselor more qualified to give intensive psychotherapy when their relationship develops to an intensity beyond the competence of the counselor.

CHAPTER
TWELVE
COUNSELING
AS A
RELATIONSHIP

225

COUNTERTRANSFERENCE

Countertransference refers to the emotional reactions and projections of the counselor toward the client. Countertransference may include conscious as well as unconscious attitudes toward real or imagined client attitudes and behavior. It may be caused by internal anxiety. The anxiety patterns may be classified into three types: unresolved personal problems, situational pressures, and the communication of the client's feelings to the counselor by empathic means. The counselor's unresolved personal problems should be worked out with another counselor.

Kernberg (1975) suggested that there are two major historical approaches to countertransference: the classical and the totalistic. In the classical approach, countertransference is regarded as an unconscious reaction of the counselor to the client's transference that interferes with treatment. The classical approach depicts countertransference as a negative aspect in treatment and distinguishes two subdivisions, direct and indirect countertransference. Direct countertransference is acknowledged as the true countertransference reaction and is regarded as interfering with the progress of treatment; indirect countertransference is defined as reactions that the analyst uses to act out his or her own impulses.

The totalistic approach regards countertransference positively. Kernberg described it as "the total emotional reaction of a psychoanalyst to his patient in a treatment situation [including reactions] to the patient's reality as well as to his transference and also to the analyst's own reality needs as well as to his neurotic needs" (1975, p. 49). In this approach countertransference is an important diagnostic tool, providing information about the client's regression, and the predominant emotional attitude of the client toward the therapist, and the changes occurring from this attitude. This concept assumes that counseling is an interaction of two personalities; in it, the countertransference becomes a mechanism for understanding the client's unconscious. Certainly, the countertransference needs to be understood to be useful.

In countertransference, a counselor's anxieties or unconscious needs and wishes may significantly color his or her understanding of a client. Horwitz (1974) found that one permanent manifestation of countertransference distortion is a tendency to understand the client exclusively in terms of a single guiding transference paradigm rather than in terms of a variety of transference manifestations.

Often, a counselor may transfer to the client feelings that really grow out of the situation. Situational pressures involve the counselor's feeling responsible for the client's improvement or believing that her or his professional reputation is involved in the client's success. In these cases the counselor may try too hard and defeat his or her purposes. Countertransference may also develop from the client's communication of feelings to the counselor. The counselor may respond overly sympathetically to the client's demand for sympathy or become angry at being provoked by the client. Horwitz (1974) reported finding support for the idea that transference lies in the counselor's tendency to overestimate the client's assets, particularly with clients who present fairly good facades despite evidence of personality weakness. It is open to question whether this kind of diagnostic error is attributable to countertransference growing out of anxieties associated with personal needs or to a technical insufficiency. In his longitudinal study, Horwitz reported that the counselors were well trained and experienced and he assumed that the countertransference was a product of some personality factor of the counselor.

Countertransference involves the counselor's value structure. Obviously, a counselor communicates some personal values even in the most objective relationship. The counselor generally conveys values about how the client should live as well as how the client should behave in counseling.

If defenses, motivations, and inhibitions central to the counselor's life are threatened by working with a particular client, the client is generally not treated. When working with unusual or difficult clients it is important for the counselor to consider his or her psychological needs as they relate to working with such clients. Karon and Vandenbos (1977) claimed that some countertransference difficulties commonly arise in working with poor clients. They suggested that all counselors come either from lower-class backgrounds and are socially upwardly mobile or from middle-class backgrounds. Either may have difficulty working with poor clients. The upwardly mobile counselor has escaped by means of impulse control, education, and hard work, and the need to maintain a view of how awful her or his life would otherwise have been may interfere with counseling a poor client. The client may stimulate an unconscious concept about the counselor's "bad self," and the counselor's projection of previously rejected impulses can lead to exaggeration of the client's weaknesses.

A counselor from an upper-middle-class background may be unable to empathize with the circumstances of the poor client. The inequity between the counselor's life and the client's is so apparent that the counselor may feel guilty and to relieve this guilt may seize on behavioral characteristics of the poor client to justify or explain the inequity. Projection of the counselor's rejection impulses may lead to exaggeration of the badness of the client's behavior.

A third, less frequent reaction to the poor client may involve counselors of any socioeconomic background: romanticizing the poor client. By romanticizing the poor client, the counselor may feel that he or she is compensating the client for the inequities of life. A well-intentioned counselor may romanticize the poor out of respect for the person's individuality or cultural heritage. Karon and Vandenbos suggested that counselor fantasies about the poor will not interfere with treatment if such fantasies are conscious and are attended to in staff meetings, supervision, and training.

CHAPTER
TWELVE

227

COUNSELING
AS A
RELATIONSHIP

Gottsegen and Gottsegen (1979) labeled countertransference as *professional identity defense*. In their view, too much of what happens in counseling involves the unconscious need of the counselor to defend a professional image at the expense of the client, claiming the client's objection to this as the client's resistance. This broader definition of countertransference can be applied to counselors from all theoretical persuasions. According to Gottsegen and Gottsegen, counselors repeatedly defend their professional images in three particular ways. The first is called data defense, which is blindness to certain client data that would require a response different from the counselor's usual behavior. A counselor's blind adherence to a particular theory requires him or her to attend to certain kinds of data and ignore others. This defense is maintained in the interest of being one's own professional person.

Another defense in this style of countertransference is a "smug attitude towards one's own understanding of the client. This would appear as flat-footedness, blaming the client, unimaginativeness about one's way of proceeding in the overall technical conducting of the therapy, a failure to utilize potentials of projective identification (an inability, in effect, to listen with the third ear)" (Gottsegen & Gottsegen, 1979, p. 57).

A third manifestation of this countertransference is structural rigidity, structuring client data to fit the counselor's view. The counselor may refuse to apply new techniques from other areas, refuse to recognize the limitations of interventions, force interpretation on clients, or denigrate other approaches, methods, and research that would require reevaluation of current methods. In Gottsegen and Gottsegen's view, the counselor's defense against defining his or her responsibility to each new client with regard to the treatment plan, structure, and method becomes resistance, a form of professional identity defense and of counter-transference.

Jones and Seagull (1977) pointed out that countertransference may also occur between the white counselor and black client, when the counselor does not fully understand or acknowledge personal feelings that will influence the counseling. According to Vontress (1971), countertransference occurs when the counselor reacts to the client as she or he has reacted to someone else in her or his past, or when the white counselor unconsciously perceives the black client as he or she has perceived other blacks. Stereotypical reactions are a form of countertransference. Counselors must understand their own feelings to deal effectively with minority clients or those different from them in other powerful dimensions such as age, sex, religion, and sexual mores.

Crowder (1972) stated that therapists who were more successful with their clients had fewer countertransference reactions. He described the counter-transference reactions as "hostile-competitive," "passive-resistant," "support-seeking." He also discussed the effect of the client on therapy. The individual who does not show much change tends to begin in counseling as more passive-resistant, less support-seeking, and less hostile-competitive. The most difficult clients show the most transference and stimulate more countertransference. Therefore, to be successful the counselor not only has to deal with her or his normal transference feelings but also, when the client is difficult, with a greater number or intensity of countertransferential reactions. Although it is not simple to assign countertransferences to one of Crowder's three categories, Pollard (1979) emphasized that doing so is important, for the more countertransference reactions a counselor has, the less likely he or she is to be successful. In addition, more difficult clients are more likely to bring on these reactions.

Pollard, in examining the impact of both sexes on the counselor, also described the importance of the sex of the client in stimulating countertransference. Readers interested in the psychoanalytic approach to counseling may wish to read his paper.

Brammer and Shostrom (1968) offered several methods for handling countertransference feelings. First, counselors must be aware that they have these feelings and begin looking for reasons for them. The counselors may need some supervisory assistance to locate the sources of these feelings and to resolve them. By discussing the problems with a supervisor, counselors may resolve their own feelings. A major source of awareness may be in audio and videotape recordings; counselors can listen to themselves and locate many of their attitudes. Or the tapes may serve as a base for supervisory discussions. Another approach to dealing with countertransference feelings is to discuss them with the client. A mild, reassuring interpretative reference may occasionally be helpful in relieving anxiety in both parties. The existential model of counseling as an encounter would permit counselors to express and interject their own feelings of anger and frustration as an open model of humanness and expression. Counselors' use of self-awareness to enhance growth and resolve their own difficulties can make them more effective in personal life as well as in professional relationships.

CONFRONTATION

Eagan (1976) described confrontation as anything the counselor does that invites a client to examine her or his behavior and its consequences more carefully. The counselor usually confronts the discrepancies in the client's thinking and action. Confrontation may be also defined as the counselor's pointing out a discrepancy between his or her and the client's way of viewing reality (Anderson, 1968, p. 411). By pointing out a discrepancy between their views the counselor is causing the client to face the situation. Discrepancies in client thinking and actions appear most frequently in three areas: between the ideal and real self; between insight and actions; and between reality and illusions. "The purpose of confrontation is to reduce the ambiguity and incongruencies in the client's experiencing and communication. In effect, it is a challenge to the client to become integrated; that is, at one with his own experience" (Carkhuff & Berenson, 1967, p. 171). The term *confrontation* frequently conjures the idea of a hostile act; however, this need not be true. Confrontation is hostile to the unhealthy patterns the client has developed, but the challenge can be considered healthy rather than destructive.

Leaman (1978) identified three purposes of confrontation. First, confrontation helps a client to recognize manipulations and ineffective communication patterns. A client may be unaware of the games he or she is playing or may not recognize the confusion produced through the conflicting messages he or she communicates. The manipulations may be an integral part of the person's defense mechanism and manipulative life-style which frustrate personal fulfillment. The confrontation can be an invitation to examine that pattern. A second purpose of confrontation is to assist the client in evaluating the consequences of maladaptive behaviors. A client may not recognize the cause-effect relationship between her or his manipulations and the responses of other people. The counselor's ability to confront the client invites the client to discover how the maladaptive behavior affects other people as well as the counselor. The third purpose of confrontation is to help clients with the ownership of feelings and with taking responsibility for their actions. A confrontation can help clients to admit personal needs and accept their emotions instead of blaming other people for what happens.

Berenson (1968) outlined the five types of confrontation as experiential, didactic, strength, weakness, and encouragement to action. Experiential confrontation is the counselor's response to any discrepancy between what the client said about himself or herself and how the counselor experiences the client. A didactic confrontation is the counselor's response to client misinformation, lack of information, or need for information regarding the educational, vocational, or social areas as well as the counseling process. Confrontation of strength occurs when the counselor focuses on the client's constructive resources; of weakness, when the counselor emphasizes the client's liabilities or pathology. Encouragement occurs when the counselor presses the client to act in life in some constructive manner or discourages the client's passive stance.

Eagan (1976) pointed out that the manner of confrontation is as important as the type of confrontation and suggested some guidelines on how the confrontation should take place. He suggested that confrontation be offered in the spirit of accurate empathy. In fact, accurate empathy is in itself often challenging to the client. If confrontation does not come from the counselor's accurate empathy, it will almost inevitably be either ineffective or destructive. Second, the counselor's confrontation should be performed tentatively, especially when offered in the early stages of counseling. The tentativeness permits the client an opportunity to hear and examine the counselor's perspective without having it forced upon him or her. Third, confrontation is a way of getting involved with the client and a way of communicating that the counselor cares enough to help. A caring confrontation presupposes that some kind of relationship has developed between the confronter and the confronted. A fourth method is to use confrontation in successive approximations. Confrontation may be more effective if it is gradual because the client has an opportunity to assimilate what is being said.

> Confrontation may range from a light challenge to a direct collision between the therapist and client. It constitutes a challenge to the client to mobilize his resources to take another step toward deeper self-recognition or constructive action on his own behalf. Frequently, it will precipitate a crisis that disturbs, at least temporarily, the client's personal and social equilibrium. Again, crises are viewed as the very fabric of growth, invoking new responses and charting new developments. Growth is viewed as a series of endless self-confrontations. Confrontation is a vehicle that ultimately translates awareness and insight into action, directionality,

wholeness, and meaning in the client's life. A life without confrontation is directionless, passive, and impotent (Carkhuff & Berenson, 1967, p. 172).

A client may feel powerless to do something for himself or herself: whatever happens to him or her is someone else's control. The client frequently searches for someone who will do something for her or him and waits for the magical moment when someone provides directionality or meaning for life. The person often knows that the life she or he is leading is miserable, but feels there is nothing he or she can do to change it. The client continues a passive-reactive stance and lives in an illusion. By the use of confrontation the counselor forces the client to choose between continuing life as it is and becoming an active force in the creation of a new life.

Leaman (1978) believed confrontation and interpretation are closely related therapeutic techniques. Both are direct statements to the client that define a specific behavior pattern. Leaman suggested that a major difference involves the source of meaning: whereas interpretation involves assigning a meaning to behavior through the counselor's theoretical framework, confrontation permits the client to assign a meaning to the behavior. When using interpretation, the counselor presents a hypothesis about what the client's behaviors mean and gives a cause-effect explanation. With confrontation, the counselor identifies the maladaptive behaviors but invites the client to interpret what the behaviors mean. The counselor does not offer an explanation of its meaning. Therefore, confrontation is not a function of the counselor's theoretical assumptions and permits greater flexibility than an interpretation does in the interpersonal encounter.

Confrontation has a number of potentially beneficial effects. It provides the counselor with a vehicle for expressing her or his real thoughts and feelings and provides a model to help the client learn to accept and express thoughts and feelings and to test perceptions against another person's reality. The client learns that there are more ways of viewing a person or a situation, and the two people may disagree without harboring hostile feelings for each other. A constructive confrontation gives clients an honest and immediate experience. Through becoming aware of their impact on another person, they begin to realize the nature and extent of their influence on themselves, a move toward self-confrontation and the ability to face themselves honestly. Confrontation also may indicate to clients a measure of respect for their capacity for self-determination. The counselor is not handling them with kid gloves for fear of overwhelming or hurting them. By directly communicating his or her own position to clients, the counselor allows them to make their own stand clear and to evaluate it. By comparing views with those of another person, clients learn to recognize and face the inter- and intrapersonal discrepancies that are inevitably a part of life (Anderson, 1968).

Counseling can be for better or for worse, and a counselor must take care that the awareness of the crisis he or she creates through use of confrontation will be resolved to the benefit of the client. Confrontation is intended to be used in conjunction with the other elements of a good therapeutic relationship. When rapport has been established and appropriate levels of empathy, positive regard, concreteness and self-disclosure are reached, then confrontation can be introduced.

Anderson (1968) studied the effects of confrontation by high- and low-facilitative counselors. High-facilitative counselors were those rated three or above on a five-point scale of facilitative conditions; low-facilitative counselors were rated below three. There were four high-functioning and sixteen low-functioning counselors in the study, which reported a total of fifty confrontations: forty-one were initiated by the high-facilitative counselors and nine by the low. There was an obvious difference between the high- and low-functioning counselors in the frequency of confrontations. Anderson also found that the high-level counselors confronted their clients more often with their resources, whereas the low-functioning counselors, when they confronted, confronted the clients more often with their limitations. Therefore, when confrontation was used by the high-functioning counselors, it led to an increased level of client self-exploration.

Berenson (1968) reported confirmation of Anderson's results and stated that high-functioning counselors employed confrontation more often regardless of the client's level of self-exploration. He also found that high-level counselors confronted strengths and confronted more often, whereas low-functioning counselors confronted weakness and confronted less often. Additional confirmation came from a study on the relationship among facilitative conditions throughout the first interview and particularly during the three minutes after a counselor's confrontation (Berenson & Mitchell, 1968). The findings indicated that counselors offering higher-level facilitative conditions confronted more frequently during the interview and continued to offer the same higher-level core conditions than did the low-functioning counselors. This indicates that counselors offering higher levels of conditions confront more frequently and yet maintain a high level of facilitative communication for their clients.

Another guideline in the use of confrontation involves timing. Leaman (1978) stated that knowing when to confront is very important. A premature confrontation may produce anger and defensiveness. In addition to having a good relationship developed and communicating with care, the counselor should remember that it is not necessary to confront every maladaptive behavior.

Friel and Berenson conducted a study to determine the interrelationship of immediacy, reference to others, and confrontation with the facilitative communications before and after confrontation (1969). They found that a counselor functioning at a given level of facilitative conditions also functioned correspondingly high or low in communication of immediacy, reference to others, and confrontation. After the confrontation, the higher-level counselors demonstrated a more clearly defined responsive, initiative, and client factor, indicating that they acted responsibly to obtain feedback from the client and then initiate direction as a result. The lower-functioning counselors did not demonstrate any consistent pattern other than asking questions, indicating that they operated independently of client feedback. Another study was conducted to investigate the effects of client confrontation of the counselor upon levels of immediacy offered by high- and low-functioning counselors. The results suggested that high-functioning counselors offered significantly higher levels of immediacy throughout the session and during a confrontation. In fact, the high-functioning counselors offered significantly higher levels of immediacy while being confronted than when they were not (Collingwood, Renz, & Carkhuff, 1969).

The counselor can never be sure that the crisis created by confrontation will be resolved to benefit the client. The crisis and the decision for handling it are the client's. The research quoted above, though not conclusive, demonstrates that the counselors who use confrontation to precipitate a crisis are probably the most capable of helping the client resolve it successfully.

COMMUNICATION

The counseling process is a relationship between the two people, rather than a meeting dominated by the counselor. As part of this relationship, however, the counselor uses techniques to help the client understand himself and the environment and reach decisions for effective behavior. These techniques affect the ways counselor and client discuss problems and the steps clients try to take between interviews. The techniques of counseling involve the counselor's sensitivity and skill both in receiving communication from the client and in communicating to the client. Each dimension of the relationship requires communication between counselor and client.

Williamson (1959) reviewed several possible modes of communication between the counselor and the client: the counselor's manner, rational use of language, and intuitional. The comment by Ralph Waldo Emerson, "What you are speaks so loudly that I can't hear what you say," pertains to the counselor's habitual and natural manner of behaving: that behavior indicates the counselor's own belief system. Certainly the counselor believes she or he will be more effective by acting in one way rather than another. In Williamson's view, the counselor's values will determine his or her behavior, and that behavior is part of the best way of communicating to the client that the latter's problems and welfare are primary considerations to the counselor.

Spoken language is the primary mode of communication in counseling. Through language the counselor attempts to communicate to the client an alternative consideration for action. Through conversation also the client reviews her or his present state of behavior, organizes difficulties, and begins to see more clearly what was once confusing. The use of language is an objective way of helping the client identify problem areas, interpret facts about the situation and herself or himself, and thereby gain a better orientation to exercise self-control. It is assumed that in a facilitative interview, the client may come to accept himself or herself. When the client clearly perceives the available options, she or he will choose those that will produce self-fulfillment.

The word *communication* comes from the Latin verb *communicare*, to share. It is similar to *communion*, an action or situation involving sharing. In other words, at least two persons, a sender and a receiver, must be involved in communication, and they share mutually in the process. Communication is talking with someone, not at someone. It is a two-way process.

What is communicated is what is comprehended by the receiver. The counselor must be concerned not only with what both people are saying, but also with what the client understands and perceives in the relationship. Words differ not only in content but also in their emotional impact on the receiver. The simplest words have emotional attachments, particularly when they are associated with beliefs, values, attitudes, feelings, and emotions presented by the client. If the counselor is unaware of potential meanings, significant misunderstandings can result.

Three major factors influence how well the counselor is understood: (1) the information's relationship to the needs of the client; (2) its relationship to existing information in the client's perceptual field; (3) and the openness of the client's perceptual field at the moment of communication. Given that an individual's needs exert a selective effect on what she or he perceives, a client will take in the information she or he has to absorb and will not use the rest.

To be effective, the information must be related to the client's current problems or interests. The individual will perceive what he or she needs, but immediate needs are always more pressing and pertinent than those of the future.

Information or an experience is more meaningful when it is related to the individual's current awareness. When someone discovers that new information or experiences relate to what he or she already comprehends, it acquires new meaning. One of the frustrations in communication occurs because one person is not successful in helping the other perceive the place of new information in present awareness. It is difficult to absorb new ideas when they are not consistent with those already present.

A major factor in the process of communication is the openness of the client. Whenever the individual feels threatened, she or he will be more closed to new communication or to exploring information about herself or himself. Selection of both what is taken in and given out will be a part of the process. The client will take in what he or she needs and defend himself or herself against what is disruptive or destructive. Various barriers to communication are used to maintain existing defense mechanisms. Most are established against some perceived threat. Combs, Avila, and Purkey (1971) described a cycle of threat that affects communication. In their view, barriers are established in response to an experienced threat, and a cycle of threat/counterthreat can spiral to destroy communication. The experience of threat may bounce back and forth from one individual to the other, spiraling upward to produce increased intensity and interference in communication. This is brought about in part by attempts at self-defense and in part by retaliatory attacks of one person against the other. To break this threat/counterthreat cycle calls for a combination of techniques. First, the counselor must pay attention to the feelings involved and the process of dialogue. He or she must evaluate personal feelings of threat and, most important, must provide a relationship for the client that reduces both internal and external threat. Second, the counselor can absorb or drain off feelings of threat. The counselor can absorb a threat by letting the client express anger or other feelings without responding in kind. Third, the counselor can contribute to the client's personal feelings of security by helping the client become aware of strengths and abilities to cope.

OBSTRUCTIONS TO COMMUNICATION

It seems a paradox that a client who comes for help and a counselor who is trained in communication have difficulty communicating with each other. Some of the obstacles to communication include motivational problems, psychological barriers, and language difficulties.

Motivational Problems

At times obstructions to communication occur because of the motivation of one or both participants. The individuals have developed habits of communicating that are not intended to facilitate the process. In fact, these behaviors are designed in large part to protect them from making some undesirable revelation or putting themselves in an unfavorable light. Clients may defend themselves against the possibility of looking ridiculous or inadequate. Hence, the motivation in communication is intended to protect oneself rather than to provide information to someone else. Another part of the motivation for clients is not to be influenced. This is a type of defensiveness that mires communication with omissions and inaccuracies. Clients may recognize that communications from another person may be an attempt to influence them in a direction they do not really want to go. Therefore, part of the communication will be defenses against permitting themselves to be influenced.

Through long experience in communication, individuals learn to anticipate what is going to be said and so don't listen attentively. Counselors may respond not to what is being said but to their own thoughts. They may hear only what they expect to. Both counselors and clients may listen for only what fits their purposes, for they have already classified the other person or information.

A part of the communication time is spent trying to evaluate the motives of the other person. Whenever the motivation is to evaluate the other person, the individual may miss part of the information being communicated. In addition, an evaluative attitude may lead to a more defensive communication from the other person.

The interview must be a process in which the forces to distort or withhold information have been eliminated or reduced as much as possible. The counselor must bear major responsibility for the pattern of interaction that occurs.

Psychological Barriers

In addition to motivational barriers, there are psychological barriers between clients and their material. There are times when clients cannot tell the counselor everything about themselves because of these psychological barriers. The simplest form of this barrier is memory failure. Clients cannot tell something because they have forgotten the material. The memory failure results not only in absence of information but also in distortion: in all innocence clients give erroneous information. People remember and forget in a selective fashion, and patterns by which memory alters or discards past events are influenced by emotional factors. Emotional forces may set up barriers between clients and the material the counselor seeks, whether the focus is on the past or on the present. The obstructions to communication exist not in the clients' wishes to withhold or distort information but in their psychological inability to produce it.

Language Difficulties

Language difficulties form another obstacle to communication. Words are only symbols that substitute for the realities they describe. However, the words chosen are frequently poor substitutes. The real world is considerably more complex and colorful than our ability to express it. How can a client describe the physical or psychological pain she or he endures with a problem? In the early stages of counseling, the client frequently talks about a problem as "it" because he or she cannot accurately define or describe the problem let alone the feelings involved with it. When the client finds words that have accurate meaning for him or her, the counselor may not be able to understand them because of his or her language decoding process. Understanding the client is certainly one of the major difficulties in communicating.

The counselor must also be aware of differences in vocabulary that may exist between herself or himself and a client from a different region, ethnic group, economic stratum, occupational specialty, or age group. Correct use of a client's colloquialisms may suggest that the client and counselor have things in common and are within range for communication purposes. But the counselor's basic skills of acceptance of understanding of the client are more important indicators of good communications.

JOHARI AWARENESS MODEL

The Johari Awareness Model, or Johari Window, is a useful concept for examining the dynamics of communication. It divides the individual into four quadrants, each of which represents an area of awareness in both the individual and the person with whom he or she interacts. This awareness involves knowledge of behavior, feelings, and motivation. Figure 12–1 illustrates the quadrants.

- Quadrant 1: The open quadrant contains material about the self that is known to both the individual and the person with whom he or she interacts. The client openly communicates some material to the counselor.

FIGURE 12–1 THE JOHARI WINDOW

Reprinted from *Group Processes: An Introduction to Group Dynamics,* by Joseph Luft, by permission of Mayfield Publishing Company. Copyright © 1963, 1970 Joseph Luft. Readers should also refer to *Of Human Interaction.*

- Quadrant 2: The blind quadrant contains material about the self that is known by others but is not recognized by the individual. This is information the counselor picks up that the client did not intend or know he communicated.
- Quadrant 3: The hidden quadrant contains material about the self that the individual is aware of but that is not known to people with whom he or she interacts. The client is consciously aware of this information but does not communicate it.
- Quadrant 4: The unknown quadrant contains material about the self that is out of awareness of both the individual and the other person.

The individual's awareness is not divided equally among the four quadrants; the relative size of each depends upon the individual's makeup. As a general rule, the more material that is contained in the open quadrant, the better the functioning of the individual will be. It follows that people experiencing some difficulty will probably have a restricted open quadrant.

Each person can be characterized by the relative size of his or her open quadrant. Although the size of the open quadrant varies, everyone is relatively stable in most communication. In a counseling situation, the size of quadrant 1 determines the degree to which the client and counselor can freely give and take, work together, and share experiences. The larger the open quadrant, the greater the individual's contact with reality and the more available her or his abilities and needs are to himself or herself and others.

The greater the client's need to protect herself or himself, the smaller the amount of material in quadrant 1 will be. A need for self-protection generally increases the amount of material in quadrant 3. Clients unsure of themselves will try to hide more of their feelings and motivations in quadrant 3. The amount of material in quadrant 2 is also increased. As a need for self-protection increases, the client will not be aware of the cues and information the counselor is seeing. Quadrant 4 is also increased as the client pushes events out of awareness. This area resembles the Freudian unconscious, containing material of which neither the individual nor others around him are aware. Figure 12–2 shows the awareness quadrants of such a client at the beginning of counseling. Because the open area is relatively small, communication will be somewhat limited; as the client feels more accepted and understood, she or he will be more open with feelings and behaviors.

One of the purposes of counseling is to help the individual move material from quadrants 2, 3, and 4 into 1. Luft (1970) described the principles of change to do this.

1. A change in any one quadrant will affect all the other quadrants.
2. It takes energy to hide, deny, or be blind to behavior that is involved in interaction.
3. Threat tends to decrease awareness; mutual trust tends to increase awareness.
4. Forced awareness (exposure) is undesirable and usually ineffective.

FIGURE 12–2 RESTRICTED CLIENT QUADRANTS

1	2
3	4

5. Interpersonal learning means a change has taken place so that quadrant 1 is larger and one or more of the other quadrants have grown smaller.
6. Working with others is facilitated by a large enough area of free activity. It means more of the resources and skills of the person involved can be applied to the task at hand.
7. The smaller the first quadrant, the poorer the communication.
8. There is universal curiosity about the unknown area, but this is held in check by custom, social training, and adverse fears.
9. Sensitivity means appreciating the covert aspects of behavior in quadrants 2, 3, and 4 and respecting the desire of others to keep themselves.

Figure 12–3 shows the relative proportions of the client's awareness quadrants as they should exist at the conclusion of successful counseling. The individual should communicate more openly about herself or himself, hence reducing the need for conscious or unconscious self-protection. Some information will remain unknown, people will pick up information the individual is not aware of, and it will be appropriate for him or her to keep some information private.

COUNSELOR COMMUNICATION

Robinson (1950) made a major contribution to counseling literature by focusing on the social psychology of counselor-client interaction. Over the years he and his colleagues have examined the counselor orientations that best help a client to discover insights into a problem and to move forward. Robinson also discussed the optimum means of treatment so a client is able to understand and carry out decisions. This involves the counselor's skill in expressing attitudes and ideas in light of the client's characteristics as the latter enters the interview, and in considering the dynamics of the interaction as it progresses. Robinson was concerned with the communication that goes on during the interview: listening, giving information, interpreting, and various degrees of leading. Early studies indicated that each counselor has a definite pattern of responses for a range of clients, but that various counselors have considerably different patterns of responding to clients.

FIGURE 12-3 FULLY FUNCTIONING INDIVIDUAL'S QUADRANTS

238 CHAPTER
TWELVE
COUNSELING
AS A
RELATIONSHIP

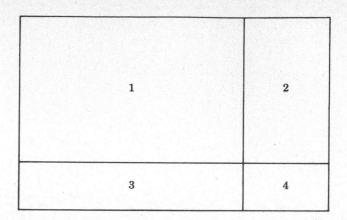

Other studies have suggested that counselors change their styles of communication as they move with their clients from responding to adjustment to skill problems.

This concern with communication involves the ways in which the counselor varies procedures to fit sensitively with the characteristics of the client. Although Robinson discussed the arrangement of the office and the counselor's own dress and manner, he focused much more on the manner of speaking. In examining the counselor's speech, four general dimensions of counselor response have been emphasized: an attitude of acceptance; a division of responsibility; responding to the core of the client's statement; and the degree of lead in the counselor's response. The counselor's communication of an accepting attitude has already been discussed as one of the facilitative conditions in counseling. The concept of responding to the core of what the client says is similar to the concreteness of communication suggested by Carkhuff. It means that the counselor responds to the central meaning the client is communicating, whether it be in content or in feeling. The counselor who responds to something extraneous in the client's statement or who introduces new material is not communicating understanding of the client or respect for what the latter is talking about. The degree of responsibility in the interview will vary with the type of problem and the client's stage in attacking it. The division of responsibility focuses on the amount of time the client is talking, either in describing his or her situation or reaching a decision, and the time the counselor takes in responding to the client. Therefore, it is a verbal division of responsibility. The techniques of communication described by Robinson involve a continuum on the degree of lead, on the assumption that counselors can be trained to be more effective in using various degrees of lead as they respond to their clients.

The counselor communicates in terms of what the client has been saying or thinking so that the latter will be stimulated to move toward effective adjustment; the counselor's remarks move the client from immediate statements toward a desired goal. The amount of leading at any given time is determined by the client's background and the amount of defensiveness or resistance that such a remark might arouse. The amount of lead may vary greatly from topic to topic or from moment to moment in the interview. The counselor's lead should move the client forward to the next stage in her or his thinking. Robinson suggested the concept of a counseling ladder in which the counselor's response would be relevant to the client's needs and interests and at the next rung above the client's thinking in order to stimulate development and lead to further insight. This next level, however, should be close enough for the client to understand easily and accept without experiencing defensive reactions. The counselor may lead too little as well as too much. If the counselor is too passive in the interview, the client may resent the counselor's use of only acceptance remarks, implying refusal to participate with the client in resolving the problem.

Degrees of Lead

A counselor can vary the degree to which his or her response leads the client toward solving problems or developing insight. Some of the earlier research indicated that counselors' verbal techniques tend to fall into definite categories. An awareness of the different degrees of lead will permit counselors to enlarge their repertoire of techniques and make them aware of their pattern of responses.

The categories of responses can be labeled and laid out on a continuum of leading. Some of the responses are quite similar and can be grouped together. Responses with the least degree of lead include silence, acceptance, restatement, clarification, and summary clarification. The counselor communicates understanding and acceptance of what the client is saying and, ideally, communicates that the client should continue in the same vein. The counselor does not introject much of himself or herself or any personal ideas but merely communicates attention to the client and encouragement to continue. By remaining silent when the client pauses, the counselor can communicate that she or he understands the client. The counselor permits the client to think and continue to talk. When the counselor wishes to communicate verbal understanding of what the client is saying without interrupting the client's momentum, he or she may make an acceptance remark such as "uh-um." Or the counselor may restate in nearly the same words the content or feeling that was communicated, thereby reflecting for the client and permitting the latter to hear what she or he has just said. With this type of reflection, the counselor does not interpret or interject anything of himself or herself. At times the counselor may wish to clarify the client's rambling comments or feelings and make a more precise statement about the problem or the client's feelings. A clarification comment should illuminate what the client has been communicating but not push the client in any direction. At the end of a series of comments on a topic, the counselor may use a summary clarification to tie together several aspects of the client's expressions. Responses in this category would be facilitative and rated around level three because they are interchangeable with the client's feelings or content.

A greater degree of lead is involved when the counselor uses a general lead. The counselor may wish to have more information from the client or to have the client go deeper into the problem. By saying, "How do you feel about that?" or "Can you tell me a little more about that?" the counselor can lead the client into the content or affective areas without developing resistance, since the client is still able to control what she or he says.

Much greater leading techniques include tentative analysis, interpretation, and urging. With these techniques the counselor communicates not only understanding of what the client has been saying, but also a desire to introduce some new ideas; the counselor goes beyond the client's present communication and puts across additional ideas. When the counselor wishes to present a new look at the problem or a new approach to the problem, he or she may do so in a very tentative manner, leaving the client free to accept, modify, or reject the communication. The counselor may say, "Do you suppose . . ." or "Correct me if I'm wrong . . ." or "What would you think about . . ." In an interpretation, the counselor states an inference from the client's communication, but not something the client has specifically said. "Interpretation speeds insight and causes little difficulty if the client was just about to state the idea anyway, would have presented the idea if he had thought of it, or if it fits a need which he has expressed" (Robinson, 1950, p. 90). A tentative analysis or interpretation response can facilitate the client's communication. If it is accurate and the timing correct, the response would be additive and rated above level three on the Carkhuff scale. However, an interpretation may cause resistance in the client if the lead is too far ahead of the client's present thinking or has negative implications for him or her. An urging comment suggests a solution for the client's problems and involves the counselor's own values. Urging the client to make a certain decision may or may not lead to a successful outcome, but the decision is the counselor's and not the client's.

In Robinson's view, techniques such as depth interpretation, rejection, assurance, and introducing an unrelated aspect of the subject are techniques with the greatest degree of lead and are frequently detrimental to the counseling relationship. A depth interpretation, made from some theory of personality dynamics, is a lead far beyond the client's present thinking and frequently touches sensitive areas in the client's unconscious. Although the counselor feels the client's attitudes or decision may be wrong, a rejection of his or her view may only hurt the client or at least increase resistance. It should be more effective to work with the client to bring about a gradual change in views. Assurance may have the same effect as rejection, because the counselor tends to belittle the client's view of the problem. By saying "I'm sure everything will work out," the counselor really denies that the client has anything to worry about and that her or his feelings are real. By introducing a new and apparently unrelated topic, the counselor may also convey rejection of the topic in which the client is interested. This certainly is not a response to the core of what the client is talking about or to the client's feelings and would not be considered a concrete statement, all of which leads to a low level of facilitation for the client.

Counselor Verbal Behaviors

One approach to studying counselor verbal behaviors focuses on specific behaviors or skills. A number of response taxonomies have been developed to categorize counselor responses. Hill (1978) developed a counselor response category system by incorporating components from eleven existing systems, refining the categories after use and having experts match examples to the definitions. The analysis culminated in the following fourteen-category system:

1. **Minimal encourager** This consists of a short phrase that indicates simple agreement, acknowledgment, or understanding. It encourages but does not request the client to continue talking; it does not imply approval or disapproval. It may be a repetition of

key word(s) and does not include responses to questions (see *information*).

2. **Approval-reassurance** This provides emotional support, approval, or reinforcement. It may imply sympathy or tend to alleviate anxiety by minimizing client's problems.

3. **Information** This supplies information in the form of data, facts, resources, theory, and the like. It may be information specifically related to the counseling process, counselor's behavior or arrangement (time, place, fee, etc.) It may answer direct questions but does not include directions for what the client should do (see *direct guidance*).

4. **Direct guidance** This consists of directions or advice that the counselor suggests for the client, or for the client and counselor together, either within or outside the counseling session. It is not aimed at soliciting verbal material from the client (see *closed* or *open question*).

5. **Closed question** This is a data-gathering inquiry that requests a one- or two-word answer, a yes or no, or a confirmation of the counselor's previous statement. The possible client responses to this type of inquiry are typically limited and specific. If statements are phrased in the form of a closed question but meet the criteria for another category, they should be put in the other category.

6. **Open question** A probe requests a clarification of feelings or an exploration of the situation without purposely limiting the nature of the response to a yes or no or a one- or two-word response. If statements are phrased in the form of an open question but meet the criteria for another category, they should be put in the other category.

7. **Restatement** This is a simple repeating or rephrasing of the client's statement(s) (not necessarily just the immediately preceding statements). It typically contains fewer but similar words and is more concrete and clear than the client's message. It may be phrased either tentatively or as a statement.

8. **Reflection** This is a repeating or rephrasing of the client's statement (not necessarily just the immediately preceding statements). It *must* contain reference to stated or implied feelings. It may be based on previous statements, nonverbal behavior, or knowledge of the total situation. It may be phrased either tentatively or as a statement.

9. **Nonverbal referent** This points out or inquires about aspects of the client's nonverbal behavior, for example, body posture, voice tone or level, facial expressions, gestures, and so on. It does not interpret the meaning of these behaviors.

10. **Interpretation** This *goes beyond* what the client has overtly recognized. It might take one of several forms: It might establish connections between seemingly isolated statements or events; it interprets defenses, feelings, resistance, or transference (the interpersonal relationship between counselor and client): it might indicate themes, patterns, or causal relationships in the client's behavior or

personality. It usually gives alternative meanings for odd behavior or issues. If a statement also meets the criteria for a confrontation, it should be put in confrontation.

11. **Confrontation**   This contains two parts: The first part may be implied rather than stated and refers to some aspect of the client's message or behavior; the second part usually begins with a "but" and presents a discrepancy. This contradiction or discrepancy may be between words and behavior, between two things the client has stated, between behavior and action, between real and ideal self, between verbal and nonverbal behavior, between fantasy and reality, or between the counselor's and the client's perceptions.

12. **Self-disclose**   This usually begins with an "I"; the counselor shares his or her own personal experiences and feelings with the client. Note that not all statements that begin with an "I" are self-disclosure; it must have a quality of sharing or disclosing.

13. **Silence**   A pause of 5 seconds is considered the counselor's pause if it occurs between a client's statement and a counselor's statement or within the client's statement (except after a simple acceptance of the counselor's statement, e.g., "yes," pause).

14. **Other**   These include statements that are unrelated to client's problems, such as small talk or salutations, comments about the weather or events; disapproval or criticism of the client; or statements that do not fit into any other category or are unclassifiable due to difficulties in transcription, comprehensibility, or incompleteness (Hill, 1978, p. 466).[1]

From a content analysis of the literature on how clients and helpers perceive particular helper behaviors, Elliott (1979) reported the following as most typical: advisements are perceived as guiding the client; acknowledgments such as "uh-huh," as reassuring the client; reflections, as communicating understanding of the client's message; interpretations, as explaining the clients to themselves; questions, as gathering information or understanding the client; and self-disclosures, as the helper's using himself or herself to help the client.

Strong, Wambach, Lopez, and Cooper (1979) discussed the importance of the type of interpretation in affecting clients' motivations to change. When clients see their problems as caused by a factor they can directly affect, such as lack of effort to do something, they are able to exert themselves to correct the situation. An interpretation that has identified causes of problems that the client can directly do something about helps the client make the necessary changes. In contrast, interpretations that have focused on causes of problems that clients cannot do anything about, such as events in their past, do not provide them with tools they can use to change. The research of Strong et al. substantiated the concept that the interpretations increase motivations to change. Students who received an interpretation rated the experience lower on an unconditionality of regard scale than did those who received a reflection, indicating that the interpretations were perceived as conditional and evaluative statements. However, the interpretations seemed to have led to greater perceived seriousnesss and motivation to change by making the problem behavior relevant and threatening to self-esteem.

1. Copyright 1978 by the American Psychological Association. Reprinted by permission.

Tracking

Kepecs (1979) discussed the importance of accurately tracking what the client is communicating. An accurate statement by the counselor helps facilitate clients' self-understanding and encourages the latter to communicate about themselves and their environment. On the other hand, errors in tracking interfere with this development. Tracking errors indicate to clients that the counselor is not following what is said and that the counselor for some reason does not want to hear them. Kepecs identified three general types of tracking errors. The first type of tracking error results from the counselor's being agitated or penetrated by the client, such as by anxiety, guilt, or anger. A second type of tracking error is triggered by the counselor's need to dominate the client. Examples of this type of error include the counselor's interests predominating over those of the client, switching the client to another track, pushing his or her own point of view, or lecturing to the client. The third tracking error is caused by the counselor's avoidance of the client by, say, not moving with a client, showing rigidity or lack of knowledge, or avoiding the client's dependency. Any of the tracking errors may lead to opposition, blocking, confusion, or a disruption in the client's flow of thought. Clients are likely to react by turning their feelings inward and making themselves feel helpless or criticizing themselves. It is important that the counselor recognize tracking errors in order to diminish their frequency and improve communication with clients.

NONVERBAL COMMUNICATION

Dittman (1963) suggested that nonverbal behavior is a way to read how the client feels at a given time. In his view, nonverbal messages are frequently different from verbal ones, and congruencies and discrepancies between the two can provide clues about what is happening in the interview. Dittman believed that nonverbal communication can give clues faster than words, for people often react sooner than they are willing or able to say in words.

Nonverbal Vocal Phenomena

Smith (1966) described the expressive levels of speech as the other vocal phenomena that accompany language. These can be systematically analyzed as qualities and noises separable from language itself. However, although they contribute to the overall meaning of the communication, they have no referential meaning by themselves. Among these expressive levels are six vocal qualifiers established on a level or baseline of any spoken communication.

1. **Intensity, or increased loudness or softness** Increased loudness or softness may affect a single syllable or a whole sentence or more. Increased loudness usually displays alarm or annoyance; increased softness might reveal displeasure or disappointment.
2. **Pitch range overall, or raised or lowered pitch** Raised pitch usually occurs in contexts of annoyance or alarm; lowered pitch might provide various kinds of emphasis, including incredulity.

3. **Spread register and squeezed register**   These are respectively, the *stretching* and compressing of the usual interval between the pitch phonemes in the utterance.
4. **Rasp and openness**   These qualities are physiologically related to the amount of muscular tension under which the laryngeal apparatus is held. The more tension, the more strained or rasping the effect. Openness or looseness results in a hollow, booming, authoritative impression.
5. **Drawl and clipping**   These reflect the tempo of individual syllables.
6. **Increased and decreased tempo**   In contrast to drawl and clipping, these are used to describe longer utterances. In many contexts, increased tempo signals annoyance or anxiety, decreased tempo uncertainty (Smith, 1966, p. 178).

When these elements occur in unusual amounts or in unusual contexts, the skilled listener figuratively perceives them with a "third ear."

Another set of vocal phenomena, called vocal differentiators, include laughing, crying, and breaking. Laughing and crying are commonly used and self-evident. Breaking is characterized by special muscular phenomena of the laryngeal machinery. There is a rigid and intermittent tension and relaxation of the vocal cords so that the voice is broken with a tremulous interruption of tone. It signifies great or deep emotional involvement in the speaker.

Vocal identifiers are considered another significant set of vocal phenomena, although so far only one has been described in the communication system. This is the interruption of a word by a glottal stop and pause, usually signifying that all or part of the utterance is negated or changed by a suddenly perceived contrasting thought or insight.

Other phenomena, usually called voice quality and voice set, are aspects of voice that seem to transcend the overall communication interchange and signify the general emotional state of the organism. An anxious or a hostile voice represents voice quality, a thin, immature, aged, or dispirited voice represents a voice set. Although these are clearly separable phenomena, they are not yet as systematically describable as the vocal modifiers.

The patterns of use of the various elements of all the vocal phenomena, singly or in combination, are recognizable as culturally, institutionally, and personally determined. Variations can be studied on individual and/or group levels.

A great deal of communication takes place without sound. We communicate with others through gestures, peculiarities in gait and dress, touch while shaking hands, mannerisms in a glance or look, condition and texture of skin, body build, and a multitude of similar bodily characteristics (Barbara, 1966).

Facial Expressions of Emotion

In everyday personal relations, the face is the primary locus of regard in identifying the nature of emotional responses (Kline and Johannsen, 1935). In the counseling process as in any interpersonal interaction, the emotions expressed through facial expressions frequently determine the direction of the interaction. For example, a client who enters a counselor's office with apparent signs of despair or torment in all likelihood wishes to discuss the problem that has brought her or him to the counseling interview—a problem that may—or may not—be easily detected by her or his facial expression. Throughout the counseling interview, facial expressions change many times. The counselor must be able to detect facial changes in emotion in order to lead the interview in the appropriate direction. If the counselor attends only to verbal communications, the client's problem may go undetected.

If people in general, and counselors in particular, can accurately identify the emotions displayed through facial expressions, better understanding and insight into the other person's particular problem can result. Discussing the emotion that the counselor sees can convince the client that the counselor does understand his or her problem—that the counselor can empathize with the client. True empathy in the counselor does not take only the form of verbal communication; verbal remarks can sound very artificial when interpreted only in terms of tone of voice. If the client is able both to hear an empathic expression and to see it reinforced by the counselor's facial expression, the client can feel that the counselor really does understand the specific situation, and because of this understanding may be able to help.

Kinesics

Although the face is the primary area of regard in identifying the nature of emotional responses, the body, limbs, and hands play an important role in communications. Kinesics is the way people communicate through body movements and gestures. Kinesics are culturally influenced systems of behavior learned informally by imitation of role models (Knapp, 1963). Because most of this behavior is learned without awareness, most people remain unaware of their participation in an elaborate system of bodily gestures and motions (Smith, 1966).

Nonverbal physical expressions include gestures and bodily postures. According to Ruesch and Kees (1956), gestures are used to illustrate, emphasize, point, explain, or interrupt and therefore cannot be isolated from verbal communication. Gestures are determined by the way the human body is constructed but are elaborated in interpersonal and social relationships. Consequently, expressions of amazement, desperation, anger, anxiety, pleasure, and indignation are similar in certain areas in all countries and cultures. On the other hand, understanding their meaning depends on familiarity with the communication system of a given culture. Gestures are necessary when verbalization is impossible, as when language barriers or hearing difficulties are present. Gestures are frequently used when verbal expression would be considered socially unacceptable. Quite different impressions are communicated by those burdened with diseases that result in involuntary movements or gestures.

An anxious person frequently will exhibit rapid, restless movement of the limbs and tremors of the hands. A depressed person moves very slowly as if every effort is a great effort. Another important factor is the physical distance a person maintains between himself or herself and other people. The withdrawn person keeps her or his arms in close contact with the body and the head lowered. As Hahn and MacLean stated, "Bodily postures, tension and relaxation of the muscular systems, gestures with head, hands and feet all have accepted symbolic value as communicated in our culture" (1955, p. 266).

CHAPTER
TWELVE
COUNSELING
AS A
RELATIONSHIP

245

THEORIES OF NONVERBAL BEHAVIOR

The counselor should have a working knowledge of nonverbal communication to perceive the myriad messages that come from a client. The counselor should also be aware of the nonverbal messages she or he is sending to the client that might facilitate understanding and indicate support.

The correct identification of expression is very important for the counseling situation, for counseling is a communicative process involving both verbal and nonverbal variables. The two theoretical models presented below may help the counselor bring order out of the myriad of nonverbal behaviors.

Kagan's Model

Through the study of Interpersonal Process Recall (IPR), Kagan et al. (1967) focused on nonverbal behavior. From the observation of clients in interviews, they inferentially developed a framework of nonverbal behavior. Through recall interviews, they found that clients frequently use nonverbal behaviors as a cue to important feelings or ideas at critical points in the interview. The topology formulated from their study is built upon three elements: the source of nonverbal behavior, the awareness of the communication, and the duration of the nonverbal behavior.

The first element in the framework is the source of the nonverbal behavior in the interview. Nonverbal behavior could be related either to verbal content or to the client's affective experience in the interview. Although these two components occur simultaneously, nonverbal behaviors seem to be related only to one and seldom to both at once. The content of the interview refers to the topic of conversation at the moment; affect refers to the feelings experienced by the client regarding himself or herself, the situation, or the topic.

The second element of the framework is the client's level of awareness of his or her nonverbal action: awareness, potential awareness, or lack of awareness. Awareness means that a client not only knows of the behavior but intends that it occur. Potential awareness indicates that a client could be aware of the actions if her or his attention were drawn to it, but involvement in the interview precludes direct awareness of the actions. Lack of awareness means that a client is entirely unaware of the behavior and would remain so even if his or her attention were drawn to it.

The third element in the topology is the duration of the behaviors. The IPR research found that nonverbal behaviors range from a motion involving a fraction of a second to one continuing for several minutes or even continuously throughout the interview.

The interaction of the source and level of awareness is described in six categories of nonverbal behavior: emphasis, facilitation, portrayal, revelation-unaware, revelation-aware, and affect demonstration. Table 12–2 illustrates the interaction of the three elements within the six categories. Each category is named in accordance with its major function.

Emphasis   Gestures used for emphasis are generally brief and forceful, accompanying a particular verbal comment. They are usually related to the content both

TABLE 12–2 NONVERBAL BEHAVIORS OF CLIENTS IN COUNSELING INTERVIEWS

SOURCE OF BEHAVIOR	DEGREE OF AWARENESS OF BEHAVIOR		
	UNAWARE	POTENTIALLY AWARE	AWARE
Content/Affect	**Emphasis:** Gestures of shortest duration accompanying particular items of verbal content.	**Facilitation:** Gestures of brief duration accompany verbal content.	**Portrayal:** Gestures of duration directly related to content, used in giving example of the topic.
	Revelation–unaware (unconscious): Unconsciously motivated body motion related to feelings.	**Revelation–aware (conscious):** Unconsciously motivated gestures revealing some degree of tension; client is aware of body motion but neither intends nor suppresses it.	**Affect Demonstration (conscious):** Intentional demonstration of client feeling.

in time and forcefulness. The client is generally unaware of this use of gestures because they are brief and associated with specific points of the verbal content.

Facilitation Gestures are often used to increase clarification. These gestures usually involve the hand and arm when a client is somewhat at a loss for words or feels that his or her communication is inadequate. The hand and arms typically move quickly in upward and outward motion as if to release words from within and speed them in the communication. The client is probably unaware of the use of facilitative gestures unless it is called to her or his attention.

Portrayal A client sometimes wants to demonstrate what he or she means and can portray it only by means of a gesture. This gesture gives an example or picture of the topic being communicated. Portrayal is generally a conscious gesture and is used specifically as an addition to the verbal communication.

Affect Demonstration A client may use a nonverbal behavior deliberately to demonstrate feelings. This behavior is intentional and fully in the awareness of the client. An example is the use of a facial expression to communicate emotional reaction to the topic being discussed.

Revelation–Aware A client may consciously make gestures that he or she attributes to habit and whose basic intention is seldom recognized: the client is aware of the activity but unaware of its motivation. These behaviors often function as pacifiers, such as ring twisting, pencil tapping, or habitual nervous gestures.

Revelation–Unaware Gestures reflecting tension-motivated behavior of which the client is totally unaware are the most frequent critical nonverbal behaviors in counseling. In the counseling interview, the client is more concerned with verbalizing content than with nonverbal behavior. In many cases, the tension in the interview motivates the nonverbal behavior. Observation of unconsciously motivated gestures may reveal a wide range of potential sources, including a client's feelings about herself or himself, the counselor, the situation, or the topics. These gestures may be continuous or repeated for an extended time.

Additional research with the IPR studies focused on the level of intensity in the client's feelings and also on how congruent nonverbal behavior was with the feeling the client was verbalizing. Researchers believed that a general awareness of the high, middle, or low affective intensity of nonverbal behavior would be useful to the counselor. The congruency dimension represents whether a statement is congruent or at variance with the nature of the affect felt. There seem to be two basic ways in which variance occurs. Either the statement is similar to the affect perceived but differs in intensity, distorting the latter through understatement or overstatement, or the verbal statement may reflect a very different emotion from the perceived affect. This constitutes denial of the situation.

Counselors must be aware of the relation between the verbal message and the nonverbal communication. The two forms of communication may be congruent; or the nonverbal communication may deny or distort part of what is being stated verbally.

Ekman's Model

Based on his research, Ekman (1973) proposed a general theory of nonverbal behavior, including a model and categories that help delineate nonverbal behaviors. First, Ekman listed the prevailing circumstances that the counselor should be aware of when observing nonverbal communication.

1. The external conditions, such as environmental setting, and the intangible circumstances, such as the emotional tone of the interaction;
2. The relationship of nonverbal behavior to verbal behavior; for example, whether a nonverbal act illustrates, repeats, or contradicts the accompanying speech;
3. The level of awareness of a client that he or she is enacting or has performed a nonverbal act;
4. The client's intention to communicate through nonverbal means;
5. The external feedback, or what the counselor did with the information the client presented;
6. The type of information conveyed, either idiosyncratic or shared (Ekman, 1973, p. 726).

Categories of Nonverbal Behavior Ekman listed five categories of nonverbal behavior. The first category, emblems, includes acts or positions that have a direct verbal translation in a word or two. Emblems typically have shared meaning and transmit an intentional message, such as a V made with two fingers upheld. A second category is illustrators, which are usually direct accompaniments of speech and serve as pictographs to shape the referent visually.

Affect displays, a third category, include all the facial behaviors. These convey more information about an emotion than do body movements. Although there are socially learned and culturally based rules of display, Ekman's theory proposes that the configurations of a face displaying so-called primary emotions—happiness, surprise, anger—are sufficiently alike to be recognizable across cultures. The affect display messages get a greater amount of attention than other nonverbal communication. The sender frequently communicates deliberately, and the receiver often comments openly on such information.

The fourth category, regulators, includes behaviors that regulate the conversational flow between two individuals. A nod of the head is a widely used regulator. Ekman's theory suggests that particular regulators are related to ethnicity, social class, and culture and that their misuse or misinterpretation is one of the perplexing but common sources of misunderstanding that can occur between individuals from different groups.

Adaptors, the fifth category, cover nonverbal behaviors that are abbreviated versions of activities originally learned in childhood for coping with needs. Three subtypes of adaptors are distinguished: self-adaptors, alter-adaptors, and object-adaptors. The self-adapting act of wiping the corner of the eye with a hand may have originated as rubbing away tears but later may be used to communicate that a person feels hurt or sad. Self-adaptors frequently involve the hand's touching the face and head. Alter-adaptors generally involve the hands' moving in space rather than in contact with the body. Alter-adaptors were learned in the course of managing early interpersonal contacts and include behaviors performed to protect oneself from attack or to withdraw. Object-adaptors are fragments of behaviors learned to perform a task such as smoking, using a typewriter, or shuffling cards. They are used when some aspect of the interaction stimulates a reenactment.

Nonverbal Leakage and Clues to Deception How does people's nonverbal behavior betray efforts to deceive themselves or another? Sometimes clients intend to deceive. Ekman called such situations deceptive interactions and tries to distinguish between self-deception and deceiving the other person.

Three characteristics of deceptive interactions differentiate them from other forms of social interaction. One is saliency of deception; that is, whether there is a conscious focus on deception by at least one of the individuals. The second characteristic is whether there is an implicit or explicit agreement between the two to be collaborators or antagonists in the deception. The third characteristic involves the adoption of either a deceptor or detective role. For example, when a client is referred to the counselor, he or she may try to deceive the counselor regarding some aspect of behavior. The counselor can decide to collaborate in that process or act as an antagonist to locate variance in the client's story. When the counselor observes nonverbal leakage to locate clues to deception, she or he must pay attention to both verbal and nonverbal behavior. The verbal behavior conveys a deceptive message, and the nonverbal behavior amplifies and enriches it. The client in essence lies with words, and his or her actions have to be consistent with those words.

In making observations to develop a theory of nonverbal behavior, counselors should note that the face, hands, and legs differ in the amount of message they send and the amount of feedback they receive. The face is the best sender and receives the most attention. The legs and feet are the poorest communicators because their transmission time is slow and the repertoire is small. Hands are somewhere in the middle range. Therefore, in deception the face is the best liar, the hands are next, and the legs are the poorest. The legs are therefore a primary source of leakage of clues to deception because leg movement is rare and seldom employed deliberately. Among hand users, the self-adaptors most often give away the deception: while chatting and smiling, the client is ripping at a hangnail or making a fist. Object-adaptors such as nervous play with a pencil may also be a giveaway. Ekman's research supported his theory: individials viewing films could not differentiate people telling the truth from those telling lies by seeing only their faces, but could differentiate by watching their bodies. Individuals not telling the truth used many more self-adaptors. Self-adaptors, touching the face or head with the hands, tend to increase with anxiety or discomfort. The level of illustrator activity increases with the difficulty of expression and to the extent the person is affectively involved in what he or she is saying.

Conclusion

Nonverbal behaviors emphasize or accent a verbal message, amplify part of the message, explain a silence, add new information to a message, or distort the verbal message. Theoretical models can help a counselor understand the contribution of nonverbal behavior in the counseling relationship. Sensitivity to nonverbal cues demands concentration and improves with training.

Several studies have investigated the importance of nonverbal clues. Claiborn (1979), in a study of verbal interventions and nonverbal behavior, found that the clients perceived the use of interpretation as more expert and trustworthy than the verbal restatement. They also perceived the counselor's use of responsive nonverbal behavior, such as more vocal variation, facial expressions, eye contact, and gestures as more expert, attractive, and trustworthy than the use of comparatively unresponsive nonverbal behavior.

Sobelman (1973) and LaCrosse (1975) reported that clients perceived affiliative nonverbal behaviors as more attractive and warmer. Affiliative nonverbal behaviors were defined as smiles, nods of the head, gestures with hands, eye contact, shoulder orientation of 90° and a forward body inclination of 20°.

Several studies have focused on kinesic nonverbal behavior. Spiegel and Machotka (1974) found that figures with closed arm positions were judged as cold, rejecting, shy, and passive, whereas those with a moderately open arm position were judged as warm and accepting. The figures with extremely open arm positions were judged as immodest and exhibitionistic. Smith-Hanen (1977) confirmed the crossed-arm position as the coldest and least empathetic position. She also studied various leg positions in terms of counselor-rated warmth and empathy, and reported that one leg crossed over the other with the ankle resting on the knee was judged as the coldest and least emphathetic position; the position with the legs crossed at the knee was not rated as cold or less empathic; and the position with the legs up on the seat of a chair was not rated as cold or less empathic.

Waxer (1977) examined the emotional leakage of anxiety through nonverbal clues. His findings generally support Ekman's. The raters were able to identify the presence of anxiety and its intentionality on nonverbal clues alone. The most important nonverbal clues in identifying anxiety were the positions of hands, eyes, mouth, and torso. The hands of anxious clients engaged in more jittery and fewer signaling gestures, their eyes showed shorter duration of contact, they smiled less, and their torso positions were more rigid. This study not only confirmed that nonverbal cues from the body leak more and give more honest information than the face, but also showed that the hand movements of anxious clients did use self-adaptors and illustrators. It also appeared that the raters concentrated more on hand movements than other nonverbal behaviors. In fact, other body areas such as the feet and legs are probably monitored less frequently by most observers.

Although class and cultural variables may interact to create difficulties in communication between a minority client and the counselor, nonverbal behaviors and conversation conventions may also contribute to difficulties. Different cultural groups expect and feel comfortable with differing amounts of personal space. Either the counselor or client may misunderstand the other's move toward distance or closeness. The meaning of eye contact is also important; although Anglo-Americans use eye contact to indicate they are listening, other cultures assign different meanings to directness or indirectness in a gaze. Some cultural groups use a more peripheral vision and avoid eye contact; in some cultural groups, avoidance of eye contact may be a sign of respect or deference. It is possible for a counselor to misinterpret a client from a culturally different background. Conversational conventions also vary from culture to culture, as do the ways in which individuals greet and address one another and take turns in speaking (Sue & Sue, 1977).

SUMMARY

In the relationship between the counselor and client, two people join in a therapeutic alliance to help the client resolve his or her problem. The relationship is the vehicle for exploring the situation, increasing understanding, and trying out appropriate behaviors. Through internalizing the relationship, the client can have a corrective emotional experience, try new behaviors, and enhance self-esteem. Counseling is a process rather than a set of techniques, although the counselor will have techniques for providing and maintaining the relationship. This chapter has suggested how to use the facilitative conditions of empathy, congruence, positive regard, and specificity of communication—concepts that embrace all counseling theories—as a basis for the counseling relationship; explored several other dimensions that appear in the counselor-client relationship; and presented methods for using and recognizing verbal and nonverbal communication to understand and help the client.

REFERENCES

Adler, A. *The practice and theory of individual psychology.* New York: Harcourt, Brace, 1929.

Alexander, F. *Fundamentals of psychoanalysis.* New York: W. W. Norton, 1963.

Anderson, S. Effects of confrontation by high- and low-functioning therapists. *Journal of Counseling Psychology*, 1968, *15*, 411–416.

Barbara, D. The value of non-verbal communication in personality understanding. *Journal of Nervous and Mental Disease*, 1966, *123*, 286–290.

Berenson, B. Level of therapist functioning, patient depth of self-exploration, and type of confrontation. *Journal of Counseling Psychology*, 1968, *15*, 317–321.

Berenson, B. & Mitchell, K. Therapeutic conditions after therapist-initiated confrontation. *Journal of Clinical Psychology*, 1968, *24*, 363–364.

Blackburn, J. R. The efficacy of modeled self-disclosure on subject's response in an interview situation. *Dissertation Abstracts*, 1970, *31* (3-B), 1529, 1530.

Bordin, E. *Psychological counseling*. New York: Appleton-Century-Crofts, 1968.

Brammer, L., & Shostrom, E. *Therapeutic psychology*. Englewood Cliffs, N.J.: Prentice-Hall, 1968.

Carkhuff, R. Toward a comprehensive model of facilitative interpersonal processes. *Journal of Counseling Psychology*, 1967, *14*, 67–72.

———. *Helping and human relations* (Vols. 1 and 2). New York: Holt, Rinehart and Winston, 1969.

Carkhuff, R., & Berenson, B. *Beyond counseling and therapy*. New York: Holt, Rinehart and Winston, 1967.

Casciani, J. Influence of model's race and sex on interviewees' self-disclosure. *Journal of Counseling Psychology*, 1978, *25*, 435–440.

Claiborn, C. Counselor verbal interaction, non-verbal behavior, and social power. *Journal of Counseling Psychology*, 1979, *26*, 378–383.

Collingwood, P., Renz, L., & Carkhuff, R. The effects of client confrontation upon levels of immediacy offered by high- and low-functioning counselors. *Journal of Clinical Psychology*, 1969, *25*, 224–225.

Combs, A., Avila, D., & Purkey, W. *Helping relationships*. Boston: Allyn and Bacon, 1971.

Crowder, J. The relationship between therapist and client interpersonal behaviors and psychotherapy outcomes. *Journal of Consulting Psychology*, 1972, *19*, 68–75.

Cullen, L. F. Nonverbal communication in counseling: An explanatory study. *Dissertation Abstracts*, 1967, *27*, 2047.

Delaney, D. J., & Heimann, R. A. Effectiveness of sensitivity training on the perception on nonverbal communications. *Journal of Counseling Psychology*, 1966, *13*, 436–440.

Dies, R. R. Group therapist self-disclosure: An evaluation by clients. *Journal of Counseling Psychology*, 1973, *20* (4), 344–348.

Dittman, A. Kinestic research and therapeutic processes: Further discussion. In P. N. Knapp (Ed.), *Expression of the emotions in man*. New York: International University Press, 1963.

Dollard, J., & Miller, N. *Personality and psychotherapy*. New York: McGraw-Hill, 1950.

Drag, L. *Experimenter-subject interaction: A situational determinant of differential levels of self-disclosure*. Unpublished Master's thesis, University of Florida, 1968.

Dreyfus, E. Counseling and existentialism. *Journal of Counseling Psychology*, 1962, *9*, 128–132.

Eagan, G. Confrontation. *Group and Organizational Studies*, 1976, *1*, 223–243.

Ekman, P. Differential communication of affect by head and body cues. *Journal of Personality and Social Psychology*, 1965, *2*, 726–735.

Ekman, P. & Gattozzi, A. A. Studies in communication through non-verbal behavior. In J. Segal (Ed.), *Mental Health Program Reports* (Vol. 6). Washington, D.C.: U.S. Government Printing Office, 1973.

Elliott, R. How clients perceive helper behaviors. *Journal of Counseling Psychology*, 1979, *26*, 285–294.

Epstein, S. Some theoretical considerations on the nature of ambiguity and the use of stimulus dimension in projective techniques. *Journal of Consulting Psychology*, 1966, *30*, 183–192.

Fiedler, F. The concept of an ideal therapeutic relationship. *Journal of Consulting Psychology*, 1950, *14*, 339–345.

Fretz, B. Postural movements in a counseling dyad. *Journal of Counseling Psychology*, 1966, *13*, 367–371.

Friel, T. & Berenson, B. The factoral dimensions of therapeutic process variables. *Journal of Counseling Psychology*, 1969, *27*, 291–293.

Gary, A. L. & Hammond, R. Self-disclosure of alcoholics and drug addicts. *Psychotherapy: Theory, Research, and Practice*, 1970, *4*, 142–146.

Giannandrea, V. & Murphy, K. Similarity self-disclosure and return for a second interview. *Journal of Counseling Psychology*, 1973, *20* (6), 545–548.

Gottsegen, G., & Gottsegen, M. Counter-transference: The professional identity defense. *Psychotherapy: Theory, Research, and Practice*, 1979, *16*, 57–60.

Graff, R. W. The relationship of counselor self-disclosure to counselor effectiveness. *Journal of Experimental Education*, 1970, *38* (3), 19–22.

Hahn, M. & MacLean, M. *Counseling psychology*. New York: McGraw-Hill, 1955.

Halpern, T. Degree of client disclosure as a function of past disclosure, counselor disclosure, and counselor facilitativeness. *Journal of Counseling Psychology*, 1977, *24*, 41–47.

Hill, C. Development of a counselor verbal response category system. *Journal of Counseling Psychology*, 1978, *25*, 461–468.

Hoffman-Graff, M. Interviewer use of positive and negative self-disclosure and interviewer-subject sex pairing. *Journal of Counseling Psychology*, 1977, *24*, 184–190.

Holland, G. *Fundamentals of psychotherapy*. New York: Holt, Rinehart and Winston, 1965.

Horney, K. *Self analysis*. New York: W. W. Norton, 1942.

Horwitz, L. *Clinical prediction and psychotherapy*. New York: Jason Aronson, 1974.

Jones, A. & Seagull, A. Dimensions of the relationship between the black client and the white therapist. *American Psychologist*, 1977, *32*, 850–855.

Jourard, S. M. *The transparent self*. Princeton: Van Nostrand, 1964.

———. *Personal adjustment: An approach through the study of healthy personality*. New York: Macmillan, 1958.

———. *Self-Disclosure: An experimental analysis of the transparent self*. New York: John Wiley and Sons, 1971.

Jourard, S. M., & Jaffe, P. E. Influence of an interviewer's disclosure on the self-disclosing behavior of interviewees. *Journal of Counseling*, 1970, *17*, 252–257.

Kagan, N., et al. *Studies in human interaction, interpersonal process recall, stimulated by video tape*. Final Report Project No. 5-0800, Washington, D.C.: U.S. Department of Health, Education and Welfare, 1967.

Karon, B. & Vandenbos, G. Psychotherapeutic technique in the economically poor patient. *Psychotherapy: Theory, Research and Practice*, 1977, *14*, 169–180.

Kell, B., & Mueller, W. *Impact and change*. New York: Appleton-Century-Crofts, 1966.

Kepecs, J. Tracking errors in psychotherapy. *American Journal of Psychotherapy*, 1979, *33*, 365–377.

Kernberg, O. *Borderline conditions and pathological narcissism*. New York: Jason Aronson, 1975.

Kline, L. W., & Johannsen, D. E. Comparative role of the face and of the face-body-hands as aids in identifying emotions.

Journal of Abnormal and Social Psychology, 1935, *29,* 415.

Knapp, P. H. *Expressions of the emotions in man.* New York: International Universities Press, 1963.

LaCrosse, M. Non-verbal behavior in perceived counselor attractiveness and persuasiveness. *Journal of Counseling Psychology,* 1975, *22,* 563–566.

Lazarus, A. *Behavior therapy and beyond.* New York: McGraw-Hill, 1971.

Leaman, D. Confrontation in counseling. *Personnel and Guidance Journal,* 1978, 56, 630–633.

Luft, J. *Group process: An introduction to group dynamics.* Palo Alto, Calif.: National Press Books, 1970.

Malan, D. *Toward the validation of dynamic psychotherapy.* London: Plenum Press, 1976.

May, R. (Ed.). *Existential psychology.* New York: Random House, 1961.

———. *The art of counseling.* New York: Abingdon Press, 1967.

May, K., Angel, E., & Ellenberger, H. *Existence.* New York: Basic Books, 1958.

McCarthy, P., & Betz, N. Differential effects of self-disclosing versus self-involved counselor statements. *Journal of Counseling Psychology,* 1978, *25,* 251–256.

Mitchell, K., Bozarth, J., & Krauft, C. A reappraisal of the therapeutic effectiveness of accurate empathy, non-possessive warmth, and genuineness. In A. Gurman & A. Razin (Eds.), *Effective psychotherapy: A handbook of research.* New York: Pergamon Press, 1977.

Myrich, R. Effect of a model on verbal behavior in counseling. *Journal of Counseling Psychology,* 1969, *16,* 185–190.

Orlinski, D., & Howard, K. The relation of process to outcome in psychotherapy. In S. Garfield & A. Bergin (Eds.), *Handbook of psychotherapy and behavior change: An empirical analysis.* New York: John Wiley and Sons, 1979.

Parloff, M. Waskow, I., & Wolfe, B. Research on therapist variables in relation to process and outcome. In S. Garfield & A. Bergin (Eds.), *Handbook of psychotherapy and behavior change: An empirical analysis.* New York: John Wiley and Sons, 1978.

Patterson, C. H. A current view of client-centered or relationship therapy. *School Psychologist,* 1969, *1,* 2–25.

Polster, E., & Polster, M. *Gestalt therapy integrated.* New York: Brunner/Mazel, 1973.

Robinson, F. *Principles and procedures in student counseling.* New York: Harper & Brothers Publishers, 1950.

Rogers, C. *Counseling and psychotherapy.* Boston: Houghton Mifflin, 1942.

———. *Client-centered therapy.* Boston: Houghton Mifflin, 1951.

———. The necessary and sufficient conditions of therapeutic personality change. *Journal of Counseling Psychology,* 1957, *21,* 95–103.

Rotter, J. *Social learning and clinical psychology.* Englewood Cliffs, N.J.: Prentice-Hall, 1954.

Ruesch, J., & Kees, W. *Nonverbal communication.* Berkeley: University of California Press, 1956.

Scheflen, A. The significance of posture in communication systems. *Psychiatry,* 1964, *27,* 316.

Shaffer, L. & Shoben, E. *The psychology of adjustment.* Boston: Houghton Mifflin, 1956.

Smith, A. *Communication and culture.* New York: Holt, Rinehart and Winston, 1966.

Smith-Hanen, S. Effects of non-verbal behaviors on judged levels of counselor warmth and empathy. *Journal of Counseling Psychology,* 1977, *24,* 87–91.

Sobelman, S. *The effects of verbal and nonverbal components on the judged level of counselor warmth.* Unpublished doctoral dissertation, American University, 1973.

Spiegel, P., & Machotka, P. *Messages of the body*. New York: The Free Press, 1974.

Strong, S., Wambach, C., Lopez, F., & Cooper, R. Motivational and equipping functions of interpretation in counseling. *Journal of Counseling Psychology*, 1979, *26*, 98–107.

Strupp, H. Psychotherapy, research, and practice: An overview. In S. Garfield, and A. Bergin, (Eds.), *Handbook of psychotherapy and behavior change: An empirical analysis*. New York: John Wiley and Sons, 1978.

Sue, D., & Sue, D. Barriers to effective cross-cultural counseling. *Journal of Counseling Psychology*, 1977, *24*, 420–429.

Sullivan, H. *The psychiatric interview*. New York: W. W. Norton, 1954.

Sundberg, N., & Tyler, L. *Clinical psychology*. New York: Appleton-Century-Crofts, 1962.

Truax, C. Effective ingredients in psychotherapy. *Journal of Counseling Psychology*, 1963, *10*, 256–263.

Truax, C., & Carkhuff, R. Toward effective counseling and psychotherapy. Chicago: Aldine, 1967.

Truax, C., & Mitchell, K. Research on certain therapist interpersonal skills in relation to process and outcome. In S. Garfield & A. Bergin (Eds.) *Handbook of psychotherapy and behavior change: An empirical analysis*. New York: John Wiley and Sons, 1978.

Van Kaam, A. *The art of existential counseling*. Wilkes-Barre: Dimension Books, 1966.

Vondracek, S. I., & Vondracek, F. W. The manipulation and measurement of self-disclosure in preadolescents. *Merrill-Palmer Quarterly*, 1971, *17*, 51–58.

Vontress, C. Racial differences: Impediments to rapport. *Journal of Counseling Psychology*, 1971, *18*, 7–13.

Waxer, P. Non-verbal cues for anxiety: An examination of emotional leakage. *Journal of Abnormal Psychology*, 1977, *86*, 306–314.

Weigel, R. G., Dinges, N., Dyer, R., & Straumfjord, A. A. Perceived self-disclosure, mental health, and who is liked in group treatment. *Journal of Counseling Psychology*, 1972, *19*(1), 47–52.

Whalen, C. Effects of a model and instructions on group verbal behaviors. *Journal of Consulting and Clinical Psychology*, 1969, *33*, 509–531.

Williamson, E. G. The meaning of communication in counseling. *Personnel and Guidance Journal*, 1959, *38*, 6–14.

Wolpe, J., & Lazarus, M. *Behavior therapy techniques*. New York: Pergamon Press, 1966.

Worthy, G. Self-disclosure as an exchange process. *Journal of Personality and Social Psychology*, 1969, *13*, 59–63.

INITIATING COUNSELING

CHAPTER THIRTEEN

"The initial interview is the hardest part of our task—the part that demands from us the most intensive concentration. Each person constitutes for us a new adventure in understanding. Each is destined to broaden our own lives in directions as yet uncharted. Each initial interview renews our appreciation of the challenge and the fascination of the counseling task" (Tyler, 1969, p. 63). The principal task in the first interview is to establish a good relationship so that the client feels comfortable enough to present and work on the problem. Many factors may affect the kind of relationship that is established. Even before the client sees the counselor, various factors may have influenced the ease with which rapport can be established. In a school or college, the reputation of the counselor and counseling center may facilitate or hinder the beginning of counseling. The degree of anxiety the client is experiencing when he or she comes to the counselor's office will also affect the ease of establishing rapport. The client is aware of a problem and wants to talk with the counselor, but even a self-referral may be struggling with whether or not to confide in the counselor. Immediate impressions of the counselor will also affect a client's early attitudes.

The counselor must be sensitive to a client's feelings, attitudes, and expectations as the latter enters counseling. This chapter explores client expectations and preferences and how they are involved in the initial interview, and the goals, phases, and some counselor behaviors in the interview.

CLIENT EXPECTATIONS AND PREFERENCES

All people approaching a new experience have preconceptions of the events before them and certain perceptions of their role and the role of others in this situation. These preconceptions influence individuals' behavior in the new environment. Both people approaching counseling have apprehensions and anticipations about the forthcoming relationship. Both will bring to the interview certain preferences and expectations of counseling that may affect their behavior.

The counselor should be aware of his or her own frame of reference and attempt to operate from it while also being aware of the client's frame of reference. The counselor must have a construct of both participants. An awareness of the client's expectations will help the counselor meet the latter at the level of those expectations.

Most writers in the field concede the importance of the client's expectations as a factor in the counseling process; however, there is conflicting evidence on the impact of those expectations on both the process and outcome. Duckro, Beal, and George (1979) commented that so much has been written about the importance of client role expectations that failure to confirm those expectations has come to be accepted as having negative consequences. They reported that despite the virtually unquestioned status of this assumption, empirical studies are evenly divided on this idea. In view of these findings, Duckro et al. suggested that the area of research on role expectations be viewed cautiously. The client's previous expectations do not have to interfere with the counseling relationship if the counselor is skilled in handling these expectations and deals with them as part of the counseling process. In Gladstein's study (1969) clients were dissatisfied only when they had received "no benefits." They were satisfied if they received some type of help, regardless of whether their stated expectations were met. Clients frequently come to interviews with more than one expectation and are generally satisfied if some of these are met. Therefore, counselors need to be alert to the multiple expectations that clients bring to the interview.

Ziemelis (1974) examined how the initial counseling interview process and outcome were affected by assigning clients to a more preferred or less preferred counselor and then giving them either a positive, neutral, or negative expectation regarding the assignment. Clients were then assigned to counselors who would be congruent or incongruent with their expectations. The clients completed a form designating the conditions they preferred in an interview with the counselor. Positive expectations of the interview were influenced and induced by an experimenter's telling clients they would receive a counselor they preferred, negative expectations by telling them they would not be able to have a counselor they preferred, and neutral expectations by not discussing the matter. The quality of the counseling relationship was rated by analyzing the counseling tapes with an interaction scale. Ziemelis reported that clients who received their preferred counselor conditions had more favorable outcomes than did those with less preferred assignments. Both positive and neutral expectancy clients received a more favorable counseling outcome than did those with a negative expectancy. Although the preferences for counselors are important, most clients showed increased preference for the counselors they saw regardless of congruence or incongruence between their expectations and the actual counseling experiences. This supports Gladstein's findings that client expectations and preferences can be changed to provide good counseling relationships.

ROLE INDUCTION

To provide a precounseling framework for the client who is beginning counseling, a counselor may use a "role induction interview." In this interview the counselor explains to the client what will take place in counseling. The client is also provided with a realistic expectation of improvement, but this is not the major purpose of the interview. Several investigations have reported positive results suggesting that role induction interviews improve the effectiveness of counseling. According to Childress and Gillis (1977), in addition to an explanation the role induction interview provides social and situational influences that increase the client's belief in or commitment to counseling.

Highlen and Voight (1978) found that cognitive and behavioral strategies combining instruction, modeling, and rehearsal resulted in significant changes in affective self-disclosure immediately following the training. Scheiderer (1977) investigated four preinterview conditions and found that detailed instructions significantly increased problem and nonproblem self-disclosure and decreased impersonal self-description and impersonal discussion. Modeling produced a significant effect in the same direction but with a lesser magnitude. Modeling produced no additional effect when combined with the instructions. The instructed clients rated their sessions as more effective and their counselors as more concerned than did other clients, and the counselors tended to rate the information given by instructed clients as more useful in developing a treatment strategy.

Another investigation that offered support for preinterview training reported that in both laboratory and nonlaboratory settings clients exposed to high-disclosing models were significantly more willing to engage in self-disclosure than were individuals exposed to a low-disclosing model. This study showed that pretraining facilitation of willingness to self-disclose can occur without the model's being in the interview with the client (Thase & Page, 1977).

Preparation programs have also been established to ready clients for the counseling process. These programs try to help clients understand the counselor's assumptions so that they will be better able to participate in the process. Many of the programs have been directed at lower-class clients to reduce the frequency with which they drop out of counseling. Heitler (1976), in a review of preparation programs designed for lower-class and unsophisticated clients, concluded that a variety of techniques held promise for facilitating a therapeutic alliance. Although these studies focused primarily on lower-class populations it seems reasonable that preparation would help all clients to view counseling as less mysterious and make them more comfortable in the counseling process.

Orienting counselors to special populations or to the special needs of their clients would further enhance improvement in counseling. Jacobs, Charles, Jacobs, Weinstein, and Mann (1972) found an increased percentage of successful outcomes when counselors were oriented to the special needs of a lower-class population in advance of treatment, when the clients were given an orientation to counseling, and particularly when both participants were given role preparation.

CONCLUSION

According to Rogers (1957), the helping relationship requires that the client and counselor be in psychological contact. A client who has certain expectations of counseling and a counselor who has different ones may be talking in the same room, but they are not in psychological contact. Clients may want information, whereas counselors may want psychological problems. For the experience to be meaningful, they must get together. It is important for the counselor to accept and work with clients even before they have become aware of and are willing to admit emotional problems. The counselor must be willing and able to talk with clients about those problems at the clients' current level of thinking.

Many counselors have difficulty grasping this point. Often their early studies have so overemphasized techniques that they enter a counseling relationship with limited knowledge of how to respond to meet the client's true needs, not just her or his initial expectations. If counselors are confused about the true nature and the controlled involvement of the relationship, and the client is even more naive, how can growth occur? It may be that counselors need a planned, gradual introduction to the personal involvement required in the counseling relationship as well as increased self-awareness before they can meet the personal needs of a client. With this preparation the counselor can structure the counseling interview appropriately for the client.

VARIABLES THAT INFLUENCE INITIATING COUNSELING

SOCIAL CLASS

Research studies on social class have found that lower-class individuals are less likely to be accepted for treatment, less likely to be assigned to intensive counseling, and are more likely to drop out early. For those who remain in counseling, however, there do not seem to be significant differences in outcome for individuals from different social classes (Lorion, 1973).

Parloff, Waskow, and Wolfe (1978), in reviewing the research on social class variables, indicated that little has been reported on the influence of the counselor's class background and characteristics, attitudes, and biases that might be related to differences in treatment based on differences in social class. Writers in this area have emphasized that middle-class counselors prefer to work with clients like themselves who share their values, speak their language, with whom they feel comfortable and able to communicate, and whom they consider good candidates for insight therapy. It has been suggested that middle-class counselors may not be able to establish rapport, understand and empathize, or communicate effectively with lower-class clients, and that most practicing counselors are middle class by reason of their educational and professional status. This has serious implications. Another perspective, however, suggests that what is significant is not the current social class of the counselor, but his or her original social class. It is assumed that counselors who have backgrounds and experiences similar to those of their clients will be able to understand and respond to them more effectively. Even so, not all individuals of lower-class backgrounds share similar experiences and values, nor do they communicate well with each other. Nevertheless, some knowledge and experience of comparable social classes may aid in communication and the counseling relationship.

Counselors who are more successful in treating lower-class clients tend to be particularly good at identifying and actively dealing with issues related to class and race differences between themselves and their clients (Terestman, Miller, & Weber, 1974).

In two approaches that have been specifically suggested for working with lower-class individuals—brief crisis-oriented counseling and behavioral counseling—counselor attitudes do not seem to be as important as they do in more traditional, insight-oriented therapy (Lorion, 1974). It is often suggested that the lower-class client responds more favorably to increased counselor activity and that the counselor should therefore use a specific, goal-oriented approach. There is concern, however, that two systems of counseling would develop, one for lower-class and one for higher-class clients. It seems more reasonable to identify differences among clients in both groups and to use treatment approaches that meet their specific needs.

SEX

Some writers have questioned traditional counseling practices, claiming that many mental health institutions and counselors perpetuate sex role stereotypes and thus may harm clients by training them to conform to socially defined roles and adjust to unhealthy life situations. Some people doubt that a male counselor can be helpful to a female client; others who are sympathetic to the feminist perspective suggest that although some males may be helpful, it may be more advantageous for a female client to be treated by a female counselor, who may function as a role model, facilitate expression of feelings, and communicate empathy. Rawlings and Carter (1977) indicated that in particular situations a female counselor is the more appropriate choice.

Although most concerns about sex roles in counseling have focused on females, some attention has been given to counseling of and by males. Toomer (1978) concluded that male clients often enter counseling expecting male counselors to be experts who will help them polish competitive skills or defenses. Clients' expectations of authority may also put pressure on the male counselor to perform early in counseling. A counselor should be aware of how he may explicitly or subtly encourage competition with male clients during counseling or encourage them to become even more controlling or emotionally stifled. The literature suggests that male dyads in counseling tend to lack expression of feeling; therefore, counselors should evaluate their own biases and comfort with the expression of feelings. Toomer suggested that male counselors ask who they are to a given client at a specific time in the relationship and decide how they can best respond to further client's growth.

The considerable research regarding sex role, stereotypes, and sex matching seems to report conflicting findings. As Parloff et al. (1978) pointed out, it may well be the attitudes and values of the counselor that are of primary importance, not the sex of the client. It is apparent that counselors need sensitivity to sex role issues and more knowledge about the psychology of females and the role of social and environmental factors in women's problems.

RACE

Concern for racial differences has become more apparent as a result of the ineffectiveness of traditional helping agencies in counseling black clients. Jourard and Lasakow (1958) found lower self-disclosure among blacks than among whites of the same class and educational level: white females disclosed most, then white males, then black females, with black males disclosing least. Wolkon (1973) presented supporting evidence. White clients manifested significantly higher self-disclosure scores than did middle-class blacks, but there were no differences between middle- and lower-class blacks. These studies support the view of Grier and Cobbs (1968) that black individuals emphasize self-expression by "playing it cool" and thus hesitate to reveal themselves psychologically.

Wolkon (1973) found that black clients have a preference for black counselors; 75 percent of the lower-class black and 70 percent of the middle-class black sample preferred counselors of the same race. Of the white sample, only 28 percent preferred a white counselor, and 72 percent claimed that the race of a counselor was unimportant. There were significant differences between middle-class blacks and whites regarding preference of the race of the counselor. However, there was no significant difference between the preferences of middle- and lower-class blacks.

In their review of research on race of the counselor, Parloff et al. (1978) stated that not much definitive information is available about the effects of race per se or of intra- or interracial matching on the outcome of counseling. Some studies indicate some benefits to communication and to feeling of satisfaction in same-race pairs in single-interview situations, and some short-term process differences in actual counseling; however, there are almost no findings on outcome. There are studies suggesting that white counselors can be of help to black clients. However, whether white counselors are as helpful as black counselors cannot be inferred, for the studies did not have comparison groups.

Research on the importance of racial similarity has frequently used single-interview or analogue studies of counselor and client race. Although there are shortcomings in these types of studies, Griffith (1977) cited some of them as major evidence for his conclusions. In his view, the limited research does support clinical observations that racial differences have a somewhat negative effect on counseling and that racial similarities lead to greater self-disclosure and higher ratings of the relationship with the counselor. In another review Sattler (1977) included some additional studies and reached the conclusion that for the most part the counselor's race is not a significant variable in affecting performance and reactions in nonclinical initial interviews. The generalizability of these results remains questionable because they are primarily single-interview, nontherapy analogues. In terms of other, established evidence on changes in client attitudes and expectations from the time of the initial interview on into the counseling process, one would expect many clients to change their preconceptions about the counseling process and the race of their counselor. What may be more important than the counselor's race is her or his attitude toward understanding people with different backgrounds and the counselor's previous experience with such individuals.

CROSS-CULTURAL COUNSELING

A counselor must guard against misinterpretation of behaviors and become aware of many aspects of counseling that may be antipathetic to the values of clients from different backgrounds. A counselor should consider the interaction of class, language, and cultural factors on client communication and behavior. The literature on cross-cultural counseling suggests that the counselor should become more action-oriented in initiating counseling and structuring the counseling interview. The counselor can also be more active in helping clients cope with social problems of immediate concern, rather than focusing on discussion, leaving later work to the client.

Because counseling is a process of interpersonal interaction and communication, the counselor and client must be able to send and receive appropriate and accurate verbal and nonverbal messages. Sue and Sue (1977) claimed that although breakdown in communication occurs among members of the same culture, the problem is aggravated among people of different racial or ethnic backgrounds. The misunderstandings that arise from cultural differences in communication may lead to alienation or an inability to develop trust and rapport. From their review of the literature, Sue and Sue concluded that approximately 50 percent of Asian Americans, blacks, Chicanos, and native Americans terminate counseling after only one session, in contrast to a 30 percent termination rate for Anglo-American clients.

Padilla, Ruiz, and Alvarez (1975) identified three major factors that hinder the formation of a good counseling relationship with a Latino population: (1) a language barrier may exist between the counselor and client, (2) classbound values may induce the counselor to conduct treatment within a middle-class value system, and (3) culturebound values are used to judge normality and abnormality in clients. All three variables interact to hinder and distort communications.

Counseling is often described as a white, middle-class activity with many values and characteristics different from those of Third World groups. Sue and Sue (1977) described three major characteristics of counseling that may act as a source of conflict with individuals from the Third World groups. First, because most approaches to counseling emphasize verbal, emotional, and behavioral expressiveness and the attainment of insight, counselors often expect clients to exhibit some degree of openness and psychological orientation. Second, counseling is usually a one-to-one activity that encourages clients to discuss the most intimate aspects of their lives, and individuals who resist doing so may be regarded as resistant or defensive. Third, the counseling situation is often ambiguous, with the client encouraged to discuss problems while the counselor listens and responds. This relatively unstructured situation forces the client to be the primary active participant.

Four additional factors identified as general characteristics of counseling include (1) a monolingual orientation in which "good" standard English is predominantly the vehicle of communication, (2) emphasis on long-range goals, (3) distinction between physical and mental well-being, and (4) emphasis on cause-and-effect relationships.

Table 13–1 presents some generic characteristics of counseling which Sue and Sue (1977) summarized and compared with the values of Third World groups: Asian Americans, blacks, Chicanos, and native Americans.

Although it is important for counselors to understand the discrepancies between counseling characteristics and Third World life values, there is a danger of overgeneralizing. It is important that each client be understood as an individual.

Three major variables are often inseparable. Those who are unable to use standard English are definitely at a disadvantage. The culture and class values that govern conversation can also operate through language to cause other serious misunderstandings. Certainly, individuals from predominantly lower-class backgrounds combine class and cultural variations in communication. Even so, Sue and Sue (1977) identified the three separate barriers as language, classbound values, and culturebound values.

Using standard English to communicate with clients may unfairly discriminate against those from bilingual backgrounds such as Asian Americans, Chicanos, and native Americans. This may be true even for clients who do not speak their group's language. Black clients who come from a subculture may use words and phrases not entirely understood by the counselor, and for some blacks nonstandard English is the norm. Their language involves a great deal of implicit communication, with shorter sentences and less grammatical elaboration. A client could be seen as uncooperative, negative, nonverbal, or repressed on the basis of language expression alone.

Class values are also important in considering counseling relationships because Third World clients are disproportionately represented in the lower socioeconomic classes. Many of these individuals have different expectations of counseling. They may be more concerned with survival or success on a temporary basis and may simply want advice and suggestions from the counselor. When the counselor attempts to explore personality dynamics or the history of the problem, the client may become confused and frustrated. It has often been stated that counselors have a preference for exhibiting the YAVIS syndrome, that is, the young, attractive, verbal, intelligent, and successful characteristics. This preference discriminates against people from different minority groups or those in a lower socioeconomic class.

TABLE 13-1 GENERIC CHARACTERISTICS OF COUNSELING

LANGUAGE	MIDDLE CLASS	CULTURE
Standard English Verbal communication	Standard English Verbal communication Adherence to time schedules (50-minute session) Long-range goals Ambiguity	Standard English Verbal communication Individual centered Verbal/emotional/behavioral expressiveness Client-counselor communication Openness and intimacy Cause-effect orientation Clear distinction between "physical" and "mental" well-being

THIRD-WORLD GROUP VARIABLES

LANGUAGE	LOWER CLASS	CULTURE
Asian-Americans		
Bilingual background	Nonstandard English Action oriented Different time perspective Immediate, short-range goals Concrete, tangible, structured approach	Asian language Family centered Restraint of feelings One-way communications from authority figure to person. Silence is respect. Advice seeking Well-defined patterns of interaction (concrete structured) Private vs. public display (shame/disgrace/pride) Physical and mental well-being defined differently
Blacks		
Black language	Nonstandard English Action oriented Different time perspective Immediate, short-range goals Concrete, tangible structured approach	Black language Sense of "peoplehood" Action oriented "Paranorm" due to oppression Importance placed on nonverbal behavior
Chicanos		
Bilingual background	Nonstandard English Action oriented Different time perspective Immediate, short-range goals Concrete, tangible, and structured approach	Spanish speaking Group-centered cooperation Temporal difference Family orientation Different pattern of communication A religious distinction between mind/body

(continued)

TABLE 13–1 *(continued)*

LANGUAGE	LOWER CLASS	CULTURE
	Native Americans	
Bilingual background	Nonstandard English	Tribal dialects
	Action oriented	Cooperative not competitive individualism
	Different time perspective	Present time orientation
	Immediate, short-range goals	Creative/experiential/intuitive/nonverbal
	Concrete, tangible, and structured approach	Satisfy present needs
		Use of folk or supernatural explanations

Source: D. Sue and D. Sue, Barriers to effective cross-cultural counseling. *Journal of Counseling Psychology*, 1977, *24*, pp. 420–429. Copyright 1977 by the American Psychological Association. Reprinted by permission.

One's culture consists in all that the individual has learned to do, believe, value, and enjoy. It includes the ideals, beliefs, skills, tools, customs, and institutions into which each person is born. Several cultural characteristics of counseling contribute to difficulties in counseling individuals from a Third World culture. First, in emphasizing clients' gaining insight into personal dynamics and verbal, emotional, and behavioral expressiveness as goals, counselors are operating from their own cultural values. Yet there are many subcultures that emphasize not revealing personal matters to outsiders. A counselor working with a client from that subculture might assume that he or she is repressed or inhibited rather than following the client's cultural standard. Second, the ambiguous structure of counseling may create discomfort and confusion for some clients. Individuals who have learned in an environment that structures social relationships and patterns of interaction will have a difficult time adjusting to the standard counseling situation. Third, the cultural milieu of some groups dictates patterns of communication different from those indicated in counseling. Counseling usually involves communication from the client to the counselor; groups reared to respect elders and authority figures, however, do not speak until spoken to, and their concepts of role behavior are in conflict with the standard counseling position. Fourth, many Third World cultures have a different concept of mental health and adjustment. Some make no distinction between mental and physical health; therefore, nonphysical problems are most likely to be referred to a physician, priest, or minister. Fifth, most counseling theories tend to be analytical, rational, and verbal and to stress discovering cause-and-effect relationships. Some cultures, however, emphasize the harmonious aspects of the world, intuitive functioning, and a holistic approach instead.

THE INITIAL INTERVIEW

Having explored some of the factors present before the interview, we will focus on the initial interview. The counselor must set goals to be accomplished in this interview. By accomplishing the primary goals, the counselor sets the counseling relationship in motion.

GOALS

Tyler (1969) suggested that there are three things to be accomplished during the initial interview. The most important goal is to lay the foundation for the counseling relationship. The relationship is one of warmth and acceptance in which the counselor communicates that he or she understands or is attempting to understand the client and responds to the client as a genuine human being. The characteristics of a facilitative relationship are covered in detail in Chapter Twelve. According to Tyler, the process of discovering the client's wants, concerns, and sources of self-esteem is likely to produce a warm feeling as a by-product.

A second goal of the initial interview is to begin opening all the psychological realities in the client's situation. Opening up marks a difference between counseling and usual conversation. When a friend expresses anxiety or doubt, the impulse is frequently to reassure the person. In counseling, however, the counselor helps the client to explore more deeply the problem or feelings he or she is trying to express. The degree of client exploration in the initial interview will depend on various circumstances. At this point the counselor will follow the client's train of thought and feelings but will not probe deliberately for hidden meanings.

Within this major goal, Wolberg (1954) listed several other important goals. The counselor will get pertinent information from the client to help establish the tentative dynamics and make a tentative diagnosis. This exploration will permit the counselor tentatively to assess the strengths and weaknesses of the client.

The third goal of the initial interview is to structure the situation for the client. Each counselor will probably give the client some idea of what the counseling is like, what is expected of the client and the counselor, and how to make plans for further work. The purpose of this orientation is to eliminate as many misconceptions as possible and to give the client some idea of what to expect when she or he begins the next interview. The counselor should give the client only as much information as the latter can use at this time.

The goals of the two participants in counseling are potentially significant factors in the counseling relationship. The counselor's goals with a particular client are indexes of the direction in which he or she wants the counseling relationship and the client to move. The client's goals may be expected to influence his or her behavior. Hill (1969) explored the perspectives of client and counselor goals. From analysis of a postcounseling questionnaire on therapeutic experiences, three clusters of counselor goals and seven clusters of client goals were identified. The first cluster of counselor goals aimed at increasing the client's self-understanding and self-awareness. This insight goal was the most frequently endorsed cluster of the counselor sample. The second cluster was described as the supportive goal, in which the counselor sought to support the client's self-esteem and tried to work with the client in solving the problems the latter brought to counseling. The third goal cluster, less frequently endorsed by the counselors, represented a second type of supportive goal aimed at helping the client maintain personal integration, including control of moods, impulses, and thoughts.

Seven clusters of client purposes emerged from the analysis of their responses to the experience of counseling. The clients' most frequently endorsed purpose for seeking counseling paralleled the counselors' insight goal. The clients' primary purpose for seeking counseling was defined as the desire for greater understanding of feelings and behavior. The clients desiring insight also included the purpose of seeking advice on how to deal with their lives and other people. The second cluster of client goals was an involvement-seeking interview which included a desire for help in talking, help in controlling moods, thoughts, and actions, a desire to work on a person-to-person basis with the counselor, and a desire for the counselor to be frank about what she or he related to the client. The third cluster of client goals aimed at catharsis, reflected in a wish to unburden themselves in relating to the problem. The fourth cluster of goals was to gain relief from tension and to get to know the counselor as a person. The fifth cluster focused specifically on support seeking; clients wanted reassurance from the counselor. The sixth and seventh clusters were infrequently endorsed intentions to demonstrate to the counselor the client's knowledge of improvement and a desire for a more personal response from the counselor. These goal clusters reflect an orientation toward self and situation understanding. Many clients will have more action-oriented goals and will want information, direct counselor intervention, or help in changing behaviors or a situation.

A periodic review of progress can be helpful in motivating the client. It is not just the final goal that is important, but intermediate goals as well. Saltzman, Luetgert, Roth, Creaser, and Howard (1976) reported that the client's sense of "movement" or progress in solving problems as early as the third session is significantly related to client improvement. The counselor and client can not only establish long-term goals but also review short-term goal attainment in the process.

COUNSELOR BEHAVIOR

Preparation for Counseling

The degree of preparation for the first interview will depend on the counselor's concept of her or his function as a counselor, the amount of time available, and, of course, whether the client appears suddenly and unannounced. Many counselors prefer to have a cumulative folder with a great deal of information about the client prior to the initial interview. Other counselors do not want previous information about the client and prefer to start with the latter's initial presentation. They assume that reading information about the client may bias their attitudes toward the client. Other counselors assume that they can learn information more quickly from written information than from talking with the client (Arbuckle, 1965).

History Taking

In some clinical situations the counselor may need a formal case history; others challenge the value of history taking with the client. Those in favor insist that great gaps in information are present when the counselor relies solely on the spontaneous unfolding of the history, and that only a careful inquiry into various aspects of the person's life will reveal a complete picture of what has happened to the client. Without an adequate history, it may take months before the client gets around to talking about an aspect of the problem that may give the counselor an entirely different perspective of the client's situation.

On the other hand, there are many reasons why counselors hesitate to take complete case histories. Exhaustive histories are not necessary from a diagnostic point of view and they are not believed to be of therapeutic value. The therapeutic value of counseling does not consist in collecting information but in helping the client to develop insight and a new outlook leading to changes in behavior (Wolberg, 1954). It may also be argued that asking the client to give a schematic account of himself or herself may increase resistance, leading the client to conceal some significant facts. A client may also assume that once the history is complete, he or she can sit back and expect the counselor to solve the problems. In circumstances that require a case history, many counselors have the client fill out a questionnaire form or have another person do the history taking.

Counselor Role

Buchheimer and Balogh (1961) described the counselor as a collaborator with the client in the process of self-exploration, problem solving, and gaining new perceptions in the client's life situation. This counseling process is both intimate and objective. It is intimate in that the two people become close to each other and the client has freedom to express her or his feelings. It is objective in the sense that the counselor will help examine and clarify the client's feelings and attitudes. For many clients this will be a new kind of experience and relationship. Counselors hope that the client will not feel the need to maintain a facade as in most social relationships. Experiencing a facilitative relationship will lead the client to be open and make self-exploration easier in this objective partnership. In this complex role as a collaborator, the counselor is not a peer, but neither does the counselor want to be perceived as a superior. This position is difficult to communicate to the client.

Saltzman et al. (1976), in a study of clients' perceptions of the counseling process, found that clients in a university counseling service who perceived themselves as expressing thoughts and feelings with greater openness early in counseling had significantly better outcomes than did clients who perceived themselves as less open in talking with their counselors. Also, clients who felt they had a better understanding of what their counselors were trying to communicate to them also had significantly better outcomes than did less comprehending clients.

It is important for the counselor to be sensitive to what is happening in the interview. The counselor must be aware that several factors are influencing the situation and must make responses that seem most likely to bring about progress. During the first interview the counselor will want to determine what type of problem the client is presenting. From his research on the types of counselor behaviors in interviews, Robinson (1950) suggested that a simple decision as to whether it is a skill or adjustment problem will affect the counselor's behavior. Experienced counselors tend to change their behavior in dealing with these two types.

The counselor will also be concerned with the motivation exhibited by the client. An anxious client who feels a need for counseling will be more highly motivated than a client who is referred or called in to see the counselor. A motivated client will usually keep the interview on the topic even when a counselor misses a point, whereas a less motivated client will be much resistant to talking about himself or herself and the situation. Working with the latter type of client constitutes one of a counselor's major difficulties. The major goal of the counselor in this interview is to overcome the client's resistance and low motivation by providing a relationship that will make the client feel secure enough to reveal her or his problems. When clients realize that the counseling situation offers no threat to their control of their own development and that counseling is a source of help but not domination, they may be motivated to express themselves.

The counselor will also want to assess the client's stage of insight. If a client has been active in thinking through the problem, his or her behavior and that of the counselor will be different from that of the client who is overwhelmed by the problem. Robinson (1950) emphasized that the counselor's communication should keep the client motivated, help the client gain insight into the problem, and make the client willing to accept what is discovered and needed.

Usually a counseling interview will be more effective if the client seeks help on her or his own rather than being referred. Once the client appears, the counselor must provide an atmosphere that makes it easier for the client to discuss the problem. Successful interviews are structured so that the client remains motivated throughout the necessary number of interviews; that is, until the client can gain insight and internalized methods to solve the problem and change behavior. The goal of moving toward self-insight suggests that the client must be provided with an optimum relationship for thinking through the problem. Under these conditions the client can frequently gain new insights independently into his or her efforts or gain help through the contribution of the counselor's ideas. Once the client has a new understanding of feelings and attitudes, he or she can slowly try out new behaviors in an effort to cope more effectively with the situation.

A client often verbalizes a personal problem vaguely and poorly, so the first step in solving the problem is to be able to see it clearly. The counselor must help the client overcome feelings of distaste and embarrassment in facing the problems, especially before another person.

Robinson (1955) stated that research studies have shown four dimensions of counselor behavior to be useful in the interview: an acceptance attitude, responding to the core of what the client says, division of responsibility, and degree of lead.

The counselor should frame remarks so that the acceptance attitude is evident. As the chart in Chapter Eleven indicates, counselors vary in their ideas from considering this the most important part of their relationship to merely calling it interested friendliness.

In dealing with the core of the client's remarks, the counselor must be sensitive to the real problems brought out by the client. The counselor must avoid responding to irrelevant cues and be careful not to diagnose the problem according to his or her thinking rather than the client's. The counselor may respond to the core of the theme beyond the content the client is communicating.

Division of responsibility in the counseling interview is determined to a great extent by the problem to be solved. Usually at the beginning of the interview the client has a responsibility for stating the problem. That responsibility continues as the client explores a personal problem, and the counselor assumes a listening role. However, the counselor follows the client's remarks closely to help the interview along as necessary. When the client has a skill problem or needs information, the counselor assumes more responsibility for the interview once the problem has been stated. The division of responsibility tends to differ not only with the type of problem but also in handling a given problem from moment to moment. As long as the client is progressing, she or he is allowed to carry primary responsibility, but when the client encounters momentary difficulties the counselor may intervene. Thus, primary responsibility shifts back and forth in a collaborative relationship in which neither person feels that he or she alone has responsibility for the relationship.

The amount of lead that a counselor assumes in her or his remarks depends upon the client's needs and interests. The situation is analogous to a ladder: the counselor's remarks should be at the next rung above the client's thinkings in order to stimulate development. This next level should be close enough that it can be easily understood and accepted by the client and not arouse resistance (Robinson, 1955). A description of various leads is presented in the section on communication techniques in Chapter Twelve.

Action Orientation

Most research studies indicate that lower-class clients are less likely to seek counseling and that, when referred, many are likely to drop out of counseling in a very short time. Given this lower rate of success and a higher rate of dropout, it is especially important in these cases to motivate the client in the initial interview. Baum and Felzer (1964) believed that early, flexible, and meaningful activity in the initial interview is essential to establishing a therapeutic relationship. Such activity should be geared to discussing the expectations of the client, as well as his or her understanding of counseling and how it works. As a result of the studies that describe the inaccessibility of the lower social class client, many authors have recommended changes in counseling technique. The concept is appropriate for all clients. Researchers believe it is wasteful to provide insight counseling to lower socioeconomic class clients. It is up to the counselor, not the client, to assess the client's motivation, work with it, and try to develop it in the initial session. The clients frequently have no clear concept about the possibility that counseling may provide help and see little relationship between talking and the resolution or elimination of their conflicts or problems. They are fearful about counseling and tend to look for direction from an authority figure. Theorists suggest that the counselor should provide more reeducation and preparatory work to stimulate the client, particularly in the initial interview.

Baum and Felzer (1964) pointed out that there is difficulty in establishing a common area of understanding. Counselors should resist trying to make a client out of someone who is not interested in becoming one. The strong tendency to let the interviews carry themselves may work with better motivated and more sophisticated clients. The counselor may not be able to persuade all clients that insight is a desirable goal. According to Baum and Felzer, there should be early, meaningful activity in the relationship. Activity means a flexible and spontaneous initiative applied to the particular needs of each client to bring about an optimum bridge of communication, whether it involves active listening and observing or explaining and educating the client about counseling. At other times the counselor may be active in describing the resistances the client has to counseling. The client must be encouraged to air her or his concept of the problem and expectations of counseling. It is important for the counselor to communicate whatever is happening in straightforward language.

CLIENT BEHAVIOR

Successful counseling requires the client's active participation. Through this participation the client expresses motivation for help. The higher the motivation, the more the client sacrifices in order to participate, and the harder he or she tries to participate adequately. The more adequate the participation, the more sensitive and attentive the client is to cues for participation, and the more opposed to disruptions of counseling. The client's performance is a measure of her or his motivation and contributes to successful outcomes.

Preparation for Counseling

Several studies have suggested that preparation of clients not only reduces attrition but also strongly affects client improvement. Parloff et al. (1979) concluded that regardless of the type of induction procedure used, some orientation regarding the nature of counseling will improve clients or involve them more in the treatment, encourage them to remain, and help them to achieve more improvement. Clients have been prepared for counseling with interviews, tape-recorded models, or filmed models.

Client Role

What constitutes a client's proper role in counseling? Krause (1967) described some of the common features of the client's role. The client's prompt, unfailing attendance and serious use of the counseling session is the first feature. A second feature of the client's role is a detailed description of the problem, its precipitating and accompanying circumstances, its consequences, the participants and their roles, the gratification and distress it yields, its course of development and the client's handling of it, and the future possibilities for its maintenance or resolution. The client may spontaneously describe the problem situation or the counselor may participate, offering some statements or clarifications to help the client with this part of her or his role. A third feature of the client's role is to be responsive to the counselor's communication. The client should listen, work to understand, and respond to the counselor's communication. Finally, counseling cannot succeed if the client restricts involvement in the counseling process to the interview hour. There are matters to think about, notice, avoid, or try out between counseling sessions. This outside work is a fourth feature of the client's role.

Appropriate motivation for counseling is identical with motivation for proper role performance: the harder a client tries to learn and enact the role, the more motivated he or she will be for counseling. Therefore, a display of motivation for a specific type of counseling requires both knowledge of one's role in it and the motivation to learn and perform it. Even though the client is motivated, she or he may have to test the counselor prior to full involvement.

Client Testing

Counselors are familiar with the idea that clients test them before divulging more personal information. Older (1972) discussed both interpersonal testing and pseudo-testing in the counseling relationship. Testing is a contrived transaction designed to secure reassuring information before trusting the counselor. It is a means of uncovering any concealed qualities to determine whether trust is warranted. Pseudo-testing is a futile and unconscious attempt to overcome feelings of worthlessness through another person's responses to a testlike manipulation. Pseudo-testing clients manipulate the counselor into acting toward them in a way that they can interpret as an indication of their own worth.

Although testing is a contrived transaction, it is not necessarily conscious. It may be a preconscious activity, for when a counselor asks the client directly if she or he has been testing, a common response is a "somewhat sheepish grin of recognition." In testing, the client extends a "feeler" to the counselor by describing something about herself or himself that the tester thinks the counselor may not be able to deal with in a way that is acceptable to the client. The counselor passes or fails the test on the strength of the response to the "feeler." The pass or fail is based on whether the counselor's response is reassuring to the client.

This procedure involves some deviousness. The test is designed so that the counselor does not know he or she is being tested because the client wants to find out about the counselor's real feelings and attitudes. The client may not accept the usual communication but designs a transaction to see if something different lurks beneath the counselor's surface communication. In addition, the tester assigns greater meaning to the response than its face value. The client gives the counselor a safe, or substitute, topic first. This substitute topic is designed to evoke the same kind of response as a more personal problem that the client is afraid to risk trusting the counselor with. If the counselor responds to the feeler in a reassuring way, she or he passes the test and opens the door to trust. If the test is not passed, one of two things can happen. If the response does not provide enough information, the counselor will be subjected to another test and possibly even another after that. If the test is failed outright, the client will postpone trust and closeness or terminate the relationship. Trust and closeness in a counseling relationship develop gradually as feelings emerge and more personal problems are discussed. Passing a test during the initial interview does not ensure against future tests.

Older (1972) suggested some typical areas of testing. One is the test of control. A client may be afraid of losing control of a decision regarding what feelings are to be discussed in counseling. Instead of confronting the counselor with the real fear, the client might ask for a change of appointment hour for an obviously trumped-up reason. If the request is granted, the client may consider that he or she has control within the counseling hour. A second area of testing involves independence. A client who fears being dominated or incorporated by others has to make sure that the counselor respects her or his wishes and needs and, ultimately, independence as an individual. The client may make a demand such as a change of interview time as a means of self-reassurance of being capable of making his or her own decisions. Another area is the test of love. In one form or another this is the most common test. A client may be afraid that the counselor does not care enough for her or him but does not trust the counselor enough to ask. Asking for a change in appointment is really asking whether the counselor cares enough to change the appointment. It is apparent that tests may have the same appearance but carry different motives.

Pseudo-testing is a client's attempt to overcome feelings of worthlessness through the counselor's responses to testlike manipulation. The client manipulates the counselor into acting toward him or her in a way that the client can interpret as an indication of his or her own worth. Like the tester, the pseudo-tester looks for a reassuring sign from the counselor, but major differences exist between the two. The pseudo-tester needs reassurance about self-worth instead of about the trustworthiness of the counselor. This need may be more conscious than the need that underlies true testing. Perhaps most important from the counselor's point of view, the sign that the client desires cannot provide the reassurance she or he wants. In the long run, the pseudo-test is almost certain to fail. In the example of asking the counselor to change the interview time, what makes pseudo-testing different from testing? No matter how many times the sign was given, the client's need for it would remain undiminished. A client testing the counselor's love could redesign and stop the tests.

When a possible testing situation occurs early in counseling, the counselor will not know if the client's behavior is a test, pseudo-test, or a legitimate request. The counselor will have to respond honestly and personally by trusting the client, whether it is a legitimate issue or a test. If it turns out to be a pseudo-test, the counselor will need to handle it in another stage of the counseling process.

PHASES IN THE INTERVIEW

Buchheimer and Balogh (1961) divided the initial interview into three phases: statement of the problem, exploration, and the closing and planning for the future. This framework represents a goal-directed approach to the interview. It is only a guide, and the counselor should not attempt to force the interview into any particular pattern. A progression through the initial interview would be from the counselor-client agreement on the problem on which they are going to work, to exploration of this problem, to the client's incentive to become involved in a counseling relationship, to resolution of the problem through self-understanding, to action based on the understanding.

Statement of the Problem

Clients are people in quest, but they may be only dimly aware of the nature of that quest or the path to attain it. They may not be able to see any way to solve their problem. The quest may stem from dissatisfaction with themselves, others may have indicated dissatisfaction with them, or they may be dissatisfied with others. Clients' concerns may be related to personal development and typical tasks related to development. It could be educational-vocational or more closely involved with personal and social concerns. The problems clients are able to state at the beginning of counseling are what they are able to acknowledge at the time; they may not represent their major concerns. It is important for the counselor to give clients freedom of self-expression, the opportunity to describe themselves in terms of environment, problems, and goals. The counselor must be careful, however, not to assume that there is always some underlying problem (Buchheimer & Balogh, 1961).

During the first part of the interview clients are given an opportunity to express their problem and what they are interested in. They may describe themselves and their view of life. If this information is sufficient for the counselor, then no further information need be gathered. However, if the counselor is concerned with doing a great deal beforehand, it is important to obtain background information in a systematic and discriminating way. The counselor may conduct a structured intake interview to elicit significant background information. This background information should deal with the specific client's self-perceptions, personal constructs, and perception of environment.

As clients begin to state their problems they will present a perception of themselves in a particular situation. There may be some hesitancy because they cannot accurately verbalize these feelings. Clients may describe one or more symptoms at this point, and some of them may not be related to the main problem. The counselor's use of general leads or reflections about the symptoms should allow clients to give a more complete picture of their main concern and the history of their problem. The clients will talk spontaneously and should not be interrupted. When there is a pause the counselor may encourage clients to continue by showing interest through careful attention and nonverbal communication.

Clients who are particularly anxious may deluge the counselor with unimportant details designed to keep the counselor off balance and to allow them to minimize their anxiety by controlling the content of the interview. The counselor may need to subtly focus clients' attention on the main aspects of their problem.

The counselor tries to indicate both verbally and nonverbally that she or he is interested in what a client has to say. This is the first actively helpful thing the counselor can do for the client. Clients frequently apologize for coming in with their problem. They may say that others have more serious problems and that theirs are really not very important. The counselor assures clients that he or she is interested in hearing more about what they have to say and communicates that he or she considers them worth the time. It is not unusual for clients to be excessively formal, restrained in behavior, to use formal speech patterns, and in other ways invest the counselor with authority (Holland, 1965). The counselor's verbal assurances and nonverbal expressions of interest contribute to the clients' sense of being of significance.

The counselor is predominantly receptive in the initial interview. A client may express uncertainty about what to say, and the counselor indicates confidence in this judgment by suggesting that the client say whatever he or she feels is important at the time. The counselor will use the communication techniques of reflection and clarification to direct the client's content and feelings to gain better understanding of what the client is experiencing.

At the first contact with the client, the counselor begins unobtrusive observation and initial assessment. Observation should include dress, carriage, walk, facial expression, and any special mannerisms. Observation of the client continues throughout the interview. Initial assessment is tentative and any conclusions are subject to later verification (Wolberg, 1954).

When opening the interview the counselor sets the tone for the rest of the counseling session. It is therefore important for the counselor to exhibit warmth and interest. What happens in the opening moments of the interview can either facilitate or hinder communication in the rest of the session.

The principal objective of the initial interview is to establish a working relationship. Without this relationship there is no counseling progress. All tasks must be subordinate to this objective and its achievement. Premature exploration of provocative conflicts will hamper the counseling process. The client will be unable to endure the anxiety or cope with the resistance that is present even in the early parts of the interviews. The attitudes of respect, trust, and confidence in the counselor must be established.

The client must be motivated to work with the counselor. If the client has been referred and has a low level of motivation, the counselor will have to concentrate on creating incentives for counseling, postponing any work on the dynamics of the client until the latter is more strongly motivated.

It is necessary to clarify the purpose of the interview so the client will be aware of the situation and his or her relationship to the counselor. When attempting to establish goals, the counselor may discover that the client's expectations are far beyond what is attainable. Some discussion of this with explorations of possibilities should take place. Resolution may have to wait until additional information is gathered later in the interview.

The counselor may also have to remove misconceptions about counseling. Movies and periodicals have depicted counselors as eccentrics, and the client may therefore be somewhat apprehensive. Others come to counseling filled with fear that the counselor can read minds. Other misconceptions may burden the counseling effort and interfere with a proper counseling relationship.

Wolberg (1954) discussed some of the resistances that frequently occur early in counseling. Clients may boycott any attempt to convince them that they can be helped. They have invested in inappropriate behavior certain needs and continue to act on them. Others may refuse to accept the counselor's ideas of counseling because they have ideas of what should happen and under what conditions they will cooperate. Probably the greatest interferences at this point are clients' habitual interpersonal activities. The client has a life-style, and even though parts of it are causing difficulty, he or she will not want to give it up. Dealing with resistances to a harmonious relationship constitutes the primary pursuit of the opening phases of counseling.

To illustrate the phases in the initial interview, we present an interview with a high school boy. Parts of later interviews with Tom are used in Chapter Fourteen.

C. Good morning, Tom.

S. Good morning.

C. I noticed that you made an appointment for this morning. Anything in particular that you'd like to talk about?

S. Well, I'm not really sure you know what, what it is, what's been happening. I've just been—I suppose some of the teachers have told you—I've been having some trouble—and my work isn't good—I've been in trouble in some of the classes. I don't really know, you know, what's, what's wrong for that matter. They told me I'd better come and see you—I'm not sure exactly what it is.

C. You sound a little bit confused—uh—maybe about what's going on inside of you and what's therefore led to the kind of behavior you're having—that other people are saying . . .

S. (interrupting) Yeah—I don't—in other words I seem to be having a problem—but I'm not sure why—I just don't know what's happened. Ah-h-h school, everything seems different just over the—probably nothing I can put my finger on, you know what I mean—but school just doesn't interest me that much anymore and I find it kind of boring—I just can't put myself into it.

C. It sounds like everything has just sort of lost meaning for you.

S. That meaning's a good—a good word, yeah, because it doesn't make sense, I guess meaning and sense are the same thing. In other words I'd—why should I be doing this, eh, where is it getting me, what for? I don't particularly like school, I always did well, although in the last year you know I haven't done well. Um-m-m, it's not any one thing I can put my finger on. It seems the classes kind of bore me.

C. Gosh, you almost sound hopeless, not just about—not just about classes or grades but—gosh I hear a hopelessness of saying what's the sense of doing anything, there's just no hope for . . .

S. (interrupting) Yeah, where does it get you—what—or not only what, eh—where do you want to go—where am I heading? Um-m if I could see where school was going to get me or why I am here or if I just enjoyed doing it but I don't, ah, you know, I don't see any—let's say that I do stay in school and graduate and go to college, you know I won't be doing it because I want to do it or because I see that it's going to get me someplace—I don't see any place that I really want to get to, I don't see where I'm going to fit in maybe.

C. If you feel this hopeless—that—that doing anything in school or making any sort of plans is so hopeless, I'm wondering if you feel the same way about talking with me?

S. Well, I don't think I would have come, you know, if I—I wasn't forced to come but I don't think I would have, um, I don't think you can answer, you know, you can't tell me what to do. But I'm willing.

C. So you feel enough hope, enough, maybe confidence in yourself or strength in yourself that you're looking for meaning for something to make sense out of life.

S. Well, you kind . . .

C. Maybe we're able to grapple with some of this here and, and maybe out of our discussions we can give you some ideas to make some steps toward . . .

S. I'd like to feel that way, but, you know, I have a kinda hard time . . .

C. I'm sure—but we can work together toward clarifying your feelings. Then maybe you can consider plans about the present as well as the future. Does that make sense to you?

S. Yes, I guess so—OK.

Exploration

Clients will explore themselves when they feel the climate is safe enough. Some clients describe things immediately, others wait until they feel more comfortable. Even when a client explores a problem and cries during the interview, she or he may still not be dealing with the core of her or his feelings or problem, but focusing at a fairly cognitive level on feelings (Buchheimer & Balogh, 1961). Rapport involves comfort in the relationship and mutual confidence between client and counselor. Many people claim that rapport must be established before counseling can begin; therefore, counselors frequently devise techniques designed to establish rapport. Rapport, however, evolves from the relationship between the two people and is not something that can be established. Many counselors begin interviews with small talk in an effort to put the client at ease. If the client has come to the counselor independently, he or she has something to say and five minutes of small talk may only get in the way. If the counselor has initiated the interview, the client is wondering why she or he was called and again has a certain level of anxiety.

The counselor will generally gain pertinent information from the client by listening to a spontaneous account and then focusing on selective information that will continue to move the client toward self-exploration. The counselor will assess the existing dynamics of the client; however, this assessment will need constant revision as new data emerge through the course of counseling. The formulation of existing dynamics will vary according to the counselor's theoretical bases, skill, training, and experience. No matter how skilled and trained the counselor may be, it is frequently impossible to gain understanding of client dynamics in the initial interview. Many of a client's patterns are not identifiable, and many clients are incapable of verbalizing sufficiently to give the counselor an idea about their dynamics. As a rule, several interviews will be required to evaluate the dynamics (Wolberg, 1954). Clients who are able to talk more freely about themselves and their feelings will be more capable of revealing sufficient clues about their problems to enable the counselor to make some tentative assumptions about the dynamics.

As clients describe themselves and their situation, the counselor should note the clients' strengths and weaknesses. It is important to note the areas in which clients are succeeding, for there will be times when the counselor will want to know the areas from which a client draws strength. It is important for the counselor to look for the positive aspects of clients' lives as well as weaknesses. All too frequently, counselors write up interviews describing only defense mechanisms and weaknesses, ignoring the positive parts of the person's life.

C.   Why don't you tell me sort of what you feel behind this hopelessness, what leads to this overall hopeless feeling.

S.   I can't say exactly what it is—it's just there all the time. You know, I used to think that I wanted to be—you know—a success. I wanted to go to college and graduate and be a success and everything just seemed to fit together and I didn't really question things but, ah, as I look around now I don't, I can't, see anything that I want to be, or to do. I don't see, ah, anything very attractive—I don't see where I fit in, I feel that there isn't anything really worth doing and then I don't do anything and then that just makes me feel worse, um, I think maybe . . .

C.   You sound, ah, really awfully lonely you know—sort of isolated, you keep saying that you don't belong—fit in—

S.   Yeah . . .

C.   There is a desperate feeling of not belonging, of not doing anything, and when you don't do anything, you sort of get in trouble.

S. Well that's exactly—where do you belong? How do you find where, who you—that's—gets to who you are—where—who—how do you know who you are and where you fit in and lonely, I don't know, I mean, I have friends and, and you know I have a good girl friend and everything but it, ah, it isn't enough, ah, you know, we do the same things and go to the same places and lately I've been drinking a lot you know and, but it's nowhere, it's just not anywhere, and it's not their fault, and. . . .

C. In playing the game, you know, studying and making those kinds of plans that you used to have are also nowhere—you don't see any sense in going through that routine again.

S. What for, I can't, I just can't do it, as I sit down to do it I can't understand why I'm doing it and you know and then I just give up, so, I guess it brings you to come around to wondering just exactly where you can find where you can find where you're going to fit in or who you are or that sort of thing and I don't know, you know, I don't know what to do—I don't know where to do—I guess I know that no one can tell me—yet—and I see everyone else, not everyone but most people just don't seem that concerned about it, they seem to know what they're doing and why they're doing it but it doesn't make it—doesn't, I don't know, I just don't . . .

C. Pretty damn confusing, isn't it?

S. I don't see what, yeah—how do ya—how do ya go about figuring something like that?

C. It sounds like you've gone along for a number of years with plans and ideas of who you were and where you thought you were going and all of a sudden the bottom fell out of that and it's not who you really are or think you want to be anyway.

S. Yeah. I guess that's—I wasn't really—that wasn't really me all that time you know—I was what my parents wanted me to be and what the teacher—everything that was expected to—you know, to what you were supposed to do—that was—it was OK—I didn't worry about it, but you know—I guess as you get really to know and you see your parents for what they really are and they're humans with their faults and they've worked hard all their lives and in any sense I guess they're successful, but they're not—that doesn't make them happy and their lives aren't—they're not really happy and they don't —I don't know, they're successful but they're not really happy and ah I find that—that's—that I was doing sort of doing the same thing—sometimes I get—you know—have you ever just felt scared that nothing makes sense and you're just all alone?

C. Yeah, it must be kind of desperate when you feel that way. I think maybe what I want to say to you is that—that—you're not alone in the sense that I'll spend enough time to try and help you in thinking through some of these because it appears you're looking for—for you—that when you say the things you used to feel and think weren't you—also saying now you don't know who you are because you haven't—you haven't worked through shedding off your parents' ideas and values. Probably you're in the process of shedding those but you haven't developed the new you yet, and maybe that's what you have to search for now, saying, "Gee, what are my values going to be, what is going to bring happiness to me and that some of the things that my folks have set up apparently aren't going to make me happy?"

S. Man, that's it—but—what . . .

Closing and Planning

Near the end of the initial interview the counselor will want to make practical arrangements for future counseling. At this point the counselor and client should establish some tentative goals to work toward in the counseling relationship.

The counselor will also tentatively select a method for working with the client. If the client is interested primarily in vocational or educational decision making, the counselor may make arrangements for testing, provision of occupational information, and later interviews for working through this information and decision making.

The counselor will probably structure the interview according to personal concepts, by explaining to the client the task that lies ahead and delimiting the problem area. The counselor may define both his or her and the client's responsibilities.

Even though the counselor will describe the situation and give some guidelines for behavior, the content of the interview will be the client's prerogative. Each interview will be structured mutually. The type of relationship that develops between the counselor and the client must be unique.

At the end of the first interview clients are concerned about closure. Holland (1965) suggested that this has several aspects. First, they have risked themselves in initiating counseling, and if they are interested in pursuing this relationship they want to know if the counselor is going to work with them. Second, clients are concerned about whether they have done the right thing in seeking counseling with this person. Third, they want to know whether the counselor thinks their problems can be successfully handled.

It is very important for the closing of the interview to be warm and friendly and communicate willingness to work with a client. The counselor's manner, speech, facial expression, and tone of voice should express there will be real satisfaction in seeing the client again.

C. You have to start saying, "What are my goals? Who am I in establishing my own identity?" you know.

S. Yeah.

C. It's going to take some time for us to—ah—sort of wrestle through and find out who you are out of this.

S. You—you mean, you think then that I—you know—you think talking about being—that—that could help?

C. Well, I think I think this is the place we have to start, that—as you grapple with this—ah—I can help you clarify some of the things that you're—that you're feeling, some of the inconsistencies you feel, and some of the behaviors you have—look at some of the things you fall into.

S. Mumble.

C. Apparently you're going to have—you're in the process of developing a new identity from what you were before.

S. Umm—can I do that?

C. Well, it's a—it's a—not a simple thing obviously. I think it's a willingness of the two of us to—to work at it. If you think you want to do that why don't we set up a couple of—of interviews a week maybe and spend some time working on it.

S. OK—well—I'm sure they'll let me out of class.

C. Let me set up a—a-an hour tomorrow—you've got a study hall tomorrow—let me set it up tomorrow—we'll start then, OK?

S. OK.

C. Very good.

SUMMARY

This chapter examined client expectations and preferences in counseling and potential methods for working with them. The goals and a three-phase model were presented, as well as counselor behavior for the initial interview. Handling the client's preferences and expectations and conducting a meaningful initial interview is a base for the counseling process. If these are not successfully managed, a counseling relationship will not develop. The next chapter illustrates how the counseling relationship continues.

REFERENCES

Arbuckle, D. Counseling philosophy, theory, and practice. Boston: Allyn and Bacon, 1965.

Baum, O. E., & Felzer, S. B. Activity in initial interviews with lower-class patients. Archives of General Psychiatry, 1964, 10 (4), 345–353.

Buchheimer, A., & Balogh, S. The counseling relationship. Chicago: Science Research Associates, 1961.

Childress, R., & Gillis, J. A study of pretherapy role induction as an influential process. Journal of Clinical Psychology, 1977, 33, 540–544.

Duckro, P., Beal, D., & George, C. Research on the effects of disconfirmed client role expectations in psychotherapy: A critical review. Psychological Bulletin, 1979, 86, 260–275.

Gladstein, G. A. Client expectations, counseling experience, and satisfaction. Journal of Counseling Psychology, 1969, 16, 476–481.

Grier, W. H., & Cobbs, P. N. Black rage. New York: Basic Books, 1968.

Griffith, M. The influence of race on the psychotherapeutic relationship. Psychiatry, 1977, 40, 27–40.

Heitler, J. Preparatory techniques in initiating expressive psychotherapy with lower-class, unsophisticated patients. *Psychological Bulletin*, 1976, *83*, 339–352.

Highlen, P., & Voight, N. Effects of social modeling, cognitive structure, and self-management strategies on self-disclosure. *Journal of Counseling Psychology*, 1978, *25*, 21–27.

Hill, J. A. Therapists' goals, patient aims, and patient satisfaction in psychotherapy. *Journal of Clincial Psychology*, 1969, *25*, 455–459.

Holland, G. *Fundamentals of psychotherapy.* New York: Holt, Rinehart and Winston, 1965.

Jacobs, D., Charles, E., Jacobs, T., Weinstein, H., & Mann, D. Preparation for treatment of the disadvantaged patient: Effects on disposition and outcome. *American Journal of Orthopsychiatry*, 1972, *42*, 666–674.

Jourard, S. N., & Lasakow, P. Some factors in self-disclosure. *Journal of Abnormal and Social Psychology*, 1958, *56*, 91–98.

Krause, M. S. Behavioral indexes of motivation for treatment. *Journal of Counseling Psychology*, 1967, *14*, 426–435.

Lorion, R. Socio-economic status and treatment approaches reconsidered. *Psychological Bulletin*, 1973, *79*, 263–270.

——. Patient and therapist variables in the treatment of low income patients. *Psychological Bulletin*, 1974, *81*, 344–354.

Malan, D. *Toward the validation of dynamic psychotherapy.* London: Plenum, 1976.

Older, J. Interpersonal testing and pseudo-testing in counseling and therapy. *Journal of Counseling Psychology*, 1972, *19*, 374–381.

Overall, B., & Aronson, H. Expectations of psychotherapy in patients of lower socio-economic class. *American Journal of Orthopsychiatry*, 1963, *33*, 421–430.

Padilla, A., Ruiz, R., & Alvarez, R. Community mental health service for the Spanish-speaking/surnamed population. *American Psychologist*, 1975, *3*, 892–905.

Parloff, M., Waskow, I., & Wolfe, B. Research on therapist variables in relation to process and outcome. In S. Garfield and A. Bergin (Eds.), *Handbook of psychotherapy and behavior change: An empirical analysis.* New York: John Wiley and Sons, 1978.

Rawlings, E., & Carter, D. Feminists and non-sexist psychotherapy. In *Psychotherapy for women.* Springfield, Ill.: Charles C Thomas, 1977.

Robinson, F. P. *Principles and procedures in student counseling.* New York: Harper & Brothers, 1950.

——. The dynamics of communication in counseling. *Journal of Counseling Psychology*, 1955, *2*, 163–169.

Rogers, C. R. The necessary and sufficient conditions of therapeutic personality change. *Journal of Counseling Psychology*, 1957, *21*, 95–103.

Saltzman, C., Luetgert, M., Roth, C., Creaser, J., & Howard, L. Formation of a therapeutic relationship: Experiences during the initial phase of psychotherapy as predictors of treatment duration and outcome. *Journal of Consulting and Clinical Psychology*, 1976, *44*, 546–555.

Sattler, J. The effects of therapist-client racial similarity. In A. Gurman and A. Razin (Eds.), *Effective psychotherapy: A handbook of research.* New York: Pergamon Press, 1977.

Scheiderer, E. Effects of instructions and modeling in producing self-disclosure in the initial clinical interview. *Journal of Consulting and Clinical Psychology*, 1977, *45*, 378–384.

Smith, E. *Counseling the culturally different black youth.* Columbus: Charles E. Merrill, 1973.

Sue, D., & Sue, D. Barriers to effective cross-cultural counseling. *Journal of Counseling Psychology*, 1977, *24*, 420–429.

Terestman, N., Miller, J., & Weber, J. Blue-collar patients at a psychoanalytic clinic. *American Journal of Psychiatry*, 1974, *131*, 261–266.

Thase, M., & Page, R. Modeling of self-disclosure in laboratory and nonlaboratory interview settings. *Journal of Counseling Psychology*, 1977, *24*, 35–40.

Toomer, J. Males in psychotherapy. *Counseling Psychologist*, 1978, *7*, 22–25.

Tyler, L. *The work of the counselor*. New York: Appleton-Century-Crofts, 1969.

Wolberg, L. *The technique of psychotherapy.* New York: Grune and Stratton, 1954.

Wolkon, G. H., Moriwaki, S., & Williams, K. Race and social class as factors in the orientation toward psychotherapy. *Journal of Counseling Psychology*, 1973, *20*, 312–316.

Ziemelis, A. Effects of client preference and expectancy upon the initial interview. *Journal of Counseling Psychology*, 1974, *21*, 23–30.

CONTINUING THE RELATIONSHIP

CHAPTER FOURTEEN

The counseling relationship evolves through various phases as clients explore, gain understanding, and work through understanding and trying new behaviors to a point of termination. This chapter presents a model of a continuing counseling relationship. Not all counseling will follow this model exactly, but we will use it to explore the developmental stages of the counseling process. Understanding these phases in the relationship can help the counselor place a single event in perspective.

This model may be more appropriate for counseling personal-social problems than for educational-vocational decision making, but there is no clearcut difference: there is considerable emotional involvement in making vocational decisions, and many decisions are made to resolve personal problems. Therefore, many of the concepts presented here can be integrated with the chapters on decision-making interviews and vocational counseling.

A number of social scientists have described developmental changes in the continuing counseling relationship. Each phase of this model is a composite of the models presented in the literature. A consensus of the literature establishes phases of initiating counseling and setting up a relationship, exploration of self, deeper exploration, and working through to termination of counseling. Although the initial interview has received separate attention, aspects of that phase are reviewed to illustrate that it is an integral part of the continuing relationship. The early phases of counseling develop the relevant problem area as it is experienced by the client. The client's self-exploration leads to self-understanding. Although the client may have stated goals when he or she initially comes to counseling, clearer and behaviorally stated goals may be better defined after the client has a more thorough self-understanding. Frequently, precise goals may not be stated but the client describes only emerging and modifiable directions.

After a client has achieved a higher level of self-understanding and has more clearly stated her or his directions or behavioral goals, she or he and the counselor can consider alternative courses of action to attain those goals. The client and counselor's consideration of the advantages and disadvantages of each alternative will lead to a higher probability of success. Incremental new behavior patterns can be established to ensure the success of the new behavior, and the behavioristic sequence used that most effectively leads to the success of that behavior pattern.

The process presented in this model does not always move in sequence through the phases, but may move backward and forward, though with a general forward movement. The phases are not discrete and have no time limit. Some clients will move quickly into self-exploration; others will experience more difficulty in overcoming their resistances. Many clients will not require the deeper self-exploration involved in the third phase but can move to working through aspects of the process. The process of understanding self and trying new behaviors will vary with each client.

PHASE 1: INITIATING COUNSELING AND ESTABLISHING A RELATIONSHIP

The first step in the counseling relationship must involve the client's recognition that he or she has a problem and motivation to work with the counselor toward a solution. The best situation exists when the client recognizes the existence of a problem and sees the counselor voluntarily. If a client is referred by someone else who recognizes a problem, it is important that the client want to work toward a resolution. A client who is unaware or unwilling to recognize the problem area will not be sufficiently motivated to work in the counseling process.

Frequently clients come to the counselor with a rather vague feeling that something is wrong but are unable to put the problem into words. It is not uncommon for clients to talk about "it." Rogers (1958) described the clients' fixity and remoteness of feelings at the initial interview. In Rogers's view, a great blockage of internal communication prevents the clients from accurately describing feelings or the problem. Frequently clients do not recognize many of their feelings, and many aspects of the problem are not apparent to them. It is not unusual for clients to be unwilling to communicate about themselves at this point and instead to describe external situations that impinge upon them instead of talking about themselves. Rogers suggested that in such cases there is no desire for change—the client wants the problem solved but really does not want to risk changing herself or himself.

GOALS

The two major goals for the first phase of counseling are to obtain a clear definition of the problem and to establish a relationship with the client. An important feature in phase one is to define the client's problem in terms as specific as possible. For example, if the client's stated problem is that school has lost meaning, she or he should try describing the behaviors that demonstrate that attitude. The client may be able to count the number of positive and negative thoughts regarding various aspects of school experience. The counselor and client can eventually use the specific descriptions and the number of behaviors to monitor changes and assess the effectiveness of the counseling process. Another way to determine the client's present behavior is to gather what is called a base line, the information about the client's behavior before counseling actually begins. For example, the counselor might have a client count the number of inappropriate behaviors he or she exhibits during the school day. The definition of inappropriate behaviors would have to be agreed upon by both client and counselor, and the client could count behaviors for several days in an effort to establish a base line.

One part of defining the problem is to examine the antecedents of an inappropriate behavior. In a behavioral approach to counseling, the antecedents refer to the stimuli in a situation just prior to the occurrence of the inappropriate behaviors, such as what occurred in the classroom, what the teacher did, what peers did, or what the client was thinking about. An awareness of the immediate antecedents to an inappropriate behavior gives the client and counselor some idea of the immediate causes of the inappropriate behavior. A second aspect of the behavioral exploration would be to determine which reinforcements maintain the inappropriate behavior: the counselor would ask the client to describe what happens immediately after the inappropriate behavior. This would include how other people behave toward the client as well as how the client feels about himself or herself. This would involve both external and internal reinforcements.

Defining the problem in behavioral terms is important regardless of the counselor's theoretical orientation. The counselor need not think in terms of base line, antecedents, or reinforcements, but all counselors examine the circumstances involved in a problem behavior.

From the definition of the problem the client and counselor can discuss desired outcomes. Although they are tentative at this stage, behavioral goals give the client something tangible to work toward.

Part of defining the problem in the early phase of counseling concerns clients' expressions of feeling about their problem. The goal at this point is to have clients maintain their expression of feelings, to confront themselves with their feelings and behaviors, and thus help them clarify their problem. At this point the counselor is able to begin formulating hypotheses about the problem area and patterns of behavior.

The other primary goal in the first phase of counseling is to establish a relationship with the client. Chapter Eleven has already discussed the facilitative conditions of positive regard, empathy, and congruence as important in establishing this relationship. The client needs to feel accepted, to experience mutual liking, and to trust the counselor. Brammer and Shostrom (1968) described this as building a pipeline between the two individuals. The client is able to trust in the strength of the counselor and will thus feel safe enough to investigate aspects of his or her personal feelings and behavior. This does not deny the strength and potential for growth within a client, but does give him or her comfort and security with a new person.

According to May (1967), the first phase of the interview consists in establishing rapport, which exists when both the client and the counselor feel at ease. This is probably best facilitated by the counselor's being comfortable and showing it. This relaxation will help break the psychological tension that the client may feel. May suggested that the counselor's attitude must be a balance between sensitivity and robustness. Sensitivity is communication of understanding of the client without letting this openness appear too obvious. When the counselor's concern becomes too obvious the client may feel that he or she is not genuine and consequently withhold confidence. Robustness is the use of a hearty voice and a good sense of humor to communicate the counselor's humanness. It is not easy to establish the balance between sensitivity and robustness, and the balance will vary with different clients. And as May suggested, one must be sensitive enough to know when to be robust.

The counselor's professional manner could interfere with establishing rapport by communicating a separation in the levels between the two people. According to Holland (1965), two kinds of relationships are apparent in this early phase of counseling: one ostensible and one hidden. The ostensible relationship is one of equality between the counselor and client in which both defend the client's inadequate self-concept. This equality demonstrates that both are equal as human beings; the counselor is not superior, because the client, too, is dealing with the problem. The counselor may have information or skills to help the client solve the problem, but this does not make the counselor a superior human being. The counselor may have car difficulty on his way home and require the services of a mechanic. The counselor is no less a person than a mechanic in needing the latter's assistance in solving the problem. The hidden aspect of the relationship is that the client does have a problem and may feel inferior because he or she has to seek help for it. Generally the client does in fact have a dependent position.

PROCESS

Early communication relates to the discrepancy between the apparent and hidden aspects of the relationship (Holland, 1965). If the counselor dominates the interview, the client may retreat even more deeply into feelings of inadequacy, and if the counselor is too passive the client may feel she or he is not getting any help. Therefore, there must be an appropriate sharing of responsibility in this early phase. The counselor wants to encourage the client to talk and to permit him or her to control the interview and the depth of self-exploration. Counselor responses will generally be restricted to acceptance, reflection, and clarification. These are the least leading responses and permit the counselor to verify her or his understanding of the client. They also serve to clarify the problem area for the client.

Counseling outcomes are dependent to a significant extent on the client characteristics. From the initial meeting with the client, the counselor seeks to define the nature of the problem requiring treatment. Counselors become diagnosticians, attempting to identify a problem in order to take appropriate therapeutic steps. The diagnostic process requires understanding the vast array of individual differences among clients as well as how to deal with them. Coming to understand individual differences is very complex. Strupp (1978) stated that it is hazardous for a variety of reasons to categorize or type clients on the basis of a presenting difficulty. The utility of the classical diagnostic categories is very limited for therapeutic practice. Other systems of classification such as defense mechanisms or ego functions may sometimes be useful but also have shortcomings. It has long been recognized by clinicians that clients differ on many dimensions.

PHASE 2: EXPLORATION OF SELF

The second phase of counseling begins when the client feels a minimal level of acceptance. Rogers (1958) described this as the point when the client feels fully received. When the relationship is secure for the client there will be a loosening and a flowing of expression from the client. This phase may occur in the first interview or it may take more than one. In the beginning the client's expression starts to flow in connection with nonself topics. Describing problems as external to herself or himself requires little sense of personal responsibility for the problem. Feelings are usually talked about rather than experienced in the present. The differentiation of personal meaning and feelings is somewhat superficial. Although the client may express some contradictions, there is little recognition of them as contradictions.

GOALS

The counselor wants to elicit and determine the client's self-evaluation, so that the client can be aware of various feelings about himself or herself and can see how these feelings and attitudes affect his or her behavior. The main objective of this phase of counseling is a clearer and more complete delineation of various aspects of the client's self-concept and situation. Holland (1965) suggested that three different self-concepts usually emerge. One is self-depreciation, in which the client points out bad characteristics and inferiority in certain areas. Closely related to this is a second self-concept representing compensatory fantasies, which tend to compensate for the negative self-depreciation. The third self-concept includes the client's contemporary attributes that constitute a more or less realistic image and an evaluation of self by reasonable standards.

Self-Exploration

Carkhuff (1969) proposed a five-point scale to examine self-exploration. In his view, the counselor's awareness of the client's level of self-exploration will aid in understanding the client and making more appropriate responses. At the first level a client avoids any self-description or self-exploration that would reveal personal feelings to the counselor. At this level the client probably does not trust his or her own feelings and may not like himself or herself well enough to offer inner feelings to the counselor. This lack of self-exploration is a common occurrence in beginning counseling. At the second level of self-exploration the client responds with discussion to the introduction of personally relevant material by the counselor. The response, however, is mechanical and does not demonstrate any real feeling. The client is answering questions, giving conclusions already reached about self-concept, but is not exploring herself or himself. At this level the counselor can learn much about the client's current self-concept. At the third level the client voluntarily introduces discussions of personally relevant material but does so mechanically and without demonstrating much feeling. This frequently is a volunteering of material that the client has already rehearsed with herself or himself or possibly has discussed with other people previously. There is no spontaneity and no inward probing for new feelings or experiences. At the fourth level the client voluntarily introduces personally relevant material in a spontaneous manner. The client is dealing with the current level of feeling. This behavior may lead to the fifth level, in which the client actively and spontaneously probes into newly discovered feelings and experiences about herself or himself and her or his situation.

PROCESS

What are some things the counselor can do to help a client in self-exploration? In addition to presenting the various levels of client self-exploration, Carkhuff (1969) suggested a number of guidelines to assist the counselor in the exploratory stage of counseling. First, the counselor must establish client exploration as the immediate goal. Without this the client will not gain new insights, gain new understanding, or be able to incorporate new behaviors into her or his pattern. Second, the counselor must initially understand the client at the presented level of self-exploration. Exploration of personal material is most likely to occur when there is understanding and a suspension of attitude or judgment by the counselor. The client will move increasingly toward initiating exploration and toward spontaneous emotions if the counselor is willing to accept him or her at each level. Third, the counselor should initially offer minimal levels of the facilitative conditions. By offering minimal levels of empathy, respect, concreteness, and genuineness the counselor establishes a relationship that the client can explore, experiment, and experience. The minimal facilitative conditions provide the client with knowledge that the counselor understands the client on the latter's terms and also provides the feedback necessary for later reformulations. Fourth, the counselor should employ the client's self-sustaining level of self-exploration as a guide for moving to the next stage in the counseling process. Within a given problem or topic area, the criterion for movement to the next stage of counseling is the client's ability to deal with his or her own explorations. When the client is able to do this, the counselor can focus on the client's self-understanding or action, depending on the client's understanding. Fifth, the counselor should recognize a repetition of the cycle of self-exploration both within and between different content areas. Having worked through the process in terms of a situation with her or his parents, for example, the client may begin at the first level of self-exploration when the topic turns to relationships with peers or a teacher.

Several studies have demonstrated that differing levels of counselor-offered facilitative conditions affect the self-exploration of high- and low-functioning clients (Holder, Carkhuff, & Berenson, 1967; Piaget, Berenson, & Carkhuff, 1967). For the higher-functioning client, variance in the counselor-offered conditions has little effect on the level of self-exploration. Such a client appears to have enough self-confidence to self-explore even when the counselor is not highly facilitative. The lower-functioning client, however, or the one with a poorer self-concept, is affected considerably by the different levels of counselor-offered conditions; self-exploration is much greater when the counselor offers higher levels of facilitation.

May (1967) called this stage of counseling the confession and assumed that two-thirds of every hour will be taken up with the client's "talking it out." It is important for the client to talk about the problem thoroughly in order to reach the essentials. In May's view, if the client does not do most of the talking in the interview something is wrong with the counseling procedure. He assumed that every word the counselor utters must have a purpose.

The counselor may employ specific or concrete communication to ensure that his or her responses will not be too far removed from the client's current feelings and experiences. Concreteness or specificity of communication serves a function complementary to that of empathic understanding. It helps the client know that the counselor is focusing directly on the former's feelings. During later phases of counseling, specific communication focuses directly upon problem solving.

Thus, it is important for the counselor to make reflections and interpretations specific, even in response to a vague and abstract client statement. This helps the counselor sharpen the client's communication and reduces the possibility of emotional remoteness from the latter's current feelings and experiences. It also encourages the client to formulate his or her own expressions in more concrete and specific terms. Developing concrete and specific communication helps the counselor emphasize the personal relevance of the client's communications. This will keep the client's focus on personally relevant material rather than on stories that include irrelevant information and keep the counselor and client away from the real problem. At times the counselor must ask for specific details and instances: who, what, when, why, where, and how specific feelings and experiences are involved. These questions serve the function of entry and should make way for the follow-through by various reflections and interpretations.

The counselor should not express shock or offense at anything the client

CHAPTER
FOURTEEN
CONTINUING
THE
RELATIONSHIP

says. Emotional upsets must be a part of this period; clients become upset because they are expressing their ideas and fears and frequently suppress information they may not have told anyone before. The client may cry, and the counselor must exercise skill in remaining calm and communicating empathy to the client. At this point we can clearly discriminate between empathy and sympathy. Giving sympathy at this point would augment emotional upsets; empathy is more objective and valuable.

Brammer and Shostrom (1968) called this phase of counseling a catharsis and pointed out that it has positive and negative aspects. First, the client experiences strong physiological relief from the burden of tension, similar to the relaxation one may feel after crying. There is also a feeling of satisfaction that comes from the control of verbalizing the material. The client feels that gaining control of the problem verbally provides a certain amount of security and control over the problem. There is also a release of emotional energy previously used for self-defense, and the client may feel considerably better.

According to May (1967), the fact that the client has talked about the problem will make her or him psychologically healthier. It will relieve some inhibitions, make possible a more ready flow of internal feelings, and help the client to see the problems with clarifying objectivity. A skillful counselor helps focus the client's confession on the core of a problem. Skill and sensitivity are required to perceive the feelings beneath the client's statements.

One of the limitations of the catharsis involves this feeling of control and exhilaration with new energy, for the client sometimes makes a "flight into health," believing the problem is solved. In many cases a client has dealt with some aspects of the problem but needs further understanding and behavior changes. Frequently a catharsis includes only material at an intellectual level that the client has already been able to think out alone while other material is still being defended. Holland (1965) pointed out that clients feel defensive when they have communicated all that they know or are willing to tell about themselves, but are aware that this is not sufficient. These clients' defensive periods usually follow one or a combination of three patterns: avoiding discussion of themselves while directing the counselor's attention to externals; denying weaknesses and inadequacies in themselves; or exposing their own concepts and evaluations of the problem.

A Critical Point

This is a crucial point in counseling, and the client may be sufficiently threatened by lack of understanding and control to drop out of counseling. The client has made a deeper exploration of feeling and this is not a pleasant experience. He or she feels less secure and comfortable and may not be sure if the pain involved in working through the process is something he or she wishes to endure. The client may be aware of other aspects of the problem, for the defense system is open enough that the client is seeing things she or he has denied before and may recognize that things may get worse before they get better. It is important for the counselor to support and encourage the client at this point. Frequently, if the counselor is able to explain to the client that these anxieties occur in many clients, the client will be able to pass through this critical point even despite the fear of exposing too much of herself or himself (Brammer & Shostrom, 1968).

Transition

There may be a transition stage in this phase of counseling. Clients become aware that they cannot account for their behavior through what they know about themselves, and the logic of their behavior does not always lead to understanding. Therefore, the clients relax some of their defenses and the counselor becomes more actively involved, using short leading techniques.

Holland (1965) suggested that clients may strongly resist dealing with feelings about themselves. Clients will reach a point of avoiding discussion of their depreciated self. They may be reluctant to evaluate their compensatory fantasies, and their real self-concept is not strong enough to provide security. The counselor will have to fulfill several client needs during this period. Because they are unable to do so, clients need the counselor to see some of the negative aspects of the depreciated self they avoid. Clients may resolve this problem with very little help from the counselor. The counselor also wants to see how much the clients can handle, and it is important to let them know that the counselor trusts them, and will enter more actively only when he or she is needed. Part of the second interview with Tom illustrates this phase. This interview follows the excerpts of the initial interview presented in Chapter Thirteen.

S. I can't—ah—I just don't—I don't have interest in anything—ah, I don't know—it's almost like rather than start something and get involved in it—it just seems easier to say the hell with it and not—ah—and not get involved in it.

C. I guess I feel—though it's sort of early today—that you're almost having the same attitude about our session—that it's just pretty hard to get into this also.

S. Yeah, maybe.

C. It's easier not to get in it—you've been round and round with yourself, you might be thinking it's going to be round and round here.

S. I guess I hadn't thought of it like that but I didn't—you know—I didn't really—huh—I almost didn't come back 'cause maybe for what you just said, I just didn't want to get involved in it—I didn't think it was going to go anyplace. Just seems like just—I don't know I can't—I can't—I don't want to do any (laugh) I don't know—I just don't like—don't—don't feel like ah doing—I guess—I don't know.

C. You seem to be asking or looking for reasons—you say you don't understand why, ah—would you want to try and start by exploring some reasons of why you feel this way—of—taking a look at what's happened to you before now that's led you this way.

S. You mean like what what is it that's ah—you know—why me (laugh) why (laugh) what's happened to me that that ah I feel this way.

C. Uh-huh.

S. You know when you say that I just draw a blank uhm.

C. You said last week that you at one time sort of accepted goals like what your family did and general societal kinds of goals-oriented behavior but, but you've ah changed from that and part of this may have been because of the maturation type thing.

S. Uh-huh. Yeah, that's, a that's for sure—what a—now that I can't—ah—I don't know I guess.

C. Maybe you can talk about how you feel about yourself.

S. Huh—I was I was going to—you know—sort of respond to what—how I felt about my parents and I guess—you know—how I feel about myself is pretty much involved with how I feel about them. Got a my par—I've always been—my parents have always taken very good care of me and, ah, I've never had to—to worry about anything in any sense I've always had everything in a sense, you know—on a silver platter—and—I don't know I'm really that's what I can't understand about myself 'cause I didn't use to be like this—I really used to—ah, to really have everything I wanted and—ah, my parents have always really taken—ah given me anything. I was, ah, I was kind of sick when I was when I was young and so my mother and my grandmother who was home a lot I think always paid special attention to me and I always I don't know (chuckle) when I look back it seems pretty rosy I always had everything that ah I could that I could want.

C. Your parents haven't rejected you lately either, have they? You could—you could still . . .

S. It's not—they don't—not at all, that's—in fact, if anything it's the other way around—you know—they still treat me like in a sense like I was still the, the I don't know, baby—I hate to say—baby—but they still treat me like I was the baby and uhm I don't know—I kind, I resent, but I don't—I resent it but I don't because I know that they—you know—that they love me and everything yet I resent being treated like that and whenever—you see I have asthma pretty badly and when I get an asthma attack, ah, I'm usually pretty sick for a couple of days—and I don't know, they treat me, they—ah, specially my mother keeps keeps that—you know she doesn't like me to do too much, a-a-a . . .

C. Sometimes they still treat you like they did when—when you were a child, when you were sick as a child.

S. Specially my mother and my grandmother, they ah—and it's in lots of little ways little things that they do—they don't, almost like they don't want me to grow up—not grow up but they don't want me to be independent of them and they, like they they like to take of me, it's important to them to be able to take care of me, so they like they keep this idea that I've, that I'm have asthma and that I should stay at home and I shouldn't do some of the things that other kids do um-m-m . . .

C. Now you're at the point where you sort of resent this kind of ah treatment. In a way though it sounds at times it's sort of comforting—possibly kind of tough to give up at other times, huh?

S. (laugh) Yeah, but I hate to admit that, but sometimes, you know—and that's the thing. I like it and I don't like it.

C. It builds up conflicting feelings in you.

S. At home sometimes—you know—I like to go home and I know that they they'll just do anything for me. I mean I still, when I get up in the morning my mother gets up and makes breakfast for me and things like that—ah—they do—any money that I need—anything like that—ah they give to me and, ah, at the same time I resent it because they don't—I don't know—I don't have a sense of independence I don't have a sense—I don't know—I just—I guess I'm pretty confused. . . . (half laugh)

C. Yeah, it sounds like you would like to have the independence—there's some comfort to the other, but you don't want to hurt your parents' feelings. As you point out, it's important to them to have this kind of relationship.

S. Uh-huh.

C. It certainly slows down your personal independence.

S. Yeah.

During these early interviews the client is communicating inadequacies and wants help from the counselor. The counselor should communicate recognition of this desire to gain something from him or her, and Holland (1965) suggested the counselor may indicate that some progress is being made and that the client has been largely responsible for this progress. This communicates that the counselor regards the client as functioning adequately. The counselor may also wish to communicate to the client that they are both personally involved in the process by trying to make this evaluation. There may also be plans of action being developed and the counselor may be able to indicate some of these to the client. Tom's counselor communicates this nicely near the end of the initial interview. In a later interview the counselor adds another.

C. In the next—in the next week before we meet again why don't you try looking at several places in which you can develop more independence, and at least—I think we may be aware now that you, that you've sort of seen some differences in your behavior pattern for what might come. Obviously as you're already aware it's not an easy thing to make an immediate change—so it's a—it's a process. I think we've reached one step in it and, ah, let's take this step and examine where we're going to go from there.

The counselor should permit clients to maintain control of themselves in the interview for as long as possible. If clients are effective in handling their problems and if the problem is not too difficult, the counselor can provide clients with labels to put on the feelings they have about themselves. It is apparent that Tom's expression of behaviors and feelings is loosening and there is some freedom in terms of his internal communication, but he still may be having difficulties tapping spontaneous feelings. The counselor will help the client by pointing out some relationships between various self-concepts and his behavior pattern.

During this stage of confrontation, the counselor concentrates on tentative formulations concerning discrepant communications from the client (Carkhuff, 1969). The counselor confronts the client with the discrepancies between the client's self versus ideal, insight versus behavior, or self versus other experiences. The counselor may employ probing questions rather than direct confrontations. Tentative comparisons of contradictory communications are both natural and appropriate for the counselor at this point. A premature direct confrontation may demoralize and demobilize an inadequately prepared client. The client needs the acceptance, approval, and support of the counselor while examining various self-concepts that she or he would rather avoid.

Holland suggested that the counselor may become more active in the later part of this phase and assume a more controlling role, thus appearing more authoritarian. If the counselor is controlling more of the communication at this point in the relationship, the client will have the greatest need for the counselor's acceptance and help. Otherwise, strong feelings about being controlled would interfere with the progress of counseling. It is important for the counselor to be gentle and provide acceptance and support for the client.

In addition to reflection and clarification, the counselor will probably be sharing information and ideas and providing some interpretation for the client. Sharing involves the client's acceptance of the counselor as a real person rather than his or her projections about the counselor. The counselor does not force information upon the client but presents it for him or her to use. The interpretation is one further step in leading in which the counselor presents some hypotheses to the client.

According to May (1967), after the client has talked out the problem, interpretation will take place. Both the client and counselor survey the facts that have been brought to light and discover through them the pattern of the client's behavior. "Interpretation is a function of both the counselor and the counselee working together." It is not a matter of the counselor's diagnosing the pattern and then presenting it to the client. The counselor may make some tentative analysis or some tentative suggestions. The counselor suggests interpretations rather than stating them dogmatically. Tom and his counselor illustrate the procedure.

C. It sounds like you may be sort of—I'm not sure you resent their behavior as much as you resent yourself behaving that way. Why—why can't you love your parents and still, and still break out of this mold.

S. Hm-m-m—never—thought of that—in a sense—you know—what the hell's wrong with me that I can't stand on my own two feet—yeah—I'm too quick to run home—I'm afraid—to ah—to try sometimes—it's too easy just to ah I guess that's that's it—it's too easy just to let things go the way they are—why get involved in something when things have been so easy like that.

C. Yeah but underneath it sounds like sort of a fear that—"Hey, if I'm not able to do this—am I ever—am I ever going to be a man? Am I always going to simply rely on the comfort of mother?" You talk about not having any meaning or—or power or control over your your future. Part of it may be the fact that you haven't really had much in the past, much of this has been controlled by your family.

S.   (pause) Yeah, you mean—ah—maybe that some of the ways—in other words the way that I was—would react at home or the way that I've been brought up at home (pause)—I see what you mean. It's just like I been—I haven't—I've just been taken care of at home rather than stand up and do anything. I've just let them take care of me and the point is that I've liked it more than try to do anything. (pause) It's so easy—too easy just to let them do—do that—I guess I can understand that—but still . . .

It is important for the counselor to read the meaning of the client's reactions to the interpretations or suggestions. If the client is indifferent, and the suggestions do not seem to make any difference, the counselor may assume that the idea was not very important. If the client rejects the suggestion or interpretation violently, protesting strongly that it is untrue, the counselor may tentatively assume that the interpretation is close enough to have struck a cord. However, the counselor must be careful not to make this assumption, for it may in fact be inaccurate and the rejection appropriate. If the client accepts the suggestion or interpretation and agrees with it, both the counselor and client can accept it for the time being. Whether or not it is accurate and meaningful may not be known until the client continues to work further on the problem and a solution. The client could have just accepted the interpretation rather than rejecting it.

Many clients' problems will move from this point to working through the behavior problems and developing the insight that leads to behavior change. Some clients, however, will go into a deeper exploration of feelings.

PHASE 3: DEEPER EXPLORATION

Some clients need more therapeutic counseling than others in order to tap feelings that will lead them to better self-understanding. These clients will be involved in a deeper exploration of feelings and attitudes. Most counselors are not equipped to deal with the intense feelings and intricate problems involved in personality reorganization that may occur at this depth of counseling. Most counselors who work in agencies, schools, or colleges will probably not have sufficient time to work through this phase of counseling. Most counseling relationships will proceed instead to the working-through phase. However, the goals and process of deeper exploration are presented here to illustrate their relevance in the counseling process.

GOALS

The counselor attempts to eliminate depreciated and fantasy self-concepts as determinants of client behavior and at the same time to complete the client's awareness of his or her real self-concept and establish reasonable standards to evaluate it. It is apparent that part of the depreciated self-concept may have been valid at one time, but because it is no longer true it must be reevaluated in terms of reasonable standards being developed for the self. As this occurs there will be a reduction in the client's need for fantasies to compensate. The client may find, however, that part of the compensated fantasies coincide with some of her or his actual attributes (Holland, 1965).

During this time the client's feelings will be expressed more freely in the present. Feelings will burst forth even though the person may fear and distrust what he or she feels. The client tends at first to realize that what she or he is feeling involves a direct referent. There is frequently surprise as well as fright at the feeling that bubbles up. The result is increasingly freer communication within the individual and increasing ownership of the feelings as a part of the self (Rogers, 1958).

As clients become aware of themselves and their uniqueness, they should establish reasonable personal standards. Such standards can be relative standards, indicative of behaviors and achievements of other people comparable to themselves. Instead of global evaluations, clients should break down these standards and examine smaller parts of the whole. This process is one of helping to fill in the details of the self-concept and the cognitive structure.

PROCESS

The counselor communicates, either directly or indirectly, what he or she considers inaccurate or inadequate in the client's thinking process. This means that the counselor is fairly active in the interview and exerts some control because she or he is involved with active emotional resistance. It always seems to amaze beginning counselors that when they are trying to help a client, the latter is resisting that help. Clients continue to deceive themselves in part, and to attempt deception of the counselor. Holland (1965) offered four reasons for this level of resistance. There may be a generalization of hostile feelings toward people who exert some control over others' lives. There are possibly negative feelings about giving up various self-concepts, and anxieties associated with depending upon a new self-concept that is not yet reliable outside the counseling situation. There may be negative feelings about the efforts and risks involved with living this new self-concept. It is this aspect that the client needs to change in order to use new behavior patterns.

Because of these feelings the client is not a passive recipient of the counselor's communication. In order to meet the objectives of this phase, the counselor may need to use persuasion. Persuasion does not entail persuading the client to do something to meet the counselor's needs. The counselor uses persuasion when less controlling techniques have not worked to help the client meet the objectives that the latter has established. Persuasive efforts should be directed toward what the client thinks, letting the behavioral responses be her or his decision. The confrontation at this point is focusing on the client's avoidance tendencies in tying things together. The counselor tries to persuade the client to give up self-defeating and self-deceptive ways of thinking. The counselor must be careful not to be too controlling in this endeavor and not to enter into persuasion too early.

According to Carkhuff (1969), the highest level of action in the counseling process consists in interpretations of immediacy. Immediacy is the counselor's ability to understand feelings and experiences that intrude between herself or himself and the client. The client may be telling the counselor something about how he or she feels about the counselor without even knowing it. The client may not be able to tell the counselor these things directly. The counselor must be able to focus on these feelings to understand the client and communicate what is going on so that the latter can gain self-understanding. Interpretations of immediacy state what the client is trying to communicate that she or he cannot say directly. These interpretations translate the counselor's immediate experience of the client in relation to the counselor directly into action. As with confrontation, there is a transition stage into direct interpretations of immediacy. With most clients the counselor will tentatively approach interpreting what is happening in the immediate relationship, perhaps with formulations that do not define precisely the counselor's experience in the moment. The formulations may take the form "You're trying to tell me something about yourself in a relation to me," which can help the client get in touch with his or her immediate feelings. This can be particularly helpful in a counseling process in which the client communicates double messages. The counselor can interpret the immediacy better by concentrating upon his or her own experiences in the immediate moment. At given moments the counselor may disregard the content of the client's expression and focus on the subverbal messages. Clients' inability to express themselves explicitly may not be a function of inability to articulate, but a result of attitudes toward the counselor in relationship to themselves. It is important that the counselor's interpretations of the immediacy not derail a meaningful experience or sidetrack the client's movement. Therefore, when movement is somewhat halting and directionless, it is a particularly appropriate time to focus on the interaction between the counselor and the client.

Critical Point

A second critical point in the counseling relationship occurs during this deeper exploration process. The client may become aware of the inadequacy of her or his defense mechanisms. They may no longer provide protection from the awareness of deeper feelings. A sudden awareness of too many impulses, thoughts, or feelings may be quite traumatic. The counselor should control the relationship to enable the client to explore these situations slowly. A client who experiences too much pain at this point may be frightened of his or her lack of control and withdraw from counseling.

PHASE 4: WORKING THROUGH

A significant part of changing one's behavior to be consistent with the new insights is involved in the process of working through. Originally used by Freud, the concept generally meant breaking down the network of resistance. Today's broader conception refers to the client's becoming aware of the meaning of past experiences and present feelings. The client develops awareness of inner feelings as well as of the external world. A rational understanding of problems, feelings, and behaviors can lead to further behavior change.

GOALS

May (1967) considered the transforming of the client's personality the final stage of the counseling process and the goal of the whole process. Although the terminology is different, the concept is very similar to working through. May assumed that during the confession-interpretation stages the client has identified the tensions involved in her or his problems and has been able to see the relationship between mistaken attitudes and behavior. He considers this phase transforming because the client now learns a new awareness of tensions and behaviors. The goals of this phase of counseling include the client's clarification and acceptance of current feelings and defense manipulations. The client will rationally understand the historical roots of the problem and will work it out in terms of the relation between past events and current experience in the relationship with the counselor. The culmination of this phase is to elicit and establish behavioral responses that are consistent with a valid self-concept (Brammer & Shostrom, 1968).

Feelings and experiences need to be worked out in all areas before the client is able to integrate feelings and behavior patterns. Working through involves resolving conflicts from many vantage points, possibly described in different words with varying degrees of insight.

Insight

The client is increasingly able to face internal contradictions and incongruencies. His or her feelings are located much more in the present instead of being postponed and thought about. The client begins to acknowledge feelings and has a freer dialogue within herself or himself. There is increasing acceptance of responsibility for the problems being faced and a concern about how he or she has contributed to the problems (Rogers, 1958).

As deeper insight occurs, feelings that have previously been inhibited are now released and experienced presently and seem to flow within the individual. Now the client is living feelings subjectively rather than thinking about them and is gaining trust in the feelings and in their momentary changes.

In the process of self-exploration, clients develop insight or become aware of other facets of their feelings that affect their behaviors. The majority of counseling approaches are insight oriented. Counselors assume that as clients gain insight or self-knowledge, they will see alternate behaviors and this new insight will lead to behavior change. This does not mean that when insight is achieved the problem automatically disappears. Most counseling, however, is still based on the concept that it is important for clients to have insight or an understanding of themselves in order to make the behavior change. Although sometimes insight occurs suddenly, more often a series of insights is involved with slow changing of behavior during the working-through process. These insights and changed perceptions of oneself become integrated into a new behavior pattern. There is a deepening in clients' awareness of what is going on, both objectively and subjectively. They are able to see relationships they have not been aware of previously. They are able to give up former defensive patterns and have greater self-confidence.

Self-Understanding

When the client is able to deal with self-exploration and immediate feelings, the counselor can help draw together the fragmented insights and help the client develop self-understanding, focusing on the construction or reconstruction of the latter's communication process. The counselor can judge the level of the client's self-understanding (Carkhuff, 1969). At lower levels of self-understanding, the client's responses or statements detract noticeably from expressed feeling and content, either in her or his own expressions or in those of others involved in the problem situation. At a minimum level of understanding the client is able to make statements about self that reflect essentially interchangeable affect and meaning; this interchange adds cognition to explorations of feelings. When the client makes statements that promote self-exploration at even deeper levels, she or he is functioning at a high level of understanding and should be able to move on to appropriate action. At this point the client can sustain the search for direction independently of the counselor.

A Critical Point

A third critical point in counseling may occur in this phase of the relationship (Brammer & Shostrom, 1968). It is another type of flight into health. After a client has explored some current feelings, for example, and understands them in terms of previous experiences, she or he may have a feeling of well-being. With this newfound insight, the client may think he or she is ready to terminate counseling. It may be that the client has the insight but lacks commitment to action. In addition, as part of the working-through process, the client may run into difficulty carrying out the decision in everyday life. The fact that the client has new insights is no guarantee that other people will change in the way they relate to the client. All of this may lead to the client's terminating counseling prematurely. The client may experience a relapse. The counselor must be careful not to keep the client in counseling longer than he or she desires but must also be careful not to terminate prematurely. It is a fine line for a decision.

PROCESS

The working-through phase involves putting understanding into action. The client's self-understanding is an intermediate goal, as well as process, that leads to constructive action. The counselor may begin by focusing on the client's areas of greater competence. The probability of the client's understanding and acting upon the situation is greatest in areas in which she or he is functioning at the highest levels. Success in these experiences will increase the probability of understanding and action in other areas. With greater exploration and an improvement in self-understanding, the counselor can increase the level of facilitative conditions. When the client is safe enough to explore herself or himself and is gaining new insight, she or he is able to handle additive responses within the given content areas. As the client gains in self-understanding and is able to sustain the level of effective understanding, the counselor can focus attention on the next stage of counseling: action. The client must recognize that the cycle of self-exploration to understanding to action is a repetitive one. For example, a client may have achieved self-understanding in relation to school situations and start constructive behaviors there, but may not have done the same in relation to parents. The counselor and client may need to start with exploration in that area and follow the cycle of exploration leading to understanding and finally to action. The early phase of self-exploration and understanding may lead to some action, which will provide feedback that can modify the original concepts, and elicit further explorations leading to a deeper level of understanding, and culminate in new action.

On the basis of what the counselor has learned from the client's exploration of the problem, the counselor tries to put the picture together. The counselor gives the counseling process direction by attempting to help the client understand himself or herself at a deeper level and finally to act upon this understanding. The conditions initiated by the counselor are called action-oriented dimensions because they involve action by the counselor and because they lead the client to initiate her or his own ideas of what is happening and to act upon these ideas.

The client gains little in the long run from an intellectual understanding of the problem unless she or he is able to try out new methods of behaving. Prior to this, the client has been behaving according to various self-concepts, and giving up those behavior patterns to adjust to the new self-concept may be quite difficult. Holland (1965) pointed out that part of this aspect of counseling involves behavioral retraining—giving up undesirables responses and trying out some new ones. Many clients can work through the understanding, gaining insight, and adapting behaviors by themselves. With other clients the counselors may need to play a more active role.

Action

The ultimate goal for the counselor should be to help the client toward constructive action. There is an interrelationship between the client's self-understanding and action, each serving to sharpen the other. The counselor emphasizes action in the area in which the client has the best self-understanding. This offers the highest probability of successful action. As the client increases other areas of understanding and approaches action, the counselor can increase the client's level of action orientation. Carkhuff (1969) suggested that the counselor begin to initiate more activities based on her or his experience in the situation, thus serving as both a model and agent for the client to do likewise. The counselor also attempts to ensure that learning and acting in relationships generalizes outside of the counseling situation. This is done most effectively when a full description of the goals of counseling has been achieved. An important aspect is the behaviorally stated objectives for the client. A behavioral objective allows the counselor to specify goals in terms of the specific extent to which a response is to be performed; thus, it provides a reliable standard for the client. The behavioral objective also specifies the criterion level—how much or how frequently the behavior is required to meet the client's objective. It should also state under what circumstances the behavior is to occur.

When the counselor and client are able to describe the dimensions desired, a plan can be put into operation to meet those goals. Based on his or her experience and abilities, the counselor should select the techniques with the greatest chance of success. In addition to insight-oriented verbal counseling, the counselor may select alternative behavior modification techniques. In any event, the counselor must tailor the techniques to each client. When operational goals have been established, step-by-step procedures for their attainment can be developed. The more fully the goals have been described, the more fully the steps can be described and implemented. Once the client is able to employ constructive action in one area, the counselor can repeat the cycle in another problem area. When the client demonstrates increasing ability to act constructively in all the relevant problem areas, readiness for termination is indicated.

One variable that May (1967) suggested in changing the client is the utilization of the client's suffering. The counselor should channel this suffering to furnish power to bring about change. An individual will not change a pattern until forced to do so by her or his own suffering. Many people prefer to endure the misery of their situation rather than risk the uncertainty of what would come with change. May believed the counselor should not relieve the client's suffering but rather redirect it into constructive channels. The client may leave the interview more courageous, strengthened with the realization that he or she must change behavior. If the counseling is more than superficial, the client may feel shaken and probably unhappy with her or his current situation. Part of what the counselor does is to indicate that the individual is suffering with inappropriate attitudes and behaviors.

To help clients confront themselves the counselor must charge them with the discrepancies in their behavior. This confrontation is most effective when the counselor concentrates on clients' verbal and nonverbal expressions. It is important for the confrontation to come when the client feels accepted and understood. The confrontation does more than communicate understanding from the client's frame of reference; it provides the experience of an external, sensitive, and accurate viewpoint of the discrepancies in behavior. At this time the counselor must focus with increasing specificity on the implications of these discrepancies. The increasing specificity will lead the client to understand the distortions in her or his assumptions and, ideally, to reconstruct both assumptions and behaviors. Directional confrontation creates a crisis that offers the client the possibility of movement to more appropriate functioning. When the counselor observes critical discrepancies, she or he confronts the client with them. The client is pressed to consider the possibility of changing and, in doing so, utilizing resources not yet employed. The client cannot avoid responsibility for choices denied so far because the counselor will not permit him or her to do so. The counselor is free to employ both a didactic and experiential form for confrontation, and may also confront the client with both deficits or assets that the client has denied. The desired outcome of the confrontation is to enable the client to confront himself or herself and to make decisions toward more appropriate behaviors.

Alternatives

At this point in counseling the client may have to look at a variety of alternative responses to a situation. Once again, the dimension of concreteness or specificity becomes a critical function in the counseling process. Concreteness is the key to consideration of potential preferred modes of treatment and involves weighing alternative courses of actions and the advantages and disadvantages of each. Concreteness during later stages of counseling makes a major contribution by requiring the client to consider specific material that is potentially relevant to the problem and to implement specific courses of action to resolve that difficulty.

When the client is unable to generate such alternative responses, the counselor may become involved by suggesting several alternatives. By offering more than one alternative the counselor is not advocating a specific behavior but continues to help the client think through various alternatives. May (1967) claimed that suggestion is often condemned as a technique because it is misconstrued to be advice. It is not. The counselor can use suggestions intelligently to lay all the constructive alternatives before the client. From these alternatives the client can select the one that will best meet her or his needs.

As Tom reaches this point in the excerpt below, it is clear that the phases in counseling are neither discrete nor sequential. Although Tom has explored himself and his problem to the point of intellectual insight, there is still resistance and a need for further understanding. Working through involves trying out some of his insights by trying to be independent in different situations.

C. This may be one of the one of the points in your life for the first time—you know, of leaving home in a way, when you've really been given an opportunity to have control over part of your life—or—sufficient power now to carry it out.

S. Hum—rather than go to college I'd just rather stay home. But what am I afraid of? Why am I—hum—seems like I'm just afraid to leave home in a sense.

C. That's probably the—the simple look at it—there may be more complex variables behind a simple answer. It may be something like that, uh-h-h—it really means truly developing a certain amount of individual behavior.

(long pause)

S. I guess I understand that but I'm not—I don't know what to do, uh—(laugh)

C. Yes [though] you can understand it intellectually it's a pretty hard to accept it and carry it out.

S. I think for sure that—for sure it is—I've been—I've just leaned on my family and let them take care of me and I think what happened is I don't dare—I—when something challenges me I'd rather just drop out of it than do it—get out before I really have to do something—so—go home and—I don't like to think about it.

C. You're sorta having the same kind of feelings right now—but by doing all that it leaves you with a sort of a—feeling of not knowing what you want to do or why you want to do—nothing seems to have meaning then—all in sort of a—running away thing. What do we—just look at a few areas in which you do have some decisions that are within your means of control and that you can carry out. What are—what are a few things that we look at now in terms of development of this?

S. I think probably the most immediate thing, the thing that I've been thinking about the most, is in how going to college next year'n like over the last couple of weeks—it's pretty—it's time now that you have to be applying and I haven't, I haven't even thought about where I want to go let alone what I'd major in or anything like that. I know I could—I could still get in if I applied—I'd pretty well decided that I wouldn't even apply.

(pause) Ya know, I'd told my parents 'n they think I should stay at home and just go and maybe go to a community college or something like that. I don't want to do that. (laugh) But I don't—you know—I've never really been away from home. It's not—don't think I'm not afraid to go away from home.

C. You're not ready to make a final decision about going away to college yet either—but it may be something we can explore in terms of different places you might want to go, or, if not to college to take a job which might permit you to live away from home—maybe not a long ways, where you still have a certain kind of security. Short of that, you may want to talk with your parents about certain areas in which you are developing some individuality. You can develop some independence yourself there.

S. It all seems so kind of—seems kind of abstract and far away from me right now—you know—but somehow I know that—somehow I know that I have to 'n what makes it so hard is—you know—my parents are so good to me but somehow I have—I've gotta actually, physically leave them.

C. It's going to be hard on both of you.

S. I think it's going to be harder on them that it is on me, almost—but I can see that—that I can't stay there—the way—as long as I stay there I'm just a little boy—you know—and I'm—I don't know, maybe it's like that with everything—I'm just—anything that's going to involve *me* having to make a decision—and—and—stand up for myself and do the work—almost seems as if everything like that I've just backed away from—I've never had—I never had to do it at home.

C. Sorta what I meant about the school work, in that—maybe you've developed this pattern of dependency. Now's the time to start working at various areas of independence.

S. I guess maybe I—I guess maybe I know that that's what I have to do and I don't—really still don't—it all seems so simple but when you come down—like when I walk out of the office now—I'll understand everything we talked about but I won't know where to start—what to do.

C. Yeah—that's the tough part. it's too easy to go back into the old pattern instead of learning a new one.

S. I know, I—huh—I just—I've worked into a point now where everything—I can see that everything that I was doing I'm not happy with anymore but I can't seem to make a step towards doing what I want to do now, and maybe like—you know—I've always (pause) I guess maybe college—I *do* want to go to college.

It is clear from this excerpt that Tom has some insight but is not ready for termination. Tom must work through to integrate the insight into new behaviors. Obviously the most important part of this integrative work is trying out these new insights and behaviors in everyday life. The personal conceptions are tentatively reformulated to be validated against further experience, but even then they are held more loosely.

The counselor must maintain some evaluation of the process. Evaluation based on achievement of stated behavioral objectives makes it possible to observe client progress. This evaluation can help the counselor decide if the selected technique is moving the client toward a goal or if the approach should be discontinued or modified. The process is not static, and a change in the client's objectives also calls for a change in the technique the counselor is using. The counselor encourages the client to live out his or her insights by trying new behaviors. The success of these experiences will reinforce new behavior patterns. Setbacks are worked through in the later sessions, and the client tries out new insights and behaviors. Counselor accountability is a critical question in the process. How stable or enduring are the effects of the counseling? Prior to termination the counselor must make provisions with the client to establish a program to maintain this newly established insight and behavior.

Termination

Termination of the counseling process may be complicated. There may be feelings of ambivalence about it. The client both desires to be free and anxious about leaving. Frequently a client will recognize that he or she is handling a problem adequately and consider termination. The counselor can discuss the idea with the client to help him or her prepare for termination. This communicates that the counselor has confidence in the client and removes any concern the latter might have about the counselor's feeling rejected by this move toward independence. Actually the relationship is never over; it may be renewed if the client desires.

TERMINATION IN COUNSELING

Hoyt (1979), in emphasizing the importance of termination, pointed out that much of what has been accomplished in counseling can be either consolidated or compromised in the termination phase. This phase is not merely a recapitulation and nailing down of the previous work; rather, all the work of the counseling sessions may be seen as prologue to the termination. With the end of counseling imminent, the client's fears or conflicts may be restimulated, especially if they involved struggles to achieve separation or independence. The manner in which the issues are handled in the termination phase will do much to determine how closely the ultimate goal of counseling is met.

Maholick and Turner (1979) suggested that termination presents a powerful analogy to how we deal with farewells in life. In their view, termination is one of the natural pausing points that present individuals with the opportunity to say goodby, and when and how to say goodby are critical issues. Termination in counseling can be thought of as a recapitulation of the multiple preceding goodbys in life; at the same time, it is a preparation for being able to deal more adequately with future goodbys.

Maholick and Turner emphasized that power exists in the ending of any relationship. A choice exists: the individual can avoid the farewell, creating a potential for destruction and continuing unhappiness, or the person can accomplish the goodby and provide for new creative experiences.

Termination is also an important aspect of the continuing process of counseling. In each counseling session and series of counseling sessions there is a need to bring closure to what has been occurring in the counselor-client interaction. Termination can occur at three points: at the conclusion of a discussion unit within an interview, at the conclusion of each interview, and at the conclusion of the counseling process.

TERMINATING DISCUSSION UNITS

Termination is necessary following the discussion of a specific client concern. Although some counselors seem to want the client to keep talking without clearly delineating or dealing with his or her concerns, most often the counselor-client interaction takes the form of a series of minisessions within a block of time. It is not always possible or meaningful to close off these segments, but when it is possible several techniques can be of value.

The unit or minisession can be terminated by a summary statement by either the client or counselor. The intent of the statement is to draw together what has been said during the unit and to help the client see what progress has been made. The client must then decide whether to move on to other areas or to continue the present discussion. The latter decision suggests that the summary or closure by the counselor was premature. The counselor must be sensitive to the client's needs in order to use the summary termination effectively, and must convey to the client that continuation of the topic is possible even though, in the counselor's mind, the discussion has been fairly completely developed.

There is a second, more direct method of stopping discussion of a topic. The counselor suggests directly that the discussion may not be as meaningful at the particular time due to client psychological condition, counselor skill, or other inner or external factors. The counselor does not eliminate the possibility of returning to the topic, but suggests that further discussion may be inappropriate or nonrewarding and that when certain other factors are present the topic can be reintroduced. The counselor will have to explain this action at times because she or he is really interpreting something in the client, the relationship, the environment, or herself or himself that may not be as apparent to the client. The crucial variable here is communication of what is happening and why it is happening.

A third termination technique falls somewhere between these two methods. This intermediate method is designed to shut off the particular topic without stopping client progress and client involvement. Several procedures can be used. The counselor may choose to alter the subject slightly so that the direction is unaltered but the intensity of feelings exhibited by the client is reduced. This is done when a client is deep in self-exploration and the counselor wants to bring him or her up and cap that emotion for the time. Old topics or new, related topics can be introduced. In another procedure, the counselor can react to different parts of client statements, leading the client into a different topical area. Or the counselor can increase the number and direction of pauses to reduce the interview's speed and intensity of affect. It is important to understand the effect of this type of activity on the client: any action of the counselor that shuts off the client's communication has an undesirable effect and should be avoided.

Termination of an interview presents dilemmas to many counselors. Those beginning their professional careers, in particular, report that the client really begins to bring up important material right at the end of the allotted interview time. Counselors are understandably hesitant to terminate at what appears to be a crucial point in the counseling session. Yet time constraints and the need to keep counseling within some reasonable boundaries forces the issue. In this situation it is often of considerable value to examine two factors: what, if any, aspects of the counselor's *modus operandi* precluded earlier client meaningful involvement, and what, if anything, stimulated the client to move at the end of the session? These factors require counselors to examine both their own motivations and their understanding of the client. Assuming that this particular area can be understood and any necessary corrective steps taken, the techniques of termination become important.

The counselor and client should establish a time limit in which the counseling is to take place. A client with a prearranged appointment should be aware of the specific limits, and in most situations the counselor can simply refer to the time factors to effect a termination. Simply saying, "Your time is up," however, will probably not satisfy the client. Someone must summarize what has occurred, what has been discussed during the session, and what the next steps might be. Often the counselor is likely to take responsibility for summarizing, but she or he should at least consider the possibility of including the client. Having the client suggest what might be done is also a valuable tool. Setting up the time and date for the next meeting as well as some of the potential discussion topics makes the termination of the interview smooth and does not leave the client without a sense of direction or accomplishment.

With some clients summarizing is not enough. They still wish to sit and talk. The counselor often has to leave the situation by standing up and moving toward the door to assist the client to get her or his coat. The counselor may use some subtle devices to suggest that it is time to end the particular interview, such as moving her or his chair or placing her or his hands on the arms of the chair as if to rise. The client usually accepts these devices without any particular stress or strain. The more nervous the counselor is about using them, the more likely the client is to resist the action.

Depending upon the type of counseling approach utilized, there are some other fairly meaningful ways to end the interview. Assigning some task to the client is one example of a general method. The counselor can phrase the instructions so as to communicate the intent to end the session, such as, "Now that we are finished for today I would like to suggest some questions that both of us should consider for next time." A related approach is to arrange for any tests or reading that may have been determined during the session.

Two or three limitations affect the termination of an interview. First, the counselor must avoid, as much as possible, leaving the client in an ambiguous situation. The more hesitancy, unsureness, or uneasiness the counselor exhibits, the less likely the client is to be able to understand or accept what is occurring.

Second, the counselor may wish to provide extra counseling time when he or she senses there is a need for the client to continue. This simply means that the counselor should have some flexibility to provide additional assistance when necessary. Some clients, however, may use this as a manipulative device to meet their own needs, wasting the scheduled session in order to effect some control or manipulation over the counselor. This tactic calls for counselor self-examination and understanding.

Regardless of the method used, the counselor should make sure that the client leaves with the most positive feeling possible about what occurs in the session and what the future activities might be. The counselor should have in mind a tentative plan and some activities to effect termination.

TERMINATING THE RELATIONSHIP

Termination of the counseling relationship involves two people, and both have potential for terminating. Clients' reasons for termination are numerous and varied and often there is nothing a counselor can do about it. Beginning counselors often feel rejected and less than competent when a client fails to return. There is a fine line between letting this affect future counseling contacts with other clients (or indeed, the same client) and developing a hardened attitude such as, "I have plenty of other people to work with; who needs him?" The preparation program should help potential counselors deal with both extremes.

The counselor's case termination skills and activities are important. Several factors may lead to the need for the counselor to terminate future contact. Time restraints or change of position may cause the counselor to end a relationship prematurely. Ideally, most of the conditions are known several weeks prior to occurrence and can be programmed into the counseling session prior to a fixed termination date. In these circumstances the counselor should arrange for referral for those who may desire further assistance. This process is discussed in another section.

Dependency activities by the client may be a clue to termination. One counseling goal is to help the client to function more adequately in her or his personal life and to begin to be an independent person. When these aims are not being met, the counselor is not being honest in continuing the relationship as it is constituted. Because the counselor may not be able to alter his or her style radically, it would appear that termination or referral is called for.

Maholick and Turner (1979) dealt with the critical issues of when and how to say goodby. Termination is indicated when the client has progressed as far as she or he wants in gaining awareness and changing behavior patterns. This is certainly a natural and desirable time to terminate, but it is important that the client leave with a respectful and genuine goodby, not a mechanical or cold farewell. Termination may be precipitated by an unexpected development such as a job change, a shift in working hours. When these circumstances are out of the client's power to manipulate, it is still important to experience closure even though the client may not have achieved the originally defined goals. This is obviously a time when individuals may be hesitant or resistant about terminating, for they have not really completed their relationship with each other. Another time for termination is when the presenting problem has been clarified with some significant resolution and there are indications that the old patterns of behaving are not returning to the same degree. It may be tempting to continue in counseling at this point because the client is becoming increasingly enjoyable to both herself or himself and the counselor. It is wise at this point to ask what the client wants to continue working on; if no new goals can be agreed upon, it may be advisable to have the client terminate and grow independently. In another situation, the client may refuse either to deal with the issues or to say goodby. This may be the least successful termination experience and is particularly difficult for the counselor. At this time the counselor must encourage the client to work on his or her problem independently, thereby decreasing dependence on the counseling situation. Another difficult time for termination occurs when no progress occurs or, even worse, a maladaptive behavior is accelerating. In some cases it may be necessary for the counselor to work through a termination into a process of referring a client to someone else.

Usually, termination comes when the client feels she or he has made the decision, has the information, or is coping adequately with the problem. The client may give clues that he or she does not need the counseling any longer. It is not uncommon for a feeling of friendship and goodwill to develop between the two people. After talking through some meaningful things in your life with another person, it is difficult to separate yourself suddenly.

Maholick and Turner (1979) suggested that there are checkpoints that clarify indications and reflect the appropriateness of termination. The counselor and client should examine the initial symptoms or problems and see if they have been resolved. This involves returning to the original point of counseling for a review. They can explore the extent to which resolution has been achieved and search for indications of improved coping ability. Other areas to check include the degree of increased awareness, appreciation, and acceptance of self and others.

The steps involved in closure of a series of counseling sessions are somewhat parallel to those used in unit and session termination. First some preparatory steps should be taken; this simply means that the counselor does not wait until the last minute to indicate inability to continue the relationship. Whatever the reasons for termination, they seldom wait to present themselves until the middle of the final interview. The counselor should provide or encourage the client to provide an overall summary of what has occurred. Sometimes, due to the nature of an extended series of meetings, both participants must be involved, and considerable clarification may be necessary.

It is important that the same conditions exist when case termination occurs as when session termination takes place. The counselor must avoid leaving the client in an ambiguous or defenseless position. The counselor must either be certain that the client can function outside the counseling situation or provide further assistance. In any case the counselor, regardless of orientation, must be able to understand the situation the client faces, understand her or his own situation, weigh the values, and make a decision.

Maholick and Turner (1979) discussed counseling as a transitional process. Initially the client relinquishes some of the responsibility but later reclaims it as he or she proceeds with less tension and anxiety and greater ability to define and fulfill himself or herself authentically. Therefore, if counseling is successful, termination can be implemented with the full knowledge that the client is now ready to take on responsibilities for his or her own counseling and to live it in life. Termination does not preclude future contact with the counselor. It is a closure of a unique interpersonal relationship that may be resumed or may be exchanged for real-life social relations. In some instances, this might be of considerable significance to each person.

COUNSELOR ASSISTANCE IN THE PROCESS

At any point in the counseling process the counselor may recognize that she or he needs assistance. A counselor cannot be expected to be able to meet the needs of all clients. Counselors must rely upon others to assist them or the client to resolve the situation better. Consultation and referral are two procedures for counselor assistance.

CONSULTATION

When a counselor experiences difficulty in diagnosis or in working with a client, he or she may seek consultation. Consultation is the provision of technical assistance by an expert. The counselor may seek assistance from other mental health, educational, or vocational specialists. Such assistance is directed to specific work-related problems, is advisory in nature, and the counselor does not have to accept or implement the consultant's ideas.

A counselor would most likely seek client-centered case consultation. This type of consultation focuses on difficulty in diagnosing the problems of the client and/or on developing an effective counseling strategy with the client. The counselor and consultant evaluate the information provided by the counselor about the client. The consultant helps the counselor define step by step any critical gaps in the information required in analyzing the problem. The issues of the client's problems are clarified; additional questions may be raised; with sufficient information the counselor and consultant may evolve a tentative suggestion regarding counseling procedures. The outcome of these procedures may be monitored in subsequent consultation sessions. The consultation sessions are best conducted face-to-face; however, client-centered case consultation may be provided by telephone.

Although the counselor may initially seek client-centered case consultation, it may become consultee-centered. In this form of consultation, the consultant listens to latent messages and metacommunications as the counselor reports the client's case. The consultant listens to what is said and how it is said in order to establish whether difficulties originate in any of the consultee-centered areas: (1) lack of knowledge or understanding, (2) lack of technical skill, (3) lack of self-esteem or self-confidence, (4) disturbance in objectivity. In other words, the difficulty the counselor is experiencing with the case is resolved by focusing on the counselor.

The counselor's difficulty may stem from inadequate knowledge about the client's problem areas, as in the case of a hyperactive child. The consultant would use the case to give generalizable information about the hyperactive syndrome, and the counselor could apply the knowledge to the client. Frequently lack of technical skill coexists with lack of knowledge. A counselor may be deficient in the basic skills of play therapy appropriate to working with a hyperactive child. The consultant may explain and rehearse with the counselor precisely what to do with the client. They should also discuss courses of action for predictable contingencies. Later sessions are used for playback and refinement of the new skills. Lack of confidence or diminished self-esteem may be indicated by the counselor's manner of presentation. The content of the counselor's presentation may reflect competence but also indicate uncertainty. The counselor's uncertainty may impair her or his capacity to act confidently on the client's behalf. The consultant's respectful listening and reinforcement of the counselor's competence can provide sufficient strength to carry out the process. A counselor may have adequate knowledge and skill but be unable to view a particular client's predicament clearly. The counselor's lack of objectivity will interfere with understanding the client and helping the latter move toward resolution. Impaired objectivity frequently occurs when the client's problem stimulates some unresolved intrapsychic conflicts in the counselor. The consultant will need several sessions to help the counselor gain perspective on the case and on himself or herself.

To receive help from the consultant, the counselor must be committed to the process. The counselor must first admit the needs for assistance to be effective with a particular client. The counselor should be aware of what she or he wants from the consultant, yet flexible enough to deal with alternatives. In seeking the consultation, the counselor should give complete, valid information about the case. Professional consultation is not a breach of counselor-client confidentiality. The counselor must be open about himself or herself because his or her knowledge, skills, and feelings relate to the case. She or he should expect to help in the diagnosis and link the understanding of the client to procedures that will increase effectiveness. Consultation is a cooperative relationship between two professionals. The counselor must cooperate in working with the consultant and also openly discuss discrepancies in their ideas. The counselor has final responsibility to implement whatever plans have been established through consultation.

REFERRAL IN COUNSELING

During the counseling process the counselor may recognize that the client would profit from working with a different professional person. Successful counseling is often related to utilizing various resource personnel. The process of referral is of considerable importance and deserves the attention of the counselor or counseling staff.

There are several dimensions of referral: the process of referral itself, the effect upon the counselor and client, and followup of the referral. The referral process should be considered an integral part of the counselor's preparation, role, and personal concern.

Each counselor will eventually find himself or herself having to call upon outside assistance for a client. The reasons frequently involve client-presented problems beyond or outside the counselor's current functional level. Another reason may be related to a long-term involvement that the counselor cannot provide. It is important for the counselor to understand and be prepared for the referral process. A number of factors must be considered, not the least of which is the counselor.

The Counselor

Whenever a person is involved as a counselor with a client there is a certain amount of ego involvement. A counselor must feel able to function effectively, yet be open to the possibility that someone else might be able to help the client more. A counselor might feel personally weak or inadequate when he or she cannot meet the task and needs to refer a client. The counselor must maintain a proper balance of confidence and judgment in knowing when to refer.

There are several ways of achieving this balance. First, the counselor needs to know what kinds of assistance she or he can provide and what degrees of client help are beyond her or his scope. Ideally, the counselor will have had the opportunity to examine personal strengths and weaknesses during training and to improve areas that may be potential problems.

Various methods are employed for counselor self-understanding and produce the desired outcomes of self-understanding, improved interrelationships, decreased defensiveness, and more adequate counseling practice. These methods include personal counseling, group seminars or sensitivity training, and supervision. Even after formal education ends, the practicing counselor profits from continued supervision. A portion of the supervisory period covers personal matters that might affect the counselor's performance. This is a mild form of counseling; perhaps the chief difference involves the intensity of the counselor's efforts to change her or his behavior. Often the supervisor helps the counselor become aware of the behavior and the assumption is made that change will take place.

The Client

The client represents another important factor in the referral process. For some clients it will be difficult to accept a change of counselors. This may be true for several reasons, some of which reside within the client and some of which are outside the client's personal situation but are nonetheless potent aspects that inhibit accepting referral.

Often the client is unable to accept the referral because of lack of mobility, scheduling difficulties, financial problems, and other factors that are in effect beyond his or her control. The person who has no transportation has a difficult time going across town to meet with a more appropriate helper. Some clients do not have the economic support to take advantage of the referral agency's service. Finally, the client may not be able to go when the referral agent is available. All these plus other external variables need to be considered by the counselor and client whenever a referral is suggested. They are not insurmountable, but they must be dealt with to ensure a meaningful referral.

The internal inhibitors that affect the client's potential for referral are more critical and crucial. A client may resist referral because of a dependency relationship that exists with the current counselor. Because the counselor has established a relationship, the client may feel more secure with her or him and not wish to move. The fear of a new situation may also be involved; though aware that the current counselor cannot help, the client may be reluctant to commit himself or herself to a new situation and an unknown, new counselor. Proposal of a referral also suggests that the problem or concern of the client is worse than originally conceived. Although this may not be the case at all, the client quite naturally may feel that the difficulty is worse than she or he thought possible. The client may realize that it is essential to seek more competent assistance and will often feel some reluctance actually to accept the additional help. Many of these anxieties can be handled by the counselor preparing the client for the referral. If the counselor is leaving her or his position or the client needs additional assistance, the counselor will know in time to prepare the client. If the client understands the reason for the referral and participates in the process, it will proceed more smoothly.

The Process

The counselor can aid the smooth transition by giving the client two or more meaningful possibilities for additional assistance. Thus, the client does not feel shunted from one person to another with little input or control of the situation. The counselor should be familiar with the referral source and promote the best possible fit for client and agency or client and other helper. In this role the counselor can help the agency to which the client is referred by providing information within the limits of confidentiality and by helping the agency mobilize appropriate resources to meet the needs of the client.

Finally, the counselor ought to have some sort of a checklist to insure that the referral is necessary and the referral agency the most appropriate for the client. The following points may be valuable in preparing this checklist.

1. List the various resources of the school or agency to be sure that all agency resources have been utilized to meet the client's needs. Often counselors are reluctant to use other personnel in an agency, when in fact these people might have the skill to provide meaningful assistance.
2. Be attuned to the continuing dynamics of the counseling situation to identify referable necessities and to develop discussion with the agency for both technical assistance and perhaps eventual referral.
3. Be as involved as possible in identifying those already a part of the problem-treatment situation. This includes knowing where other family members fit in and what agencies are already involved so that there is minimal overlapping and personal feelings are not strained.
4. Understand the agency, its limitations and strengths, and be particularly careful in communicating these to the client and others involved with the client.
5. Be certain that a balance exists between dependency of the client on the counselor to do everything and the real needs of the client for assistance in accepting the referral.
6. Develop communication lines with the agency so that both the referring counselor and the person in the agency have contact possibilities. Obviously some involvement of the client and her or his family may be included in this step, but the counselor should avoid coaching or supporting illicit methods of obtaining services.

SUMMARY

This chapter has presented a descriptive model of a continuing counseling relationship. Not all relationships, and probably no single one, would follow this model exactly. However, it is a guide to the various stages of counseling that we have observed. Clients frequently enter counseling with apprehensions and talk about their problem, move to some exploration of themselves, gain some understanding of themselves and the problem, work through the understanding and trying of new behaviors, and then terminate counseling. The process does not move in sequence but with stops, starts, and regressions through various phases. The various aspects of termination occur through the process and provide closure of the various points in time. Because a counselor may not be able to help a client through the entire process, referral is a part of the continuing relationship.

REFERENCES

Brammer, L., & Shostrom, E. *Therapeutic psychology*. Englewood Cliffs, N. J.: Prentice-Hall, 1968.

Carkhuff, R. *Helping and human relations* (Vols. 1 and 2). New York: Holt, Rinehart and Winston, 1969.

Holder, B., Carkhuff, R., & Berenson, B. The differential effects of the manipulation of therapeutic conditions upon high- and low-functioning clients. *Journal of Counseling Psychology*, 1967, *14*, 63–66.

Holland, G. *Fundamentals of psychology*. New York: Holt, Rinehart and Winston, 1965.

Hoyt, M. Aspects of termination in a time-limited brief psychotherapy. *Psychiatry*, 1979, *42*, 208–219.

Maholick, L., & Turner, D. Termination: That difficult farewell. *American Journal of Psychotherapy*, 1979, *33*, 583–591.

May, R. *The art of counseling*. New York: Abingdon Press, 1967.

Osipow, S. H., & Walsh, W. B. *Strategies in counseling for behavior change*. New York: Appleton-Century-Crofts, 1970.

Piaget, G., Berenson, B., & Carkhuff, R. The differential effects of the manipulation of therapeutic conditions by high- and low-functioning counselors upon high- and low-functioning clients. *Journal of Consulting Psychology*, 1967, *31*, 481–486.

Rogers, C. A process conception of psychotherapy. *American Psychologist*, 1958, *13*, 142–149.

Strupp, H. Psychotherapy research and practice: An overview. In S. Garfield and A. Bergin (Eds.), *Handbook of psychotherapy and behavior change*. New York: John Wiley and Sons, 1978.

DIAGNOSIS IN COUNSELING

CHAPTER FIFTEEN

Strupp (1978) contended that whatever the counselor's background or level of training, he or she cannot escape the necessity of forming some notions or hypotheses about the client's problem or difficulty and deciding what needs to be done to improve the client's condition. In other words, counselors must first become diagnosticians before they engage in some activity they consider therapeutic.

The concept of diagnosis has its origin in medicine, where it is defined as distinguishing an illness or disease and identifying its symptoms. Diagnosis is the attempt to classify illness or disease in discrete, mutually exclusive categories, each of which is characterized by a common origin or cause, a common course, and a common prognosis, or outcome (Patterson, 1959). The concept of diagnosis was brought into counseling through the influence of psychiatry, a branch of medicine that deals with social and emotional problems. Classification of disease and treatment, however, does not seem to apply to counseling with normal individuals. This has caused some controversy about the function of diagnosis in counseling. Advocates of diagnosis suggested that it plays a central role in counseling; opponents claimed that problems were not sufficiently discrete nor techniques specific enough to be effective. Diagnosis for classification is still used, but the concept of diagnosis as understanding is more useful in the counseling program. This chapter discusses some of the major concepts of diagnosis in counseling and some ideas regarding the process of diagnosis.

THE PURPOSE OF DIAGNOSIS

The purpose of diagnosis in counseling is to identify the client's life-style of functioning, or more specifically, the disruptions of the life-style. By identifying the problem area, the counselor and client can establish the goals of the counseling process. Diagnosis can serve different functions in the counseling process. It can be used to categorize the problem of the client and therefore label the problem area. This is a carryover of the medical model, in which the first step is to diagnose the problem in order to prescribe appropriate treatment. Because most of the labels in counseling are not sufficiently discrete to suggest differential treatment, a diagnosis that gives a comprehensive picture is frequently used. Drawing together all the information about a client and his or her situation as a basis for decision making is an important part of educational and vocational counseling. Another concept of diagnosis is the use of a working hypothesis to understand the client. The counselor develops a model of the client or an individual theory that changes as the counselor learns more about the client. This moment-to-moment understanding is particularly important for both personal and social problems. The model is usually based on the counselor's counseling theory as it is applied to the individual client.

In some clinical settings, a counselor may hold a diagnostic interview in which he or she evaluates the current psychological status of the client and the causal factors of behavior, which leads to suggesting treatment and a prognosis of future adjustment. Such an interview is used only for evaluation; the counseling process begins later and frequently with a different counselor. In most settings, however, diagnosis and counseling are interwoven as the counselor begins the process with an initial interview and continues working with the client. With this approach, diagnosis is not a judgment at a specific time but an intricate part of the continuing process of counseling.

Proponents of diagnostic evaluation base their support on the assumption that diagnosis brings clarity and order into a very complex field. They contend that diagnosis enables the counselor to fit many diverse items of information into a pattern, which then allows the counselor to make a prediction about the client's behavior. This procedure subsequently gives the counselor a firm basis on which to construct plans for handling the case. A second factor in support of diagnostic evaluation is the assumption that it will aid in the selection of clients for treatment or continuation of treatment. The counselor must decide whether she or he or the agency can provide the kinds of treatment appropriate to help the client. It is generally accepted that counselors are not equipped to work with severely disturbed clients suffering from psychotic manifestations such as delusions and hallucinations, or with those clients requiring hospitalization. These cases, it is felt, should be referred to a psychiatrist. A third reason for using diagnosis in counseling is to aid the counselor in determining what the client seems to need most. Is a client lacking information, or insight? Is he or she in need of clarification or support? of a combination of these? Is the client's stated reason for seeking counseling the real problem or is it a facade? These are questions the diagnostician feels must be answered before the appropriate treatment can begin (Weiner, 1959).

The existing diagnostic schemes are helpful but inexact. The same can be said for theoretical formulations of client problems in terms of presenting symptoms. Diagnosis is a process that calls for an exercise of keen clinical skills. It should be systematic and lead to prognostic judgments that are translated into a plan for treatment. The personality and behavior pattern of the individual client is the single most important aspect of understanding for the counselor in formulating an individual program of counseling.

DIFFERENTIAL TECHNIQUES

Underlying diagnosis is the assumption that different problems require different treatment. Callis (1960), for example, theorized that new experience, perception, and generalization develop a behavior repertoire, whereas inadequacies in a behavior repertoire are due to lack of experience, distortion in perception, and errors in generalizations. There are two basic approaches in counseling to deal with these problems. Callis suggested that lack of experience is most effectively dealt with by the method of counselor discovery and interpretation to the client. Distortion in perception is most effectively handled by the client's self-discovery.

Although much of counseling is remedial, it may also include developing the client's potential. The counselor can be effective in bringing about positive aspects of development in the client's life. Developmental goals can be reached without seeking causes and remedial counseling. The counselor and client must state these goals carefully so that learning efforts can be directed efficiently. Defining the areas of positive development is one aspect of the diagnostic process. Table 15–1 presents Robinson's (1963) two types of goals: remedial and developing strengths. Robinson suggested that the counselor's techniques would vary not only with the type of client problem but also with the goal. These are gross areas of diagnosis and very general approaches to the counseling process.

Because diagnosis and treatment remain nonspecific, many counselors have not regarded diagnosis as an essential part of counseling. Diagnosis was considered one of the most important skills of a counselor until the rise of the nondirective movement. Since then the proponents of diagnosis in counseling have done much research and writing in an attempt to demonstrate the positive contributions of counselor diagnosis. Two major conceptions of diagnosis approach it as either classification or understanding.

DIAGNOSIS AS CLASSIFICATION

Many proponents of diagnosis maintain that it is possible to classify psychological problems and that each category will indicate different treatment. This hypothesis has led to many attempts to develop a series of diagnostic constructs for counselors to use in their work. Acceptable constructs have four characteristics: (1) the system must result in a reliable classification of the subjects among its categories; (2) the categories must be mutually exclusive: each class should be identified by constant, discrete symptom clusters; (3) there must be greater variance among the constructs than within each category; (4) each construct should form the basis for the choice of treatment (Bordin, 1946). These four criteria can be used to evaluate the following proposed systems.

TABLE 15–1 A CLASSIFICATION OF CLIENT NEEDS THAT AFFECT COUNSELING METHOD

	PERSONAL ADJUSTMENT	RELATING TO OTHERS	KNOWLEDGE	MATURITY	SKILLS
Remedial	Motivational conflicts Poor self-insight Neurotic tendencies	Conflict with authority figures, peers, spouse, children Loss of loved ones	Lack information about environment	Dependence	Reading disability Speech disability
Developing Strengths	Personality integration Self-insight and acceptance Educational and vocational planning Philosophy of life	Cooperation Loving	Competence	Independence Civic and family responsibility Breadth of interests	Dev. higher-level skill SQ3R study method Use of semantics Use of resources Discussion Cl. use of Co.: Discussing plans As a resource

CATEGORY SYSTEMS

Several categorization systems of diagnosis have been proposed over the years. Most of them have been established for educational, vocational, and personal problems in school or university settings. Although these systems may be appropriate for many community clinical settings, some clinics and most hospitals use a psychiatric classification. The psychiatric classification system is based on a Freudian theory of personality; the other systems do not use theory to understand the client behaviors but merely describe the area of the problem behavior.

In 1937 Williamson and Darley identified the diagnostic categories that they felt would encompass all problems dealt with by the counselor: vocational, educational, personal-social-emotional, financial, health, family. Bordin (1946) viewed the Williamson-Darley diagnostic constructs as sociologically oriented and as excluding psychological dynamics, describing the difficulty but ignoring the source. He suggested that these categories overlapped and did not lead to differential treatment. Bordin proposed instead his own system of classification, a "psychological description which starts at the individual describing the organization of his behavioral characteristics and predicting what his reactions will be to his social environment (1946, p. 169). The list below summarizes Bordin's set of diagnostic concepts with the common cause and suggested treatment.

- **Dependence** The client has not learned to take the responsibility for solving her or his own problems. The counselor aids the client in gaining insight into feelings of adequacy to cope with everyday problems and to obtain experiences that will make her or him independent.
- **Lack of Information** Past experiences have not provided the client with the knowledge necessary to cope with the situation. The counselor must give the client the needed information or direct the client to the appropriate source.
- **Self-Conflict** Two or more conflicting feelings are motivating the client. The counselor helps the client to recognize and accept conflicting feelings so that he or she may resolve the conflict.
- **Choice Anxiety** The client is unable to face and accept an inevitable unpleasant situation. The counselor helps the client realize and accept the problem and subsequently make a decision.
- **No Problem** The client is in need of support in following through on a decision already made, or wants to determine whether the decision leads in the right direction. The counselor should lend the client support.

In evaluating Bordin's constructs, Robinson (1963) contended that the categories do not give any diagnostic indication of the specific cause of the frustration and, therefore, little indication of the treatment to be used.

Pepinsky (1948) made the next attempt to define and to differentiate empirically among the causal categories of client problems. Pepinsky based his diagnostic categories on Bordin's set of constructs but expanded the construct of self-conflict to include three subcategories: cultural, interpersonal, and intrapersonal self-conflict. Pepinsky replaced Bordin's no-problem category, which did not explain the reason the client sought counseling, with lack of assurance, and added a sixth category, lack of skill.

Pepinsky evaluated his system by studying intercounselor agreement in applying the constructs to 115 cases. Each counselor based his or her diagnosis on an analysis of the individual's record blanks, test scores, and other available reports. There were three important findings: (1) the constructs of interpersonal self-conflict, intrapersonal self-conflict, lack of assurance, lack of information, and lack of skill, which were used with consistency by the counselor, were relatively mutually exclusive and seemed to identify important cause factors; (2) counselors were unable to distinguish clearly between cultural self-conflict and dependence; and (3) choice anxiety was not studied systematically because problems of this type were rarely observed in the cases used.

Byrne (1958) replaced the construct of self-conflict and its subcategories with the categories lack of insight and lack of information. Byrne also replaced the category of dependence with that of immaturity, believing dependence to be only one expression of immaturity. He dropped choice anxiety because anxiety is a symptom, not a cause, but retained the category lack of assurance. The construct lack of skill was altered to lack of problem-solving skill. Byrne added a new category, domination by authority, persons, or situations, to include clients who are unable to make a choice or plan for the future because of pressures from the environment to do something other than they want to do.

Robinson (1963) revised the Bordin, Pepinsky, Byrne, and Callis (1960) systems of classification and proposed the following categories: (1) personal maladjustment, (2) conflict with significant others, (3) discussing plans, (4) lack of information about environment, (5) immaturity, and (6) skill deficiency.

Callis (1965) subsequently described a departure in diagnostic divisions with a two-dimension diagnostic classification plan. Along one dimension are three of the Williamson-Darley categories: (1) vocational (VOC); (2) emotional (EM); and (3) educational (ED); this dimension is labeled problem–goal. Along the cause dimension are: (1) lack of information or understanding of self (LIS); (2) lack of information or understanding of the environment (LIE); (3) motivational conflict within self (CS); (4) conflict with significant others (CO); and (5) lack of skill (LS), such as poor reading skills or poor study habits. The cause dimension attempts to focus on what is lacking in the client's personal resources that causes the inability to solve the problem.

This system of classification makes fifteen diagnostic hypotheses possible. The counselor places a client into one category from each dimension and can record a diagnostic hypothesis by using the symbols from each dimension. The problem–goal dimension is written first, with the cause dimension second. Callis's system of classification has been successfully used in record keeping.

In many clinical settings, the counselor may need to make a diagnosis of mental disorders or may receive a client case history with psychiatric diagnostic nomenclature. The American Psychiatric Association's most recent effort to categorize mental disorders, the *Diagnostic and Statistical Manual of Mental Disorders* (DSM-III) is generally used for this purpose (APA, 1980). The DSM-III is larger and more comprehensive than its predecessors and is intended to be inclusive; that is, whenever a clinical condition can be described with clarity and relative distinctness it is considered for inclusion. The overall goal of DSM-III was to develop a classification system that reflects the current state of knowledge about mental disorders. This was to be accomplished by clear and brief professional communication facilitating professional inquiry; providing a guide to current differentiated treatments; providing information concerning likely outcomes with and without treatment; reflecting current knowledge of theory and pathophysiology; and meeting the needs of practitioners and administrators in various settings.

Diagnosis in the DSM-III takes a multiaxial form. Each diagnosis contains information on five predetermined axes designed to be of value in planning treatment and predicting outcome as well as categorizing. The five axes are: (1) clinical psychiatric syndromes and other conditions, (2) personality disorders (adult) and specific developmental disorders (children and adolescents), (3) nonmental medical disorders, (4) severity of psychosocial stresses, and (5) highest level of adaptive functioning in the past year.

McLemore and Benjamin (1979) pointed out some of the advantages of this new diagnostic system. The practice of focusing on psychiatric symptoms in isolation from psychological substructure and personality is lessened by relating those symptoms to more enduring aspects of personality. Second, establishing the current level of functioning in relation to maximum personal effectiveness in the recent past places diagnosis in a time perspective, particularly useful for prognosis and for planning treatment. It also allows for multiple ideologies by coding current environmental precipitants as well as physiological ailments and by distinguishing tentatively between physical and nonphysical causes. Even so, diagnosis is still partly an impressionistic clinical judgment, including, for example, global ratings of the "severity" of the psychosocial stresses and of the client's highest level of adaptive functioning during the past year. The system also still categorizes people in terms of very broadly defined illnesses. Particularly important, DSM-III shows nearly total neglect of the sociopsychological variables and interpersonal behavior.

SEPARATE DIAGNOSTIC INTERVIEW

The large number of individuals seen in some agencies necessitates some form of diagnostic workup. Many agencies use a separate diagnostic interview, separating the diagnostic from the counseling process. Shectman, De LaTorre, and Garza (1979) discussed some of the advantages and disadvantages of a system in which intake interviews are separate from the counseling process.

A particular advantage to the client is that theoretically she or he can obtain the best person the institution has to offer. Through the diagnostic interview the client may be placed with the staff counselor most likely to be able to help. It is possible to match the client with the appropriate counselor and treatment modality.

The referral of a client to another counselor after the diagnostic interview has the potential disadvantage of interrupting a relationship that has just begun. The client could feel rejected by the diagnostician or by the institutional machinery. It is therefore important when using a diagnostic interview to prepare the client to give information to the diagnostician and to begin counseling with another counselor.

Another possible disadvantage of conducting the diagnostic interview separately occurs when the client is aware that the relationship is limited by time and might consciously or unconsciously stall in order to save more important information for the "real" counselor. In other cases, the client might try to cram long-term counseling into a short time. In some cases the client may resort to premature closure as a way of easing the transfer from one person to another, dealing with an issue only intellectually rather than with feeling.

One advantage of the separate diagnostic interview is that it allows the counselor to circumscribe the task and separate diagnosis from treatment. Therefore, issues can be clarified before treatment begins. It is often easier to clarify issues in advance; neutrality can be much more difficult to maintain once the client-counselor relationship is under way. Menninger, Mayman, and Pruyser claimed that diagnosis

> is not a search for a proper name by which one can refer to this affliction
> in this or other patients. It is diagnosis in a sense of understanding just
> how a patient is ill and how ill the patient is, how he became ill and how
> his illness serves him. . . . It is still necessary to know in advance, to plan
> as logically as we can, what kind of interference with a human life we pro-
> pose to make (1963, p. 103).

A major function of a diagnostic study is to improve the accuracy of clinical prediction about the client's probable response to possible treatment situations. The diagnostician, then, focuses on assessing the variables about the client and makes predictive statements that will help in deciding the treatment procedure. Therefore, the counselor has an opportunity to use the diagnostician to help in planning. The way in which the client responds to the diagnostician can provide good information in predicting behavior and issues in counseling. The diagnostic interview, therefore, is a brief experiment, a kind of trial counseling and a preview of what will occur with the counselor.

A diagnostician who has a short-lived diagnostic involvement with clients before referring them to a counselor may feel drained or threatened and may avoid the openness required to help the clients optimally and perform the diagnostic task. It is obviously important for the diagnostician to balance diagnostic interviews with counseling clients on a longer-term basis. In most agencies there is a rotation system whereby all counselors perform some diagnostic interviewing as a part of their regular case load.

A diagnostician can serve an excellent role by preparing the client for counseling. Some counselors, however, experience a disadvantage when they begin counseling a client in the middle of an experience between the client and the diagnostician, particularly if the counselor has begun with a client in a different way or has suggested a different procedure. The counselor also relies on the diagnostician for a type of testing out of how the client may respond to or deal with the counselor's mode of counseling.

CONCLUSION

Although many systems of diagnosis have been formulated, revised, or modified, no one has met all four of the desired characteristics mentioned earlier. Diagnosis by classification has received considerable criticism. It usually focuses only on the client's weaknesses and fails to look at the strengths that can be used. There is a preoccupation with the client's history. The classification oversimplifies the client, creating the possibility that the counselor may conceptualize and treat the client as a stereotype of the label and miss the client's individuality. The classification systems are not reliable enough to lead to differential counseling plans. The label suggests a final judgment indicating the diagnosis is an act that is not tentative.

Classification systems have failed to relate classification to differential counseling procedures. Menninger conceded, "I am somewhat ashamed to admit that it has taken me a quarter of a century to realize that this formula [treating the patient according to his diagnosis] rarely works out this way in actual experience" (1968, p. 8). It seems clear that a classification bearing no relation to counseling procedures is of little value. It has been assumed that there should be different counseling methods associated with the various categories of client problems. The attempt to look at the diagnostic categories with this in mind has led to persistence in attempts at classification.

The difficulty of classifying client problems is evident from the initial interview with Tom. He was having problems in course work and was considering whether or not to attend college. The college-or-work choice would involve a vocational decision. It was clear that Tom had an internal conflict that he could not describe clearly. There was the additional possibility of conflict with his parents. Should the counselor categorize Tom's problem in each area or seek the one major cause? How might counseling differ with his various problems? Do these classifications help a counselor understand Tom?

Over the years, the opponents of diagnosis, frequently Client-Centered theorists (Rogers, 1951), did not stress structure of any sort, including diagnosis or assessment. In their view, diagnosis is palliative and superficial and sometimes restricting and negative to the counseling relationship. The basic reason for Client-Centered theorists' rejection of diagnosis was their position that the client is the only one who can fully understand the dynamics of her or his own behavior. Change in behavior comes only through a change in perception of the self. Rogers claimed that the client will deal with or explore problems "as soon as he is able to bear the pain, and that he will experience a change in perception as rapidly as that experience can be tolerated by the self" (1951, p. 222). Diagnosis places evaluation in the hands of someone else, which may foster feelings of dependency and interfere with the empathic relationship. Patterson (1959) also suggested that diagnosis is not necessary because all maladjustment is similar in origin and the technique of counseling is not dependent on the nature or content of the conflict.

Many have been concerned that psychiatric diagnosis leads to labeling clients and may, in fact, hinder the individual's chances for change. Sometimes clients as well as professional workers accept the labels. Monahan (1977) studied the effects of using psychological labels on the expectations for clients' change and recovery. Because initial diagnosis is required in many outpatient agencies as well as in hospital settings, the importance of preliminary labels may affect the way staff members behave with clients. Thirty-nine staff members were given a description of a client and asked to indicate the expected length of stay in the hospital, chance of readmission, chance of leading a normal life, and overall prognosis. The findings indicated that staff members working in acute treatment areas were significantly negatively affected by the diagnosis when rendering a prognosis. Although the results of this study are tenuous, they do suggest that using labels in diagnosis requires caution.

DIAGNOSIS AS UNDERSTANDING

The impact of client-centered theory challenged the concept of diagnosis by classification. Diagnosis, however, may also be viewed as a process of understanding and entails a very different approach: "In a very meaningful and accurate sense, therapy 'is' diagnosis, and diagnosis is a process which goes on in the experience of the client, rather than in the intellect of the clinician" (Rogers, 1951, p. 223).

We suggest that diagnosis is a process that involves both the counselor and the client. Diagnosis as understanding uses working hypotheses that are constantly subject to revision by any new cognitive and affective factors introduced in the interview by the client and by other sources.

How does the counselor establish the working hypothesis? In a statement challenging the use of categories, Bordin advocated understanding the client, suggesting that it seems more fruitful to rely on a well-differentiated theory of personality as a basis for trying to understand a particular person (1955). This concept bases diagnosis on the counselor's understanding of the client in accordance with the counselor's philosophy of human nature, personality theory, and counseling theory.

The concept of the counselor as hypothesis maker and model builder has received wide support. Pepinsky and Pepinsky (1954) proposed that the counselor be a model builder by forming a "micro-theory" of the client's behavior. They contended that the counselor must distinguish between observation and inference; state testable hypotheses; test them; and reconstruct the microtheory in light of new information. It is clear that the counselor's responses in the interview result from her or his understanding of the client.

Similarly, Meehl (1954) viewed the process as one in which the counselor brings events and immediate circumstances together into a "conception of this person." Wrenn (1951) characterized it as "process diagnosis" while Super (1957) talked about the counselor's "picture of the client."

These early writers embraced the idea of diagnosis as understanding. The counselor maintains continuing understanding by formulating a personal theory for the client. That personal theory is generally based on some larger theory of personality development, maladjustment, and counseling theory.

With this approach to diagnosis, in the initial interview with Tom the counselor can only begin to establish some working hypothesis. There is no need to make a judgment—only to understand the client.

DIAGNOSTIC PROCESS

To use diagnoses effectively as understanding, the counselor remains open to himself or herself and to new information. The process of diagnosis is complex and calls for understanding as many facets of the client as possible.

Robinson (1963) contended that at least four aspects of client analysis are needed in formulating a diagnosis that is to serve as a basis in selecting appropriate counseling methods. The first aspect follows the traditional concept of looking for the cause of difficulty to determine the treatment. An intensive case study is necessary to understand the complex pattern of causal factors as well as the client's previous dynamics of adjusting to his or her situation. Much of this will be gathered in the counseling interview; however, testing may contribute valuable information.

Psychological tests present problems to be solved by the client under specified interactional conditions. Compared with usual interview procedures, most psychological tests provide greater standardization of stimulus conditions. Test results should represent objective material; the subjective element consists in the client's interpretation of the factual results. Psychological tests are an objective aid to observation in the diagnostic process.

All too frequently, testing is conducted in a separate interview and the results of the tests communicated to the counselor for implementation of the diagnosis. However, there is much to be gained from having the counselor making the diagnosis administer a test during the interview. In addition to the specific answers given in the test, the counselor can thereby obtain a behavioral sample of the patient's reaction to a problem situation in a relatively stressful interpersonal situation. The use of tests in the interview can be considered a miniature life experience, yielding information about the patient's interpersonal behavior and variations in behavior as a function of the stimulus conditions (Kanfer & Saslow, 1965).

The client's modes of achieving adjustment reflect a range of responses, from reliance on particular defense mechanisms and selective responses to stimulation associated with those defenses. Responses to various test items are verbalized end products of thought processes initiated by the items. A test response, then, is more than just a score, although scores may be helpful in making comparisons with other persons or with the same client after therapy. Because it represents the individual's characteristic style of thinking, a test response allows inferences concerning the client's predominant behavior pattern. Hence, the person administering the test may learn more from the client than just the test score.

The client must be made to think in a variety of problem situations so that the counselor can distinguish the pervasive aspects of her or his efforts at adjustment. It is important for the counselor to learn about the client's past adjustment efforts (including his application of assets and liabilities) to new problems. Usually there is considerable continuity between past and present adjustment behavior, but it is possible to have a discrepancy. From the test responses, the counselor can form a picture of the characteristic efforts at adjustment. It is imperative that the counselor check the implications of any one response or pattern against the implications of all others. When enough patterns have one or two major implications in common, an interpretation is possible. The counselor seeks as few general conclusions as possible that embrace all the significant patterns. An interpretation is a prediction that certain behavior or thinking will be found by direct observation to characterize the individual. The interpretation applies to thinking or behavior that can be immediately apprehended and does not commit the counselor to any diagnosis. The counselor incorporates test data, case experience, and observations into a set of diagnostic hypotheses about the patient.

The second focus of client analysis looks for the client's positive characteristics. It emphasizes describing the goals involved in building the strengths of a client, thus giving direction to counseling. The diagnosis is focused on identifying the positive areas of the client's life that he or she would like to strengthen.

A third focus of the process involves discovering the manner in which the client responds to stimuli so that the counselor can select appropriate counseling methods. The counselor looks for the client's adjustment techniques so that they can be reinforced. The counselor studies how the client responds to certain situations and why certain responses make it possible to develop a model of the client. This is helpful in understanding the client and determining which methods will be effective.

The fourth aspect involves the moment-by-moment responses of the counselor to aid the client in learning more appropriate behaviors. With the conceptualization of the client—the problem area, the client's dynamics of adjustment, and the counseling goals—the counselor selects the techniques that best suit the goal being worked on at the time.

THOUGHT PROCESS

In the counseling interview the counselor's thought processes can involve various diagnostic styles. Gauron and Dickinson (1966) investigated diagnostic decision making in psychiatric interviews and then described six approaches. Their illustrations seem appropriate to the processes that might be found in counseling. In the intuitive-adversary approach the counselor commits himself or herself to a diagnosis on an intuitive basis early in the interview and then challenges the information to disprove this diagnosis. This approach, dependent as it is on intuition, is vulnerable to attitude, bias, or distortion.

In another approach, the overinclusive-indecisive, a counselor starts in one direction and drifts into a different one when information that suggests another potential direction is presented. The final result is a decision maker in conflict with no apparent confidence in his or her ability to form conclusions. Diagnosis is impulsive and probably arbitrary.

The textbook approach is used by a counselor who follows a rigid format, asking for information as it appears in written records and case history writeups. This counselor has no concept of the relative value of the information and ignores information with potential diagnostic clues in favor of a predetermined course. The bibliography approach is closely related, though not as structured. Information is not requested in any predetermined order but apparently on the basis of whim. A counselor using the bibliography approach is compulsive in obtaining all the information but impulsive in getting it.

Two other approaches result in more meaningful processes. In a diagnosis-by-exclusion approach, the counselor lists several broad diagnostic possibilities. As the counselor gathers information, she or he excludes these possibilities one by one until the most meaningful one remains. This approach is inductive in nature: the counselor infers conclusions on the basis of information and functions as a data gatherer and excluder. This approach might be an effective process if a counselor has to diagnose for classification.

In the flexible-adaptable approach, the counselor has no preconceived ideas about the order in which information is requested but goes where the information leads, modifying ideas as he or she receives data. The counselor's current thinking, derived from the impact of the combined information, determines what she or he responds to next with the client.

If diagnosis is viewed as a continuous process to understand clients—where they are at the moment as well as where they have been—the last approach would be most helpful. It seems that a relatively unstructured method of gathering information would permit clients more freedom to explore themselves and their environmental situation. This will yield more meaningful information and help the clients gain self-insight. The thought process of the counselor could extend from the inductive-logical to the intuitive-alogical. The inductive thinking would probably be more productive. The logic might follow the inductive process rather than a prescribed set of questions.

Used in the capacity of a working hypothesis, diagnosis seems valuable. The following excerpt from Kell and Mueller (1966) describes how to make the best use of diagnosis:

> Diagnosis . . . is an interpersonal process in which the sole purpose of the diagnosis is to understand the relationship well enough to be able to help the client to change. . . . The initial diagnosis is only one of the means that the counselor has of setting the counseling relationship into motion. As the counseling process continues to progress appropriately, the process of diagnosis becomes a more intimate, idiosyncratic one. . . . Whether the counselor's diagnosis changes will be a function of whether the relationship becomes closer, because only in an intimate relationship is it safe for the client to talk about the meaning that his behavior has for him. . . . As the relationship grows stronger, the diagnosis necessarily becomes more specific to this person, and the counselor leaves the generic ideas farther and farther behind him as he and the client delve more deeply into the meanings of his experiences (pp. 16–17).

How successful are counselors in the process of formulating a personal theory for their clients? Several studies have examined this question. McArthur (1954) had counselors predict behavior over a ten-year period. All the counselors tended to use a variety of data and formulated hypotheses from several theories regardless of their theoretical orientation. They were operating from some conception of the person. Two early studies pointed out the problem in the process. Koester (1954) recorded counselors' thought processes and found they did interpret data, synthesize the data, make hypotheses, and evaluate their hypotheses, but were reluctant to accept negative information that would refute the hypothesis. A similar finding by Parker (1957) suggested that although counselors did make a conceptual model of the client, they did not increase the richness of the model from interview to interview. Gauron and Dickinson (1966) reported that clinicians were influenced by their initial impressions. They compared the initial and final diagnoses and found that in eighteen of thirty-six cases they were the same. It appears that counselors make hypotheses in building a model of the client but often do not modify them. The result is a judgment, not a fluid, changing process.

A related area involves the controversy regarding the effectiveness of a counselor's clinical prediction compared with using data in a formula to make a statistical prediction. Meehl (1954) reviewed nineteen studies that predicted success in some kind of training, education, or recovery from psychoses. He reported that ten studies found no difference in the effectiveness and nine found that the statistical method was more effective. For years this information was used to suggest that the counselor should use a statistical formula for prediction whenever possible. In educational and vocational counseling this is frequently possible.

Watley conducted two studies on counselors' predictions on student grades in college. In one (1966a) he investigated the predictive validity among individual counselors and tried to identify factors that differentiated between the most and least accurate predictors. He found that increased amounts of data did not affect the predictive accuracy of the counselors as a group. Predictive ability was highly individual. Although no counselor was able to predict better than the average of the statistical predictions, some consistently equaled it. The counselors who were the best predictors obtained significantly higher Miller's Analogies Test mean scores and had a higher mean P+ score on the Minnesota Multiphasic Personality Inventory. These scores suggest the better predictors were better able to understand abstract concepts and had stronger needs to develop knowledge of the constructs with which they worked.

A second study by Watley (1966b) investigated the counselors' confidence in the accuracy of their predictions. These findings suggest that counselors who lack confidence in their predictions are more often correct than those who express the most confidence in their judgments. Educational and vocational counseling relies heavily on the accuracy of counselor predictions. The results of these studies indicate that counselors arrive at inaccurate conclusions and that unless they recognize how inaccurate their predictions are, their efforts may be detrimental to a client.

MODELS OF DIAGNOSIS

There are models of diagnosis that help the counselor by providing a structure for his or her thought processes. The task of diagnosis is essentially to answer the following three questions: (1) What specific behavior patterns need changing in terms of their frequency of occurrence, intensity, duration, or in the conditions in which they occur? (2) Under what conditions was this behavior pattern established and what factors currently maintain it? (3) What are the best methods to produce the desired changes in this client (Kanfer & Saslow, 1965)? A model can serve as a guide for gathering information, but the counselor will still rely on a personality and counseling theory.

We present three models of the diagnostic process: a medical model, a cyclical interpersonal conflict model, and a behavioral model.

MEDICAL MODEL

There is no uniformity among medical models. In fact, Nathan (1967) believed the lack of common diagnostic purposes and procedures in psychiatry raises questions about the possibility for future advances in the field.

Someone using a medical model generally gathers a history of the problem to discover its origin and evolution. The classification system is used to summarize observations and relate them to other conditions. The clinician uses this knowledge of the client's assets and liabilities to make a treatment plan and predict chances of success.

Ledley and Lusted (1959) analyzed the rationale for the traditional medical model of diagnosis. They differentiated between a disease complex and a symptom complex. The disease complex describes known pathological processes and their correlated signs; the symptom complex represents particular signs present in the individual client. The bridge between these two complexes is provided by available medical knowledge, and the final diagnosis is tantamount to labeling the disease complex. Because of the current gaps in medical knowledge, it is necessary to use probability statements when relating disease to symptoms, thereby admitting a possibility for error in diagnosis. Once the diagnosis is made, decisions about treatment still depend upon other factors including social, moral, and economic conditions.

Noyes and Kolb (1963) offered a medical model for diagnosis that leads to a multiple diagnosis. They suggested that a counselor construct a diagnostic formulation of three parts: etiology, behavior, and prediction. The etiology is a genetic diagnosis incorporating the constitutional, somatic, and historical traumatic factors involved as primary sources or determinants of the mental illness. The behavioral aspect is a dynamic diagnosis describing the mechanisms and techniques unconsciously used by a client to cope with anxiety and enhance self-esteem. This dynamic diagnosis essentially traces the client's psychopathological processes. The predictive part is a clinical diagnosis of the reaction syndrome, the probable course of the disorder, and treatment methods that would most likely prove beneficial.

The kind of information communicated in each type of diagnostic label is specifically adapted to the purpose for which the diagnosis is used. This triple-label approach attempts to counter the criticisms aimed at the use of a single classification system, in which a diagnostic formulation intended to describe current behavior may be found useless in predicting the responses to a specific treatment.

Because of its reliance on a classification system, probably not many counselors will use the medical model. Awareness of this model, however, may be helpful for working with a client referred with this type of diagnosis.

A CYCLICAL MODEL OF INTERPERSONAL CONFLICTS

Walton (1969) proposed a cyclical diagnostic model to understand interpersonal conflicts. Although the model was designed for third-party consultation between two people having conflicts, it also seems appropriate for use in counseling, for many clients present problems that are essentially interpersonal conflicts. Figure 15–1 suggests that the client may occasionally engage in a manifest conflict and at others in a latent conflict. Something occurs to trigger opposition between the client and other individuals, and they engage in conflict-relevant behaviors. After they experience the consequence of their interchange, the conflict between them becomes latent again. Interpersonal conflicts tend to be dynamic and may escalate or deescalate from one cycle to the next. The figure shows that if the client does not understand the situation and make some resolution the conflict may go on repeatedly. The implications are that the counselor must help the client understand not only the conflict behaviors and the triggering event, but also the underlying issues that lead to the difficulties. To diagnose a client in a conflict situation, the counselor must search for the issues involved in the problem, the triggering event, the interpersonal conflict behaviors, and the outcomes or consequences of the conflict.

FIGURE 15-1 A CYCLICAL DIAGNOSTIC MODEL OF IN-TERPERSONAL CONFLICTS

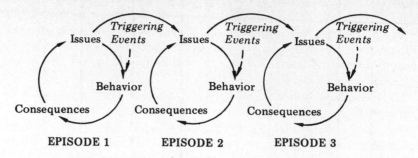

Source: Richard E. Walton, *Interpersonal Peacemaking: Confrontations and Third-Party Consultation*, © 1969, Addison-Wesley Publishing Company, Inc., Chapter 5, page 72, figure 5-1, "A Cyclical Model of Interpersonal Conflict." Reprinted with permission.

Issues

A major distinction must be made between substantive and emotional conflicts. Substantive issues involve disagreements over policies, practices, and rules; emotional issues involve negative feelings between the individuals. The substantive issue is basically cognitive; emotional conflicts are affective. The client and counselor should not focus on one aspect of the issue while ignoring the other. Issues of conflict between an adolescent and his or her parents regarding rules of behavior appear to be substantive; however, there may be emotional issues as well.

Diagnosing the conflicts requires determining which issues are basic and which merely symptomatic; the latter represent a proliferation of the basic issues. Walton (1969) maintained that a person may inject a second or a substitute issue into a conflict because it provides a more legitimate issue for the conflict. Substantive issues are often injected into a basically emotional conflict because the latter sometimes risks so much embarrassment for one or both individuals. The eventual resolution of the symptomatic issue may lead also to a resolution of the basic issue.

Defining the issues provides better understanding of the individual in the situation. Substantive conflicts require bargaining and problem solving between the individuals. Emotional conflicts require restructuring of perceptions and then working through the feelings between the individuals involved.

Triggering Events

As Figure 15-1 shows, the issues can and do exist as latent conflict for certain periods. Latency is maintained with barriers to overt conflict, but certain circumstances are capable of precipitating action. Frequently clients will present a problem by describing the triggering events that set off the conflict and then describe the conflict behaviors between themselves and another. Through understanding the triggering events and conflict behaviors the counselor and client may be able to understand the issues in the conflict situation.

Various barriers can prevent a person from initiating or reacting to a triggering situation. Among these barriers are internal forces such as attitudes, values, needs, fears, habitual behaviors, or perceptions of the other's or one's own vulnerability. Despite these barriers some events or circumstances are able to precipitate an open conflict. With the underlying issue always present, a vigorous disagreement, problem-solving interchange, or candid confrontation may serve as a triggering event to break through the barriers and establish conflict behaviors.

An important aspect of the diagnosis is understanding which types of barriers are customarily used and what triggers the open conflict. This level of understanding can be used in several ways to handle the conflict. First, by understanding the barriers she or he and the other individual are using as well as what triggers the conflict, the client is better able to choose the right time and place as well as an appropriate issue for dealing with the conflict. If the client prefers to prevent an open conflict, at least temporarily, he or she can take steps to maintain the barriers and head off triggering events. Second, for a particular conflict, certain events will trigger conflict tactics that initiate a bad cycle, whereas others may initiate a benevolent type of conflict. Diagnosing a particular conflict involves distinguishing between these two circumstances. Third, an analysis of the events that surround and precede a conflict may provide clues about the basic issue in a recurring conflict. Fourth, the frequency of conflicts may be systematically controlled by operating on the barriers or triggering events.

Conflict Behaviors

Conflict behaviors involve both the tactics used in the conflict and overtures toward resolution. The conflict tactics may include expressions of feelings of conflict, such as anger and attack or avoidance and rejection. The behaviors also include competitive strategies intended to win the conflict such as blocking, interrupting, depreciating others, forming alliances, and outmaneuvering the other. These are sometimes demonstrated by arguing in front of neutral people, criticizing the other person, blaming the other person for the problem, challenging his or her judgment, and forming an alliance with someone in a superior position.

Overtures toward a resolution involve cooperative strategies intended to end the conflict, such as a unilateral or reciprocal concession and a search for integrated solutions. These behaviors include agreeing to meet, listening to the other side, expressing regret about the difficulty, and acknowledging blame in the situation.

The diagnostic aspect of the conflict behaviors involves helping the client understand her or his own feelings and behaviors when the conflict comes into the open as well as developing an understanding of the other person's feelings and behaviors. This approach contributes to the client's insight into himself or herself in situations and can lead to behavior change.

Consequences

It is important for the counselor and the client to understand the consequences of the conflict—the potential costs and benefits of conflict that affect the individuals, their work, and others around them. What does the conflict cost the other person? Do the costs of the conflict outweigh the gains? Does the potential improvement justify the risk? An analysis of the particular consequences of a recurrent conflict will provide an understanding of why the conflict is escalating or deescalating. Understanding the consequences of the current conflict and appreciating the issues involved will enable the client and counselor to identify desirable and realistic outcomes and to map strategies for achieving the outcome.

A BEHAVIORAL MODEL

The growing popularity of behavioral counseling has led to an increased use of behavioral analysis as a means of diagnosis. Behavioral counseling is aimed toward problem solving, decision making, and overt behavior change. When the behavioral counselor asks questions of clients, he or she is actually helping them identify questions to ask themselves. These questions may lead to a productive accumulation of data about the individuals, their world, and how they interact with it. The behavioral analysis concept of diagnosis is not based on a disease model that assumes that behaviors are overt symptoms of an underlying problem. Instead, it views behavior disruptions primarily as problems of human learning. Diagnosis consists in eliciting data from clients about the development of the problem behavior, on the assumption that identifying original learning conditions will be helpful in developing procedures to remedy the inappropriate behaviors. The purpose of the diagnosis is to identify the antecedent events that cause the problem behavior to be maintained.

With the behavioral approach, an effective diagnostic process includes specifying therapeutic methods on the basis of information obtained from a continuing assessment of client behaviors. A behavioral analysis has the advantage of specifying the causes of a behavior in terms of environmental events that can be objectively identified and possibly changed. A behavioral diagnosis assumes that a description of the problem behaviors, the controlling factors, and the means by which they can be changed are the most appropriate explanations of the behavior pattern. Diagnosis, then, consists in focusing on specific problem behaviors, identifying their environmental and personal antecedents, and developing procedures to extinguish old behaviors and/or acquire new ones.

COUNSELOR BEHAVIOR

The counselor operates on two levels during the diagnostic process. On a conceptual level, the counselor develops hypotheses and makes inferences based on observations and reports of the client's behavior. At the same time, the counselor's overt responses communicate positive regard, empathy, and genuineness to the client, who otherwise might not provide the necessary data for the inferences.

Blackham and Silberman (1971) suggested that four steps are involved in formulating change strategies. First, the counselor defines and analyzes the problem behavior. Second, the counselor secures a developmental and social history to delineate further the problem and its present adaptation. Third, the counselor and client establish specific goals for behavior change. Fourth, the counselor and client identify and implement methods of modifying the behavior.

Definition of the Problem

Analysis of the problem begins with the statement from the client or the referral agent. Once the problem is stated, it is desirable to expand the analysis: when, where, and with whom is the problem behavior exhibited? It is important to know how pervasive the problem behavior is; that is, does it occur frequently? is it a new behavior the client wishes to initiate? or does it occur only in specific situations with specific people?

The counselor seeks to identify the antecedents as well as the consequences of the behavior. By making a systematic analysis of the problem behaviors, she or he is able to determine which stimuli or events may be evoking the behavior. The most productive approach is to search for specific behaviors and events in the client's history that might have originated the current disruptive or ineffective behaviors.

It is important also to know the situational factors of the client's living conditions that may be helpful in effecting change. This knowledge involves analyzing the conditions under which the inappropriate behavior pattern originated and is maintained.

The client's inappropriate behavior may be widely separated in time from the originating situation. The counselor should distinguish between originators and maintainers of behavior. Even though the client perceives a problem behavior, it has persisted because the client has been receiving some type of reward. Therefore, the counselor explores possible reinforcing elements in the problem situation. Whenever it is possible, careful observation of the client's problem behavior in the appropriate situation helps to determine the reinforcing contingencies. If the client is in school, it may be possible to observe classroom behavior. In family situations, a family group process may permit analysis. It is important to determine who else is helping to maintain the client's behavior or could be helpful in modifying the behavior. If the client and counselor understand the reinforcements that are maintaining the inappropriate behavior, those reinforcements can be changed. Once a behavioral response has been acquired, it is subject to modification and shaping by means of new and partially relevant reinforcements.

The Developmental and Social History

The developmental and social history is useful not only in identifying health status and physical deficiencies, but also in obtaining a picture of the child's general developmental pattern. The developmental history should reveal the client's intellectual, social, and emotional development. Through the developmental and social history the counselor should gain a comprehensive picture of the client. The client should reveal areas of success and failure, competencies and deficiencies, social relationships, coping behavior, and areas of conflict.

For clients whose problem behavior has physical or organic determinants, the developmental history identifies these conditions for consideration in behavior analysis. The social history reveals the social reinforcement of the problem area—the stimuli, events, and conditions that serve as reinforcers. The counselor identifies these reinforcers by inquiring about the activities or things that the client selects when free choice is possible. The counselor then examines the extent to which the problem behavior may be resistant to change and which social reinforcements the client prefers. The counselor should be alert to the relative reinforcement properties of significant individuals in the client's life and how they might be utilized in a strategy to modify the behavior. In many cases it may be useful to interview other people in addition to the client, after securing the client's permission to do so.

Kanfer and Saslow (1965)* proposed a guide for the analysis of individual behavior to serve as a working model for the client's behavior. This guide covers the statement of problem as well as the developmental and social history. They organize a series of areas to analyze that yields immediate implications for a plan of treatment. The following seven categories briefly outline the diagnostic areas:

1. **Analysis of a Problem Situation**† The patient's major complaints are categorized into classes of behavioral excesses and deficits. For each excess or deficit the dimensions of frequency, intensity, duration, appropriateness of form, and stimulus conditions are described. In content, the response classes represent the major targets of the therapeutic intervention. As an additional indispensable feature, the behavioral assets of the patient are listed for utilization in a therapy program.

2. **Clarification of the Problem Situation** Here we consider the people and circumstances that tend to maintain the problem behaviors, and the consequences of these behaviors to the patient and to others in his environment. Attention is given also to the consequences of changes in these behaviors that may result from psychiatric intervention.

3. **Motivational Analysis** Since reinforcing stimuli are idiosyncratic and depend for their effect on a number of unique parameters for each person, a hierarchy of particular persons, events, and objects that serve as reinforcers is established for each patient. Included in this hierarchy are reinforcing events that facilitate approach behaviors as well as those which, because of their aversiveness, prompt avoidance responses. This information has as its purpose to lay plans for utilization of various reinforcers in prescription of a specific behavior therapy program for the patient, and to permit utilization of appropriate reinforcing behaviors by the therapist and significant others in the patient's social environment.

4. **Developmental Analysis** Questions are asked about the patient's biological equipment, sociocultural experiences, and characteristic behavioral development. They are phrased in such a way as (a) to evoke descriptions of his habitual behavior at various chronological stages of his life; (b) to relate specific new stimulus conditions to noticeable changes from his habitual behaviors; and (c) to relate such altered behavior and other residuals of biological and sociocultural events to the present problem.

* Reprinted from the *Archives of General Psychiatry*, June 1965, *12*. Copyright © 1965, American Medical Association.

† A detailed analysis is required for each patient. For example, a list of behavioral excesses may include specific aggressive acts, hallucinatory behaviors, crying, submission to others in social situations, etc. It is recognized that some behaviors can be viewed as excesses or deficits, depending on the vantage point from which the imbalance is observed. For instance, excessive withdrawal and deficient social responsiveness, or excessive social autonomy (nonconformity) and deficient self-inhibitory behavior may be complementary. The particular view taken is of consequence because of its impact on a treatment plan. Regarding certain behavior as excessively aggressive, to be reduced by constraints, clearly differs from regarding the same behavior as a deficit in self-control, subject to increase by training and treatment.

5. **Analysis of Self-Control** This section examines both the methods and the degree of self-control exercised by the patient in his daily life. Persons, events, or institutions which have successfully reinforced self-controlling behaviors are considered. The deficits or excesses of self-control are evaluated in relation to their importance as therapeutic targets and to their utilization in a therapeutic program.

6. **Analysis of Social Relationships** Examination of the patient's social network is carried out to evaluate the significance of people in the patient's environment who have some influence over the problematic behaviors, or who in turn are influenced by the patient for his own satisfactions. These interpersonal relationships are reviewed in order to plan the potential participation of significant others in a treatment program, based on the principles of behavior modification. The review also helps the therapist to consider the range of actual social relationships in which the patient needs to function.

7. **Analysis of the Social-Cultural-Physical Environment** In this section we add to the preceding analysis of the patient's behavior as an individual, considering the norms in his natural environment. Agreements and discrepancies between the patient's idiosyncratic life patterns and the norms in his environment are defined so that the importance of these factors can be decided in formulating treatment goals which allow as explicitly as possible for the patient's needs as for the pressures of his social environment (p. 532).

Stating Behavioral Goals

Setting specific behavioral goals with a client is a major part of the diagnostic task. From observation of the client's behavior or from the client's self-report, the counselor is able to determine the number of the client's specific behavior patterns that cause difficulty. The counselor helps the client describe which appropriate behavior patterns the latter would prefer.

According to Krumboltz (1966), the goals of behavioral counseling must be stated in specific terms if modification is to occur. Because the goals are stated in specific terms, they will be different for each individual. It is important for the client and counselor to agree on the goals of counseling. If the client's goal is outside the realm of the counselor, the latter must tell the client so. The counselor and client must work together in setting the behavioral goal for counseling and must agree that through counseling there is a possibility of achieving it. The behavioral goal is the basis for the strategy to modify the behavior. The methods the counselor utilizes to help each client may differ with the client and the problem he or she brings to the counseling situation.

Strategy for Behavior Change

The diagnostic process is intended to suggest specific behaviors as targets for modification and a specific treatment plan to be used. Therefore, the diagnostic formulation is action oriented. It is a guide for the initial collection of information, for organizing additional information as it is gathered, and for treatment. The formulation of the treatment plan follows this diagnosis as a series of goals. The attainment of these goals can also serve for evaluation of progress.

The behavioral analysis concept of diagnosis assumes that a diagnosis is never complete; additional information about the circumstances of the client's behavior pattern, the relationships among her or his behaviors, and the controlling stimuli in the client's environment is obtained continuously until it proves sufficient to change the client's behavior and resolve the problem. It is therefore necessary to maintain a continuing evaluation of the client's behavior pattern and its controlling variables, concurrent with attempts to change these variables by reinforcement and direct intervention until the changes in the client's behavior permit more appropriate behaviors. Thus, there is constant interplay between the diagnosis and the counseling strategies. The initial diagnosis seeks to understand the variables that can be directly controlled during counseling or outside treatment. Throughout successive phases of treatment, additional information about the client's behavior, reinforcement history, pertinent controlling stimuli, and other sociological limitations within both the client and the environment will possibly enlarge the initial diagnosis.

SUMMARY

This chapter has examined and evaluated the major concepts of diagnosis. The controversy about the role of diagnosis in counseling has concerned the process of classification, not diagnosis by understanding. Several classification systems have been proposed to identify client problems and help differentiate treatment. A classification system is helpful in research and record keeping but generally neutral in the counseling process.

Establishing working hypotheses to build a model or microtheory of the client seems more appropriate to achieve deep understanding of the client. This approach permits the counselor to make a series of tentative diagnoses rather than rendering an inflexible judgment. This diagnostic approach involves the counselor's counseling theory. There are models to guide a counselor in gathering information, in helping the client select goals, and in establishing a preferred mode of treatment.

REFERENCES

American Psychiatric Association. *Diagnostic and statistical manual of mental disorders.* Washington, D. C., 1980.

Blackham, G., & Silberman, A. *Modification of child behavior.* Belmont, Calif.: Wadsworth Publishing, 1971.

Bordin, E. S. Diagnosis in counseling and psychotherapy. *Educational and Psychological Measurement,* 1946, 6, 169–184.

———. *Psychological counseling.* New York: Appleton-Century-Crofts, 1955.

Byrne, R. H. Proposed revisions of the Bordin-Pepinsky diagnostic constructs. *Journal of Counseling Psychology,* 1958, 5, 184–188.

Callis, R. Toward an integrated theory of counseling. *Journal of College Student Personnel,* 1960, 1, 2–9.

———. Diagnostic classification as a research tool. *Journal of Counseling Psychology*, 1965, *12*, 238–243.

Gauron, E., & Dickinson, J. Diagnostic decision making in psychiatry. *Archives of General Psychiatry*, 1966, *14*, 233–237.

Kanfer, F., & Saslow, G. Behavioral analysis: An alternative to diagnostic classification. *Archives of General Psychiatry*, 1965, *12*, 529–538.

Kell, B. L., & Mueller, W. J. *Impact and change: A study of counseling relationships.* New York: Appleton-Century-Crofts, 1966.

Koester, G. A. A study of the diagnostic process. *Educational and Psychological Measurement*, 1954, *14*, 473–486.

Krumboltz, J. D. *Revolution in counseling.* Boston: Houghton-Mifflin, 1966.

Ledley, R. S., & Lusted, L. A. Reasoning foundations of medical diagnosis. *Science*, 1959, *130*, 9–21.

McArthur, C. Analyzing the clinical process. *Journal of Counseling Psychology*, 1954, *1*, 203–207.

McLemore, C., & Benjamin, L. Whatever happened to interpersonal diagnosis? *American Psychologist*, 1979, *34*, 17–34.

Meehl, P. E. *Clincial versus statistical prediction.* Minneapolis: University of Minnesota Press, 1954.

Menninger, K., Ellenberger, H., Pruyser, P., & Mayman, M. The unitary concept of mental illness. *Bulletin of the Menninger Clinic*, 1958, *22*, 4–12.

Menninger, K., Mayman, M., & Pruyser, P. *The vital balance.* New York: Viking Press, 1963.

Monahan, L. Diagnosis and expectation for change: An inverse relationship? *Journal of Nervous and Mental Disease.* 1977, *164*, 214–217.

Nathan, P. E. *Cues, decisions, and diagnoses.* New York: Academic Press, 1967.

Noyes, A. P., & Kolb, L. C. *Modern clinical psychiatry.* Philadelphia: W. D. Saunders, 1963.

Osipow, S. H., & Walsh, W. B. *Strategies in counseling for behavior change.* New York: Appleton-Century-Crofts, 1970.

Parker, C. A. A study of clinical diagnosis and prediction by means of verbal report. Doctoral dissertation, University of Minnesota, 1957.

Patterson, C. H. *Counseling and psychotherapy: Theory and practice.* New York: Harper & Row, 1959.

Pepinsky, H. B. The selection and use of diagnostic categories in clinical counseling. *Applied Psychological Monographs*, 1948. *15.*

Pepinsky, H. B., & Pepinsky, P. *Counseling: Theory and practice.* New York: Ronald Press, 1954.

Robinson, F. P. Modern approaches to counseling diagnosis. *Journal of Counseling Psychology*, 1963, *10*, 325–333.

Rogers, C. R. *Client-centered therapy.* Boston: Houghton Mifflin, 1951.

Schacht, T., & Nathan, P. But is it good for psychologists? *American Psychologist*, 1977, *32*, 1017–25.

Shectman, F., De LaTorre, J., & Garza, A. C. Diagnosis separate from psychotherapy: Pros and cons. *American Journal of Psychotherapy*, 1979, *33*, 291–302.

Strupp, H. Psychotherapy research and practice: An overview. In S. Garfield and A. Bergin (Eds.), *Handbook of psychotherapy and behavior change.* New York: John Wiley and Sons, 1978.

Super, D. E. The preliminary appraisal in vocational counseling. *Personnel and Guidance Journal*, 1957, *36*, 154–161.

Walton, R. E. *Interpersonal peacemaking: Confrontations and third-party consultation.* Reading, Mass.: Addison-Wesley, 1969.

Watley, D. Counselor variability in making accurate predictions. *Journal of Counseling Psychology*, 1966a, *13*, 53–62.

———. Counselor confidence in accuracy of predictions. *Journal of Counseling Psychology*, 1966b, *13*, 62–67.

Weiner, I. B. The role of diagnosis in a university counseling center. *Journal of Counseling Psychology*, 1959, 6, 110–115.

Williamson, E. G., & Darley, J. G. *Student personnel work.* New York: McGraw-Hill, 1937.

Wrenn, C. G. *Student personnel work in college.* New York: Ronald Press, 1951.

DECISION MAKING IN COUNSELING

CHAPTER SIXTEEN

Much counseling is related to helping clients make decisions. The choice of an occupation, the selection of courses of study, choosing between several life alternatives, and personal problem solving are examples of the decision-making dimension of counseling. Decision making is a skill and can be learned, modified, or improved, and the counseling process offers an ideal situation for the counselor to help the client learn. The counselor should know about decision making to be of maximum assistance to the client. The ultimate decision must be made by the client, but the counselor creates the decision-making environment and assists the client in learning the process.

The counseling situation offers an ideal setting for making educational decisions, vocational decisions, and personal decisions. In the actual counseling setting these areas are often interrelated.

THE COUNSELING SITUATION

The counseling setting offers an ideal situation for facilitating decision-making skills. All the principles of the counseling relationship, the counselor's value system, and her or his activity or inactivity are important. Counseling principles apply to any of its specific purposes. The counseling setting should be as free as possible from threat to clients as they attempt to deal with themselves and their concerns. Any counselor action that demeans the client inevitably reduces the number of possible effective outcomes. The counselor should respect clients, their feelings and values, and must like clients as fellow human beings regardless of unpleasant facets of their personalities. The attitudes that clients bring to the session must be recognized, accepted, understood to the greatest degree possible, and clarified when appropriate.

The decision-making relationship has some unique aspects. For one thing, the counselor must know whether a decision has actually been made. This may involve distinguishing between real and unreal decisions. Making the distinction is a counselor skill that necessarily improves with training and practice. The counselor must take care not to accept a decision that in fact either has not been made or has been made in order to avoid pressure from someone, perhaps the counselor. For example, when a student comes to the counselor and states a desire to go to college, the counselor asks certain questions to determine whether this is really the case and then decides that the client does indeed want to go to college. This settled, the counselor moves on to more important areas, namely type of college, college requirements, and so on. But in the midst of deciding between state colleges or private colleges, the client suggests that he or she is not really sure about wanting to go to college; it just seems to be the thing to do. This situation illustrates two important aspects of counseling decision making. First, a premature decision by the counselor is not wise. Premature decisions usually relate more to the counselor's needs and are of little value to the client. Second, even after the client has made a tentative decision, the counselor must continue to listen for cues that support or refute the earlier position. Kell and Mueller (1966) suggested that the client will raise important topics several times in the face of counselor avoidance or failure to respond to a cue.

It may be essential for the counselor to deal with indecisiveness or inability to make a decision. The counselor should be willing to help the client examine some of the causes for this behavior, especially when the reasons for this indecisiveness surface. This type of examination by counselor and client in a nonevaluative light can often move the client toward more productive activity.

THE DECISION-MAKING PROCESS

Much counseling is concerned with deciding on a course of action that is appropriate for the client. Both the counselor and the client participate in the process, in which the client's aspirations, self-understanding, interests, or values are interrelated with the rational process or sequence of decision making. The decision-making process is one that can be described and ideally will lead people to reasonably adequate outcomes. The counselor can deal with the process, but cannot control outcomes.

When the counselor has a client who wishes to move from indecision to decision, the counselor's job is often twofold: to teach decision-making skills and to help the client make a decision as a result of the process. In addition to variables in the counseling relationship, steps in the decision-making process include: (1) defining the problem, (2) generating alternatives, (3) gathering information, (4) processing information, (5) making plans and selecting goals, and (6) implementing and evaluating plans.

ESTABLISHING THE RELATIONSHIP

The need to establish a working relationship with the client is as important when the client's decision is vocational or educational as when the decision is an outcome of some personal type of counseling. The value of the relationship is equivalent throughout all types of counseling. Without a good one, the chances are less of working through the steps of the process toward successful outcomes.

DEFINING THE PROBLEM

The initial step in decision making is to define the client's problem or problems. The counselor and client work toward clear delineation of the client's needs. This is an extremely important but sometimes difficult step. The client may be reluctant to discuss concerns until she or he is more certain of the relationship and the counselor. The counselor must be willing to be patient and must behave in ways that indicate concern and a desire to be of assistance. Under these circumstances the counselor must take care not to misinterpret the client's actions.

A second impediment is the inability of some clients to verbalize their concerns. Young children often cannot tell the counselor directly, but may be able to show the counselor, as in play diagnosis. Other clients may be unable to describe their concerns or feel comfortable in describing the concern. The counselor's job is to be attuned to the characteristics of the client and to help him or her express concerns or decisions that the client feels are important.

Assuming that these impediments are overcome, the counselor's task is to listen to and understand what the client is saying. The counselor clarifies by focusing on the individual's perceived concern or need. The counselor allows sufficient time for the client to delineate the concerns or problems.

The counselor should monitor very closely the issues the client raises. Robinson (1950) suggested two ways for a counselor to deal with the clients' concerns: The counselor can deal with them one at a time in which case as each topic is raised the counselor attempts to work through it with the client until both are agreed that full knowledge is shared. The other method is to allow a fairly long listing of topics and then a working-through process. Both approaches have strengths and weaknesses. Cutting the client off before he or she has raised all topics may cause the client to misinterpret the counselor's attitude and to hesitate to raise further issues. Allowing a number of topics to be raised may tax the ability of the counselor and client to remember everything that is said. One aid is to tape the session if possible. This allows for a more thorough review of the topics and allows the counselor to formulate some questions for later sessions. Somehow the counselor and client must arrive at a definition of the problems, concerns, or decision-making areas. The counselor should be concerned with helping the client define her or his particular needs and the details of the decision. The counselor provides clarification statements to help the client make as clear a statement as possible about the possibilities. This may lead to one or more specific statements of the decisions that the client perceives as relevant.

GENERATING ALTERNATIVES

Together the counselor and client must identify the alternatives that are available and acceptable to the latter. The development of alternatives is crucial to the process. The counselor's job is to help the client learn ways of identifying and considering the greatest range of possibilities. First he and the client simply discuss possibilities. What has the client considered? What can the counselor add? Second, the counselor and client identify areas that seem crucial but for which there are insufficient data available. Various material may be necessary to expand the alternatives, perhaps published material or interviews with people related to the alternative under consideration. College catalogs, career guidance materials, and agency directories are examples of prepared materials. All these tools are designed to provide as wide a spectrum as possible of alternatives for the client.

Normally the process of generating alternatives will stop when the client stops discussing alternatives or pushes to move ahead. The counselor's sensitivity to the client's wishes ensures that the development of alternatives does not go too far and cause a breakdown of the process.

GATHERING INFORMATION

The client needs specific information about at least two things: the alternatives identified earlier and his or her own self. Information may not guarantee a good decision, but without it the chances of a good decision are greatly diminished. Herr and Cramer (1979) grouped the factors into four categories: (1) inner-limiting factors, such as ability and skills; (2) inner-directing factors, such as values and interests; (3) outer-limiting factors, such as accessibility and scope of educational and occupational opportunities; and (4) outer-directing factors, such as social class expectation and familial aspirations.

Within this framework the counselor and counselee work together to identify what is known and to gather information to fill in what may not be known. Tests of ability, interest, and aptitude may be administered or previous records searched to provide information to the client about these areas. Prepared materials, such as college catalogs, the *Occupational Outlook Handbook*, or the *Dictionary of Occupational Titles*, may be obtained to provide information on available occupations, educational opportunities, requirements, and so forth.

Previous academic and personal histories are utilized when necessary to provide information about the client. A work history may be developed. Specialized reading can be identified for both counselor and client to become more familiar with some of the less known aspects of the alternatives. Arrangements for the client to talk to people closely related to specific alternatives provide an opportunity to discuss pertinent questions with a knowledgeable source. Gathering information includes not only the more traditional aspect of counseling, discussion, but also activities designed to provide greater client self-understanding. The counselor must monitor and clarify the various pieces of information, which may mean doing outside reading and research on the client and the alternatives.

PROCESSING INFORMATION

Processing the information is an important and difficult step for the client and counselor. The client must now assess the alternatives that were generated and the information that was gathered. It is a difficult point for the counselor, who may assume that because the client has reached this point he or she can also follow through on the processing.

In most cases the client needs assistance in developing an effective method of completing this step. First the client must organize the information to determine value or relative status. The counselor now begins to help the client determine which factors from the information are relevant to the decision. The counselor uses this information in at least two ways: to develop predictions about the client's probabilities of success in the various alternatives, and to help the client better understand himself or herself and the probabilities of success (Brammer & Shostrom, 1977). Ideally the kinds of probabilities that emerge from the counselor's examination of data are roughly equivalent to the client's examination. If these are too divergent, the decision-making process may have to stop until this discrepancy is resolved.

When the data are gathered and examined for relevance between client characteristics and the probabilities, the counselor begins to provide interpretation to help the client understand the various aspects of the decision and any data not readily understood. The counselor begins integrating client data, outside information, and client characteristics.

MAKING PLANS

The next step translates the integrated information into a tentative plan of action. In this step it might be possible to provide the client with some practical experience, such as role playing, actual experience, simulation, or some mechanical manipulation of the factors that have been identified. The methods used will depend in part upon the general model the counselor is using.

There is some merit in focusing on the tentative aspect of the client's plan. The client must decide and thus move toward some specific course of action, but that course must be tentative to permit adjustments. Establishing both short- and long-term goals will enable the client to organize the goals or objectives in an order of hoped-for accomplishment.

Next, the client must implement the decision and develop some method of evaluation. It is important that the client be involved in both processes, for he or she must eventually take responsibility for the consequences. This involvement also helps the client learn the decision-making process for future critical or complex decisions.

Quite often the process stops after a decision is made. If so, the counselor should indicate interest in the evaluative aspect and should be available to review the outcomes at some not-too-distant time. The counselor should be able to help the client change direction when appropriate. Maintaining this availability poses some difficulty for the counselor, who usually has many clients and little time for the evaluation. The counselor may also find that the client is sometimes being manipulative and react negatively. If the client pressures the counselor to rearrange things so that a previous, less-than-adequate decision can be wiped out and something else substituted, the counselor should deal with this aspect before any further decisions are allowed or fostered.

ASPECTS OF DECISION MAKING

MODES

Decision making is an activity that leads an individual to choose how she or he will act on or react to an environment. The decision maker receives information from the environment, processes that information into a pattern, gives meaning to the data, and translates the information into an action, a reaction, or does nothing. Decision-making behavior is the product of years of learning and using appropriate skills. Several behavioral processes are involved depending upon the form, content, or meaning of the decision.

Washburne (1975) maintained that there are four modes of decision making. The first is puzzle solving. This mode is appropriate when the decision requires manipulation of environmental elements that behave in predictable ways. In puzzle solving the problem is defined in terms of outcome or goals. Courses of action are considered, and each is judged on a logical basis in terms of its applicability to goal attainment. Then the decision is made. The necessary skills for puzzle solving are the abilities to search through a wide range of possible courses of action, to evaluate correctly the available data, to select carefully, and to move toward implementation of the decision. Puzzle solving is active when the individual manipulates the environment toward the selected goals. It is passive when the individual seems to be swayed by the arguments of others.

Chance taking, the second mode of decision making, is appropriate when the goals of the decider are achievable only by external action of people, events, or organizations. The orientation of the chance taker has an important relation to this type of decision making. The decision maker may believe that the outcomes will be positive because past experiences indicate that most things turn out all right. Or, he or she may be pessimistic and believe that nothing will turn out right. The active chance taker seeks out and seizes upon situations in which, despite the risk of the unknown, the possibility of continued good luck exists. The passive person in this mode accepts whatever happens and tries to make the most of it.

The third mode is interactional decision making. It involves dealing with others who have their own goals and who may have some effect on the outcome through their behavior or lack thereof. Interactional decision making requires understanding of both oneself and others, of social norms, and a sensitivity to the interaction of people in a social setting. It involves the ability to see oneself through others' eyes. This mode also requires a degree of compromise or flexibility and the ability to give and receive communication. The counseling dyad provides a good opportunity for the individual to work through the various requirements of this mode of deciding.

Evaluative decision making involves responding to aesthetics, ethics, and values; that is, selecting one thing because it is "better" than another. The assessment and subsequent decision are made in terms of a set or system of values.

Often the decision-making process is reflexive or habitual, regardless of the particular mode in operation; a decision is called for and made with little concern about the reasons or consequences. When this is not the case the individual must choose a method of deciding and apply it to the problem or concern at hand. Inappropriate selection of a mode or its improper application to the problem results in ineffective or inefficient decision making.

REQUIREMENTS

The value of the decision-making process relates to satisfaction with its outcomes. The required skills can be learned, used, and evaluated. Gelatt et al. (1973) suggested that there are three major requirements of decision making.

1. **Examination and recognition of personal values** Values determine the satisfactions that can accrue to the individual. Examining and understanding one's values enhances the process of setting goals or objectives. The more clearly the person understands what these values are, the greater the potential for setting and reaching objectives with satisfactory results.

2. **Knowledge and use of adequate, relevant information** It is essential for the individual to have information and know how to locate and use information. Accurate information is necessary for developing alternatives, identifying possible outcomes, establishing the probabilities that certain action will lead to certain outcomes, and evaluating the desirability (personal preference) of the outcomes. The counselor helps the client examine each of these aspects and develop reasoned statements related to each.

3. **Knowledge and use of an effective strategy for converting the information into action** Eventually the individual must put the decision into action. Most often the decision maker integrates information and personal values into strategy. The strategy is the plan for deciding upon and implementing the action.

The strategy adopted will depend on the degree of risk or seriousness of the decision and on the person who must implement it. The counselor can help the client examine several strategies and to choose one that seems to offer the greatest potential for a successful outcome.

Sometimes it is possible to make a decision with little or no consideration of the process, as when a consumer shopping for vegetables in a supermarket selects a particular package of carrots. The decision can be accomplished through a variety of processes. The shopper may pick up the package without applying any criterion for selection, reject certain packages after applying negative criteria, or choose the package that most closely meets positive criteria. Probably the consumer could not specify which of the three processes he or she uses; yet over time that person is probably consistent in the way she or he chooses packages of carrots.

This example illustrates some of the major considerations in the decision-making process. Decision making can be accidental, can be based on negative decisions, or can employ selection criteria to guide the choice. In addition, decisions are distinguished by the existence or nonexistence of risk. In the example, the shopper probably was in a no-risk situation. It really did not make much difference which package she or he chose because all were approximately alike. There was also probably a guarantee that if the purchase proved unsatisfactory it could be returned.

ACCIDENTAL DECISIONS

A large percentage of the many decisions people make each day fall into the accidental category. Faced with the need to decide something, people decide. They may choose clothes because they were the first ones they saw. With this type of decision perhaps the most effective approach is the existential: do whatever seems right. But it is possible to use this process at the wrong time. Sometimes decision makers need to gain a clearer understanding of the process because the consequences of the decision are greater.

NEGATIVE CRITERIA

Decisions are often based on negative criteria. In effect, ruling out certain choices restricts what is actually available to the decision maker. A person looking at a menu in a restaurant, for example, must make a decision about what to order. Some would begin by eliminating items that are perceived negatively: "I don't like seafood" and "The roast duck costs too much." The individual is narrowing the list of available possibilities. The final choice may be the result of successive eliminations or of reducing the list to a number of equally attractive items. The customer has moved toward the selection by applying negative criteria.

POSITIVE CRITERIA

An individual often uses positive criteria to choose between equally attractive items: "I like item X because I've had it before" or "I think I will try item Y because I've heard others say how good it is." This person is establishing positive criteria for selection of the item. He or she decides to select the item with the most positive value without regard to negative feelings about the remainder of the items.

NO-RISK VERSUS RISK DECISION MAKING

If a decision presents no risk, the decision maker probably does not need to feel much concern. When risk is involved, however, the person needs to be aware of probable outcomes and of alternatives. The decision maker may need outside assistance to bring all critical elements into focus on the decision. Perhaps no-risk decisions can be valuable as learning experiences for later, more important decisions involving risk.

RISK TAKING

Making any decision involves a lack of certainty, the possibility of loss or failure as a result. Kogan and Wallach (1967) pointed out that risk taking refers to behavior in situations in which there is a desirable goal and lack of certainty that it can be attained. The situations may require a choice between more or less desirable goals, with the former having a lower probability of attainment than the latter. A possible, but not necessary, characteristic of such situations is the threat of negative consequences or failure; an individual might find himself or herself worse off after making a decision than he or she was before making it (Kogan & Wallach, 1967).

Counseling helps clients develop accurate predictors on which to base relevant decisions. Many models for prediction involve some sort of mathematical probability. Because less information is available about the risk-taking propensity of the client, the counselor must develop a method of determining both the client's level and the meaning risk has to the client. In doing so, it is important to understand the difference between chance outcomes and skill outcomes. A prediction involving a chance, such as gambling, requires a different set of dimensions from those used in predicting an outcome that involves some specifiable or learned skill. The decision maker will react differently when she or he can manipulate success than when chance is at issue. The problem is to specify the direction of this response. Some clients are gamblers and thus will take chances; others are more certain that the skills they possess are most important.

Thus, several situational and personal factors are related to risk taking and decision making, among them the client's propensity to take a chance or to use a skill. Kogan and Wallach (1967) suggested that the skill context stimulates a moderate level of risk taking, whereas a chance context induces avoidance of intermediate in favor of extremely risky or conservative strategies.

A second factor related to risk taking is the type and range of information available to the decision maker. The amount of information available and the degree of importance of the decision combine to determine what kind of decision is made. Although it is obvious that a purchase in the supermarket is less consequential than buying a house, most decisions are not as easy to differentiate, and the counselor may be called upon to provide information and promote the decision. There are probably more individual differences involved in seeking information than in other areas. However, it may be true that decision makers consider interrelated material more valuable than data that seem to have little internal consistency. It is also probably true that each individual has a fairly consistent pattern, so that once the client has given an indication of his or her proclivities the counselor will have a reliable base on which to build.

Gain or cost is also related to the individual's willingness to take a risk. In general, the greater the value of the goal, the greater the potential risk-taking behavior. As gain increases in value to predominate over costs, risk taking also increases. The converse is also true. Nevertheless, individual differences continue to require that the counselor understand the client's mode of action.

A fourth aspect of risk taking involves real incentives. It is easy to make decisions in hypothetical situations, but when real outcomes are involved, behavior is usually different. Conservatism is likely when real incentives are offered.

Finally there is some evidence that previous gains or losses affect the individual's willingness to take risks. However, although one would assume that prior successes with various models would lead the individual to utilize a similar model for all decisions, the evidence indicates that in some gambling situations previous losses seem to increase betting. The individual's reactions to prior losses or gains constitute important data for the counselor and client. The counselor should not force a method of risk taking or decision making upon the client, but should develop a more appropriate strategy by building upon or altering previous methods that are understood.

Although little substantive evidence is available about the relationships between the variables described above and risk taking, it is important, for certain decisions, that clients understand both the variables and their inclinations toward the variables. The counselor needs to know about variables in order to provide intelligent assistance to the client.

THE SEQUENTIAL NATURE OF DECISION MAKING

Many decisions are sequential in nature. The process extends over time, and previous experiences and decisions influence and direct the outcome. In some cases previous experiences and decisions lead to irreversibility. The vocational theory of Ginzberg et al. (1951) illustrates this point.

The important aspect to be considered here is that the client should be aware that the decisions he or she is called upon to make are for the most part not single events but rather part of a series of events that occurs over time. It is therefore important to analyze, organize, and synthesize (Gelatt, 1962) information at each point along the way. The counselor should provide assistance in monitoring these processes.

INFORMATION

Understanding decision making requires understanding the role of information in the process. The decision maker may use only minimal information in the decision process, or a great deal of information combined with feedback and prognosis. Hollis and Hollis (1969) described this as personalizing information. The individual internalizes the available information to make it usable. The counselor helps the individual select the information that is most relevant.

The availability of continuous information is also important in the decision-making process. The decider must understand that most decisions are avenues to later, more difficult decisions. The information available and used at one time may be far from adequate for future decisions. In addition, the information should be up-to-date so that decisions are as accurate as possible.

Many decisions that people are asked to make relate closely to activities several years in the future. In school, a decision made in the eighth or ninth grade to select one type of high school curriculum instead of another directly affects college plans and occupational choices; but the information necessary to help the individual make the decision is based on current conditions. It is difficult to know what the situation will actually be when the decision maker graduates. Information must be continuously updated, and the client may need to review the decision on a regular basis.

Some decisions are really not decisions but foregone conclusions. If there is a decision to be made, however, and if the client comes to a counselor, it is safe to assume that either the individual does not know what information she or he needs, does not have the information he or she wants, or is unable to use the information available.

PERSONAL PREFERENCE

People need to understand their personal preferences so that their decision will both move them toward a goal and meet their needs. Personal values are important in making any decision. In retrospect they often help decision makers understand why they did certain things when objectively the decision did not make much sense. To reach a meaningful personal decision, clients must understand what personal values they attach to any possible outcome.

VALUES

The values that people hold affect their decisions even though the decision makers may not be able to verbalize them. The counselor's job may include helping clients to be more aware of the relationship of personal values to the decision-making process.

Values are seen as representing a desirable condition. Interests, preferences, attitudes, and opinions contribute to the value structure.

Much has been written about the relationship of the counselor's value structure to that of the client. Counselors are sometimes told that they should not indicate their own values in an interview. At other times, counselors are told that they should reveal their value structure so that clients can either reject the values and/or the counselor or work within a known framework. How does the counselor deal with his or her own values as well as those of the client in helping the client reach a meaningful decision?

It is essential to the success of the counseling relationship that the counselor understand his or her value structure as well as the client's. Ideally the counselor will have had the opportunity to examine personal values during the preparation period. The counselor also needs to learn methods of identifying the client's values and to bring both together in a counseling relationship.

Values or beliefs are very personal matters, and the client probably will not be willing to discuss them openly at first. He or she will test the counselor to see if it is safe to talk about values or beliefs, to see if confidentiality is maintained. Most decisions will emerge from the interaction of the decider with various elements in her or his environment: values, significant persons, and meaningfulness of alternatives, among other aspects. The process usually involves the client's exposing herself or himself to changing values or beliefs, to a changed style of life, to the possibility of loss as well as gain. The counselor's job is to help the client deal effectively with the wide array of factors involved, make a decision, and follow through with it.

ALTERNATIVES

Decision making requires identifying and sorting through various alternatives. For example, a high school student may need to decide which college to apply to and, eventually, which college is the best for her or him. The student may use various methods of eliminating colleges, but in the end develops a list of several reasonable choices. The process involves weighing both the characteristics of the colleges and his or her strengths and weaknesses. By identifying certain factors about more than one college that are within the acceptable alternatives, the alternatives themselves become clear. The student may like the breadth of offerings at one college but not the size of its student population, the size of another but not the scope of courses. The student may be able to afford college Z but is concerned about its academic reputation. From all these alternatives the decider wants to select the college most appropriate for her or him.

Yet another factor comes into the decision-making process at some point: control of the decision by someone else. The college, for example, also exercises choice through admission or refusal. The same factor affects other types of decisions and introduces the element of compromise. The counselor should help the client recognize the existence of these external controls.

PROBABILITIES

The client must understand how certain actions or their omission affects the probabilities of success. This amounts to considering the degree of risk involved in some decisions. When risk is present, the notion of probability becomes important. Much information is available about probability. Many school counselors have data available on the probability of student success in certain courses. Expectancy tables also provide data that are helpful in college selection and evaluations of jobs. The college boards and American College Testing (ACT) programs provide basic probability information for potential students. Employment services often have information on the relationship of the client's performance to her or his characteristics, tested and otherwise. These figures are meant to be applied flexibly. Expectancy tables provide additional probability data for the student to analyze, organize, and synthesize for the final decision.

COMPROMISE

Allowing for compromise is basic to any decision and involves the ability to conceive of various levels of value or meaning. Super (1957) suggested that vocational development, including choice, involves a compromise between personal and social factors, self-concept and reality, newly learned responses and existing patterns of reacting. It is unlikely that any important decision can fulfill every possible value and personal need of the individual. Thus the need for compromise.

The counselor provides an opportunity for the client to consider various facets of the available alternatives. For example, a student may be considering attending a state college or university although the first choice may be a local university. The student's own values, his or her parents' desires, and other factors may preclude the possibility of choosing the local school. On the other hand, the small student population, the ratio of students to instructors, and the location of a private college may fit the value outcome of the student, but cost may preclude this choice, and the process of compromise may lead the student to choose another college that comes close to both values but does not meet either completely.

Society today tends to regard compromise negatively, in the belief that compromise constitutes giving in to the system and thus is an undesirable action. Both the counselor and the client should recognize the prevalence of this point of view and when necessary spend some counseling time discussing the meaning the client ascribes to compromise.

Other meaningful persons in the client's life may make a compromise necessary, for often their preferences are interjected into the decision-making process. The counselor should realize that the process of selection and the decision itself often involve more than one person's values and attitudes. In these cases it is necessary to include these people, either directly or indirectly, in the decision-making process.

OUTCOMES

Any decision is made to move toward desirable outcomes. In many instances previous experiences—in effect, decisions—play an important part in the outcome. For example, the student who earned top scholastic marks in high school has many potential outcomes available that the average student may not have. The decision to work hard enough to earn good grades contributed to potential outcomes.

It may be important for the client to deal also with suboutcomes, or outcomes of a lesser magnitude than the ultimate outcome. People need to have reinforcement along the way to the desired outcome. It is difficult to maintain a direction if the goal is so far away that it becomes meaningless. Subgoals may be necessary to keep the person moving steadily toward the final goal.

THE DECISION

The final decision must be the responsibility of the client. The counselor is responsible for fostering the investigation of alternatives, bringing relevant information to the problem, and involving people who are interrelated with the client and his or her decision. Nonetheless, the final decision is the client's.

In some cases the counselor's most difficult job is to get the individual to accept responsibility for the decision. Many people's perception of the counseling process is that the counselor can in some way force or coerce the client to move in different directions than she or he would independently. Although it might well be possible to help the client move in different directions, it is probable that the client has greater insight into his or her own behavior and can be helped to see new and more meaningful directions. This is not accomplished in a short time and, with some minor exceptions, does not come about because the counselor told the client to change. It involves a process of close interaction and involvement between the counselor and client.

GENERAL NOTIONS OF DECISION MAKING

Some general concepts apply to the decision-making interview. First, clients must develop the general direction in which they wish to move. They should have rather definite ideas about what purposes the decision may serve. Second, clients must be able to consider the extent of their freedom of choice. These may be external or internal in nature. Normally these parameters serve to restrict the range of possibilities and thus reduce confusion. Understanding the parameters may amount to understanding what one cannot do, leaving only positive actions from which a selection is made.

Third, clients need to understand themselves as persons. A counselor should not assume that clients have the ability to gain this understanding outside of the counseling situation, nor should the counselor accept all client statements about themselves. Often subsequent information suggests that the clients' understanding was partial at best. The decision makers may need help in gaining further understanding of their abilities, needs, goals, potentials, and other aspects in order to move toward the decision.

Decision making is continuous, tentative, and psychological (Hansen, 1965). Almost always there are prior factors or antecedent conditions related to the decision. Educational preparation is often closely related to vocational choices. The earlier selection of a specific educational course of action relates in a continuing way to the possible alternatives, and thus, to the choices available.

Fortunately, many can later be altered to some degree. Although there is a degree of irreversibility in any decision, since some alternatives may no longer be available, clients should realize that their decision does not bind them forever to the outcomes.

Very often outside factors are more deeply involved in the decision than is apparent. Hoppock (1957) described a man choosing an occupation well below the level of his abilities as an example of this situation; the moral factor of providing for his family was an unknown but very potent aspect in the life of the chooser. Other psychological factors, external or internal, may not be immediately visible, but are nevertheless closely related to the decision-making process.

MODELS OF DECISION MAKING

A model can help the client and counselor determine what steps need to be taken and what informational input related to decision making is needed. Several models have been developed for understanding the decision-making process.

AUTHORITARIAN MODEL

The authoritarian model of decision making posits a situation in which an expert advises the decision maker. The resultant decision is fairly predictable and, in some cases, is ensured by the authoritarian. For example, a young child about to cross the street may be given the important facts of the situation: Watch for the green light because this means you have the right-of-way; look out for cars; and so forth. Many of the elements can be described, but even more important, the child can be forced into the "right" decision by the parent's physical intervention. This does not mean that the authoritarian model always entails physical intervention. On the contrary, the expectation is that the individual will act reasonably or decide reasonably when he or she knows the facts.

LAISSEZ FAIRE MODEL

At the other extreme is the laissez faire model, in which the helping person gives very little information or direction. The decision maker is expected to sort out the important factors independently and to move in a reasonable direction because of the innate predominance of reason. The model calls for little involvement by the adviser.

MATHEMATICAL MODEL

Another type of model, the mathematical, approaches the decision by way of probabilities. The model presented by Katz (1966) in Table 16–1 is an example.

Two factors are important in this model: values and options. The individual determines three aspects of values important to her or him, such as money, power, and authority. Next, the client identifies the magnitude of the dimension. Finally, the client assigns a level of importance to the dimension with an arbitrary sum. These numbers can be altered; the only criterion for the original assignment is that they be manageable.

The client must also select a series of options, the possibilities within a given situation or a series of possibilities that may or may not be related. The client might list the curricular offerings at a particular high school or want to examine a variety of jobs available to him or her. The coefficient listed in the chart may be calculated according to some pattern of value magnitude; for example, the percentage of people earning a particular amount of money can provide the coefficient. In other cases the coefficient may result from an educated guess by the counselor concerning the probability that a certain percentage of people will attain a particular level of operation.

One other aspect must be determined: the probability of the client's success in the option. This figure is derived from expectancy tables, tests, and characteristics studies. The counselor may not always have complete prediction information and may have to supplement it with soft data such as counselor impressions.

The client performs the mathematical computations called for to get the expected value or success outcome available to her or him. These numbers, though tentative, provide the decision maker with information about continued exploration, changes in values, greater self-understanding, or the actual decision.

The mathematical model is more accurate when hard data are used instead of soft data. The desired outcome is to promote the deliberation of the decision maker through acquiring and processing relevant information. According to Katz, "This model of guidance for career decision making first assists the student in taking full cognizance of the range of values in the culture and encourages him to make his own values explicit" (1966, p. 9).

GELATT'S SEQUENTIAL MODEL

Gelatt (1962) proposed a decision-making framework in which objectives are defined, data collected and analyzed, possible alternatives studied, and conse-

TABLE 16–1 MODEL OF GUIDANCE FOR CAREER DECISION MAKING: ILLUSTRATIVE CHART FOR JOE DOE

| | VALUES | | | OPTIONS STRENGTH OF RETURN | | | | | | | |
| | | | | W | | X | | Y | | Z | |
DIMENSION	MAGNITUDE	IMPORTANCE (SUM=100)		COEFFICIENT	PRODUCT	COEFFICIENT	PRODUCT	COEFFICIENT	PRODUCT	COEFFICIENT	PRODUCT
A	A_1 A_2 A_3 A_4 A_5	30		5	150	2	60	4	120	2	60
B	B_1 B_2 B_3	20		4	80	5	100	5	100	3	60
C	C_1 C_2	10		5	50	1	10	3	30	1	10
D	D_1 D_2	5		5	25	3	15	1	5	1	5
E	E_1 E_2 E_3 E_4	35		3	105	2	70	3	105	4	140
Sum of value returns					410		255		360		275
Joe's probability of success					0.7		0.8		0.7		0.5
Expected value					287		204		252		137.5

Source: Martin Katz, A model of guidance for career decision-making. *Vocational Guidance Quarterly*, 1966, 15, 2–10. Copyright © 1976 by American Personnel and Guidance Association. Reprinted by permission.

quences evaluated. Figure 16-1 shows the framework of Gelatt's sequential model. First a purpose or objective is established. Then data are gathered from various sources, leading the client to a strategy that includes a prediction system, a value system, and the criterion for evaluating or selecting a decision. This process leads to a decision that may be tentative or final. In either case recycling may occur.

The importance of the Gelatt model is that it delineates possible involvement by a counselor. The counselor can provide specific assistance at each level, but avoids making the decision or framing personal input to lead to a specific decision.

STOCHASTIC MODEL

The stochastic model presumes that after a decision is made there are two separate, independent paths to be followed. A decision to follow one course denies the facts or probability of the other. Reversibility is not possible. This seems to be the type of situation that most people would prefer: to be able clearly to define the various paths to be followed and make a decision on the basis of knowing just what to expect. However, this is not usually the case. There is usually an element of risk involved, and the counselor and client must deal with this risk factor.

FIGURE 16-1 THE SEQUENTIAL DECISION-MAKING PROCESS

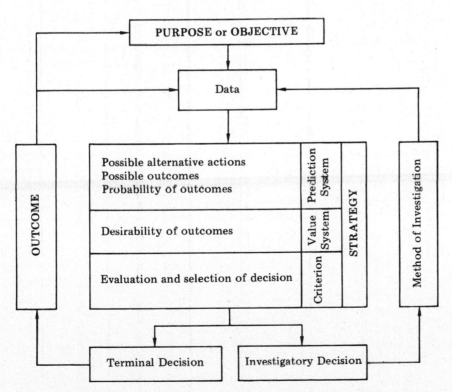

Source: H. B. Gelatt, Decision-making: A conceptual frame of reference for counseling. *Journal of Counseling Psychology*, 1962, 9, 240–245. Copyright © 1962 by the American Psychological Association. Reprinted by permission.

TRAIT AND FACTOR MODEL

The trait and factor model of decision making assumes that each individual has certain traits or characteristics. The choices available to the individual have certain identifiable factors or requirements. When these are known the individual can match her or his traits with the choice requirements, compromising when necessary. This essentially is the earliest model of vocational choice espoused by Parsons (1909), and it contains some major weaknesses. First, it describes a generally static process in which neither the individual nor the choice can change. In addition, though admitting that change can occur, the model does not effectively handle out-of-date material.

GOAL ATTAINMENT SCALING

A promising method for helping clients identify problems and develop goals is goal attainment scaling (Kiresuk, 1973). Table 16–2 (pp. 362, 363) shows the format of Kiresuk's *Goal Attainment Follow-up Guide*. The client is asked to select at least three potentially changeable problems or concerns and describe them briefly in the first row of the guide. The client then assigns a weight to the importance of the concern. These numbers allow the client to select priorities for the counseling interaction by indicating that certain problems are critical and need more immediate attention than others. The counselor can aid the client throughout the process by helping to clarify or answering some of the client's questions.

The third step is to choose a method for measuring how well the problems are being handled. In some cases there may be countable methods, as when the client is to talk to a given number of people each day. In other cases the measure is more subjective, as when the client wants to do something. The more objective the statement of measures, the greater the probabilities of showing some success.

In the next step the client or counselor—usually the client— fills in the levels of predicted attainment. It is often better to use different terms from those in the attainment column and to treat these attainments as distinct segments. Thus, the first question might be, "What do you expect for your own results in a specific period of time?" This is written into the row labeled "Expected level of success." The counselor must help the client develop a statement of what can reasonably be expected without over- or underestimating the success factor. Again, numbers for the measures are valuable because they allow for more clearcut evaluation of outcomes. The client may list two or three social activities per week for this level of success.

The next step is for the client to develop what she or he perceives as the most favorable outcome. Thus, the client enters the specific results of doing much better than he or she expects. Again, specifying the number of activities is helpful, such as "I will have at least six social activities per week" if we follow the same concern area as above. The counselor can provide assistance by helping the client develop realistic numbers or predicted outcomes. To do so the counselor must have an understanding of the client, his or her concerns, and the desired outcomes.

The client should also list the outcomes perceived as most unfavorable. When this step is completed, the client and counselor have an idea of the parameters in which the client wishes to work. Two other parts of the process still need completion. First, the client may wish to list intermediate outcomes in the rows "Less than expected success" and "More than expected success." These steps provide additional indications of the client's anticipated progress. Finally, the client needs to indicate which steps seem closest to the way she or he is currently behaving.

With this material the counselor can begin to provide assistance to the client. The following data are available: a list of the client's concerns; a ranking or priority assigned to those concerns; statements of hoped-for outcomes ranging from highly unfavorable to highly favorable, with intermediate steps specified; and a starting point.

DECISION MAKERS

Recent evidence (Mintzberg, Raisinghani, and Theoret, 1976) suggests that decision makers, when faced with complex situations, tend to subdivide the decision into more manageable segments, then to use procedures that may have served well previously in completing the process. Often the decision maker falls back on previous behavior to deal with new and perhaps more complex tasks. A systematic study of previous behavior often helps to determine what processes the client is likely to use. The counselor can use this information to aid the client in making decisions. The client may need to learn new methods or to alter previous ones to complete the current process successfully. Thus, the counselor and client must have some knowledge of the skills the client has, how these relate to the new situation, and ways of modifying them to meet the new situation.

Decisions may be classified in several ways. Mintzberg et al. used the categories of stimulus, process, and solution (1976, p. 251). Stimulus decisions are those made as a result of some event that triggered the need for the decision. For example, if a company decides to move to another location, workers must decide whether they wish to relocate. The stimulus, the proposed move, forces a decision by the worker.

Process decisions involve understanding the various factors that need to be considered in any decision. In the example used above, the workers may begin to examine the advantages and disadvantages of moving, visiting the new location and investigating other factors. They may investigate other job possibilities in their current area or consider retirement. Thus, in response to an external stimulus the workers enter a process to reach a decision that makes the most sense to them.

Solution decisions relate to outcomes of the decision-making process, to the potential solutions for the problem. The crucial variable is the actual decision. Success or failure is determined by whether the decision was a "good" one, not by the original stimulus or by the process through which the decision was reached. A solution decision poses the difficulty of postponing evaluation until after the decision has been made. Once the decision has been made, the counselor may need to help the client live with it.

Obviously, these decisions are interrelated. Many decisions are stimulated by outside events. In some cases the process, old or new, becomes an important aspect of the decision making. The person may look to outside sources for assistance in ordering the process or learning new ways of making decisions. The outcome, too, is important. The counselor can play an important role in helping

TABLE 16-2 GOAL ATTAINMENT FOLLOW-UP GUIDE

SCALE HEADINGS AND SCALE WEIGHTS

LEVELS OF PREDICTED ATTAINMENTS	SCALE 1: ($WEIGHT_1 = $)	SCALE 2: ($WEIGHT_2 = $)	SCALE 3: ($WEIGHT_3 = $)	SCALE 4: ($WEIGHT_4 = $)	SCALE 5: ($WEIGHT_5 = $)
Most unfavorable outcome thought likely					
Less than expected success					
Expected level of success					
More than expected success					
Most favorable outcome thought likely					

PROGRAM USING G.A.S. _____

1. _____ Client name

2. _____ Client number

3a. _____ Date of intake interview(s)
   b. _____

4. _____ Intake Interviewer

5. Persons involved in construction of the goal attainment follow-up guide:
   a. _____ Both clinician and client
   b. _____ Client only
   c. _____ Clinician only
   d. _____ Family member
   e. _____ Other:

6. _____ Recommended follow-up time

7. _____ Approved for follow-up

8. _____ Follow-up interviewer(s)

9. _____ Date of follow-up

Reminders for Follow-up Guide Construction

1. *Scale headings* are optional conceptual guides used to communicate general dimension of change to the follow-up worker. They identify the aspect of client functioning that the scale is intended to measure.

2. *Scale weights* are numbers assigned to the scales which reflect the relative importance of each scale. Large numbers should be assigned to the more important scales. Weight numbers may be any numbers from 1 to 100. (They need not sum to 100 or any other number.) Weight assignment is optional, but without specific weights all scales are weighed equally.

3. For each scale, weights from three to five *scale levels* must be defined by statements of behavioral or social events which correspond to levels of attainment. These events must be specific and well defined so that the follow-up worker may accurately determine levels will not overlap and the position on the scale.

4. Scales should generally not include more than one variable per level.

This form was developed under Department of Health, Education and Welfare Grant Number 5 R01 MH1678902 and 1 R12 MH2517901, by the Program Evaluation Project at 501 Park Avenue South, Minneapolis, Minnesota 55415.

the client devote time and energy to ensuring that the appropriate steps are identified, that the process is adequate to the situation, and that the final decision has a potential for a positive outcome in the life of the client.

It is clear that the counselor can have the greatest input during the process stage or when process is the mode of behavior, because the counselor knows something about decision making. The counselor does not make the decision, but fosters the climate for decision making by understanding the process, working with the client, and providing any necessary materials.

Often the process mode is very complex because the decider is not free to move in ways that meet her or his needs. Family, environment, training or lack thereof, developmental factors, and health are all related to decision making. The counselor can work with the client to identify as many of these factors as possible. The counselor also helps the client develop a strategy for integrating as many of the factors as is realistic into the process and final decision.

When available, a computer can be programmed to provide output that helps the client. In the model presented by Katz (1966), for example, the decider can identify factors, weight them, identify outcome variables, and receive a number of outputs that allow her or him to see the desirability of certain combinations. Because the computer can store data, the only limitations to output are time and money. The counselor and client can spend their time discussing the potentialities that have been identified. The decision is still the client's to make; a computer, the counselor, and other outside aids only foster the process.

In a recent article Johnson (1978) suggested that individuals have unique styles of collecting and analyzing data. His examination seems to show that there are four styles of decision making. The important characteristics are shown in Figure 16–2.

Spontaneous people tend to react in a holistic way: things are wonderful or lousy, hardly ever in between. They tend to ignore segments of the experience and to react as they feel about the total situation. This may involve a majority reaction; that is, when more negative things occur than positive, the total reaction is negative. Because decisions are based on how he or she feels about something that has occurred, this type of decider needs to experience things.

FIGURE 16–2 STYLES OF DECISION MAKING

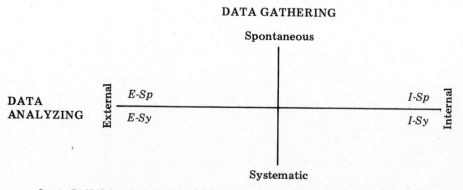

Source: R. H. Johnson, Individual styles in decision making: A theoretical model for counseling. *Personnel and Guidance Journal,* 1978, *56,* 533. Reprinted by permission.

Spontaneous people also commit themselves quickly to an alternative. Because they tend to react at one end or the other of a continuum, it may not take long for them to decide to invest energy and commitment into specific alternatives. Thus, they may pick the first or second choice they investigate because they wish to move toward resolution. They also react just as rapidly to new data and changes in decisions.

Systematic people react to the components of an experience. They evaluate experience by responding to a variety of parts and then give an overall reaction of good, pretty good, or not so good. Systematic decision makers usually require a lot of information about a particular idea or factor before taking any action.

Systematic people are cautious in their commitment to something new. They usually want more information or time before making the decision. After deciding upon an action they tend to stay with their decision rather than changing when new data are presented. In addition, systematic decision makers tend to move from task to task in a very methodical way. They establish goals and work toward them regardless of the time involved.

Styles of data analysis are external or internal depending upon the degree to which communication with someone else is necessary. External people tend to want to talk about the data or decision. They are best able to complete the process if they are allowed and encouraged to talk out the matter with someone, such as a counselor.

Internal processors prefer to think about data or decisions before talking about the subject. According to Johnson (1968), external processors think out loud and internals talk about things following a time of thought.

Understanding an individual's particular style will allow the counselor to be more effective in providing assistance in the decision-making process. It will not be helpful to force clients with an internal style to talk when they are in the thinking stage. In contrast, it will be helpful to allow external clients to think out loud about the various factors and to include new variables whenever possible. Usually it will be possible to determine which styles exist. Some clients wish to talk about a number of factors; others wish to think about material before talking.

Johnson's conceptualization provides a method for the counselor to follow in aiding clients. First the counselor and client identify the style of deciding. Then appropriate materials and the proper climate are provided. The client is encouraged to process the data in the style he or she finds most helpful in order to move toward the decision. The counselor helps the client by evaluating and following up on the outcomes that result from the decision.

A decision may involve a choice between alternative behaviors, between ways of organizing information, or between ways of perceiving the environment. People want to be able to look into the future and choose the best possible outcomes for themselves. Decision makers want to know whether if and when they do something they will receive the appropriate rewards or reach the right goals. One approach may be to move through a series of activities related to the decision-making process.

1. **State the problem as clearly and completely as possible** A counselor can provide assistance in clarifying the actual statement. The problem can be a relatively simple concern, yet it is something with which the client wishes to deal.

2. **Examine previous decisions and the processes used in reaching the decision** It is essential that the client understand previous decision-making behavior(s). These may have had negative effects on the current concern or on the client. On the other hand, they may have positive effects in that the processes that worked before are appropriate for the current concern.

3. **List the outcomes** The client should be encouraged to look closely at the potential outcomes. Gains or losses of various things such as money are important determinants. Which outcomes are related to the various alternatives?

4. **Choose the alternative and implement action** It is easy to choose an alternative, much more difficult to activate the decision. In losing weight, for example, it is comparatively easy to decide that this is important and that the rewards and reinforcements are positive; if the decider does not stop eating, however, the process is incomplete.

5. **Find support systems for the decision and action** Support systems may be external or internal or both. In some cases it is enough to know and be able to say that one's health is better, one looks better, or the like. Often, however, external support is just as important. The decision maker wants and needs others to see that he or she is attempting to implement a decision and to provide positive feedback about both the decision and the changes that are occurring.

COMPUTER-ASSISTED DECISION MAKING

There is much interest in the use of computers as aids in counseling. When decision making is the focus of attention computers, properly used, may be of considerable benefit to the client. This does not mean that the counselor becomes less important in the relationship. The assistance offered by the counselor during the process of counseling continues to be necessary regardless of the sophistication of the computer.

Some methods suggested earlier could be integrated with the computer or computer-related activities. Gelatt's (1962) original concept, for example, could make use of computer assistance in working through the various steps. The more recent exposition by Gelatt et al. (1973) involves using programmed materials for helping clients understand and implement a decision-making paradigm. Various on-line computer terminals in schools and other agencies allow immediate access to and feedback from a data base related to colleges, technical schools, and job information. The advantages include immediacy of feedback, more efficient updating, and the ability to manipulate a variety of measurable factors to look at a number of possibilities.

Counselors can use computers in several exciting ways. Computers can screen data about the client and assist the counselor in diagnostic work. They can score tests and furnish almost instantaneous interpretation in visual and verbal form for use by the client and counselor. Computers can alert the counselor to changes in behavior, however defined, for the counselor and client to examine together in a counseling session.

The personal involvement of a counselor is still of prime importance, but judicious use of the computer may prove helpful to the client in such areas as decision making, where data can be combined and recombined in numerous ways and where suggested alternative behaviors can be generated for use by the client as she or he attempts to move toward the action so essential in decision making.

There are, of course, limitations to computers. As most people know, using computers effectively depends on proper input and programming. Without these elements computers provide little or no assistance. Also, not every counselor has access to a computer. The cost is coming down and counselors may wish to consider acquiring one of the new computers, which have great potential for storing and processing data of the type necessary for assisting in the decision-making process.

SUMMARY

Decision making offers the counselor and client an important milieu for counseling. In the process the counselor provides a situation in which the client can examine herself or himself and the available possibilities. The client must understand such personal variables as risk-taking propensity. The client should also have as much accurate information as possible about alternatives so that he or she can make the best decision possible. The counselor should be a potent contributor to the decision making of the client.

REFERENCES

Brammer, L. M., & Shostrom, E. L. *Therapeutic psychology* (3rd ed.). Englewood, Cliffs, N.J.: Prentice-Hall, 1977.

Gelatt, H. B. Decision making: A conceptual frame of reference for counseling. *Journal of Counseling Psychology*, 1962, 9, 240–245.

Gelatt, H. B., Varenhorst, B., Carey, R., & Miller, G. P. *Decisions and outcomes*. New York: College Entrance Examination Board, 1973.

Ginzberg, E., Ginzberg, S. W., Axelrad, S., & Herma, J. L. *Occupational choice*. New York: Columbia University Press, 1951.

Hansen, L. S. How do they choose a college? *College Board Review*, 1965, 57, 35–37.

Herr, E. L., & Cramer, S. *Career guidance through the life span*. Boston: Little, Brown, 1979.

Hollis, J. W., & Hollis, L. V. *Personalizing informational processes*. New York: Macmillan, 1969.

Hoppock, R. *Occupational information*. New York: McGraw-Hill, 1957.

Johnson, R. H. Individual styles of decision making: A theoretical model for counseling. *Personnel and Guidance Journal*, 1978, 57, 531–536.

Katz, M. A model of guidance for career decision-making. *Vocational Guidance Quarterly*, 1966, 15, 2–10.

Kell, B. L., & Mueller, W. J. *Impact and change: A study of counseling relationships*. New York: Appleton-Century-Crofts, 1966.

Kiresuk, T. J. *Goal attainment follow-up guide*. Program Evaluation Project, U. S. Department of Health, Education and Welfare. Minneapolis, 1973.

Kogan, N., & Wallach, M. A. (Eds.). *New directions in psychology II*. New York: Holt, Rinehart and Winston, 1967.

Mintzberg, H., Raisinghani, D., & Theoret, A. The structure of "unstructured" decision processes. *Administrative Science Quarterly*, 1976, *21*, 240–275.

Parsons, F. *Choosing a vocation*. Boston: Houghton Mifflin, 1909.

Robinson, F. P. *Principles and procedures in student counseling*. New York: Harper & Brothers, 1950.

Super, D. *The psychology of careers*. New York: Harper & Row, 1957.

Washburne, N. F. Decision making in a dyad. Paper presented at the annual meeting of the Southern Sociological Society, April 9–12, 1975, Washington, D. C.

USING TESTS IN COUNSELING

CHAPTER SEVENTEEN

It is often important to help a client to obtain information about themselves in order to meet the counseling goals established. Although the counselor and client may be able to gather the data in a series of interviews, it may be more efficient to utilize data from tests previously taken by the client or from an appropriate set of tests completed during the counseling. In addition, integration of test data into the client's informational system may be necessary for counseling to be of value.

Tests are designed to provide samples of performance in skill areas or to identify important personal data in nonskill areas. Although tests have limitations, these limitations should not preclude the use of tests, when appropriate, as part of counseling. The counselor must be familiar with tests and testing so that their selection and the interpretation of their results will be as meaningful as possible for the client.

Appraisal and test information can be useful, but they may not be as valuable as one might hope. Appraisal is a helping process that should enhance personal effectiveness, but it remains for the practitioner to provide the basis for the effective use of data. The client, if allowed to take control of appraisal data, may be able to take responsibility for planning and decision making, and thus, responsibility for his or her own outcomes.

Testing in counseling involves many considerations, such as selection for validity and relevance, test administration and scoring, and interpretation of the data. Although the counselor can and probably will handle most of the decisions requiring expertise, it is essential to involve the client as much as possible.

FUNCTIONS OF TESTING IN COUNSELING

Tests can serve a number of functions. Tests can provide data to help the client increase self-understanding, self-acceptance, and self-evaluation. In addition, test results can be used to challenge the client's perceptions of herself or himself and the world and can promote exploration of a number of areas. The test can aid in prediction, reinforcement, and reassuring the client (Layton, 1972). In serving these functions the test is a predictive tool, a diagnostic aid, a monitoring device, and an evaluative instrument. Normally prediction and diagnosis have greater counseling value than do monitoring and evaluation. Each function, however, can be part of the counselor process designed to aid the client in self-understanding, decision making, or any of the several other goals of counseling.

PREDICTION

The results of tests can aid in predicting an individual's success or degrees of success in a specific course of study, job, career, or other endeavor. Tests in this category are often used to select certain people for jobs or placement. Colleges, for example, have utilized test results as part of the selection process because there is evidence that tests can help predict which students may be successful in the program of study and learning environment of the college. Counselors are called upon to provide information about predictive tests for clients assigned to them. The more information the counselor has about the predictive value of the test, the better his or her chances will be of helping a client understand the test results and make reasonably sound decisions within existing parameters.

DIAGNOSIS

Tests can be used diagnostically to help a client to understand better the skills and knowledges he or she possesses and to gain insight into areas that are below acceptable levels. Then the client can decide which areas need greater concentration or attention. The diagnostic use of testing can provide information to persons working with the client outside of the counseling setting. It allows for greater concentration of effort by teachers, parents, or other helping persons. These tests can also provide information that may not previously have been part of the client's awareness. Interest tests, for example, may identify previously unknown areas of the client's interest and thus involve the client in exploration of the identified interests.

MONITORING

Tests can fulfill a monitoring function by helping the counselor and others see what progress (or lack of progress) the client is making. Achievement tests, for example, make it possible to observe academic progress over time; the counselor can investigate any unexpected change. Other measures can provide similar assistance to the counselor and client as they attempt to promote some sort of change in the client's behavior, attitudes, or personal skills.

EVALUATION

Tests can be used to evaluate the client's growth, the counselor's success in the counseling setting, or the achievement of certain goals. Whenever there is a possibility of some statement concerning the relative worth of a particular course of action, implementation of program or change, tests can aid in the evaluation.

When the client's behavior is being evaluated, the counselor and client should have agreed upon the valued outcomes. How this occurs is usually a function of the counselor, his or her feelings toward the process of evaluation, and the client's willingness to be involved. One of the counselor's jobs may be to establish some reasonable goals with the client and then devise some way of ascertaining the degree to which the goals have been met. Accountability, another aspect of evaluation, is becoming important to many people involved with counseling, especially those paying for the service. However, as Wesman suggested, "information obtained from well-chosen and properly administered tests, when integrated with all other relevant information about a student that a counselor can obtain, will improve the quality of the service the counselor gives and the decision the counselor makes" (1972, p. 398).

USES AND PURPOSES OF TESTS IN COUNSELING

Goldman (1971) differentiated tests on the basis of noncounseling and counseling uses. He categorized the noncounseling uses as (1) selection of candidates for the institution, (2) placement of individuals within the institution, (3) adaptation of institutional practices to meet the needs and characteristics of particular individuals, and (4) development and revision of institutional practices to meet the needs and characteristics of students or employees in general (1971, p. 19). These categories are largely self-explanatory. Noncounseling uses of tests may lead to concerns or problems that induce the individual to seek counseling. For example, a student who has been denied admission to a class, program, or institution on the basis of a test may seek out a helping person in order to discuss her or his concerns about tests, goals, and other topics. Thus, the noncounseling use of tests is related to the counseling interaction.

INFORMATIONAL PURPOSES

The counseling uses of tests described by Goldman (1971) fall into two broad areas: provision of information and other purposes. Under the information category we can differentiate information the counselor needs from information the client needs. Sometimes tests help the counselor make decisions about the appropriateness of counseling to meet the identified needs of the client. The counselor may choose not to accept the client or may use the data to effect the best possible referral. Quite often this procedure is separate from the counseling process.

At other times the counselor needs to make decisions about the best methods, approaches, or techniques to use to provide maximum assistance to the client. It is difficult to defend inappropriate counseling strategies, yet lack of information about the client often results in ineffective counselor activity.

The use of tests in counseling is related to the needs of the client. Tests provide assistance to the client in making plans and decisions. This assistance is not exclusively cognitive in nature. Regardless of the techniques or materials used, counseling also deals with the client's feelings about methods and facts. Thus, when tests appear to be of value the task of the counselor is to help the client to identify the information the test provides, to understand the limitations and implications of the test results, and to integrate the test information with the client's existing perceptions and behaviors (Layton, 1972).

Information fills the client's needs in one of four modes (Goldman, 1971). In the first, the client may be interested in identifying one or several courses of action. The client is trying to reduce the universe and seeks assistance in answering such questions as "Of all the possible things I might do what list can I develop?"

A second mode involves evaluating a more narrowly defined set of alternatives. The client has reduced the universe of possibilities and now wishes to examine more deeply the implications of a few. The client is now asking, "Which one or two of these few possibilities is better for me?"

In the third mode the client narrows the choices even more, seeking input from the counselor on the realism of a tentative choice, plan, or decision. Even within this restricted range the potential for counseling is great and, when appropriate in the process, tests can be helpful. The client is asking the counselor to help determine whether the decision is right for her or him.

In the final mode of information processing for client use, the purpose is to develop self-concept. Tests may help the client to clarify self-concept by sharpening the focus of the individual's self-knowledge. Under these circumstances the client is indirectly asking, "Who am I?"

NONINFORMATIONAL PURPOSES

Tests can also be used for noninformational purposes in counseling by stimulating interest in areas that were previously unknown or not considered. A test given for information purposes may raise client questions about her or his potential in educational and vocational areas. Or the results may provide an opportunity for the client to consider higher goals. Without test data the client may believe in and live a life without goals, achievement, and success.

Tests may also promote counseling at a later time. This is especially true when tests are administered to a group of persons and some group or individual interpretative effort is made. Often these circumstances motivate an individual to seek additional opportunities to review test results and other personal topics with a counselor. The group interpretative session provides the counselor with an opportunity to indicate an interest in the person and a willingness to meet with him or her at some future time on an individual basis.

Testing can promote decision making by the client. Instead of merely developing a testing program and administering it to the client, the counselor can use the situation to help the client learn decision-making skills and to understand that whereas some decisions result in positive gains, others may not work out as well. In either case the client learns that a decision is not always final.

When a client tends to talk only about impersonal matters, tests can promote movement toward more personal interaction between counselor and client.

SELECTION OF TESTS

Proper selection is crucial to the use of tests in counseling. Tests should be selected to measure the content areas that the counselor is concerned with and, at the same time, contribute as much as possible to the client's growth and development.

There is a continuing interest in the issue of client involvement in test selection. Each counselor will develop the plan that is most effective for his or her practice. As with all other aspects of counseling, the counselor's unique characteristics play a part in test selection.

INVOLVING THE CLIENT IN SELECTION

Client participation seems justified for several general reasons. First, the motivation to complete a test accurately and honestly seems enhanced when the client knows the purposes of testing as well as some specifics of the tests that might be used. In addition, when the client understands the reasons for the use of the test, the test itself can be a learning device.

Clients who are involved in the test selection are more receptive to the interpretation of test results. The clients are less likely to need to rationalize their performance and can be more involved in applying the results to their needs.

The client often needs experience in decision making. Helping to choose a test can be a learning situation for the client. Ideally the counselor serves as a model for discerning not only the existing alternatives but also the reasons for choosing certain tests and rejecting others.

Because the discussion of tests includes some description of test content the counselor can expect the client to verbalize positive and/or negative feelings about tests. This provides additional information for the counselor's use either then or later in the counseling process.

There are two other reasons for involving the client in test selection. First, it helps avoid an increase in the client's dependency. Although independence is not necessarily the goal of all counseling, anything that fosters increased dependence should be thoroughly examined. Second, involving the client in the selection process could make areas of accurate measurement available and thus eliminate the necessity of taking the test, avoiding the delay in counseling that test administration normally causes.

Many counselors, however, do not want clients to participate in test selection. Their reasons include the following:

- It is very important that the most appropriate tests be administered and interpreted. The counselor is more skilled than the client in selecting tests and time taken to improve the client's test selection skills could be better spent in counseling or test interpretation.
- The counselor can be more objective than the client in selecting appropriate tests. The types of problems that are identified in the test selection process, often dependency or inability to make decisions, may be more appropriately dealt with in ways other than attempting to remedy the problem through involving the client in test selection.

There are arguments for both positions on client involvement, but in general the client's participation in the selection of tests does not seem to have an adverse effect on the relationship. It is probable that the counselor is an important variable in the process. It is also likely that some clients' skills are more adequate than others' to the task of participating in test selection. The key factor here is the counselor's sensitivity to the needs and characteristics of the client. Through clinical observations the counselor should be able to identify those clients for whom participation would be unwise. In the remaining cases the counselor ought to encourage as much participation as possible in any activity related to the client's growth.

There are other factors involved in this process. Key among these are the situation in which the counseling takes place, the characteristics of the client, and the availability of tests and/or testing specialists. The structure of the institution is an important consideration when test selection is involved. Some schools, for example, disapprove of tests that might be labeled personality inventories. It is usually unwise for the counselor to try to include these tests in any package offered the client. An abundance of material on testing, such as Banish Hoffman's "The Tyranny of Testing," has revealed some of the problems and misunderstandings associated with tests. There is no need to create additional problems.

It is also probably unwise to spend a considerable amount of time with very young clients in test selection, for they are not sufficiently well informed about many factors of tests.

Counselors must understand themselves well enough to know how much involvement they want to allow the client. The type of cooperative and sometimes long involvement necessary for successful collaboration on test selection may not suit the personality characteristics or role enactment of some counselors.

TYPES OF TESTS

Proper selection of tests requires knowledge of the types of tests available. One simple distinction is between standardized and nonstandardized tests. The term *standardized* has generally been used to describe a test, or more specifically, a measuring instrument, with these characteristics:

- A standard administrative process has been developed for the test, including instruction and specific time limits. The standard process allows for similar administration and measurement regardless of the administrator or the place of testing.
- There is provision of scoring instructions or keys designed to eliminate scorer errors on the test. Thus, every scorer records the same results and is not influenced by any personal bias.
- Various normative data are made available with the test. These data allow for comparison with a wide variety of groups and provide information beyond the actual score, however recorded.
- A manual with technical testing data, such as validity and reliability, is included. This provides information for realistic selection of a test that will provide the most meaningful data. (The manual does not address the test-nontest issue, for most standardized tests are commercially prepared and among other purposes are used to provide income for the publisher and author.)

Another distinction is between group tests and individual tests. The difference between them, obviously, is in how many people can take the test at one time with one examiner. Generally group tests require less formal and supervised preparation for administration than do individual tests.

There are also distinctions between pencil-and-paper tests and performance tests. The latter require the use of objects and physical skills and generally provide more direct data for skill area judgment than do pencil-and-paper tests. The latter, however, require less time and cost to administer.

A final distinction can be made between speed tests and power tests. Speed tests are designed to measure the examinee's speed of accomplishment; most are so long that no one can finish them in the time provided. A power test measures the level of performance. Test items are usually arranged in increasing order of difficulty and, because the examinee is given sufficient time to finish, performance depends upon the degree of successful completion of items.

All these distinctions are important if test selection is to be effective. Each should be considered in relation to the need of the client. Some of the aspects have built-in rejection probabilities: counselors who must be their own psychometrists, for example, should not select tests that they are incapable of administering. Counselors who do not have the required administration skills should not use individual tests.

SELECTION FOR CONTENT

Tests should be selected on the basis of content. The following types can be identified: mental ability, achievement, aptitude, interest inventories, personality inventories, and special tests (such as creativity).

There may be no clear differentiation between various types of tests. A mental ability test that purports to measure intellectual functioning, for example, may in fact be an achievement test that measures specific things the examinee has learned. The counselor should examine the tests carefully to determine which category they belong to.

Mental Ability Tests

Mental ability tests are usually designed to measure individual intellectual functioning, such as spatial relations, abstract reasoning, verbal and mathematical competence, or even performance on certain given tasks. In general the examiner hopes to assess the functional level of the individual taking the test in order to provide the latter with the most appropriate educational experiences. The intelligence test should give the examiner and examinee a notion of how the latter functions relative to the norm population. Both individual and group intelligence tests are available; group tests are most popular because they require less administrative time and fewer specific administrative skills.

Achievement Tests

Achievement tests measure knowledge of specific content areas. Samples of behavior from a given amount of materials indicate the amount of material the examinee has learned. Various methods are used to obtain this sample. Usually, however, the test has a multiple-choice format in which the individual is asked to choose the best response. Several test-taking skills can significantly affect the outcome of achievement tests. Those who are interested in a "true" measure of achievement must try to avoid tests that penalize certain students or overly reward others and, most significantly, do not measure achievement (that is, learning) in the content areas. Achievement tests usually are more teaching than counseling oriented. Counselors who are interested in examining achievement, however, need to know about these tests.

Aptitude Tests

Aptitude tests measure sample behaviors in areas for which the examinee has certain potential. As such they serve a predictive function for the examinee by relating to a specific task area. The General Aptitude Test Battery (GATB), used by many employment services, includes verbal and numerical tests combined to indicate a measure of mental functioning. The remaining subtests are directly related to skills that might be necessary to perform certain employment tasks, such as clerical, eye-hand coordination, or manual dexterity. These aptitudes can be related to specific job categories and provide information either about what field the client may wish to enter or in what skill areas certain training might increase his or her performance level.

Specific tests for single area skills are called special aptitude tests and include fields such as music or art. These tests can be helpful in their particular area, but the examiner should investigate their validity and reliability. The fact that a test is called an art aptitude test does not necessarily mean that it will accurately predict success in art. If the test and artistic talent are not related, the predictability is meaningless.

The remaining type of aptitude test is prognostic, aimed at learning areas such as reading readiness or algebra. These tests can be valuable in helping place students in the most appropriate learning situation. The test results should be meaningfully reported to a number of people, including the test taker. Often these tests are used in a negative way to reject people who do not meet requirements, with little or no explanation offered to the examinee.

Interest Inventories

Whereas mental ability, achievement, and aptitude tests are designed to measure some maximum performance of the individual, interest tests are used to measure typical performance. The examinee's involvement in this testing situation is crucial: if he or she has little or no motivation to take the test, the result will not be a typical measure. Also, it is usually possible for the examinee to answer in a way more acceptable to someone else, whether counselor, parent, or teacher, than in the way that is closest to his or her feelings.

Interest inventories attempt to measure one of the four types of interests identified by Super and Crites (1962): expressed interest, manifest interest, tested interest, and inventoried interest.

In general, expressed interest is the verbal expression of liking or disliking something. These expressions often are related to maturity and experience.

Manifest interest is what is observable because of the individual's participation in a given activity. A boy or girl voluntarily playing basketball can safely be assumed to have an interest in basketball. This type of interest, however, can also be misleading, for participation in a given activity may be necessary for certain fringe benefits to occur. It is usually valuable to observe the activities related to the event as well as the individual's participation to determine the degree of manifest interest. Furthermore, lack of participation may not mean lack of interest. Factors like cost or time may affect participation and manifest interest.

Tested interest can be ascertained by measuring the knowledge of vocabulary or other information the examinee has in a specific interest area. These measures are based on an assumption that interests result in the accumulation of relevant information as well as a specialized vocabulary.

Inventoried interests are those determined by interest checklists. Usually an examinee is asked to check whether she or he likes or dislikes certain activities or situations. Patterns of high and low interest normally result so that the test taker can begin to determine areas of liking or disliking.

Inventoried interest is the basis of most published tests. The Kuder Personal Preference Inventory and the Strong-Campbell have dominated the measurement of interest. Textbooks such as Cronbach (1970) discuss the philosophy and construction of these instruments. Each has a specific value: Kuder's and other inventories identify basic interest groups; the Strong test relates specific patterns among people in certain occupations to the pattern of the examinee's responses.

Personality Inventories

Personality inventories are used to identify various facets of an individual's personality structure. Because human personality is multifaceted, no instrument can do more than explore a few areas. It is possible, however, to assess some major areas of the personality. On certain inventories, for example, truthful responses can indicate a dominant, assertive type or a submissive dependent type.

In other cases the inventory can provide a measure of the resemblance between the response pattern of the examinee and the response pattern of certain personality types. The Minnesota Multiphasic Personality Inventory (MMPI), for example, provides scores in a number of areas associated with specific personality disorders such as paranoia.

With personality inventories it is especially important to exercise caution in the interpretation and use of results. These types of tests were used during the 1960s as ammunition for antitesting arguments. Because the tests include certain items that in isolation are somewhat unacceptable, they can be misused for many purposes. The counselor should be completely familiar with the test items, be selective in using the results, and certain that the test will be properly explained and interpreted before and after administration.

The reliability and validity of personality tests are questionable because the possibility of faking or creating positive or negative images is high. Many inventories attempt to deal with this problem by using faking scales or truth scales to determine whether the examinee is responding to certain items in a significantly different way than the standardizing population did. There is no guarantee that this will eliminate the attempts of the examinee to present a more or less favorable picture. Therefore, administrators of personality inventories must exercise great caution.

Special Tests

Measuring creativity is a relatively new concept in testing. The creativity test usually asks the individual to respond to certain situations and presumes that those who respond in a unique or different way are demonstrating creativity. Again, the test highlights patterns rather than specific characteristics. One test, for example, asks the respondent to list the uses of a brick. Those who list the normal uses such as building a wall or as a doorstop are not considered creative. Those who say that it could be hollowed out and made into a boat would be considered potentially more creative because they are not restricted by a set of assumed rules and outcomes. No test requires that the use of the brick result in some successful or positive outcome; thus, even though the brick boat would probably sink, the respondent does show creative tendencies.

CLIENT ORIENTATION

A person's performance on any test is affected by a number of factors. Understanding these factors is essential to using test results to derive an accurate appraisal of the test taker. One area sometimes overlooked is the client's feelings about testing. Once it appears that a test is appropriate the counselor should devote some time to dealing with the client's attitude toward testing. Previous experiences with tests may exert a significant influence on test-taking skills. The prospect of psychological testing may have a negative effect on the client. The counselor can help the client understand these factors and thus increase the potential for accurate measurement of client performance and the ultimate helpfulness of the test results. This orientation phase can help not only to reduce the client's negative feelings about testing but also to promote a positive attitude toward the proper use of test results. The client's perception of tests and counseling as aids in meeting her or his needs increases the potential benefits of the testing and counseling process. The orientation of the client may well develop with the selection and administration process.

TEST ADMINISTRATION AND SCORING

Test administration and scoring procedures affect the usefulness of test results. The test or tests should be administered with standardized procedures in an environment that minimizes distracting elements. The test developer's instructions should be followed closely so that when the counselor and client use the results they can be relatively certain that their interpretation is valid. Often other personnel administer the tests. Whether the tests are given in classrooms, counseling agencies, vocational and employment offices, or rehabilitation settings, the counselor should ensure the accurate administration of whatever test is used.

Test scoring has become quite mechanical. The use of computers for high-speed, accurate scoring is an important development in testing. Computers, however, are capable of performing only what they are programmed to do. They cannot pick up or deliver test results for use by the counselor. The counselor's job is to develop questions for the programmer to feed into the computer. These may be diagnostic questions related to clusters of activities, such as academic competence. Or they may be comparison or discriminant questions designed to note how the client responds in two or more areas of the test or how the client's responses compare with those of a norm group.

Thus, although scoring is a mechanized process the counselor should ensure that the data received from the scoring service are useful to the client. The computer or scoring service should provide as much assistance as possible based upon interaction of the counselor and programmer. The counselor should work closely with the computer operator to insure rapid turnaround for the test results. Outdated scores have no value, no matter how nicely they are prepared.

INTERPRETATION OF TEST DATA

Once the tests are administered and scored the counselor develops a package of information to present to the client. A meaningful presentation of the test data is necessary.

First, the counselor must determine the relevant outcomes of the tests. Skill is necessary to examine data and educe important factors. The counselor who does not feel competent to do this should seek outside assistance so that the results presented to the client are manageable and meaningful.

During the interpretative session the counselor should not move too rapidly through the material; she or he must ensure that the client understands what the test measured, how he or she did on the test, and what predictions, evaluations, or future activities seem indicated. Using interpretative concepts such as percentiles or deciles is likely to confuse the client. The counselor's skill in translating the results into understandable terms will often make the difference between meaningful use of tests and an extremely unproductive session.

The counselor should also use caution in presenting certain types of data. Actual I.Q. scores, for example, have too much related affect to be presented solely as numbers. The client with a 95 on a given test probably never hears any remarks that the result is "average" or that "the score is an estimate" or other interpretative statements. The presentation of test data is usually general, expressed in such phrases as "about average." Otherwise the more important uses of tests can be lost.

The counselor faces a number of dilemmas when interpreting tests. If all clients scored well on tests it would be pleasant to be able to use very positive statements concerning performance. However, clients are prone to score below average, to be under the acceptable score for placement in various programs; in short, to perform less adequately than they would like. It is necessary for the counselor to interpret these data as objectively as possible. Often the client has some idea of his or her level of performance and is not as discouraged as the counselor might assume. Moreover, a great deal of client behavior is related to the behavior of the counselor. If the counselor conveys a negative reaction to the test performance the client will probably react in kind. Nonobjective presentations are of little value. Tests results are meant to contribute to self-understanding, prediction, or client movement. They are not goals of the counseling situation. The counselor uses the foundation that test results and other data provide to move farther in the process of counseling.

Finally, it is probably wise to avoid giving any type of advice with the results of the test data. Statements such as "if I were you with these test scores" tend to promote defensiveness or dependence in the client. Sometimes giving advice is unavoidable because the counselor must make a placement decision based upon her or his understanding of the client. In such cases the client as well as the counselor should understand that this sort of decision is necessary.

COMMUNICATION OF TEST RESULTS

Whenever counselors and clients interact the potential exists for misunderstanding. This potential is greater in situations involving test interpretation. It is incumbent upon the counselor to ensure that the client knows the meanings of words, phrases, and sentences connected with testing. The counselor must monitor the client's understanding and correct or expand his or her own communicative skills when the client seems to misunderstand. The following rules should apply.

1. Keep the statistical reporting as simple as possible. Most clients understand expressions such as 8 out of 10 or 25 out of 100.
2. Give the client a chance to react to whatever data are presented. Although this may entail either pauses or extended periods of silence, the client's response helps in the monitoring process.

3. Help the client move toward self-evaluation and expression of feelings. A statement such as "It's hard to accept these results" may help the client move toward expressing his or her feelings.
4. Help the client relate test data to other data. For example, tested interests should be related to expressed interests so that a combination of data eventually becomes part of the interpretation.

The counselor should develop some specific approaches for interpretation. Goldman (1971) listed four kinds of interpretation: description, genetic, predictive, and evaluative. He described these approaches, summarized below, in terms of questions related to each interpretative type.

- Questions for descriptive interpretation. What kind of person is the client? How well does the client do on certain tasks? What does she or he like to do?
- Questions for genetic interpretation. How did the client evolve to this point with these characteristics? What background—parental, experiential, or academic—does he or she have?
- Questions for predictive interpretation. How well will the client perform in the particular course, sequence, or college? What differential success patterns appear to be possible?
- Questions for evaluative interpretation. What should the client do? Should he or she become a teacher or tradesperson?

The proportional use of hard data decreases from the descriptive through the evaluative questions. The counselor will use each of these in counseling and should be aware of the specific value each has and plan accordingly in preparing the test data package.

GENERAL MODES OF TEST INTERPRETATION

Interpreting test scores in such a way that they acquire meaning for the client amounts to establishing a bridge between hard data and human characteristics or set of behaviors (Goldman, 1971). These bridges are either statistical or clinical in orientation. Norms, discrimination, and regression are statistical bridges.

In comparing an individual's score with a norm group, reporting is in terms such as seventy-second percentile, third stanine, or fourth decile with appropriate interpretations. Norms indicate the test taker's relative placement in the norm group. Interpretations of norms are useful for prediction, placement, self-understanding, or any other objectives of the tests.

Sometimes a test provides more than one score, making possible a profile or multiple relationship to the norm group. Comparison of the client with the norm group is possible in each subtest. Examining these multiple levels reveals the internal, more personalized data from the test. Interpretation of the norm helps the client begin to internalize the test results but may not provide all the data the client needs.

The discriminant bridge allows for comparison with more than one norm group at a time. Information from the comparison permits the client to discriminate between two or more alternatives. Various tests emphasize this approach, including the Strong Vocational Interest Blank. A high score in any particular area allows for differentiation between the identified occupational group, people in general, and various occupations.

Like other interpretations of testing, bridges omit some important information. The results on the Strong test, for example, do not provide much assistance in determining satisfaction or potential success. The results suggest only that the test taker is similar to or different from a given population in the areas, activities, and other measured aspects included by the test developer.

The regression bridge indicates the degree to which people show promise for a particular activity. This information has been used in at least two ways. One use establishes a cutoff score below which or, in some cases, above which the client is refused admission. The other use, more closely related to counseling, provides data for the numbers or percentage of people who succeeded or failed at the task with scores similar to the client's. The client is expected to make wiser decisions when provided with this information. The regression bridge may be dependent upon and developed by an outside source. The counselor's job is to provide data concerning probable access to or success in a particular area. The client decides whether to pursue the situation further. The counselor must make it clear to the client that regression interpretations cannot be final until all the people or agencies involved have completed the process.

It is possible to combine more than one set of data to determine potential success. Quite often the combination is provided by an outside source that has access to sufficiently large populations to develop the necessary formulas. Prediction of college success, for example, might be enhanced by developing a formula that includes a scholastic aptitude test score, high school rank, an English usage test, and a grading of the high school, perhaps based on the success of previous graduates. A multiple regression formula that assigns weights to the variables provides the client with better prediction possibilities.

Much of this information is used by outside agencies that make a decision about the client. The information is useful to the client in determining probable success in the institution, so that theoretically a good decision occurs. The advent of computers has increased the potential for multiple regression; computers can process large amounts of data, manipulate the various factors, and determine the weights and the best combinations to use in the prediction formula.

The second type of bridge is clinical interpretation which develops a mental picture of the client so that the counselor can help the client move from data to activities or personal involvement. This hypotheses development or model-building concept has been part of the counseling process since at least the early 1950s (Pepinsky & Pepinsky, 1954). Implementation of the concept today incorporates test data with model building.

Typically, the counselor's task is to describe the client in terms of ability, aptitude, interests, needs, and the like. Test data can help the counselor and client answer some of the important questions that this process raises. Discrepancies often exist in the model building, and test data can help explain or diminish these discrepancies.

The counselor or client might be asked to describe where the client wishes to go, what he wants to do, or similar questions. On the basis of the answers to these questions—both where he is and where he wants to go—the counselor and client can develop some specific steps to move across the bridge. There is a prediction of the possible outcomes once the client is across the clinical bridge.

The process is not as static as this description indicates. The client is a dynamic person whose goals change, and the prediction about various outcomes is less than perfect. But the skilled counselor can continue to monitor and assess the situation. By keeping in touch with the dynamic nature of the client, the counselor can help the client reach her or his personal, educational, and vocational goals. Tests are a way to manage the multitude of variables that are part of the client and his or her world.

INTERACTION

Using tests in counseling includes at least two distinct types of interaction with the client. First, before testing occurs the client should understand why tests might be meaningful and what their general limitations are. This means that the counselor and client understand the latter's needs and the potential value of tests. The partial dialogue that follows illustrates the kind of exchange that might encourage this understanding.

C. Perhaps it would be of value to talk about the kinds of ideas that tests can provide and see if you think these would be helpful to you.

S. Yeah, I'd like to know if I can make it in college.

C. That's asking an ability question. Maybe you're asking whether you can be accepted into college as well as whether you can pass the courses there.

S. I think I'll be accepted but I'm kinda worried about whether I can do college work.

C. So it would be helpful if we had an idea of how your ability to learn compares with other college students'.

S. Yeah.

C. One way of getting at that would be to look at your scores on a college entrance test. Have you taken the college boards?

Later in the interview, after discussion of the college entrance tests, the conversation turns to interests.

C. You know that interests are important to examine before you make very many decisions.

S. Well, I'm interested in college.

C. I was thinking about the kinds of things you like to do. What are you interested in and how might these things be related to the curriculum you choose in college?

S. I can tell you that I don't like English and social studies.

C.   OK. This helps. Maybe we can spend some time getting a clearer picture of what you might like to do. It might be of some help for you to complete an interest checklist. This would give you a chance to respond to a large number of activities.

S.   OK.

C.   One thing, though, that you should remember. The checklist can only provide an accurate picture if you try to respond as honestly as possible.

The second type of interaction occurs in the interpretation of test results to the client. In addition to communicating clearly the statistical concepts involved the counselor should be attuned to client responses that signal a personal reaction to the tests. The counselor should maintain a balance between a dry academic reporting of test data and sensitivity to the client's reactions. The excerpt below illustrates how test interpretation can lead to personal exploration by the client.

The student has completed the tests and returns for interpretation of the interest checklist. The results suggest an interest in public service and math. The student does not appear to be interested in activities that require selling or aesthetic appreciation.

C.   Here are the results of the checklist. Remember this means that you have indicated an interest in the activities. The items you check point to working with people or in a job that relates to math as something you might like. You don't seem to want to work as a salesman and you have little interest in art or music. How does that fit into your own ideas about yourself?

S.   I guess about right.

C.   You're not sure about the results.

S.   I don't know. I never really did that well in math.

C.   You're questioning whether you would be able to succeed in a job that required math?

S.   Yes.

C.   That's a good thought. You have been able to differentiate between interest and ability. Although you might like math you have not done as well gradewise as you think would be necessary.

S.   I do OK in the math part like adding and subtracting but algebra was really hard.

C.   It might be valuable to talk about algebra a bit more right now.

The more the client knows about testing, the greater the likelihood that the results will be meaningful to the client. Because the counselor is more expert in testing and communication, she or he must accept the responsibility for preparing the client well for testing.

Like all other aspects of counseling, test results are confidential. The client's rights should be protected by ensuring not only that each client receives his or her own test package but also that the client has the final control of how the test results are used and made known, if at all, to others.

Rapid communication of test results is of considerable importance. The administration, scoring, and interpretation of results should occur as quickly as possible.

CLIENT INVOLVEMENT

The most crucial period of client involvement in testing is during interpretation. Some counselors wish to hurry through test interpretation to get to more "pertinent" topics. This demeans the testing and creates a negative client attitude toward why tests were administered in the first place.

The task of the counselor is to fulfill the client's attempts at self-appraisal and understanding rather than the more mechanistic and often counselor- or agency-pleasing behavior, diagnosis. The objective is to devise ways for clients to obtain information, to process it in personally meaningful ways, and to integrate it when appropriate. Incomplete understanding of test data reduces the value of testing and, more important, arbitrarily restricts freedom of action and choice. The interpretation of test results should relate to helping clients learn about talents, potentials, personal strengths and weaknesses, decision making, or any of the several other important aspects themselves. Therefore, the test interpretation process should be viewed in developmental terms. The counselor should avoid the notion that test results provide input for only a single choice, at one time, and for a static situation and should take care that the client understands this perspective.

During the process of interpreting tests it is wise to use the information the client brings to the interview. Because the counselor's task is to ensure that information from any source is as valid as possible, some monitoring of the validity of these personal data is necessary. The counselor can use personally supplied data when he or she and the client begin to identify the areas of concern or lack of knowledge. The client is an active participant throughout this questioning process. The counselor must realize that the client is not expert in the technical aspects of testing and data processing. It is the counselor's job to determine the client's degree of skill in understanding test data, personal data, and other information that may be relevant. The counselor ensures that data are used meaningfully by clarifying, teaching, and restating the data to the client.

Once the client understands the implications of the data, he or she is responsible for deciding how, or whether, to use them. The counselor continues to monitor the situation so that any event related to the goals of the counseling interaction is based on self-understanding and the client is able to process the data meaningfully.

The counselor can facilitate client self-evaluation and involvement by her or his method of data presentation and test interpretation. Tentative statements such as "You really did not expect the results that occurred" can help clients to think further about themselves, the test results, and the decisions or activities they face. Clients put the data to use with the aid of the counselor rather than the reverse; the counselor does not use the test data to tell the client something.

DEVICES

Several devices can be helpful in the interpretation of test results to clients. These devices usually provide a graphic presentation of data and, more important, a fairly clearcut idea of the individual's relative position within one or more tested dimensions. These devices include the scattergram, a test profile sheet, or a histogram.

Each device makes a particular contribution to a test interpretation, but in general they are more meaningful for younger clients because they help maintain interest during the presentation of data. All are designed to help clients clarify their understanding and thinking.

There are several limitations on these types of devices. First, the form of the presentation sometimes distracts clients from the content of the data. Second, these devices tend to be oriented to presentations in a noncounseling context. The scattergram, for example, has been called a teacher-centered instrument because many teachers have used it to understand a group of pupils. When used with care, however, such devices can add another dimension to test interpretation.

THE EVALUATIVE ROLE

One persistent problem of using tests in counseling is the counselor's evaluative role. Whereas some accept this role as a legitimate one, others believe the counselor's job is instead to help the client to become more self-evaluative. If counselors are to provide little or no evaluation, they can make only limited use of tests.

Tests can be helpful in promoting client self-evaluation. They can provide additional information for the client as he or she moves toward self-understanding. When the client does need accurate information, tests, judiciously used, can be an efficient, objective tool.

Tests must provide data that clients need and want. Although it may be more convenient to administer tests prior to counseling, the data gathered then may not be as meaningful to the client as those gathered when the client identifies a need for additional information during the process of counseling.

Clients may not always express the need for tests directly. Some may know enough about testing to request one as part of counseling, yet not know about specific tests. In such cases, the counselor provides help in identifying possibilities, in arranging for the client to take the test, and in interpreting the results.

Other clients need more assistance in identifying the need for a test or tests. The counselor might note this need during the course of the counseling session. At an appropriate time the counselor can offer the possibility of testing and explain the types of tests and potential outcomes. The client is responsible for deciding whether testing forms a part of her or his counseling needs.

Because this need may arise at different times for different clients, the counselor must be ready to offer testing whenever the need occurs. This individual timing seems to meet the needs of clients better than a precounseling battery of tests designed to provide information more useful to the counselor than to the client.

Tests can help clients define and achieve personal goals if the counselor is willing to assist in identifying what information is needed. Layton (1972) suggested that under these circumstances tests can be helpful to the client in "increased precision of information, self-evaluation during the course of the counseling process, self-understanding and self-acceptance, challenge, exploration, prediction, reinforcement, and reassurance" (1972, p. 404).

SUMMARY

The following list summarizes the important facets of test interpretation and should help the counselor develop a method of integrating tests into counseling.

1. **Be thoroughly familiar with the test** The counselor should know what the test measures from reading the testing information in the manual and critiques of the test in various journals or the *Mental Measurements Yearbook* edited by Buros. She or he should have taken the test and verified its weaknesses and strengths. Only with this level of familiarity can the counselor interpret the test meaningfully to the client.

2. **Develop a rationale with the client for administering the test** The counselor must spend time with the client to determine the latter's feelings about tests. Does the client react to testing in ways that will make the results of little or no value? Does the client put too much faith in the test? The counselor should know how well the client understands tests and what his or her feelings are, whether those feelings are negative or positive.

3. **Provide a model for interpretation that the client understands and accepts** The counselor should spend some time discussing general test information so that the client knows the limitations and strengths of the particular tests under consideration. The counselor should stress the fact that test results may provide important information for the client but that the use of tests and test results should grow out of the expressed needs of the client during interaction with the counselor in the counseling session.

The counselor should ensure that the client understands the type of test and the meaning of its scores. Is the test an achievement test? an aptitude test? a personality inventory? What do the scores signify? The norm group, or referent group, should be clearly defined so that the client knows with whom he or she is being compared and why the particular group is being used. This knowledge helps the client interpret the score.

The style of presenting data is important to realistic use of test results. Results rather than scores should be given. Numbers tend to keep the client from focusing on the real meaning of the test. Statements like "You seem to have above average (or average) capacity to use language" are usually more meaningful than "Your high scores on the language test are ———." The latter tends to focus on the score; the former focuses on the construct being measured.

4. **Use tests within the limits for which they were designed** The counselor must verify both tests and test results, making certain that the test being used is current and that the appropriate background material is available. In addition, both the counselor and client should seek other data that provide information about the validity of the result. Seldom should any test be used in isolation. Other tests and self-reported data are essential for the client in attempts to determine her or his needs, skills, prospects, and chances of success.

5. **Keep interpretation as nonevaluative as possible** Reporting on test scores is not an appropriate occasion for evaluative, reinforcing statements such as

"You really did a great job on the test." It is better to report, "People with scores like these seem to be able to do well in foreign languages." This allows the client to do the evaluation, that is, to say, "I am going to do well in French next year." The counselor can then help the client focus on the meanings of the nonevaluative counselor statement and the more properly evaluative client statement.

6. **Present the data in clear and meaningful ways** The counselor can use a number of aids to present test results. These might include charts and diagrams that show the normal curve or profiles. To be certain that the client has grasped the material, the counselor might ask him or her to summarize the interpretation at various points. If there is some misunderstanding, the counselor can provide additional material.

7. **Use tests for prediction** Tests, though not always as good as one would like, may nevertheless help a client examine future potentials and probabilities of success. In prediction, the counselor should use the data tentatively and in conjunction with other data. The counselor should help the client interpret results with such statements as "People with scores like these tend to do well in ———" or "With scores like these the chances are high that one could succeed in ———."

8. **Involve the client** Anything that occurs in counseling should aim toward helping the client reach his or her objectives. The client should be involved in the decision to use tests, in their selection (to the degree possible), in the interpretation process, and in the final use of test results for prediction or whatever outcomes or uses are desired. The counselor, as the expert, usually takes the lead in involving the client. Often this means that the client expects the counselor to "tell" him or her something. The counselor, in test interpretation and other phases of counseling, should help the client learn something.

SPECIAL POPULATIONS

One crucial issue related to testing and counseling is the meaningfulness of tests for special populations whose background, social situation, current living status, and needs are different from some norm population from which the test data were derived. Goldman put this issue in perspective thus:

> Tests reflect the mistreatment which many disadvantaged people have received and reflect it all too accurately, so the test is unfair only when used improperly; when used to deny opportunity once again to those whose previous deprivation led them to their present underdeveloped status (1971, p. 441).

The improper use of tests must, then, be the concern of counselors and psychometricians. Because the counselor's clientele often come from a range of ethnic, racial, and religious groups, he or she should be aware of factors related to the use and interpretation of tests with differing populations.

PREDICTION

Using tests for prediction with minority clients poses a problem because the prediction quite often involves activities, outcomes, success, or placement into groups similar to the norm groups of the test. Thus, a college admissions test is used to predict academic success in higher education. Previous educational success contributes to the score on the test, and the test does in fact predict equally well for minority populations as for the norm group. The usual prediction is that given the opportunity to attend college the minority population will have limited success; the prediction is usually accurate for a wide variety of youths.

Another problem is that some see the test results as below the "actual" skill level of the student. He or she knows more than the test reveals. Usually there is no question that this is true. Most people know more than tests of achievement reveal. However, this clouds the issue, for what is being asked by the test user relates to prediction of later success. It will be helpful for the counselor to understand this point clearly and be able to explain it to the client when necessary.

We do not expect all readers to accept this point. We are suggesting that in the area of prediction of future success tests are often not discriminatory. One may wish to argue about the future success but prediction in terms of the current definition of success will be about the same for all people taking the tests.

The counselor can be helpful in ensuring that the client knows what the tests are about, how they are to be used, and, perhaps most important, how to ensure the best possible outcome in the predicted behavior. Thus, the counselor might spend time helping a client learn about what is expected in college so that once the student is accepted her or his chances of success are related to skill rather than to self-defeating behaviors.

In short, when discussing the predictive use of tests the counselor is to help the client understand the setting in which the prediction is made. The counselor should try to provide ways for the client to learn to maximize this understanding. The counselor may wish to become involved in changing the setting aimed at. The critical problem is not to modify tests but to develop procedures suitable for people who are not prepared intellectually or motivationally for the situation for which the prediction is made.

DIAGNOSIS

It is in diagnosis that the counselor and others involved with clients may have the greatest impact. Test diagnosis can be used to describe the client. It can be helpful in providing inferences about motivations, interests, and reactions to persons and things. It can help locate the client in some category. The testing situation promotes diagnosis by providing observations of style, content responses, and patterned responses to various tests or subtests.

The counselor and client can select and use appropriate tests to provide information in the areas of achievement, aptitude, interest, ability, and perhaps creativity. The results of these tests can be discussed with the client without undue concern about whether the test has a cultural bias. The interpretation should be factual, covering both strengths and weaknesses. In reviewing the results of an aptitude test with a student, for example, in the diagnostic area the counselor can provide assistance in describing aptitudes the client already has and those that are not currently at a level acceptable to the client. Because there is no need for prediction at this point in the relationship, the discussion can center on the results of the test, and there is likely to be little client affect.

The counselor and client can decide in what directions the client wishes to move. The client may be happy with the current situation and see no particular need to set up a program for improving skills. On the other hand, the test results may be used to encourage the client to undertake certain personal, academic, or practical tasks to incorporate some of the activities found lacking.

Many people tend to utilize all test data in evaluative or predictive ways. The counselor and client should spend time discussing this issue, and the client should be willing to examine other data in a diagnostic way. This does not preclude eventually using the data in other ways. Diagnosis should be the first priority of counseling at this point.

Tests can be used for specific diagnostic purposes with all clients. They provide additional information that should contribute to self-understanding and help the client develop methods of improving or building upon current skills and behaviors. Used properly, diagnostic tests results can also provide information to others in the client's life. Teachers can use the data to develop classroom and curriculum assistance. Parents can use them to promote activities that help the client move toward desired goals. The counselor should make sure that teachers, parents, and clients understand that the test is being used for diagnosis, not for evaluation or prediction.

MONITORING

Tests can serve a valuable monitoring function for the culturally different client. If the client has developed a plan of action or decided upon some acceptable short- and long-term alternatives, tests can help indicate the progress the client is making. The counselor should help select tests that can serve this function, adding to other types of information.

In addition to being familiar with types of tests that can provide the necessary information, the counselor should establish a good relationship with the client so that the latter's emotional response to tests is minimal.

The monitoring function, as an extension of the diagnostic function, can be used by others in addition to the counselor. Teachers, parents, and other helping professionals are potential monitorial aides. The counselor should lead the way in ensuring that the client's wishes are known and met. If the client wishes to keep the process anonymous the counselor should ensure that confidentiality is maintained. If the client wishes to have others involved in the process, the counselor should take care that the communication to others is clear, understood, and accepted. Unless the counselor is sure of these dimensions he or she should be reluctant to provide information to the outside monitors.

Although this care should apply to all clients, not just those from a minority group, the precautions necessary for the selection, use, interpretation, and sharing of tests are greater for minority populations because the tests often are not geared as closely to their needs.

EVALUATION

Tests in counseling may have an evaluative function both within and outside the counseling setting. Evaluations may range from specific career concerns such as "Should I be a teacher?" through general normative concerns such as "How do I compare with others on this test?" During the counseling session the counselor may attempt to avoid answering certain direct questions of the client, but the latter may then infer some answers instead. The client is asking for an evaluation of potential, and it is easy to misinterpret the counselor's silence or evasion of the issue as a reply. The counselor must attempt to aid the client in answering these questions. Depending on his or her theoretical framework, the counselor may be direct, nondirect, or somewhere in between but cannot shirk the responsibility of helping the client search for answers.

Outside the counseling setting, evaluation becomes more difficult, for it sometimes involves personnel who do not know as much about the tests as the counselor does. Most parents, for example, do not understand tests, test terminology, and the interpretations that counselors prefer. All they seem to understand is that their child is below average, above average, can or cannot do something. Teachers and other professionals may have more understanding of tests, but blind spots can lead to inadequate understanding of the results and thus to insufficient interpretation and use of the test itself.

The counselor can provide technical assistance to outside personnel in all areas of test usage. The evaluative function is perhaps the most important because emotional overlay and potential for misuse are greatest at this point. The counselor must ensure that the evaluative function is as free of misinformation and bias as possible. Careful selection of tests and communication with clients and others will ensure the highest degree of accuracy.

INTERPRETATION

In the interpretation of tests, the counselor, among others, can be helpful in minimizing misuse. Whatever the client's background, tests can provide helpful additional information when properly understood and used. The counselor can help prevent their misuse and misinterpretation by a process of explaining tests, discussing their selection, seeing that administration is standardized, and ensuring that the results are clearly interpreted, understood, and used.

Group Interpretation

Although individualized interpretation of test results is generally preferable, there are times when group methods can be of value. On these occasions it is especially important to maintain the confidentiality of test results.

In general there are several possibilities for group test data presentation. In the preliminary presentation of reasons for testing, a skilled counselor can usually deal with a small group because much of the information is not personal. The presentation can be fairly straightforward, describing the objectives of the test, what the test measures, and how it will be used and interpreted. The counselor can encourage questions from individuals in the group.

Preliminary test interpretation following administration can also be done on a group basis, especially when a profile sheet or similar device is part of the test score. The counselor can explain what the profile is, how the scores are presented, and even begin some explanation of test results. This should be a general approach and must not replace individual interpretation.

In group interpretations it is essential for the counselor to select his or her words and phrases carefully. The listeners will not always understand the total context and yet may not feel free to ask for clarification in the group setting. Some clients may leave the setting with misinformation. The counselor should look for input from the group and encourage as many questions as possible. Premature termination of the interpretation can quickly undo the value that accrues from testing.

The skilled counselor will be alert to individuals within the group. He or she must avoid putting people on the spot but elicit as many questions or comments as possible. This type of alertness permits the counselor to transfer the reactions of the client from the group to individual interpretative sessions. Group sessions should be seen as occasions with the potential for future individual involvement with the client.

The counselor should remember that any group situation increases involvement, potential problem areas, and misunderstanding at perhaps geometric rather than arithmetic rates. Because of the hazards involved in this type of interpretation, other types of settings are more appropriate for tests such as interest or personality inventories, which have a close relationship to personal feelings and are better interpreted on a one-to-one basis.

Reflection of Feelings

Test interpretation does not differ greatly from other types of counseling. Although some focus is upon the test, the test is really an extension of the individual so that the focus is still on the client. When counselors forget this, the client derives relatively little value from the test.

During and after whatever technical involvement there is the counselor helps the client deal with the meaning of the test results within her or his own life. The counselor listens for the client's personal feelings about the test-taking experience, about the outcomes of the test, and about future life meanings attached to the results. The counselor should respond to the client's feeling rather than to the actual scores or results.

Testing is only an extension of the real core of counseling: the aid one person can provide to another for living a more satisfying life. Although there is sometimes an inclination toward a sterile interpretation of tests, the counselor must constantly attempt to help the client focus on meaning and his or her own feelings about the topic of the session.

Prior Experience of the Client

During the counseling session it is important for the counselor to be aware of potential input from the client's prior experience. In a cooperative model of test interpretation the client is deeply involved in the process and her or his feelings and attitudes are relevant variables. The counselor should be willing to postpone testing or test interpretation if it becomes apparent that the client has to work through some feelings beforehand.

The client's prior experience also determines his or her possession of test-taking skills. Any testing program is selected to provide an accurate appraisal of the client's performance in various areas. Any known effect that causes an increase or decrease in performance must be taken into account. Observation of the test-taking situation and the characteristics of the test taker can provide important information for interpretation. For example, any physical defect that affects performance should be noted. Obvious defects usually preclude involvement in normal testing. Minor defects, however, often go unnoticed and the obtained score is used as if it were an accurate measure of performance.

Finally, some clients may not have experienced some of the newer methods of testing and scoring and are not always aware of the differences that can result from faulty responses. Others take the instructions too literally and the resultant score is below what might be predicted. If the counselor is going to set up a testing program for the client, he or she has an obligation to investigate the client factors that will influence test results.

The Involvement of Others

Counseling does not exist in a vacuum. The counselor and client are the major participants in the process but many others may have an important place in it, too. Outside personnel may be able to contribute meaningfully to the success of counseling by providing specialized information and assistance.

In addition to counseling interaction by teachers in a classroom setting, various professionals can contribute to the understanding the client derives from the counseling process. The counselor must be aware of the types of personnel who can help and the specific skills that might contribute to the goals of counseling. Most political agencies have already prepared general directories of available services. Within the counseling agency or setting there are also usually professionals with skills in a number of areas. The counselor should identify these professionals so that reasonably rapid involvement is possible. The counselor also should be willing to share his or her expertise with other professionals.

Whenever outside personnel are involved in the counseling process, the ethical, moral, and confidential standards of the profession apply. Any communication within the counselor-client relationship must be guarded, and either the client or counselor has the right to maintain the confidentiality of the interaction. Usually, however, when both realize the potential benefits that outside experts can provide and the fact that confidentiality can still be maintained, the help of others is more readily accepted.

Others may have more competency than the counselor in some of the areas under examination in counseling. Under these conditions the counselor is encouraged to draw upon their professional knowledge, thus minimizing errors caused by a limited perspective. The client will receive more accurate information, which in turn can be processed into meaningful self-understanding and action.

One of the better-known consultation methods is the case conference. Data are presented to a group of people who have potential to help in diagnosis, remediation, information processing, and other, similar areas. The focus of these conferences is the client and his or her attempts to work through a variety of needs. As the contact person the counselor is attempting to provide the best possible situation for the client by utilizing the thinking of several people to work through a specific problem. For the use of test data the counselor may be able to secure assistance prior to the counseling interaction. Outside personnel can provide insight into the test meanings and can assist the counselor in the presentation of data and interpretative activities with the client.

Each counselor probably arranges for a case conference differently. In addition to providing for the special requirements of each client, identification of the appropriate personnel and the counselor's style are important. Success is related to the interpersonal skills of the counselor. If the counselor approaches the use of outside personnel in a positive manner the client will probably be more accepting. If the counselor indicates reasonable interest in the skills of the assisting person the chances are good that the consultant will be helpful.

SPECIAL CONCERNS

One of the concerns related to using tests for clients from special populations is that tests have been misused to label people. This will be a problem as long as tests are used, but the counselor can make certain that the test selected is not a device to label or separate people. It is the counselor's responsibility to ensure that tests used in the counseling dyad are properly administered and interpreted and that they add information for the client's use.

A second concern is that tests are unfair to special populations. Although it is true that scores vary and that some groups seem to score higher than others, this does not necessarily make the test invalid or unusable. The counselor must provide interpretative assistance throughout the testing process—from selection, to understanding the test, to interpreting and using the data.

A third concern is that tests do not measure some of the important aspects of a person, such as creativity. Tests do not provide answers about every aspect of people; if one needs to know about such aspects as creativity, testing is not the way to find out. For many other aspects, however, tests can be valuable adjuncts to counseling. The counselor makes the best use of results and understands and communicates the test's strengths and weaknesses.

Whenever a client sees actual test questions that raise issues in her or his mind, the counselor should eliminate testing altogether. There is negative potential in most parts of human interaction, including the counseling process. But the answer is not to throw the process or materials away; rather, it is to make the situation as positive as possible so that the client receives the greatest possible assistance. When tests can be helpful they should be used. When they may not contribute to the process, either by way of increasing efficiency or adding data, they should not be used. The counselor and client should focus on the data necessary for the client's needs regardless of the source of the information.

COMPUTER ASSISTANCE FOR TEST INTERPRETATION

One issue that is comparatively recent in counseling involves the use of computers for providing assistance to individuals in a wide variety of ways that might be described as counseling. Computer dating services, job search processes, and other enterprises involving decision making have used computer technology to aid individuals in resolving concerns. For some clients this is a valuable service and when combined with interaction with a counselor works well for certain concerns.

Many counselors are wary of the computer as an adjunct to counseling. They sense that the potential for depersonalization is great and believe that this may be too big a risk to take. Other counselors have used computers for certain aspects of their counseling with clients. It seems certain that there will be increasing use of computers in counseling. The devices are becoming affordable, the technology is improving, and people are increasingly accepting the possibilities. Just as counsel- ing itself expanded when the cost, financial and psychological, became lower, so computer-assisted counseling will expand to meet the needs of those inclined to use it.

The computer has already been utilized in testing. It has provided high-speed scoring and profiling; diagnostic information to teachers and counselors involved in academic placement and remediation; and interpretative protocols for certain tests, such as the Minnesota Multiphasic Personality Inventory (MMPI). In most cases this has not interfered with the counselor's provision of personal assistance to the client.

For counselors who wish to use tests as part of the counseling process, access to a computer can provide immediate scoring, profiling, and visual and/or printed information for use by the counselor and client as part of counseling. The com- puter can arrange data in a number of ways for client use, providing predictive in- formation about each of the manipulations.

As with any aspect of counseling a major concern is the proper use of the computer. It should serve as an aid to, not a substitute for, the counselor.

The scenario that follows may be commonplace in the near future. The counselor and client have worked through the testing issue and decided that a test would be helpful. The appropriate test is selected and the client makes an appoint- ment at the test center. (Or the counselor may have the hardware in the suite as part of a complete counseling program.) The program for the test is put into the computer; when the questions are presented, the client responds either on an answer sheet or directly to the computer by use of the keyboard or perhaps ver- bally. Once the testing is completed the client receives immediate feedback from the computer in the form of appropriate profiled data, interpretative data, or pro- tocols among other types of data. The computer may suggest additional activities for the client such as examining other materials or looking at data stored in the computer or available from data cards. This can expand the data the client has and needs. Once this interaction is complete, perhaps in a very short time, the counselor and client complete the counseling process in whatever ways were sug- gested during the original interaction. The computer has assisted the client and counselor by speeding up the assessment process and by providing information that might not otherwise have been available.

Properly used, the computer can be of assistance to clients in their attempts to deal with concerns that brought them to the counselor in the first place. The counselor and client will benefit more from proper utilization of the device than from trying to deny its usefulness in the counseling process. The counselor can maintain professional involvement and increase his or her effectiveness in helping clients.

SUMMARY

This chapter has discussed the potential uses of tests in the counseling process. In addition to understanding the technical aspects of tests, the counselor needs skill in selection and interpretation. Tests can be a valuable addition to the client's self-understanding. They can provide information for prediction, diagnosis, monitoring, or evaluation of the client. Proper use of test data can help the client establish, move toward, attain, and judge reasonable outcomes. It is the counselor's responsibility to provide specialized assistance to the client when tests are included in the counseling process. In addition, the counselor must ensure that the test and its results are understood and properly used.

REFERENCES

Aiken, L. R. *Psychological testing and assessment* (3rd ed.). Boston: Allyn and Bacon, 1979.

Belkin, G. S. *Practical counseling in the schools*. Dubuque, Iowa: William C. Brown, 1975.

Brammer, L. M., & Shostrom, E. L. *Therapeutic psychology* (3rd ed.). Englewood Cliffs, N. J.: Prentice-Hall, 1977.

Cronbach, L. J. *Essentials of psychological testing* (3rd ed.). New York: Harper & Row, 1970.

Goldman, L. *Using tests in counseling* (rev. ed.). New York: Appleton-Century-Crofts, 1971.

Hoffman, B. *The tyranny of testing*. New York: Harper & Row, 1962.

Ivey, A. E., & Simek-Downing, L. *Counseling and psychotherapy: Skills, theories, and practice*. Englewood Cliffs, N. J.: Prentice-Hall, 1980.

Layton, W. L. Symposium: Tests and counseling II: The basis for a lasting connection between tests and counseling. *Measurement and Evaluation in Guidance*, 1972, 5, 403–407.

Pepinsky, H. B., & Pepinsky, P. N. *Counseling: Theory and practice*. New York: Ronald Press, 1954.

Shertzer, B., & Stone, S. C. *Fundamentals of guidance* (3rd ed.). Boston: Houghton Mifflin, 1976.

Super, D. E., & Crites, J. O. *Appraising vocational fitness*. New York: Harper & Row, 1962.

Tyler, L. *The work of the counselor* (3rd ed.). New York: Appleton-Century-Crofts, 1969.

Wesman, A. G. Symposium: Tests and counseling I: Testing and counseling, fact and fancy. *Measurement and Evaluation in Guidance*, 1972, 5, 397–402.

VOCATIONAL COUNSELING

CHAPTER EIGHTEEN

Work occupies an important place in U.S. society. Despite concerns about high unemployment, usually around 90 percent of the employable population hold jobs. There are many others who work but are not included in the employable population, such as teenagers still in school. The great majority of our population works in some capacity. Many of these people are happy and productive in their jobs and in many cases seeking the job, taking it, and progressing in a career were accomplished without the assistance of a vocational counseling specialist. In other cases getting and holding a job seems to be enough, and the worker may not consider utilizing a vocational counselor to help him or her find more meaningful positions. The need for vocational assistance within the working population has not been established or understood.

Yet almost from the beginning of counseling as a profession, vocational assistance has been an accepted part of the counseling process. Theorists have researched the process and developed approaches that can be of value to clients in career decision making.

Providing assistance in several aspects of vocational development has long been an accepted part of the counseling process. In too many cases the focus of the process, the client, has not recognized the need for or value of a counselor's assistance. Yet the vocational counselor can help the client in several ways. For the person who has not yet entered the workforce, many counselors are involved in job analysis, job development, or job searches that provide information about where potential employment exists or will shortly be available. Second, vocational counselors can aid in the process of job adjustment, which may make the difference between advancement or stagnation, or between having a job and being without one. Third, the counselor can provide assistance in the area of job satisfaction. This can occur prior to job entry, through discussion and understanding of the good and bad aspects of the job. Or it can occur at various points in the career development process, when the counselor and client identify and discuss the positive and negative factors related to a job. Finally, the counselor can aid in job or career change for the individual who is forced out of or decides to move away from his or her current position. In short, the skilled counselor can provide assistance to the individual as he or she develops vocationally, seeks and chooses a job, advances in a job, and at points when he or she may change or leave employment.

CAREER EDUCATION

Career development and vocational assistance are lifelong processes. This already established concept received support from Sidney Marland during his tenure as U.S. Commissioner of Education. He suggested that "all educational experiences, curriculum, instruction, and counseling should be geared to preparation for economic independence and an appreciation for the dignity of work" (*Career Education*, 1971). Unfortunately, the institutions to which the individual is normally exposed (Herr, 1974) have rarely facilitiated systematic choice-making competencies.

Career education is a process that occurs over an extended period to help the individual learn about work alternatives and make a career choice leading to a satisfying, productive vocational life. Consequently, career education demands self-understanding, the development of a method for moving toward reasonable outcomes, and the acquisition of skills identified in the process of vocational counseling.

Attention to career development is important in elementary and secondary schools, institutions of higher education, and other agencies whose mandate for service includes job placement, development, or assessment. The attitudes, knowledge, and skills necessary for choosing, preparing for, and pursuing a career are stressed at all levels. It is clear that the integration of learning, doing, and knowing about work is essential throughout each person's vocational life. Counselors trained in each aspect must accept a major role in ensuring that this integration exists in career opportunities for vocationally oriented clients.

Hoyt et al. (1972) identified five basic components of career education that focus on the major aspects of career needs. First, there are career implications in every learning experience. Each person—teacher, counselor, adviser—should integrate knowledge of work and work values. Counselors must look for and point out the work-related factors in any activity in which a learner is involved in interaction with an instructor, regardless of the latter's specific title.

A second component is the skill training that is necessary for entry into an occupation. Counselors, teachers, and others will try to maximize the quality, appropriateness, variety, and level of skill training available to each person. A variety of methods exist to reach this goal; the skilled counselor must be ready and able to work closely with clients to ensure the successful working through of the necessary tasks.

A third component is the provision of cognitive and experiential ways for the client or student to understand the values of a work-oriented society. The helping person's job is to ensure systematic and continuous assistance in the career education and development process. Self-understanding and knowledge of the alternatives available to each person must be a focal point during this phase. Finally, this component includes providing assistance for intelligent decision making. Counselors should be available to the individual throughout this process, for these activities are essential to intelligent career choices and job satisfaction.

The fourth component involves the individual's movement from the abstractness of the classroom or counseling dyad into the actual world of work. The individual must have opportunities for observing work and the people who do it and, eventually, work experience. In our society the individual often has few opportunities to observe work situations and to question others about their work. When the opportunity arises, the individual may not know which questions to ask, and there is little assurance that the answers will be helpful. The fourth component includes the identification of the nature and needs of an occupational society in which the roles of workers are somewhat hidden; and a knowledge of the economy, of production, of human interaction, of technology, and of the many other problems that the industrial and occupational sectors of our complex society face and will face in the future. Education and business must cooperate to make this knowledge available. The counselor should lead the cooperative efforts and the implementation of activities.

The fifth component involves identification of the interrelationship of the home, family, community, and occupational society. The importance of parental values, work opportunities, and societal attitudes are emphasized at this time.

These components are not necessarily sequential. Rather, they specify the major aspects of a career education model whose goals are awareness of work; the exploration and decision making necessary to develop a personal value system related to work; and the preparation, placement, and advancement that indicate successful completion of a career education sequence. This is the important sequence in vocational, occupational, or career assistance. As Hoyt et al. suggested,

> This three-step process is a continuing one which most individuals will experience more than once in their lives. Indeed, it must occur whenever the individual is faced with choosing or changing his occupation. It is tied as intimately to why an individual chooses to work as it is to why he chooses one form of work over another. It is a concept appropriate for all students at all educational levels and in almost all kinds of educational settings. It is not a process that can be assigned to any one part of the educational establishment but must, rather, involve all educators at all levels in all kinds of educational settings. Similarly, it is not a process that education, as part of the total society, can accomplish by itself. Rather, it will demand the active involvement of the total community of which the school system is a part (1972, p. 11).

This model provides a basis for the examination of vocational assistance in this chapter. As Hoyt suggested, the task is not for one person or segment of society. The focus of this chapter, however, is the involvement of one professional, the counselor, as he or she functions in the vocational process, regardless of the institution where the counselor works or the client's vocational developmental level.

Professional counselors are involved at numerous points in career development. Their task is to promote each client's self-understanding, using a variety of techniques and materials. Counselors can help the client develop or refine her or his strategy for moving toward the desired job or career. This requires a variety of involvements on the part of the counselor, depending on such factors as the client's age, previous experience, crucialness of need, and skill factors. Finally, the counselor's involvement assures the client of help in identifying the skills required by his or her choice. These skills may include educational preparation, personal improvement, specific work tasks, and value development. Whereas it is always possible that a client will accomplish these goals independently, there is no doubt that an involved counselor can provide valuable help.

This formalization of the tasks in the vocational area simply focuses again on the client's needs. Counselors have always known about the value of counseling in meeting vocational needs. Many counselors, however, have not given vocational counseling as high a priority as the leaders in career education programs believe is necessary. Professional counselors must not only recognize but also act upon the fact that vocational, educational, and personal counseling are necessary for the client to lead an effective life. Neglecting or ignoring one of these factors makes counseling less meaningful than it might be.

Since Parsons' (1909) involvement with the problems of out-of-work individuals early in the century, there has been ambivalence about vocational counseling. On one hand, many people seeking counseling assistance need help in some aspect of vocational decision making. At the same time, practitioners have characterized vocational counseling as a rather low-level activity that counselors like to avoid. Vocational choice and satisfaction, however, are important aspects of our society and the process of vocational development should be respected and used well.

There are several basic ideas that the vocational counselor should understand, including vocational development theory, the organization and use of occupational information, and the world of work. In addition, certain topics are having an effect on vocational counseling. These include women and work, nonwork, and the impact of technology on the workforce.

A rationale for career guidance is that work meets a basic need in humans, the need for positive self-concept. For most people several types of work leading to any of several careers can serve this purpose. For others this may not be the case. For any person knowledge of self, of skills, of attitudes, and an understanding of work are essential elements in entering the world of work. As Herr and Cramer (1979) pointed out, these dimensions should be fostered and acted upon rather than left to chance.

The counselor and other people involved in the client's life must understand the process of career development. Because it is normally a process, certain aspects can be anticipated and assistance offered to each person at critical points along the way. Career development is a process of helping individuals deal with potential and probable outcomes in a way that is most beneficial to them. In career counseling, clients are given assistance in making choices that help them begin, manage, and finalize a career or careers. Career counseling transcends age, educational level, and setting.

A number of factors have been identified as part of career development. Interests, values, and significant others play an important role in the individual's decision-making process. The more the person knows about these factors, the better related the ultimate decision or set of decisions should be to career and life.

ABILITIES

It is clear that the individual needs to know what his or her abilities are. This knowledge will help the person identify potential job areas and/or methods for increasing her or his abilities to the level necessary for job entry or advancement. The individual who has had career development assistance will have less of a problem in dealing with this aspect of the career guidance process. If the previous work has not been completed, the counselor may have to provide information about possibilities for training and education. In some cases the counselor may become directly involved in providing this help. For example, if the client cannot use the various materials that are necessary and available, the counselor may help the client learn whatever is necessary. The counselor may have to adopt this teaching function in order to aid the client in job decision making.

INTERESTS

The client must also know what her or his interests are so that appropriate matching can occur with occupational choice. Most people are likely to change or expand their interests. The counselor should be prepared to include this fact in discussions with the client during counseling. The counselor must help the client determine his or her interests or pattern of interests so that the client can see and understand the relationship between interests, jobs, and job satisfaction. The counselor should also help the client realize that interests and abilities are not always as nicely interrelated as one might like. Interests do not predict ability. Ability does not mean that the person will be happy in a position requiring those abilities.

VALUES

Values are closely related to the decision-making process. Like interests, values exist prior to contact with a counselor and may be well defined or ill defined depending on the developmental stage and maturity of the client. The relationship between values, especially work values, and reward systems is a critical area for the counselor and client to discuss. The better the client understands his or her values, the greater the potential for good decisions and job satisfaction.

Values may be positively related to vocational maturity. The vocationally mature person has given time and thought to her or his values and how these relate to life as well as to work. The greater the level of vocational maturity, the more likely the client will be to choose appropriate jobs and careers. Dealing with values, interests, and abilities during the process of choosing a vocation increases the chances that career advancement will occur.

The counselor should be ready to help the client deal with values. There are a number of ways this can occur, including direct counselor-client discussion. In direct discussion the counselor may experience some anxious moments, for often her or his values will come under scrutiny. This is especially true when the counselor's values are in conflict with those of the client. Values about education are an example. Because most counselors have a significant amount of education, often successfully completed, it is difficult for them to work with a client who disparages the value of education or sees little value in doing well or making a real effort in school.

DECISION MAKING

Decision making is an important element in the career choice process. Without skills in decision making the client is inadequately prepared to move toward choosing a career. A client who cannot combine information about himself or herself with information about jobs and make a decision receives little benefit from career assistance.

The decision-making process usually involves several steps: defining the problem, developing alternative solutions, finding appropriate information, using the information, developing plans and objectives, following through (implementation), and evaluation. The counselor's job is to provide assistance when the client is unable to handle portions of the sequence. Indeed, the counselor may have to teach the client the sequence.

Defining the Problem

Defining the problem entails identifying client's concerns and placing them in an understandable frame of reference. This might include establishing priorities with the client or clarifying the problem(s) as presented by the client. This activity is continual, for concerns related to problems recur throughout the counseling sequence.

Developing Alternative Solutions

In this activity, the counselor and client attempt to identify several solutions for the concerns the client has raised. At some point closure and establishing priorities become necessary so that the larger process can continue. One of the counselor's tasks is to monitor the counseling process, moving on to another topic or developing one further when appropriate. Sometimes the counselor will want to return to previous levels or topics. This additional dimension in the counselor's role helps furnish guidance to the client.

Finding Appropriate Information

Information should be as readily available to the client as possible. Because it is impossible to anticipate every informational need prior to the session, it is sometimes necessary to stop for a time or to direct the client to specific information to examine for later use. The counselor should attempt to have current vocational, occupational, and educational information for client use. Only with accurate, up-to-date information can the counselor help the client find appropriate data.

Using the Information

The client needs an opportunity not only to discuss the available information but also to use it in the process of choosing an occupation. Whenever possible, the counselor provides this opportunity both within and outside the counseling setting. For example, the client may have found some data on the job she or he is interested in. Discussing the information with the counselor clarifies some points and answers some questions. However, the client may not be satisfied with the outcome. The counselor can help the client develop outside possibilities for additional opinions and data gathering. In some cases the counselor might arrange these contacts, inviting the outside person to the school or agency to provide additional clarifying data for the client or for others who might be interested in the information.

Developing Plans and Objectives

Once the informational phase is completed or nearly completed the client should be ready to develop some plans. These may be tentative or firm, depending on the status of the client and on his or her need to move forward. A high school junior's plans may not be as firmly developed as a college senior's. At this point the counselor helps the client focus on realistic objectives. The method for the reality focusing will flow from the counselor's orientation. This planning stage is important in any vocational choice, and the counselor must ensure that the client has dealt with the stage and that her or his plans are reasonable.

Following Through

Following through is largely the responsibility of the client. He or she must now implement the plan, perhaps by simply applying for a job or enrolling in appropriate preemployment education or obtaining more and perhaps different counseling assistance. The client may have developed a plan to attend college as a prelude to going to work. However, the client may not have developed the personal discipline necessary to complete the educational process at the performance level called for by the employer. The client must deal with this aspect of her or his personal status, either by changing personal characteristics or rethinking the plan. In either case additional counseling of a personal nature may be necessary.

Evaluation

Evaluation gives the client an opportunity to see the success of his or her endeavor. As a result of evaluation the client can reassess the decision or move toward subsequent decisions in vocational and career development.

The purpose of any vocational counseling process is to help the client maximize her or his potential and goals. Many factors influence this process. In all cases, however, the counselor and client try to make decisions that provide the greatest potential for success in light of personal characteristics, time, skills, salary, and long-term potential.

For most people, the choice of a career begins early and continues throughout life. A number of crucial points in people's lifetimes have been identified by society or through observation of developmental sequences. Providing assistance at these points will increase the probability of good decisions and, it is hoped, satisfactory careers. The involvement of a counselor can occur at many points. Other people, such as teachers or parents, can also provide input. The counselor may interact with these people to help them maximize their input. There may also be others who probably want to help but who are unable to do so and may even inhibit the client's progress. Wanting to help is not a sufficient qualification in counseling. Skill and understanding are essential.

Choosing a vocation is a highly complex process that often appears simple. Many people have chosen and will continue to choose an occupation without counselor assistance. In their case it is difficult to know whether involvement with a helping person during the critical periods of career development would have resulted in increased job satisfaction, productivity and appropriateness. Most people work. Are most people satisfied with their jobs? Did most make the best choices? What can people do after the choice has been made and some degree of flexibility seems to have disappeared? This is the challenge for the vocational counselor: to offer opportunities to many people to examine their skills, values, interests, and potentials and to move through the process toward a productive working life.

THEORY OF VOCATIONAL DEVELOPMENT

Since the end of World War II there has been increasing interest in the process by which people approach, enter, and exit from the world of work. A number of theories have been developed and some have been tested over an extended period of time. Some theorists postulate a sequence of steps or stages through which individuals pass vocationally (Super, 1957). This developmental notion provides an excellent perspective for viewing vocational counseling.

THE SEQUENCE OF STAGES

The earliest stage is often a nonrealistic conceptualization of one's potentials and the world of work. A child thinks about many glamorous types of work or imagines himself or herself as a multitalented person. Although either of these activities carried to an extreme might eventually lead to psychological problems, they are desirable ones during the first four to six years of schooling. At this stage the counselor's job is to encourage wide-ranging vocational thinking in students.

In the second phase a narrowing of possibilities occurs; the individual begins to be more realistic in investigating potential jobs. This narrowing of choices may represent the elimination of jobs with negative valence or it may indicate the child's more realistic understanding that he or she is unable or unwilling to do certain kinds of work. This phase normally extends from about the end of elementary school into high school. Again the counselor's job is to promote the narrowing of vocational choices and to provide materials and discussion periods that focus on career or vocational potential.

The third phase of vocational development might be labeled realistic choice making. In this stage the potential field becomes quite restricted. The individual is faced with several decisions that are no longer simply intellectual; these choices will affect his or her life-style. Several factors become important in this phase. First, there is an interrelatedness of choice. Educational decisions are interrelated with vocational decisions because they represent intermediate steps in the vocational choice process. Moreover, the individual's understanding of the interesting vocation is interrelated with self-understanding. A number of factors may imbue the potential vocation with more meaning for one person than for another. The counselor provides materials that discuss the various aspects of jobs. There are other equally important aspects that may not be covered but should be. For instance, many people fail in jobs for psychological reasons; having the requisite skills is not a sufficient condition for success. This phase is extremely important, and counselor input is crucial at this point. The counselor should be deeply involved in the decision making.

During the fourth phase, often identified as maintenance, the individual settles into the pattern of his or her vocational life, perhaps moving from one position to another within an organization or from one organization to another. Generally, though not always, this is a quieter and smoother vocational period than other phases. Several potential pitfalls do exist.

Economic conditions may restrict or eliminate occupational advancement. The individual may have the requisite skills, but if no job is available the person may have some difficulty dealing with her or his personal and vocational life. As one gets older and settled into a position, irreversibility may interfere with the upward advancement that was predictable from the earlier vocational pattern. In completely negative terms, the employer may be relatively certain that the employee is probably not going to seek other employment, and the employer may not be as concerned with the employee as he or she was earlier. In these circumstances the employee may need some personal as well as vocational aid. Finally, physical condition often forces change in activity or a geographic move. In either case adjustment is often difficult.

Thus, the maintenance period has the potential for either great trauma or little effect on the life of the worker. The relationship between counselor and client will be quite different at this time from other times in vocational development.

In the final phase the worker moves to terminate vocational activities and enters, it is hoped, a period of meaningful retirement. For many people now completing their formal vocational lives, retirement is an undesirable prospect. The prevailing work ethic makes it difficult for some older workers to deal with nonwork as a way of life. The individual has developed a pattern of life that includes working, and this pattern is difficult to break. Retirement or nonwork forces disruptions, and the individuals often begin to manifest personal behaviors that are not pleasant to them or those around them. At this point, the counselor can provide a great amount of aid. Members of the profession are beginning to gather data to understand the situation and to develop processes and materials for counseling.

Most people move through the stages of vocational development with relatively little difficulty. The uniqueness of each phase demands that the counselor provide individual assistance and information whenever appropriate. There are no clearcut times when one phase ends and the next begins, but the counselor should quickly learn to recognize the referents of each phase and the characteristics of the client (Super, 1957).

THE WORLD OF WORK

In our society work provides ways for meeting a number of psychological needs. It may be an outlet for the expressive drive that is a major source of energy. It may provide an opportunity for the individual to win approval from others. Work promotes the development of satisfying social relationships and provides a way for a person to feel that his or her life counts for something. The worker's role as a leader, a director, a creator, a server, or a teacher is meaningful to both the worker and society.

The array of available jobs is immense and sometimes bewildering. People are faced with finding jobs they can do, in which they have an interest, and that are available. When making a selection individuals find that the job itself may have several facets that are important for advancement, promotion, increase in salary, and job satisfaction. They may find that their selection is not particularly satisfying and must begin the process again. Assistance should be available to help individuals make important vocational decisions.

When a person enters the world of work, one area of major importance is the relationship of the individual's education to the vocational choice. Another is the utilization of practical work experience as a foundation for more realistic choices (Brammer & Shostrom, 1977).

EDUCATIONAL INFORMATION

In an increasingly complex society, vocational choice demands sophisticated training or education prior to entry into a particular position. Educational choice becomes one step in the vocational choice process. The counselor can assist the client in several areas of educational counseling.

First, the counselor can help the client in planning for educational experiences. The activities of a secondary school counselor are an example of educational planning. A second type of activity is educational placement. Many employment counselors are involved in selection of educational opportunities. Because this choice often is prerequisite to job placement, it is a very important factor. A third area of aid is remediation of educational deficiencies. This type of activity occurs usually in educational institutions where the counselor, as an instructional staff member, uses special skills in diagnosing students' educational problems and understands the institutional offerings enough to offer the client the most meaningful remediation possible. A fourth area is preventive educational assistance. The counselor might be more of a coordinator in this area, identifying students who appear to be headed toward difficulty and coordinating school and outside personnel facilities to reverse the student's movement toward inadequate levels of achievement or personal functioning. A final area is direct counseling concerning the reasons for inadequate educational performance. In this case the client would be facing academic difficulties that are rooted in lack of motivation, lack of interest, or other psychological and nonintellectual factors. The counselor helps the client understand his or her problems and begin to function more adequately by eliminating the problem or bypassing the affect of the problem.

Quite often the initial interview begins as an examination of vocational choice and evolves into an interview about educational planning or choice. The following dialogue shows how the client and counselor move from vocational choice to examination of both educational and vocational information.

After some preliminary conversation the counselor begins:

C.   When you were here the other day for next year's schedule you thought it might be helpful to meet again and discuss your future plans.

S.   Yeah, I don't know what I want to do.

C.   And you would like to find out.

S.   Yeah, why not.

C.   OK, let's try to find out some things about you and what you have been thinking about, because these are important facets when one thinks about a job or career. The first thing that might make sense is for you to tell me about yourself.

The client responds with descriptions of what he likes to do and what he does not think he likes. At some point the following statement is made.

S.   I kind of like school but I think that something like being a dentist would be interesting.

C.   Right now you have a couple of interests but you are not sure which is most attractive.

S.   I guess. My dad says that I should keep all the doors open that I can. It's just that I don't know what my chances are. I sure don't want to spend a lot of time taking courses that aren't going to help me.

C.   You would like to be sure that what you decide is right for you.

S.   Yeah.

C. But I think I hear that you would like to know more about you before committing yourself to a plan of action.

S. I suppose. I mean, what can I do and what do I want to do?

C. Let's look at dentistry for a while. Maybe this can help focus on you and your interests. What do you know about being a dentist?

S. I know you have to go to dentist school and that science is important. I think most dentists make pretty good money but sometimes the things you have to do are not very pleasant. But I guess I really don't know very much.

C. Perhaps you could talk to a dentist to find out some other things.

S. Like what?

C. Well, several things. First, what does one have to do to become a dentist? What education is necessary? What subjects are required? Questions like that. Second, what does a dentist actually do? What possibilities exist in the field of dentistry? Is it a good field to enter? These are a few of the questions that are important.

S. Well, we do have a family dentist. Maybe I could talk to him.

C. I think that would be helpful.

S. Could you help me with this?

C. In what ways?

S. Well what other questions should I ask? What should I know before going to see him?

C. We listed several questions before, like what preparation is necessary and what he does. We can work on several others but first I think that it will be good to talk about you a bit more so that you do know about yourself prior to talking with the dentist.

S. What do you mean?

C. Well, for example, have you thought about education, if you would like to go on to college and where you would like to go.

S. I'm interested in a small college somewhere but I haven't really looked at college.

C. What kinds of things do you want to know about college before you enter?

S. I'd like to know what I need to get in and I'd like to be sure I can make it through.

C. Anything else you can think of?

S. No, I guess not.

C. OK, those are good topics and perhaps we can get started on those. Have you looked at any college catalogs?

S.   Yeah, but I don't understand them.

C.   Let's take a look at some we have here and see whether we can learn a bit about colleges from them.

This counselor has chosen to wait to discuss some topics that others may find more important. The point is that many vocational decisions include educational decisions and they should be discussed. The timing may be left to the counselor and client.

Planning Educational Experiences

The counselor is probably most comfortable in this area of counseling because her or his experience as a student is often directly related to the client's goals and objectives. The counselor may not have experienced the same concerns as the client, but he or she does have a general idea of the educational world.

The counselor is called upon to help the client select an educational goal that is attainable and in line with the client's aptitudes and interests, and also the best educational experience to meet this goal. College placement, though important, is not the only type of planning necessary. The need for noncollege educational prerequisites in many occupational areas suggests that most clients will need information about various types of educational experiences.

In general, the following factors are important. First, the client needs to understand himself or herself and what he or she wants to do. This may require some assessment by the counselor. It also means that the counselor should help the client develop alternatives. The counselor may be called upon to confront the client at certain points if it becomes apparent that the client is moving in an unproductive direction. There is nothing to be gained by discussing avenues that the client has little potential for completing successfully. In such confrontations the counselor should rely on fairly hard data and cite the sources verbatim. For example, it is not fruitful to spend time with a client exploring the possibilities of matriculating at a very selective college if the client does not have the characteristics that the college requires in its student population.

For counseling assistance in college planning much information is available and surprisingly up-to-date. In exploring many other types of educational opportunities, the counselor must develop strategies for meeting the needs of the clients. Probabilities of successful completion of a given course of study, relationship to job opportunities, and job factors are important types of information that both college and noncollege bound clients need.

Educational Placement

Many counselors in educational institutions are called upon to recommend levels of placement within the institution. In these circumstances, counselors should understand the multiple aspects of the educational situation to be effective in providing meaningful placement assistance. They should know what courses are offered in various areas of the curriculum and what differentiates levels of content. In secondary schools, counselors ought to be thoroughly aware of content areas so that the client can be well informed about what is being offered and what is going to be expected of him or her.

At the same time the client should know how educational experiences relate to her or his life and goals. He or she needs to know the requirements for completion of a specific set of experiences and must develop awareness about which curriculum offerings meet personal needs and abilities. The client must know how to move into and out of various experiences to take full advantage of what is offered.

Most educational institutions do not provide students with complete freedom of movement in the curriculum. The counselor should help the client adjust to the limitations or restrictions that exist in the institution. The counselor also ought to be active in changing institutional practices that inhibit students' growth. This requires the counselor to determine how much variability in student characteristics the institution can tolerate. Yet it is part of the counselor's role to identify institutional strengths and weaknesses and utilize them to the greatest benefit of the client.

The placement activities of the counselor also deal with opportunities outside the institution. Because the counselor often serves as a resource person to clients who must seek specialized education, the counselor should know something about the various agencies and methods for taking advantage of their offerings. Similarly, the counselor needs to know about other levels of the educational enterprise. She or he should be familiar with the previous levels of client experience and help the client relate these future experiences.

The counselor's involvement in educational planning can be very meaningful when approached correctly. If a counselor is interested only in getting students accepted into classes or institutions, she or he has failed to fill an important role in educational planning.

Remediation

The counselor's primary involvement in remediation is to diagnose and then make an appropriate recommendation or referral. There are several means of making the diagnosis. Appraisal instruments are available in such areas as achievement, attitude, and general study methods. They provide data about areas in which the client may be experiencing difficulty. The counselor ought to be the most skilled person in using these assessment instruments but eventually instructional personnel will also have to be involved. Communication with instructional personnel concerning these results is important.

A second area of diagnosis deals with the client's physical and psychological makeup. In diagnosing physical aspects the counselor will depend on those more skilled in the area. But he or she should be able to utilize information from specialists to help the client understand the cause and some potential remedies. To diagnose psychological factors the counselor should be skilled in the use of clinical processes. Common factors such as motivation or lack of interest are usually easily recognizable. These types of problems usually demand depth-oriented counseling rather than remedial educational processes. In short, the counselor's involvement in remediation is to diagnose the area of concern and assist the client in understanding what the concern is, what kinds of assistance are available, and how the student utilizes the referral specialist who might most closely meet his or her needs.

Prevention

In general, counseling can be more successful if preventive aspects are involved in the process. The counselor's goal is to identify as early as possible the characteristics that might predict inadequate development or functioning. It is then possible to introduce preventive measures.

For example, because future success in a subject like reading is tied to previous reading accomplishment and to age, it is important to provide as much assistance as possible as early as possible to promote adequate development of reading skills. Providing reading aid can help the client avoid later academic difficulties. This concept can be applied to other levels of the educational enterprise. A client needs to understand the relationship between what she or he is currently doing or not doing and future goals. Although the counselor has no instant way of changing the client's present behavior, he or she can help the client see the potential difficulty and understand how it can be prevented.

Inadequate Performance

A counselor, regardless of the educational level he or she is working at, should be available to help the client understand and deal with inadequate academic performance. Usually this type of counseling activity involves underachievers or bad achievers who need to improve. The counselor can provide a relatively safe place for investigation of inadequate performance. Because the counselor is not called upon to evaluate performance, the counseling environment ought to be more conducive to exploration and resolution of the problem.

Not all clients identified as having inadequate academic performance actually have this problem. Many people achieve at about the level their ability predicts even though it might be below where parents, teachers, or school staff want them to be. These students are not bad achievers but do have a problem with the demands that others make on them. This situation again provides the counselor with an opportunity to work closely with people to understand needs and aptitudes better.

Practical Experience

It is desirable for the client to have an opportunity to gain experience in various areas of vocations. Although it is impossible to provide trial experience for every client in every area of interest or aptitude, until the person has had some practical involvement with the specifics of the vocation all choices remain tentative. It is possible to help a client adjust to a position after she or he is faced with some negative factors. Many employers are beginning to recognize that job satisfaction, the adjustment of worker and job, is important to productiveness and are providing counseling assistance to employees to aid in this process.

In providing assistance to the worker who finds it difficult to adjust to the job, followup and development of alternatives are important. When the problem is the job, not unwillingness to work, the vocational counselor can provide valuable service to the client in this often neglected area of followup and redirection.

THE COUNSELING PROCESS

Vocational counseling helps people develop an accurate appraisal of themselves in relation to the world of work. Clients may need help in integrating their desires and abilities with the realities of the job market. Because this process is developmental, clients may need assistance at several points. Their needs will differ depending on their progress through the sequence. Several elements in this process are important considerations regardless of the counselor's theoretical viewpoint.

1. The vocational counselor can provide the greatest assistance to the client by keeping pressure and negative aspects at a minimum. The client will respond more favorably to positive counseling conditions that permit open communication of characteristics and needs.

2. The client needs to understand both the facts about vocations and how his or her perceptions about self and job interrelate with those facts. Even when the counselor does not hold a client-centered view, it remains a necessary condition of counseling to help the client understand how her or his world relates to another world, the world of work.

3. The counselor should help the client obtain and use information, whether by selection of and interpretation of tests or by contact with outside agencies and work opportunities so that data are available. There are many ways of gathering data and making them available to the client. The counselor must be involved in providing this information and in helping the client clarify it.

4. The vocational counselor should help the client make necessary decisions, accomplish appropriate tasks, and move into the next phase of vocational development. These activities may involve education, preoccupational training, and/or job seeking. The process is designed to culminate in the best possible alignment of worker to job and to provide the worker with the requisite skills to advance in the job, to evaluate progress and performance, and to be as successful as possible in the chosen career.

The steps above indicate that vocational counseling is an important facet of the work of most counselors. The professional counselor will accept this responsibility, realizing that the complexities of vocational choice require as much assistance as other personal client needs. Vocational counseling is an important task. For many clients the vocational choice is and remains the most important aspect of their lives.

Throughout life certain activities are considered the job or occupation of a specific portion of the population. These activities illustrate the nature of appropriate involvement by helping persons. Play is the young child's work. When the child attends school, learning is added to his or her job. During high school and thereafter the individual works in more commonly accepted types of jobs. Retirement becomes the work of the older citizen. Vocational assistance all along the way helps the individual take advantage of the benefits that his or her work offers, personally, professionally, and psychologically.

Counselors must therefore be aware of the needs and problems of these different populations and communicate this understanding to the client and to the society. Counselors must see the possibilities as well as impediments and develop strategies for helping clients cope with these many facets.

Vocational or educational counseling is generally an orderly process, beginning with the development of the relationship and ending with followup and potential change of plans. Along the way the counselor is involved in helping the client develop understanding of problems or concerns, gathering data from several sources and presenting the information to the client. The counselor and client work to apply the appraisal process and individual client study to a plan of action or a choice.

These steps will never be as clearly definable in reality as they are in the discussion below. Nevertheless, after the counseling relationship is established the counselor should be aware of the six factors: appraisal of the client's characteristics, introduction of outside information, exploration, clarification, integration, and the decision (Brammer & Shostrom, 1977).

WORKING WITH SELF-AWARENESS

One of the most important factors related to vocational choice is knowledge of self. The individual needs to differentiate a number of facets of self and relate these to choices or alternatives. The counselor begins early in the relationship with the client to help identify values, interests, personal strengths, and personal weaknesses. The counselor uses a variety of techniques to accomplish this goal, including counselee reporting, tests, previous client information, and observed characteristics within and outside the counseling session. One of the counselor's tasks is to monitor the data to ensure the greatest accuracy for the client.

This process should be part of the assistance provided to individuals from early in life throughout their vocational history, although at present much of the process occurs during the end of the teen years and the first half of the twenties. Parents, teachers, counselors, and others aid in the process and the individual begins to sense his or her individuality and to see a unique pattern of interests, values, and abilities. This process should be part of any counseling interaction but it is especially important for vocational assistance.

APPRAISAL OF CLIENT CHARACTERISTICS

The client needs to examine her or his interests, aptitudes, achievement, aspiration, skills, values, and other characteristics. The methods for doing this process include checklists, inventories, tests, previous records, interview data, and work history. There may also be focus on special aptitudes, personality traits, and educational attainment.

One of the first tasks of the counselor is to determine the client's aspirations; limitations in training, skills, educational background, and experience; and special aptitudes or skills. The counselor provides assistance for the client to discover as many of these "facts" as possible.

Ascertaining these characteristics may complicate the counseling situation. Some clients are only seeking affirmation of a decision already made. The counselor, however, is unable to affirm the rightness or wrongness of the decision without knowing the client's characteristics. At other times the counselor must try to help a client who appears to lack some of the required skills or characteristics. This client might have specific, though unrealistic, expectations. Other clients are confused by an overabundance of talents and available choices.

The counselor's job is to help sort out these facts. He or she may need to work with the client to develop hierarchies related to jobs and needs or may help the client accept certain restrictions related to job opportunities. The counselor may also broaden the scope by introducing new materials or concepts. All represent efforts to help clients understand who they are and what characteristics they have.

During initial contacts with the client the counselor is involved in developing predictions about the client's probabilities. She or he is learning about the client not to force a decision but to be in a position to provide meaningful assistance later in the process. The counselor listens to determine where the client is in the process of choice, learns whether the client has relatively accurate information, and remains aware of the counseling interaction. These activities reflect attempts to determine where the client is, where he or she wishes to go, what the probabilities are of getting there, and how the counselor can be of most assistance.

Client Objectives

The client and counselor need to agree upon objectives for the counseling process based on the data gathering and interpretation in the early interviews. The counselor helps the client begin to specify possibilities. They establish methods of further exploration of these possibilities. (In the case of behavioral counseling a method of reinforcement or learning is established.) At the end of this step the counselor and client should have a clear notion of the existing alternatives and should move toward establishing a hierarchy of possibilities for further exploration.

In some cases the client will not be able to reconcile the data with his or her desires. Many clients are unwilling or unable to accept data that predict unacceptable outcomes for them. Although predictive powers are not as refined as one would like, the counselor may have to confront the client at certain points in the process.

Interests

The fact that a client has the aptitude to perform certain tasks does not guarantee that a client has an interest in the task area. The counselor can help the client to determine whether the potential position or area is within her or his pattern of interests. Job satisfaction has become an important aspect of vocational adjustment, and interests have a significant influence on satisfaction.

The client must also reconcile interests with personal values by understanding how those values fit with the demands of the position. The client may be expected to perform certain tasks that are outside his or her value system. This type of information is important for the client at this stage because it can affect choices.

It is also necessary to relate the physical demands of the job to the characteristics of the client. If these are in conflict the counselor should help the client avoid what will probably be an unsatisfactory situation.

Sometimes the client is forced to compromise in selecting jobs. Interests may not match aptitudes; the employer's or the client's prerequisites may not match interests or skills. The client may need the job; the counselor's role is to help the client find the best situation available.

LEARNING ABOUT THE ENVIRONMENT

Concurrently with learning about self the individual must learn about the environment in which she or he will eventually seek employment. Early in life the home and school represent the major components of the individual's environment. The client needs to understand how these influences relate to vocational choice. Field trips and career days provide opportunities for exposure. Counselors at various levels must also provide a way for the client to discuss his or her concepts of the world of work, to clarify and expand these concepts, and to explore new ideas. The counselor must provide an opportunity for the individual to learn about the environment and its relationship to career planning and decision making.

The counselor provides information about vocations that the client does not have but that he or she needs in order to make a meaningful decision. Various types of information are available. Commercially published material lists the important aspects of a vocation, including entry characteristics, salaries, structure of the vocation, and relationship to other vocational fields and levels. Judicious use of the this type of information can help a client work through a vocational decision. The counselor should also make some personal information available to clients. This would be more specific information, dealing with a particular position at a specific moment in time. The counselor must be cautious not to overpersonalize this process by responding to a client's chance remark simply because the counselor has some knowledge about the area. The counselor should be sure that the client does want to know about the topic.

The counselor is responsible for keeping informational sources up-to-date and relevant and for clarifying the material in various sources so that it is relevant to the local situation.

EXPLORATION, CLARIFICATION, AND INTEGRATION

Once the client has begun to focus on values, interests, and self-concept and to relate these to the environmental factors in her or his life, the counselor should provide an opportunity for exploration of vocational possibilities. For clients aged ten to twelve, the emphasis is upon talking about and trying out as many possibilities as the clients are willing to consider. The task at this time is simply to expand horizons so that the young client's vocational experience, either vicarious or actual, include a spectrum of activities. The counselor's task here may be to develop activities, to work closely with significant others to implement this stage of vocational development, and to involve clients in as many of these opportunities as possible. The greater the involvement in activities prior to vocational decision making, the greater the potential for viable vocational choice.

For some people the expansion of choices will be the extent of their vocational counseling. Many others, however, will need to go beyond exploration to phases that will culminate in a vocational choice. The decision-making aspects of this process are covered elsewhere. Occupational information provides avenues for further exploration, and this exploration is most effective when the clients themselves use the material. Being told something is not as meaningful as finding out for oneself.

In exploring vocational possibilities, the client needs to understand thoroughly the various possibilities available to her or him. To develop realistic choices, the client needs to delineate clearly the various possibilities and their characteristics. The counselor should be active in this process and be as factual and neutral as possible. Often counselors reveal the decision they have made for the client in the way in which they present information and clarify what the client says. The decision, however, is the client's to make.

Finally, the client must integrate the material into his or her decision or choice. After exploration and clarification, successful counseling should lead to a choice that incorporates as much personal, vocational, and occupational information as possible. Although compromise is usually part of the process this should be held at a minimal level.

INFORMATION PROCESSING

The counselor-client interaction should have generated a great amount of information. Ideally, the counselor has helped the client learn about self, the environment, and occupational opportunities in which she or he is interested. Both participants have verified this information at several points along the way. Now the client and counselor must begin to process the information.

A number of factors, largely to be introduced by the counselor, become important. First, some probability of success should be established. This step does not remove risk entirely but helps the client understand the degree of risk that exists. The counselor must remain objective at this point, resisting any tendency to "protect" the client from any risk of failure. The counselor should consider what effect trying and failing might have upon the client. When it is clear that it would have long-range debilitative effects the counselor may wish to intervene. Other effects must be carefully considered.

Clients need assistance in processing information as well as in gathering it. The counselor's responsibility does not end when there seem to be sufficient data for the vocational choice. The tasks of estimating probabilities of success and developing alternative strategies are necessary and occur with the counselor's assistance.

MAKING A VOCATIONAL CHOICE

At this point the counselee may be ready to choose among the available alternatives. The counselor, who has provided the opportunity for gathering, exploring, and processing the data, should now help the client make a choice. First, the client needs to understand that this is not the end of the process, that the choice is tentative. Whatever the choice, the client then must act upon it. The counselor provides supportive assistance as the client begins to implement the choice. The counselor attempts to remain available for further discussions about the job the client takes and tries to help the client make one major and perhaps one or two minor choices.

If the client is not ready for the decision the counselor may have to spend some time helping the client understand what has occurred. When more than one possibility exists the decision is the client's to make. The counselor may provide some further assistance during the decision process and in a followup later.

The process of making a vocational choice can become routinized if the counselor is not alert to the unique interaction that is occurring with the client. The client is not a set of data to be intermingled with a set of job characteristics; she or he has values, individuality, needs, and aspirations. Super (1957) suggested that vocational choice is an implementation of the client's self-concept. The closer the chosen occupation is to that self-concept, the more meaningful the position will be.

IMPLEMENTATION EVALUATION

Once the client has a job the counselor normally becomes less involved with the process. However, when the choice and degree of commitment are tentative the counselor should remain in contact with the client so that the decision can be evaluated. Evaluation at this point is not a value process; it is a method of assessing the extent to which the client has reached her or his goals and either determining what alternatives will help in reaching the goals or establishing different goals. The issue is not how good or bad the goals were; it is how to reach the goals or establish new ones more clearly related to the individual's needs. Because the actual experience of work may impinge on the client differently than previous cognitive activities, the counselor should allow for additional planning, decision-making, and data-gathering sessions.

The concept that educators and counselors have an obligation to place students and clients and determine the degree of success requires consideration. Given that the process of vocational development is lifelong, the assistance offered by counselors should probably be lifelong. Measurements of success will include not only job placements or choices but also career movement, degree of job satisfaction, and other equally important factors.

Depending on their approach and experience, some counselors would relate more closely to some phases in the developmental model described above than they might to others. However, unless each phase is completed at some time during the vocational selection process the outcome may not be as meaningful to the client as it might be.

In the following dialogue, a counselor is trying to keep the client moving toward a decision about his vocational future. It is obvious that two or three variables are intertwined, as they are in any counseling relationship. It is difficult, for example, to separate decision-making counseling from vocational counseling, and it is probably unwise to do so. Most vocational counseling includes implicit educational assistance because our society usually has educational requirements for the vocation that the individual might choose. The dialogue below shows how one counselor handles the elements of this vocational counseling process.

Cl. I'm still lost. I don't know what I want yet.

Co. You're concerned about what's going to be best for you in a job.

Cl. Yeah.

Co. The idea is that for you you're better off if you have a definite goal.

Cl. Yeah, right. I like several things and I just can't be sure. I'm kinda lost in the middle someplace you know.

Co. You've stated that you have spent a lot of time on art and to throw that away now would kinda bother you.

Cl. Yeah—I'm not sure exactly, you know, if the change would stick—if I'd stick to it, you know, as far as that goes. If I took law for a career and art for a hobby. But it wouldn't work the other way around you know.

Co. This thing about changing your mind bothers you. You would have to go to college and then to law school and that would take a long time.

Cl. Yeah, seven years, isn't that right?

Co. It seems like a long time.

Cl. Yeah, especially three years of law school. I'd better pick up on my grades next year too.

Co. Seems like you're in the middle of a lot of things and don't know which way to go.

Cl. I just want to be sure. I feel more secure with a definite goal in mind.

Co. I kind of sense that you are saying the most important thing is that you want to be happy with your choice. What would be important to your choice?

Cl. Everyone wants to make as much money as he possibly can. How hard do you have to work and how much you get out of it. If you didn't have much interest it wouldn't be much fun. I think the more schooling you have the more money you make.

Co. So money and interest are important.

Cl. Oh yeah—I don't want to point toward something which I don't like.

Co. It's better to have something to point toward and to be sure you will like it. If you really have a goal you may work harder when the going is tough. You've talked about this decision several times but you don't seem to be able to set a goal. You say, "I need a goal but I can't pick one."

Cl. Well, I don't know which is best. Should I choose one field and then look at colleges?

Co. You seem to be waiting for something or someone to come along and make you feel sure.

Cl. I just want to make the best choice between these two.

Co. So whatever you eventually pick you're going to have to stick with it.

Cl. I just want to be sure so I don't go halfway through and find out something I didn't know.

Co. You don't want to consider the possibility of change somewhere along the line.

Cl. Right.

Co. Has this been a pattern in your life, starting something and sticking to it?

Cl. No, but this seems so big and important that I want to be sure.

Co. And you're not sure about the decision. Between now and the time to choose a college are you going to be able to make the decision?

Cl. I just want time to think. I'd just like to work it out now and let you know in the fall so we can work on colleges.

Co. Well, what can we do now?

BEHAVIORAL COUNSELING IN VOCATIONAL CHOICE

Among the several approaches to counseling used in vocational assistance, behavioral counseling may be especially effective. Krumboltz and many of his students (1969) have demonstrated the effectiveness of the behavioral approach in decision making, vocational exploration, and vocational choice.

In any counseling situation one goal is to have the client change behavior in her or his normal life to resemble the changed mode of behavior with the counselor. This concept is especially necessary for the behaviorist, who is able to elicit certain responses within the counseling setting. Unless these responses lead to changed behavior outside the setting, counseling has demonstrated only that people can be influenced by other people.

VOCATIONAL DIAGNOSIS

Vocational diagnosis is an important activity for counselors in a variety of counseling settings. The counselor in a high school, college setting, rehabilitation agency, employment service, and a number of other public and private counseling agencies must try to determine what the client wants, what his or her vocational problems and assets are, and what services are available to meet these needs.

The counselor has several ways of obtaining this information, depending on her or his level of competence. Paper-and-pencil methods include questionnaires, standardized tests, or projective methods. The counselor may also conduct an interview specifically designed to obtain vocational information from the client. The techniques of interviewing are similar to counseling skills. The interview may be more specifically structured, but the nuances of response pattern, nonverbal cues, or priority setting are important for the counselor to observe and deal with.

The interview helps the counselor reach several goals that are important to successful vocational assistance. First, the counselor can obtain information that she or he might not receive from other sources. Because the client is responding directly to the counselor, clarification and more intensive development of topics are possible. The counselor can verify information received from other sources by observing whether the client's responses are consistent with that information and by following up on these and other confirmational points. On some subjects the client's information may be very shallow or narrow and supplementary data may be necessary.

STRUCTURING THE INTERVIEW

More than any other diagnostic instrument, the face-to-face interview gives the client and counselor an opportunity to discuss topics thoroughly. This opportunity can help the client define his or her vocational concern more accurately. The counselor asks the client to identify his or her vocational needs and helps clarify these by focusing on them during the interview.

During the interview the client provides additional information verbally and nonverbally. This extra information makes the interview a meaningful tool for the counselor.

The format of the interview can vary according to the needs of the client and counselor, but should always be aimed at attaining certain goals normally related to the client's needs. These goals may include determining what the client expects as a result of contact with the counselor and/or agency. The counselor can help the client form a clearer idea of what he or she is looking for. If it becomes clear that the client's needs are not compatible with the counselor's role or the charge of the agency, a referral is necessary.

Another goal is the identification of vocational concerns, their security, and the client's strengths. Eventual job selection, placement, or development of an educational plan all depend upon the client's traits. Therefore, the more that is known about the client, the more meaningful the eventual vocational choice will be.

FACTORS INFLUENCING VOCATIONAL SUCCESS

Once the vocational concerns, goals, assets, and liabilities are identified, the counselor can help the client understand the important roles of several other factors. Is there sufficient motivation to achieve the vocational goals? The high school student who wishes to enter a professional field may lack the sufficient motivation to attend the necessary educational institutions. The client may not lack the skills, intellectual capacity, or job knowledge, but may consider eight to ten years of education an unacceptable requirement.

A second factor is the amount of experience necessary for a particular occupation and the client's willingness to get it. Often the situation is circular: getting a job is sometimes based on having experience, and breaking into the circle may be difficult.

A third factor is the client's mental and/or physical ability. Some clients will be unable to fulfill the physical, mental, or psychological demands of their desired job, and the counselor does a disservice to such clients by avoiding a realistic assessment of the job's requirements.

One outcome of this evaluation process is the identification of alternatives related to the stated goal but not requiring the same degree of motivation, training, experience, and/or personal qualifications. When discussing alternatives the counselor should spend additional time on the same items as for the original goal, perhaps in another interview or counseling session.

For vocational or educational counseling to be of value the client should know something about himself or herself, about the job or occupation under consideration, and how to bring the two into alignment. The counselor and client should examine some of the factors that relate to getting and keeping a job. Although counselors may consider some of these factors unfair, it is unrealistic to think that employers and their agents do not have certain expectations for potential employees. The personal traits of the potential employee are important.

The skilled counselor will help the client to understand the importance of these factors. If the client agrees that these factors are important, the counselor will help the client change any that the latter thinks are important to alter. Often this part of the counseling experience focuses on the negative, such as why people lose jobs, and it is not unusual to see the client and counselor in adversary roles. Instead, the counselor should help the client look at the positive factors too.

Employers have identified several factors that are closely related to holding a job. The person who comes to work regularly and on time tends to remain on the job. The client whose life pattern indicates irregular attendance patterns should realize the potential they have for jeopardizing long-term employment.

The importance of interpersonal relations between the worker and coworkers and supervisors is another fruitful area for discussion. A realistic appraisal of the client's interpersonal behavior will help the client determine which, if any, aspects she or he may wish to change.

Finally, performance and productivity are important factors. At a time when performance evaluation occurs in almost every occupation the potential worker needs to understand that certain expectations will affect her or his advancement in a particular occupation. This too is a fruitful topic for discussion during the interview or counseling sequence.

COUNSELOR INVOLVEMENT IN THE INTERVIEW

Thus, with the focus on the client and his or her input to the vocational interview, the counselor has helped the client clarify certain areas and factors about herself or himself and the world of work. Ideally, the counselor will also provide assistance in finding a job. In addition, the counselor has several other tasks in the vocational interview.

One potential difference between vocational counseling and personal counseling is that the counselor should already have read and understood records and materials on the client prior to the contact. This prereading reduces the redundancy that often occurs in informational interaction and identifies areas that need further exploration.

Second, when the client seeks information from the counselor, the latter should be certain that it is factual. If the counselor does not know the answer to a client's question he or she should say so and perhaps develop a plan for obtaining the information. When the counselor is unable to answer the client's questions, he or she should give the reasons for not answering, such as "I don't know" or "I do not have that information."

Third, when giving information, the counselor should make certain that the client receives the information accurately, perhaps by asking the client to summarize it during the interview. In this way the counselor can see whether the communication was successful.

The vocational interview, as a specialized form of counseling, provides the opportunity for the client and counselor to identify and discuss factors that will aid or impede the client's vocational progress. The counselor may use a prepared form as a format for the interview. Table 18–1 depicts such a model form. It includes a wide variety of factors that relate to self-understanding, job understand-

TABLE 18–1 VOCATIONAL ASSESSMENT OUTLINE

A. GOALS
1. Experience
2. Training
3. Education
4. Skills
5. Interests
6. Expected salary
7. Expected duties

B. PHYSICAL ATTRIBUTES

C. EDUCATIONAL ATTAINMENT
1. Verbal skills
2. Math skills
3. Other

D. JOB POTENTIAL
1. Current status of labor market

E. EMPLOYMENT RECORD
1. Current employment if any
2. Length of time from last job
3. Reasons for leaving previous job
4. Knowledge of jobs
5. Readiness for employment
6. Personal appearance

F. WORK HISTORY
1. Relations with coworkers
2. Relations with supervisors
3. Quality of work
4. Quantity of work
5. Work habits
    a. Absenteeism
    b. Tardiness

G. PERSONAL FACTORS
1. Health
2. Transportation possibilities
3. Family
4. Financial
5. Legal
6. Residence
7. Other Factors
    a. Leisure activities
    b. Drugs, tranquilizers

H. CLIENT'S PERSONAL STATEMENT
OF CONCERNS AND NEEDS

I. COUNSELOR'S COMMENTS

ing, and getting a job. Topics identified in this rather structured way can be followed up in later counseling sessions to improve the client's ability to seek, obtain, and retain a job. Although there may not be information for every part of the outline from every client, the data gathered from as many topics as possible will provide additional positive input into the counseling and decision-making process.

Another format that might be helpful is the outline for vocational appraisal prepared by Crites (1974), shown in Figure 18–1. The subtopics and questions are related to the vocational needs of clients. Accurate answers and data in the various categories will lead to more realistic appraisal of the vocationally oriented client and her or his problem and prognosis. Although the information-gathering process of either format may take time, the result will be better self-understanding, better knowledge of jobs, and a better decision about how to reconcile personal and vocational needs.

ORGANIZATION AND USE OF OCCUPATIONAL INFORMATION

Because the client's knowledge and skill are closely related to occupational information, counselors must ensure meaningful delivery of relevant materials for client use. Much commercially published occupational material already exists. Usually these are written at a level accessible to all but a few clients. Even with well-prepared materials, however, there are always some problems. First, reading does not necessarily guarantee understanding; the client may have various difficulties in accepting what is said, in understanding the materials clearly, or in ex-

**FIGURE 18–1 OUTLINE FOR A VOCATIONAL
APPRAISAL**

This outline is applicable to either a counseling or a personnel situation. Also, it might be used for research purposes. It is designed to summarize background, interview, and test data on an individual in a systematic fashion. Changes in the outline may be necessary, however, to adapt it to special problems or situations.

TITLE ("VOCATIONAL APPRAISAL OF _____")

PERSON APPRAISAL

(Description of the individual in terms of his status on psychological, sociological and physical dimensions.)

Present Status and Functioning. (1) How does the individual "stand" on the various pertinent dimensions? What are his general and special attitudes? Interests? Personality characteristics? Attitudes? Educational background and achievement? Socioeconomic status? (2) How is the individual adjusting to the various aspects or areas of his physical and psychological environment, including himself? What is his "self-concept?" Daily pattern of living (sleeping, eating, personal hygiene, study, work and recreational habits)? What are the nature and quality of his relationships with peers? Family? Teachers? Superiors and subordinates? General authorities (administrative officers, police)? What is his general level of adjustment? Personality integration? What are his predominant adjustment mechanisms?

Developmental History. (1) Has the individual had any significant physical illness which either affected his psycho-social development or left him with special disabilities and handicaps? (2) What is the family background of the individual? Intact or broken home? Number and order of siblings? Parents? Parental attitudes (acceptance, concentration, avoidance)? Parental identification? What were the individual's relationships to peers (accepted as equal, leader, follower, isolate, etc.)? (3) Early interests and abilities (hobbies, sports, organizations, etc.)? (4) Early vocational choices and plans (preferred occupations, age of first choice, motives for choices, indecision, etc.)? (5) School achievement and adjustment (grades, attitudes toward school, best and least liked subjects, favorite teachers, etc.)?

PROBLEM APPRAISAL

(Identification of the individual's problem; assessment of his strengths as well as his weaknesses, e.g., motivation to change self or assume responsibility for problem solution, adaptability and flexibility, equanimity and sense of humor, constructive and integrative behavior.)

Vocational Problem. (1) Classify according to one of the currently available diagnostic systems. (2) Assess the individual's vocational thinking. How involved is he in the decision-making process? How does he perceive occupations—as ends in themselves or means to other ends? Does he think in "either-or" terms about occupations? How does he "reason through" the problem of vocational choice? Is his thinking logical or does it have "Psychological" fallacies in it, e.g., parataxic distortions? (3) Evaluate whether the individual's vocational problem arises because of immaturity or maladjustment. Does he simply not know how to choose an occupation, or is he conflicted to the extent that he cannot make the appropriate response?

Factors Related to Vocational Problem. (1) What part is played by the individual's family in his choice problem? (2) What is the relationship of his personality to his choice problem?

FIGURE 18–1 *(continued)*

(3) What other factors, such as financial resources, military obligations, marriage plans, academic achievement, etc., are relevant?

PROGNOSTIC APPRAISAL

(Predictions about the individual's future behavior in counseling or on the job.)

Vocational Counseling. (1) Motivation: How well will the individual respond to counseling? Will he "work" on his problem, or will he want the counselor to solve it for him? Why did he apply for counseling? What are his expectations? (2) Interview behavior: How will the client respond verbally? Will he talk readily or not? Will he be verbally hostile or not? How will he relate to the counselor? Will he be dependent, aggressive, aloof, etc.? (3) Counseling goals and plans: What can be achieved with this individual? Should the counselor simply give him test and occupational information, or should he try to "think through" the vocational problem with the individual? Should the counselor focus only upon the specific choice problem of the individual, or should he help him learn how to solve other vocational problems which he may encounter in the future? Can the counseling be primarily vocational in nature, or should personal adjustment counseling precede a consideration of the individual's vocational problem? How can the counseling best be implemented? What techniques should be used?

Vocational Adjustment. (1) Success: Which occupations are within the limits of the individual's capabilities? (2) Satisfaction: In which occupation is the client most likely to find satisfaction? What problems might his personality create for him on the job with respect to doing the work itself, getting along with others, adjusting to the physical conditions of the work, and in realizing his aspirations and goals (material rewards, recognition, prestige, etc.)? (3) Contingencies: What factors which are known might either facilitate or adversely affect the individual's future vocational adjustment if they should occur (for example, military service, marriage, change of job duties, transfer to another region of the country, slow or fast promotion, incompatible social life and obligations, etc.)?

SUMMARY

(A "thumb-nail" sketch of the individual which pulls together the various parts of the vocational appraisal.)

Source: J. O. Crites, Career counseling: A review of major approaches. *Counseling Psychologist,* 1974, *4*(3), 14–15. Copyright 1974 by the American Psychological Association. Reprinted by permission.

cluding aspects that interfere with goals. The counselor may have to spend some time teaching the client how to read these materials. Second, much of the published material is out-of-date. This does not mean that the materials are not valuable adjuncts, only that some monitoring is necessary. Perhaps material more than five years old should not be utilized. Finally, because most material is general in nature to cover a broad potential market, its relevance to an individual client could be tenuous. As is the case in test interpretation, group data may not be particularly valuable to an individual. Thus, the counselor should individualize the occupational material available.

There are also mechanical aids for the presentation of occupational information. Clients can avail themselves of these for exploration activities and then move to the counseling setting for more specific aid. For example, it is possible to use computer assistance in selecting a college. The client can identify areas of interest by making some preliminary choices about the types of courses desired, the characteristics of the student population he or she thinks would be most compatible, cost factors, location, and so on. Once the client has indicated these parameters, the computer can provide a list of specific colleges and additional data about them. The client can manipulate the parameters to receive additional feedback from the computer. Until the output of the computer is related to the client, however, the process is incomplete.

This approach can also be used in selecting potential job areas (Katz, 1966). In this process the computer helps the client to understand various characteristics of the job and to assess some probability of success based upon his or her needs, interests, skills, or characteristics. The counselor helps the client integrate this information into his or her own vocational decision making.

The counselor's involvement in the organization of occupational information is trifold. First, the counselor must be familiar with available materials. The materials must be chosen for their overall relevance to the needs of the client. Second, the counselor must be certain that whenever necessary the client receives specialized interpretation and integrative assistance. When the client raises questions, the counselor or someone knowledgeable should be available to answer them. Third, the counselor or a surrogate should be aware of the specific local situation. It is of little value to a client to read about some position that simply is not available.

USES OF OCCUPATIONAL INFORMATION

Clients generally have a variety of reasons for seeking out occupational information. Tyler (1969) identified these as exploratory, understanding, and elaboration, depending on the type of information that might be used and the sequence in which it generally occurs. Exploratory use involves the search for potential alternatives to action, usually as part of the discussion in which the counselor and client try to list alternatives. Or it may involve the assignment of reading outside the session.

Available information also leads to a clearer understanding of the specifics of the occupation or self. Several potential exercises might aid the client in this use of information. Talking to a practitioner should help, although there are some limitations in this area: the worker may have such a negative feeling that no positives are listed, or positive characteristics may be so meaningful that the worker cannot provide any other information. The counselor should act as a balancing agent in these cases. The counselor should be skilled in helping the client gather information and relate it to self and occupation.

The final use of information involves the elaboration of whatever plan has been made, planning the details of a particular position or decision. Once a client has made a decision, she or he must begin to determine what to do next. For a client wishing to become a skilled tradesperson, information might be necessary about entry into the job, advancement, working conditions, and so on.

TIMING

Timing is of critical importance in supplying occupational information. The counselor must be aware of the particular needs of the individual in order to avoid introducing information prematurely.

Usually the counselor should allow the client to take the lead, offering certain information and observing the client's response. If the client seems to want to continue the exploration, the counselor should try to help the client develop the direction and indicate the amount of information he or she wants. Above all, the counselor should avoid overpowering the client with information. It is wiser to say too little and have the client ask for more than to lose the client because too much was said.

EVENT VERSUS DEVELOPMENTAL COUNSELING

The previous sections have described the sequential presentation of information, on the assumption that the vocational decision is developmental rather than a series of discrete events. The client's previous history—various aspects of the client's life, important earlier decisions, and background data—provides a basis for current and future decisions. The counselor will use this and other information to achieve relevance and understanding rather than to focus on some specific area mentioned by the client.

Second, the client's decisions are related to future activity instead of being viewed as final. The counselor does not preclude the possibility of future counseling because certain decisions have been made; rather, he or she helps the client consider the relationships of the decision to future potentials and alternatives.

Third, any decision may limit the range of behaviors or alternatives available to the client. Some clients see this as a desirable condition: limiting decision-making possibilities creates a more acceptable world. Some clients want a stochastic situation, in which the decision rules out all other possibilities. This client has no doubts because she or he has eliminated all alternatives. Other clients see so many attractive possibilities that they cannot choose. Regardless of the situation, various vocational decisions engender limitations, and the counselor and client should try to deal with them as much as possible.

VOCATIONAL COUNSELING AND SPECIAL POPULATIONS

Counselors especially must understand the characteristics of the population and people with whom they work. Today a number of special populations are demanding attention—native Americans, blacks, women, the handicapped, and others. They are appearing more frequently as clients in general and vocational counseling. The vocational development, vocational maturity, needs, desires, and decision making of these populations are different from those of the majority population. Therefore, the counselor serving such clients should be attuned to their special needs, learning how each client is like all other clients, like some other clients, and like no other client (Shertzer & Stone, 1974) and applying this knowledge to counseling with them.

One major concern is the difference that exists between the client and the counselor. Resolutions of these issues involve individuals rather than global decisions by all counselors. A counselor needs to know himself or herself, be willing to admit that he or she will have difficulties dealing with certain clients, and find a compatible setting in which to work.

Evidence suggests that some counselors can counsel with fairly diverse populations. In these cases the counselor is aware of the characteristics of the clientele. He or she maintains this sensitivity in all phases of the counseling process, focusing on what he or she can do to help the client. This counselor recognizes her or his own values and limitations and is willing to include others in the process or to transfer the process to others when appropriate. In short, the counselor knows who he or she is, who the client is, and what possibilities exist in the counseling relationship.

In relation to counseling special populations there have been suggestions that the successful counselor should be like his or her client. This resemblance alone is not a sufficient condition for successful counseling. In fact this consideration may interfere with the counselor's ability to focus on resolution of the client's concern or need, with seeing and helping the client deal with his or her uniqueness.

SOME PROBLEMS FOR VOCATIONAL COUNSELING

WORK AND TECHNOLOGY

The Industrial Revolution changed concepts about work in terms of both performance and meaning. The work ethic is changing today as alienation, lack of commitment, less intrinsic values, and the possibility of automation increasingly affect the world of work. Career guidance and early vocational assistance must deal with these issues. Those who are about to enter the workforce at any level should understand what the growth of technology means and what effect it may have upon future work placement. Counselors are in a position to assist in the learning process.

Many workers are finding themselves out of work due to unemployment or abolition of a job. The transitional problems they face may be very debilitating. The counselor who considers job placement as her or his only function fails to meet these people's psychological and personal needs. Counselors in employment service agencies or rehabilitation settings will face this problem most often, and even under the press of extremely high loads must provide opportunities for clients to deal with comprehensive concerns.

NONWORK

Today nonwork is a reality in some form or another. The counselor interested in working with vocational decision making should understand this phenomenon.

In one form nonwork is a feature of lack of job identity. According to Warnath, "The system within which those workers are engaged responds to factors quite unrelated to the welfare of the individual worker and can fulfill the needs of individuals only insofar as those needs support the needs of the organization" (1975, p. 427). This may become one of the long-term concerns for which the counselor has to provide assistance. When a job no longer provides psychological support, something must replace it. Counselors will need to be part of the search for replacement while working closely with workers who are currently experiencing the loss of meaning in their life. Employment will continue but the person will be seeking other ways to confirm herself or himself. The client will need assistance in dealing with the new alienation: jobs that are at best bearable, and at worst, intolerable.

There are increasing numbers of unemployed people who are looking for work but are unable to find it. These people may seek out a variety of helping persons and desire assistance for the wrong reasons. On March 10, 1975 the *New York Times* discussed an increase in the numbers of out-of-work people who were becoming taxi drivers. The people were interested in work but would not be prone to work through a vocational counseling relationship without fairly firm assurance that a job would be forthcoming. Under these circumstances a counselor would work closely with the client and job sources to provide as much assurance as possible that the counseling would be meaningful.

A third form of nonwork relates to retirement. As people live longer the years spent in retirement become more important. The switch from work to retirement is a very severe shock to many people because their jobs have occupied an important portion of their lives. Vocational development includes awareness of the retirement years. As the number of retirees increases, more attention will be given to helping them make this important transition. Some form of the halfway house concept, used in other transitional areas, may become part of society's assistance. Until that occurs, counselors may need to fulfill this need during the counseling relationship. Many centers are currently operating to provide activities for the retired person. These centers can be used to promote vocational assistance to the older worker as he or she moves into retirement. Many retirees, however, do not attend these centers, so that some form of assistance may be necessary in the work setting prior to retirement. Rehabilitation counselors, industrial consultants, vocationally oriented personnel, and the prospective retiree will need to become actively involved in the process.

Many current workers now face early retirement. Some may openly desire this, but many others do not want to leave work. Counselors can help these clients plan for adequate medical assistance, financial security, and use of leisure time. Although counselors may not be the only people involved, they will have the requisite skills to deal openly with the problem and to serve as coordinators for mobilizing service personnel who may be able to provide specialized assistance.

Finally, many people are part of the counterculture and see societal structure as harmful to their life-style. They may be forced to work from time to time to support their modest needs. At some point a variety of counselors will be involved with this clientele, and a clash of values may ensue. These clients' problems may not seem relevant to the counselor, but the need for understanding, a hearing, and assistance still exist. Although the outcome may not be traditional job placement or job satisfaction, the process of working through to an outcome will be similar, regardless of the type of client.

WOMEN

Current vocational counseling for women is generally lukewarm, indifferent, unfocused, negative, or nonexistent. Counselors will be interacting more often with women seeking assistance in dealing with sexual discrimination, social stereotyping, familial pressures, and personal feelings as they relate to their ability to lead productive personal, vocational, and professional lives. Although some current general information is helpful in providing vocational assistance to women, there is much to be learned about their vocational development. Among the issues to be resolved are education and work positions. For example, although the number of women in the work force has increased, the proportion of women in upper-level managerial or professional jobs has remained constant. Education as a route to vocational success does not seem to be working for women.

Because of societal notions about women's place in society, the woman who attempts to move outside the confines will face a number of personal and interpersonal problems. She may have to deal with other women who do not wish to understand her needs. She is often supported less by a number of significant people in her life, personal or professional. These pressures may lead to the need for vocational as well as personal counseling assistance.

Households in which both adults are trained for and work in relatively responsible and well-paid jobs pose a number of difficulties for both partners. The strain often weighs most heavily upon the women. Some resolution of this problem must be found, and the counselor's involvement may prove to be considerable.

Finally, there are many areas of discrimination against women. Business firms still have few, if any, women in top management positions. Women are often paid less for equivalent responsibility. Despite increasing use of women as professional and administrative personnel, there is ample evidence that discrimination continues to exist. The same is true of the professions, where women continue to face exclusion solely because of sex.

The counselor must be concerned with the numbers of women now wishing to enter the world of work. The counseling process must include personal understanding, family involvement, vocational experimentation, planning, and implementation. Premature vocational decisions will not help. The vocational counselor will need training, self-understanding, and an understanding of the resources, talents, and commitment that women can bring to any job.

Schlossberg (1972) suggested that women need assistance in dealing with societally imposed restrictions related to vocational growth. They must be given the opportunity to raise their aspirations to a level more congruent with their needs as these emerge during crucial stages of development. Schlossberg advocated an activist role for counselors, involving intervention at significant points in the developmental stages. The counselor becomes an agent of change to help modify or remove the policies and practices that discriminate against any portion of the society. The critical tasks are to help women continue to examine their potentials and to make the greatest possible use of these potentials. Sometimes the effort is directed toward helping the individual, sometimes toward institutions and society.

BURNOUT

Another phenomenon, burnout, involves a growing lack of interest and activity by persons currently employed. Most of these people will continue to hold jobs, but their productivity and effort will be minimal. They may not know exactly what is happening to them, but they will not perform as they did before, and they will develop problems and concerns in other parts of their life.

Some have suggested that burnout is the result of the stress that is a normal part of some jobs: day-to-day involvement creates such pressure on the worker that a variety of negative things begin to occur, such as absenteeism, lack of motivation, or a dislike of work. The worker must continue the job but receives little or no satisfaction from working.

Others explain burnout as a feature of people's recognition that fulfilling the so-called American dream is a remote possibility. The worker sees that he or she has reached the highest possible level and begins to look elsewhere for continued satisfaction. This may have important effects upon the personal and social life; family relationships become strained, and the incidence of broken marriages and disjointed families increases.

Inflation may be another cause of burnout: working may no longer provide the money necessary to purchase the things that have become important to many persons, such as houses or cars. When the worker cannot see some meaning within or outside work the labor loses its value: why should a person work when he or she has no better life than the person who does not work?

Regardless of the causes, burnout is an important phenomenon for vocational specialists to understand. Some companies are attempting to provide ways to moderate this effect at all occupational levels. Some allow workers increased flexibility within the job: the tasks of the job remain the same, but the worker's method of completing the tasks may vary. Some are providing professional counseling assistance to employees. Often this occurs only at the upper managerial and supervisory levels, but it is a step toward accepting the reality of the situation.

Counselors have a preventive and remedial involvement in this area. At appropriate times they can help clients understand that workers often remain at plateaus for some time. This knowledge need not have a negative effect. The counselor can help the person affected by burnout by offering counseling assistance to the worker and his or her family to understand the problem and to develop ways of resolving the difficulties.

SUMMARY

Counselors are increasingly called upon to provide vocational counseling. The changing number and types of jobs available and the increased necessity for education prior to job entry and advancement have increased the importance of vocational counseling. In many cases the client's initial contact with a counselor is related to an educational or vocational decision. This chapter has listed some steps in the process as well as some sources for information. The personality of the counselor remains an important factor in the process. Regardless of the client's need, the counselor's commitment to the client is an essential aspect of successful counseling.

REFERENCES

Brammer, L. M., & Shostrom, E. L. *Therapeutic psychology* (3rd ed.). Englewood Cliffs, N.J.: Prentice-Hall, 1977.

Career education. DHEW Publication No.

(DE) 72–39. Washington, D.C.: Office of Education, U.S. Department of Health, Education and Welfare, 1971.

Cramer, S. H. (Ed.). *Pre-service and in-service*

preparation of school counselors for educational guidance. Washington, D.C.: American Personnel and Guidance Association, 1970.

Crites, J. O. Career counseling: A review of major approaches. *Counseling Psychologist*, 1974, *4*, 3–32.

———. Career counseling: A comprehensive approach. *Counseling Psychologist*, 1976, *6*, 2–11.

Herr, E. L. (Ed.). *Vocational guidance and human development*. Boston: Houghton Mifflin, 1974.

Herr, E. L., & Cramer, S. H. *Career guidance through the life span*. Boston: Little, Brown, 1979.

Hoyt, K. B., Evans, R. N., Mackin, E. F., & Mangum, G. L. *Career education: What it is and how to do it*. Salt Lake City: Olympus, 1972.

Ivey, A. E., & Simek-Downing, L. *Counseling and psychotherapy: Skills, theories, and practice*. Englewood Cliffs, N.J.: Prentice-Hall, 1980.

Katz, M. A model of guidance for career decision-making. *Vocational Guidance Quarterly*, 1966, *15*, 2–10.

Krumboltz, J. D., & Sheppard, L. E. Vocational problem solving experiences. In J. D.

Krumboltz and C. E. Thoresen (Eds.), *Behavioral counseling*. New York: Holt, Rinehart and Winston, 1969.

Mathews, E. E. The vocational guidance of girls and women in the United States. In E. L. Herr (Ed.), *Vocational Guidance and human development*. Boston: Houghton Mifflin, 1974.

Parsons, F. *Choosing a vocation*. Boston: Houghton Mifflin, 1909.

Schlossberg, N. K. A framework for counseling women. *Personnel and Guidance Journal*, 1972, *51*, 137–143.

Shertzer, B., & Stone, S. *Fundamentals of counseling* (2nd ed.). Boston: Houghton Mifflin, 1974.

Super, D. *Psychology of careers*. New York: Harper & Row, 1957.

Tolbert, E. L. *Counseling for career development*. Boston: Houghton Mifflin, 1974.

Tyler, L. *The work of the counselor* (3rd ed.). New York: Appleton-Century-Crofts, 1969.

Warnath, C. Vocational theories: Direction to nowhere. *Personnel and Guidance Journal*, 1975, *53*, 422–428.

ETHICS, LEGALITIES, AND VALUES IN COUNSELING

CHAPTER NINETEEN

438 CHAPTER
NINETEEN
ETHICS,
LEGALITIES,
AND VALUES
IN
COUNSELING

Ethics, legalities, and values are important features of counselor understanding and action. Professional organizations have developed statements of ethics that are valuable for the counselor as she or he attempts to function in ways that are personally and professionally ethical. As counselors begin to work with broader segments of the population, client rights and legal protection become even more important. The values of the counselor and client also have important relationships to the counseling process. Regardless of their level of preparation or functioning, counselors have an obligation to be aware of existing ethical and legal standards and values and to function within the established parameters.

Sometimes the counselor finds that situations do not fit neatly into existing categories or fall under existing rules. Statements of ethical behavior developed by professional organizations, though valuable, do not always provide a clear direction for the counselor. Likewise, whereas some legal responsibilities are specific, there are many unresolved issues that are important to the professional activities of all counselors. Because the law is dynamic, there is a possibility that what is acceptable at one time may become less acceptable later. Values and perhaps value systems also seem to change rapidly, constantly challenging what people know and believe.

The counselor must act ethically and legally with clients. This requires awareness of existing standards of ethics, such as those developed by the American Personnel and Guidance Association (APGA) and the American Psychological Association (APA). The counselor also must understand not only her or his legal responsibilities and obligations in the professional involvement with the client, but also the client's rights.

The counselor is aware of how values affect the counseling interaction, especially those of clients with backgrounds different from the counselor's. The counselor must be able to help clients identify their values or value systems. Although most people behave consistently in relation to a value system, some may not be able to articulate the values that influence their behavior. The counselor may be called upon to help clarify client values as part of counseling interaction. Some clients know a little about their values but find they need to clarify and perhaps change them. The counselor can help the client in this process. If the client needs to develop a method for changing, the counselor can help identify a process and work through it with the client. Thus, the counselor helps identify, clarify, and change values and helps develop the processes for change because values are part of the client's life.

ETHICAL CONSIDERATIONS

Ethics are suggested standards of conduct based upon an agreed-on set of values. A profession attempts to translate as many values as possible into structured expectations of behavior as its members relate to one another, their clientele, and the public. These usually take the form of statements that constitute complete codes of ethics. National professional organizations such as APGA and APA have developed ethical standards and make these available to practitioners. Some state and local groups have elaborated or modified these standards to bring them into closer alignment with the specific populations served by the professionals. Knowledge of these standards can provide the counselor with a method for dealing with various difficult situations. But many situations arise for which no ethical statement has been developed or for which only a tangential relationship exists to current statements.

All statements of ethical standards define certain areas of professional activity. The APGA standards, for example, discuss several specific areas of professional activity and are intended to serve as guidelines for ethical professional practice. Each counselor should obtain copies of current standards and utilize them when ethical issues arise. In the area of professional assistance to a client, for example, the APGA's *Ethical Standards* specifies the following conditions:

> If the member is unable to be of professional assistance to the counselee, the member avoids initiating the counseling relationship or the member terminates it. In either event, the member is obligated to refer the counselee to an appropriate specialist. (It is incumbent upon the member to be knowledgeable about referral resources so that a satisfactory referral can be initiated.) In the event the counselee declines the suggested referral, the member is not obligated to continue the relationship (1974, p. 3).

Thus, the counselor has a statement about current and future responsibilities, including provision for client nonacceptance of the counselor's ethical resolution.

Making ethical decisions when conflicts occur is difficult. The codes furnish only broad guidelines. The counselor must base choices on perceptions of the counseling dyad and the society in which the client lives. Unethical behavior sometimes occurs when the counselor's communication to the client establishes a particular set of expectations for the latter that are inconsistent with the counselor's actual behavior. The counselor must be able to verbalize and live within a reasonable ethical hierarchy.

Van Hoose and Kottler (1977) pointed out that ethical codes clarify the responsibility that a practitioner owes the client and society: they provide the latter with some assurance that the counselor will not act in ways detrimental to the profession and also give the professional assurance that his or her own freedom and integrity are considered important.

Several topical areas may be helpful to counselors evolving an ethical position or strengthening an existing one.

MORAL RULES

Society provides a number of rules, implicit and explicit, that relate to the life of the counselor and client. These rules are determinants for developing or refining an ethical position.

In our society, honesty is considered better than cheating. Honesty leads to positive outcomes; cheating leads to punishment. Honest persons are more mentally healthy than persons who cheat. Yet many clients enter counseling with conflicts about these concerns. What society says is not always completely true, and clients often seek clarifications or justification of society's rules, wishing to order their lives according to the "real" rules of society. One counselor task, therefore, is to help clients sort out these rules and integrate them into their behavior and value systems. The greater the understanding of the rules, the greater the possibility that clients will be able to resolve these value dilemmas.

PERSONAL GOALS

The professional needs to examine his or her position in terms of qualification for the activity, violation of standards as they relate to the good of the client, society, and the profession. During the course of any counselor's professional life she or he must inevitably assess her or his qualifications to handle a particular client. Even though the client may be willing to continue, the counselor may feel a lack of sufficient skill to continue and may need to refer the client to another professional. The counselor may be forced to decide when and if truth is most helpful to a client. The decision and the process of decision making will provide the counselor with a better understanding of ethical and personal goals.

BEHAVIOR

Sometimes counselors must monitor their own activities and those of other professionals in the counseling relationship. How does one react to and deal with a colleague's incompetency? How does one deal with one's own mistakes in the counseling interaction? To what extent does one use the counseling relationship for personal gratification? This is a crucial area, for it is the basis for potential legal action against the counselor. Some self-monitoring of personal behavior is essential to all counselors to ensure awareness of what is going on and of its effect on the needs of the client.

CHANGE OF BEHAVIOR AND EXPERIMENTATION

Professional counselors should be alert to and involved with new ideas in counseling. They should be aware not only of the activities of a variety of professional groups but also of the interactions of each counseling contact so that evaluation and change can occur when appropriate. This process must be continuous to ensure that assistance offered to the client is appropriate to the latter's needs. Experimentation for its own sake is of questionable value and is sometimes unethical. Counselors have an ethical position to maintain regardless of how much time they have spent developing it. It is advantageous to make this an active process. Counselors should study statements of ethics and continue to examine and reevaluate their ethical position as revealed within the counseling dyad in terms of its effects on clients.

> By committing himself to upgrade his ethical behavior and working diligently to assess his current levels of functioning, desired goals, and courses of action necessary to meet moral responsibilities to himself, his clients, and his profession, the therapist can refine his competencies and protect himself against outside interference, legal suits, and a guilty conscience (Van Hoose & Kottler, 1977, p. 44).

CONFIDENTIALITY

Confidentiality involves the retention of information received in a personal interaction with a client. A dilemma exists because not all such information or data can be treated as completely confidential. Understanding what information is confidential and what is not is crucial. In addition to the ethical aspects, there is a legal element related to confidentiality to be covered later.

There are several levels of counselor-client confidentiality. The first involves professional use of information. All discussion at this level occurs with others who have a degree of understanding of the meaning of the information, and with the client's consent. Information at this level would include test data, records, and other information about and outside the client. A second level involves information that is transmitted by the client on a personal basis in the counseling interview. The client should be aware of the degree to which confidentiality can exist prior to communication within the counseling situation. The counselor must be able to discern when the information is going to pose a confidentiality problem. He or she must be able to communicate a structure that helps the client understand the possible consequences, good or bad. The counselor should also know the constraints under which he or she works in order to develop a way to deal with this type of information. In such cases the counselor should have a plan of action before the interview but should introduce the material at the appropriate time rather than making a structuring speech early in the series of interviews.

At the third level of confidentiality the counselor does not divulge any material given by the client. Two exceptions are when clear danger to human life exists or when the client consents to divulging the information. The counselor who refuses to communicate any material may be involved in a legal problem, for it is not always clear whether the counselor has legally privileged communication.

LEGAL ASPECTS

The legal aspects of the counseling relationship are not as clearly defined as one might like. Few laws relate directly to the counseling process, and even when laws do exist their interpretation and enforcement may vary widely from place to place. A few court cases have begun to establish precedents. But the absence of laws or precedents should not be interpreted to mean that the counselor is under no legal restraint. There are several areas of legal responsibility that are important for the counselor to observe.

COUNSELING RELATIONSHIP

The counselor has a legal responsibility to inform clients what her or his skills are, perhaps indicating extent of preparation, experience, and limitations. The counselor should make certain that the client knows the conditions under which the counseling is taking place, discussing such aspects as fees, scheduling, and client and counselor obligations. This means that the counselor and client are establishing a contract, albeit unwritten, defining the conditions in which counseling will occur and the ends toward which the counselor and client are working. If the conditions are not met, either party may have recourse to legal action. The client, for example, may be expected to pay for the session whether or not it occurs; failure to cancel an appointment within a reasonable time may impose a financial obligation on the client.

This emphasis upon the legal aspects of the counseling interaction is necessary so that the client understands what and how much the counselor can provide. It also ensures that the client knows what will be expected of her or him within the counseling setting.

CHAPTER NINETEEN ETHICS, LEGALITIES, AND VALUES IN COUNSELING 441

CONFIDENTIAL INFORMATION

442   CHAPTER
NINETEEN
ETHICS,
LEGALITIES,
AND VALUES
IN
COUNSELING

When a client enters a relationship with a counselor, he or she has a right to expect that the content of the interaction will remain confidential. Confidentiality relates to the degree to which either person in the relationship can divulge exchange of information. Confidentiality usually is taken to mean that the interchange took place in a relationship that is recognized by legal statute or judicial precedent. Over the years this relationship has come to include physician and patient, lawyer and client, minister and parishioner, husband and wife, and, in some cases, psychologists and clients.

Most counselors do not have legally protected confidentiality; however, there is still a legal requirement that the counselor maintain the confidentiality as long as possible. As Goldman (1969) suggested, the privilege of confidentiality resides with the client. It is the professional duty of the counselor to maintain confidentiality.

There are some exceptions to this rule. When it appears that the client is going to harm herself or himself and/or society, the counselor may be required to contact appropriate authorities. In addition, many states are requiring that any professional report evidence of child abuse. At such times, even though confidentiality in counseling may not exist, the counselor has an obligation to report the information only to appropriate and legally authorized personnel. The counselor must be aware of who the appropriate personnel are so that the information remains as confidential as possible. It is also essential that the counselor report the information accurately.

LIABILITY

Liability deals with the responsibility that one person has in a relationship with another person when he or she was or still may be directly involved on a personal level. Liability can attach to acts of negligence, malpractice, libel, and slander.

Burgum and Anderson (1975) listed three principal areas in which the counselor may be held liable for injury to a client through failing to exercise proper professional care: when the counselor performs an act that exceeds the limits of her or his professional training; when the counselor defames the character of the client; and when the counselor invades the client's privacy through illegal search.

In general, the counselor is expected to exercise the care and prudence that any reasonable person would exercise in a similar situation. The counselor who does not may become liable for any injury or harm that might result from imprudent actions if he or she is negligent. In general, the courts emphasize the principle of foreseeableness: a counselor will be held guilty of negligence if he or she pursues a course of action from which any reasonably prudent person would have foreseen that some kind of injury might result.

It is difficult to develop a firm statement of what this definition might mean to counselors at various professional levels. One case used as a precedent is that of *Bogust* v. *Iverson*. In this case the counselor was charged with negligently and carelessly failing to perform his duties. Three specific charges were brought against a counselor in a college counseling center because his client had committed suicide approximately six months after the counselor terminated counseling. The parents charged that the counselor failed to secure emergency psychiatric treatment after he was aware or should have been aware of the client's inability to care for her own safety. Second, the counselor was charged with failing at all times to advise the parents or contact them concerning her true mental state and emotional condition, thus preventing them from securing proper medical aid. Third, the parents suggested that the counselor failed to provide proper student guidance.

The case was finally resolved in favor of the counselor. The court ruled that before liability can be attached a duty must rest upon the person against whom recovery is sought. Because the counselor in this case was not qualified as a medical doctor or as a specialist in mental disorders, the requirement to recognize in the student a condition of the type mentioned was adjudged a duty beyond reason. The court said further that the suggested termination of the interviews, which was advanced as a cause for suicide, did not in fact cause the injury or place the client in a condition worse than she was before the interviews began. There was no duty on the counselor's part to continue the interviews; therefore, the termination could not be considered negligence.

A substantial reason for denying recovery for mental distress or its physical consequences was that the judicial process is not well adapted to distinguishing valid from fraudulent claims in this area. Because causation is difficult to prove, the court was reluctant to extend recovery for mental distresses or even its physical consequences when the defendant is charged with ordinary negligence. Finally, even if the jury assumed that the counselor had secured psychiatric aid or that he had advised his client's parents of her emotional condition or that he had not secured termination, it would have required speculation to conclude under these circumstances that she would not have taken her own life. This was beyond the duty and power of the jury or a court.

In general, then it is safe to assume that counselor liability will be related to personal injury when the counselor does not act as a reasonably prudent person could be expected to act. The counselor is not generally liable for the actions of his or her client outside the counseling session. Despite the lack of counselor involvement in litigation of this nature there is a high degree of vulnerability implicit in the counseling relationship. There will probably be an increase in attempts to bring suit for personal injury or harm in the future as a result of counselor negligence.

LIBEL AND SLANDER

Libel is a false written or printed statement that injures the reputation of a living person. With the advent of the open records law in some states the potential for libel action has increased. Counselors' statements included in the records of clients or written statements or recommendations related to the individual's obtaining a job or gaining admission to a specific educational institution may be used to bring court action against the writer.

Slander is defined in the same manner but is confined to defamatory spoken words. Slander is a more tenuous concept than libel because the permanency and thus possibility of examination are considerably less. In each case malice is an element. Malice may be personal ill will or a reckless disregard of the rights of others.

Regardless of the extent of malice or any other action related to libel or slander, there are defenses against an action in either area. If the statement was true or the individual had consented to the statement, in effect accepting the truth of the matter, then no libel or slander exists. There is also a possibility of qualified

444 CHAPTER
NINETEEN

ETHICS,
LEGALITIES,
AND VALUES
IN
COUNSELING

privilege, which implies that the communication was made in good faith by a person having an interest or obligation in the matter to a person with a similar interest or duty. The effect is to eliminate the presumption of malice.

Because counselors must prepare written statements about clients for required records or for subsequent educational or vocational opportunities, they will be faced with the possibility of action for libel. In addition, because feedback to other persons who have some relationship to the client is essential, counselors may also find that action for slander is possible. The obvious way to avoid losing a court case in either area is to utilize the guidelines of truth and good faith. Increased communication with the client may also deter potential libel or slander charges.

Sometimes the counselor may have to put himself or herself on the line and take the chance that court action may ensue. If the counselor has well-established data about a client's physical, mental, moral, or psychological health, he or she is obligated to report this information to various significant people in the client's life even though in the process some statement might be construed to be slanderous. Thus, if the counselor has good evidence that a female client is pregnant he or she should attempt to ensure that her health is protected by examination and medical care. If the client will not see the doctor voluntarily, the counselor may have to involve her parents even though this means that the counselor is violating the girl's confidence and revealing information about her sexual activities. Because the counselor and parents share an interest in the client, this is an area of qualified privilege.

Counselors have a grave professional and moral responsibility not to defame and injure the reputation of others needlessly. This is true whether the individuals are students, parents, or other associates. Counselors must take care that communications are related to the needs of the client and that they accurately reflect the truth.

MALPRACTICE

Malpractice generally refers to any professional misconduct, carelessness, or lack of skill in the performance of an established and socially imposed duty (Huckens, 1968). For many counselors the "established and socially imposed duty," or role, is not clearly defined, and malpractice is difficult to determine. The case of *Bogust* v. *Iverson* serves as an example of malpractice as well as negligence. If the counselor had the well-defined and clearcut social role that professional colleagues would generally assume him to have, he probably did practice his profession badly. The court, however, ruled that the generally accepted counselor role was not a reality and the idea that counselors are adequately prepared to furnish services of a therapeutic nature was probably untrue. Although these guidelines provide margins of safety in the area of malpractice, they also suggest that there is no profession of counseling.

Three conditions exist when malpractice is possible. First, the counselor must have responsibility or duty to the client. Second, damages must result through the counselor's negligence or improper action; the counselor must practice badly the duty she or he has to the client. Third, there must be a link between the departure from practice and the physical, mental, or monetary damage that occurred; there must be a causal relationship between what the counselor did badly and the resultant harm to the client.

Although the number of malpractice suits is low, some events suggest that this may not continue to be the case. Trent and Muhl (1975) suggested three.

1. People are becoming more aware of the potential for malpractice in all professions. They are apt to be more familiar with lawyers and thus apt to hire them to try to obtain compensation for damages.
2. The trend toward more active therapies increases the potential for claims, for the activity of the counselor may be more open to examination and the relationship between the counselor's actions and the client's resultant behavior may be clearer.
3. The public is more aware of what constitutes bad practice in many professions and can translate this awareness to the activities of counselors.

To this list one might add another: malpractice insurance is available to counselors, and many have been forced to purchase policies. Whenever money is available, especially from insurance companies, there are people who will seek ways to get those funds. As long as the insurance company is paying it is less personal and more acceptable to try to collect.

This does not mean that the majority of clients enter therapy to look for and exploit the malpractice potential. Clients are seeking assistance. The counselor can diminish the potential for malpractice suits by being open in communication with clients, especially in terms of the skills, methods, and limitations of the counseling that he or she can provide. The best way for the counselor to avoid malpractice is to understand her or his limitations, communicate with the client, and practice well the counseling skills within these parameters.

In many ways this area is a crucial one for counselors. They must evaluate their own activity, be aware of what others are doing, and be willing to be involved with other counselors. In evaluating their own activity, counselors must clearly understand themselves and what they are doing, including the seriousness of interaction with clients. It is also important for counselors to have sufficient self-understanding and knowledge of personal limitations to prevent acceptance of tasks and counseling responsibilities that could lead to charges of malpractice.

Second, counselors may need to be involved with other counselors. Traditionally, counselors have tended to avoid confrontation with colleagues because there is no single definition of what constitutes good counseling. It may be possible, however, to establish what constitutes bad counseling. Any profession must have internal controls on the behavior of its members. Unless counselors are willing to be involved, internal control will not occur and the professional status that counselors need and want will not exist. Even though there are few, if any clearcut statements of legal behavior and few precedent-setting cases to determine counselors' legal standing, this tenuousness does not excuse behavior detrimental to the client and the profession. It suggests that different kinds of behaviors on the part of the counselor and profession are necessary.

PRIVILEGED COMMUNICATION

A privileged communication is anything said by a client to a counselor in a counseling interview with the understanding that the counselor will not be called upon

446 CHAPTER
NINETEEN
ETHICS,
LEGALITIES,
AND VALUES
IN
COUNSELING

to divulge the information, regardless of its nature. Privileged communication has long existed for ministers and individual parishioners, for lawyers and clients, for husband and wife in any legal case involving one or the other, for physicians and patients, and, in some cases, for counselors and clients. It is not always clear whether counselors, therapists, and clinicians have privileged communication. There is little consistency among the states in this area. Counselors should not assume that in the absence of legislation to the contrary they have privileged communication.

Privileged communication is divided into three separate classes: privileges protecting the individual client, such as those precluding any forced self-incrimination; privileges protecting systems within society, such as those related to jurors; and privileges that protect functions of importance to society, such as counselor-client communication. Although the privilege of the individual is important, the third type of privilege is of principal concern to counselors.

There are two types of privileged communication: absolute and qualified. The best most counselors can expect is qualified, which means that exceptions are possible and in some cases specific.

Some conditions should be made clear before any exchange of privileged communication. First, there must be an understanding that the communications will not be disclosed. It may be necessary to be straightforward with the client about this, or the counselor may need to indicate sometime in the interaction that the material being discussed may be outside his or her protected area of privilege.

Second, confidentiality must be deemed necessary to the maintenance of the relationship. This becomes an ad hoc factor which may pose some difficulties: the counselor may not know until after the communication took place that confidentiality (or at least some degree of it) is essential. The counselor should be wary of the intensity of the interaction so that any potential problem area can be anticipated and a satisfactory method devised for dealing with it.

Third, the relationship between the privileged parties must have support or be fostered by the community. Counseling generally comes within this category, but there is sufficient doubt in some people's minds to render this condition ambiguous.

Fourth, there is a concern over the extent to which disclosure would harm the communicant. The benefit that accrues to the client by maintaining confidentiality must be greater than the benefit gained by disposition of information.

There must be legal recognition of privileged communication before it can exist. There is little current support outside the counseling profession for granting this privilege, based on the argument that counseling is not a profession and thus not worthy of the privilege. There is also a contention that few confidences are shared and thus there is no real need for the privilege. Finally, there is a lack of professional standards by which a person becomes a counselor. If the profession does not have or enforce standards there is little to justify granting privileged communication to its members.

On the assumption that most counselors do not have privileged communication, the counselor must perform several actions before counseling and after a call has been made for material gathered in a counseling session.

The counselor should inform the client, at an appropriate time, what the status of privileged communication is as he or she understands it. This suggests that the counselor is alert to the possibility that various statements of the client may need to be discussed later with others. Examples might be statements concerning a client's proclivity to violence, reports of what he or she had done, and similar statements. The counselor may eventually be asked to repeat, under oath, the statements made by the client.

Any written or taped recording of the counseling session could be subpoenaed in a court case. It is the counselor's responsibility to keep careful records and to provide protection for the client in relation to these records. Thus, the counselor may wish to purge the records from time to time to eliminate material that may no longer be relevant to the counselor-client interaction. The counselor may also wish to keep records that require his interpretation to maintain some control over the interpretations by people who have not interacted with the client. It is clear that some method of ensuring the highest degree of confidentiality is necessary. When communication in turn becomes necessary, the clearest communication of specific points is essential.

The counselor should be alert to client statements that might require testimony by the counselor. At that point some structuring is necessary to protect the client, who may not be aware of the possible outcomes of this interaction. Careful records should be maintained to ensure that the client is protected within the legal interpretations of the counseling process. The counselor should be certain that records supplied to a court are truthful and made in good faith for the interest of the client.

When a counselor is called upon to testify in a court case involving a client, unless privileged communication exists the counselor has several alternatives. First, she or he can give the testimony, in effect acknowledging that the issue is best settled by due process rather than by an individual decision. Or the counselor may refuse to testify, claiming violation of confidence and conscience or infringement of rights. The counselor who does this may be held in contempt of court and face a lawsuit. The counselor may feel compelled to do this even with the potentially damaging consequences. Finally, the counselor may develop a compromise activity for a court appearance. Two possibilities exist. First, the counselor may be relying on memory, especially if the records are no longer available, and this can pose a problem for any witness. It is usually difficult to remember specifics well enough to be of value in any court of law. The second type of situation is that often the material the court is interested in is hearsay from the counselor's point of view. The counselor did not actually observe the activities reported by the client. All the counselor knows is what the client said, and this is usually not admissible evidence. The counselor can handle both sides of the question even after the fact of some court action.

When facing the serious occasion of presenting client data in a court, the counselor can legitimately deal with these problems within the context of law.

RIGHTS OF THE CLIENT

Many of the legal aspects of counseling relate to things the counselor should know to ensure compliance with the law. In the past few years the rights of the client have emerged as an important issue. This issue centers on due process. Due process refers to individuals' rights to certain legal actions as part of any complaint against them. This has been applied primarily to various rules and regulations established as part of a particular institution or agency.

448 CHAPTER
NINETEEN
ETHICS,
LEGALITIES,
AND VALUES
IN
COUNSELING

There are two separate types of due process: substantive and procedural. Substantive due process relates to whether there has been a deprivation of the individual's constitutional rights. Any rule that arbitrarily limits the freedom of an individual is a violation of substantive due process. Procedural due process relates to the procedures that apply when some rule is broken. Thus, the client may know the rule but is often uninformed about the process necessary to initiate or complete any action.

The counselor's first task may be to ensure that the client knows both substantive and procedural material. The counselor may be called upon to be an advocate for the client to see that his or her rights are upheld. The counselor must know the rights of clients, know what constitutes due process, and be prepared to work with the proper personnel to ensure the application of due process to any action that may be instituted against the client.

Confidentiality of records also relates to the client's legal rights. The legal aspects of this change rapidly, but in general the counselor should avoid revealing data in client records unless he or she has the client's permission. Within this legal extensive area the counselor may utilize the following guidelines:

1. Avoid revealing any data from client records without the client's specific permission.
2. When it is no longer possible to avoid revealing data, present the data with appropriate interpretative material.
3. Under extreme pressure release the data if the law so states.

Counselors should seldom be forced into the final step if they ensure that their records are accurate and known by the client and if they present material so that misinterpretation is minimal. As Burgum and Anderson (1975) suggested, the counselor should take care to enter accurate information where required and to disclose the information to those who have a legitimate rationale for receiving it.

VALUES IN COUNSELING

The life of each individual reflects her or his values or value orientation. Counselors and clients demonstrate the quality and quantity of their values in many diverse ways. Both participants in the counseling process should understand the diversity of their values as clearly as possible.

Lowe (1976) pointed out that the critical nature of values in counseling has resulted from at least two significant societal changes. First, there has been a decline in the influence of traditional religion on the value development of the individual. With the movement away from inner orientation toward more outside impingement of societal values, the individual knows more about what others are doing and this often affects his or her values. When this outer orientation causes a dilemma for a client, the counselor needs to understand the values of the client, the society, and herself or himself to provide assistance in some sort of value reorientation or clarification.

Second, there has been a shift from counseling for the few, usually the mentally disturbed, to more general counseling for a more diverse clientele. The focus of treatment has expanded to more general types of individual needs, often related to problems in everyday living. This process forces both client and counselor into a more overt choice of values, especially the counselor who works with clients from a population that was not much considered during the development of her or his particular system of counseling.

Thus the client comes to the counselor with a need to clarify and, perhaps, develop an internally integrated system of values. The development of this system allows the individual to move from a confused life to one with some order, or at least allows the imposition of order on his or her life as a member of society with all its complexities.

Another implicit aspect of value clarification is societal involvement. Almost all societies and subsections of society have moral codes. These are consentually accepted expectations for the members of that society. A delicate balance exists between the need to allow each person as much freedom as possible to select values and the assumption that there is a set of expectations that will be transmitted to the younger members of society with the idea that they will accept and abide by the code.

There has been a breakdown in both aspects of this process. Society often does not seem to have provided a set of morals that its members can clearly discern and understand. Perhaps people now know too much about others' societies and try to include or preclude the good and bad aspects of other social codes. As a result, it is difficult to determine what is acceptable and unacceptable in society. In addition, even in those areas that are relatively clearly defined, the traditional ways of passing values on to the younger members of society have decreased in potency or disappeared. Churches, schools, and the family do not have as much input into the process as formerly. Moreover, the messages from these and from other portions of society are often in conflict, and the individual becomes more confused about his or her values and value system.

The counseling setting becomes a place where clients seek to develop and understand values and to learn ways of implementing this newly developed or reorganized system in everyday life. The counselor, in focusing on the ideas, concerns, hopes, and values of the client, acts as a catalyst and explorer. She or he avoids judging, criticizing, and evaluating in this process of value development.

The counselor's role raises several issues concerning the whole area of values. Obviously the counselor's values have some part in the counseling process. What values does the counselor have? How aware is he or she of that value system? What feelings does a counselor have concerning imposition or nonimposition of values in the counseling relationship? Another area relates to the values imposed by the institution or system within which the counselor works. Does the counselor understand the mores of the school, the counseling center? Does she or he accept them? Can the counselor change them? How does the client fit into the setting?

Finally, there is the whole area of client value orientation. How do the client's values relate to the counseling topic under discussion? Can the client be helped to understand values and change those that bring unhappiness? What outside forces impinge upon the client, especially as they influence values?

These questions and many others have emerged in recent years as our society and its people change their outlook on values and mores formerly considered acceptable or good. These changes lead to difficulties for many people. Many clients come to counseling for assistance in dealing with value development or clarification or problems related to values.

450　CHAPTER
NINETEEN
ETHICS,
LEGALITIES,
AND VALUES
IN
COUNSELING

Values that emerge from self-examination provide a background for interpreting the many new experiences and events that greet each person daily. This explosion of data, experiences, life situations, and human events requires interpretation to provide integration and meaning. The materials necessary for this interpretation or integration are found in personal values and beliefs. Counseling may be defined as a search for values because the search reflects the development of personal values both intrinsically and authentically.

Values are criteria that include ideals, goals, normative action, and standards of behavior. Values are learned and help the individual develop a concept of what is desirable. In today's world the quest for purpose, meaning, and identity is a major concern. The counselor must be aware of and concerned with his or her own values, the client's values, and how both relate to the counseling process.

Peterson (1970) suggested that values represent the desirable. Values help the individual to perceive or decide what he or she ought to do or what is "right" in the given circumstance. As such, values can be motivational in nature, helping the client during and as a result of counseling. Often some portion of the client's value system is out of line and the job of the counselor is to assist in the realignment process.

A recognition of the importance of values is crucial to human development, and so is the recognition that values cannot be handed to individuals or placed within a final experiential framework on the assumption that the individual will find them meaningful. In the process of choosing and owning values, the individual must be willing to question and then, having questioned, to act in constructive, purposeful ways (Peterson, 1970).

There are two general aspects of values in the counseling process. The first is the degree to which the personal values of the counselor should or do affect the counselor-client relationship. The second aspect is the values that the client holds and their effect on counseling process and outcomes.

THE COUNSELOR'S VALUES

In the professional literature, there has been little disagreement concerning the need for the counselor to understand his or her value system. The counselor's value system has influenced the important decisions of her or his life. Some counselors seem unaware of the values they espouse, but observation indicates a consistent reflection of values. The counselor's value system is critically important to his or her interaction with the client. However, success in counseling may be related less to the nature of the counselor's personal and professional values than to the degree of control the counselor has over them and to her or his ability to use them in a systematic way.

Values are the inferred criteria by which choices of objects or goals are justified. There is a distinction between the desired and the desirable: the desired is tied closely to physiological needs; the desirable seems to transcend mere physiological needs. Values are related to imitations of action and to setting directions for action.

Value Orientations

Lowe (1959) identified four value orientations that compete for the commitment of the counselor or therapist. The problem of selecting values is compounded by the demands made by society, the organization, the client, and the counselor himself or herself. Each orientation has merit and followers. Each has critics who disclaim the orientation.

Naturalism   One orientation assumes that scientific laws account for all phenomena. Things that can be measured or defined operationally constitute naturalism. This orientation has been manifested most clearly in behaviorism, which has become an important factor in counseling. The behaviorist can report striking evidence of successful outcomes in counseling based upon various methods of manipulating behavior to ensure effective living for the client and cultural survival. While you may not wish to go to the extent implied by Skinner (1948) in *Walden Two*, note that the manipulation of the client by the counselor can be toward values espoused by the majority with less concern over the client's understanding of how his or her value system meshes with that of the larger society.

Culturalism   Culturalists develop their value orientation from the social nature of people and the needs that result from particular cultures. Thus, the client is in need of help because he or she is isolated from other people, unable to relate to others, or unable to adapt to what others in the culture are doing. Again, the value is outside the individual, and he or she must move toward it through an adjustment, adaptation, or learning process. The cultural values are clearly delineated and the therapist's ultimate allegiance is to society. Culturalism disavows individual moral responsibility, allowing instead the substitution of value establishment and perhaps behavior responsibility to reside outside the individual.

Humanism   The humanist moves the locus of concern to the individual. Humanists assume that people can control their own destiny and realize their own potentialities through rational thought processes. People should move toward their highest level of being without particular concern for the values that others establish for them. Therapy is designed to foster the individual's ability to solve personal problems.

Theism   The theist believes that loyalty to and dependence upon God constitute the major values of life. Although beliefs can be as broadly defined as religions are, the one central value deals with loving God and finding and accepting the will of God in all of life. People find resolution of their problems because of faith in God, who has a purpose for all people and to whom people must eventually return.

Each counselor must gain understanding of his or her own values as well as the values of others. No one value orientation seems to be better than the others. However, as Lowe pointed out, "As psychologists familiarize themselves with the value orientation under which they operate . . . they confess their philosophic biases and then turn those biases to fullest advantage by being of professional assistance to the special interest groups with which their values coincide. In such ways . . . the public will receive more of what psychology has to contribute . . ." (1959, p. 692).

Values serve as reference points for individuals. They provide a basis for deciding which course of action to take. People have always needed these guidelines in order to continue their existence. However, values change, and what was prescribed as absolute and final at one time becomes tenuous at others. People may not be able to adjust to rapidly changing value systems; the result is guilt or anxiety. Although some may question the psychologist's involvement in developing value orientations, few would suggest that counselors can avoid values, either

452   CHAPTER
NINETEEN

ETHICS,
LEGALITIES,
AND VALUES
IN
COUNSELING

their own or their clients', in interaction with the clients. Values are the core of the counseling relationship. They are reflected by the content and the interaction. Thus counseling, which promotes modification of behavior, also provides a basis for the client to change attitudes and values.

Belkin (1975) suggested that a value system permeates the whole of a person's life. The client brings a system, developed to some degree, to the counseling setting. The counselor brings a system that will affect her or his interaction with the client. It is important to know how the latter contributes to the counseling process and its outcomes.

The Role of Counselor Values

The counselor's value system may serve any of several roles. At one level, a counselor or therapist knows her or his own value system but avoids introducing it into the counseling interview. The counselor does not indicate his or her own position in any of the moral or value questions raised. The goal is to provide a situation in which the client can move from a position of external evaluation and valuing to an internalized locus of evaluation. Any value input by the counselor would work against this objective.

A second role makes it impossible for the counselor to remain neutral or not have an influence on the client. The client has come to a counselor for assistance that often relates to values. A major question is raised by this general position; namely, if in fact values and moral stance are inherent in any relationship, to what degree are they used or abused by the counselor? Most persons who adopt this role want to avoid manipulating values. They suggest that the individual's philosophy is and must remain his or her own.

A question that this second position on values often raises is whether the counselor ought to provide instruction to the client in developing a value system, clarifying personal values, or any of several related value-learning activities. Some counselors reject this teaching function in the counseling session, contending that there are more appropriate things to do and more appropriate ways to learn whatever might be taught in the counseling session. Others suggest the opposite: for some clients the first and most appropriate objective of counseling is learning or developing a more comprehensive and acceptable value system.

Given that various types of values or morals are introduced into the counseling setting, there may be some areas in which the counselor's own thoughts or development of an acceptable system is incomplete. This counselor cannot help the client in the realm of values because the latter may already be beyond the reach of the counselor, say, in the area of religious values.

The third role entails the active imposition of values upon the client. Intervention by the counselor is necessary and should be an identifiable part of counseling. The counselor must first deal with the values of the client: values about himself or herself, about the various prospects available, and about life and its interrelationships. Until these are known and accepted the client will not be able to make a decision, move in meaningful directions, escape therapy, or whatever the more cognitive objectives of counseling might be.

This role tends to suggest that the counselor has greater intelligence, skill, or knowledge than anyone else and is entitled to a superior position toward others.

This is not acceptable to some counselors, who would characterize this as a dehumanizing process. Regardless of criticisms, however, there is some evidence that many clients want and readily accept this more directive assistance without regard to the topic or area of concern. In effect, the client comes seeking help and wants the counselor to provide the assistance. More cynical observers suggest that these clients are only seeking justification from someone else for what they have already done or are contemplating. as long as someone agrees with them, the action is more acceptable to their own value system.

In contrasting the views of value introduction into counseling, Peterson (1970) suggested that if people are basically good nothing need be added to the counseling session, and thus, nondirection is logical; most value questions can be ignored because once the obstacles are removed the client will move toward and arrive at proper values. On the other hand, with a view of people as evil or with the potential for evil, the counselor cannot allow the client to move in other than positive directions; value questions are not self-resolving because the client's proclivity would be toward even greater manifestation of socially unacceptable behavior.

It is difficult to believe that the values and moral attitudes of the counselor can be hidden from the client. The counselor is better advised to recognize and accept his or her values, using them to promote greater awareness in the counseling relationship and expressing them when it appears that doing so will improve or further the relationship. When this occurs the client will feel less coerced into defending his or her own values and will be able to examine them in the privacy of the counseling session. This openness in sharing values will shift the emphasis to the act of valuing instead of evaluating the content of values. The client will be able to mature or function more effectively when the emphasis is on decision making. Valuing can thus help the client relate to a situation and then form a commitment to a course of action.

CHAPTER
NINETEEN   453
ETHICS,
LEGALITIES,
AND VALUES
IN
COUNSELING

THE CLIENT'S VALUES

There are several ways of categorizing values. Belkin (1975) suggested five categories.

Cognitive Values

Cognitive values assign a relative worth to things or belief, such as the belief that better cars are built outside the United States than inside the country. There may be data available to support this point of view or belief, and the person holding this belief is unlikely to change it. If this type of value exists the counselor may experience difficulty fostering changes, and if the change seems necessary for client growth, an impasse is likely to occur.

Preference Values

Preference values reflect personal preference without much evidence to back it up. Thus, "Broadway musicals are more pleasing to me than opera" expresses a preference on the part of the chooser but does not suggest that musicals or opera are better. The possibility of changing preference values is greater than for cognitive values.

Moral Values

Moral values derive from a larger set of society and represent the expectations of the specific portion of society so identified. People who hold moral values tend to be inflexible, either accepting a moral statement or disagreeing so much that change is unlikely. Moral values are often a major topic for the counselor and client as they interact in counseling. The client may not know what the expectation is and needs to learn, or may misinterpret the expectation and cling so tightly to the position, rightly or wrongly, that change is difficult at best. The client may rightly interpret the expectations but be unwilling to accept the restrictions imposed during his or her interaction with society.

Cultural Values

Cultural values are values shared by certain identifiable cultural groups, such as religious groups. A client coming from that group experiences difficulties as a result of interactions with other populations, when her or his value comes into conflict with theirs. For example, a client may come from a cultural milieu in which intense competition is expected on almost any dimension. When the client cannot or will not accept this value, the conflict affects her or his personal and social life. The counselor faces a difficult task in helping the client deal with this impasse. Help must be available so that the client can resolve the dilemma and return to the social setting or find a new place to live where the expectations are different. Often this type of dilemma leads to a potential inferior-superior situation: cultures that are different and the person from those settings are seen as inferior. The counselor must take care that neither he or she nor the client accepts this position.

Self Values

Self values relate to feelings about one's person, one's self-esteem, and one's feelings of worth. These values have a strong influence on client choices and personal difficulties. They are often the basis of counselor-client interaction.

The interface of the client's and counselor's values in any or all of these categories requires the counselor to be aware of and willing to deal with values in the relationship. If the interactions are conflictual, the counselor is obligated to arrange for a referral. The counselor must be committed to providing a forum for the client to examine his or her values and the elements that may be producing conflict. The counselor must value freedom of choice for the client even though the choice may be quite different from the one the counselor would make. The counselor must value the client and bring a sense of trust into the session. Unless there are very strong indications that the client is unable to choose, to reorient her or his value system, and to deal with the relationship of personal values to cultural mores, the counselor's main job in terms of values is to provide information, be a sounding board, and be supportive to the client among any other tasks that become essential for the latter's welfare.

CLIENT CONCERNS ABOUT VALUES

The client typically brings certain concerns about values to a counselor. Sometimes the categories are hazy and often the client and counselor are not certain of the need. Many problems, however, seem to belong to one of the following types.

Understanding Life

Most people go through a process of questioning the meaning of life in general and individual life specifically. Whether they attempt to derive meaning from a theological, rational, intellectual, or human framework, they are attempting to understand the totality of life and where they fit into the picture. Most people face this problem and are able to work through to some satisfactory solution. They may receive help from a religious leader or from a trusted friend, or they may mature through the process and one day find an acceptable meaning to life and understand themselves. People who do not accomplish this often seek the assistance of a counselor, either during adolescence or sometimes not until much later in life. There are generally predictable times when this problem will occur in the lives of almost everyone in our society.

Certain age groups may have greater concerns about understanding life than do others. Adolescents find conflicts between what they have been told and what they observe in much of society. They are faced with the dilemma about what is right and how to handle the guilt that accompanies the rejection of a previously accepted set of values. Students often have conflicts during their years at college. The freedom they gain in contrast to previous situations poses difficulties for some students in maintaining a way of life or even understanding the life they live. Adults at certain ages are also subject to this pressure. As people grow older they may find less and less meaning to life and begin to search for some other meaning.

Various occurrences tend to generate the same type of problem. The outward movement of family members cause some problems for adults, such as the mother who has devoted her life to raising a family and maintaining a home. The death of someone near often triggers feelings of misunderstanding about life. New experiences in the world often lead people to examine the meaning of life. In contemporary society the drug culture provides a potent reinforcer for all types of people to reexamine what life is all about. The counselor's first job in working with this problem is to help the client become aware of his or her current value system, by providing a situation in which clarification can occur. The counselor should avoid pontification in this process: the client needs assistance in developing a personal system, not in implementing some outside system. Eventually the counselor should help the client deal with beliefs and how they can be most effectively implemented in life. Finally, the client should move into a period of a more acceptable understanding of her or his own life and the meaning attached to it.

Many factors are interrelated with this process, including forces of a physical, psychological, or familial nature that affect the freedom of the individual. Although it is probably true that people can do most of what they want to do in life, these factors play an important role and must be recognized by the counselor and the client. In all cases the counselor should be alert to the possibility that other, more competent assistance might be necessary.

Problems of Interrelatedness

A second area of value counseling involves the relationships people have with others. People are basically social animals and need to feel wanted and needed by others. When this does not occur they develop all kinds of methods for handling the situation.

Satisfaction is often achieved by belonging to identifiable groups in society. Political groups, work groups, and family units all can be helpful in meeting individual social needs. But in certain situations these groups pose problems for the individual. For example, people who devote time and energy to getting ahead in the business of their choice may, upon reaching certain levels, find that they, too, are a product and not the significant people they thought. If these people did not have a relationship in the most important aspect of their life, where does this occur? How do they handle this, especially if future conquests do not seem as meaningful or available as they were in the past?

In most such cases, clients need to develop a balance in their relationship endeavors. They begin to learn to invest themselves into other activities that provide a broader base for the generation of relationships. They must learn where other potential relationships exist and how to take advantage of them. The counselor can help these clients by simply creating a counseling relationship in which the latter see themselves as meaningful people who can change and can be more effective in interrelations. They are helped to see how their own behavior or personality may be related to the problem and that when they are less manipulative, others tend to respond more favorably.

Life Traumas

Various life traumas, such as loss of job, retirement, death, some physical problem or change of geographic location, can bring the individual into a counseling relationship. Sometimes the crisis is not as bad as the thoughts the client has about it. In all of life many things occur or statements are made which are misinterpreted by the hearer. For example, many students hear about a change in the curriculum in which they are involved and, without checking the truth of the situation, become quite anxious about their own situation. Eventually learning the truth does not automatically and completely relieve that anxiety.

The counselor tries to resolve the dilemmas in both the trauma itself and the words that accompany the trauma. Often people use earlier experiences with less traumas to cope with the greater traumas in life. Sometimes, though, the person either has not faced the lesser trauma or has not learned from the experience. This person enters counseling with a need to learn how to cope with the specific problem he or she is presently facing.

The counselor provides a counseling relationship to deal with the doubts and inadequacies facing the client. The client begins to examine his or her own life and begins to learn strategies for dealing with the particular event that led to counseling. In this case the counselor may not know whether he or she was instrumental in helping the client change or whether the passage of time was sufficient to block out whatever was related to the dilemma. The counselor should still strive to help the client work through self-understanding and learning effective strategies for dealing with future situations. The counselor's goal is to help alleviate the present condition and to provide assistance for generalizing to other situations in the future.

MORAL PROBLEMS

Moral problems often cause people to seek counseling assistance. Whenever individuals are behaving in a way contradictory to the mores of their society they may eventually seek assistance. At this point clients either want someone to say, "What you're doing is all right" or to find the set of circumstances under which the behavior would be more acceptable. They are not interested at that point in changing behavior.

On the other hand, the guilt generated by this behavior can be the focus of attention of the counselor and client. Part of the difficulty in contemporary society is that mores sometimes change more rapidly than people can adapt; yet their behavior may be in line with the new mores. They are torn between doing something quite acceptable in society but living with previous strongly held values.

Two types of guilt may exist in this kind of situation. First, clients may feel they are not doing as well as they would like to. Quite often this is related to a value system oriented to outside people. Parents, for example, are prone to pick out the negative aspects of the child's behavior and bypass any positive aspects. This tends to generate a feeling of inadequacy or guilt for not doing better. Often this is translated into "I am a bad person."

A second type of guilt is related to breaking a specific moral code, social rule, or legal law. These activities tend to create an emotional reaction, which the client may not be able to cope with. As a result the person turns inward and does nothing to prevent the guilt feelings from recurring.

Guilt and its accompanying feelings pose a difficult problem for the counselor. First, the counselor must help the client reduce the tensions and anxieties related to the guilt by creating a relationship in which the client is free to express her or his feelings and begin to deal with them objectively. Then the client can move toward understanding the motives behind what he or she has done, beginning to understand defense mechanisms and to develop sufficient strength to examine needs and values. The rest of the process involves the development of responsibility and positive self-regard so that the client is able to function more effectively. Effective functioning may entail a change of behavior that causes the guilt or an acceptance of the behavior as appropriate to self-understanding. The former is probably more desirable because only one person is affected. The latter solution may affect several people in the life space of the individual in various ways. Acceptance of the behavior should be examined as part of the process, and the counselor probably should not impose her or his own moral position on the situation. This type of outcome might be contrary to the counselor's values or those of the institution he or she represents.

Helping clients in areas of value is a very tenuous and ambiguous task. Although it is possible to define many of the problems, the process of helping the client understand and resolve these problems is not as easily defined. As a result, the counselor's primary task should be to offer a relationship environment that allows for client freedom and depth of feeling. Once this is done, the resultant steps will be easier regardless of the theoretical counseling position. The outline below lists possible steps for value clarification for the client derived from the work of Thomas (1970).

1. **Identify the value conflict.** A conflict occurs when a problem is

not solvable within the client's behavior repertoire. A conflict may suggest that various equally attractive alternatives exist.

2. **Identify live options to the conflict.**   A live option refers to the fact that a portion of the population in the society is dealing with an alternative in a specific identifiable way. The option represents a judgment of value on the part of someone.

3. **Compare and contrast the various options.**   When several options are identified the client and counselor compare and contrast them for strengths and weaknesses. The question usually is: What are the consequences associated with this option?

4. **Rank order the various options.**   The counselor and client begin to work out a listing of options based upon merits, good outcomes, lack of bad consequences, and so forth. The selection of the best option should be the natural result of this ranking.

5. **Select the most attractive option.**   The selection process includes commitment on the part of the client. Values, in this case, are commitments to standards of what is personally believed desirable. Until the selection and commitment occur the process is largely intellectual.

6. **Live the choice.**   Values and thus the selection of the best option are normative. Public commitment is a necessary experience for value clarification.

A counselor can indicate his or her values within this framework but should avoid making the decisions or ranking the options for the client. According to Glasser (1965), a counselor helps patients decide about the moral quality of their behavior. The use of the Thomas model is appropriate in this process, for it helps the client develop acceptable outcomes for specifically identified problem areas.

SUMMARY

It seems impossible to avoid the influence of values in the counseling situation. The counselor has values that are identifiable whether they are presented covertly or overtly. The client has values and value dilemmas. Society supports certain value systems more than others, despite the appearance of increased flexibility, the client who is too remote from the socially held values faces adjustment difficulties for which he or she will seek counseling help.

In terms of the values of the counselor Rogers contended, "One cannot engage in psychotherapy without giving operational evidence of an underlying value orientation and view of human nature. It is definitely preferable, in my estimation, that such underlying views be open and explicit rather than covert and implicit" (1957, p. 199).

REFERENCES

American Personnel and Guidance Association. *Ethical standards*. Washington, D.C., 1974.

American Psychological Association. Revised ethical standards of psychologists. *APA Monitor*, March 1977.

Belkin, G. S. *Practical counseling in the schools*. Dubuque, Iowa: William C. Brown, 1975.

Bogust v. Iverson, 192 N.E. 2d 228 (Wisc. 1960).

Brammer, L. M., & Shostrom, E. L. *Therapeutic psychology* (3rd ed.). Englewood Cliffs, N.J.: Prentice-Hall, 1977.

Burgum, T., & Anderson, S. *The counselor and the law*. Washington, D.C.: American Personnel and Guidance Association Press, 1975.

Glasser, W. *Reality therapy*. New York: Harper & Row, 1965.

Goldman, L. Privilege or privacy l. *Personnel and Guidance Journal*, 1969, *48*, 88.

Huckens, W. *Ethical and legal considerations in guidance*. Boston: Houghton Mifflin, 1968.

Lowe, C. Value orientations: An ethical dilemma. *American Psychologist*, 1959, *14*, 687–693.

———. *Value orientations in counseling and psychotherapy* (2nd ed.). Cranston, R.I.: Carroll Press, 1976.

Matthews, F. Values and counseling: One perspective. *Counseling and Values*, 1974, *19*, 37–41.

Nygaard, J. M. *The counselor and student legal rights*. Boston: Houghton Mifflin, 1973.

Peterson, J. A. *Counseling and values*. Scranton: International Textbook, 1970.

Pine, G., & Boy, A. Counseling and the quest for values. *Counseling and Values*, 1974, *19*, 42–47.

Rogers, C. R. A note on the nature of man. *Journal of Counseling Psychology*, 1957, *4*, 199–203.

Skinner, B. F. *Walden two*. New York: Macmillan, 1948.

Thomas, W. L. *Toward a concept of affective education*. Chicago: Combined Motivation Education Systems, 1970.

Trent, C. C., & Muhl, W. P. Professional liability insurance and the American psychiatrist. *Brief Communications*, 1975, *132*, (12), 1312–1314.

Tyler, L. *The work of the counselor* (3rd ed.). New York: Appleton-Century-Crofts, 1969.

Van Hoose, W. H., & Kottler, J. A. *Ethical and legal issues in counseling and psychotherapy*. San Francisco: Jossey Bass Publishers, 1977.

Wrenn, C. G. Psychology, religion, and values for the counselor. *Personnel and Guidance Journal*, 1957, *36*, 326–334.

AUTHOR INDEX

SUBJECT INDEX

Incompatible behaviors, reinforcement
of, 149
Incongruence, 100
Incongruity, 98
Independence, 273
Individual tests, 377
Inferiority, 58, 59
Information, 105, 232–233, 287, 349,
352–353, 374, 410–411, 420,
426–429, 441
and decisions, 346–347
integration, 349–350
processing, 347
Initial interview, 258
research, 259
Initiating counseling, 260–265
and race, 262–263
and sex, 261–262
and social class, 260–261
research on, 261–263
Injunctions, 76
Insight, 186–189, 267, 270, 300
Insight-affective dimension of counseling,
188–189
Institute for Advanced Study in Rational
Psychotherapy, 168
Institute for Child Guidance, 92
Integration, 419–420
Interest checklists, 379
Interest inventories, 379
Interests, 405–406, 418
expressed, 379
inventoried, 379
manifest, 379
tested, 379
Intermittent reinforcement, 134
Internalization, 201–202
Interpersonal process recall, 246
Interpersonal relationships, 62–63
Interpretation, 36, 51–52, 65, 86,
185–186, 188, 220, 239–240,
241–242, 291, 296, 297, 327,
381–382, 391–392, 393
in Adlerian psychology, 65
and confrontation, 230
clinical bridges, 384–385
descriptive bridges, 383
discrimination bridges, 383
evaluative bridges, 383
genetic bridges, 384
predictive bridges, 383
regression bridges, 384
statistical bridges, 383–384
Interrelation of counseling theories,
178–181
Interrelationships, 456
Interrogation, 85
Interview termination, 308–309
Intimacy, 75
Irrational beliefs, 169–171
Irrational thinking, 173

Job development, 402
Job satisfaction, 402

Karpman triangle and transactional
analysis, 87
Kinesics, 245

Labelling, 318
Lack of information, 321
Latency stage, 32
Learned behavior, 184
Learned needs, 137–138
freedom of movement, 138
need potential, 138
need value, 138
Learning, 131–132
behavioristic principles of, 131–137
cognitive, 152
imitative, 132, 149–152
Learning theory, 139, 181, 184
approach to personality, 137–139
behavioral counseling, 131–137
development of complex behaviors,
134–136
Legal responsibility, 441–448
Levels of facilitative communication,
210–211
Liability, 442–443
Libel, 443–444
Libido, 28
Life goals, 57, 58–60
and Adlerian psychology, 57
Life meaning, 455
Life positions, 75–78, 82
Life script, 76–77
Life-style, 63–64
analysis, 63–65
Life traumas, 456
Little Professor, 71

Maladaptive behavior, 60–61. *See also*
Abnormal development
anxiety, 98
and behavioral counseling, 139–140
defense mechanisms, 98
development of, 183–184
estrangement, 97–98
Gestalt counseling, 121–123
incongruity, 98
rational-emotive therapy, 170–171
reality therapy, 160–161
self-theory, 97–99
Malice, 443
Malpractice, 444–445
Manipulation, 147, 273–274
Mediating responses in behavioral
counseling, 136–137
Mental ability tests, 378
Mental defects, 60
Mental health approach, 11
counseling, 10
Modeling, in behavioral counseling,
149–151
Monitoring clients, 373, 392
Morals, 439, 449, 457
Motivation, 227